# Raising Livestock

*The Ultimate Guide to Raising Horses, Donkeys, Beef Cattle, Llamas, Pigs, Sheep, and Goats*

# Contents

# Part 1: Raising Horses

*The Ultimate Guide To Horse Breeding, Training And Care*

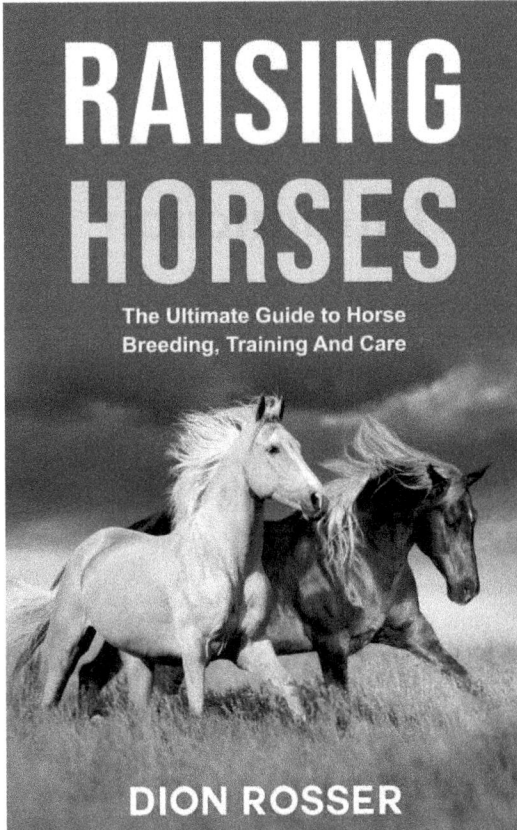

# Introduction

The horse is one of the most versatile and beautiful creatures in the animal kingdom. It has been a faithful companion of man for centuries and will surely continue to be. This majestic animal serves so many important purposes, and today, it is not uncommon to find people raising them.

If you have even the slightest interest of raising or breeding one, this book is definitely for you. Everything you need to know about horses, training them, understanding their behavior, caring, and creating a lifelong relationship with them is all written here.

Whatever reason you may have for wanting to be a horse owner, you will find this guide to be the perfect book to assist you on your journey.

Pick it up, read it, and share it with other horse friends!

# Chapter One: Why Raise Horses?

The relationship between horses and men began over 3,000 years ago. Surprising, right? The domestication of horses dates to 3,500BC. Horses have been such versatile creatures that raising them provides a ton of benefits – companionship being one of such. It is interesting to note that the horse has not always been the sturdy, large, hoofed animal you see and know today. Fifty million years ago, it was a tiny multi-toed mammal – no larger than a medium-sized pup. Since its evolution, humans have recognized and have taken advantage of the great power and strength the horse possesses, putting it to use for various purposes.

## Reasons For Raising Horses

Horseback riding is one of the oldest uses of horses since its domestication. Horses were also used to pull wheels of chariots, carts, and wagons in medieval times. Horses were a predominant means of transportation and communication in ancient times. It was also commonly used in warfare and had increasing relevance in society as it became a standard of wealth.

In the past, movement on foot was the only means of transporting resources and communicating with other people. So, you can imagine how revolutionary it was when horse riding came on the scene. Goods and places, once inaccessible or too time-consuming to transport, quickly became available as riders can move easily and faster than people on foot.

Fast-forward to the present day, and horseback riding is still very much relevant. They might not have as much social importance as they did back then since they were the only means of transportation, and ow, we have various vehicles and machinery to replace them. However, there are still a lot of uses for horses that technology is yet to replace. For example, mounted police are still in use by various countries in the world. Although their work is sometimes ceremonial, they are often used by the police for other functions such as crowd control or patrol in places inaccessible for police vehicles.

You may have seen one or more mounted police in your vicinity or at an event. During crowd control, mounted officers are more visible than those on the ground or in cars and inform people of the presence of the police. This helps to deter crimes and helps officers easily spot offenders as the height of the horse allows the police to see farther and wider.

In today's world, equestrian sport is perhaps the most notable application of horses. There are two major styles of riding horses: the English riding style and the Western riding style. You might be wondering what makes them different. Well, history helps provide an answer.

The Western riding originated from the ranches and was practiced by cowboys of mid and southwest United States. Cattle ranchers used horses in controlling the cattle, and this required the rider to be skillful at controlling and maneuvering the horse while riding at high speed. Specialized heavy saddles were created for the riders to help spread their weight on the horse and allow them to ride for long and across uneven roads without feeling uncomfortable.

The reins tied around their neck and a bit in the horse's mouth enabled the rider to control the horse with just one hand. Some equestrian disciplines that require western riding style include roping, reining, trail-riding, cutting, speed games, and so on.

The English riding style, on the other hand, originated from England and has its root in military and cavalry training. As equestrian sports competition began, this riding style was passed down and adopted for sporting purposes. Over the years, there have been changes to the style – but the basic principles remain the same.

Since the primary purpose of the English riding style is competitions, the saddles are designed to aid mobility for both the horse and its rider. They are lighter and smaller than the western saddles. The reins are directly connected to the horse's mouth and are to be held with both hands. Examples of equestrian competitions in which this riding style is used are dressage, show jumping, hunting, polo, mounted games, and many more.

# Use of Horses For Their Therapeutic Benefits

Horseback riding is not only fun but has been proven to be therapeutic. It is a form of recreational therapy aimed at improving an individual's mental, physical, and emotional health through different horse riding techniques.

Since riding a horse can obviously be done only in an outdoor environment, you are bound to spend more in the open, breathing in nature's fresh air. The feeling of freedom and independence that accompanies riding your horse in the wild is stimulating and second to none. Horse riding is a creative and helpful way to take a break from your typical everyday routine.

Coupled with this, horses are intelligent and emotional creatures capable of developing a bond with their owners and caretakers. Raising, riding, and caring for a horse avails you the opportunity to form a pure and unadulterated bond with it. These gentle yet majestic creatures are faithful and trustworthy and can easily become a man's best friend.

# Additional Health Benefits Associated with Horse Riding

### Core Muscle Strengthening

Consistently riding horses is a form of exercise for your core muscles. Your chest, abdomen, and lower back make up your core muscles. By engaging them while riding, you are actually strengthening the muscles present there. This simultaneously helps you stay balanced on the horse.

### Flexibility and Balance

Balancing is one of the first skills to master if you want to ride a horse properly and avoid falling off. The more accustomed you get to riding your horse, the easier it becomes to balance yourself either on a saddle or bareback. This balance is usually evident in the improvement of your body posture. The continuous exercise of galloping helps to improve your body flexibility, even when you are not riding.

### Improved Coordination

First-time horse riders will find it difficult to move or direct the horse as they please because of the high level of coordination required. You will need to apply leg pressure, rein pressure, and move your body all – at the same time – when riding and directing your horse. The more consistently you ride, the more your coordination skills improve. Soon enough, you will learn how to simultaneously use individual parts of your body to move your horse in any direction, and this can be applied to other activities as well.

### Enhances Mental Strength

Horse riding is extremely beneficial for your mental health. For starters, it is a soothing and relaxing exercise that clears your mind and improves your mood. Horses are emotional creatures with stress-relieving abilities. Also, interacting with the horse will require you to learn different cues that aid in directing and understanding your horse. Your confidence level can significantly improve just by gaining mastery over this huge and beautiful animal. Besides all these, raising a horse is a great feat and gives you a sense of fulfillment.

### Muscle Tone and Stable Strength

While riding a horse, your inner thighs and pelvic are engaged the most as you need to position yourself constantly in rhythm with the horse's cadence. Taking care of the horse in the stables requires you to lift heavy items that can be initially tasking. Still, as you engage in these activities, you can increase your cardiovascular capability and build what is popularly known as *stable strength*.

### Improves Problem-Solving Skills

Problem-solving is another skill associated with raising horses. This is because horses can be quite challenging and unpredictable sometimes, especially if it is unfamiliar territory. As a rider, you have to learn to think critically and come up with solutions that allow you to safeguard yourself and keep your horse under control. Each problem you can solve with your horse helps you develop a reservoir of skills that can come handy soon.

# Use of Horses for Farm Work

In some parts of the world, horses are raised strictly for farm work purposes. Although machinery and other forms of equipment have taken over much of farm and agricultural related labor, horses are still the preferred means of work in certain places. A common reason for this is the type of land or soil present. Some terrains can easily be destroyed by the use of machines or vehicles; to preserve such natural reserves, animals are used.

Also, in cases where the land is too rough for vehicles to pass through, horses or other farm animals are employed. Last, specific agricultural practices like cultivating and logging are best carried out by horses or other working animals to prevent loss of natural habitat through the use of fossil fuels.

Historically, farm animals have been in use for centuries. Long before any technological advancement was made in agriculture, animals were used in carrying out farm labor. Due to the hard labor required on the farmlands, a specific horse breed was desired for this cause. While the lighter and spirited horses were suitable for riding, the bulkier and patient ones were preferred by farmers to be used on ranches and farmlands. These horses are called *draft horses*. Plowing and transportation of heavy loads are some tasks of a draft horse.

Raising and caring for draft horses differs somewhat from raising a horse for leisure. Because they are work animals, your main focus will be on grooming them to work efficiently. Shoeing and feeding are essential and costly because, as opposed to riding horses, draft horses require their shoes for labor. Draft horses have a slower rate of metabolism in comparison with riding horses but need a large amount of food due to their bulky size.

### Fertilizer

Here is a fascinating fact about horses you probably did not know. The average horse eats 2 percent of its bodyweight and excretes about 50 pounds of wet manure between 4 to 13 times daily. Add that all up, and in a year, you will have about 9.1 tons of manure. However, the waste product of your horse does not necessarily have to *go to waste*.

Horse feces contain a lot of nutrients beneficial for plant growth. As a horse owner, you need not worry much about buying fertilizer for your grass. Your horse is a convenient source of fertilizer! Horses are herbivores, and so their manure contains necessary nutrients and organic matter that plants require for growth. It is an economical way of getting fertilizers for plants, and you can also produce enough to sell.

Composting the manure helps to keep the nutrients in and gets rid of bacteria or weed seed present. Compositing the manure simply means allowing it to sit for a while before use, which ensures the proper breakdown of the organic matter present in it.

Horse manure comprises nitrogen, phosphorus, and potassium, with nitrogen produced in the highest amount. Although these nutrients are extremely beneficial for soil and crop production, if not properly managed, they can also have adverse effects on the environment.

As a horse owner, you will need to acquaint yourself with your state regulations guiding proper management of horse manure to ensure its optimal use and reduce pollution. The best way to do this is by having a plan for horse manure management. Consider the number of horses you have per acre of land, the estimated amount of manure produced yearly, and the means of manure storage or removal.

# Horses for Entertainment and Ceremonial Uses

Horses are also used for entertainment, in the form of shows and to portray historical or past events. These are regal and handsome creatures whose gracefulness is unparalleled with any other animal, with a majestic appearance that makes them very suitable for royal or official ceremonies and functions.

A horse-drawn carriage and riding horses are especially useful for these occasions. Weddings, inaugurations, and tourist attractions make up some functions you will find horses being used in present-day society. In some other cultures, horses are usually the main events at parades and festivals. Circuses and theater shows also make use of horses in some of their performances. These horses are often trained to perform various tricks solely for entertainment.

Films and literature set in historic or medieval times often make use of horses while trying to re-enact the way people lived in bygone days. Horses were the most common means of transportation for many centuries, and so their presence in historical films are pivotal. Unsurprisingly, warfare has also witnessed the uniqueness of the horse from other animals. Like other human activities the horse has participated in, it played a huge role at war fronts, transporting both goods and men and even engaging in the bitter rivalry and bloodshed.

# Horses As Companions and Pets

Of the different roles that horses play in man's life, being a companion is one of the most revered positions. When you ride a horse frequently, over time, as you get used to each other, there is a high tendency of becoming attached to the horse and forming a bond. Most often, this bond is based on trust. The horse is an intelligent animal with a mind of its own, so for you to train, control, and ride it, mutual trust is required on both sides.

Coupled with this is the emotional quality horses possess. If you spend time petting and being around your horse, it can improve your emotional health and be a stress-reliever. Horses have an uncanny ability to recognize emotions and empathize with you.

Horses are social animals, and so it is not uncommon to find them moving in herds, especially feral horses. If you are raising a working horse alone in a barn or stable, there is a tendency that your horse may feel lonely or isolated. As a horse owner, you can try to recreate this need for a social structure by rearing what is commonly known as companion horses. Companion horses do not necessarily need to be ridden as they mainly provide company and succor to the working horse. The companion horse also doubles as a pet.

# Horses For Leisure and Sport

There are many leisure and sporting activities within which horses play primary and pivotal roles. Equestrian activities are fairly common today and serve as a major reason to raise horses. There are different equestrian sporting activities, each with its specific breed of horses. Some of the competitive equestrian sports include events, horse racing, dressage, rodeo, polo, reining, tent pegging, and many more. These sports are very different and require a varying number of technical and specialized skills for each one, so different breeds of horses are used in different sports.

You might be surprised to know that most of the horse breeds today came about because of well-ordered specific breeding. To raise a sports horse, there are so many breeds to select from. As you read further in the book, you will get to know more about the different horse breeds.

There are also non-competitive sports that you can train your horse to participate in and if you are not a sports person, simply riding your horse in the open field or ranch is adventurous and exhilarating.

# Important Considerations Before Purchasing a Horse

People raise horses for one or more of the reasons listed above, but whatever your reason might be, you will need to consider important factors before purchasing a horse. A horse is a big investment you most likely cannot return, so it is wise that you carefully weigh your options before making a selection.

**1. Cost:** Taking care of horses is quite a responsibility. Before you buy a horse, you need to consider the total costs required to raise it – and not just the initial purchase cost. The average horse has a lifespan of about 20 to 30 years, and so you will be taking care of the horse for a long time. Feeding, shelter, health care, riding equipment, hoof care, tack and supplies, training and riding lessons, emergency expenses, and many more make up the long-term cost you will need to spend to care for and raise a horse.

**2. Commitment:** As previously stated, horses are a great responsibility, and so raising one will require care and attention. Be ready to commit enough time to care for the horse. Riding, grooming, feeding, and training your horse is part of your duties as a horse owner, and they need to be done often. You should not leave your horse without attention for more than a day, as they require frequent exercise.

**3. Shelter:** Depending on how many horses you plan on buying (and their purpose), you will need to provide suitable shelter for it. Housing your horse on your own land gives you the advantage of easy access to feeding and daily grooming, but the daily maintenance of horse care is a daunting task that comes with this choice. Local stables offer boarding facilities to horse owners that assist in horse care and offer other amenities. There is also the added advantage of meeting other horse owners at the stable. Consider which option works best for you before buying the horse.

**4. The Horse:** Horses come in various breeds, sizes, ages, pedigree, and levels of training, and each feature should be considered e before making your purchase. The purpose you want to use your horse will help you narrow down your options. For riding horses, you will need to be more specific as there are various riding styles suitable for different breeds. Preferably, purchase a horse that has a significant level of training, unless you plan on doing that yourself. Horses have different personalities, so select a horse that suits your temperamental preference.

Once you can select the horse most suitable to your liking, the next thing to do is to ensure a thorough and complete health examination is carried out by a certified veterinarian. The veterinarian should be well acquainted with the specific breed and designated purpose. This examination is very important as you will be provided with an in-depth knowledge of the horse's medical history. Such information will aid you in making your final decision.

Raising a horse is a rewarding yet challenging task. As a horse owner, you have a lot of responsibility to ensure you groom and care for your horse properly. Horses may be huge and stubborn sometimes, but they still need a confident, tender-yet-assertive owner to direct and take care of them. This book is focused on making you that kind of owner.

# Chapter Two: Selecting The Right Breed

There are about 400 horse breeds known to man, each one with its own uniqueness and specializations. Equestrian competitions capitalize on these differences and can thus engage in a variety of sporting activities. As a horse owner, you must know the differences between breeds and their specializations. In this chapter, we will describe some of the most popular horse breeds, their qualities, and their usage.

### Arabian

With its unique arched shaped neck and high graceful tail carriage, you can easily identify the Arabian horse anywhere. It originated from Arab and is one of the oldest breeds whose lineage dates to over 4,000 years ago. It is versatile, has strong stamina, and is popularly known for its endurance riding.

The Arabian has a height of 14 hands to 16 hands, (56 inches - 64 inches), and a light bodyweight of 800 - 100 pounds. Arabians are also known for their amicable temperament, which makes them quick to learn and easily attached to humans. They are widely used in many equestrian activities like horse racing, dressage, showjumping, endurance riding, and many more. They are ideal for leisure riding and can be found on ranches, when not in sports competitions.

### Thoroughbred

Have you noticed a very popular fast and specific breed used in various equestrian competitions? It is very likely to be a fierce and agile Thoroughbred. Thoroughbred horses come from a lineage of likewise agile and swift stallions like the Arabian and the Turkoman. It is considered a part of the "hot-blooded" breed of horses because of its strength, agility, and speed. They mostly come in dark or gray colors and have a height range of about 15.2 hands (62 inches) to 17.0 hands (68 inches).

Some easily recognizable features of the Thoroughbred include a well-chiseled head, long neck, deep chest, short back, lean body, and long legs. The Thoroughbred is a very spirited and athletic horse, which makes it a perfect fit for various equestrian sports competitions. It is also commonly used to bred horses for other riding sports like polo, dressage, showjumping, and others.

### Appaloosa

Best known for its spotted and brightly colored body, the Appaloosa is a very popular breed in North America with a unique heritage. Originally domesticated by the Nez-Perce natives, it was used in hunting and as a war animal. Its distinct spots and color resulted from different cross breeds over the centuries. Uneven skin color, striped hooves, and visible white sclera in the eyes are traits that identify an Appaloosa.

There are various body types attributed to an Appaloosa breed because of the different other breeds that make up its lineage. Still, the average size is usually between 950 – 1250 pounds and 14 hands (56 inches) to 15 hands (60 inches) in height. It is commonly used as a stock horse for controlling cattle on the ranch, and it also features in various western riding competitions. Leisure riding, trail riding, and middle distance are a few other uses this versatile and intelligent horse is great for.

### Morgan

The Morgan Horse is a fine and peculiar horse with a regal carriage that makes it befitting for various ceremonial functions and as coach horses. It was named after its first owner, Justin Morgan, and has been used for breeding other horses. You can recognize a Morgan horse with its confident gait, refined and muscular build, strong hindquarters, and high tail carriage. Morgan breeds are very strong and have a standard height of 14.1 hands (57 inches) to 15.2 hands (62 inches). The Morgan is commonly used for both English and Western riding sport, leisure riding, and also in equestrian sports competitions. It is renowned for its distinct personality, quiet disposition, intelligence, and boldness.

### American Quarter Horse

The quarter horse is one of the most popular horse breeds in America. It was bred from the Thoroughbred horse and is very versatile. You may recognize it at rodeos or racehorse shows by its ability to move swiftly across short distances. It has a short but refined head, sturdy body structure, and rounded hindquarters. The height of a typical Quarter horse ranges from 14 hands (56 inches) to 16 hands (64 inches). It is best known on the sports field as a sprinter, outrunning other breeds in races of a quarter-mile distance or less. It is also commonly used as a ranch horse, and its petite body makes it very suitable for technical and skillful activities like barrel racing, calf roping, and other western riding competitions.

### Standardbred

A Standardbred horse is a versatile North American horse breed whose prowess is evident in horse harnessing and several other equestrian disciplines. Like other horse breeds, it comes from a lineage of other stallion breeds, notably the thoroughbred and Morgan, among others. It is agile, swift, and has a muscular, strong build slightly heavier than the thoroughbred.

Standardbreds have an average height of 14 hands (56 inches) to 17 hands (68 inches) and weigh between 800 to 1000 pounds. You will find them easily in harness racing competitions as they are the fastest trotting horse breed known to man. Other uses of the Standardbred include leisure riding, horse shows, ranch horses, and, most important, they are used for breeding other horses.

### Percheron

The Percheron is a French horse that belongs to a popular breed of horses known as draft breeds. They are peculiar for their rugged and sturdy build. They have served as war horses, stagecoaches, and farm animals because of their great strength and muscular bulk. You can easily tell a Percheron horse out by its bulky and muscular legs, broad chest, huge size, and docile personality. They are commonly called "cold-blooded" because of their calm disposition.

The height and weight of the Percheron differ for various countries, and they are widely used as workhorses. They are used at parades, for agricultural purposes, to pull heavy loads and are crossbred with other lighter horses to improve stamina and produce medium-sized horses for other purposes.

### Welsh Ponies

Most people know what a pony is, at least by their description. Ponies are miniature horses. They are a class of horse breeds with a height that is not over 14.2 hands (58 inches) at maturity. They are thus shorter than the average horse and preferably the best option for children riders. They have their origin from Wales with the Arabian and Thoroughbred horses as part of their lineage.

They come in four types distinguished by their height, the shortest being about 11 hands (44 inches) and 16 hands (64 inches) being the tallest. Their strong and easy gait movements often characterize them. Welsh ponies are highly intelligent animals with great speed and endurance. They are used for many purposes, namely as work animals, for leisure riding, and in equestrian sports competition. They are especially good at dressage, endurance racing, and driving.

### Tennessee Walking Horse

Also known as the *Tennessee Walker*, this unique horse breed belongs to a class of horse breeds commonly known as gaited breeds. The gaited breed is a distinct class of horses bred for their ability to go at an easy pace with a four-beat rhythm. Their sauntered gait makes them ideal for older riders or just anyone looking for a smooth ride.

The Tennessee Walker is an elegant and sturdy animal with an average height of 14.3 hands (59 inches) to 17 hands (68 inches) and a weight of about 900 to 1200 pounds. They are most popular for their calm nature and running-walk ability. They are commonly used in horse shows, trail riding events, and for pleasure riding.

### Hanoverian

The Hanoverian horse falls into the category of "warm-blooded" horse breeds. They are usually developed by breeding a "hot-blooded" type with a "cold-blooded" stallion. The Hanoverian is a special warmblood that originated from Germany. It was refined with Thoroughbred blood to make it more agile and athletic. The result turned out to be utterly successful.

Elegant, strong, and athletic, the Hanoverian breed is a versatile, spirited horse with a pleasant ambiance. It was formerly used in the military and as a coach horse. Today, it is one of the most popular and widely used sport horses as it holds medals in all equestrian Olympic sports. The average height of a Hanoverian breed is between 15.3 hands (63 inches) to 17.2 hands (70 inches). It is used mainly as a sports animal but can also be ridden for pleasure.

### Mustang

Mustangs are breeds of horses you will mostly find in the wild. They are free-roaming horses originally brought to North America by the Spanish. You can effortlessly recognize them by the short but sturdy frame, wide head, and small muzzle. The typical Mustang has a height of about 14 hands (56 inches) to 15 hands (60 inches). They are best known for their endurance, strength, and surefootedness. They are used in horse race competitions, trail riding, pleasure riding, and also as farm animals.

### American Paint Horse

One of the first things you will notice about the American Paint Horse is its rich and colorful coat. Every paint horse has a unique color of white and another equine color. Its lineage can be traced back to the Thoroughbred and Quarter horse breed.

A typical American Paint Horse has an average height of 14 to 16 hands (56 inches to 64 inches) and a weight of about 950 to 1,200 pounds. Some of its other distinctive features include a muscular body, a low center of gravity that allows easy maneuvering, and strong hindquarters for swift movement. It is frequently used in western equestrian competitions like show jumping and reining.

### Haflinger

If you see a group of somewhat short horses all chestnut in color, they probably are the Haflinger horse breed. Originally from Austria, the history of the Haflinger can be traced back to the middle ages. They are strongly built, elegant, and have a beautiful flaxen mare.

The average height for the Haflinger is 13.2 to 15 hands (54 to 60 inches, respectively), and it mainly exists in chestnut color. It has a smooth, rhythmic gait that allows it to provide an energetic yet soothing ride.

It is suitable for under saddle activities and can also be used as a draft or packhorse. Some of the equestrian competitions you will find a Haflinger engaged in include show jumping, vaulting, dressage, endurance, and trail riding. It is also suitable for therapeutic and leisure riding.

### American Saddlebred

Another member of the gaited breed, the American Saddlebred Horse, is a brilliant horse breed that originated from the United States. Its lineage can be traced back to riding horses of ambling gaits in the British Isles. It has the Morgan and Thoroughbred blood as part of its ancestry. The Saddlebred is characterized by the regal carriage of its muscular and lean frame.

A very beautiful and lively horse, the typical Saddlebred has an average height of 15 to 17 hands (60 to 68 inches, respectively). Gentle and elegant, you can clearly spot a Saddlebred by its superior movement and smooth gait. It is best used as a show horse but also features in other equestrian competitions such as combined driving, dressage, and saddle seat riding.

### Hackney Horse

The Hackney horse breed has its roots in Britain and was developed to be a riding horse with a perfect trot. It has strong stamina and an attractive frame. It is popularly used as a carriage horse due to its stylish and superior movement.

The height of a typical Hackney horse is between 14. 2 to 16.2 hands (58 inches to 64 inches respectively), and they weigh about 1000 pounds. Its high-speed trot and elegant appearance usually characterize it.

You can differentiate a Hackney horse from other similar breeds by its well-defined features, attentive ears, eyes, and a naturally high tail carriage. It is mostly used as a carriage horse and in competitive sports, can be found in harness racing and driving events. Its powerful hindquarters help provide a comfortable and rhythmic stride that allows for pleasure and therapeutic riding.

# Selecting The Right Horse Breed

Horses are emotional and intelligent creatures with a personality and mind of their own. When selecting a horse, you need to consider your preferences alongside the horse's temperament and disposition. The purpose for which you want to raise the horse, your level of expertise and your riding experience should all be considered.

If you are a beginner just starting out with horses, you will need a patient and willing horse; one that is intelligent, learns easily, and has a pleasant ambiance. The American Quarter Horse, Tennessee Walking Horse, Shire Horse, and Morgan all fall into this category. Ponies also make great beginner horses for children or those under 5.5 ft.

Cold-blooded horse breeds are calm, approachable, and friendly. They are often very huge and lack the excitement you will normally find among sports horses. Their gentle disposition makes them ideal for farm work and labor. Examples of cold-blooded breeds include coldblooded trotter, Percheron, Belgian Draft, and Clydesdale.

Warm-blooded horse breeds are versatile and vivacious animals. They are a combination of cold-blooded and hot-blooded breeds, with the friendly and approachable ambiance of cold-bloods and the strength and agility of hot-bloods. You can train and use them for sports competitions with little difficulty. The American Quarter Horse, Appaloosa, Tennessee Walker, Mustang, and Cleveland bay are examples of warmbloods.

If you are looking for energetic and fast-paced horses, go for hot-blooded breeds. They are frequently used as sports horses because of the high level of energy and agility they possess. They are hard to control, highly temperamental, and are more suited for experienced owners. Examples of hot-bloods include Arabian, Thoroughbred, and Morgan. They are often used in systematic breeding to produce other horse breeds with specific features.

You can check out the Hanoverian, American Saddlebred, Paint horse, Arabian and Morgan, if you are looking for horse breeds with poise and elegance. These breeds have a muscular and well-defined frame, have a majestic carriage, and are ideal for pleasure riding.

# Chapter Three: Bringing Your Horse Home

Having completed the first stage of selecting and purchasing your dream horse, it is time to begin your role as a horse owner. Understandably you will be feeling nervous and excited about the prospect, so the best way to deal with those nerves is by proper planning. In this chapter, you will learn about the necessary tasks involved in bringing your horse home and what to do once it arrives. Remember, your horse is moving into new and unfamiliar surroundings, so you need to ensure it feels safe and comfortable.

## What to do before your Horse comes Home

Before your horse arrives, prepare a form of shelter for it. You can use either house the horse on your property if you have enough land or in a local stable nearby. If you have the stable on your property, you will need to clean and inspect it before the horse arrives. The fence, stall walls, and gates should be in good condition and free of any hazardous item. The stall should not be too tight or cornered so as not to make your horse feel trapped. It is a new environment, and it is important to lessen the anxiety of your horse. Make repairs where necessary and ensure the fences are visible and of adequate height for the horse, especially if it is an outdoor enclosure. Your horse can try to jump over the fence, so you need to take all precautions. The stall door should be strong and sturdy enough to hold the horse in. If you plan on boarding your horse at a local stable, make proper inquiries to ensure your horse will be kept safe and comfortable.

**Ready Stable Checklist**

✔ Select appropriate shelter

✔ Clean and inspect stable

✔ Make necessary repairs

✔ Purchase Necessary Equipment

The phrase "*necessary equipment*" varies based on your purpose of raising the horse, but there are essential items every horse owner must-have.

●Feed and water basin.

●Lead rope and head collar

●Saddle, bridle, and bit.

●Splint and tendon boots.

●Horse grooming kit. This should include a curry comb, water, and body brush, mane comb, hoof brush, sponge, hoof oil, fly repellent, and sweat scraper. You can put them all in a single box to ease convenience.

●First aid kit. In case of any injury or emergency, be ready to attend to your horse before the veterinarian arrives. Your first aid kit should contain bandages, cotton wool, tweezers, wound cleanser, scissors, antibiotic spray, thermometer, and veterinarian emergency numbers.

**Vaccinations**

Before bringing your horse home, make sure a certified veterinarian thoroughly examines it, preferably one familiar with the breed. There are different vaccinations available for horses to help them maintain good health. As a horse owner, you must ensure the protection of your horse by keeping it up to date with vaccines, even before it arrives at your home. Horses, if not well cared for, can fall ill due to infections or diseases. Your horse will rely on you to keep it in good shape.

### Update Vaccine Checklist

✔ Find out the necessary information on horse vaccination.

✔ Get your horse thoroughly examined.

✔ Get your horse vaccinated.

### Feeding

If your horse has a previous owner, it will be wise to get all the information about your new horse from him/her. Discover what kind of feed your horse prefers and how much hay and feed it consumes daily. Purchase the hay and feed for your horse before you bring it home. If you have a particular feed you want your horse to eat, do not force it on your horse. Instead, gradually introduce the feed, and with the time, you will win him over.

Water is essential to horses of all breeds. The average horse consumes about seven gallons of water each day. It is, therefore, imperative you provide access to fresh and clean water for your horse. Because your horse is new to your environment, there is a tendency for it to react negatively to drinking foreign water. One way to combat is by using the same or a similar basin that your horse is familiar with. If your barn or stable has an automated water system, your new horse might be unfamiliar with it, and can take a while to figure it out. During that period, you will need to provide clean water in a means that your horse is familiar with, such as a basin or tub.

### Feeding Checklist

✔ Ask the previous owner for feed preference.

✔ Buy enough hay and feed.

✔ Provide access to fresh water.

✔ Put fresh water in a familiar basin for the horse.

# Transporting the Horse

So, you have gotten the stable set up, purchased the equipment, vaccinated your horse, and bought essential food items. Now, it is time to bring the horse home. Depending on the distance between your horse's location and your home, you can transport your horse via land or air. Whichever means of transportation you use, try to take the shortest route possible to make the journey less strenuous. The best way to transport your horse on land is by using a horse trailer. You can always rent one if you don't have one of your own. Employing the services of a professional horse moving company will help reduce the stress on your horse during the travel.

Check the trailer before the travel day to make sure it is in good condition and comfortable for your horse. The size of the trailer should be big enough for your horse to lower its head, and the floor should be non-slip. Stop the vehicle at intervals for the horse to feed and rest if it is a long distance. For safety and to also aid you in loading the horse, make use of a lead rope or halter to tie the horse, but not too tight, so it does not get uncomfortable. Hauling a horse in a transport vehicle can be really stressful as horses are wary of confined spaces. To avoid such, train your horse to climb in and out of the trailer before the traveling day.

**Transportation Checklist**

✔ Research the best mode to bring the horse home.

✔ Hire a professional horse moving services.

✔ Inspect the transportation vehicle.

✔ Plan the trip taking the shortest route possible.

✔ Carry enough water and feed for the horse.

✔ Get travel boots for your horse.

✔ Train the horse to load in and out of the trailer before moving day.

# Settling The Horse in its New Home

After a long trip (or maybe a short one), you have finally arrived at your destination-home, with your horse. The first few days and weeks of your horse's arrival is important in helping it adjust to its new home and getting familiar with you. Here are important steps that can help you settle your horse in its new home.

**Step 1**: Getting your horse out of the trailer can be a daunting task as the horse is bound to be nervous and reluctant. If you have trained your horse on how to load and offload a trailer, it might not be as hard. Preferably - and especially if this is your first horse - have an experienced person around to guide and assist you.

**Step 2**: Gently and patiently guide your horse to the barn and remove his traveling boots. Provide clean water and hay in his stall. If you have other horses, position your new horse so that he can see the other horses.

If you will be placing your new horse in a pasture with a padlock, consider walking him around the fence, so he becomes accustomed to the boundary and knows where to find feed and water.

**Step 3**: When you want to turn out your horse for the first time, protect him with boots, so he doesn't hurt himself or get hurt by other horses. Keep your horse in a closed stall or pasture, facing other horses. This will help him interact with the other horses.

Leave your new horse in his stall for the first few days. This will help him relax and feel safe. Ensure he is feeding and drinking water properly. Check his temperature regularly and if you have any worries, consult a veterinarian. Since he is not exercising, you can reduce his feed to avoid him having colic.

**Step 4**: While he is in his stall, you can get more familiar with him by grooming and spending time with him. After a few days, you can take your new horse out for a walk around the grounds. Use a rope and bridle to lead him. Allow him to explore his new environment while keeping an eye on him.

If you have more than two other horses, it is advisable not to introduce your new horse to the whole herd all at once. Rather, as the weeks go by, introduce to them one after the other. Keep him away from the others but not totally isolated, as horses are social creatures and need company too.

**Step 5**: Once you are certain your new horse has spent considerable time with you and is more familiar with the grounds and other horses, you can consider letting him out with the whole herd. Before doing so, make sure there is enough pasture for all horses to graze comfortably. If the pasture is too small, there is likely to be a fight for space and grass among the horses – you don't want that! The general rule of thumb is to have one acre of land pasture per horse.

**Step 6**: When you decide to let your new horse out with the whole herd, you will need to be around and watch carefully, so there are no brawls or injuries sustained. There is no need to rush with the introductions. Observe your new horse for any signs of stress or mistreatment by the older horses.

Spend time with the new horse by grooming and getting more acquainted with what he likes.

**Step 7**: Riding your new horse for the first time is usually a thrilling experience for any horse owner. Before you start riding, your horse should already feel comfortable with you and the environment. Do not force it but be slow and gentle with the horse.

This is still part of the process of getting to know your horse and vice versa for him. Ride just a short distance for the first few times, doing your best to keep it simple. In time, you will both get used to each other.

**Step 8**: Owning a horse creates an avenue to make new friends - fellow horse owners! Get to meet other horse owners, trade stories, and get tips and insights on how best to care for your horse. Borrow from the experience of seasoned horse riders in training and keep your horse safe.

You can learn a lot by listening to other people's stories and experiences.

**Step 9**: Most important, keep in touch with your horse's previous owner or seller. Let the person know improvements the horse is making and ask questions when unsure of certain behavioral traits.

Keep a close eye on the health of your horse and consult a veterinarian when necessary.

# Chapter Four: Horse Handling And Bonding

Before going further, it is paramount that you understand the mindset and behavioral patterns of the horse to improve and develop your relationship with it. As it was stated earlier in the book, horses are highly intelligent animals with a mind of their own. When you can grasp the way a horse thinks, you can then modify its behavior and train it.

The first – and most important – thing you should know about the horse is that it is a *prey animal.* This means that its actions and thought pattern is predicated upon staying alive. Consider other prey animals you know, rabbits, sheep, and so on; they all possess a common instinct to survive, and this is often seen in their behavior and reaction to what they consider as threats.

The horse, like these animals, understands that to stay alive, it has to be vigilant and watchful of perceived threat or danger. This is why you can find your horse becoming anxious at seemingly unimportant things like walking through a small pool of water, climbing into a trailer, being in a novel situation, or hearing unexpected sounds in the environment. Their first instinct is to flee to protect themselves. This is an example of the self-preservation skills they have acquired over the years.

To the horse, the human is a predator, unless proven otherwise. Predators, unlike prey, are less focused on surviving and more on achieving their goal. The prey (the horse), on the other hand, just wants to live. He runs away, not necessarily out of fear of getting hurt but to save his life. Knowing this about your horse can help you relate better with him. Now that you know how the typical horse sees you, your aim should be to gain his trust by building a relationship with him. This is usually the first step towards training your horse.

Horses are social animals who live in packs and have a hierarchical structure. This structure is pivotal because it allows for a dominant and reliable leader who makes the horse feel safe. They all respect the leader because he provides food, guidance, and safety for all. He eats and drinks first, while the others wait, and he exerts his dominance assertively by claiming his space. The other horses understand this assertion and submit them to the authority. If you have more than one horse, you can take time out to study your herd and try to identify the dominant one.

You need to know that horses naturally desire leadership, whether they are alone or in a herd. As a horse owner, you must provide such leadership, or the horse will take the reins. The bedrock of a successful horse-human relationship begins with you taking the lead. When the horse sees you as a reliable leader, it respects your authority and follows your direction, just like the social hierarchy of the herds. Asserting dominance is how you become the leader of the herd. This assertion is not done with violence but calmly and firmly. This is most often done by either inhibiting or allowing movement. For instance, if your horse wants to move in a certain direction, you can stop his movement by applying pressure using his reins and releasing it when he does your bidding. It must be you who controls its movement and not the other way around.

The more dominance you exert, the more willing your horse will be to follow your leadership. When your horse is willing to follow you, training it for any purpose will not be difficult. Your horse must see you as a confident and consistent leader. Take charge when situations arise and give direction to your horse. Horses have two major needs; safety and comfort. Lack of comfort for the horse can range from mild things like a piece of moving plastic to dangerous situations like a predator threat; both are equally terrifying for him. He does not feel safe and will seek to get rid of the discomfort. But when there is a clearly defined leader, the horse feels safe and secured. As a horse owner, aim for making your horse feel safe.

# Safe Handling of Horses

Safe handling of horses refers to guidelines and rules. Every horse owner has to know, for his/her own safety and the safety of the horse. The horse is physically stronger than a human, so it is very important to take safety measures while tending to him. Like it was stated earlier, horses are prey animals whose first instinct to an unfamiliar stimulus (puddle, enclosed space, unexpected noise) or discomfort is to defend themselves and flee. Therefore, they should be handled calmly and gently. These safety guidelines help a horse owner attend to his/her horse in the best way possible so as not to get hurt by the horse. They might seem like a lot initially for the beginner horse owner, but not to worry; you will quickly get used to them with time.

1. Always approach the horse from a visible point, preferably the front, so he is not caught unaware of your presence. Avoid touching or patting him from behind as this can easily startle or scare him, causing him to react aggressively.

2. Wear strong and protective footwear while attending to your horse to avoid getting hurt if he steps on you. Causal, open, or thin shoes should not be worn in the barn, stable, or around your horse.

3. When cleaning your horse's stall, grooming, or preparing for a ride, keep your horse tied up. It is dangerous to let him freely roam the barn.

4. Horses are much different from dogs or other pets that can be fed with your hands. They can mistake your hands for food and bite you, along with whatever you are feeding them. To feed your horse treats, do it from a bucket.

5. You should never stand directly behind a horse. It has powerful hindquarters that can knock you out with a single kick. To clean his tail, stand at one side, and carefully pull the tail to you.

6. If you are cleaning the hooves of your horse or you want to put bandages on, do not kneel or squat; bend low instead. If the horse makes any movement, you can quickly get out of harm's way.

7. Tie your horse with simple and easy to remove knots like the quick release knot so that if your horse feels uncomfortable or threatened, it can quickly break free. Hard or complicated knots can make you feel constrained, and he might react negatively.

8. Use a lead rope and halter to safe lead and direct your horse. Do not place your hands or fingers through any of the tack equipment as you can easily get injured by sudden movements of the horse.

9. Do not stand beside your horse unseen. Always make sure your horse sees and knows who you are while grooming or just talk with him.

10. Do not clean out the stall of your horse while your horse is inside. Put him in another stall or take him to pasture.

11. Understand your horse's body language while interacting with him. Horses communicate with their eyes, ears, and tails. Continuous movement of their ears signals nervousness, while flat ears indicate annoyance or anger, which can lead to an attack. If his ears are relaxed, he is relaxed also.

12. Horses learn a lot from their owner's overt and covert behavior. They are good judges of mood and can detect fear and anxiety. While handling your horse, you must be confident and bold.

13. Do not tie the lead rope or reins around your hands or body part. It can be disastrous if the horse moves suddenly without direction. Never tie yourself in any way to a horse.

14. Stall and barn doors should be wide enough for your horse to pass through without feeling crowded or tight. If you have to pass through a narrow door with your horse, lead the way by going in first, then stand at one side and allow him to come in.

# Bonding with Horses

Horses make excellent companions. They are emotional, therapeutic, and easy to talk to. While this easy camaraderie seems enchanting, it does not come with little effort. For a horse owner, bonding with your horse begins with a mutual trust from both sides. Your horse has to learn to trust you to keep him safe and comfortable. You, the horse owner, have to handle your horse in a gentle, caring, and sincere manner.

If you are a beginner with horses and you are wondering why you do not seem to bond with your horse, maybe you are not doing things correctly. While interacting and spending time with your horse, there are tips and tricks you can employ to aid foster the relationship between both of you. These tips, when implemented, help you and your horse develop a close and long-lasting relationship.

### Be a Firm, Open-Minded, and Assertive Leader

The importance of you being a leader to your horse has been explained earlier, so it should not come as a surprise to you how pivotal this is. Being a firm and assertive leader makes your horse respect your authority and dominance. He will treat you like the head of the herd and follow your lead. Notwithstanding, be open-minded and fair. Treat your horse right by using consistent cues he can understand and follow. Horses are not logical thinkers, so don't have unrealistic expectations from them. Horses have a good memory and can tell when they are not being treated right. They can become resistant and stubborn in such cases. It is best to begin your relationship on a good foot.

### Spend Quality Time with Them

Your relationship with your horse should go beyond work or training hours. To develop a bond with your horse, you need to show him you are interested in him and not just the work he can do. Visit him in the stable often and take him out for walks to serene environments. Horses relax and spend time together when they are out grazing. You can also reenact this practice by sitting out in the pasture with him while he grazes leisurely beside you. This is similar to two friends chilling together. Match your pace with his, and don't be afraid to talk to him. Let him hear your voice often so he can get used to hearing you and can recognize you. Exercises like this reduce tension between you and are also beneficial health-wise for you both.

### Engage in Routine Training

Horses are adventurous creatures who enjoy challenges. Engaging in rigorous and routine training with them helps you develop the bonding process. You need to be careful not to overwork or drain your horses with too much training. Take breaks when necessary and be watchful of the health of your horse. On some other days, you can simply do groundwork maneuvers with your horse. It is necessary to have a balanced training routine, and sometimes, you can add a new activity to challenge your horse.

### Groom your Horse Regularly

Grooming is an important way to bond with your horse. Horses in the wild also engage in a similar practice; they groom each other. This is, of course, not done with brushes but by nuzzling their necks against each other. This is a show of affection, and more importantly, they help each scratch those spots they otherwise can't reach on their own. So, when you groom your horse, you are not only keeping it clean, but you are also scratching parts of his body he will not have been able to reach on his own. Horses have "sweet spots," and regular grooming helps you discover them. Some horses like to scratch while others prefer a gentle touch. Discovering your horse's preference comes in handy when you want to appreciate your horse or help it feel less anxious.

### Massage with your Hand

If you have been to a spa or massage, then you know how relaxing massages can be. A good idea for relaxing your horse is by using your hands to softly massage him, preferably in one of the sweet spots you recently discovered. Equine massages are very beneficial and therapeutic for horses, especially when they are feeling nervous or agitated. This also helps to develop a stronger bond because, in time, your horse will associate positive feelings with you. He will look forward to your arrival because your horse knows that when he is with you, he will feel good and relaxed.

### Understand the Physical Cues of your Horse

Horse, like humans, engage in non-verbal communication. Since they cannot talk, they express feelings and emotions with non-verbal cues. Often, your horse communicates with you this way, and so as a horse owner, you need to read your horse's body language to know what he is trying to tell you. Their ears, eyes, and tails indicate when the animal is tensed or frightened, happy or relaxed, tired, or ill. There are also times when your horse wants to play, and that is frequently expressed in body language. The more time you spend with your horse, the easier it gets for you to read his body language and attend to his needs.

### Explore and Experience Things Together

Sharing an experience with someone has a way of bringing you closer; it's the same with horses. As you explore with your horse, riding or competing, facing different challenges and triumphs, you build a close bond. So, do not fear sharing your emotions with your horse. The bond you can create with your horse can last for a long time.

### Respect your Horse's Space

Horses are social animals who thrive when they are together. If you only have one hour, you should allow your horse to mingle and meet with other horses. If you have a herd, create ample time for them to ride and explore together. This will help improve your horse's mood, disposition, and overall health. Horses only have an interest in safety (food and shelter), comfort, and companionship. When you can provide all these for your horse, he will learn to trust and depend on you.

# Chapter Five: Housing and Fencing

Before you bring your horse home, you will need to sort out is a place for it to live. Unless you intend to board your horse at a stable, you must have a stable built on your premises. Boarding is a more expensive option, although some people might find it more convenient. You will also miss the pleasure of having your horse around you. Depending on the stable service you choose, you may spend between $200 to $450 per month to keep your horse as a boarding facility. You may even spend more on extra care and training. However, you will free yourself from the stress of daily chores by choosing this option. But what's the fun in that?

If you prefer to have your horse close to you at home, then you must build horse housing and a fence around your property. You will need a lot of space for this. This project will also take some time and, of course, money. Keeping your horse at home also means it will depend on you for daily care, and you will need extensive knowledge of horse care. Eventually, the cost of keeping your horse at home is most likely going to be cheaper than housing it in a stable. So, a house housing and fencing project is a good investment. Still, you will need to plan carefully for shelter, fencing, equipment, storage, bedding, hay, manure disposal, and management of the facility.

Generally, prepare to spend about $1100 annually on the maintenance of a mature horse on your property. This is significantly lower than the cost of boarding. You may spend more if you intend to breed, train, or compete with your horse.

# Horse Housing

Building a horse housing facility involves providing everything your horse needs to be safe and comfortable. This includes shelter from the weather and wind, a place to eat, and sleeping facilities. A horse's basic needs differ from those of humans. You have to understand this in planning for your horse housing.

Most times, these basic needs depend on what you intend to do with your horse. If you intend to go for shows, for example, then you will need a place to ride the horse built into your housing facility. But if you are keeping a horse for just casual riding or leisure, then a barn or three-sided shed may be enough.

The truth is that you can spend as much as you want to build a horse housing facility, depending on your budget. You may estimate at least $7 for every square foot of space if you are building an enclosed barn. You may spend even more depending on the bells and whistles you intend to install.

Generally, you need to build an indoor shelter, an outdoor unit, and a walking or grazing area. You will also need one or two storage rooms for food, drugs, and other equine needs. Finally, you will need to install a fence to keep your animal enclosed properly. Let's go over the process of constructing each of these in greater detail.

### Indoor Shelter

Your horse needs a place to sleep and rest (typically from 8 pm until 7 am). Generally, each horse will need as much as 16 square meters (or 170 feet) space to stay. This indoor shelter also has to have bedding facilities (usually sawdust), constant access to fresh water and hay, good ventilation, and proper cleaning and maintenance. While designs may vary slightly, this stall will generally have the main door, with an upper half, which opens like a window. This allows you to look into the stall without letting the horse out.

### Stall Sizing

The size of your stall depends largely on the size of your horse, among other factors. For a miniature horse, the stall can have a dimension of 6' x 8' per horse. For small horses and ponies that weigh less than 900 lb., a stall with a 10' x 10' dimension is good. You will, of course, need more space for larger horses. A 12' x 12' size is the industry standard. You will need a lot more for a larger draft horse (as much as 16' x 16'). For a stall intended for foaling, you will need a size twice that of a single stall.

# Types of Indoor Shelters

Horse stalls can be designed in various ways, depending on your preferences and needs. Some common indoor shelters for horses include the following.

### Tie Stalls

This is the most basic type of indoor shelter. In a standing stall, the horse is simply tied forward using a rope or chain. Sometimes, the horse may stand loose with chains across the open ends of the stall. Horses housed this way must have been trained to stand quietly. A tie-stall should be at least 10 feet long and 5 feet wide.

Horse stalls are not very comfortable as they provide very limited space for movement, although they can serve to accommodate in cases where you have limited space available. Tie stalls are less popular these days than they used to be in the past.

### Box Stalls

Another option for housing horses is an open-sided or free box stall. This provides a form of protection and shelter for your horse by also allows you to keep it in an open-air area. This type of housing is commonly used to house a group of horses that get along with each other well.

### Open Shed Stall

These are similar to box stall but designed in a row with doors that open outdoors. The doors are typically the Dutch-door type with an open top-half for ventilation. Open shed stalls work best in areas with mild-climatic conditions.

# Horse Housing Construction Materials

For all stall types, hardwood is the common material used in construction. This hardwood is commonly treated to discourage the horse from chewing the wood. While pine and other softwoods may be used, your horse is most likely going to chew through quickly.

The stall flooring may comprise a crushed rock base, which is typically covered with field lime or clay. Hard surfaces like asphalt or cement may be used for stall flooring. The flooring can also be made of sand. The latter option is less stable and durable than packed lime or clay, although it does allow better drainage and is more comfortable for the horse than harder surfaces that are slippery and hard on a horse's legs.

However, hard flooring is easier to clean than bare sand. You can use hard flooring along with sufficient bedding and some sort of mat, which helps to ease some problems associated with hard flooring options.

### Stall Ceiling and Doors

A stall should provide sufficient clearance from the floor. You need a height of at least 10 feet or even higher for good air circulation and safety. Stall doors should be at least four feet wide. *You will need larger doors for a draft horse.*

Generally, you have two options for stall doors. You can either have Dutch doors or sliding doors. If a Dutch door occurs, it should swing open into the aisle and not into the stall. Sliding doors are generally easier to maneuver, but they are generally more expensive.

You must choose between shutting your horse in or having a top window over which the horse can hang its head. Horses not shut in are generally happier, although this also carries the risk of biting passersby.

Doors can be made of a wide range of materials (commonly wood). But steel or wire mesh doors are popular in places with hot climates as this promotes better air circulation. However, the mesh may allow some of the bedding to spill out into the aisle. Generally, your stall horse stall should be well built, rugged, and secure with a "horse-proof" latch with no dangerous or protruding edges.

### Bedding

One of the final considerations for indoor housing is the bedding options. Various types of bedding materials can be used, from straw to wood shavings. Which one you go for depends on the availability of material in your area, cost, and suitability for your needs. Straw and wood shavings can be purchased from local lumber manufacturer or furniture makers around you. Other possible options for bedding include rice hulls, sawdust, peanut hulls, paper pulp, and peat moss.

The thickness of the bedding depends, to a large extent, on the flooring. For a dirt floor, be good with just 3 to 4 inches of bedding. For harder floors made with cement or asphalt, the bedding should be at least 8 to 10 inches in depth.

# Outdoor Housing

You should be good with a simple three-sided shelter with a sturdy roof. An outdoor shelter houses your horse on hot or rainy days. On average, target a size of at least 170 square feet *per horse* for your outdoor shelter.

The construction cost of an outdoor shelter is generally lower than that of indoor housing. They come in different designs, from three-sided barns to open-ended bars. It is recommended to feed your horse in your outdoor shelter rather than in the barn. This will reduce manure in the barn, and your horses are less likely to fight over food in an open area than they will in a confined space.

### The Outside Grazing/Walking Area

Part of your outdoor housing facility is a grazing or walking area. Experts recommend that you allow your horse to graze or walk around for better health and well-being. A space of at least 1,5 acre (6.000 square meters) per horse is recommended for outdoor grazing. There are no strict rules about how this should be designed. However, ensure that you remove foreign objects and rock from this area to avoid injuring your horse.

# Feed And Tack Storage

You will also need to consider storage facilities in your barn for hay, commercial feeds, drugs, and other health kits. You need a dry, shadowy room, designed so it keeps your horse feeds fresh and free from pests. The feed storage room should also be out of reach of the horses. How large this will be, and the method of storage depends on how many horses you have to feed. You will also need to plan for a space to store straw and bedding materials.

You will need a special tack room to keep valuable equipment you use on your facility safe and dust-free. You may also add in a few other features to your tack room that makes it more livable like a comfortable chair, storage cupboard, or even a small fridge. Depending on your needs and preferences, you may even go all out with some extra luxury features like a coffeemaker, washer or dryer, microwave oven, and a water heater.

# Horse Fencing

Another vital component of horse housing is the fence. In ancient times, those who owned horses were limited to stones and sticks as materials for making fences. Today, thanks to modern technology, modern fences are now made from a wide range of materials. Still, it is impossible to claim one fence type as the only perfect one. Choosing the ideal fencing material involves balancing aesthetics, cost, and safety concerns.

# Horse Fence Safety Considerations

Fencing for horses has peculiarities that cannot be ignored. While it is possible to keep pastures of cattle and other farm animals enclosed with a barbed wire fence, this cannot be done with horses.

Fencing for horses is subject to various factors, including the building code of wherever you live. However, there are still major considerations that apply to horse fencing everywhere. For instance, it is generally recommended that horse fencing should be at least 54 to 60 inches high. You may need to make it taller depending on the breed of horses or if your property is next to a highway, or anywhere else that an escape from your premises may be of major concern. Here, a minimum height of 5 feet is recommended for a field fence while at least 6 feet is recommended for stall paddocks and runs.

Experts also recommend that your fence bottom should have an opening of 8 to 12 inches. This opening should be the right dimension to prevent your horse's legs from getting trapped under the fence or foals rolling out. The opening should be wide enough to prevent the hoof from getting trapped or simply too small for the hoof to pass through.

With wire fencing, visibility is one of the major considerations. A wooden fence or one made with PVC material is easily distinguishable for a horse. But wire fences are almost invisible, and in a panic, your horse might run into the fence and risk injury. The visibility of a wire fence can be improved by adding a top rail made of other materials like PVC or wood. Wire fences also tend to be electrified, which helps to create a psychological barrier keeping horses in check.

No matter the type of material used and how it is constructed, present a smooth side of the material to the horse. Also, boards and other fencing materials should be mounted inside and not outside the fence posts, as this makes it more difficult for the horse to knock them loose. Also consider the angle of the fence corners, especially when you have horses that do not get along with each other. With an acute corner angle, a bullied horse is likely to get entrapped. A simple way to solve this is to make the fence corners curved or simply block the corners completely.

### Fence Posts

Perhaps the most important part of a fence is the post. This determines the integrity and strength of the fence since the gate and other parts of the fence assembly are braced against it.

### Wood Posts

Traditionally, wood is the most commonly used material for making fence posts. The choice of wood in all cases depends largely on the local availability of materials. For instance, in most parts of Western USA, softwood is the most abundant. Similarly, hardwood is more commonly used for fencing posts in the East, Midwest, and Southeast.

Some of the common softwood that may be used for fence posts include redwood, cedar, and cypress. However, they are very expensive, so most people simply go for treated fir or pinewood, which costs less and has been impregnated with chemicals that prevent rust and insect or fungi-damage.

Wooden posts are most commonly driven into the ground. This is a more reliable technique that produces stronger results than digging and back-filling. Wooden posts are commonly used combined with wire materials (like V-mesh wire, high-tensile wire, woven wire, etc.) to reduce the overall cost of the fence. Other materials like vinyl-covered wire products and PVC vinyl-and-wire planks may also be used in combination with wooden posts.

### Metal T-Posts

Horse fence posts may also be made from metal materials. These are generally cheaper and easier to install compared to wooden posts. However, metal T-Post offers little in terms of aesthetic appeal.

If you are choosing metal T-posts, make them as safe as possible for your horse. To minimize the risk of having your horse impaled by the pole, top them with plastic caps. The caps to install on your metal T-post should allow the installation of electrified mesh ribbon. This helps to increase the visibility of the fence and prevent socializing or grazing over the fence, which is a common cause of fence damage.

### Fence Barriers

The functional part of a horse fence is the barrier, and the quality of the barrier determines how sturdy your fence will be. Ultimately, no barrier is impenetrable, especially if your horse is bent on escaping. However, the goal is to create a fence barrier that is strong enough to keep your horse contained without causing harm to the animal if it charges at the fence. A fence barrier should also serve as a psychological deterrent that helps to keep the horse from escaping. Fence barriers can be made from a wide range of materials, and this includes:

**Wood board:** Wood is a much-desired material for fencing mainly because of its aesthetics, strength, and enhanced visibility. However, wood is more expensive and high maintenance since they are prone to weathering or horses chewing through them. Spooked horses may also break through wood barriers, and splinters or nails can cause injuries. If you are choosing a wood board barrier, you can expect to spend between $4 to $5 per linear foot of fencing.

**PVC board fence:** Another visually appealing option for horse fencing is a PVC board. It is just as aesthetically pleasing as wood but without the maintenance headache. But a PVC barrier is even more expensive. You can spend as much as $10 per linear foot of fencing. A PVC material (even when reinforced by internal ribbing) will still break away under pressure. Hence, they are commonly rigged with electricity to keep the animal in check within the enclosure.

**Pipe steel:** This is an exceptionally strong material for making horse fencing. However, their limitation is also in their strength. Pipe steels rarely give, which means your horse risks serious injury if it runs into this kind of fence. However, since pipe steel fences are highly visible, the risk of this happening is minimal. Pipes are generally cheaper to purchase but difficult to install. Hence labor costs may drive price high since we must hire a professional installer. Modifying this fence barrier will be difficult. Hence, they must be properly planned and installed correctly.

**High-tensile wire:** This refers to wire under tension, and it is one of the most commonly used materials for fencing barriers. There are different high-tensile wire fencing, which includes smooth wire and woven wire fencing. In these types, the wire is pulled tight against posts and corner assemblies placed intermittently along the lines of the fence to counter the pulling forces.

Hire tensile wire barriers are typically professionally installed since they require the knowledge of various professional techniques that keeps the fence braced properly. Springs and tighteners may also be installed on the fence to ensure that it maintains the right tension despite changes in temperature and stretching.

**Smooth wire:** This wired fencing is like barbed wire but without the barbs. They are the least expensive wired fencing barrier. The wires are not only cheaper, but they can also span a longer distance and thus can take wide pole spacing of up to 20 feet, which further helps to cut costs. Visibility is a major problem with this wire. To solve this problem, they are typically wrapped in PVC coating that comes in a wide range of colors. It is also recommended that they are rigged with electricity to deter horses from trying to push through or run against them.

**Woven field fence:** This is another commonly used wire fencing material that finds application in various forms of livestock management. It is inexpensive and effective for keeping horses in check while keeping unwanted wildlife out. Woven field barriers are made from cheap fabrics that have been pot welded or brazed to create a woven effect. The best types use knots at the intersection of the wires. Due to their design, they are more visible than smooth wires, and visibility can be further enhanced by having a top board installed or electrifying the fence.

**V-mesh barrier:** This is a type of wire fencing material made up of meshes of diagonal and horizontal wires woven to create a diamond or V fabric pattern. Like the woven fence, they not only keep horses in check but also lock out unwanted wildlife and predators effectively. They are thus the top choice for foaling facilities and small paddock enclosures. But they are more expensive with a cost similar to traditional wood fencing.

### Electric Fencing

Horse fencing is designed to physically deter horses from escaping and also present a form of psychological barrier that keeps them in check by making them think escaping is too difficult or impossible to achieve. While the fencing materials discussed so far help to achieve the former, an electric fence system provides the psychological deterrent effect.

Electric fencing may be combined with all types of conventional fencing materials, including wood, PVC, and wire fencing. They help to reduce the risk of damage and improve the effectiveness of your barrier. The cost of adding electric fencing to your fence barrier is about 15 cents for every linear foot of fencing.

Typically, an electric fence dispenses a high-voltage but low amperage current. This safely shocks the horse when they lean in, run into, or try to graze over the fence and serves as psychological deterrence. The system typically consists of a charger that dispenses the current, conductive wire materials, and the poles sunk into the ground that completes the circuit. The system must be properly installed and well-maintained to prevent failure in the circuit due to broken wire or poor grounding. Besides professional installation, routine inspection and damage repairs must be carried out regularly to keep the electric system in working condition.

# Chapter Six: Horse Nutrition and Feeding

Like all living things, horses eat. This is a no-brainer!!! If you're going to be a conscientious and caring horse owner, it's essential that you become familiar with is horse nutrition and feeding. To stay healthy and strong, your horse must be fed with the right supplement and hay choices needed to maintain good health.

There are several myths and differing opinions about how horses should be fed and what they should be fed with. This makes it all the more difficult to decide on the right nutrition and feeding choices. In this chapter, we will discuss all you need to know about horse nutrition and feeding from the basic nutritional requirements of horses to some of the common guidelines you must be familiar with in meeting those requirements.

## Understanding The Digestive System Of a Horse

You need to fully understand horse nutrition and feeding; this means learning about how the digestive system of a horse works. Horses differ from other farm animals and must not be treated the same way in terms of feed.

A horse is an herbivore, but they are hind-gut fermenters rather than multi-gastric non-ruminant animals. This means that they have only one stomach. Horses have a small stomach capacity (usually about 2-4 gallons for an average-sized horse). Because of this small size, the feed your horse can consume at any single time is limited. That they are non-ruminant also affects their feeding habit.

Equids are naturally grazing animals. They may spend as much as 16 hours of the day grazing on pasture grasses. Their stomach can secrete digestive enzymes like pepsin and hydrochloric acid, which breaks down the food in their stomachs. They do not regurgitate food, so overeating is not really an option for horses, and eating something poisonous can be fatal since they cannot vomit whatever they eat.

Another peculiarity about the digestive system of a horse is the absence of a gallbladder. This makes it difficult to digest and utilize foods with high fat content. They only digest about 20% of the fat in their meals, and this can take as much as 3 or 4 weeks to take place. Due to this, normal horse feed is expected only to contain a limited quantity of fat (about 3-4%).

In horses, most nutrients are absorbed in the small intestine, which can hold up to 10 to 24 gallons of food. After the protein, fat, carbohydrates, vitamin, and minerals are absorbed here, most of the liquid portion of the food will be passed on to the cecum where detoxification takes place. This is also responsible for the digestion of soluble carbohydrates and fiber.

This is a general overview of how the digestive system of a horse works. By understanding the peculiarities of these systems, it is easier to understand some of the basic nutritional requirements of horses and how to handle them properly.

# Horse Nutritional Requirements

Horses require six main classes of nutrients to survive and maintain good health. These nutrients include water, carbohydrates, fat, vitamins, proteins, and minerals. These nutrients must be combined in the right quantity and proportion for a balanced horse diet.

### Water

Water is the most vital nutrients required for a horse's survival. You must maintain a supply of clean water for your horse at all times. On average, they need up to 2 quarts of water with every pound of hay they eat. They will need even more under special conditions like high temperatures, periods of high activity, or hard work, and for lactating mares.

When horses are deprived of water, it may lead to reduced food intake and decreased physical activities. If your horse is passing dry feces or you notice dry mucous membranes in their mouth, they may be dehydrated. Keep a healthy supply of clean water and ensure that the water is palatable and accessible for your horse.

### Carbohydrates

The main source of energy in horse nutrition is carbohydrates. The basic building block of carbohydrate is glucose. Starches and sugars are broken down into glucose and absorbed in the small intestine of a horse. The non-soluble carbohydrates are passed into the large intestine, where they are fermented by microbes to release their energy constituent. Most horse feeds contain soluble carbohydrates to varying amounts. Corn is the highest source of carbohydrate or horses. Oats and barley are also great sources, and forages may contain about 8% starch.

Horses need the energy supplied by carbohydrates in order to sustain life. All of your horses' basic functional activities require a supply of energy that is most commonly supplied by soluble carbohydrates and fibers. Signs of energy deficiency in horses include weight loss, low growth rate, low physical activity, low milk production in lactating mares, and so on. Excessive consumption of high energy foods can lead to obesity and increase the risk of conditions like laminitis and colic.

### Fat

This is another vital source of energy in a horse's diet. Fat supplies up to 9 MCal of energy per kg of food. This is up to three times higher than what you get when you feed your horse carbohydrates. However, horses have a hard time digesting and absorbing fat. Therefore, only about 2 - 6% fat is contained in pre-mixed horse feeds as higher may be difficult to digest and cause problems eventually.

### Protein

This nutrient is crucial for growth and for muscle development in horses. Proteins comprise amino acids and are sourced from food like alfalfa and soybean meal, which are essential parts of a horse's diet. Protein is easily incorporated, and most adult horses need only about 8-10% of the protein in their ration. However, rowing foals and lactating mares may require more than this.

Protein deficiency in horses can lead to weight loss, reduced growth, low milk production, and rough or coarse hair coat. It can also affect the performance of your horse. Excessive consumption of protein can cause electrolyte imbalances and dehydration in horses.

### Vitamins

Vitamins are vital parts of a horse maintenance diet. They are in two main categories. The fat-soluble vitamins include vitamins K, E, D, and A. Vitamin C and B-complex are the water-soluble vitamins. Vitamins may be supplied by premixed rations or in fresh green forage. Vitamin supplements may also be given to horses directly during periods of high activity or prolonged stress or when the horses are not eating well due to sickness or any other condition.

The different vitamins can be sourced from various natural sources, especially in green and leafy forages. If your horse is kept in a stall throughout the day, it will need to be given Vitamin D supplement since this nutrient is sunlight is the main source of this nutrient. Vitamin K, B-complex, and C are produced in the horse's body but are also contained in fresh veggies and fruits. These vitamins are not essential requirements in a horse's diet except under conditions like severe stress.

### Minerals

This group of nutrients is required for the maintenance of a healthy body structure, nerve conduction, and fluid balance in the cells of the body. Most minerals like calcium, sodium, phosphorus, magnesium, chloride, and sulfur are required in small quantities daily. If your horse is being fed good quality premixed rations or a fresh green pasture, they will get all the supply of minerals they need for health and growth. However, supplementation may be required under special conditions like the restoration of electrolyte balance in horses that sweat excessively – and in young horses.

# Horse Feeding Requirements

In this section, we will discuss what to feed horses to get the needed supply of food that meets their nutritional requirement.

### Forages

This includes grasses or legumes and makes up a large proportion of a horse's diet. It is difficult to predict the exact nutritional composition of forages since this tends to vary based on the maturity of the grasses, environmental conditions, and the management of the forages. Only a detailed lab analysis can accurately determine the exact nutritional composition of forages. The various types of horse feed in this category are discussed below.

### Legumes

Legumes have a high proportion of protein in their composition. They also serve as a good supply of energy and minerals like calcium. To supply the needed nutrients, legumes need optimal growth conditions like good soil and warm weather. The most popular legumes used in feeding horses are alfalfa and clover.

### Hay

This refers to forages harvested and dried for later use in feeding horses. It can be in the form of legumes or grasses like orchard grass, bluegrass, timothy, and fescue. Legume hay contains more protein than grass, but they tend to be more expensive. Grass hays have longer leaves and stems than legumes and are most nutritious if they are cut earlier in their growth stage. Although not a sure sign of quality, appearance is one of the main indicators of good nutrition in the hay. This is why you should avoid feeding your horse moldy or dusty hay.

### Concentrates

The Association of American Feed Control Officials (AAFCO) defines concentrate feed as one used with another to improve the nutritional balance of the total feed. Typically, a concentrate is intended to be further diluted or mixed to produce a complete feed. While forages/hay is the most common natural source of nutrition for horses, specially formulated concentrates supply specific nutrients like protein, carbohydrates, and vitamins and are intended to be mixed with other feed ingredients based on the recommendation of the manufacturer.

## Grains

This makes up another category of ingredients used in feeding horses. Grains can be given alone or mixed with concentrate feed. Some of the most popular grains used in feeding horses are listed in detail below.

Oats: This is arguably the most popular gain used in feeding horses. However, oats are quite expensive. It is typically rich in fiber but has a lower digestible energy value than most of the other grains. Horses also find oats more palatable than most grains and are easily digestible for equids.

Corn: This is another popular grain used in feeding horses. It contains twice as much digestible energy value but is typically low in fiber. You should feed your horses only the right quantity of corn. It is palatable, and given it has a high energy content, it is easy to overfeed corn, which can lead to obesity. You should never feed your horse moldy corn, as this can be lethal.

Sorghum (Milo): This is high energy and low fiber grain for feeding horses. It is typically in a small hard kernel that has to be processed to make it palatable for feeding horses and for efficient digestion. Sorghum is hardly edible as a grain on its own and is most commonly mixed with other grains.

Barley: Barley has moderate energy and fiber content, and it a palatable grain for feeding horses. Like sorghum, it has to undergo some form of processing for easier digestibility.

Wheat: Although wheat is a high energy grain that horses can eat, it rarely is served as feedstuff due to its high cost. It has hard kernels as well and must be processed for easy digestion and must be mixed with other grains to make it palatable.

## Supplements

Nutritional supplements are not main feedstuffs. Instead, they are given as an addition or replacement for nutrients that may not be available in sufficient quantity in your horse's regular diet. There are various supplements for horses.

Protein Supplements: The most common protein supplement is soybean meal. It contains high-quality protein and is typically administered to supply essential amino acids. Cottonseed meal and peanut meal are other examples of protein supplements. They contain about 48% and 53%

of crude protein, respectively. Brewer's grain (a by-product of the production of beer) is another nutritious and highly palatable protein supplement. Brewer's grain is also commonly used as a fat and vitamin B supplement.

Fat Supplements: Fat supplements can also be added to horse feeds to provide an additional source of fat in horse feeds. Vegetable oil is the most commonly used fat supplement for horse feeding. Rice bran is another ingredient that has become popular in recent times as a feed supplement.

# The Rules Of Feeding Your Horse

It is not enough to know what to feed your horse; there are basic rules and considerations for horse feeding to ensure optimum results as far as the nutrition and health of your horse is concerned. Understanding these rules is crucial to your overall knowledge of horse care. Below are some of the most important things to remember when feeding your horse.

### Feed your Horse a Lot of Roughage

The bulk of your horse's daily calorie intake should be from roughage. While grain may be given as additional feed for your horse, good quality hay or pasture legumes and grass is just enough and should be the main thing you feed your horse. The digestive system of a horse is best suited for digesting roughage. Always ensure that you have a good supply of roughage available and only serve grains as supplementary feeding.

Generally, a horse will need up between 1 to 2% of its body weight in roughage per day. Grazing horses will typically feed for up to 16 hours of the day. If you keep your horse in a stall for most of the day, you can try to replicate this natural feeding pattern by having hay available in front of them for most of the day. This will maintain a supply of roughage for its digestive system.

### Feed Grain Often but in Small Amounts

As earlier explained, grain should not be the main feed for your horses. Instead, you can feed them small amounts of grains multiple times in a day. Small and frequent grain meal replicates the natural feeding pattern of horses better than giving them large quantities of grain at a time. Your horse can digest better this way, and you get much better results.

### Change Feed and Feed Schedules Gradually

If you are changing what you feed your horse, you should make such a change gradually rather than switch suddenly. Sudden changes in nutrient supply can cause conditions like founder or colic. The same applies to if you are changing how much feed you give your horse. Increase or decrease your meal food little at a time over a period of several weeks, not suddenly. A simple technique for changing your horse's feed is to replace just 25% of the current feed with the new food every two days. Watch for serious changes and adverse effects so you can make adjustments accordingly.

### Feed with an Accurate and Consistent Feed Measurement

One of the most important rules of horse feeding is to ensure that you feed your horse consistently with an accurate measure of feed. Averagely, a thousand-pound equid will need about 15 to 20 pounds of hay daily. Although hay is typically dispensed in flakes, the amount of hay in a flake can vary considerably. It all depends on the kind of hay and the size of the flakes. You should measure the portion of hay you intend to feed your horse and only feed the portion that your horse needs.

### Don't Feed your Horse Right Before or After Exercise

Horses are active animals, and they do a lot of physical activities daily. If you have plans to ride your horse, wait for an hour or more after it has finished its meal before you proceed. For even more strenuous activities, a three or four-hour wait is recommended. Also, allow your horse to cool down after work (with the breathing rate fully restored) before feeding. With a full stomach, your horse's lungs (which are essential for all rigorous physical activities) will have less room to expand, and this will make exercise a lot harder for them. Also, during rigorous activities, blood flow will be diverted away from organs in the digestive system, and this can slow down gut movement.

### Stick to a Routine

Horses do better when fed on a routine. They have an amazing internal clock that will adjust to feeding time. Therefore, we recommend that you maintain a consistent feeding schedule for your horse at the same time daily. An abrupt change in the feeding schedule can be annoying and may trigger serious health conditions such as colic.

# Additional Rules for Horse Feeding

• The needs of every horse differ. Hence, consider the size, age, and other peculiarities of your horse in deciding what to feed it with

• Consider the hay or pasture balance: if your horse is grazing, with access to good pasture, then you need not feed so much hay anymore. Similarly, horses that don't get enough good pastures will need more hay.

• Feed only a minimal amount of grain.

• Adjust your horse feed based on the amount of work it does and the level of physical activities.

# Chapter Seven: Horse Health and Disease Prevention

Horses are strong animals; however, they are not impenetrable. They can suffer from various types of illnesses or one injury or the other. Even with the best of care, occasional bouts of ill-health cannot be entirely avoided.

Your role as a horse keeper is to reduce the risks and occurrence of these ailments. And even when they do occur, be able to recognize the signs of ill-health in your health and attend to the injuries or disease in time and ensure that your horse receives the treatment it needs.

## How To Recognize When Your Horse Needs Care

As a horse owner, recognizing if your horse needs care is an essential skill. Although a horse cannot speak to tell you when it is sick, by knowing the signs to watch out for and carefully observing your horse for these signs, you should be able to identify when your horse is not in good condition and learn the correct ways to care for it. The following are signs that something might be wrong with your horse.

- Fever
- Irregular breathing and heart rate (too slow or too rapid)
- Loss of appetite

- Excessive heat in the feet or limbs

- Discharge from nose, mouth, or eyes

- Swelling on various parts of the body

- Sensitivity and exercise intolerance

- Colic

- Flared nostrils or a frightening appearance

- Breathing difficulties

- Chronic coughing and unusual sounds

- Limping or lameness

- Body sores

- Constipation and diarrhea

- Muscle spasms

These are some signs to look out for. While having these signs does not positively confirm that your horse is sick, it is sufficient reason to invite a vet to take a look at your horse and carry out a comprehensive diagnosis.

# Skin Conditions

### Ringworm

Ringworm is a type of fungal skin infection that occurs in various animals, including horses. It is so named due to the circular-shaped lesions that occur on the skin. These lesions vary in their density and size and may appear on various parts of the horse's body like the neck, saddle region, neck, or girth regions. Initially, the infection may show as tufts of hair, which eventually fall off and leave behind weeping lesions.

Ringworm is a contagious skin infection that may be spread by direct contact with an infected animal. It may also be spread indirectly since the immediate environment of an infected horse may become infected.

How to prevent and manage ringworm: if you notice a ringworm breakout on your horse, you should isolate the infected animal as much as possible. Items like bedding materials used by the infected horse should also be disposed of. Strict hygiene is important to prevent the spread of ringworms. Also, seek the help of a vet on how to treat the infection.

## Rain Scald

This is a skin infection that occurs because of a softening of the skin due to persistent water saturation. It is characterized by patchy hair loss along with the hindquarters and back of your horse. The hair on the site of infection may become matted, and weeping lesions and sores may appear on the spot.

Horses with an already-weakened immune system suffer more from this condition. It may also occur in horses that lack natural lubrication that keeps their coat dry and warm.

Rain scald may also be caused by non-breathable or leaking blankets, which may expose a horse's back to constant moisture.

How to prevent and manage rain scald: keeping moisture away from your horse is the most effective way to prevent rain scald. Ensure that you have a shelter for your horse away from the field and ensure that you used the right type of horse blankets. Keep your horse stall well maintained, clean, and as dry as possible.

## Mud Fever and Cracked Heel

Muddy or wet conditions cause this skin condition, characterized by skin inflammation on the legs and stomach of the infected horses. The inflamed area may also be scaly. Severe cases of mud fever can also cause fever or high temperature. Mud fever is a bacterial infection. The bacteria may enter under the skin when it is muddy or waterlogged. Cracked heel is similar to mud fever, as the same factors cause both conditions.

How to prevent and manage mud fever and cracked heel: to prevent this disease, you should clean your horse's legs whenever you bring it in from the field. To get rid of the mud, you can either leave it to dry off before brushing it off or simply wash off the wet mud with water and dry it up. You may also apply a barrier cream, which helps to prevent the horse's skin from getting waterlogged.

## Sweet Itch

Also known as Summer Seasonal Recurrent Dermatitis (SSRD), *sweet itch* s a type of allergic reaction characterized by inflammation of the skin. Often, the affected area of the skin may also become itchy. The back, mane, and tail of the horse are the most commonly affected area. A type of midge ("no-see-ums" or gnats) called Culicoides causes it, leading to irritation and an allergic reaction to the saliva of the midge. In serious cases, the horse may rub itself raw against surfaces in other to relive the itch.

Although the appearance of symptoms of this condition depends largely on environmental conditions, a horse that develops this condition as a youngster will suffer from it continually.

The most effective way to prevent sweet itch is to get rid of midges or avoid grazing your horse in areas where they are likely to encounter them. Midges are attracted to areas with a lot of decomposing vegetation, typically in woodlands or areas near the water. Avoid these areas entirely. Avoiding grazing at certain times of the day (midges are more common at dusk or dawn) can also help manage and limit encounters to this insect.

# Respiratory Conditions

### Common Cold

Horses may suffer from a common cold, characterized by a white or yellowish discharge from your horse's nose. This may also come with a slight fever and swollen glands in the horse's nose. Flu is a viral infection that can be easily spread through contact with an infected person. Horses kept in a poorly ventilated stall for a long period are likely to come down with an infection. If you take your horses on shows, their proximity with other horses may increase the risk of catching a cold.

How to prevent/manage common cold: if your horse comes down with a cold, isolate him from your other animals and call a vet immediately. Keep your horse in a well-ventilated area at all times. Feed infected horses with soft and easy to swallow hay (preferably soaked). When at competitions or public shows, limit your horse's contact with other horses and try to avoid letting the horse drink from public water troughs.

### Cough

Various factors can cause coughs. The most common cough is typically associated with the common cold and is characterized by the watery discharge from the horse's nose. This type of cough may span for about two weeks, with the cough gradually increasing in frequency. An allergic reaction is also another likely cause of coughs, as well as bacteria and viruses.

How to treat/manage coughs: if your horse has a cough, get stop the animal from working or any other rigorous activity and get a veterinarian immediately. Treat a viral or bacterial infection if it is the cause. With cough caused by allergic reactions, ensure that your horse's immediate environment is clean and well-ventilated. Bedding and other stable materials should be dust-free, and hay should be soaked in water to limit dust. It is always recommended to keep the horse away from other animals until you have determined the exact cause of the cough.

# Other Conditions

## Colic

This is a term used to describe abdominal discomfort and pain in horses. Colic is an indication of a problem in the gut or any other abdominal organs. Symptoms of colic include restlessness, pawing at the ground or excessive attempts to roll, labored or rapid breathing, unusual irritability, unsuccessful attempt to pass dung, and elevated pulse rates. Colic can be caused by a wide range of factors, which can be as simple as indigestion or, in more serious cases, a twisted gut. Call in a vet immediately if you notice any sign of discomfort or suspect that your horse may be suffering from abdominal pain.

## Laminitis

Also called *founder*, laminitis is an inflammation, weakening, swelling, or even death of soft tissues in the horse's hoof. It is a serious problem that is usually very painful and debilitating. Laminitis is better prevented since it can be difficult to cure. Laminitis can be linked to a wide range of causes, including obesity, insulin resistance, poor nutrition, metabolic syndrome, excessive weight-bearing, cold weather, and serious cases of colic, among others. You may notice an increased amplitude of the digital pulse in the horse's lower limb. This is an early indicator of laminitis. Other signs to watch out for include shifting weight from one foot to the other, inability or reluctance to move, outstretched limbs while standing, and so on. If you notice any of these signs, call for a vet immediately.

## Arthritis

Bone arthritis or degenerative joint disease is a fairly common condition that affects horses. It is a common reason horses have to be retired or even put down. Joints affected by arthritis may swell and appear larger than they are supposed to be, which will cause serious pain and make the horse act stiff. Unfortunately, there is really no cure for arthritis. So, it is better to prevent it entirely rather than let it happen. Taking preventive measures as early as possible is the best way to keep arthritis in check. Basic precautions to take include ensuring that your horse always gets sufficient warm-up before any activities, avoiding harmful, hard, and uneven surfaces for riding, and watching your horse's weight, as this may put a lot of pressure on the joints.

### Poor Dental Care

Horses may also suffer from dental issues, many of which are commonly associated with poor dental care. A foul odor from your horse's mouth is a clear indication of dental problems. If you notice your horse is behaving abnormally (especially during feeding), their teeth may be the problem. Taking precautions and ensuring proper dental care from an early stage is the best way to prevent dental problems in your horse later on. Schedule annual oral and dental exams for horses older than five years. When left to linger, oral problems can lead to other serious problems for your horse later.

### Back Issues

The back of a horse comprises a complicated system of bones, muscles, nerves, and tendons. It is crucial to a horse's comfort, activity, and general well-being. Back issues are one of the major problems frequently encountered by performance horses. If your horse competes often, it is likely to develop back issues. For performing horses, a sudden drop in performance is a likely indicator or back issues. Often, a simple rest for a few days should be able to fix the problem and relieve back pain. In extreme cases, a vet must come in to treat the back problem through mesotherapy or other forms of medical interventions. There are injections, foams, or spray that may be administered to help relax your horse's tired muscles and for a cool and soothing effect. Braces may also be put on your horse to hasten recovery.

# Horse Parasites

Horses can be affected by a wide range of parasites. This can be internal parasites like lungworms, ascarids, strongyles, threadworms, tapeworms, and pinworms, or external parasites like ticks, mosquitoes, lice, or horse mange. These parasites are causative organisms or vectors of various common horse diseases. For dealing with horse parasites, prevention and treatment should go hand-in-hand. No horse in the world avoids being plagued by one type of parasite or the other. Regular checks at intervals and seasonal or daily care are needed to keep these parasites in check and prevent various health issues that may be associated with them.

Regular deworming of your horses is one way to deal with various worm parasites. Speak to your veterinarian to help develop a deworming plan for your horse. All the horses on your premises should be dewormed simultaneously and at regular intervals. A single warm specie should be targeted at once for effectiveness, and a correct dosage of dewormer should be used. New arrivals to your premises should be quarantined and dewormed as well before they are allowed to join the other horses on your premises.

Environmental control is an effective way of taking care of insect parasites on your premises. This involves keeping your premises clean and getting rid of conditions that may make it easier for insect parasites to thrive. Targeted insect control and fumigation using insecticides and pesticides may also be carried out to remove specific insect species that may attack your horses. As a horse keeper, be familiar with various insect parasites in your area and learn about how to deal with them effectively and prevent the diseases they spread.

# Chapter Eight: Horse Grooming and Daily Care

To keep your horse healthy and strong, regular care is vital. You are not ready to be a horse owner if you are not willing - or you do not have enough time – to carry out the stressful and potentially time-consuming chores of caring for your horse. Horse care chores can be categorized as daily, weekly, monthly, or seasonal care required to keep your horse healthy and happy. Falling behind or failing to carry out any of these tasks can make your horse stall unsafe and unsanitary for horses, leading to a wide range of health problems.

## Basic Daily Tasks

Some of the basic daily tasks that should be carried out by a horse owner include:

• Feeding: Ideally, your horse should be fed on a forage-based diet at least twice or more throughout the day with the right type of feed and accurately measured quantity. See the previous chapter for guidelines on proper feeding practices.

• Watering: Your horse should always have a healthy supply of water available. Horses need about 10 gallons of water per day in warm weather. More or less may be required depending on the activity and general weather conditions.

- Cleaning: Regular cleaning of horse stalls, including removing wet or soiled bedding from the stall and getting rid of manure piles from paddock areas.

- Exercise: Horses are high-activity animals. They need at least 30 minutes of exercise daily.

Keep an eye out for your horse and look out for any signs of injury and illness so it can be identified and treated immediately.

# Weekly Tasks

These tasks should be carried out at least once per week or multiple times in a week based on your schedule and the specific needs of your horse

- Bathing and grooming the mane, tail, hooves, and other parts of your horse's body

- Cleaning the water trough or buckets

- Several hours of exercise or workout

- Maintenance clipping

# Other Periodic Tasks

Other important tasks should be scheduled and carried out periodically either at a specific season, after a certain period of time, or as your horse requires them. These general preventive care steps help prevent a wide range of preventable conditions and diseases. These include:

- Pest control and routine control of internal and external parasites

- Vaccination

- Dental checks and general oral care

- Maintenance and checks of horse shelter and fencing

- Power-washing stall walls and floor

These are a few activities that must be carried out to keep your facility running and maintain the health and wellbeing of your horses. While these might seem like a lot of chores, most horse owners find these activities enjoyable – even therapeutic. If the work required is less than the time you have on your hands, you may consider hiring extra hands to assist you. Do not raise horses if you don't have plans for handling these responsibilities.

# Horse Grooming

Grooming involves a series of activities aimed at taking care of the coat, hooves, and the hair of your horse. It provides an opportunity to bond with your horse. Grooming also allows you to look closely and check your horse for injuries or signs of irritation. Hence, it is a chore that must be performed regularly. Ideally, groom your horse daily. However, even if daily grooming is impossible, you should at least spend some time grooming your horse before riding. Taking time to groom your horse will help get rid of grit n your horse's back. Having grit underneath the saddle will be quite uncomfortable for your horse and will lead to sores.

## Grooming Tools

There are several tools you will need for horse grooming. You should always have them available and arranged in a convenient shelter. Some tools and materials you will need for horse grooming include:

- Curry comb

- Body brush (with stiff bristles)

- Tail or mane comb (plastic is preferable to metal)

- Finishing brush (should be soft and fine)

- Clippers or scissors (not compulsory)

- Hoof pick

- A soft cloth or clean sponge

- Grooming spray (not compulsory)

- Hoof ointment (not compulsory, but may be recommended by your farrier)

You can gather all of your grooming tools in a wide bucket or buy a grooming box to keep them all organized.

# Instructions For Grooming

Before you groom, tie your horse safely and securely using a quick-release knot or cross ties. Below is a basic guide for grooming your horse.

### How To Clean Your Horse's Hooves

Begin by sliding your hand down your horse's left foreleg and squeeze the back of the leg just along the tendons. Instruct your horse to raise its legs up by saying "hoof," "up," or whatever word your horse responds to. When your horse raises its hoof, raise it up and pry away any grit, dirt, or manure that may be lodged in the sole (or frog) of the horse's foot. While doing this, also check for injury, grease heel, or thrush. Pay attention to cracks in the hoof and consult a farrier if you notice any problem. Once you are done cleaning and inspecting the hoof of the left foreleg, you can repeat the same for the remaining three legs.

### How to Curry Your Horse

The next task will be to curry your horse. Beginning from the left side (offside) of your horse, gently use your grooming mitt or curry comb to loosen and remove any dirt on the horse's coat. Currying also helps to remove any grit, mud, and other debris. Gently curry the horse's coat with circular sweeps over the horse's body. Be extra careful when currying bony areas of your horse's hips, shoulders, and legs. Also, be careful when brushing the belly and back legs of your horse. Some horses are sensitive to this and may react violently to rigorous brushing. If you notice that your horse is swishing his tail in an agitated way or he lays back his ears, then the brushing is probably too rigorous.

Currying is an opportunity to inspect the skin of your horse for signs of injury, wounds, and skin lesions. Watch out for these as you carefully curry your horse's coat, and if you notice any, check the injury and decide if it is something you can treat on your own, or you must invite the vet.

### How to Comb-Out Tangles

Combing your horse's tangles helps to give your horse a flowing and shiny mane and give it a full and healthy look. To comb the mane, begin with a mane brush or comb and brush at the bottom of the mane strands. Brush downwards until the mane is untangled, and you can smoothly comb the mane from top to bottom.

Be careful when you do this and position yourself correctly. For safety, stand to one side of your horse then pull the tail gently to your side. This way, you stand completely clear should your horse decide to kick. Having a grooming spray as part of your grooming collection is a good idea. This helps to detangle the hair effectively and makes brushing out the strands of mane a lot easier.

### Using the Body Brush

When you are finished brushing, use the body brush to get rid of dirt on your horse's body. A body brush is a stiff brush with loner bristles that will help to get rid of dirt and grit you missed with your curry comb. Begin from one side of your horse in gently sweeping strokes toward the hair growth. The curry brush is generally considered more effective for cleaning parts of the body like the legs than the curry comb. While using the body brush on your horse, check for signs of skin irritation and lesions on the knees and legs. Also, watch out for small nicks and cut and assess the severity of the injuries.

### Using the Finishing Brush

The finishing brush has softer and softer bristles and helps make your horse's coat smooth and shiny. Most people also use a finishing brush to clean their horse's face if they do not have a brush specifically for that.

With the finishing brush, gently remove dust that might have been missed by the body brush. Gently use this brush to remove dust from areas like the horse's throat, face, or ears that were most likely missed by the other brushes. The fine and soft bristles of the finishing brush will help smooth the hair and leave your horse with a glossy and shiny coat.

When finished, you can apply a grooming spray. This is not compulsory, but it can help to shine your horse's coat and may also serve as a form of sun protection. Some grooming sprays can make the horse's hair slippery. Avoid using products like this in the saddle area, especially if you intend to ride soon.

### Cleaning the Ears, Muzzle, Eyes, and Dock Area

When finished with the rest of your horse's body, it is time for more detailed cleaning. Using a soft cloth or a soft damp sponge, gently wipe clean the area around the eyes and muzzle of your horse to get rid of any dirt that may be present. Doing this also allows you to observe your horse's eyes closely and check for signs of injury or infection. Look out for symptoms like redness, swelling, or excessive tearing.

Do this for the ears, but be careful. Some horses are fussy about having their ears handled. Be careful not to pinch or pull the hairs when you clean it. With time and special care, your horse may come to love having its ears groomed.

# Chapter Nine: Horse Breeding

If you raise horses, one of the main things you will need to be familiar with is horse reproduction. While some parts of the reproduction process depend on the attending veterinarian, the efficiency of a horse breeding operation depends largely on your understanding and management of the process.

Horse reproduction aims to produce healthy foals after each successful mating. There is an elaborate process leading up to foaling, and the success of the breeding stage depends on your understanding of your mare and stallion's reproductive performance. In this chapter, we will discuss some essentials of horse breeding and reproduction you are expected to be familiar with as a horse owner. While you can simply have a vet handle or advice you on some of the reproduction processes, it will be better if you also have some of the information necessary for successful horse breeding. This will help you make the right decisions and get the best results.

### Horse Selection

One of the most crucial aspects of horse breeding is choosing a horse for breeding. Usually, this is one of the major factors that will determine the success of the breeding process. The probability of getting a healthy and strong foal is also subject to your horse selection process.

It pays to have the progeny information of your horses, as this will help to identify the superior breeding stock. Your vet can assist you with selecting a healthy stallion and mare for breeding. When this is done right, the breeding process is likely to yield better results leading to a successful pregnancy and a healthy foal.

# The Reproductive Examination of the Mare

A reproductive examination is necessary to ascertain the reproductive state of your mare. This process involves rectal palpation and ultrasound examination. In a reproductive examination, the mare's vagina, cervix, and vestibule are examined by your vet to determine if they are in a good reproductive state.

Reproductive exams are better done in a stall or the stall entrance rather than in an open field. This helps to keep the horse restricted and also provides some degree of protection to the vet and other personnel handling the horse. If your mare has a foal, they should be not be separated as this will only make the mare agitated and make the examination difficult. Besides having the horse properly restrained, it will also be helpful to have one more person available to assist the vet.

To prevent the spread of disease from one mare to another, disposable equipment should be used. The mare should be washed to get rid of fecal material and dirt from the vulva before examination. With an ultrasound examination, it is best done indoors, away from sunlight, so the vet can easily read the screen of the ultrasound machine.

# Understanding the Mare's Estrous Cycle of the Mare

Like all animals, a mare goes through a monthly fertility cycle in response to fluctuations in hormone production. This reproductive cycle is completed in about 21 days. In horses, the reproductive cycle takes place in two phases. There is a continuous cycle during which the mare is in heat (or in season), typically lasting about 5 to 7 days. There is also the dioestrus cycle, which is the period in-between successive heat periods, lasting for about 14 to 16 days).

In non-pregnant mares, the estrous cycle is typically stimulated by increasing daylight. Hence it coincides with the early spring season. There is usually a transitional phase that may persist for a few weeks and might be characterized by short irregular cycles. However, after the first ovulation period, the estrous cycle will become more balanced and regular until autumn, when the mare will enter into an anoestrous cycle again, and ovulation stops.

Hormonal changes in the mare cause the estrous cycle. The hormones produced during the various stages of the estrous cycle include progesterone, prostaglandin (PG), luteinizing hormone, estrogen, and follicle-stimulating hormone (FSH). The production of these hormones determines the progression of the estrous cycle, and some are necessary for the maintenance of pregnancy.

# Mare Management

Breeding in horses is relatively inefficient compared to breeding in other domesticated animals. Generally, about an average of 50 percent of mares sent to a stud ever get to produce a foal. This is a hugely inefficient and wasteful process. One factor that probably affects the success rate of horse breeding is a poor selection process of mares for breeding. As a horse breeder, you must identify some of the possible reasons and factors that contribute to wastage in horse breeding and work around them.

An effective mare fertility assessment is important for successful breeding. This practice is used to determine if a mare is suitable for service. Fertility assessment will also help to identify the factors that may contribute to reduced fertility. It will rate mares and place them in order of priority based on the probability of the success of the breeding process.

Proper fertility assessment will also ensure that a mare is served only when it is an estrous period, as this gives it a better chance of conception. At the end of every breeding season, detailed veterinary inspection and a series of examinations should be performed for your mares. Mares that fail to conceive should be assessed and problems identified and rectified before the start of the next breeding season.

# Stallion Management

Managing a stallion depends largely on the purpose for which it is being raised. Stallions can be raised for show, racing, or for breeding. This will determine how the stallion will be managed in terms of handling, exercise, health care, and of course, fertility assessment.

If you are raising your stallion for breeding, then a basic understanding of the reproductive system is required. A stallion reproductive system consists of the scrotum, testes, penis, the accessory glands, epididymis, and spermatic cord. These organs must be in a healthy condition for a stallion that is being raised for breeding.

## Horse Teasing

One of the essential stages of horse breeding is the teasing process. It will be nearly impossible for your mare to conceive if you do not have an efficient teasing program. The effectiveness of this process depends largely on how well you can determine if the mare is in heat and will be receptive to stallion service. Typically, once the breeding season starts, you have a narrow window of 5 to 7 days within a 21-day monthly cycle. The remaining 14 to 16 days of the estrous cycle are off days during which conception is unlikely.

Although some mares will show signs they are in an "on" season in the absence of a male horse, most mares must be stimulated by a stallion or colt before they show they are on heat. Teasing can be done in various ways. However, no matter how it is done, you must have a flexible and systematic approach since each mare is unique, and the same approach cannot work for all mares.

Some signs that are mare is an estrous period include:

- Accepting the teaser

- Lifting of the tail

- Urinating

- Winking

- Squatting

If a mare is not estrous, it will show the following signs:

- Rejection of the teaser

- Kicking the teaser

- Pulling back the ears

- Clamping her tail down

### Interfering in the Horse Breeding Process

Sometimes, human intervention may be required to achieve some control and improve the chances of success of a horse breeding program. This can be in the form of hormone therapy and artificial lighting programs.

### Hormone Therapy

Hormone production is one of the critical factors that influence the horse breeding process. Hormone therapy is usually carried out as a way of manipulating barren or maiden mares to improve their chances of conception. Foaling mares may also undergo hormone therapy. When done correctly, hormone therapy can improve the reproductive performance of your mare quite significantly.

### Record Keeping

Another essential aspect of a horse breeding program is record keeping. Keeping a complete and comprehensive record of your horses will play a major role in helping you make educated decisions about the chances of a breeding attempt. Aside from the progeny record of the individual stud and mare, you also need to keep a teasing record on all your mares and have it available to your vet during a mare fertility assessment.

### Artificial Lighting Programs

Light plays a significant role in the estrous cycle of horses. The onset of the breeding season is typically determined by longer periods of sunlight. Therefore, a properly implemented artificial lighting program can improve the performance of mares since the breeding cycle is influenced by periods of daylight. By increasing the length of daylight using artificial light, mares can be encouraged to come into season earlier than they will normally do. Artificial lighting can also help improve productivity in foaling mares.

### Laboratory Aids to Improve Reproductive Performance

Besides simple fertility assessments and tests, several laboratory tests may be carried out to understand fertility in your horses, diagnose problems, and deal with medical issues. Some tests that may be carried out include bacteriological examinations, biopsy, cytology, hormone assays, and endoscopic examinations.

### Serving the Mare

Now that you understand the basic principles of horse breeding and the factors that determine the success of a breeding exercise, you can now proceed with the mating of the horses. Remember that the success of this stage depends on the efficiency of your selection process and the horse teasing itself. The four major ways of getting your mare to foal include hand service, paddock mating, artificial insemination, and embryo transfer.

# Chapter Ten: Foaling and Weaning

Once a mare has been successfully impregnated, the pregnancy lasts for approximately 330 to 342 days. You must understand how to accurately diagnose pregnancy early, as this will ensure that you do not return a pregnant mare for servicing. Pregnancy can be diagnosed manually, using an ultrasonic examination, or by a laboratory test.

A pregnant mare requires good quality care, as this can significantly influence if the pregnancy will be carried to term and the health of the foal produced. Basic care for an expectant mare includes:

• Provision of nutritious forage

• Reduce exposure to other horses to reduce the risk of injury and disease

• Vaccination and deworming

• Additional care by a veterinarian

• Do not transport your mare during pregnancy unless it is absolutely necessary.

Twin conception is typically problematic for mares. This is one reason why early pregnancy detection is important. An ultrasound exam should be carried out a about 14 to 16 days post ovulation, and one of the embryos should be eliminated to allow the other to develop normally.

# Signs Of An Impending Birth

Typically, pregnancy will last for about 330 to 342 days. A birth approaches, there are some signs to watch for that indicates that a birth is imminent. While the time-frame of these signs varies from one mare to the other, prepare for an impending birth. Some of the most obvious and reliable signs to look out for include:

- Filling of the udder (occurs at about 2 to 4 weeks pre-foaling)

- Distension of teats (this occurs about 4 to 6-day pre-foaling)

- Waxing of the teats (occurs 1 to 4 days pre-foaling)

- Obvious dripping of milk

- Increase in calcium content of milk (this can be detected with a stall-side test kit)

Other less obvious signs include relaxation of the vulva, changes in the position of the foal, and softening of the croup muscles.

It is difficult to pinpoint an exact day of foaling. However, during the final stage of pregnancy, the mare will begin to show some signs of labor. The signs to watch out for at the onset of labor include:

- Restlessness

- Getting up and down

- Curling of the top-lip

- Weight shifting and picking up the hind legs

- Frequent urination & defecation

- Tail swishing

# Foaling

When a mare is ready to foal, it will be advantageous to have an attendant present. Usually, the mare will get only a little or no assistance. But it will still be beneficial to have someone at hand to offer assistance if needed.

During birth, the chorioallantois ruptures, and the foal begins to move through the pelvic canal. The foal should present with two forelegs with its nose resting in-between them. Uteri and abdominal contractions will push it out, and this should take about 10 to 20 minutes.

Usually, the mare should be able to have its foal without assistance. If assistance is to be given, then it has to be in the form of gently holding the feet of the foal and letting the mare push on its own. The attention of a vet should be *required* only in cases of abnormal presentation of the foal.

### Care of the Newborn Foal

Within 30 minutes of its birth, a healthy foal should be able to stand on its feet after some failed attempts. Once steady, it will seek out the mare's teats to nurse. This is somewhat random, but with gentle assistance from the mare, the foal will eventually find the teat and suckle on instinct.

Following below are the expected behaviors within the first two hours of a foal's birth:

•Foal breathes (immediately after birth)

• Lifts its head (within five minutes)

• Attempt to rise within 10 minutes and successfully does so within 55 minutes.

• Vocalize (within 45 minutes)

• Defecates (within 30 minutes)

• Suckles (Within an hour)

• Starts walking or running (within 90 minutes)

• Take a nap (within 3 hours)

Understanding normal foal behavior is essential to diagnosing possible problems and seeking help if you need it.

Within the first few weeks of its birth, the foal will nurse quite frequently at an estimated range of one or two 3-minutes sessions within an hour. With time, the duration and frequency of suckling will decrease, and they eat other feedstuffs more. The foal will remain close to its dam for the first few weeks but will gradually explore its immediate environment further.

Right after the delivery of a foal, the first thing to do is to ensure that the foal is breathing. Approach the foaling area quietly to check if the foal is breathing and remove the birth sack from the foal's head if you need to. Once you have confirmed that the foal is breathing, your work is done for the moment. Leave the foaling area and only observe from a distance.

However, if the foal is not breathing on its own immediately, you can tickle its nostrils using a piece of straw or grass or blow into its mouth. If these do not work, shake and rub the foal vigorously, squeeze its ribs gently, or lifting it off the ground slightly and dropping.

Do not cut the umbilical cord immediately after birth. Rather, wait for the mare or foal to break it off as they move. Once the cord breaks, add 1 to 2% mild iodine to the stump to dry it and prevent a bacterial infection, which can lead to severe illness or even death in foals. Continue to observe this naval stump for a few days to ensure that it closes, and if it doesn't, call in a vet.

Usually, the foal should be able to stand on its own within an hour of its birth. The first few attempts may be unsuccessful, but with time, the foal will get the hang of it and should become steady after a while. Let the foal stand by itself, as lifting it onto its feet before it is ready can lead to a strain the tendons and ligaments.

The foal should instinctively search for the udder within an hour of its birth. Again, this is an exploratory process that might take a while for the foal to get used to. Resist the urge to intervene as this can affect the bonding between the mare and the foal. An intervention will be required only if the foal has not nursed within two hours of its birth – or if you notice that the mare is rejecting the foal's attempt to nurse.

Gently help the foal stand on its feet and guide it towards the udder. Sometimes, a mare with a swollen udder or a young and inexperienced mare with sensitive teats must be restrained before she willingly allows the foal to nurse. In extreme cases, the mare may have to be tranquilized by a vet if it continually rejects the foal's attempt to nurse.

### Colostrum

The first form of fluid produced by the mare immediately after the birth of the foal is known as *colostrum*. This milk contains antibodies for disease protection and other essential nutrients. Hence, it is vital that your foal receives colostrum soon after it is born. The foal's ability to absorb these essential antibodies will reduce drastically after 12 hours of birth. Ensure that you get your foal to nurse from the mother within this time.

You can increase the number of antibodies present in the mare's colostrum by vaccinating it about 30 days before foaling. If this is not done, then you have to give the foal a tetanus shot at birth. This will help protect the foal for about two to three weeks while its umbilical stump heals.

Colostrum also has laxative effects, and it will help the foal to pass fetal excrement (also known as meconium) shortly after taking it (usually within four hours). Constipation may occur if the foal cannot defecate within the stipulated time.

# Common Foal Health Problems

Diarrhea: this is an uncommon problem in foals and may indicate a more serious underlying condition. Severe cases of squirting diarrhea can cause dehydration, weakness, or even death of a newborn foal. Older foals (about one to two weeks old) may experience mild cases of diarrhea. Foal heat scours may also cause diarrhea. This is caused by a parasite known as Strongyloides westeri, which may be transmitted from an infected dam to a foal through breast milk. For a healthy foal, a mild case of foal heat course rarely causes serious harm. However, if you notice that the foal is dehydrated or weak, then you should call in a veterinarian immediately.

Limb weakness & deformities: foals can be born with deformities in the limbs like crooked legs, knuckling, weak pasterns, and general limb weakness. While most of these conditions are likely to correct as the goal grows, you can call in a vet to have it checked just to be sure and recommended treatment if any is required.

Hernias: hernias are defects in the body wall, which leads to the extrusion of part of the horse's intestine under its skin. This defect can occur around the scrotal area or naval of the horse. Mild cases of hernia are self-corrective; surgery may be required in severe cases.

Entropion: this refers to a condition where the foal is born with its eyelids and lashes turned out the wrong way. This can cause tearing or irritation. Often, it is possible to roll the effected eyelid with your hands. But sometimes, special eye treatment may be needed to correct the defect.

### Jaundice Foal

Jaundice is a rare condition caused by an incompatibility in the mare and foal's blood group leading to a formation of antibodies in the mare's breast milk. When the foal nurses, these antibodies can be passed to their bodies, and this can have debilitating effects – and may even be fatal without prompt treatment. Call a vet for help immediately if you suspect the foal might have jaundice. Also, discontinue nursing from its mother's milk until treatment is administered.

### Caring for Orphaned Foals

In the unfortunate event of a mare's death after foaling (or due to maternal rejection), a foal may require extra care from you. Orphaned foals can still be raised successfully when you know what to do. Absent a mother, one of the first things to do is to ensure that you get the foal colostrum soon after its birth. You may be able to purchase frozen colostrum from a large breeding farm or vet near you. Thaw the frozen milk (do not heat or microwave) and feed your foal with it. A vet can also administer oral colostrum or carry out plasma transfusion as a replacement for regular colostrum.

The easiest way to care for an orphaned mare is to transfer it to a nursing mare. But you must disguise the mare using any strong-smelling liquid like whiskey, milk, urine, or linseed oil. You may also have to restrain or tranquilize the adopted nursing mare until she willingly accepts the orphaned foal. An alternative is to allow the foal nurse on goat milk, although it will be difficult to find goats than can produce enough milk to meet the nutritional needs of a foal. Bottle-feeding or bucket-feeding the foal is the next best alternative if the other options are not available. You can find nutritionally balanced mare replacer milk at feed stores and feed it to your foal.

If you bottle-feed or bucket feed an orphaned foal, try to introduce it to other horses soon so it can learn normal equine behavior and it does not become attached to you. You can place your orphaned foal next to a gentle gelding or mere in a pen if the older horse can be trusted not to hurt the foal.

Before we look at how to wean a foal, here is a checklist of the things you need to do right after the birth:

1. Ensure that the foal is breathing

2. Put iodine on the umbilical cord stump

3. Ensure that the foal gets colostrum as soon as possible

4. Give the foal a tetanus shot if colostrum is not available right away

5. Ensure that the foal passes meconium and treat diarrhea if any

6. Check the umbilical stump to ensure it closes

7. Continually check the foal for several days for signs of infection and call a veterinarian immediately, if necessary.

### Horse Weaning

In the first few months of its life, a foal will spend most of its life close to its mother and will depend fully on the mare for its food. By the end of the third month, only about 60% of its time will be spent with the mare. Milk production in the dam will typically continue until the dam is about five to seven months old. At this point, 70% of the foal's nutrients will come from non-milk sources. At this stage (at about five months), you should begin plan to wean your horse. Here is a checklist of things to do to:

1. Gradually increase the foal's feed ration over a period of two to three weeks.

2. Although the dam's milk will start to lose its nutritional value at about three months, you can further reduce milk production by reducing the mare's feed ration.

3. Watch your foal closely during the weaning period. Do not wean the foal if it is ill or isn't thriving well, if it is still attached to its mother, or not eating enough of the feed ration.

4. Your foal has to be halter-broken for a successful weaning.

Weaning a foal can be done gradually or abruptly, depending on factors like the mare's temperament, facilities you have available, and the presence of other horses.

# Chapter Eleven: Basic Horse Training

One of the most interesting aspects of horse raising is horse training. It can be challenging, especially for a beginner. Horse training (especially for young horses) is best left in the hands of experienced trainers since young horses tend to be unpredictable, and you need the right skills and experience to handle them.

This training requires time and patience, and it is also about bonding with your horse; still, it is a rewarding experience. As you train your horse to do something new, you also learn something too. It's not all of that cowboy-style horse breaking that you see in old wild west movies!

Basic horse training is about teaching your horse to be ridden the *right way*, and it is not as dangerous as typically portrayed. It cannot be rushed; neither can you train your horse all the skills it needs to learn all at once. Below, you'll find the simple steps of basic horse training.

### Take Time To Build a Bond

The first – and perhaps most important – step of basic horse training: taking time to build a bond with your horse. If a horse is not comfortable around you or does not trust you enough, it will be difficult, if not impossible, to teach it anything. You need to give your horse time to get used to you for effective communication between both of you. Building a bond with your horse involves spending time with the horse, creating a positive association, and learning how it communicates with you.

### Spend More Time with your Horse

To develop a solid bond with your horse and train it effectively, you must spend more time with it. Horses learn better by routine and repetition. The more time you spend on bonding, the more likely the horse will get comfortable around you. You spend more time with your horse when you groom, bath, or braid their mane. You can also hand-walk your horse around your property.

### Creating Positive Associations

To train your horse, you have to teach your horse to associate your presence with positivity. If your horse is always agitated in your presence, you cannot teach it anything. At the start of training, begin with low-stress and pleasurable activities. Doing this will help the horse associate your presence with a sense of calmness. Maintaining a positive attitude and rewarding your horse when it gets the smallest things right will help associate training with positivity.

Most horse trainers subconsciously switch into training mode when they are instinctively demanding for too much from their horse. When you do this, you not only stress the horse, but you are also not allowing the horse to enjoy your presence. The focus should be on building a relationship with the horse rather than merely training it to do your bidding. Both you and your horse will become frustrated if you do this.

### Learn How Your Horse Communicates

Taking time to bond with your horse will help you learn more about your horse and how it communicates. This is not about telling your horse *what to do*. As you communicate with your horse, it will communicate back, and you must learn to watch out for these cues. Every horse is unique, so even as an experienced horse trainer, you will learn new things when you train a new horse.

Learning about your horse involves their likes and dislikes, what it fears, and what encourages it to learn better. Doing this will help you learn how to handle your horse the right way.

How long this entire process will take (of getting used to your horse) depends on various factors. Your commitment to training and the horse's personality will affect how fast you can build a bond and get started with riding and training your horse.

# Horse Training Groundwork

The very foundation of any horse training routine is groundwork. This basically refers to the art of training your horse *on the ground.* There is a popular saying among horse enthusiasts that "Whatever you cannot get your horse to do on the ground, it will not be able to do it with you in the saddle."

Horse training groundwork involves several simple training and exercises which include:

- Training your horse to stand still

- Flexing

- Properly leading your horse

- Softening

- Getting your horse to move in a circle

- Basic motion (hind-end and shoulder movements)

Although it might be tempting to skip this step and move straight to saddle training, this is not recommended. Groundwork is the first place to start to introduce new training to your horse.

### Standing Still

One of the basic things you have to train your horse to do is stand still. When you train your horse to stand still, it can pay attention to you as its training and look to you for the next instruction.

*How to:* Have the horse on a halter and lead, then stand facing the horse while holding the lead rope. Allow the lead to slack and stand still. Shake the lead rope each time the horse steps out of its original position. If the horse does not back up immediately, shake the rope harder until it gets the message and responds. With continuous training, your horse should learn to back up when you shake the rope as it realizes that walking off is wrong.

### Properly Leading

While leading a horse is a fairly simple task, a horse not trained will have some trouble with leading. Leading your horse properly will help establish that you are the one in charge. You will need a halter lead rope for this exercise. A lunge whip will also be necessary.

*How to:* The correct position to lead your horse is at your elbow. The horse should walk behind you on the side where you are leading it. If the horse is falling behind, you can encourage it to maintain pace by simply waving the lunge whip at it behind you. If the horse is being pushy and is trying to walk ahead of you, stop immediately and get the horse to back up. Repeat this as many times as possible until the horse learns to respond correctly.

### Flexing

A horse flexes when it bends its neck to either side. This exercise trains your horse to respond when pressure is applied at the reins. At the end of the flexing training, your horse should turn its neck so that its nose touches its right or left shoulders.

*How to:* Hold the lead rope and bring your hand to the horse's withers. Apply some pressure on the rope. Your horse should bend its neck towards the source of the pressure. And even when it does, you may need more time and training to get it to bend its neck all the way until you no longer feel pressure on the lead rope. Hold the pressure continuously until the horse eventually dips its nose further, and the pressure on the rope is released. Reward your horse once this is completed. Repeat the exercise for the other side.

### Softening

The goal of this drill is to get your horse to lower its head when you apply pressure to its lead rope. This will help your horse to accept a bit more conveniently later. It will also train your horse to respond to pressure on the bit.

*How to:* For this drill, grab the base of the horse's lead rope, and apply some pressure to pull it down towards the ground. Your horse should respond by lowering its head. If it does not do this right away, maintain steady pressure on the rope and release it as soon as the horses dip its head even slightly.

# Desensitizing Your Horse

Asides groundwork, another aspect of training your horse is desensitizing it. This involves getting your horse used to certain things it is not normally used to. Throughout its lifetime, your horse must get familiar with otherwise unfamiliar things like having a saddle on its back or having someone sitting in its saddle. An untrained horse will react strangely. Desensitizing helps to build trust in your horse and prepare it for pressure and some form of discomfort, so it does not react strangely in certain situations.

### Desensitizing your Horse to a Saddle

There are a lot of things you have to desensitize your horse to, but top on the list is saddling. Without training, the first instinct of your horse when you place a saddle on it will be to flee. Saddle training will make your animal more trusting and better prepared for saddling for the first time.

The goal of this exercise is to prepare your horse to have things placed on their back, around their stomach, or touching their sides. To desensitize your horse to saddles, you will need a saddle pad, tarps, or plastic bags.

One way you can prepare your horse is by rubbing these materials all over the horse's body. This will help prepare your horse for when the tack is actually placed on it. When you rub your horse with these materials, if it attempts to move away, simply stop and hold the material on its body until it stops moving.

You will also have to desensitize the horse to pressure. A saddle will apply pressure to the sides and back of the horse. You should start getting the horse used to this pressure before you actually start riding it. Other parts of the horse's body where gear will be worn like the legs and face, should be desensitized to pressure. Let your horse get used to having a bridle and bit, so the horse gets familiar with what it feels like.

### Putting the Saddle On

Once your horse has been trained and desensitized, you can put the saddle on. Remember that putting the saddle on is still a new experience, so your horse can still get frustrated and react unpredictably. Saddle training your horse helps it become comfortable having a saddle on its back.

Repetition is one of the most effective ways to get your horse used to saddling. Practice putting the saddle on and pulling it off repeatedly. Repeat this as often as you need to leave the saddle on for longer each time. With time, you should be able to let the horse move around the pen with the stirrups at its side for a while before pulling it off again.

Practice throwing the saddle over the back of your horse from both sides. This will ensure that the horse gets completely comfortable with having the saddle thrown from either side.

The most challenging part of getting your horse familiar with the saddle is attaching the girth. Once your horse shows it is comfortable with having the saddle on its back, you can now gently attach the girth to the saddle on one of its sides. But don't leave it hanging on the side as this can make the horse nervous.

To avoid this, attach the girth on one side then gradually rub the other end of the girth over the horse's belly and legs. Swing the girth back and forth under the horse's belly until it feels comfortable. You can then proceed to the other side of the horse and pull the girth and tighten it properly. Once you have been able to do this, undo the girth and allow it to fall to the side of the horse again. Repeat this action until your horse gets used to it. Some people just tighten the girth and let their horse buck around to wear itself out. *This is not good practice.*

**Desensitizing your Horse to Having Weight on the Saddle**

Once your horse has gotten comfortable with having a saddle on its back, the next step is to get it accustomed to having weight added. This will prepare your horse for an eventual ride - which is the ultimate goal.

You cannot simply proceed to sit on the back of an untrained horse. You need to patiently get him used to having weight on its back. Once you have the saddle on the back of your horse, you can begin weight desensitization by putting your arm gently over the back of your horse to mimic the feeling of having weight on its back.

You can also try jumping up beside the horse like you are about to mount up, but you do not mount yet. Do this gently, and in a relaxed and playful way, so your horse does not feel threatened and take off. Next, you can try laying across the back of your horse on your belly. This position is great since it also allows you to get off the horse fast if you need to.

Now you can sit on your horse. But do this carefully. As a precaution, turn your horse's nose towards you as you try to mount, so it doesn't freak out on you. To start, place one foot on the stirrup and put some of your weight on it without swinging your leg over the horse's back yet. If your horse seems calm about this, then proceed to stand in the stirrup. Wait for your horse to adjust before finally swinging your leg over to sit in the saddle.

You should sit for a few seconds, then dismount. Do this repeatedly while gradually increasing the time so you don't overwhelm your horse. Finally, when your horse is comfortable with you having you sit in the saddle, you have to train it to get familiar with the application pressure under the saddle (which is crucial to riding it) further. This is the stage where you will see the full benefits of good groundwork. You will also have to train your horse to get familiar with various types of movement in the saddle, so it doesn't freak out with any slight movement.

### Be Patient and Reward the Smallest Tries

Throughout the entire process of training your horse, be patient. You don't want to rush your horse through the processes. Throughout your training, reward your horse for even the slightest tries, especially when you begin riding. You want your horse to associate an action with a positive reward.

Do not put too much pressure on your horse or ask for too much, especially if the horse is newly-trained. The horse might have a hard time understanding what you are trying to do. But if it shows any positive sign, rewarding it will let it learn that that was the correct response. Training a horse is simple and fun. You have to understand only your horse's actions and reactions and figure out how to use his training effectively. If you are new to horse training, you can either get someone else to train your horse or have a professional trainer you can call for help every step of the way.

# Chapter Twelve: Training Athletic and Show Horses

Horses are kept for a wide range of reasons. For most horses, basic training is enough. But if you are raising your horses for special purposes like racing or shows, then your horse will need additional training. We cannot fully cover all horse training in this book, but this chapter will run you through the basics of horse training for athletic purposes and shows.

## Horse Training for Races

Before you train and condition your horse as a racing prospect, you should first evaluate it objectively. This involves both physical evaluations of the horse's gait and structure and psychological evaluations of its attitude. Is your horse well-built enough to handle the stress of moving at a great speed? Will your sweet colt, easily pushed out of the way by other horses, have the drive to become a top racehorse? There is no sure way to tell, but an objective observation and evaluation will guide you in choosing the horse to train.

Once you have carefully evaluated your choice of the horse to train, you can condition your horse for racing. There are multiple factors to consider as far as training racehorses is considered. This includes respiratory conditioning (aerobic and anaerobic conditioning) and physical conditioning - or fitness training.

### Aerobic Conditioning

Horses depend on both aerobic and anaerobic respiration during rigorous physical activity. Aerobic respiration refers to regular respiration in a resting state or during low energy activities. As the rigor of physical activity increases, the horse will switch from aerobic to anaerobic breathing. The importance of aerobic conditioning is to delay how long your horse can depend on aerobic respiration before it needs to switch to anaerobic energy sources. Aerobic conditioning also helps to shorten recovery time after a race or workout.

The main exercise involved in aerobic conditioning is slow, long-distance work. This is an ideal way to begin aerobic conditioning for your horse or whip it back into shape after a long period away from training. Aerobic exercises basically consist of walking and trotting routines, and some cantering exercises.

In aerobic training, the horse may be galloped for a few minutes, then allowed to recover by walking or trotting. The longer the workout, the longer the recovery time required. The amount of bouts the horse will take per day depends on the horse's response and your desired progression.

During aerobic workouts, track the heart rate of your horse; you may do this manually or simply use a heart rate monitor for this. The normal resting heart rate of usually about 40 beats per minute. While walking or trotting, the heart rate may be raised to about 80 to 140. A heartbeat rate between 150 to 160 per minute (or less) should be targeted.

Depending on factors like age, condition, and response rate, this initial period of aerobic conditioning may last for about six to eight weeks or more before you switch to intense exercises and race training. With horses being trained for shows, skill work is introduced after the period of aerobic conditioning has been completed.

### Anaerobic Conditioning

Horses rely on both anaerobic respiration and aerobic respiration for high-powered activities like racing. Horses will typically switch from aerobic to anaerobic energy consumption when their heart rate exceeds about 150 beats per minute.

Sprinting or breezing exercises are required to improve the anaerobic capacity of your horse. These exercises also work to improve bone structure and strength. Anaerobic conditioning for horses can be executed in two ways. You can increase the speed of the horse over a short distance or increase the workout distance it has to cover and gradually push for more speed.

Horses should not be pushed for maximum speed capacity during a workout. In fact, your horse simply needs to go at about 70 to 80% of its maximum speed during all workouts; the same is true for race distance. This is important to avoid overwhelming and overworking your horse.

Most trainers follow an "interval training" plan. This involves working out two days in a week with the horse making multiple short sprints on each day with rest periods of rest in-between those sprints. The horse is expected to reach a maximum heart rate of 200 to 250 per minute during this training.

A sprinting horse should be observed closely and evaluated for signs of respiratory distress, bone or muscle soreness or other problems, and workout should be discontinued to allow the horse to recover if any of these are observed.

### Pay Attention to Your Horse's Weight and Diet

During these respiration training routines, you must evaluate the physical condition of your horse. An overweight horse must lose weight during its workout, and you must focus on routines that make this possible. Similarly, if your horse is underweight, you must increase its food ration, especially with fatty foods. However, the fat should be introduced slowly to avoid adverse effects on your horse's digestion. The diet of a horse in training should also contain minerals, and vitamins, and access to clean and fresh water at all times.

### Horse Training for Shows

If you are training for shows, your horse needs to learn specific tricks. Many showmanship competitions are for showcasing the ability of a handler to perform skills with the horse. However, no matter the handler's skill, only a well-trained horse can perform the intricate moves that win shows.

Showmanship training also offers additional benefits, even outside the show ring. Basic show training will improve the horse's manners and respect. It will also improve its ability to maintain control over its pace and position. Some skills may also be useful for real-life scenarios.

## Basic Horse Training for Shows

There are six major maneuvers involve basic showmanship training. You can teach your horse these basic maneuvers, and these techniques can be combined in different ways and serve as the basic foundation for more advanced techniques.

- Leading at a walk

- Backing up

- Leading at a jog

- Pivoting

- Stopping

- Setting up

Before we describe these maneuvers in greater detail, you must understand basic things about training your horse to perform these skills. To train these maneuvers, you apply pressure on a lead chain. You also direct your horse with pressure from your own body sometimes. Reward every correct response by releasing pressure and pausing briefly before you give your horse the command for another maneuver.

Some exaggerated body movements or verbal cues may be required in training, especially for beginners. However, as your horse progresses, you must refine or adjust these cues until they are virtually non-existent or subtle as these cues and train your horse to adapt and follow instructions without them.

Note that progress in horse training is slow and steady. Your horse may not produce the results you want right way, but consider any close approximation to what you want as a desired response and reward accordingly.

### Leading at a Walk

*Goal:* This drill is aimed at training your horse how to lead calmly at the same pace as you are moving while maintaining its body on a straight line.

*How to:* The starting position of this drill is such that the offside of your horse is positioned close to a fence or guardrail to align its motion. The trainer should be positioned between the middle part of the horse's neck and its throatlatch. Start off on a quick walk without moving your arms. Incline your shoulders in a forward direction to serve as a visual command for a forward motion for your horse. Also, apply some pressure on the chain to get the horse to follow you as you move.

### Leading at a Jog

*Goal:* This exercise trains your horse to step into a trot or jog when you start running, all while keeping its body straight.

*How to:* The starting position of this drill is the same as the previous ones. Start with a walk with your elbow positioned on your side and your lead-hand anchored. With your body tilted forward, step forward and break into a small jog or run. Keep your elbow and lead hand steady as you run. If the horse responds accordingly and can adjust its pace to yours, relieve some of the pressure on the chain. You can also return to a brief walk after some seconds of jogging or trotting. If it does not break into a jog as expected, you may need to use verbal cues.

### Stopping

*Goal:* The goal of this training is to get your horse stopped in a balanced and soft manner and with its body straight and properly aligned.

*How to:* Maintain the same starting position as the previous training and start with a walk. As your horse walks with you, give a stop command softly, such as "whoa." Stand still immediately as you give this command. This verbal cue will help your horse associate the command with the action. At first, your horse may go past you a bit but will stop moving when the rope tightens against its chin. After a while, your horse should be able to respond to the stop command. When it does, reward accordingly by releasing the rope pressure. Repeat the command as many times as possible until your horse is used to it. With time, you should be able to eliminate the verbal cue entirely.

### Backing

*Goal:* This training is aimed at getting your horse to back up smoothly and calmly and with its body aligned properly when a command is given.

*How to:* Begin this training in the lead position earlier described. Turn your body to the opposite direction (now you should be facing the rear end of the horse). Align yourself with your arm or shoulder level with the muzzle of the horse. While still holding the lead rope, take one step forward (use your left leg first) and apply a rearward pressure on the chain. With this motion, you should be invading your horse's space. This training is to get your horse to step back when you do this. Usually, the horse will only move one of its legs out of the way. With time, it should adjust fully and back up properly with both legs.

### Setting Up

*Goal:* The goal of this exercise is to train your horse to set itself up with its legs under him. Your horse will learn to maintain this position until you give it another command.

*How to:* These techniques can be taught in various ways, so the method we will describe here is just one of the many ways it can be done. Start this training in the standstill position earlier described, then turn to face the horse. In this position, be positioned on the left side of your horse's head. Hold the lead chain close to the juncture of the chain and leather parts.

The first step is to control the movement of your horse's feet. Begin by making the horse move its left hind leg close to the right hind leg. You can control the horse to push its foot forward or backward, depending on the initial position of the right leg relative to the left. Pull-on the chain until you get your horse to respond appropriately. Reward a correct response with a pressure release.

### Pivoting

*Goal:* This training is aimed at getting your horse to anchor itself on the spot on its right hind-foot. The horse will then pivot around that foot by crossing its left leg across the right one.

*How to:* Begin by facing the left side of your horse and position yourself just across the throatlatch. With your left hand, hold the shank at the point where the chain and the leather meets. To initiate movement, apply a light forward pressure to the chain and step forward step with your right leg. This will encourage your horse to step his left front leg in front of the right. Raise your hand slightly to tap the horse on its left shoulder. This cue and body language should make the horse move its legs and shoulders in the right direction. Take the training one step a time until your horse can complete a 360-degree full pivot.

Beyond these basics, your horse must learn more advanced maneuvers that cannot be covered in this book, especially if you intend to go fully into showmanship. However, this is a good basic foundation to start with. You can find additional materials at a feed or tack store, or contact a professional trainer for help.

# Conclusion

Raising horses is no easy job, which is why many people choose boarding facilities instead. If you raise your horses on your own land, then you have to be ready to commit and put in the required work. This includes preparing housing facilities, proper nutrition, health, grooming, and daily care for your equine friend.

Raising horses also requires an in-depth knowledge of horse breeding, foaling, and weaning. Depending on your purpose for raising horses, you must learn about training your horse. This includes basic horse training and advanced training for athletics or showmanship.

Horse raising is a highly beneficial venture. Horses serve many purposes, including simply human companionship, helping you make the best use of your free time, and as work animals on farming facilities. Keeping horses can also be beneficial for your health.

You may also raise horses for commercial purposes or train your horse for equestrian sports. No matter your reason for raising horses, this book summarizes all the things you need to know about breeding healthy and strong horses. I hope you have learned enough in this book to set you on the right path on your journey to becoming an expert hostler.

# Part 2: Raising Donkeys

*The Ultimate Guide to Donkey Selection, Caring, and Training, Including a Comparison of Standard and Miniature Donkeys*

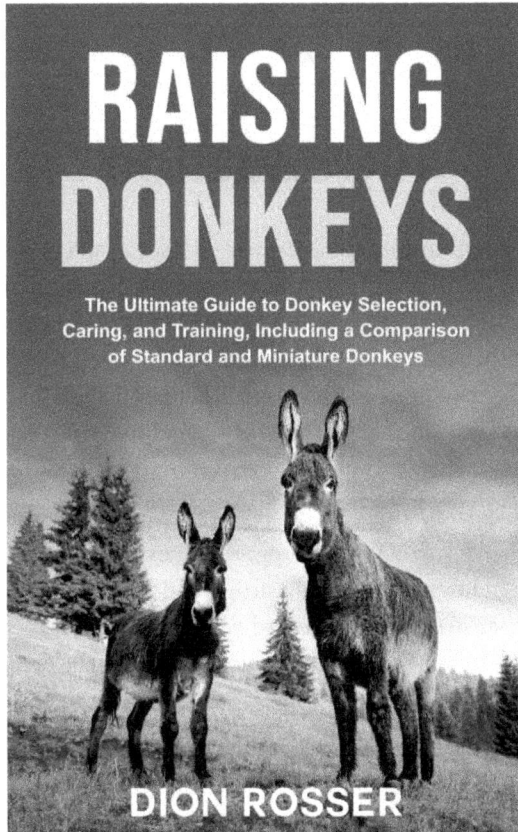

# Introduction

Donkeys are unique creatures that evolved and adapted to live in harsh environments with rough terrain and without a lot of nutrient-rich forage. This makes them hardy animals and good for a variety of agricultural and other types of physical tasks. Many use donkeys as guard animals for livestock; others use them to carry small loads on their backs or to pull carts. They can provide manual labor for grinding stones and even make their way between narrow rows of produce with more ease than a horse.

Many people keep donkeys as pets or companion animals. Raising donkeys can be a lucrative and rewarding experience that provides a decent income. They are incredibly strong and have a great temperament, and are less expensive to purchase and care for than horses. Their smaller size makes them suitable for tasks that horses cannot perform.

Like with any animal, though, there is care involved, and these animals must receive regular care and maintenance to thrive. Knowing what all donkey ownership entails and how to care for your animals is the point of this guide.

## What This Guide Contains

First, we briefly introduce the social and evolutionary history of the donkey - from their time in the wild to human's early use of them for a variety of labor functions. Then, we will touch on some of the major breeds, temperament, physical differences, and the like. Next, we will move on to tips and information you need to purchase healthy animals that meet your expectations and needs.

### Training and Management

Once we have gotten through the basic information you'll need, we will turn to the care of donkeys, including feeding and maintenance, such as grooming and hoof care. You'll learn the best ways to train donkeys with tips and hints on how to get the success you desire in this process is provided in detail. Everything you need to know about donkey breeding is reviewed. Common diseases and issues that can plague donkeys, how to avoid these problems, and how to diagnose them are also covered.

We then have a brief aside on the milking of donkeys, which isn't all that common but *perhaps should be.*

Finally, we round out the book with a discussion of mules and end with information about how to create a business raising and caring for donkeys.

# Chapter 1: Purpose and Benefits of Raising Donkeys

## Donkeys and Humans: A Longstanding Relationship

Donkeys have first domesticated some 6,000-years ago and have had a long and beneficial relationship with humans ever since. Known scientifically as Equus asinus and descended from an African wild ass, they have been a well-loved work animal since early in human civilization. Males are called jacks, females as a jenny or jennet, and their offspring as a foal. They have served several purposes for humans during their long history with us, including companion animals to other farm animals, protection, riding, and even as a work animal or beast of burden.

The donkey has a long and storied history alongside humanity and is a great animal to have with other equines, like horses. Interestingly, donkeys can also mate with several other equine species, including horses and zebras. Their offspring are called hinny or mules and zedonk (or zebrass), respectively.

This humble and unique animal was also prized for its working power and even healing power. For a long time, donkey milk was used as a medicinal substance for a variety of circumstances. This included feeding premature babies, sick children, and there is even evidence it was thought to be an effective treatment for tuberculosis patients. Their milk is higher in sugar and lowers in fat than cow's milk.

Like other equine, donkeys are also long-lived animals. They tend to live to at least 25-years old, and it's not unheard of for a donkey to live as long as 60 years in some cases. At 40, a donkey would be considered elderly and thus unable to work with the same vigor and ferocity as a younger donkey can.

# Benefits of Donkeys

There are a lot of misconceptions about donkeys that may make one think that they don't make good animals for pets or as a farm animal. However, they have a huge number of positive behaviors and traits that make them highly desirable as farm animals, whether for their power to work or their power to protect. Let's take a look at some of the biggest benefits of raising donkeys on your property.

### Temperament

Donkeys get a bad rap for being stubborn, which is largely not true. They are highly intelligent animals that learn and react in different ways than, say, a horse might. They can be taught several valuable behaviors and tend to be gentle – even affectionate –animals that show a wide range of positive social skills, both with people and other animals. They have a good attitude about most things, and unless they feel threatened, they tend to be rather quiet animals. This means, if your donkey is braying loudly, there is probably something afoot.

Especially when gotten as foals (babies), they will often grow up to be sweet and affectionate towards people. They are very social and will need a lot of social interaction with both people and animals, and they can even be taught to eat out of your hands. Donkeys get on well with other donkeys and horses (particularly mares) and can be taught to tolerate other animals like cows, sheep, goats, etc. While they will bond with livestock, it is important to understand that they are territorial animals.

When introducing a donkey to livestock, it needs to be supervised to ensure the safety of the stock animals, as donkeys can be extremely aggressive if they feel threatened. Most often, the process of introduction takes place over several weeks and starts with a fence or some sort of guard between the donkey and the stock animals. Once the donkey is used to the stock animals, they will typically be gentle and friendly towards them.

Since they are so social, they can develop deep bonds with people or other animals. This means they can experience great distress if a companion animal dies. Though rare, this can, in extreme cases, lead to a condition called hyperlipemia, which can even cause death.

Donkeys also do prefer a calm and quiet environment. Loud noises and a lot of rackets are likely to stress or irritate the animal, and they have been known to bite the animal or person who is the source of loud noises - something to remember if children are going to be around the donkey.

### Intelligent

Donkeys, like other equine species, are known for their intelligence. They are highly curious creatures who can learn a wide range of different behaviors and reactions to stimuli. They not only crave, but they also need mental stimulation and can act out and develop unwanted behaviors if they aren't given enough space or ways to fill their time. Like humans, they act out when they are bored.

Since donkeys are such social creatures, they thrive best when raised with other animals, particularly donkeys or mares (female horses). They are also less likely to develop undesirable behaviors when raised with adult animals like other donkeys who have been properly raised. It seems they can learn both good and bad behaviors from other animals.

While they are incredibly intelligent, it is important to note that there are sharp distinctions between them and humans. They do not possess a "moral compass," nor do they take cues from their social surroundings as to what is or is not acceptable behavior. In short, they don't know the difference between right and wrong, as that is a human construct. This is something to remember when training a donkey.

A donkey simply responds to what works or doesn't work, not whether the action or behavior is desirable or wanted. The type of reinforcement you give the donkey is key, and they learn much better with clear and simple communication from the trainer or owner. As with most animals, unnatural behaviors, such as being ridden, take longer for a donkey to learn. They will pick up on their surroundings much faster, making it easier for them to learn proper interactions with other animals. With this in mind, you must stay patient when training a young donkey.

As the owner or trainer gets to know the donkey, both will learn to better "read" each other. The way an owner or trainer treats the donkey will have a huge impact on how well and how quickly they learn to do desirable behaviors. Again, communication is key, and donkeys with a good rapport with their trainer or owner tend to pick up new skills more quickly.

Horses are well known for having highly expressive body language, which can give owners and trainers clues as to the mindset or emotional state of the animal. This isn't the case with donkeys, and it can take longer to get to know and understand the actions and behaviors of the animal. To many, they are "hard to read" when it comes to their emotional state, and they've been said to have a very stoic temperament that gives little emotion away. This doesn't at all mean they don't have emotions - they most certainly do - it just takes longer and is more difficult to ascertain.

Since they can be a little hard to read, this can cause some miscommunication between animal and owner or trainer. Since humans best understand human body language, we can often misread a donkey's behavior in ways that don't apply to the animal. For example, sometimes, when a donkey is highly stressed, their eyes will widen. To a human, this may indicate curiosity and interest, but it is a sign of distress.

Their cool demeanor is also why so many people use them as guard animals, though this might be surprising to some at first. They are less prone to the "flight reaction" than horses and other equines, which means they are more likely to stand up to predators. This lowered flight reaction makes them stand their ground in potentially threatening situations, which will be discussed in more detail below.

You'll get to know your donkey's personality better with time, which will lead to more effective and positive interactions and communications with the animal. As you learn about their personality, you can learn better to communicate your wants and desires to the animal, and they are more likely to understand what you want from them. Like humans must get to know each other to have effective communication, so to do humans and donkeys.

Being social and highly intelligent, donkeys make great animals for younger people or others with limitations to learn to ride. They can also be put to work in a variety of ways, which is discussed below.

## Behaviors

As intelligent creatures, donkeys can exhibit a huge array of different behaviors and can learn how to perform several tasks, but some of their natural behaviors should still be understood. Donkeys are known for being pretty "chill" creatures. One reason many people choose them over horses is that they tend to have a calmer and more laid-back demeanor. They are also curious, gentle, and will often be affectionate with trusted humans.

Training is key for achieving desired behaviors and minimizing the expression of undesirable behaviors. Patience is important when training a donkey. The adage that they are stubborn is not as true as some might think, but it definitely has some merit. Since they are social creatures, they will feed off signals we give them, whether intended or otherwise. It is vital that trainers know their body language and verbal cues they may be giving to the animal, as this will affect how well (or not well) they pick up the behaviors one is attempting to teach them. Good or desirable behaviors need to be rewarded and encouraged quickly.

Their behavior is reliably stable, so any dramatic or noticeable change in behavior may be an indication of a larger problem. If the donkey is acting markedly different than normal, it is recommended to have them looked at for potential health issues. If they start to develop an undesirable behavior, address it immediately, as the behavior is more likely to be expressed (and harder to eliminate) the longer it is allowed to continue.

While we do know a lot about donkeys, there is still a lot we don't know. For example, there is a question as to whether behavioral traits can be passed from one donkey to another; right now, the proverbial jury is still out on that one. Since a lot is unknown about their genetics, but we do know that their surroundings and environment are largely indicative of their behavior and attitude, how they are raised becomes ever more important.

Trainers will have the best results in terms of the donkey's interaction with and relations to other animals when they are socialized from a young age with other animals. They learn for their surrounding environment, and so only trained animals that exhibit the desired behaviors should be kept with a donkey in training. Often, donkeys are kept with mares and foals. Well-trained mares will help create the environment for a well-trained donkey. It is vital to start interacting with them and working with them at a young age. Behaviors are far more difficult to get rid of once they emerge rather than reduce the likelihood of their occurring, to begin with.

Donkeys can also be very vocal when they want to communicate something, and, though it will take time, you will learn what the different noises mean or what emotions they indicate. This will also help you more effectively communicate with your animal and determine what is wrong in the event the animal is showing distress.

Chewing is an incredibly common behavior for donkeys. They are known to chew on anything from wooden fence posts to items of clothing that may have been left around. They are also known to escape, so keeping fences properly closed and latched is also important.

### Environment

Donkeys can live in a wide range of different environments and terrains, which can make them more versatile than other equines with more limited environmental requirements. If, for example, you live on difficult or uneven terrain, a donkey is an option much better than a horse as they can more easily navigate an uncertain environment and are far more nimble.

The donkey evolved and selectively bred to withstand long journeys with scarce forage for them to eat. This means they can function on far fewer resources than, say, a horse can. Due to the environment they evolved in, they are lean but also amazingly smart and cunning, able to find food to browse on even in seemingly inhospitable environs.

In the wild, it is easy for a donkey to stay trim and fit, often hailing from the desert or other harsh types of environment where there simply isn't enough food for them to become overweight. However, if they are given too much access to food or forage as farm animals, they can easily become overweight, and a lot of negative health problems can result from this. A strict feeding schedule is recommended, and they require little supplemental feeding if provided a decent amount of area to browse.

Donkeys also evolved to be highly active animals and thus require a decent amount of physical and mental stimulation, or they may begin to act out or show signs of mental distress. They need to have a proper amount of space to move about it.

They also aren't that great with changes, particularly large environmental ones. While these changes cannot always be avoided in certain circumstances, it is important that, if possible, any change is introduced slowly to allow the donkey to acclimate.

## Low-Maintenance

One of the most important reasons to own donkeys is that they are relatively low maintenance, especially when compared with other equines known for having finicky dietary needs and often requiring lots of veterinary care. They tend to be healthy, robust animals that rarely have issues. Not that donkeys can't get sick or never experience negative health, but comparatively speaking, they are far less hassle than a horse.

Donkeys require a lot fewer inputs than other equines. They can largely browse for their food and need only a little supplemental hay or straw to get by. They also eat, by volume, far less than horses and other equines, which makes them an economical choice for sure. They are also not nearly as expensive from the outset. They are well known to require less food than even an equally-sized pony.

As grazing animals, donkeys will eat almost any fiber-rich vegetation and can find sufficient nutrition off a relatively small plot of fallow land. Since they can eat nearly anything, they find much of their nutritional needs from wild foods. They may browse vegetation for up to 16 hours a day. They prefer browsing on higher fiber plants, but as stated above, just about any vegetation is fair game. Each animal requires about a half-acre of land in order to graze.

They need a bit supplemental hay only or straw, most often in winter, when forage is harder to come by. They will need regular access to water and do drink more than some other equine animals. They thrive best when given daily trace mineral salts, which will be discussed in depth in the chapter on feeding.

Donkeys are hoofed animals, like all other equines, and thus, at times, will require foot maintenance. They do not get nearly as many feet issues as horses are known to get but will require hoof trimming about every 4-8 weeks. And the donkey will also need to be regularly drenched (dewormed). Like most equines, they will require regular vaccination against things like influenza, and when this basic care is provided, they rarely need any more medical treatment than this.

Unlike horses, donkeys do not have an undercoat. This leaves them more vulnerable to rain and cold and will require protection from the elements.

### Protection/Companionship

The donkey is growing in popularity as a companion animal due to its highly social and affectionate nature. They tend to be calmer and laid back than horses and will often become so affectionate with people as to eat from their hands and greet them when they come into their living space. While they may be a little stubborn when it comes to learning new things, they really do tend to be quiet, gentle animals, but at times, donkeys will snap at other animals for being too loud or to protect their environment if they feel threatened.

Not only do donkeys make good companions for people, but they also make even better companions for other animals. They get on very well with other equines, including mares and foals. They are often introduced as a companion to a horse mare after her foals are taken from her. They almost always get on well with other donkeys, especially if they are raised from foals together.

Perhaps less commonly known is the highly territorial nature of donkeys, which is both a positive aspect of this animal and can be a downside. It's positive in that they will protect flocks and can even run off predators if they feel their environment is threatened. They have huge ears and are known for their great hearing, so they will often hear any potential intrusions well before any other animal and certain people.

They don't distinguish, and dogs may be included in animals that are run off from the yard. If they are raised with puppies, they will be more used to them and, thus, will be less likely to bite them. However, they are famous for nipping to keep an unruly pup in line. And it should also be said that all donkeys are different, and some simply won't abide by a dog, any dog, regardless.

Due to their highly territorial nature, donkeys can be used to guard livestock like sheep, goats, cows, and the like. However, the introduction needs to be gradual. As we noted earlier, donkeys don't like a drastic change, and they are territorial, so they have to be introduced to new animals slowly. This often takes place during several weeks, first through a fence or some other form of protection, then supervised, until finally the donkey can be left alone with the livestock.

To the donkey, the livestock simply becomes part of its environment. While they will most certainly protect the livestock in their territory, they are more protecting the territory than the animals, though the result is the same. Though it takes time, the donkey will often bond with the other animals and spend much of its time browsing near the rest of the crew.

Donkeys won't bother with small animals like birds or raccoons, but they will run off dogs, foxes, and coyotes. They are always listening and amazingly attentive to their surroundings; they often investigate unknown noises or commotion. Unlike horses, donkeys are not as prone to running at signs of a potential threat. They will stand their ground and even attack if running the interloper off isn't successful. Kicking and biting are their two most common forms of defense. They will also use auditory threats like loud braying.

If possible, it is best to raise the donkey with other animals in the area. Then, it is less likely to ever turn against the family pet or livestock, and the animal will bond more solidly with the livestock.

Here, we should point out that intact jacks are not the best choice for this purpose. Most often, jennies or gelded (castrated) jacks are used for guarding and protection purposes.

### Work

During their millennia-long partnership with humans, donkeys have been prized for their low maintenance and ability to work. Donkeys are very hard-working animals, and though not as common today, they were once the primary work animal in several, largely inhospitable environments. Their hardiness and ability to work in rough conditions is part of what made them so attractive to man all those thousands of years ago.

Though many keep them today as companion animals, donkeys are great to work animals and can provide for several functions. As we mentioned briefly earlier, donkeys can be great to ride. This is especially true for children, older adults, or those with disabilities. Donkeys, of course, are not large and intimidating, have a good demeanor, and are often less scary to young children than horses. Most important of all, donkeys are very patient, which is huge for teaching a child to ride. Since they are so gentle and often affectionate, they just interact better with children besides being a more reasonable size to ride.

Though riding is what they are most used for in a work setting today, they are also great to pack animals and can even haul small loads in carts. They can carry up to 100 lb. on their back and can pull twice their body weight at ground level, for example, using a cart.

# Chapter 2: Donkey Breeds: Standard vs. Miniature

As with many animals, there are a lot of subspecies, or breeds, of the donkey, ranging in size, color, temperament, ability, and more. The word "donkey" is an English term that is most often used, as it would stand to reason, in English-speaking parts of the world. The word "burro" is another commonly used term to refer to animals in the Equus asinus genus, and it derives from the Spanish word "borrico," which simply means "donkey." Many people in non-English speaking parts of the world use the term burro to refer to miniature donkeys. In the American southwest, it is becoming increasingly common to hear donkeys called burros.

The American Donkey and Mule Society use the term "burro" to refer to mid-sized animals who descend from wild species of donkey and don't use it in relation to miniature donkeys or exceptionally large breeds. This semantic difference can cause a little confusion, depending on the origin of the website, book, or person you are talking to. Their place of origin is likely to affect the terms they use to refer to this animal.

Donkeys have been selectively bred for thousands of years to bring out a variety of features or behaviors. Predecessors to this species can still be found in the wild in many places, though they are becoming increasingly rare. Domesticated standard donkeys have been known to escape and revert to a more wild or feral state, living out their days in the wild.

Miniature donkeys are fully-domesticated animals and are not found in the wild and would not fare particularly well if they escaped.

Estimates suggest there are 50 million donkeys worldwide, making them a popular equine species though many are unfamiliar with their use as work or companion animals.

# History and Types of Donkey

As stated in the opening chapter, humans have a longstanding relationship with the donkey that goes back some 6,000-years. This long history has seen a lot of change not only in human culture and society but in the look and temperament of the donkey. The different breeds of donkey will vary in size, color, and temperament, but the general history of the donkey is roughly the same regardless of breed.

### A Brief History of the Donkey

Donkeys are equine species, and millions of years ago, the donkey, the horse, and other equine species all descended from the same ancient animal. Their genetic paths have diverged greatly since then, but they are distant relatives in the genetic family tree. Horses and donkeys, though related, have very different biology and temperament, so the similarities end at the fact that both are hooved equine species.

Donkeys have two distinct genetic lineages. These lineages evolved in quite different climates, and their differences are very important to their temperament and the care they need. The main lineages are Asiatic and African, which we will look at, in turn.

The Asiatic lineage of donkeys includes several species, but they all came from roughly the same area between the Red Sea and Tibet. This is a huge demographic range with vastly different environmental conditions. Asiatic donkeys evolved to deal with a huge range of environments, from a more typical desert environment to high altitudes and unsteady terrain, such as what is found in Tibet. There is a range of different species derived from the Asiatic ass.

The African lineage doesn't include as many species and covers a large, but more environmentally similar ecological niche. African asses are found between the coast of the Mediterranean Sea to the south of the Red Sea, usually in incredibly dry regions like the Sahara Desert. The two African species are the Nubian and the Somali wild ass. This is the lineage of most modern domesticated donkeys.

Donkeys have been domesticated for some 6,000 years, and it is believed that domestication originated in North Africa. The animals were originally domesticated for meat, milk, and hides. They weren't used as beasts of burden until about 2,000-years ago, at least from the evidence we have found.

The domesticated asses first used as draught animals were put to work, making the long 4,000-mile journey across the Silk Road, loaded down with cargo. This journey, since done on foot, could take a couple of years to complete. This long-distance travel resulted in breeding between disparate breeds that were once geographically far apart, helping to create the complicated assortment of donkey varieties we see in modern times.

Their use for carrying cargo on the Silk Roads exposed other peoples to their myriad of uses. The Greeks found that donkeys were ideal for traversing the narrow and rocky paths that make up the Greek lands and are small enough to navigate between grape vines - grapes being a very important part of Greek life and economics. Since they were such a good animal for working grapevines, the donkey spread to other wine-growing regions like Spain. While it seems like an unbelievably long distance, somehow getting from Africa to Spain, the coast of Spain and the coast of North Africa are only a few miles apart in certain areas.

We can thank the Romans for the entry of the donkey into mainland Europe. The Romans used donkeys for farm work, typically using them as agricultural inputs or to haul produce. Wherever the Romans would plant vines in the places they conquered, which is basically wherever they would grow, the donkey was brought. There were vineyards as far north as Germany and France during the empire.

When the Romans invaded England, they also brought the donkey along with them. Historians dated this introduction to around 43 AD when the Romans invaded Britain. While there were a few scattered donkeys in use in this area at the time, it wasn't until the 16th century that they became commonplace in the British isles.

With the invasion of Ireland by Oliver Cromwell, more donkeys were introduced into the area to assist with the war effort. They weren't used as the primary animal of burden, but they were able to make up for the shortfall of horses with their labor. It is estimated that there were some

250,000 donkeys owned by the British Army at the end of the first World War, showing just how useful they proved to be for the military.

With a long and storied history, evolving and being selectively bred alongside humans as they developed more and more complex and global civilizations shows just how close the relationship is between the evolution of the donkey and human intervention.

# Standard Donkey Breeds

There are tons of different breeds of donkey. According to country reports tallied by the International Domestic Animal Diversity Information System within the Food and Agriculture Organization of the United Nations, there are some 172+ breeds of donkey worldwide - most of which are very rare and region-specific, and a few breeds thought to be extinct.

While there are a variety of donkeys, the most commonly-owned breeds of donkey are the Grand Noir du Berry, the hinny, the mule, the Poitou, and the miniature, which will get its own subsection below. Let's look at each of these common breeds in turn.

### Grand Noir du Berry

This donkey breed takes its name from the Berry region of France from which it originates. The males are generally around 135-145 cm at the withers (the tallest portion of the donkey between the shoulder blades) and females around 130 cm. As the name implies, their coats are typically black but can be other colors like bay brown, dark bay brown, or grey.

This breed of donkey often has a grey belly, muzzle, thighs, and portions of their leg. They do not have the typical cross that many people associated with donkeys and also have no stripes present on the legs. Grand Noirs have a great temperament and are incredibly strong for their size.

Early on, they were found to be more useful than other animals in working with grapevines and were thus the primary animal used for this type of agriculture in the region. Their size makes it easier for them to travel between the narrow rows of vines better than horses. In the 19th century, the donkey replaced human power for pulling barges down the Berry Canal and, once approaching Paris, their usual destination, the Briare Canal.

The Grand Noir has been standardized as a breed by local organizations that promote their breeding and use. They have great temperaments and are often chosen as companion animals or pets. To this day, the Grand Noir is still used by small-scale farmers and to carry tourist packs while hiking in the region.

### Hinny

A hinny is a cross-breed between a female donkey and a male horse. They most often have the external features (for example, facial features) of a horse, but the body type and size of a donkey. This is a smaller and rarer breed than a lot of the others, and it can often be confused with a mule. This breed is also genetically rare. Horses have 64 chromosomes, and donkeys have 62; the hinny has 63.

The coat color and pattern can vary widely among hinnies. The coat and type of pattern the hinny will have depend highly on the coat and markings of the parents, more so than with other breeds of the donkey.

Intact male hinnies are known to be very aggressive, and extreme caution should be used when interacting with them. They also should not be kept around livestock or other animals. You should choose a gelded male to avoid potential problems.

### Mules

We won't spend much time talking about the mule in this section as we dedicate an entire chapter to them below. This breed is very common in America and is much more common there than in Europe and elsewhere.

The mule is a mix between a male donkey and a female horse.

### Poitou

This is another donkey breed that takes its name from the region in which it originated, in this case, Poitou, France. The Poitou is one of the larger breeds of donkey and is distinguished by its size and its unique thick, often tangled coat.

Adult males are called *baudet* and range from around 142-153 cm in height, though they can be bigger. Females are called *anesse* and are usually about a hand (about 4 inches) shorter, and their coats don't tend to be as thick.

In earlier times, this was a breed commonly used for the breeding of mules, and their genes traversed the planet through this process. Now, they are less commonly used to breed mules, like any breed of donkey is suitable, and their population went on the decline. There wasn't much of a demand for purebred Poitous, so there was a tremendous drop in their population, and they went into a significant decline in the 1950s.

Worried that the Poitou might go extinct, studies were commissioned in the 1970s, and they showed that females were having fewer pregnancies and also fewer pregnancies that were able to come to term. This led to the launch of the Save the Baudet (SABAUD) movement, which continues to this day. This organization was launched in an effort to keep the animal from going extinct and finding ways to boost their population numbers.

Stud books have been opened, and information is shared to help encourage the breeding and continued existence of the Poitou breed of donkey. Experimental breeding programs have also been set up to find more effective ways for successful breeding. Though the process is slow-going and arduous, the population climbed again in the mid-90s, and the effort is ongoing.

### Miniature Donkeys

Also called a Miniature Mediterranean Donkey, this is a totally separate breed from what are considered standard donkeys. They originate from the islands of Sardinia and Sicily.

For the animal to truly be considered miniature, it cannot be any taller than 91 cm at the withers. Their parentage will also need to be documented as a miniature for them to be officially considered part of this breed.

These are uncommonly small and sweet animals and are one of the most well-known breeds of donkey for their cuteness. They come in a wide variety of different colored patterns and may or may not have markings. They range between black, grey, brown, cream, chestnut, spotted, and skewbald (animals with patches of white and another color, but typically not black).

The history of these animals is interesting. As they are so small, peasants found them very useful for turning grinding stones inside the home to grind grain. They became so well known for this use that in the 18th century, this task took on more industrial proportions. The animals were used in large scale grain mills and would be blindfolded, left to turn circles for hour after hour, grinding massive quantities of grain. Thankfully, they rarely serve this function anymore, especially not in an industrial capacity.

As with other breeds of donkey, they can also be used for small scale agricultural work. They also proved especially useful at carrying water and other supplies through mountainous or otherwise inhospitable regions. Today, they are most commonly kept as pets since they are known for gentle and sweet temperament, and their size is more conducive to being a pet.

# Chapter 3: Purchasing Your Donkeys: Selection, Cost, and Other Tips

The actual purchasing of donkeys might seem like the easiest part of the ownership process, but it actually comes with a ton of important considerations. These animals require special care and are long-lived, which shows why it is so important to carefully consider a variety of aspects before buying a donkey. Some important steps in the buying process can help to ensure that you make a good decision and investment with your money.

## Considerations to Address When Buying Donkeys

It takes a bit of research and some due diligence to ensure that you get animals that suit your specific needs and abilities. This isn't like making an impulse purchase of something that doesn't matter; donkeys are living creatures with emotional and physical needs that you will be responsible for providing it with. You must clearly understand what is involved with owning and raising donkeys for any purpose, but also the specific purpose with which you intend to use them.

There isn't really a pet store where you can go buy a donkey, so you will need to do some homework, and what follows are tips as to how to look for the right donkey for your needs. You will need to do a lot of legwork, but these animals are an investment, and a long-term one, so it just makes plain sense to ensure that you know what you are getting into and that you get a healthy animal that is trained or well-suited for your intended uses.

### First, A Warning About Buying Online

Just like with most things today, you can look at and purchase donkeys online, but you should use a lot of caution when doing this and it is not advised that you purchase animals online, without having physically seen them first. As great as the internet is, it is also a place where scams and shady people run rampant. It is far too easy to make a professional-looking website and grab pictures of healthy, happy animals from elsewhere on the web and use them as your own.

Customer testimonials can also be faked and easily bought online. This is why it is imperative that if you are looking at donkeys online, you do that extra homework to make sure that the breeder or vendor is actually legit and who they say they are. You can make successful purchases of animals online, and many people do because of the convenience, but you shouldn't shop for and buy animals online, sight unseen. Never ever deal with someone who is reluctant or simply refuses to let you see the animals in person before purchasing. This is a huge red flag that the operation is not legit and that you may either get scammed out of your money or end up with an unhealthy or ill-tempered animal for which you will then spend time (and often, money) figuring out what to do with.

The internet can be a good starting point when shopping. It can be a great source of information for anything you need to know about donkeys and their care, but it is not the ideal place to carry out the entire purchasing process as there is a lot you need to see in person when deciding on which animal or animals to buy.

# General Considerations

As we briefly touched on in the introduction, some homework is required in determining what kind of donkey to purchase and where to purchase it from. You need to consider your expectations, your skill and knowledge level, the amount of space you have available. There are resources involved with the long-term ownership and care of donkeys, and you should be able to manage these and not just the initial purchase. You can make money raising and using donkeys for specific activities, but it still requires regular inputs, training, medical care, and so on.

Remember, donkeys often live into their 30s and beyond. It isn't like buying a fish; it is a long-term investment and commitment. You need to be able to commit to decades of care and ownership.

Unless you are keeping the donkey as a pet, and sometimes even in that case, you will want your donkey to have other donkeys for companions. They are incredibly social animals and rarely fare well and have a lot of emotional distress without contact with other equines.

Consider the space you have to dedicate to the donkeys. You might look around and think you have plenty of space for 'x' number of donkeys, but they need to have plenty of room to run and have adequate space for browsing. Each animal will need at least half an acre for browsing, so you will need to plan the size of your brood.

Since we can get flustered when put on the spot, have a list of questions prepared in advance, so you don't forget to ask all pertinent questions of the breeder or vendor. Know what type of animal (breed, temperament, or training, etc.) you are looking for, so the breeder has the information they need to help you choose the best animals. When you have narrowed down your selection, ask to see the animals in a variety of settings. Ask to see them in the stables, in the pasture, being groomed, and ask to see their feet to ensure their hooves are well-trimmed and in good repair.

You mustn't make an emotional purpose because you think an animal is cute or sweet. You want the animals for a specific purpose, and you want to make sure that you choose an animal-based on those needs and desires. It's easy to get caught up in the sweet eyes of an affectionate donkey, but if that personality or skill set doesn't serve the purposes you are getting the animal for in the first place, it won't be a good fit. This isn't something you want to have buyer's remorse over.

## Physically Go See the Donkeys for Yourself

Whether you scope out a potential breeder or vendor online or you simply connect with someone local, it is vital that you physically go out and see the animals so you can make sure you are getting what you are being told you are getting. Though there are plenty of great, knowledgeable, and reputable donkey breeders, there are also people just looking to make a quick buck. They perhaps don't know what they are doing or simply cut corners to save on costs, which can lead you to be saddled with a subpar or unhealthy animal.

When possible, take someone with you with in-depth knowledge and lots of experience with donkeys. They will know what to look for, questions to ask that you might not have thought of, and red flags that may indicate that things are not what they seem.

Especially when buying a purebred or miniature donkey, you want to make sure that you are actually getting what you think you are getting. Purebreds and miniatures come at a higher price tag than other donkeys, so you want to make sure you are actually getting an official, legitimate breed.

By going to look at the animals, not only can you be sure that you are getting the breed you wanted, you can see the conditions the animal is kept in. You want animals that are kept in clean, healthy, and safe conditions, so they don't come to you sick or stressed out. Setting up an appointment for viewing is imperative, but experts recommend you visit more than once.

If at all possible, show up unexpectedly on your second visit, so you know they haven't created a fake or idealized environment simply for your behalf. You want to know what the actual conditions the animal is kept in are like.

In addition, to make sure you are getting the breed you expect and that the animals are in good condition physically, you also want to make sure that you are getting an animal with the right temperament and/or training for your desired needs. You will be looking for quite different things when looking for a donkey to be a pet as opposed to a donkey used to guard livestock. Clearly understand your expectations and needs when deciding which breeds or specific animals will be best suited for you.

For example, if you want a donkey that will be good for young children learning to ride, you don't want a fresh, untrained animal. It takes a lot of skill, experience, and years of training to prepare a donkey to accept and tolerate being ridden in order for it to be safe for children to ride them. Don't take the breeders word for it; it is always better to demand evidence and be sure.

If the breeder or vendor tells you the animal has been handled or trained, request a proof. Ask to see the animal interact with people and being ridden so you know that you are getting an animal that will be safe for your children to ride on.

### A Note on Males

Intact males are well known for being quite aggressive and difficult to handle and train. They can be unpredictable and may be dangerous for people who lack experience. Most experts recommend getting gelded males unless you plan on breeding them. Even if you plan on breeding them, you will need to keep the intact male away from other animals and use extreme caution when handling them for care. It is best to get a gelded male or make sure that you have the costs of castration included in your purchasing figures.

Gelding can be a complicated process that involves someone with experience and specialty, and it's expensive to have a male gelded after purchase. Many breeders and vendors will have already gelded males for sale, and choosing these is recommended.

### A Note on Miniatures

We should also touch on the particulars of purchasing miniature donkeys. Since this is a specialty breed, they typically command a price higher than other donkeys, even some purebred varieties. The animal, as we noted above, must meet certain criteria to be officially a miniature and thus command the higher price tag. If you are in the market for a miniature donkey, make sure the breeder can provide you with proof of age and parentage.

Though it isn't all that common, people have tried to pass off smaller donkeys or even ailing, malnourished older donkeys, like miniatures, so you want to have the proof for the peace of mind it provides.

## Cost

Since any animal will require regular and ongoing care, you will want to know all the costs involved not only in the purchase of the animals but their care. You will need to budget for hay, water, protection from the elements, trace mineral salt supplements, drenching, and regular hoof trimming. To keep donkeys healthy, annual vaccinations for things like influenza are recommended. Breeding animals will come with a whole range of costs too detailed for this kind of basic overview.

Typically, depending on the breed, age, and training of the animals, donkeys will range in price from around $500-2,000.

After choosing your animals and making the purchase, ask for a written receipt with as much pertinent information as possible documented on it. The receipt should include the following information:

- Vendor's name

- Vendor's address

- Vendor's phone number and email address (if applicable)

- Date of sale

- Cost of sale

- Any additional information such as the inclusion of tack or transport

## Equine Passports

To legally purchase a donkey, you will need to have a certificate of sale and an equine passport. All donkeys should come with an equine passport, or it will not be a legally-recognized purchase. First, you want to confirm before visiting that all their animals have legitimate equine passports. You will also want to ask to see the document before you finalize the purchase.

Since there is a legal element to this, you will want to make sure all your proverbial ducks are in a row. It isn't enough just to have the breeder's word that all the animals have an equine passport; you will want to see the document and make sure it is official.

When shown the passport, you will want to verify that the breeder or vendor information is correct and what you were given when working with them. You may also consider checking with the issuer of the passports to make sure that they are valid. If you don't have the certificate of sale and equine passport, not only can you end up being fined in certain areas, you will have no legal recourse if there is a problem.

Once you have done your homework, made a visit or two, and chosen your animals, it is time to make the purchase final and decide how you will get the animals home. Some breeders and vendors will include transport in the cost of the animal; others expect you to find your own transportation, which will involve the use of a trailer and a truck suitable for pulling an animal trailer.

If the cost of transport is included in your purchase, ask to see the trailer the animals are being transported in. You want to make sure that it is in good repair and a safe space for the animals to travel in. You don't want to have too many animals in one trailer where they may be unsafe, uncomfortable, and overstressed. That doesn't start the animal off on a particularly good footing at their new home. It is best if there can be as little stress as possible, which, of course, isn't easy, especially if the animals have to endure long-distance travel to get to their new home.

If you are responsible for their transport, you will either need to own or otherwise obtain access to a truck suitable for hauling an animal trailer. You will then need a trailer adequately sized for the number of animals you intend to transport. You will need to make sure the animals are properly protected and secured in the trailer, so you don't risk injury during the journey from one place to another.

# Chapter 4: Housing Your Donkeys

While donkeys are hardy animals, they evolved in warmer climates that don't get a ton of rain, may have unstable terrain, and often have very nutrient-poor forage to eat. This is the climate across large swaths of the world, but in places like the United States and Europe, the climate can be much different, with long periods of cold and, sometimes, a lot of rain. As we noted in an earlier section, donkeys do not have an undercoat as horses have, so they have no protection from the rain or cold weather and cannot tolerate being left exposed to either for long.

Basic shelter is necessary for any place that sees regular rain or has winter. The shelter need not be huge or anything extremely complicated either. Simple structures made from basic materials will work just fine. You just have to make sure that the animals have the correct space, adequate protection from the elements, and a safe environment to seek protection from the elements.

You don't have to be a builder or a professional carpenter to build a simple shelter. With just a basic understanding of how to use basic tools and the right supplies and you can put together a nice shelter that will keep your animals safe, even in harsh conditions. Below are some basic instructions on how to build a simple shelter for your donkeys. You may need to research some of the terms if you are unfamiliar with them, but we use a simple language as possible to explain the steps needed to build a shelter.

A plan and a trip to your local hardware store are all you need to get started. That, and some good old hard work, because building a shelter, even a simple one, is hard work. Most people, even those with rudimentary building skills, can put together a simple shelter in just a few days. If you are building an enclosure for just a couple of animals, you can likely get the project complete over a weekend if you have a bit of help.

# How to Build a Basic Donkey Shelter

You want to create a safe and comfortable enclosure for your animals that provides them with the amount of space and things they need to stay safe from the elements. You will want to make sure that your shelter is large enough for your animals. Most of the time, donkeys prefer to be outside, so they will likely spend most of their time outside of the enclosure, but you will want to make sure there is enough room should all the animals need to seek shelter simultaneously.

If you just have a couple of animals, an 8' x 8' enclosure will suffice. If you have many animals, you will want to make sure that you are providing adequate space for the animals. Most experts recommend giving about 40 sq. ft. of space per animal.

The basic instructions we use in this guide use the assumption that only donkeys will be kept in the enclosure. You will want to find more specific guidelines if you are looking to house your donkeys with other equines or other animals as their needs are a bit different. It will require more complicated planning to keep all the animals safe while still providing for their individual needs.

When deciding on a plan for your shelter, consider your landscape and the weather in your area. This will determine what you will need to include in your designs.

Once you have decided how large you want the structure to be, you will want to write out a simple plan with the appropriate measurements for your enclosure. The size of the space will not only depend on the number of animals you have but the open space you have available on your property.

Having a good plan will make it much easier to find what you need at the hardware store, so you don't get stuck making multiple trips because you keep forgetting something. You will need tools like a mason line, hammers, nails, and screws; a power drill can be very helpful. For the building itself, you will need:

- Properly-sized wooden poles for a frame
- Properly-sized lengths of wood to build the sidewall frame
- Wood for the roof
- Joist holders
- Shingles
- Glue for shingles
- Nails or screws
- Concrete (optional, some build wood floors since they are easier on the hooves)
- Framing for the door
- Chipboard or sheets of wood to line the framed walls and seal up the enclosure

To start, you will need a foundation. It is best if the foundation of the shelter is as level with the surrounding ground as possible. You will likely want to dig out the foundation so that after the wood or concrete is laid, it will be mostly flush with the ground. The foundation is one of the most important elements of the shelter, and great care needs to be taken to make sure the structure is on a level base.

Most people measure out their foundation using a mason's line as it is a simple and effective way of creating an evenly-sized space. Some people use concrete in the foundation, but this can be rough on the hooves of the donkey, so it should be lined with earth or hay. Others will make a wooden floor (be careful there isn't enough space between the boards for a hoof to get caught), while others just simply leave the floor earthen. It just depends on your land and your preferences; you just want to make sure they aren't standing for extended periods of time on hard and rough surfaces.

After you have your foundation built, it is time to make a pole frame for the building itself. Pole frame buildings are simpler to build than any other style, and they are known for being very sturdy and durable. They are also cheaper to construct than many other types of buildings. Especially if you don't have a ton of building skills, this is the building for you.

A pole frame consists of thick, sturdy, upright wooden posts that will bear the weight of the structure and thus need to be firmly rooted in the ground. It is recommended that your posts be placed around 2 feet (24 inches) in the ground to give them the strength they need to hold the roof on solidly.

Most woods made for outdoor use has been treated, and donkeys chew on pretty much anything, but wood especially. You will want to make sure that you restrict access to any treated wood to ensure that the donkey doesn't get sick.

After you have your major load-bearing uprights in place, you will use horizontal wooden lengths to frame the rest of the shelter around its perimeter. This will finish out the basic framing of the enclosure and will be where you attach walls and/or siding to the outside of the shelter. This step comes after the roof supports and joists are in place.

So, naturally, next, we come to roof supports. To keep the roof upright and stable, you will need roof joists. You will want to install joist supporters along the top edge of your wood frame in the spots where you will be putting wooden joists. Once the supports are in place, you can install the wooden joists.

When building the roof, you need to consider the amount of snow that you regularly receive and ensure that the roof can bear that amount of weight. If you aren't sure that it can bear the weight, you may have to come out and regularly clear the snow off the roof, which can be a real hassle.

Once your roof boards and materials are laid, shingle the roof as this will help to protect the wood from rotting, and from excessive expansion and contraction with changes in temperature.

Before you begin to shore up the sides and inside of the structure, you will want to consider the door. Some people have a typical stable door in their shelters. This is fine, but you want to make sure that the door is tall enough that the donkey can't jump over it and short enough that they can see over it. Some people simply don't have a door, which gives the donkey free reign to come in and out as they please. If you choose not to have a door, consider the most common direction the wind comes from and face the door away from the wind as best as possible.

A lot of longtime donkey owners claim that their animals prefer the open style rather than having a traditional stable door, but it just depends on the animals and the preferences of the owner. Since donkeys typically prefer to be outside in natural settings, it can be easier not to have a door and allow them to choose whether they want to be inside or not. However, the stable door will give you control over when they are in the shelter or outside. Again, it just depends on what you prefer. The ideal size for a door for the donkey enclosure measures 4' x 3'6".

Once this decision has been made, you will want to put up your outside walls. You can use weather-treated boards if you wish to keep the entire structure in a simple slat board style, or you can line outside walls with siding of your choice. One thing to note is that no treated wood should be accessible to your animals as they chew on wood. Many veterinarians argue that treated wood can make animals ill.

You will need to shore up the inside of the structure to keep your animals away from treated wood and to have a place to attach food and water holders. Many people just line the inside of the structure with chipboard sheets to provide a more finished look and to keep the animals from chewing the treated boards and posts.

Ventilation and airflow are also important, so some people leave a little clearance between the foundation and the walls of the structure to allow air to flow more easily through the shelter. You can also leave a bit of space between boards in the walls if you choose not to side the building, but you want to make sure that it isn't wide enough for an animal to get their hoof caught between boards.

Some use exhaust fans with locking shutters as a means of ventilation, and this is an excellent choice, especially if you are keeping a larger number of animals. Humidity can quickly get out of hand in a poorly-ventilated enclosure, which can make the animals sick.

# Other Shelter Elements

In the wild, donkeys graze with their heads down, so eating from the ground is their natural means of eating. A floor-level feeder for supplemental hay is a great way to provide the animals with forage while still using their natural mode of consumption. The Donkey Sanctuary recommends a feeding trough that measures approximately 2' wide by 3' x 2'3" deep.

Your animals will always need easy access to forage in the winter and clean water.

We briefly noted earlier that many would line the floor of the shelter with some sort of bedding. It is important that clean straw is used and that the material is water-resistant or is frequently changed. Donkeys can become ill if left with a rotting or overly-moist straw, so it is vital to clean the enclosure regularly and to replace the straw; otherwise, the animals may become ill.

Some people will use wood shavings as bedding, but most agree that straw is the best choice. There are products that you can buy that will help reduce moisture, such as Stall Dry or Sweet PD2.

Lighting may also be a consideration. Since most donkey shelters have one side open, this isn't often a problem, but in certain areas or with certain types of enclosure, it can get pretty dark in these enclosures, and donkeys don't like to be kept in the dark. If so, you will want to provide some supplemental lighting. Make sure that all cords are kept out of reach of the animals, and guards are installed on any lights that they can reach.

# Winter Donkey Care

Before we dive into winter donkey care, we should make a note about shelters in the summer. Though donkeys prefer to stay out in the open, they may seek shelter on days that are incredibly hot and sunny to avoid dehydration or heat exhaustion. They should have access to shelter year-round and always have ready access to clean water. If you choose to use misting fans, make sure that all cords are secure and out of the donkey's reach because they will try to chew on them.

Some people will put misting fans in the shelter during the summer to help keep their animals cool or will hose donkeys down with water on particularly hot days. If you use either option in the shelter, remember that this will cause the bedding to become moist. This can then cause bacteria and fungus to grow, and it will need to be replaced after each misting or hosing down.

Now onto winter. If you live in a cold area, you may want to insulate the shelter to help protect the animals from intense cold and wind. If you notice any condensation in the structure, it is a sign you do not have adequate ventilation, and you will need to address this since moisture can cause a host of different issues in donkeys.

As with any season, donkeys in winter will need to be provided with adequate supplemental food and water. It isn't recommended to keep the enclosure warmer than 50 degrees. Water, naturally, is prone to freezing in the winter, so you will need to make sure that the water you leave for the donkeys doesn't get so cold it freezes and is inaccessible to the animals. Some people will use an automated water heating system to keep the water free of ice.

You will also want to supply the animal with a vitamin and mineral balancer or a mineral salt lick.

If you have only a few animals, try to keep the space suitable to that number as it will be much harder to keep an overly-large enclosure warm enough during the winter months to protect the animals.

For those who live in areas that have bitterly cold winters, donkey rugs and protective ear coverings may be necessary to ensure they are protected from the cold. If you use these, you will need to remove them daily to brush the animal and occasionally change it if it becomes soiled or wet. Older and underweight animals are most likely to need this additional protection.

It is advised to be prepared for winter by laying in a supply of supplemental hay and bedding to make sure you have what you need for the cold months ahead. Before the weather gets cold, it is a great time to make sure your animals are current on vaccinations, has their teeth looked at, and to either have a farrier come out or inspect and trim hooves yourself if you have the proper skill and tools.

Rain Scald and mud fever are two common conditions that can plague donkeys during the winter, especially if the donkey doesn't have access to a dry environment. Rain Scald typically affects the shoulder back and rump. Mud fever affects lower extremities.

# Outdoor Space Considerations

Donkeys are known to wander away from their home territory, so fencing is an important element to ensure you don't have a bunch of escaping donkeys you have to track down and return. Enclosed spaces work best, and typically most pasture is fenced in. Wood makes good fencing, but as we have mentioned numerous times, donkeys are likely to chew on the material, so if you use wood, it will occasionally need to be replaced or repaired. The fence should be at least 4' tall, so the donkeys cannot jump it.

Regular inspections are recommended to ensure your fence stays in good repair, especially if it is made from wood.

You will need to consider the type of vegetation on your land as there are plants that are known to be toxic to donkeys. Remove any poisonous plants from their pasture area, or keep the animals from accessing this area. Your local agriculture department can tell you if any poisonous native plants should be removed from your property before letting donkeys graze.

You should not graze donkeys on alfalfa grass as it is rich food, and donkeys are evolved to survive on nutrient-poor forage. Alfalfa is remarkably high in certain nutrients that donkeys aren't used to consuming in such quantities, and this can lead to stomach upset or other gastrointestinal issues.

Donkeys, as we have mentioned a couple of times, cannot have sudden changes in their food source. This will lead to gastrointestinal issues. Any new food or forage will need to be introduced slowly, usually over a couple of weeks, to allow them to adjust to the new food source.

You will need to provide numerous places to access clean water, and if your pastureland is large, you will want to place water troughs in various places around the property.

Mud is something that you will also want to keep an eye out for. Donkeys left standing in muddy areas can develop a range of different foot issues, so they should spend most of their time on dry ground.

Many people will use de-icers or other salt-based products to keep down on the ice during the winter, but this use is not recommended around donkeys. Salt will accumulate on surfaces, and this can cause problems with their hooves.

If your animals are getting the bulk of their calories from the pastureland itself and not from supplemental feeding, it is important to leave certain sections fallow. This will ensure that it can regenerate after significant grazing; otherwise, the land will quickly be exhausted and unable to support forage growth.

# Chapter 5: Feeding Your Donkeys

Though donkeys are a species of equine, they have hugely different nutritional needs than horses or other equines. Due to the environment they evolved in, they are accustomed to a diet of nutrient-poor forage, and rich foods that are high in nutrients will cause colic, stomach upset, and potentially a host of other gastrointestinal issues. This is why you must keenly understand the nutritional needs of these animals so you can provide them with appropriate food for their needs.

## Donkey Eating Habits

In their natural environment, donkeys are grazers. This means that they will browse a small amount of forage often throughout the day. They will consume roughly 1.3-1.8% of their body weight in forage daily. They are not used to - or meant to - eat food in large quantities. These animals will overeat, which can lead to a whole host of issues, so you will need to control their access to supplemental forage. Restricted grazing is also a means to help control the amount of food the animal eats at a given time. There are many different kinds of supplemental forage you can give to donkeys, which we will look at below. Still, the Donkey Sanctuary recommends barley straw as the best source of supplemental nutrition.

In the winter, donkeys will not likely have access to the forage and natural browsing they get in the summer, so they may largely or exclusively subsist off supplemental foods. This means you will need to provide them with a controlled amount of food daily, most often straw or a substance called haylage, which we will discuss below.

If any of your donkeys are ill or underweight, they will need extra high fiber forage, and you may want to consider supplementing their forage with vitamins.

For those with decent pasture, donkeys will require little supplemental feeding during the summer, but if your land is poor, more will be required.

As we have noted numerous times, donkeys will overeat. An overfed donkey is more prone to issues such as laminitis and hyperlipemia. These can be serious conditions and is further proof of the necessity of controlling the amount of food they have access to.

Barley straw, as we mentioned earlier, is the best source of supplemental nutrition for donkeys since it is low in sugar and high in fiber. Oat straw can be used and may actually be preferable for underweight or ill donkeys since it is higher in nutrients than barley straw. Use caution when feeding oat straw to healthy animals, as they can over-eat.

Younger animals or those with strong teeth can eat wheat straw, but it is not recommended for older animals or those with poor teeth. Wheat straw is lower in nutrition than the other types of straw we discuss here, so it isn't ideal. You will want to avoid linseed straw completely. Animals can safely eat the straw, the seeds are poisonous, and it is almost impossible to ensure that there are no seeds in linseed straw. It can be boiled to help reduce the toxicity of the seeds, but again, it can still cause issues that lead many to avoid this straw type entirely.

Hay can also be used as a food supplement besides being a great source for bedding for a donkey enclosure. Like straw, different types of hay are more or less suitable for donkeys. Make sure that any hay used for feeding or bedding is free of moisture and fungal growth.

What follows are the most common types of hay:

> • Meadow hay - this comprises a mix of natural grasses and is safe to use for feed.

- Seed hay - this is usually made from rye or timothy and refers to the stems that are left after the seeds have been collected. It is also suitable for use as a supplemental feed.

- Hay from cow pastures - since this hay tends to be rich in nutrients, it isn't the best source of supplemental food for donkeys.

Ragwort can be found in many different types of hay, and it is poisonous to equine. This is why you must have a trusted and quality source of hay.

Many people grow their own hay since it isn't too difficult and can make more financial sense than buying it from a third party. Most often, hay crops are harvested between late May through July. Though it can be harvested later, the later you harvest, the lower the nutritional value of the hay will be. Once the hay is harvested, it will need to be kept in a dry, well-ventilated space for at least three months.

Freshly-cut hay shouldn't be offered to donkeys as it can cause stomach upset like colic. Hay is considered ready for use when it reaches 85% dryness.

Haylage is another source of supplemental food sometimes given to donkeys for feed. Haylage is partially-wilted grass that has been dried, but not to the level that hay is dried. Typically, haylage is about 55-65% dry. To make haylage, once the grass is baled, you will want to seal it with strong plastic that is free from tears. If there are any tears in the plastic, dangerous mold can develop in just a few days, ruining the crop for use with donkeys and most other livestock animals.

Never feed donkeys silage (grass or other green fodder compacted and stored in airtight conditions, typically in a silo, without first being dried, and used as animal feed in the winter) as it has a much too high level of moisture and is far too low in fiber to make proper food for these animals.

If you don't have a good source of hay or haylage, high fiber pellets are another way to supplement your donkey's diet. It may also be preferable for use with animals with laminitis or need to put on weight. Since they are so much higher in nutrition than natural forage or hay, you will want to give the animals small amounts at a time, so they don't overeat.

If you are feeding a donkey with bad teeth, soaking the pellets in water will soften them and make them easier to eat. You will want to avoid pellets from mixed sources as they may be high in cereal grains, which aren't good for donkeys and do not provide their ideal nutrition.

Now, let's consider a substance called *chaff*, which can be used as a supplemental food source. Chaff is a mixture of chopped hay and straw and often has oils or other supplemental vitamins and minerals added to it. Animals with bad teeth or that struggle to eat straw may find this a preferable food source that is easier for them to manage. It is also a good choice in supplemental feed for donkeys that suffer from laminitis.

Chaff should have a sugar content of less than 8% and will often be listed as laminitic safe on the packaging.

Old or sick donkeys may benefit from supplemental feeding of small amounts of dried sugar beet pulp, which is a byproduct of the sugar production process. This is not a replacement for hay or other supplemental food but is an excellent source of fiber and is more nutritious than hay or straw.

Sugar beet pulp tends to come in shreds and should not be given to the animals straight. It needs to be soaked before it is safe to give to your donkeys. Most often, it will need to be soaked for about 24-hours, but there are now varieties that offer a quick soak method. Some modern, quick soak varieties can be ready to eat in as little as ten minutes. The proper means of soaking will be listed on the manufacturer's instructions.

# Additional Food for Donkeys

Some people will give their animals a few fruits and vegetables as a supplement for their diet. Not only is this a great way to give the animals some variety, but it is also known to help spurn appetite in animals that may be struggling to eat. Fruits and vegetables are often given in winter but make an appropriate treatment at any time of year. Late winter and early spring are "lean times" for sources of hay and other supplemental forage, making this a good way to keep the animals healthy and full, even if hay or straw isn't readily available.

You shouldn't give animals any stone fruits (fruits with a large seed in the middle), potatoes, garlic, or any type of spoiled produce. Donkeys enjoy things like carrots, apples, bananas, pears, and turnips. The produce should be cut into small chunks to make it easier for the donkey to manage.

# A Note On Vitamins and Minerals

If your animals subsist entirely or largely on natural pasture, it is possible that they aren't getting all the vitamins and nutrients they need for optimal health. Vitamin and mineral supplements often called *balancers*, are a great means of providing any nutrients they may lack their daily diet.

Some people prefer to use mineralized blocks to provide needed supplemental vitamins and nutrients but is it vital that you don't get a mineral block intended for horses. Horses have quite different nutritional requirements, and these blocks may contain substances that are toxic or unsuitable for donkeys. There are mineral blocks made especially for donkeys, which is used if this is the form of vitamin and mineral supplementation you choose.

For animals that need to lose weight or maintain their current body weight, there are several supplements recommended by the Donkey Sanctuary for this purpose. TopSpec Donkey Forage Balancer is highly recommended. If you are dealing with pregnant, older, or ill animals, products like TopSpec Comprehensive Balancer are a great choice.

# Final Thoughts On Feeding

The following should be adhered to for feeding your donkeys:

- All food should be free of mold and fungus
- Feed the animals the proper foods for their nutritional needs
- Feed the animals small amounts, regularly, and control the amount of food they have access to.
- Any dietary changes should be made slowly, over time, typically over a period of 7-14 days.
- Avoid foods high in sugar.
- Make sure nutritional supplements are suitable for donkeys and readily available.

• Never feed your donkeys grass clippings.

We have stressed several times and will stress again, that while donkeys are equine, they are not horses. They have quite different needs, and requirements and some things that are safe and suitable for horses are not so for donkeys. Never assume that something meant for horses is okay to use on a donkey. For example, horses eat nutrient-rich feed which, if given to donkeys, is likely to cause colic or a range of other gastrointestinal issues.

Vitamin supplements for horses are also not suitable for donkeys as they often contain nutrients at higher levels than are suitable for donkeys and may contain substances harmful to them.

Part of their physical adaptation to their environment, and what makes them so popular in harsh climates, is their ability to subsist on sparse, low-nutrient foods, quite different from what a horse needs. It takes donkeys longer to digest their food than other animals, including horses, as this allows them to derive as much nutritional value from their food as possible.

Donkeys, unlike ponies and horses, can recycle nitrogen, which is a unique adaptation to a low nutrient environment. In horses, nitrogen is expelled as urea by the kidneys and released from the body via urine. Donkeys can reabsorb the urea, which allows them to reuse the nitrogen. This process is naturally regulated in response to the amount of nitrogen available in their food supply, and how much protein they are getting.

Crude protein requirements are much less for donkeys than they are for horses. A donkey only needs a daily intake of about 3.8-7.4% crude protein, whereas a horse requires between 8-12%. This figure alone shows that what is good for a horse may well not be for a donkey and vice versa.

Donkeys will browse on more than just grass, which can become a frustration for people with a lot of trees or shrubs on their pasture. Donkeys eat trees, shrubs, flowering plants, and well, pretty much any vegetation that may be growing on your land. If forage is limited, but other types of plant material are not, a donkey can quickly destroy the other vegetation.

Some people provide brambles or shrubs intended for the donkey to browse on to try to keep them from destroying surrounding trees or other desirable vegetation and can be an effective deterrent.

Overall, with a donkey's diet, foods high in fiber and low in sugar are most important. Some animals get the bulk of their nutrition from browsing and need truly little supplementation in their diet. Others that are housed on grounds with poor forage or pasture may rely largely or even entirely on straw or other forms of supplemental foods.

Pasture is ideal as it is more akin to their natural environment. It allows them to graze slowly and makes them less prone to overeating than animals fed largely on supplemental hay or straw. Animals on pasture also get more exercise, and this is vital to keeping them healthy and maintaining a healthy weight. Whether they are fed exclusively on hay or straw, forage, or a combination of the two, provide the appropriate amount of supplemental vitamins and minerals to ensure they get a fully balanced diet that meets all their nutritional requirements.

It is incredibly important, hence why we repeat it, to understand that donkeys have evolved to consume foods low in nutritional content. Their digestive systems are even designed for this purpose, allowing them to get every possible amount of nutrition from the poor-quality forage they consume. This can be a concern for land that has been improved as it may grow higher quality pasture than donkeys are accustomed to consuming.

If your property has forage that is too high in nutritional value for the donkeys, one way to accommodate the animals is to let the grass go to seed before allowing the donkeys to feed on it. This lowers the nutritional quality of the grasses, which makes it easier for the animals to digest properly. You may also want to consider sowing the land with lower nutrient grasses that are more suitable to the needs of donkeys.

# Chapter 6: Training Your Donkeys

Donkeys are known for being stubborn, but this isn't the fairest criticism. Donkeys are cautious animals that like to think about what they do before they do it. This means it can take them longer to learn certain behaviors or skills, but it shouldn't be seen as the animal being obstinate. They need time to understand what you are asking them to do and how to do it. Yet, while it may take them a little longer to pick up on a skill or behavior, they are more likely to remember and retain it than a horse. Basically, this means that you won't have to keep working with the donkey on the same skill for as long as you would a horse.

Understanding how your donkeys learn will better help you to develop a training routine that makes sense for the animal you are training and is more likely to succeed.

Different types of training will be employed depending on what you plan to use the animals for. It is best to start with some general or basic training and then move on to more difficult moves and maneuvers.

# Basic Training

Though it isn't always possible, it is best to train donkeys as foals. The earlier training can begin, the easier it is to develop the bond with them that is needed for them to follow your orders and perform certain tasks. You want to imprint on the foal. This means they learn your physical presence, smell, sound, and touch when it is possible to do so. The earlier a bond can be developed, the easier it is to train your donkey later.

Sometimes, though, the jenny isn't entirely comfortable with someone coming in and handling her foal. If so, you may need to socialize the jenny before you can approach the foal. She needs to be comfortable enough with you that she will let you near her foal without causing her undue stress or making her aggressive.

Even if you aren't starting out with a foal, socialization is an important part of any training routine. The animal needs to trust you, and you both need to know each other well enough to take verbal and nonverbal cues from each other. The more time you spend with the animals, the better the bond will become. The process for socialization - spending time with the animal, letting them get used to your scent, talking to the animal, and handling the animal - will be the same, whether you are working with a foal or an adult animal. Just know the older the animal is, the longer it may take to socialize them.

There are several ways that people train donkeys, but the most effective way is through positive reinforcement. This reinforcement utilizes positive rewards as opposed to negative actions or punishment. Different types of reinforcement have long been studied, and science has shown this is one of the most effective means of teaching donkeys new skills. They respond far better to rewards than the removal of something unpleasant (like in negative reinforcement) or punishment.

All donkeys are unique creatures and learn in slightly different ways, so while positive reinforcement is the most commonly used and most effective way to train donkeys, with certain animals, a different mode of reinforcement may be necessary.

With positive reinforcement, you are essentially offering the animal a reward for following command or request. The animal is more likely to perform if they know the result is getting something they like.

Most often, treats, sometimes paired with a clicker, are used as the reward in a positive reinforcement schedule. While food works best, some animals will respond well to physical praise and thus may not require the treats to learn certain skills. You are likely to get better results if you go the treat route.

Positive reinforcement has numerous benefits. Besides it being a proven and effective way to teach an animal new skills, it will also help to strengthen your bond with the animal, which will help in later training.

Before we move on to specific modes of training, let's take a quick look at the other types of reinforcement that may be employed in donkey training.

### Negative Reinforcement

This type of reinforcement is often called the Natural Horsemanship process and seeks to train animals using their basic natural instincts and modes of communication. Pain is not used in this type of reinforcement, but discomfort is. For example, unpleasant pressure may be used, followed by the release of said pressure when the animal performs the desired task.

This, as it's the alternative name implies, works decently with horses who are well known to perform a task to get relief from unpleasant pressure. It has less success with donkeys, but you may run into certain animals that will best respond to this mode of reinforcement. Horses do better with nonverbal communication than donkeys do, so donkeys are not as likely to respond well to this as a horse would be.

### Extinction

We won't spend long on this reinforcement schedule as it isn't recommended for use with donkeys. The basic idea is to extinguish an undesired behavior through the removal of a particular stimulus.

### Punishment

This is the least effective means of training and donkey, and many avoid it because it can be considered cruel. As the name of this schedule implies, punishment entails the introduction of something unpleasant if the animal fails to perform the desired behavior. Most people avoid this type of reinforcement with all equine, but especially donkeys, where having a close, positive bond with their trainer is so vital to the success of training efforts.

These training schedules and the means of teaching donkeys that follow rely on both main types of animal conditioning: classical conditioning and operant conditioning. Classical conditioning involves animals learning to make associations between a particular stimulus and its response. Operant conditioning relies more on trial and error. The animal learns that behavior "x" is followed by the response "y," and through this will learn the most effective means of achieving the desired result.

Regardless of the type of reinforcement you employ, the reinforcement schedule is very important. Usually the reinforcement schedule will be every time the animal performs an action or every certain number of times the animal performs the action. Training tends to work better when rewards follow the completion of every task rather than intermittent reinforcement. It can be more difficult for a donkey to pick up a skill with this schedule.

We should also point out that the age, temperament, and health of the animal will have a profound effect on how training's effectiveness. The sex of the animal can also have an impact. These things will help you determine what you should be able to expect from a given animal and the best way to achieve the desired results.

As is probably understood, older animals do not learn as fast and will not pick up as much as younger animals. This doesn't mean they can't or shouldn't be trained, but this should alter what your expectations of the animal are. Jennies in heat or intact jacks will need to be handled very differently than a foal or a gelded jack.

Like humans and most other creatures, donkeys build and strengthen neural pathways as they develop a new skill. Learning something new is harder for anyone and takes longer as no path has been developed. Conversely, a skill that builds off a simpler skill the animal always knows will likely be picked up far more quickly than a completely novel behavior.

We noted earlier in this guide that donkeys don't have nearly as strong of a flight response as horses do. This means that, while it can take longer to train a donkey, it can actually be easier than training a horse, which is naturally frightened and has a strong flight response.

Before you start any training routine, you need to have a plan set out with clearly-defined goals. This will help to ensure your training sessions are more fruitful and effective. None of the experts think it is a good idea to "wing it" for training any animal, but especially donkeys.

Finally, let's discuss equipment. All donkeys are differently sized and proportioned. It is imperative that you use gear that properly fits the specific animal. Equipment meant for horses will often be too large or too heavy to use with donkeys. You must choose a saddle or bridle that fits the animal as well as possible. Though costly, if you can afford to do so, having a custom saddle or harness is a great idea.

# General Verbal Commands

The most effective way to communicate with your donkey is through the use of short, clear language. This will help them understand what you are asking them to do. You can come up with your own short verbal commands, but what follows are some of the most commonly used.

- Whoa - means stop
- Stand
- Step - this is the command for the animal to start walking
- Trot - walking at a faster clip
- Back up
- Gee - a right turn
- Haw - a left turn
- Canter
- Easy - this is telling the animal to slow down

As we mentioned, you do not have to use these standard commands, and most trainers have their own ways of making commands. Whatever you choose, short, single word commands are easiest for the animal to learn and thus most effective.

### Haltering and Leading

This is one of the most basic skills to teach your donkey, as this will be required for several tasks. The first step is to get the animal used to wear a halter. You can acclimate the animal to the halter by simply letting them wear it for a while, allowing them to get comfortable having something unfamiliar on their back. This may take a few days, but once the animal can wear the halter without issue, you can move on to the next step in the training process.

Once the donkey is comfortable being harnessed, you will want to train the animal to lead or walk with a rope and follow quite simple verbal commands. First, you will want to put the lead on the animal and let it get used to it as you did with the harness. Tie the lead to something like a fence. Let the animal stay there for about 10-15 minutes and then come back and take the lead off whatever it was tied to.

Give them words of encouragement and see if they move in your direction (or at all). Even if they just move a single step, give them verbal and physical praise along with a treat they enjoy. If the donkey doesn't move, tie the lead back to the support and come back again in 15 minutes and try the same process.

It can be a slow process that requires time and quite a few treats, but this is a proven and effective way to get them accustomed to leading. Each step forward is a step forward and means you are closer to moving on to more complex training. Always offer treats and praise whenever even the smallest amount of progress is made.

Call the animal when trying to get it to come to you and reward every step they take in your direction. Once you get the donkey to come all the way to you, you can take them on walks but remember to bring plenty of treats to reward their progress. It might seem like bribery, and in truth, it is; but it is also effective, *so bribery it is!*

Sometimes unfamiliar objects will startle or scare the animal, and they need to be reassured there is nothing to fear before trying to get them to move on from whatever frightened them. Console them and try to show them there is no danger in whatever the unknown object is. Communication is vital when it comes to the successful training of donkeys.

When the animal has developed some confidence and is good at being led on walks, you will want to introduce some simple obstacles such as logs or tires. This will teach the donkey how to walk around or maneuver over obstacles that may be in their way. They probably will be reluctant at first, but with coaxing and praise, they will gain confidence and move over or around these obstacles.

You will want to slowly introduce the animal to more complicated moves like backing up or turning around once the animal is comfortable and confident with obstacles. It is important that you don't try to move this process along too fast as it may not be as successful as if you display patience.

Experts at donkey training recommend about a year of this type of training before you attempt to ride or haul things with the animal. The animal needs a lot of practice, and it needs to develop a close and positive relationship with its trainer. This means that besides working on skill development, you will also develop an emotional bond with the animal, both learning the communication style of the other, which will, in turn, make it easier to teach the animal other skills.

### Driving

Training gets more complex when you introduce the donkey while driving. This complexity is why you so should develop a positive relationship and effective communication with the animal before moving on to the more complex elements of training. To learn driving, the animal must learn to stand still and respond to basic verbal commands.

Donkeys learn in a variety of ways, and part of how they can be acclimated to and become comfortable with a new skill is to see other animals performing said skill. It might seem a bit strange, but this will help the donkey get used to this being a normal occurrence and shouldn't be frightened.

And the animal will also need to get used to wearing a bridle, and the best way to do this is to acclimate them to it in the same way you got them used to wear a harness - simply put the bridle on them for periods of time so they can get accustomed to wearing it. They will also need to become acclimated with the long reins used to guide the animal and a guide whip. We will note here and other places that the whip is meant to be used as a guide, not as a punishment. You don't want to hit the animal hard with the whip, even if they aren't following your commands. Use firm but gentle pressure when using the whip.

Leaving the animal's cart somewhere on your property where he regularly goes; this is a good way to get them used to seeing it and thus will make it less likely they fear it when you go to introduce it. Some people will leave the cart on their grounds somewhere and reward the donkey if they see it investigating the cart. This will help the donkey develop a positive association with the cart.

If you are new to donkey training, you should have someone with experience with you the first time you hook your donkey up to a cart. You need to make sure that it is properly hooked up, and it can be a little complicated the first time you do it. All equipment used needs to be of appropriate size for the donkey and that the cart is properly hitched to avoid injuring the animal or yourself. Often, people will bring in outside help from someone who has successfully taught donkeys to drive to get a feel for how the process works and the best course of action for training animals in this skill.

Once the animal is comfortable being hitched to a cart, acclimate it to having the cart hitched to them. If possible, take the animal on a short, leaded walk with an empty cart. When the animal is comfortable being led with an empty cart, add some weight to the cart so they can get used to pulling as well.

After you have gotten the animal comfortable with being hitched to a cart with some weight in it, you will want to begin ground training the donkey to make different maneuvers with the cart. As the animal's level of skill develops, you can introduce more complex moves such as turning and backing up while pulling the cart. These are sophisticated moves, and you shouldn't expect that the animal will learn how to do these things overnight. This process will take time to become perfect for both you and the donkey.

### Riding

We have mentioned several times in this guide that donkeys are great for teaching kids how to ride. They are also suitable for older people and those with certain disabilities. They even take regular-sized adults in certain areas with difficult terrain that are tourist attractions, such as at the Grand Canyon.

The donkey should be large enough to be ridden. Miniatures are generally only recommended as proper riding animals for children, given their small stature. Both children and adults can ride most standard donkeys.

Ground driving skills are especially important for both hauling material and being ridden. It not only gets them used to follow basic commands, but they will have learned more complex moves like turning around or backing up, which can be particularly useful and necessary when being ridden.

Like with most other things we have discussed here, you will want to let the donkey become acclimated to the new equipment they will have to wear. Putting all riding equipment on the donkey and letting them wear it for short periods of time is a highly effective way to accomplish this.

Next, you will want to spend some time mounted on the animal without it walking to allow both the animal and you to get used to being on the back. Practice mounting and dismounting on both sides of the animal to help them get used to this part of the process.

Once your animal is comfortable with the equipment, being mounted, and dismounted, it is time to get the animal used to walking with someone on their back. This is best done with another person who can lead the animal on short walks (with lots of praise and treats) while you are on the animal's back.

At every step of the way, you will want to communicate with your donkey, giving them verbal cues and praise. For example, you can say "walk-on" while gently tapping the side of the donkey with your foot to get the donkey to continue walking. Any progress should be rewarded both verbally and with a treat or physical praise like petting.

Donkeys aren't good long-haul trainers. They do best in shorter sessions of about 20 minutes, performed frequently. The process of training will follow a very similar path to that of horses, with the exception that it can take a bit longer to train a donkey to be ridden than a horse.

### Lifting Feet

Donkeys, like all equine, are hooved animals, and they will require regular foot care and maintenance. This means that the animal will need to let you pick up their leg so you can clean and examine their feet regularly. Most donkeys aren't fond of this at first, but with some patience, you can acclimate the animal to let you manipulate their feet.

If the animal tries to pull away while you are working on the food, don't let go, but give the animal a lot of praise, so they know not to be alarmed or scared. This will also teach the animal that trying to pull their leg away is ineffective.

You will want to start with the front legs, but we should note here you need to use extreme caution when you start this training. Donkeys that are resistant have tried to kick the person training them, which is why it's better to have a trained professional or farrier with you the first time you start this kind of training.

Over time, the animal will get accustomed to having their legs lifted, and their feet messed with.

### Guard Donkeys

Though it is less well known, as we mentioned above, donkeys are very territorial and will be aggressive with anything they see as a potential threat to their area. This is why many people choose to use donkeys as guard animals over the more traditional dog. With proper socialization and training, donkeys are an incredibly effective means of protecting flocks of livestock like sheep, goats, and cows. Once the donkey has become established with the flock, they will guard almost any kind of livestock.

The more comfortable the donkey is with the flock, the more time they will spend in and among the flock, often spending much of their day grazing alongside them. If the donkey and the flock are well bonded, the donkey will spend much, if not all, of their day with the livestock. Donkeys have a natural herding instinct and rely on keen sight and sound for detecting potential threats or predators.

If an intruder is spotted, a well-bonded donkey will physically put themselves between the flock and the potential threat. They will bray loudly, which is often effective at scaring off the potential trouble source. Not only does this distress call scare off predators, but it can also alert the owner that something may be upon the property.

Should braying prove unsuccessful, the donkey has more proverbial ammunition. The animals will rear up and attack the animal with a swift kick, which will deter and sometimes even kill the predator.

Jennies and foals raised with sheep or other livestock will have a stronger bond with the livestock and thus be better protectors to the flock. Once a foal is weaned, the jenny can be removed, and the foal left with the livestock. This is the best way to bond a donkey to the livestock they are to protect.

Even if the animal is not raised with the flock, it can be successfully introduced and become bonded with the flock. This needs to be done under close supervision. First, housing the donkey near the livestock they will guard, but not with it, will help both get used to the presence of the other.

You can then move on to having the donkey in an enclosure with the flock, but this will need to be closely supervised. Remember that donkeys are very territorial and aggressive, and it isn't all that uncommon for a new donkey to see the livestock as a threat and to act accordingly. In order to keep everyone safe until you can trust the donkey understands its role in the flock, this needs to be closely monitored, and the donkey shouldn't be left alone with the flock until you are sure they are well bonded and won't attack.

Most donkeys, even those raised apart from livestock, can be successfully bonded and become good guard animals for the flock. However, remember that donkeys, like humans, have very distinct personalities, and sometimes, certain individuals just aren't well-suited to guarding livestock.

In tack, males should not be used as they are too aggressive and can behave unpredictably. Certain donkeys can become overprotective of the flock they guard and will, at times, mistake foals for threats and can injure or kill the babies. Many people remove the donkey from the pasture when the livestock give birth to allow the foals to gain some strength and size, making them less likely to be seen as a potential threat by the guard donkey.

Donkeys have a strong dislike for any and all canines, so this is something you will need to remember if you also keep dogs on your property. For the safety of the dog, it is best to keep them away from the donkey unless they were raised together. It is not unheard of for a curious family dog to get a good kick for their efforts from an unsuspecting donkey.

One donkey can guard anywhere from 100-200 animals, depending on the size and terrain of the property in question.

## Benefits of Clicker Training

Many people swear by the use of clickers for training all different kinds of animals and this method has the benefit of being both effective and straightforward to learn. Using a clicker involves operant conditioning with positive reinforcement and should be performed on a regular rewards schedule.

It seems to be so effective because it pairs a consistent sound with the reward given after the performance of the desired behavior.

First, you will need to employ a little classical conditioning to get the animal to associate the sound of the clicker with getting a treat and praise. Once the animal responds to the sound of the clicker, even when distracted, the association has become ingrained. Once this happens, the operant conditioning can begin, and the sound of the clicker will be paired with a command which will be rewarded if successfully completed.

Once it seems like the donkey has developed an association between the verbal command and reward, you can stop using the clicker and stick to only verbal cues. The length of time it will take to get to this point will depend on each individual animal.

# Chapter 7: Grooming and Caring for Your Donkeys

Donkeys, like any other animal, require some basic grooming and care to keep them looking and feeling their best. While known for being low maintenance, this doesn't mean that these animals are no maintenance. They require minimal regular care, most of which is related to grooming. This helps keep their coats looking their best and keeps their eyes, nose, mouth, and hooves free of debris, which can cause discomfort or health issues.

With donkey grooming, there are a few basic tools that are required, which we will touch on below, but the toolkit most people use for grooming is specialized over time, depending on the needs and preferences of the owner and the animals.

## General

Donkeys need to be kept clean and their coats free of debris, which is why you should brush them regularly, every day if possible. Grooming will be especially important in the winter for donkeys that are wearing rugs to keep them warm. The hair under the rug can easily become matted and tangled, leading to discomfort and the potential for skin issues.

Brushing donkeys dry is far preferable to brushing them wet, which can irritate their skin. Donkeys aren't very fond of getting wet, of beginning with. Most donkeys actually enjoy being groomed and will appreciate the daily care. It is also a great bonding opportunity for you and the donkey, so take advantage of this.

It should be mentioned that if you have any expectations of keeping your donkeys fully clean, you will need to let that go. Even with regular brushing, donkeys get dirty, especially as they are known to roll in the dirt, and unlike horses, don't shake it off when they are done. The main goal of grooming is to keep their hair and skin free of debris and other substances that can cause sores or irritation, not to keep them looking showroom clean (though we will touch show donkeys briefly below).

Their hooves will require regular and specialized care, just as horses do. Daily, it is recommended to clean mud, dirt, and other debris from the hooves using a hoof hook, which we will discuss below. You may want to consult the chapter on training to see how to get the animal to become used to having their feet lifted and messed with.

Like other equine, donkeys' hooves grow continuously and will need to be trimmed regularly roughly every 4-8 weeks. Failure to properly care for their hooves can lead to a range of problems that can become serious. Trimming hooves is not something everyone is comfortable doing or has the tools and skill to perform. Many rely on the occasional visit by a professional farrier for this maintenance.

Every time you groom your donkeys, take a minute to look them over and check for any cuts, skin or hoof issues, injuries, or any sign of illness. Catching problems early will help reduce the likelihood that the animal will experience major problems. You will also want to consider their teeth for any signs of rot, damage, or sharp edges. Donkey's teeth are always growing, and they get worn down by the coarse forage they eat. This can lead to sharp edges on the teeth, which can then lead to mouth sores. Have your donkeys looked at if you notice any issues. You will want to have their teeth looked at professionally about once a year.

If a donkey has poor or damaged teeth, switch them to a soft diet of wet, mashed, or soaked food that is easier and less painful for them to eat.

Donkeys also need regular vaccinations against distemper, the flu, and tetanus. There may be other recommended vaccinations depending on the area you live in.

Like other equine and most outdoor animals, donkeys can suffer from intestinal parasites, particularly intestinal worms. Donkeys should have fecal checks about four times a year to look for parasites and treat them when found. Many medicines are not as effective as they used to be due to overuse and pest evolution, making it harder than it used to be to successfully treat many of these pests as they have developed resistance.

Because many pests have become resistant, you should have the animal checked after a course of treatment to ensure that it actually worked. Keeping your donkey's shelter and living space clean is the best way to avoid worms and other parasites, to begin with. Worms, like all parasites, have a unique life cycle that requires time for them to develop from one stage to the next. Regularly removing waste (largely donkey feces) a few times a week is a great way to reduce the animal's exposure to worm larva.

In the summer, you will want to groom the donkeys pretty much every day. In winter, you can scale it back to every other day. Air pockets naturally form in their coats, providing a degree of insulation from the cold, and brushing will break those air pockets.

Since donkeys have long, thick, coarse hair, it is much more prone to gathering dirt and debris than a horse, which is why they require more regular grooming. During the spring months (when the animals are molting their winter coats), you will need to groom them more often than usual to help get rid of the excess hair they are shedding.

# Basic Tools

You don't need a ton of expensive specialty tools to keep your donkey looking and feeling good. Using a damp cloth, carefully clean any dirt or debris out of the animal's eyes, ear, nose, and mouth. This helps prevent infection and other issues that can result from dirt or debris build-up in these orifices.

A stiff round-headed brush made from metal, rubber, or plastic will be the most important tool to use for grooming your donkeys. Brush the animal with a body brush from head to tail, applying even pressure as you do so.

To keep the hooves clean and free from debris, you will need a hoof pick, which is an important grooming tool that allows you to remove safely and easily caked in gunk or debris. When cleaning the hooves, work from heel to toe, making sure you get all the crevices clean. You will want to keep an eye out for the back of the hoof (called the frog), turning black or even oozing. This indicates a bacterial infection called *thrush*, and it will need to be addressed immediately.

Keep your grooming tools clean, as this will help prevent the spread of germs. After each use, sanitize the grooming equipment using a mild detergent and warm water. You can let them air dry until their next use.

A basic grooming kit for donkeys will include a coarse curry comb brush, which is good for breaking up clumps of mud or debris. A short-bristled curry comb is an excellent all-purpose comb that can be used in most areas of the body for general brushing. Groomers gloves may be worn, but most animals prefer being groomed bare-handed, so this isn't required and is more of preference. A hoof hook will be needed for cleaning the coat.

A lot of donkey owners will use a rain rot prevention spray, insect repellent (especially for flies), and a coat conditioner of some sort to help keep their coats in good repair. All of these products can be bought from most outdoor farm stores, or you can even make your own. Skin conditioners are the most common product people make at home because it only requires basic ingredients. You can also make your own rain rot prevention and insect repellent, and recipes for these can easily be found online. Since skin conditioner is so easy to make, let's consider a recipe kindly provided by the Donkey Listener.

# The Donkey Listener's Skin Conditioner

½ cup apple cider vinegar

½ cup water

3 drops of peppermint essential oil

3 drops of essential oil of your choice of scent

1 tbsp vitamin E oil

Mix all these ingredients and shake well before each use.

# Clipping Donkeys

Occasionally, like most animals, a donkey may need a bit of a coat trim. Their coats are incredibly important to their bodily comfort and should never be fully trimmed. Their coats allow them to regulate their temperature properly and helps to protect against insect pests, especially flies, which pester pretty much all farm animals.

Sometimes, elderly or ill donkeys will experience a condition that causes an excessive overgrowth of their coat, leaving them matted and tangled, which can be painful and make the animal more prone to skin conditions. A donkey is most likely to need a coat clipping in late spring and early summer. This differs greatly from horses, which tend to be clipped in the winter.

Most donkeys need not be clipped often, but there are certain conditions and issues that can make this a necessity more often than is typical. Sometimes, donkeys will experience a greater than usual amount of hair growth during a winter, and they may be slow to molt the excess hair in the spring. When this happens, targeted light trimming is a great way to help the donkey's natural process along.

Certain skin conditions or a wound may also necessitate clipping a donkey to keep the area free of hair and debris. Many donkeys will experience lice infestations, which can often be addressed by bathing but may require some clipping in really severe cases. There are a variety of pest control products you can use that will make a lice infestation less likely to occur.

## Hooves

The hooves of your donkeys are vital and keeping them healthy and in good shape is part and parcel to keeping your animals in top shape. Any time you groom your donkeys, you will want to clean out their hooves and check for any signs of injury or possible infection.

As we have noted a couple of times, it will be necessary to trim your donkey's hooves about every 4-8 weeks to keep them from becoming overgrown. You should only do this yourself if you have the proper tools and know-how.

## Show Donkeys

Though not something commonly is known, some people keep donkeys as show animals, and these will require a much higher level of grooming than animals kept for work or milk. For show donkeys, you will want to bathe them regularly, and grooming will be more complex than it is with regular donkeys. You will need to clip the coat more often than a work donkey to keep it in good shape, and as a result, they will need to wear a rug in winter and perhaps even on cooler summer days.

Before a showing, it is advised to clip the donkey about once a week to allow unevenly shorn hair to grow back and look less shaggy. Using scissors with long blades and round ends is a good way to reduce uneven trimming and unsightly shag. The longer the blades of the scissors, the more even and smooth the resulting cut will look.

People who show their donkeys will also use hoof polish to make the hooves shine.

# Chapter 8: Donkey Breeding

Though not as common as they once were, there are still places today where donkeys are used for transport, hauling cargo, and as the primary beast of burden for agriculture or small-scale industry. They are becoming more attractive today due to their hardiness and the low level of inputs required when compared to other equine species. They are more resilient for traction than oxen power, which can make them a more attractive animal for agricultural work than oxen.

Jennies and horse mares are similar with reproduction, but there are some key differences. The same is true for jacks and stallions - overall, the process is roughly similar, but there are some important differences that will affect breeding.

## Basic Reproduction

A donkey reaches "puberty" at around two-years old, and jennies are in estrus (heat) for shorter periods of time than most horses. The estrus cycle in jennies tends to last between 23-30 days. Estrus itself, at its peak, lasts between 6-9 days, and jenny will be ovulating for about 5-6 days after the onset of estrus.

Jennies can be in heat more often than horses, which is beneficial for breeding since jacks can be finicky about mating. This means that the jenny has more opportunities to conceive than her horse counterpart.

Common symptoms of jennies in estrus include:

- Standing with legs apart in what is often called the breeding position.
- Excessive urination
- Tail raising
- Winking
- Drooling

The gestation cycle for a pregnant jenny is typically about 372-374 days, so a little over a year. Foal heat, or heat after the birth of a foal, sets in within 3-13 days after the jenny has given birth.

Jennies are extremely protective of their young and typically have a strong maternal instinct than mares do. You should keep this in mind when considering how you will go about socializing and handling foals. Jennies need to be comfortable with you in order to let you near their offspring, so you may have to socialize her and get her comfortable with you before you can safely touch the foal if this process of socialization wasn't already performed.

Jennies have a higher rate of fertility than horse mares, which makes them more likely to conceive. The conception rate for jennies is about 78%, compared with about 65% for mares.

A jenny is more likely to have multiple ovulatory periods than a mare, which makes the phenomena of twinning more common in them. This will need to be addressed by a vet, as twinnings present greatly increased risk of complications for the jenny. One embryo is typically destroyed for the safety of the jenny and to increase the likelihood that she will carry her pregnancy to term and birth a healthy foal.

Since jennies have narrower and longer, often protruding vaginas than mares, it can be more difficult to artificially inseminate a jenny than it is a mare. This can also put them at more risk for issues like cervical lesions and may have a harder time giving birth than a mare, which is why someone should be present when a jenny goes into labor.

We noted the signs above of a jenny in heat, and they are obvious, so it will be somewhat easy to know when she is ready to breed. The sound of braying jacks is said to cause them to go into heat faster. Jennies also become more vocal while in estrus than at any other time. If your jenny is more talkative than usual, this may be a sign that she is ready to breed.

As we noted above, jacks have a similar reproductive system to stallions, but there are some key differences. For one, the penis on a jack is larger than that of a similarly-sized horse. This means that if you geld any of your jacks, be aware that they will bleed more than horses tend to.

Accessory sex glands are also larger in jacks than in stallions. Unlike horses, it takes donkeys longer to achieve an erection and climax, about 15-30 minutes, compared to about 10 minutes for stallions. Jacks use something akin to foreplay, called teasing, with the jenny to "get in the mood." Breeding attempts, due to the time it can take for the jack to get ready and do its thing, maybe unsuccessful and take multiple tries. It should also be noted that the entire process can last as long as a couple of hours.

Young jacks will have a libido lower than their horse counterparts and won't reach sexual maturity for a few years after puberty.

Jacks can use artificial donkey vaginas, and this is a way to obtain sperm for artificial insemination, which is often the preferred method of breeders. It can be safer for the jenny, with a longer and narrower cervix than a horse mare.

Donkeys can be bred naturally, bred on a schedule, or bred via artificial insemination. Jacks and jennies can be kept together and allowed to "do what nature requires," or you can put the animals together at a specific time when the jenny is in the optimal state to conceive.

In natural systems, the jenny is most likely to conceive during what is called standing heat, referring to a 48-hour period after the onset of estrus.

# Mule Breeding

A mule is a cross between a jack with a female mare (we will devote a short chapter to the mule below), and the pairing is not a natural one, but rather one that must be contrived or coaxed. If you want to breed jacks and horse mares, it is best to raise the jack in the company of horse mares and not jennies, as they will prefer their natural mate over horse mares. Raising the jack with horse mares will not only get him used to being in their presence; they will be his only source of "relief" for an exciting jack.

Jacks that are brought up in horse-like environments are far more likely to be receptive to breeding horse mares, but it will still have to be encouraged. Some have noted that farms with multiple jacks used for breeding with horse mares may encourage new jacks to mate with mares more readily. But, as we stated, you will have to cultivate a jack to breed with horse mares, and it isn't usually possible to have a jack that will mate with both horse mares and jennies. You will need to use separate animals for these purposes. To breed a specific jack with both horse mares and jennies, artificial insemination is the best route.

Mares are also not naturally drawn to jacks, and this can lead to distress at the presence of a braying jack. This further illustrates the importance of early socialization between the jack and mare. This will be less likely to happen between a pair that was raised together. A mare won't always stand to be mounted by a jack, and sometimes, she might even kick the jack, potentially injuring him as he tries to mount.

Restraints called breeding chutes or hobbles are often used to help ensure the safety of both animals in the process.

# Breeding Miniature Donkeys

Miniature donkeys are affectionate and cute animals that have become increasingly popular as pets. These are much smaller than a standard donkey, standing no more than 36 inches tall. Besides being cute and having great temperaments, miniature donkeys also don't require as much space or input due to their smaller size.

Their size does present a limitation in the amount of work they can do, the amount of weight they can hold, and the size of rider appropriate for their stature. You will want to remember this when considering breeding miniatures as if you are breeding for work animals; the miniature is not likely the best choice.

The first thing you will need to do is find a jack and jenny that are good representations of the miniature breed in terms of size, coat, having long, straight legs, and so on. A jenny with wider hips and ribcage will have an easier time giving birth than one with more narrow hips and ribs.

You will want to have a potential breeding pair checked out by a vet to ensure they are healthy and have no diseases they could transmit in the process of breeding. Both Jenny and Jack should be at least three years old before any attempts of breeding begin. This is to make sure that both animals are fully sexually developed.

Wash both animals before bringing them together, and many people will pin up the jennies' tail to make it easier for the jack to mount her. It is recommended to wash their genitals with iodine soap to ensure that both are free of any bacteria or potentially harmful pathogens.

You may need to hold or restrain the jenny while the jack sniffs and inspects her. It is an important part of the mating process for jacks, but it has a tendency to make the jenny a bit nervous. If her tail isn't already tied back, a receptive jenny will raise it up to indicate her interest.

Once the breeding process is complete, you will want to separate the pair and release the jenny's tail if it was tied up. The jenny should be taken to a quiet, calm place for the year (roughly) it takes her to gestate a foal. Keeping the jenny calm and stress-free will help ensure she has a healthy pregnancy.

A pregnant jenny shouldn't be exercised vigorously, but she should be encouraged to move around each day when she feels the desire.

During the last three months of pregnancy, you will want to increase the amount you feed the pregnant jenny by about 50% to account for the needs of her growing foal. In the last month of her pregnancy, place the jenny in a foaling stall, which is specially designed to be away from other animals and provide her a safe and private space to give birth.

The foaling stall should be covered with clean thick bedding made from straw or wood shavings (straw is preferable). It is important that the jenny be away from other animals and as far away from loud noise as possible; she should be kept in as little stress as possible during labor. While known for being affectionate, jennies about to give birth are less friendly shortly before entering labor, so if your usually-loving jenny cops a bit of an attitude, it is a good sign that she is going to give birth soon.

About 48-hours before giving birth, you will notice the jenny's udders begin to swell, and there may even be a slightly waxy secretion coming out of her teats. This is perfectly normal.

You will want to be nearby when the jenny goes into labor in case you need to provide assistance but try to give her as much space as possible, so she doesn't feel crowded or confined. You don't want to cause her any unnecessary stress. This can prolong the time it takes for her to give birth and increase the chances of complications. She will begin to roll around and pace the stall right before she gives birth.

Once the jenny's water breaks, the foal will begin its appearance; further contractions will allow her to push the baby the rest of the way out. This can take a little while, but if about 20 minutes pass by with no progress or contractions, it is best to call in a vet to see if there are issues with her pregnancy that you aren't suited to handle.

After the foal is born, the jenny will sever the umbilical cord herself and clean the foal. The foal, if healthy, should stand shortly thereafter and begin to nurse. Though not all that common, sometimes jennies fear their foal at first. If this happens and she won't let the foal nurse, hold and comfort the jenny until the foal can approach the jenny and nurse.

If possible, have both the jenny and the foal examined by a vet a few days after the birth. This will allow the vet to determine that both mom and baby are in good condition. The vet will look for any remaining placenta that may need to be removed, as well as signs of mastitis. This is an inflammation of the teats that can lead to discomfort and even the avoidance of nursing and should be quickly addressed. There are a lot of different treatments that are effective for mastitis.

The vet will also check to make sure the foal is getting an adequate supply of milk. If the foal cannot get enough milk from the jenny, it may be recommended that you give the foal supplemental food to make up for calories and needed nutrients it isn't receiving from its mother.

# Chapter 9: Donkey Milking (and Why You Should Consider It)

Milk probably isn't the first thing you associate with donkeys. Yet, donkey milk is becoming a lucrative field; it may be, perhaps, something you consider becoming involved with if you are going to raise donkeys. Donkey milk has been used since ancient times for a wide range of uses and is becoming popular again today.

In fact, donkey milk is becoming a highly sought ingredient for a number of different health and beauty products. This has led to a dramatic rise in the price the milk fetches on the open market. Prices can be as high as about $50 a liter, which is, indeed, an extremely high price for milk!

## Benefits of Donkey Milk

In ancient times, donkey milk was used medicinally to treat many different ailments and as a beauty enhancer. Legend states that Cleopatra, the famous Queen of Egypt, took baths in donkey milk to help maintain her youthful appearance and glowing skin. Modern science shows that there is a lot to this legend, even if it didn't happen as historical fact.

It was long used as a medicine for a range of ailments from an upset stomach to allergies.

We have numerous ancient accounts for the use of donkey milk beyond the Cleopatra legend. The father of medicine, Hippocrates, writes one of the oldest known accounts about the benefits of donkey milk. Also, ancient Roman records attest to its fairly widespread use. Napoleon's sister is known to have included it in her skin care regimen. Also, in France, donkey milk was used until the twentieth century to feed orphaned infants and as a cure for the sick and elderly.

# Common Uses of Donkey Milk Today

Even today, some people still argue for the medicinal value of donkey milk, claiming it can help people with issues such as bronchitis or asthma. This should not replace modern medical treatment and medication, and a lot more study needs to be done to determine the true efficacy of donkey milk as a good treatment for these conditions.

People with severe allergies may benefit from the consumption of donkey milk. Many people claim that by simply drinking a little milk each day, they saw dramatic reductions in their allergy symptoms. Like with other health claims made about donkey milk, there needs to be more research to determine how well it actually works for these conditions and to understand what it is about this type of milk that makes it useful.

Serbia is one of the largest producing regions for donkey milk and what is considered to be the most expensive cheese in the world - made from donkey milk - is produced there at Zasavica Nature Reserve. The cheese sells for about $48 euros per 50 grams of cheese. Indeed, pricey, with a unique taste and texture that people swear cannot be rivaled by other types of specialty cheese. Other nations with decent-sized donkey milk production capabilities include South Korea, Belgium, and Switzerland.

Scientific studies have shown that, chemically, donkey milk is the closest to human breast milk and is lower in fat and much higher in Omega-3 fatty acids than cow's milk. There have been recent studies published in the professional journal, Current Pharmaceutical Design, that demonstrates_that_donkey milk has the ability to dilate blood vessels and can reduce the hardening of arteries. Another recent piece in the Journal of Food Science has described donkey milk as a "pharmafood" for its myriad of benefits in terms of both health and nutrition.

More and more, donkey milk is used in skin products helpful in treating a variety of skin conditions like psoriasis and eczema. It is also safe for use on overly sensitive skin and can be made into a gentle soap. Some say that donkey milk contains anti-aging properties, and its fat content makes it great at skin hydration, helping improve the look and elasticity of the skin. It is also known as a great skin cleanser.

This milk can also be beneficial for infants that suffer from gastric issues since, at a chemical structural level, it is so close to human breast milk. It is also high in much-needed vitamins and minerals, and it may be a better alternative than formula or cow's milk. Donkey milk has a comparable level of protein to cow's milk but is much higher in vitamin C.

As more research continues to identify the widely varied benefits of donkey milk, many expect to continue to see it rise in popularity and demand.

### Considerations

In terms of animals that can be milked, the donkey isn't high on the list of good sources since they produce so little milk. While donkey milk, when compared to that of cow's milk, is far more scarce, it is used for far more specialized purposes than cow milk, so the scarcity isn't as much of an issue as it might immediately seem.

Because they produce so little milk, specialty products are the most common that use this unique and rare substance. Jennies can only be milked for about 2-3 months after giving birth. They rarely produce more than about 400 mL of milk a day, a very tiny amount when compared to cows.

# Chapter 10: Identifying and Preventing Donkey Diseases

The donkey is known and prized for being a hardy and durable creature, but this does not mean they never suffer from health issues. Their hardiness is, of course, one reason they were so popular historically and one of the main reasons they are growing in popularity today. However, even though they are hardy and can live in challenging environments, they remain faced with the risk of several different health problems.

As we noted earlier, donkeys tend to hide their emotions, and this is also true when they are ill. There is a good chance your donkey won't display obvious symptoms of illness until the illness has progressed to a point where it is impossible for the animal to hide any longer. This can often result in letting something small and simple fester to where it becomes a larger issue.

## Basic Health Considerations

The more time you spend with your donkeys, the better your relationship and understanding of them will be. It will also help you to learn the personality, temperament, and particular behaviors of each animal, which can make it a lot easier to tell when something isn't quite right with them. It is highly recommended that you do regular body checks to look for any potential issues and address them as soon as you notice anything. These checks are great to do in tandem with daily grooming.

# Common Donkey Ailments and Their Symptoms

Like any animal, donkeys can get a wide range of diseases that can be mild to even life-threatening. What follows are some of the most common ailments that donkeys suffer from, and symptoms associated with these conditions.

### Abscesses

An abscess is caused when an outside source – often a pathogen or an injury – spurs the overproduction of white blood cells, which can lead to painful sores, which then rupture and exude pus. An abscess can show up in any number of places on the donkey from inside the body, in the mouth, or even on the hooves. They can rupture, causing the expulsion of a large amount of unpleasant smelling pus.

If left untreated, especially on the hooves, it can lead to chronic sores and an infection that can spread up into surrounding tissues, causing a lot of discomfort and even risking permanent damage. You will need to consult a vet to diagnose and properly treat abscesses.

The abscess may be lanced, and a sample checked for bacteria that could necessitate the need for a course of antibiotics. The wound may also be irrigated or deeply cleaned to help avoid future infection and to aid in the healing of the wound.

### Anthrax

Anthrax spores are commonly found in soils in most areas of the world. Known as Bacillus anthracis, this toxin can lay dormant in the soil for many years, becoming "activated" during certain climatic conditions such as cool and wet weather that is immediately followed by very hot and dry weather. The spores can live in the soil for as long as 48 years!

Animals can then eat grass that has been contaminated with anthrax spores and become ill. Common symptoms of anthrax include mood changes like depression, lack of physical coordination, uncontrollable tremors, and even random bleeding. You will want to contact the vet immediately if they display any of these systems and may have been exposed to contaminated soil as it can be fatal.

Anthrax is highly spreadable and can easily be spread from an infected donkey to other animals and even humans. This is why any confirmed cases of anthrax must be reported to appreciate local government officials.

There is a vaccine available to inoculate against anthrax, and it is highly recommended, particularly if you live in an area where anthrax has been known to be found. If caught early, anthrax poisoning can be treated with antibiotics, but since the toxin can often prove fatal, it is better to rely on the vaccination.

### Arthritis

Like humans, donkeys can suffer from arthritis as they get older. Arthritis is also caused by certain genetic predispositions and can also be caused by poor nutrition and inadequate space. The symptoms of arthritis in donkeys can vary but most commonly include changes in the animal's gait, swollen joints, weight loss, and changes in the condition of their coat.

There are a variety of ways to treat arthritis in donkeys, but the proper course of treatment will depend on the underlying cause of the arthritis. You will want to contact a vet on the appropriate treatment plan for your animal.

Especially for older animals, you may have to modify their environment to make it safer and easier for an arthritic animal to get around. This can include reducing the grade of the terrain if it is steep, moving food and water closer to where the donkey spends its time, and more. A donkey with arthritis can still live a long and happy life; it just takes a bit of ingenuity to figure out ways to make life easier on the animal.

### Brucellosis

This condition typically presents in *poll evil* (a painful condition) and *fistulous withers* (another inflammatory condition). The poll of the donkey refers to the space between the ears down to the back of its neck. Poll evil occurs when this area is injured and swells, becoming inflamed and infected. This can lead to the waning and even the necrosis (death) of the affected tissue.

Fistulous withers refers to a similar condition in which the supraspinous bursa (which is located near the withers of the animal) becomes infected. This can occur because of an injury or an infection, most commonly Brucella abortus, hence the name of the condition.

Symptoms of these conditions include swelling, noticeable tenderness, heat emitting from the area, new sensitivities in the animal, as well as fever and listlessness. The bursa, if left untreated, can rupture and leak infectious fluid.

Both poll evil and fistulous withers can be treated, but if left untreated, they can easily turn into chronic conditions that can lead to even further inflammation and permanent scar tissues.

Bursas that haven't ruptured are often treated with antibiotics. A ruptured bursa is treated by removing tissue in the affected area and cleaning the area with a betadine solution. A course of antibiotics will also often be given to help ensure that all infection has been killed off.

Donkeys do not spread this condition to other animals nor to humans, so no separation or extra caution will need to be taken. It should be noted that cows suffering from these conditions can spread it to other animals, though.

### Cataracts

This is another common issue that plagues both aging humans and donkeys alike. It is marked by the increasing opacity of the lens of the eyeball, which reduces sight. This is often a congenital issue that develops in the animal as it ages. However, it can also be caused because of trauma, radiation, toxins, or other eye conditions.

The issue is most noticeable by the steady increase in the cloudiness and grayness of the lens of the eye. You will want to contact your vet to determine the source and treatment for cataracts. Surgery is the only known cure for cataracts, but this can also lead to permanent vision loss – but either way, cataracts may cause blindness in the end.

If surgery isn't recommended or doesn't seem like a good option, you may need to modify their surroundings to make it easier for a poorly-sighted animal to get around, eat, and drink with relative ease.

### Conjunctivitis

This is a common condition in donkeys that is often a result of an injury to the eye. Virus and fungal infections are another cause of this condition. Eye irritants like dust and dirt can also lead to minor cases. This occurs because of the inner eyelid and surrounding soft tissue becoming inflamed.

Symptoms include redness and swelling around the eyes, often with a mucus-like discharge coming from the eye.

Treatments for this condition will depend on the source of the irritation. If the issue results from an eye irritant or foreign body, you will want to flush the eye with water thoroughly. In the event of this being caused by fungal infections, viruses, or injury, you will want to contact the vet to determine the proper course of action.

### Cystitis and Pyelonephritis

Cystitis is a common type of equine urinary tract infection. Infections like this are most often a result of some condition that is restricting the flow of urine and may result from bacteria such as E. coli Enterococcus app, or Streptococcus app.

Pyelonephritis is a urinary tract infection that has spread to the kidneys and gotten more severe.

The symptoms most commonly associated with these conditions are similar to human experiences, including frequent urination and blood in the urine. If the infection has spread to the kidneys, they may begin losing weight and exhibiting certain behavior changes, like depression.

You will need to contact your vet for proper diagnosis and treatment of either of these issues. While you are waiting to take the animal in, make sure they stay well hydrated, as this can help reduce the severity of some of the symptoms.

### Colic

This is actually a more general term than the name of a specific condition. The word simply refers to abdominal or stomach pain and discomfort and can be a result of a variety of different issues. Colic can often be detected by sounds from the gut, an increased heart rate, and even increased respiration.

Impaction is a type of colic that results from something in the gut, most often undigested food. Cramps are called spasmodic colic and often cause general discomfort. Flatulent colic is a fancy name for stomach or gastrointestinal discomfort that results from excess gas. Tumors, which are most often seen in older animals, may also be a cause of colic. Torsion is a very painful condition in which the donkey has a twisted gut, which will naturally cause a lot of pain. Ulcers may also be a source. Worms, such as tapeworms or roundworms, will also commonly cause colic. Pancreatitis, which is caused by the swelling and inflammation of the pancreas, can also result in colic and can be a serious issue.

Most often, the donkey will display symptoms such as a refusal to eat. There are a variety of ways that this condition can be treated, from treating the underlying cause or even providing the animal with additional fluids through a tube in the nose. An intravenous drip may also supply the animal with extra fluids. In rare cases, colic can necessitate surgery and may even be fatal.

Dirty or inadequate water can be a cause of colic and issues with the feed. This is especially true if you change the animal's diet suddenly, without allowing them to become acclimatized to the new food gradually. Grazing on sandy soils may cause colic and eating non-food materials like rope, wood, plastic, or other materials.

The diseases and ailments we have listed here are, of course, not an exhaustive list of conditions that can affect donkeys, but they do cover the range of the most common issues that they are likely to experience. The longer you raise and care for these animals, the more familiar you will get with some of the main issues that may be a problem with these animals, what to do, and when to call in a vet or other professional.

# Chapter 11: A Word On Mules

Mules are, for all intents and purposes, a hybrid creature. Many confuse donkeys with mules, but they are different. Donkeys descended from wild asses in Africa and Asia, whereas a mule is a cross between a female horse and a jack.

There are also crosses between male horses and jennies, but these are called hinnies. They are very similar to mules but are a bit smaller and shouldn't be confused for the same animal.

A mule is a unique animal genetically, being a cross between a horse with 64 chromosomes and a donkey that has 62. Both mules and hinnies have 63 chromosomes, making them incredibly unique.

Basically, this means that mules and hinnies are sterile and unable to reproduce sexually. The female mule, called a molly or a molly mule, has an estrus cycle, which would make it theoretically possible for her to conceive. Still, since males are usually 99.9% sterile, there are few records of any actual pregnancies or births among mollies - most often, the rare birth of a foal results from an embryo transfer. The mule is desirable because they tend to be healthier and much hardier than comparably-sized horses and require less food and care.

# Similarities and Differences Between Mules and Standard Donkeys

Though they are easily confused for donkeys, a mule actually has more physically in common with a horse than a donkey. When it comes to body size, shape, teeth, and more, they are morphologically more similar to the mare than the jack. There are different types of mules, including miniatures. A typical mule, because of the horse side of their genetics, is a bit larger than a standard donkey.

Donkeys have very long ears, which is one of the most clearly identifiable features of the animal. However, a mule will have ears that are smaller and more like a horse than a donkey.

Vocalizations are another significant way to distinguish between a donkey and a mule. A donkey is well known for its hee-haw call, whereas a mule has something that is more between a whinny and the hee-haw. It is a distinctive sound that isn't likely to be confused with a donkey – once you are used to it.

Mules, like donkeys and horses, are long-lived animals and typically live between 30-40 years, though working or breeding animals may have shorter lifespans.

One of the things that make mules more attractive to some than donkeys is that they are more intelligent - which says a lot, seeing as how donkeys have amazing intelligence, as well. Mules also seem a bit less stubborn than donkeys; mules, quickly pick up skills, more like horse, than do the thoughtful and cautious donkeys.

A mule will typically weigh between 800-1000 pounds, but miniatures can be so small as to weigh less than 50 pounds. Miniature mules are super cute and sweet creatures that make great pets or companion animals.

Though half-descended from a mare, the skin of a mule isn't nearly as sensitive as horse skin; it is more like donkey skin, resistant to both sun and rain, making them a hardier animal than their horse counterparts. This doesn't, of course, mean they require no shelter from the elements, but rather that they are less sensitive and more adaptable to their environment than a horse is.

Like a donkey, a mule is better for navigating complex and uneven terrain. They have hooves much harder than horses, and thus they are much less likely to crack and can handle rocky or uneven terrain. Since they don't typically have shoes, they are easier and less expensive to care for than horses.

Just as with donkeys and horses, the mule is a great animal for carrying small loads. They can carry about 20% of their body weight on their backs and much more when pulling a cart over the ground.

Just like a donkey, a mule is not a horse, even if half of its genetics come from them. They have very different nutritional needs and requirements and shouldn't be treated as a small horse, but rather a unique creature in their own right.

As with donkeys, mules' digestive system is far better suited to pasture that is of low nutritional value. It takes them longer to digest their food, which allows them to get as many nutrients as possible from feeding. Food that is too rich or high in nutrients can cause a range of gastrointestinal issues, just like it will with donkeys.

You will need to remember that they do not share the same requirements as horses and, in terms of maintenance and care, and are more akin to the donkey side of their ancestry – and should be dealt with as such.

Feeding a mule should be approached in the same way you would approach feeding a donkey. Their food needs to be appropriate for their nutritional and digestive needs, and the amount that they eat needs to be controlled. Like donkeys, mules are known to overeat when given an overabundance of food, and this can cause problems like obesity (or even diabetes), which mules are more susceptible to than horses.

Never use equipment meant for horses with mules. While they have a similar body type, they aren't the same, and using inappropriate gear can harm and injure the animal. If at all possible, get halters and other equipment especially suited for mules. There are many places where you can have a custom halter, or other equipment made that is exactly to size for your animal. Though this is more expensive than buying a halter from a farm store, it will fit better and likely lead to better results with the animal.

Mules, like both donkeys and horses, come in a wide range of sizes and colors, and what will work best for you will depend on the intended use of the animal and your personal preferences. A mule comes with a heftier price tag than a donkey since it is a crossbreed, and it takes more skill to breed and raise them. You can expect to pay somewhere between $1,200-5,000 for a mule, perhaps more if you are looking at getting a miniature.

# Interesting Facts About Mules

Militaries around the world have long relied on mules as they are hardier, require fewer inputs, and can handle a more diverse range of terrains and environments than horses can. They are cheaper and easier to care for and maintain, making them superior to the horse for many applications.

The mule has even been used in more modern warfare. In the 80s, when the US army was working in Afghanistan, mules were used to carry weapons and supplies over the harsh terrain. Estimates are that as many as 10,000 mules were used in these operations.

There is a long historical tradition of both mules and donkeys being used in wars, from ancient warfare to major world wars. They made better assistants than horses because they require less food and other inputs, are tougher, and can navigate a diverse range of terrain types, whereas horses need to have smooth, flat ground, which can't always be found in a warzone.

Mules are predominately bred in China and Mexico, though there are known breeders on almost every continent and in every country.

Like the donkey, a mule will resort to kicking when threatened. They can kick both front and backward, but it's unusual that they can also kick sideways – certainly something that many people don't expect to see when dealing with these animals. Their hind legs are amazingly strong, and a good kick can both hurt and do serious damage. Keep this in mind when dealing with mules and try to steer clear of those powerful back legs!

# Breeding and Raising Mules

We touched on some of the basics for breeding mules in the chapter on reproduction. The cross between a horse mare and a jack is not the easiest to produce since donkeys and horses, being different species, don't mate naturally. The exception is apparently with jacks that are raised *exclusively* with horses. It is far easier to get a jack – raised with horses only, rather than with other donkeys or a mix of both - to breed with mares, as it seems more natural to them.

Donkeys and horses have similar but different sexual reproduction systems and different ways of approaching breeding, which makes it more difficult to have successful intercourse, but it is not impossible. Many people choose to use artificial insemination as the key means for reproduction as it is easier to accomplish and requires a lot less effort on everyone's part. However, as we noted in the chapter about breeding, it is not impossible, and with some know-how and skill, you can get mares and jacks to breed naturally.

As we also noted, most male mules are sterile, though females are still known to go into heat and, on rare occasions, give birth to a foal. Most often, though, they cannot reproduce, and thus the only way to get a mule is through the direct breeding of horse mares and jacks.

Though they have the morphology more akin to a horse, their care is more akin to the donkey portion of their genetics. They can live in a far more diverse range of environments than horses can, and their hooves are much more like a donkey than a horse, making them easier to care for and less demanding - shoes are not usually necessary for mules. Their dietary needs are very similar to their donkey counterparts.

They need to be fed on high fiber vegetation or supplemental hay or straw that is low in sugar. Rich forage or nutrient-dense vegetation is not ideal for those animals. For the best results in terms of proper nutrition, please consult the chapter on feeding donkeys for more information.

For best results when training your mule, get involved with them as soon as possible after they are born. The earlier you can start to socialize them, the better your relationship with them will be, and the easier they will be to train. Since they are a little less thoughtful and contemplative than donkeys, they tend to pick up on skills and training a little faster, but like the donkey, they don't need as much repetition to learn the task as a horse would.

You can develop something closely akin to a friendship with a mule, just as you can with a donkey, and this is not only regarding, but makes it easier to give them the care they need. Since they, like donkeys, aren't as expressive as horses, knowing them well makes it easier to read their emotions and body language. This is especially important if the animal is sick or injured. They enjoy social interaction with people and other animals, and as a result, they may make a better companion animal than a donkey.

Your mule's body language should not be read exactly as a horse's body language; mules are likely to display different emotions or desires. They may approach humans with their ears turned back, which, like a horse, is an indication of aggravation or aggression. But in a mule, it could mean they are asking for a treat. It takes time to get to know what the different body cues mean, and it helps to consider what the rest of the body is doing and the context the action is taking place in. That will help you better determine what their desires or intentions are.

Mules are territorial in much the same way as donkeys are, and this can be both a good and a bad thing. Like the donkey, a mule can be trained to watch over the livestock and chase predators. However, also like the donkey, they are not fans of any canine species, so their interaction with a family dog may be less than ideal. Whether you are raising and keeping donkeys or mules, use caution when letting a dog near them.

Mules have a different smell than either a donkey or a horse, and this can lead to some confusion if mules are kept with other types of equine. It seems the other animals have a harder time figuring out what exactly the mule is. Mules can be kept with other mules, horses, donkeys, or livestock. They are versatile animals that can take on a range of jobs on a farm and simply keep a person company.

A mule, like a donkey, will require regular grooming to keep them in good shape. Their coat is smoother than a donkey but caring for it is very similar. They need regular brushing to get rid of mud and other debris that collects in their fur. They will also need to have their eyes, ears, mouth, and hooves cleaned out regularly in the same manner as a donkey. Like a donkey, their hooves continue to grow throughout their lives and will need to be trimmed regularly, but they do not need shoes or the same level environment a horse requires.

# Conclusion

Donkeys are unique and hardy creatures that evolved to live in harsh and unforgiving environments. As a result, they are prized for their relatively low-maintenance care, good demeanor, and hard work ethic. These animals, when cared for and trained properly, can perform several functions from being ridden to protecting livestock.

Raising donkeys can also be a lucrative business idea as the donkey is ideal for certain activities and environments. As we close this brief guide to owning and raising donkeys, let's look at a couple of ways you can turn to raise donkeys into a lucrative money-making venture that provides a valuable service and is rewarding for both you and the donkey.

Since donkeys are such emotional and social creatures, some raise donkeys, particularly miniatures, to be petted. Since they are small and very friendly, miniature donkeys are great family animals for people with a small amount of land and a desire for a companion animal less common than the humble dog. If you are raising donkeys and selling them to be pets, you will want to do your homework when determining who to sell animals to.

As we noted numerous times in this guide, donkeys are long-lived animals, and anyone who is interested in adopting one needs to understand this, and the fact that they require some specialized care; they are not cared for exactly like horses. You might do background checks or even checking out the property of potential owners to ensure that they are a good fit for owning a donkey (or donkeys) as pets.

Since these animals are so social, anyone interested in buying one as a pet needs to know just how much time and socialization is necessary for their animal to be happy and fulfilled. Many get a pair of donkeys so they can keep each other company and maybe a suggestion to give a potential adopter of donkeys.

You will need to check with your local government offices to learn of the rules and regulations required for selling donkeys as pets and ensure that you follow the proper channels of providing equine passports for any donkey you sell.

Some people will raise and sell donkeys as light work animals. Though this isn't as common as it once was, donkeys are a great investment for a variety of different work activities, from agricultural work to hauling goods or people. Many tourist locations use donkeys to carry the packs of hikers or even for tourists to ride to a particular destination (recall the Grand Canyon, which relies on donkeys - especially mules). You may also want to check out your local laws to ensure that you are following all the rules and regulations that required for selling donkeys in your area.

Finally, this is perhaps the most lucrative way of using donkeys, and that is selling their milk. As we touched on in the chapter about donkey milk, it has been proven to be highly useful for a variety of conditions. People still use it to treat a variety of health ailments from eczema to allergies. More commonly, though, donkey milk is used in high-end beauty products.

Known and lauded for its myriad of benefits to the skin, such as anti-aging properties, advanced hydration, and the ability of people even with sensitive skin to use products made from donkey milk, beauty products made with it are becoming increasingly popular. Due to the high demand and the relative scarcity of donkey milk, the milk sells for a premium; cheese made from this milk can go for as high as $1,000 per pound, making it one of the most expensive milk products in the world.

Donkey milk is also used for a variety of other purposes, including giving it to sick or fussy children and even making cheese from it. The world's most expensive cheese is made from donkey milk.

Since donkeys don't produce large quantities of milk, you will need a decent number of animals to get enough milk to make it worth your while. Still, there is such high demand, and this might be the best business opportunity related to raising donkeys. Many farmers who raise donkeys for their milk work directly with a particular business or beauty company and sell their milk exclusively to said company. If you have enough animals, you may be able to produce enough milk to supply more than one small company. This isn't something that can be done on an industrial scale, and chances are, you will be servicing just one or two small companies.

Regardless of what you choose to use the donkeys for, they are great animals that provide a ton of work power and can even guard livestock. They are highly intelligent creatures who can adapt to a wide range of environments and can learn to perform a range of different skills, depending on your needs and expectations.

Understanding the emotional nature, temperament, and special needs of donkeys will make it easier to raise them healthily and happily. Keeping donkeys for any reason is a rewarding endeavor that allows you to develop a deep bond with an affectionate and loving creature that can also provide work power and more.

Raising healthy, happy, and well-trained donkeys will earn you a reputation far outside of your local area. People interested in buying donkeys will come from far and wide to obtain animals that have a solid pedigree and are from a trainer/owner who is well known for providing the animals with the best possible care, training, and socialization.

Donkeys may not be the most common animal anymore, but they have a long and storied history of living alongside humans. For some 6,000 years, donkey and man have lived and worked together in a variety of ways, working the narrow rows between vineyards or teaching a child how to ride.

They have evolved and been selectively bred to have several traits that make them more adaptable and useful to humans in a variety of climates and types of terrain. Donkeys are known for being affectionate and sweet to humans when they have been properly socialized. These are highly-intelligent creatures that need a decent amount of mental stimulation to keep them at their happiest and healthiest.

This guide has sought to provide those interested in raising donkeys, whether for commercial or personal reasons, the information they need to make an informed decision on the type of animal to get. It also covers the care they need, how to train them in basic skills, and an overview of different ailments common to the animals and how to spot or prevent these from occurring to begin with.

While this isn't a completely comprehensive guide, it should give you the knowledge you need to get started on your journey with the humble donkey. Given a bad reputation for being stubborn, this thoughtful animal just needs the right kind of training and can learn several skills and behaviors, providing you with companionship and animal power for many years to come.

# Part 3: Raising Beef Cattle

*An Essential Guide to Raising Cows, Calves, Bulls, Steers and Heifers in Your Backyard or on a Small Farm*

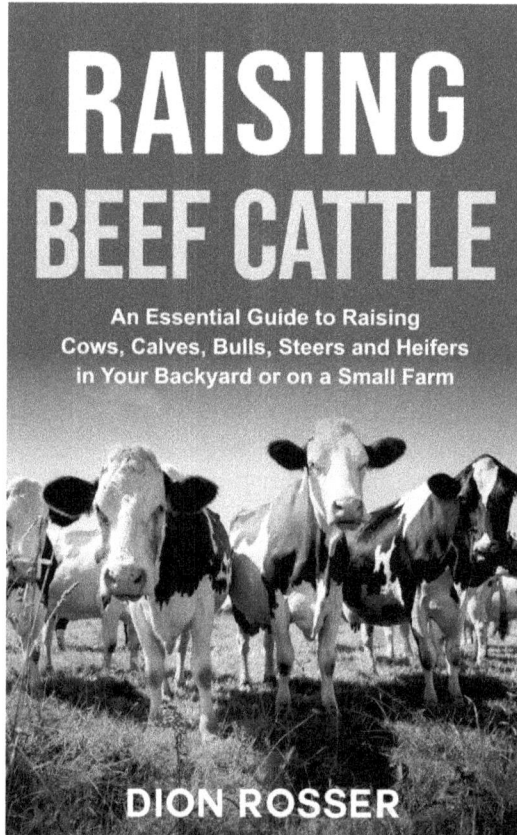

# Introduction

Americans love beef - so much so we consume 25 billion pounds of it each year. But there's something far more interesting and fulfilling than eating the juiciest medium-rare steak on a Friday night, and that is raising your own beef.

The satisfaction of knowing that the beef you eat is obtained from cattle raised in a safe, healthy, cruelty-free environment is better experienced than explained. You probably agree, and that's why you have this book in your hands.

In the pages that follow, you will gain in-depth knowledge on topics ranging from breed selection to cattle psychology to housing, nutrition, reproduction and calving. Smart tips for your beef cattle business are also included in this book to help make sure your new venture is as financially rewarding as it is satisfying.

Are you ready to take a leap into your new adventure? Then flip the page and let's begin!

# Chapter 1: The 6 Benefits of Raising Beef Cattle

Did you know that every 14th day of July is Cow Appreciation Day? No, it's not a national holiday, but Chick-fil-A did launch this event in 2004 as a way to get people to spare a thought for the cows that provide us so much.

On Cow Appreciation Day, people are encouraged to hug cows, thank dairy farmers in person, or buy locally made milk and dairy products. On the fun side, certain Chick-fil-A branches also offer a free meal on this day to any customer that comes into their restaurant dressed as a cow. Sweet, right? And it's the least we can do considering how much cows do for us, often at the cost of their lives.

Over 98% of a beef animal will be used when processed. Beef, cheese, milk, ice cream and yogurt are delicious consumables that come to mind when we think of cows (or cattle more correctly. Not every animal that looks like a cow is a cow. But more on that later). From cattle, we get about 25 billion pounds of beef annually. That's huge!

But there's so much more that cattle do for us. About 45% of a cow's body is used as meat and the other parts go into the production of glue, leather, soap, gelatins, pharmaceuticals, china and even insulin. Picture this: one bovine animal provides enough hide to make about 144 baseballs, or 20 footballs or 12 basketballs.

Cattle are also wonderful recyclers as they feed on many of the by-products from manufacturing products like potato chips, candy, and beer. We haven't even mentioned the amazing benefits their dung provides in manure. One bovine can produce up to 80 pounds of manure every single day! That's more manure than even scientists or farmers know what to do with.

There are many benefits we enjoy from rearing cattle, and so it's difficult to think about them beyond all the ways they are useful to us as humans. But on their own, cattle are fascinating animals worth looking closely at. Here are just a few fun facts to make you look at cattle a little differently.

# A Dozen Things You Didn't Know About Cows/Cattle

### 1. Cattle Have Nearly 360-Degree Vision

This means it's practically impossible to sneak up on them. It also means that cow tipping is mostly wishful thinking. Besides their nearly panoramic vision, they also never zone out.

Plus, come on, these animals are massive! We are looking at about 1500 pounds average effectively balanced on four legs. What are the odds? Watching someone try to trip a sleeping cow might be funny if it wasn't so dangerous.

### 2. The Word "Cattle" has its Roots in the Word "Chattel"

Yes, the same Anglo-French term that means "personal property." Back in the day, cattle were considered valuable property and a person's wealth was measured by it.

### 3. Every Cow is Female

Every cow is a girl or more correctly, a female that has birthed a calf. Those that haven't are called heifers. Males, on the other hand, are called bulls. If they are castrated so they can no longer breed and are reared for their beef alone, then they are called steers.

There are also those called veal. These are specifically raised to reach a maximum weight of about 500 pounds.

Other names used to differentiate members of a herd include:

**Stag:** A stag is just like a steer except that it is also used as a "gomer bull." Gomer bulls are used to detect heifers and cows in heat.

**Ox:** These are raised specifically to do draft work. Draft work includes pulling farm and travel machinery such as wagons, plows, or carts.

Oxen are mostly castrated male bovines, but they can also sometimes be bulls or even female cattle.

**Freemartin:** Freemartins are infertile heifers. Infertility in heifers is usually the result of sharing the womb with a bull calf. The testosterone levels produced by the bull calf in the womb affect the production of estrogen in the female calf.

Freemartins can be born in one of two ways. They can have underdeveloped reproductive organs, or they might have both male and female parts (such freemartins can also be called hermaphrodites).

Hermaphroditic freemartins will usually develop secondary male characteristics as they mature, such as a wide forehead or a muscular crest around their neck.

**Cattle:** A plural term used when there's more than one bovine, especially when the genders are mixed or uncertain.

### 4. Cows are not always Black and White

Bulls are not always solidly colored either. With cattle, color is determined by breed and not by sex. Cattle can literally come in many colors and these are varied by different markings. You can find cattle in brown, yellow, white, black, red, gray, and even orange. They can also come in a variation of these colors (most times mixed with white) such as speckled, pointed, patchy, dorsal-striped, white-faced or white-tailed.

Generally...

Friesians, Holstein-Friesians and Purebred Holsteins, male and female, are always black and white.

Dairy cows such as Jersey, Guernsey and Brown Swiss cows are usually either solid red or solid brown.

Beef cows such as the Limousin, Gelbvieh, Red Brangus, Red Angus, Simmental and Santa Gertrudis breeds are also usually red or brown.

Belgian Blue cattle, though, are not actually blue. They are more bluish roan than blue. They only appear smoky-blue because of the way the white and black hairs on their coats are mixed.

### 5. Both Sexes of Cattle can either be Horned or Polled or Both

So, it's not a great idea to rely on the presence or absence of horns or polls in determining the gender of bovine. To tell the gender of a bovine accurately, look behind the animal's hind limbs to see if there's a scrotum or an udder.

### 6. Bulls Cannot See Red

Like their other bovine brothers and sisters, bulls are red/green colorblind. So, why do they charge at the matador then? It turns out all flapping in the breeze that aggravates them, which is understandable, right?

So, even if the matador used an indigo flag, the bull would still charge. But why have they continued to use red flags? Well, it isn't ignorance. It's actually a more "sinister" reason - to hide the bull's blood.

### 7. Named Cows Produce More Milk than Nameless Ones

This suggests that the more emotionally invested a farmer is in their relationship with their cows, the more milk the cows produce. A good relationship with humans means that cows are less stressed when milked, which means more milk for the farmer. A cow called by name will produce nearly 500 more pints of milk in a year!

But if the cow feels jittery around their human, she gets stressed, and her body produces cortisol. This hormone inhibits the production of milk, which means less milk. But even more important, a happy loved cow is less likely to hurt her human when being milked.

### 8. Cows are very Social and even have Best Friends

It's hard for you to find cows all alone except when they are ill or about to give birth. Separating a cow from her best friends could cause her to become stressed. The body secretes more cortisol (the stress hormone), and heart rate goes up when you put them with random bovines rather than their preferred partners.

## 9. Cows can Swim

Cows are excellent swimmers, believe it or not. After Hurricane Dorian, three cows were found at the Cape Lookout National Seashore. They were believed to have swum all the way from Cedar Island, where they lived before the hurricane-ravaged their home.

Swimming about 4 to 5 miles might seem astonishing, but experienced farmers won't find this information surprising.

## 10. Surrogacy is a thing Among Cows

There are such things as surrogate cows. Surrogacy is becoming more common these days, especially with dairy cows. The process involves moving embryos from genetically superior cows to other less superior cows.

Naturally, cows produce only one embryo at a time, but when surrogacy is the plan, the cow gets injected with a hormone triggering the production of many eggs, which are then fertilized.

The fertilized eggs (embryos) can be as many as 80 or even 90 but, in the end, only about 6 to 7 end up being usable.

The vet removes the embryos from the cow, employing a process called an embryo flush. These embryos can then be transferred to the less superior surrogate cows so their offspring are of better genetic quality compared to what they might have produced on their own.

Surrogacy among cows is a genius innovation, and not just because you get to "create" your preferred, desirable, genetically superior cows. Through surrogacy, farmers in other countries with inadequate resources to meet dairy-cow demands can improve their own bovine gene pool, producing quality cows to meet their lack.

## 11. Aurochs Are Cattle's Earliest Ancestors

Aurochs were huge, wild beasts originally located in the Indian subcontinent before they spread to China, the Middle East, North Africa and then Europe. After a while, about 8,000 to 10,000 years ago, people domesticated aurochs.

In 1493, Columbus introduced these domesticated aurochs, now known as cattle, to the western hemisphere. Later, in 1519, Hernando Cortez, a Spanish explorer, took the offspring of these cattle to Mexico. In 1773, Juan Bautista de Anza supplied the early California missions with

200 head of cattle. And this was how cattle evolved and spread around the world.

Cattle are raised and bred globally, in widely varied settings and climates. This is possible because cows can survive and even thrive eating only low-quality grasses and feed. For most cattle, grazing would be on steep, hilly, rocky or dry grounds, unsuitable for cultivating crops or building houses.

## 12. Cattle Have 32 Teeth in Total but Have no Upper Front Teeth

So, how do they cut grass? Well, to cut grass, they join their lower front teeth to the hard upper palate. After doing the cutting, they then chew their food roughly 50 times in 60 seconds. This means they move their jaws close to 40,000 times per day!

It's common knowledge that cattle have four-compartment stomachs, the rumen being the main stomach. The rumen is the part of the stomach that holds the partially digested food called the cud. From this part of the anatomy the cud goes back into the cattle's mouth when regurgitated.

The rumen can hold about 50 gallons of partially digested food. If you want to feel small, the human stomach can only hold 1 quart of food, which is just about a quarter of a gallon!

A bovine typically spends a third of its day eating, consuming about 40 pounds worth of food and about 30 to 50 gallons of water each day. Naturally, cattle pass out large amounts of dung and urine daily. It is estimated that cattle produce about 60 pounds of manure and roughly 30 gallons of urine every day. In one year, we are looking at over 20,000 pounds (or 10 tons!) of manure!

This makes an excellent point to segue into the next part of this chapter. Let's see all the reasons you should raise your own beef cattle.

# 6 Reasons You Should Consider Growing Your Own Beef Cattle

### 1. Raising Your Own Beef Cattle Can Help Improve Your Land

When done properly, grazing your cattle can help improve the quality of your land. Here's how that works.

Plants need leaves to photosynthesize. When they do that, they release sugars into the soil, which soil microbes then use to break down soil nutrients, making these nutrients available for the plants to use. By grazing on the grass, cattle break up the ground and remove the old foliage so that the grasses have room to germinate and photosynthesize.

Also, by indirectly laying plant debris on top of the soil, cattle assist in the maximizing of the life cycle of soil minerals. As the debris composts, it makes it possible for these nutrients to properly cycle and enter the root nodules of plants.

Plus, don't forget their urine and manure, which supply nitrogen, additional microorganisms, and more partly decomposed grass to the soil. Thanks to this natural fertilizer, your soil will be infiltrated and hold water better for future plants. This means that your land will be less vulnerable to drought.

Another very important thing your grazing cattle do as they improve your land is to sequester atmospheric carbon in large amounts. This creates a safer ecosystem for us all.

### 2. You Get Access to Healthy Meat

From a single cow, you can get over 500 pounds of beef. Even if you eat that in one year, you'd still get to eat 1.3 pounds of beef each day, and that's substantial. Killing one cow to get that much beef is much more efficient, plus more humane, than killing the required number of chickens it would take to get the same meat.

Also, raising your own beef cattle, you get access to the choicest, healthiest parts. There's the liver, for instance, which is the most nutritious food you can find. You should eat about 1 to 3 ounces of liver per week, at least. Other parts like shanks, brisket, and oxtail, when made into bone broths, are also super healthy for you as they provide rare nutrients you can't get from other sources.

Furthermore, beef from grass-fed cattle is richer in healthy fatty acids, which are important for proper immunity, heart and brain function. Research shows that the fat ratio you find in grass-fed beef is very similar to the ratio found in the ancestral human diet.

Pasture-raised cattle also contain the highest levels of conjugated linoleic acid, which has been known to have anti-cancer properties. And compared to grain-fed beef cattle, they supply 7 times more beta-carotene, 2 times more vitamin B2, and thrice as much vitamin B1.

### 3.   You Get More Nutritious Crops

In recent years, nutrient density in vegetable crops in America has witnessed a steady decline. As of now, nutrient density in crops has dropped by up to 40% because livestock is nowhere to be found on our farmlands anymore.

Removing livestock from the land means you no longer get the benefits explained in the first point. Therefore, there would be a decrease in the available soil nutrients for plants, which will, in turn, affect the quality of the crops you harvest.

### 4.   It's a Blossoming Income Stream

Pasture-raised cattle beef is not mainstream or even popular yet. Of the 30 million cattle we see on the market annually, just 1% are grass-fed. But from all indications, the market for grass-fed beef is growing, as consumers are becoming more aware of the positive benefits. Plus, grass-fed beef tastes sublime when people use the best methods to produce them, and the demand for these flavorful delicacies is on the rise.

To correctly breed your cattle, it's important to feed them in the fields or in the feedlot with high-energy feeds. This is the only way to make them fat and delicious. Feeding them on lush, delicious high-protein green grass will affect the flavor of your beef. It might seem counterintuitive, but it's the way it works. High-energy, carbohydrate feeds are much better at preparing cattle for processing than high-protein feeds.

High-protein will give your cattle stronger frames and better yield, but the luscious fat that gives beef its great taste, that's the work of carb diets. This is the key to producing the "best-beef-you-ever-tasted" kind of grass-fed beef.

### 5.   Carefully Planned Grazing Increases Biodiversity

If cattle are properly grazed, their grazing activity can increase the biodiversity of the pasture in which they feed. This improves the ecosystem for millions of other critters found in that biome.

### 6.   It's a Fun, Educational Project for the Whole Family

Nurturing cattle involve activities that can be carried out by different family members of different ages and skill levels. Raising cattle as a family can foster family bonding. And then there's all the fun of traveling around the country exhibiting your animals in cattle shows.

But showing cows isn't the only way raising cattle can be great for your family. The venture of raising cattle all on its own is rewarding. Everyone gets to learn dependability and develop a great work ethic.

Cattle are demanding animals, requiring care every single day in the sun and in the rain. Together, your family can work out the kinks of caring for them by drawing up budgets, making purchasing decisions, assigning responsibilities and managing money and other resources.

It's inevitable that doing all these things together as a family will bring you all closer and increase your love and appreciation for other living creatures with whom you share this planet.

# Chapter 2: Beef Cattle Breeds and Selection

Beef cattle are specifically bred for their meat because of how efficiently they convert feed into meat. When feeding, they absorb the minimum amount of nutrients they need to carry out basic physiological functions. After that, they begin to gain weight, which is mostly muscle and not fat or bone. Thanks to this genetic predisposition, a newborn 90-pound calf only needs as little as 12 to 13 months to achieve butchering size.

Beef cows do produce milk - just not in large amounts. They produce just enough to keep them in tip-top physical shape as they rear their young calves.

That said, efficiency in growth isn't the only reason they are reared. There are other important qualities for which such herds are raised. These attributes include reproductive superiority, efficiency in the feed, and hardiness, which are critical traits when raising and breeding the best with minimal care and maintenance.

Genetics aside, they are also identifiable by their looks. Good quality herds look rectangular with broad chests, wide shoulders, a thickness along the top of their backs, and round and full stomachs and ribs. Good beef herds are never bony or skinny. They always look plump and robust but such animals typically cost more than the skinnier ones. So, remember this when shopping.

When it comes to color, they almost always come in solid colors. This can range from solid black to white to gray to red. It's rare for them to be spotted, although they do exist. Nonetheless, because more buyers prefer solid black, even preferring to pay a premium price for them, spotted cattle are becoming rare.

The first step in any venture is to select a breed. We've talked a bit about the breed in general, but these guys come in many breeds. Choosing the right one that matches your goals and objectives as a farmer is critical to enjoying a more profitable herd-growing experience.

Now, pay close attention because, in this chapter, you will be getting key pointers for picking the best breed for your needs. But, before that, let's look at the most common beef in the United States.

# The Top 9 Most Common Beef Cattle Breeds in the United States

### 1. Black Angus

The Black Angus is the most popular breed in America. There are more than 330,000 of these animals currently registered, and the reason for its popularity is the value of its carcass. It is commonly touted knowledge that the cadaver of the Black Angus is well-marbled and very flavorful. They don't need a high level of maintenance, especially during the calving season. They are very efficient with feed and are excellent mothers too.

### 2. Charolais

There are many who believe that introducing the Charolais revolutionized the North American beef industry. Before the breed was introduced, American farmers were in search of heavier, larger-framed cattle, something they were not getting with traditional British breeds. But with introducing the Charolais, that problem was solved immediately.

Charolais are usually creamy white, or white. In the summer, their hair is short, and as the weather gets colder, the hair thickens to protect them.

### 3. Hereford

Herefords are desired for their fattening ability and early maturation. They are usually reddish yellow to dark red and have a white face. They are also quite docile, great mothers, good milkers, and typically live longer.

### 4. Simmental

The Simmentals are an old breed, widely distributed across the globe. They are usually white and red. They first entered the United States in the 19th century and have been a part of the American beef community since then.

Simmentals have a large frame with an impressive ability to gain weight.

### 5. Red Angus

The Red Angus is a less popular breed than its cousin, the Black Angus, but both breeds share the same favorable characteristics, like amazing marbling and terrific flavor. These cattle are docile, excellent mothers, and can tolerate hotter climates better than the other breeds accustomed to Highland conditions in Europe.

### 6. Texas Longhorns

Texas Longhorns are white and red with characteristically long horns. They have great calving ability and hybrid vigor when crossed with other varieties.

Texas Longhorns beef is choice meat because it's lean and low in fat, cholesterol and calories when compared to other kinds.

### 7. Gelbvieh

The Gelbvieh is European, but it got introduced to the US via artificial insemination. The breed is typically red and horned, although there are polled varieties that came about from crossing with hornless female cattle.

Many of the breed's best attributes include their great fertility, ease of calving, good mothering ability and impressive growth rate for calves.

### 8. Limousin

The Limousins are golden red and are mostly found in south-central France — Marche and Limousin, to be precise. The carcass merit of this breed is top notch, making it another popular beef in the industry.

### 9. Highlands

Highlands are known for their double coat and longhorns. These herds are super easy to keep as they often go by with the minimum in terms of feed, shelter and the likes. They do nicely in colder climates and are found thriving in Alaska and Scandinavian countries. They also succeed in southern climates like Georgia and Texas.

This breed is practically immune to eye infections and diseases such as pink eye and eye cancer, thanks to the forelocks and long lashes that protect their eyes.

Beef from Highland cattle is rich in flavor, well-marbled, and with only little waste fat.

# Beef Cattle Selection

Selecting the right ones to raise will depend on your personal goals. Many people prefer to raise them to graze their pasture. Others want to sell feeder calves or raise them for showing. The most popular reason for keeping them is to get quality beef either to eat or for sale. So, you need to clarify your cattle-raising aspirations first before deciding on which breed to select.

Once you've done that, the following are a few factors you want to consider when selecting a breed.

### 1.   Local Availability

It will be much easier for you if you get cattle common to your locale, except for when your heart is set on a particular type. So, check on neighboring farms in your vicinity and discover the breeds they raise when making your selection. There are several advantages to this.

First, if you go for those that are popular in your region, you'd have a larger pool to select from, which gives you more options. Plus, you won't have to spend big bucks moving them from one part of the country to the other. Considering the size of these animals, transportation costs can be large.

Also, because they are "natives" of your region, you won't need to pass them through the rigors of adapting to a new climate and new feed. Buying similar product to your neighbors' means you begin your enterprise with an already proven track record of success.

### 2.   Hair Color

Hair color varies widely, as we discussed earlier, but following current trends, solid-colored cattle sell for prices much greater than the spotted varieties. While solid colored cattle are the priciest, they are most common in this industry due to higher demand. As with human fashion, black hides flaws like lack of muscle or fat and gives the bovine a more flattering look, hence their desirability.

Uniform color is more attractive to potential buyers. Many believe that a uniform herd grows, feeds, and attains butchering size at the same rate, even though this isn't necessarily always true. Whatever the case, achieving a uniform look is probably a good idea if you plan to sell, and much more easily achieved if all your cattle are a solid dark color.

There's a small catch, though. Black cattle do not stay cool as easily as lighter-colored cattle. So, offer plenty of water and adequate shade for them.

### 3.   Horns

Generally, raising them without horns is often easier than those with horns. There's the danger factor — they can be sharp and tough! Then you also must consider all the space they require, both during transportation and at the feeding bunker.

For these reasons, horned cattle sell for a price considerably lower than their counterparts (polled cattle). But especially if you're working with limited space - perhaps just your backyard - you might have to spend the extra bucks and choose the hornless varieties.

Now, remember that once dehorned, they are different as hornless (polled) cattle. Dehorned are considered bovines who have had them physically removed. If you don't want horned offspring, then you shouldn't get dehorned cattle as they still have the genes to produce calves with horns and can pass this trait on. Polled cattle, on the other hand, are bovines born without horns. These do not have these genetics, and won't pass them down to their offspring.

Breeds like the Angus, Polled Hereford, and Polled Shorthorn are naturally always polled but, for other varieties, horning, while possible, should be avoided using selective reproduction.

Now, since we're here, it's important to talk about the dangers of dehorning. Dehorning causes a high level of stress to the animal, plus the potential complications. A much better and safer way to remove horns remains through selective breeding.

## 4. Breed Characteristics

Having looked at all other factors like horns, hair color and local availability, it's time to check out the characteristics of the cattle. Your knowledge of these features and how they are affected by environmental changes can be helpful to determine the best breeds you want to raise in your situation.

The following are the important qualities to consider thoughtfully:

**Carcass Merit**: The carcass of an animal includes all that's left after the hide, head, and internal organs have been removed. It typically consists of fat, bone and muscle.

Carcass merit refers to an assessment of the yield (also known as lean meat) and its eating quality. If you plan to sell your animals on the grid, this determines the price offered for the beef. The higher the value, the higher the prices you're offered, and the more satisfied customers you'd have.

Pick those that are identified for their lean meat. No one likes to drain grease from meat. Also, it is very important to look for their eating quality and tenderness.

**Body Size:** Specifically, this refers to adult body size. Large parents mean large calves, which usually means birthing difficulties most of the time. But  large cattle mean you get calves with heavy weaning weights, which can be a great if you plan to sell feeders by weight.

But do remember that with a large size comes an even larger responsibility. These guys sure do eat! If you live in an arid climate with little grass, you probably shouldn't be thinking of getting a 1,500-pounder. It's not a good idea to get large cattle if you're working with a small space.

**Milking Ability:** This refers to just how much milk a cow can produce to feed her calf. The more milk, the heavier the weaning weight of her calves, but cows that milk heavily are often skinnier because their bodies direct all the calories toward milking. Therefore, these cows take longer to rebreed.

If you have a heavy milking cow, the quality and quantity of feed you give your cow really matters. These cows do not do well with a meager pasture.

**Growth Rate:** A measure of how much a bovine can grow during a period, as well as how much feed is required to produce one pound of weight gain. This rate is expressed using the unit, ADG, which stands for "average daily gain."

To calculate the average daily gain of a cattle animal, simply divide the pounds gained over a period by the number of days. An ADG of 3 or more is considered high.

Cattle with a high ADG, naturally need high-quality, high-energy feedstuff to achieve their fullest growth potential.

**Adaptability:** How well the breed thrives in challenging environmental conditions such as sparse feeds, or extreme weather, or in the presence of insects should be considered. This is the cattle's adaptability.

Although this factor has been mentioned last, it's important because what's the point of having a fantastic calf with a high ADG and carcass merit that dies because it can't cope with the challenges of the environment? Exactly.

# Purebred vs Crossbred

Purebreds are cattle with parents from the same strain, while a crossbred will have each parent from different or unknown breeds. Both have their strengths and demerits. Let's look at each in detail.

### Purebreds

With purebreds, you can be part of a recognized breed association like the American Angus Association, for example. The benefit of being part of such organizations is that they promote and help you raise your breed by providing the right education and supporting your marketing effort.

If you're going into the raising and selling of your reproductive stock, then purebreds are your best bet. You may come to where you want to sell crossbreeds too, but even at that, you'd still need your purebreds to serve as the foundation breeding lines. Also, shows, fairs and competitions are more open to purebreds than to others.

Looking at the marketing angle, it's a broader space for purebreds. For instance, you can only find registered trademarks (like Certified Angus Beef, for example) for purebreds and not for crossbred animals.

Now, if you do go for purebred cattle, you must be on top of all things that are data and paperwork-related. You need to do this because it's the only way to register your animals.

Registration papers contain information on the animal, including its parentage, and expected breeding performance. Without registration, your cattle will not be eligible for shows, but when your animals are properly registered, you'll be offered greater prices for them as having a registered animal increases its resale value.

### Crossbreeds

Crossbreeds have the advantage of heterosis or hybrid vigor. This refers to how they excel in key performance areas such as fertility, growth and longevity. They typically do a lot better than both their purebred parents in these areas. This often is to be expected, seeing as the main aim of crossbreeding is to obtain the best traits of two purebreds in one superior offspring.

Certain features have low heritability; they are not easily passed to the next generation. Examples of such attributes include mothering instinct, reproductive performance, and environmental adaptability. Crossbreeding can help to improve such features to increase their heritability.

Should you get crossbred cattle? Why not? Well, that depends on two things. If your cattle-raising goals involve purebreds and purebreds alone, you should stay away.

Now, if the aforementioned isn't your plan, then it is okay to choose crossbred cattle. They have are advantages over purebreds. Superior mothering instincts, excellent fertility, longevity, and calves with heavier weaning weights are things you want in a cow, and crossbred cattle provide these traits and skills better than purebreds.

With crossbred bulls the benefits aren't as clear-cut. Mating these cows with crossbred bulls does not always go as expected. Often, variations are too wide, and the calves obtained differ widely in size and weight, which you don't want. So, to improve certain traits in your herd using breeding selection, it might be better to use a purebred bull.

A quick tip if you're going for crossbred cattle. Like George Orwell said in <u>Animal Farm</u>, all crossbreeds are equal, *but some are more equal than others*. If you missed it, the point is that all forms aren't all created equal. So, when buying this type of cattle, confirm from the seller that they are an offspring of different purebred breeds, not just a calf with unknown ancestry.

# Chapter 3: Cattle Psychology and Handling

While animal cruelty and abuse are usually a result of terrible motives on the side of the handler, sometimes a handler uses cruel actions because they are frustrated and have run out of ideas.

In this chapter, you'll be exposed to how cattle behave and why they behave the way they do. Once you understand normal cattle behavior, you can learn to handle them without having to resort to cruel and dangerous measures. Let's get started.

## Vision and Cattle Behavior

Cattle eyesight differs significantly from that of humans. And this difference is probably most evident in the relationship between their eyesight and their movements.

Cattle have a wide angle vision that allows them to see things happening beside them. So, if your cattle notices movement from the corner of their eye, regardless of how subtle the movement is, it will most likely balk and stop moving. Worse still, the perceived movement can frighten them and cause agitation that you'd rather not have. Introducing a paddle at this point or forcing them to keep on moving can lead to very unpleasant circumstances.

Besides their wide-angled vision, cattle do not have a good depth perception at ground level. For them to figure out how deep a hole is, they must lower their heads, so they can see the ground.

So, if your cattle are walking and notice a dip or hole, like a drain or even a change in ground texture, they'll most likely stop moving. You might even notice a few of them checking out what is on the ground.

If your cattle suddenly stop walking, your first instinct shouldn't be to force them to keep moving but to discover why they've stopped moving.

However, this sudden stop can be prevented if you consider the suggestions made in the next section.

# Vision and Cattle Handling

Let's start with paying attention to their wide-angle vision. Because cattle can perceive movement from the corner of their eyes, and that movement can prevent them from moving, so eliminate distractions.

So, in building your handling space and/or loading ramp, add in a few side slabs high enough to keep the distractions out.

Besides ensuring the free flow of movement, blocking out the distractions can contribute to making your cattle less agitated. Make sure that they can't see people and things they can't control, as this will help keep them calm.

Building solid ramps that will block out the distractions is especially important for new cattle breeders because, as a new cattle breeder, your cattle are not familiar with your farm and are not used to those distractions. They have also most likely not yet been trained to ignore the distractions.

Something else you should do as regards your cattle's wide-angle vision is to remove anything around them that moves.

So, there should be nothing hanging anywhere or flapping in the breeze. Coats, hangers, and even tree branches should be removed. If you pull off your coat because the weather is too hot, do not hang it on the fence or anywhere within your cattle's line of sight.

If you have a barn, consider other ventilating mediums besides fans because fan blades can be distracting for your cattle.

Now, let's look at their depth perception. Make certain that the path that your cattle will be walking is free of any obstacles. Your cattle must be able to sense that walking a particular path will not be dangerous for them.

Make sure there are no drain chutes along the path. Also, make sure that the ground texture has the same consistency; there should be no ridges or crevices. There should also not be any puddles of water, as these can be perceived as a potential drowning site.

If your cattle suddenly stop to check things out on the ground, allow them to satisfy their curiosity. They will be more willing to listen to you if they have confirmed that they are not in danger.

# Light and Cattle Behavior

Cattle find it easy to move from a place that isn't properly lit to one that is, but they will not go toward a brightly lit place if it's too bright.

Also, cattle rarely take well to shadows, whether those are on the walls or on the floor. Shadows confuse them as the shadows make it difficult for them to see what's ahead of them.

# Lighting and Cattle Handling

Make sure that the destination (most likely a loading ramp or trailer) you want your cattle to move onto is better lit than the loading chute (race). You can do this by beaming light directly on the loading ramp.

This light should not be too bright, as that can deter your cattle. And the light should also not be shined directly into your cattle's eyes, as that can make them agitated.

As for the chute, make sure that the entire chute is evenly lit. There should be no shadows or dark spots. These make your cattle feel uneasy. The idea is just to make sure that your cattle know that what they see is all that is there.

# Noise and Cattle Behavior

Cattle do not like loud sounds. And probably unfortunately for them, they have good hearing. To put things in perspective, in the best-case scenario, humans hear at 3000 hz while cattle can hear at up to 8000 hz. So, it makes sense that noise easily irritates them.

However, the emphasis here is on loud because cattle have no issues with white noise and random radio talk, provided the sound is at a reasonable volume. In fact, consistent white noise can help your cattle relax.

Cattle are disturbed by loud and sudden noises. The sounds from bells, trains, heavy-duty trucks, firecrackers and even sounds of heavy-duty machinery at a slaughterhouse is auditory sensory overload for your cattle.

Something else that they do not take well to shouting. So, whether it's being shouted at or just generally having humans screaming and shouting around them, you want to keep your vocalizations down when you're in their presence.

Now, cattle that generally have a calm disposition might not seem agitated at the sound of something loud and foreign, but this does not mean they aren't. Cattle that are calm will usually tilt their ears in the general area of foreign noise, as if they are trying to figure the sounds out.

Now that you know all that about how noise can affect your cattle's behavior, what can you do about it?

# Noise and Cattle Handling

First, if you are running a slaughterhouse, make sure that the barn or wherever your cattle are housed is far from the slaughterhouse; far enough away that your cattle cannot hear the activities going on in there.

Also, if you love firecrackers, you must sacrifice for your cattle. Make sure that everybody knows that your property is a no-firecracker zone.

However, if you have a small farm, it might be difficult to cut out every source of noise completely. Here, having constant white noise play in the barn can help make your cattle less susceptible to reacting loud noise. You can use a radio to play talk show stations in your barn with the volume set to normal.

Make sure that you do not shout at your cattle. Not only will the shout not be effective, but it can also make the situation worse.

You also want to make sure that whatever disagreement you are having with anyone is away from your cattle's range of hearing, especially if you feel that the disagreement could lead to a shouting match.

And in rounding up your herd, whistling or shouting should not be considered, as those are classified as a sudden noise. But (and this might seem like an antithesis of all that has been said) blowing a horn to call your cattle could be a good idea. But you need to know if you want to use a horn, your cattle must be trained (with rewards) to come to the sound of the horn.

Moving on, you want to avoid using mechanical doors that make noise as they open. If doors squeak, you can use rubber stoppers to minimize the sound.

Finally, you can take advantage of the calm ones among your cattle. Seeing as the calm ones are more likely to turn their ears toward the sudden loud noise than to show agitation, you can look toward their ears to figure out what the source of the noise is. And removing that source should help the other cattle remain calm.

# Touch and Cattle Behavior

Probably the most well-known facts about cattle are that they are herd animals. And the implication is that they usually move in groups. As a result, cattle and other animals that travel in herds are accustomed to the feeling of having bodies around them.

Furthermore, cattle are sensitive to touch. And much like they do not like sudden noise or sudden movement, they certainly do not like to be touched unexpectedly. They can react violently if they misinterpret a particular touch as harmful. This is especially true if they have a history of being abused.

In building your chute or any other structure that your cattle must walk through, it's important that you make it narrow enough they can feel the pressure of bodies against them as they walk.

Aside from the fact that the feeling of the nearness of other bodies helps the cows to stay calm, they cannot turn around and go in the opposite direction. So, building a compact chute allows you to kill several birds with one stone.

As for touch, use firm strokes on your cattle. Firm strokes communicate to them you are not only intentional, but that you also mean well. Avoid using uncertain or sudden strokes as those could convey the exact antithesis of what you want them to. Pats are something you want to avoid as your cattle could confuse them for hits.

Finally, when dealing with day-to-day activities, it's important to consider whether any of your cattle have been abused because cattle rarely forget the abuse, and this might translate into their overreaction to your touch.

If any of your cattle have been abused you have to be careful and, more important, extremely patient and calm when touching them.

# Health and Cattle Behavior

An animal that isn't at peak health could be difficult to manage. Unfortunately, a lot of factors can make your cattle sick. Many of these health issues are things you have control over, and a few others aren't.

For one, extreme weather conditions can put your cattle under the weather. And for cattle, heat is a bigger threat than cold. Other factors that can affect your cattle you have little control over include parasites, diseases and predators.

However, there will be things you have control over, like food. Your cattle must be properly fed (food and water) if you want them to be agreeable. But you do not want them to be overfed as that can make them bored and lethargic, making it difficult for you to get them to do anything.

Undergoing certain procedures can also affect your cattle's response. For example, having your testicles ripped off will bring any man down and make them uncooperative. So, expect that from your cattle that have just been castrated!

As much as it's within your control, make sure your cattle are in optimal health. And even those factors you can't control, you can try to manage. Here are a few tips:

Feed your cattle promptly and appropriately. Give them enough food as and when due.

Cattle don't take well to being isolated. So house them in herds.

If you just castrated your cattle, you must allow them time alone to heal. They might need to be isolated during this period, but make sure they are in a place where they can see other cattle.

Remember the high wall slab mentioned earlier? The one that should help keep out distractions? It could also help to keep out predators. Having a herding dog can also be useful.

# The Flight Zone

From all that has been mentioned, it's easy to conclude that it doesn't take much to spook a herd of cattle. In fact, because of how easy it is, you must pay attention to their reactions.

In simple terms, the flight zone is your cattle's personal space. It is the distance and space from the cattle you can stand and move within without making your cattle becoming violent.

The interesting thing about the flight zone is that getting into it makes the cattle walk away from you. And you could use this to get them to where you want them to go.

To get a cow or bull to move forward, you must stand at the edge of its flight zone. And to get it to stop moving, you must get out of its flight zone but make sure that you are still within sight.

Now, the flight zone distance differs from one animal to another. And this difference could result from temperament or even training.

The calmer an animal is, the shorter the distance of their flight zone, if docile cattle have almost no flight zone (which would make herding them difficult). Also, as your cattle get used to having you around, they get more comfortable and this will diminish their flight zone distance.

Now, how do you figure out your cattle's flight zone? Just try walking gently toward them within their line of sight. When they walk away from you is the edge of their flight zone. If you keep getting closer, your cattle might get really agitated. So, you want to work with that spot where they moved away from you.

Also, if you want them to move forward, use the flight zone behind their forelimbs as they will try to distance themselves from you by moving forward. If you come from their front, they'll most likely go back to where they were coming from.

Finally, cattle can see 300 degrees around them. So, their blind spot is directly behind their head, and that is a place you do not want to be.

Remember that cattle do not like surprises, so standing in a spot where they can't see you but can feel your presence will spook them. And cattle spooked like that can get aggressive, leading to serious injuries for you.

# Chapter 4: Facilities, Housing and Fencing

Now, it's time to think about where your cattle will stay and what facilities you'll be using for your operation. And it goes without saying that these housing and operating facilities must be in place a couple of days before your cattle arrives.

However, the facilities you need to operate your cattle rearing outfit depends upon the outfit you want to run. Basically, there are three types of cattle rearing outfits:

- Cow-Calf Outfit: You are breeding cattle.

- Feeder Outfit: You are raising cattle to be sold as meat.

- Combination Outfit: A combination of both.

While a cow-calf rearing outfit requires roofed living quarters for the cattle, it's unnecessary for a feeder outfit. And while a feeder outfit requires a lot of confinement pens and automated feeding systems, a cow-calf outfit doesn't need as many pens. As far as the handling facilities, you'll need the same things no matter what sort of cattle rearing business you want to run.

With all that said, let's see what facilities you'll need to run a successful business.

# Beef Cattle Handling Facilities

### Headgate

The headgate is a gate device used to hold the head of cattle in place. The idea is to hold the animal in place so the cattle can be accessed to receive veterinary treatment.

There are four broad types of headgates. The self-catching kind automatically closes immediately after the cattle step in, but if that doesn't work too well for you, you can get a version that can also be operated manually.

The scissor stanchion comprises two pieces with a pivot at the bottom. The full opening stanchion comprises two pieces that slide open to allow the cattle in and then slide shut to keep them in. The positive control headgate, which isn't very safe, locks the standing cattle in firmly (but maybe too firmly).

In choosing a headgate, you want to remember the following things:

● An automatic headgate usually locks either too tightly or too loosely. So, it might not always be a good choice.

● If you run a small farm with agreeable cattle or the cattle you want to work on are sick, the automatic headgate will work well.

● However, if you want to get an automatic headgate, it's best to get the kind that allows you to run it manually.

### Holding/Squeeze Chute

The holding/squeeze chute is typically attached to the headgate. Many people do without this and just stick with the head gate. If yours is a small outfit, that could work.

But if you have the cash to spare, the holding chute is a good idea. It basically holds the rest of the cow's body so you or the vet can work on the animal without the risk of injury to the cattle or the handler.

### Working Chute (Race)

The working chute is a passageway from the crowding pen into the squeeze chute or the headgate (depending on which one you have). A working chute is usually wide enough for just one head of cattle. So, your cattle must pass through the chute in a single file.

### Holding Pen

The holding pen is that area where your cattle will stay, pending being taken through the working chute and into the squeeze chute.

Your holding pen should be able to hold as many cows as you'll be working on in one session. This means that if you have a five headgate - holding chute combos (or singles), the pen should accommodate five cows. The reason for this? So your cattle do not get restless waiting in the holding pen.

### Loading Chute

The loading chute is used for moving cattle to a trailer. This loading chute should be able to move the cattle quickly enough so those that have entered the trailer do not get restless and moving about.

Also, your loading chute must hold as many cattle as your truck can accommodate.

A loading chute looks like a mobile passageway with raised walls and comes in various sizes.

### Scales

You also want to consider getting scales. While you might not need scales, if you are not running a commercial outfit, you'll need them for weighing feed and the calves when they are born.

If you'll be weighing your cattle, placing the scales close to your chute system (basically every facility we just talked about) would be more effective than anywhere else. This way, you can weigh them before you work them.

# Beef Cattle Feeding Equipment

### Feed Trough

A feed trough is usually a rectangular trough into which you'll pour feed for your cattle. It is typically wide enough to allow several cattle to feed simultaneously.

There are different kinds of feed troughs made of different kinds of materials; plastic, wood, and even metal. If your feed trough is outside, plastic and wood are good choices.

Whatever material you decide on, though, make sure that the trough is tough. Recycled car tires are good material for feed troughs because they are tough and won't harm your cattle.

If you have a lot of cattle of different sizes and ages, it's important to get more than one feed trough.

The idea is to be able to feed your herd by using different troughs according to their age and/or size. This is important because cattle of different ages and sizes have different feeding needs.

By feeding them in different troughs, you'll be able to feed them according to their various needs. Also, the bigger cattle won't be able to oppress the smaller ones.

If you are raising feeder cattle, consider getting automated feeders. Feeder cattle must be fattened up, which means they must eat a lot.

Using automated feeders helps ensure that your cattle are fed often, on schedule, without causing you extra stress.

### Feed Carts and Scoops

You need carts to move the feed from where it's kept to the trough. You also need a scoop to put feed into the trough. But you can just carry a bag of feed and pour it directly into the trough if that works better for you.

### Hay Feeder

A hay feeder is optional if you already have a feed trough, but it's a good idea. Hay feeders typically look like the bed of a truck. There is a handle attached to the feeder that releases the hay.

That said, other kinds of hay feeders that are smaller and more portable; a few are even collapsible. This is a better option to start a small farm.

### Water System

You also need to have a water trough on your farm. Now, this water trough is basically a large water bowl with a few additions, and it has quite a few benefits.

First off, a good trough will have a ballcock valve (the ball-like thing in your toilet tank). The ballcock valve helps to control the water supply. Water will come in, but because of the ballcock value, the water will stop at a set point to prevent waste.

Something else you'll find is a stop valve. The stop valve stops the flow of water into one trough. You'll need this if you want to clean out just one trough and leave the others active.

A check valve is something to look out for if your water line is connected to the main house water line. The check valve will help make sure that water from the trough doesn't find its way into the main waterline of the house.

Here are a few other things to think about in picking out water troughs:

- The water trough should be easy to clean. Troughs rarely have a drain, so you cannot just pull out a plug and easily empty the water. You also must consider that you need to clean your trough as often as every three months. So, pick a trough easy to clean.

- Since you must clean your trough, consider getting more than one, regardless of how many cattle you have. This way, you always have a trough full of fresh water for your cattle, even when one is being cleaned.

- Trough size is an important consideration. When picking the right size, you want to consider how many cows you have.

- If you have only one animal, you want to pick a trough just a little bigger than its head so it will not accidentally fall into the trough and drown.

- If you have more than one cow or you have a herd, consider getting a trough about 20 centimeters in depth.

- The water supply hose should be large enough to supply water quickly into the trough so the trough will not run out of the water as your cattle drink. Cattle can become angry if the trough is out of water.

- The water pipes must be covered so your cattle do not trip and fall and/or damage the system.

- Also, make sure that the trough is anchored firmly to the ground.

# Beef Cattle Housing

Cattle housing doesn't have to be complicated. If you have a grassy area or a pasture and your cattle are feeder cattle, they can just live in the field in the summer. But it doesn't hurt to have something constructed for them.

Now, here are a few things to remember in constructing housing for your beef cattle:

1. One of the most important things is to construct something that is easy to clean. To do this, you can either make sure that your barn or cattle house has a drain, or you can erect the structure on an elevated area.

Either of these will make it easier to drain the floor while cleaning or if it rains into the structure.

If you'll be installing a drain, make sure that it isn't in an area where your cattle will be walking. Remember, they are not good at depth perception.

2. Make sure that space is properly ventilated and well-lit with natural light. If the entrance to the shelter faces south, that will work well.

Avoid artificial lights as much as possible as cows do not like areas too brightly lit. Allowing for natural lighting will ensure that the cattle are receiving this important light in a uniform manner.

3. Make sure that the ground is level and uniform because various or changing textures can be stressful for cattle.

4. Create a separate space for birthing.

There are several housing options you can consider.

The first choice is an open-sided plan or the closed-sided barn structure. If you chose the open-sided structure, erect a small fence around the sides. It should be small enough so it doesn't obstruct the view, but high enough to prevent your cattle or other outside animals getting over it.

Whichever style you use, the interior is important. Inside the cattle house, it's important that each head of cattle has its own space and doesn't roam freely.

If you have a small amount of cattle and enough space, one row of stalls should be fine. Make sure that the cattle have enough space to be in their stalls. Consider a 105-centimeter side space and 165-centimeter standing space.

But if you do not have that much space or you are running a large outfit, consider doing two rows of stalls, with the cattle facing each other.

Now, if you want to run a fixed housing system where the cattle remain indoors all day, each stall must have its own feeding and water trough.

If you are running a two-row system, on the other hand, the two cattle facing each other can share a feeding and water trough.

### Fencing

If you'll be running an open housing system, it is very important that you pay attention to fencing. In the open housing system, your cattle spend most of their time outside, feeding, grazing and resting.

You want to make sure that they do not wander off or get attacked by other animals. So, here's what you need to know to keep them safe.

### Choosing The Right Fence

The type of fence you'll want to use depends on the breed of cattle you're rearing and whether you have a predator problem. Different kinds of fences range from barbed wire with woven wire to high tensile and electric fences.

Most cattle eventually hurt themselves on barbed wire. If you are raising beef cattle, predators might not be a problem because of how large and heavy the cows are. So, you could investigate the high tensile or woven wire fence types.

### Fence Post Spacing

The general rule of thumb says to space your fence posts 8 to 12 feet apart. The idea is to have enough fence posts so your fence is solid and braced for impact. The posts help anchor the wire and keep it grounded. Too few posts will give you a weak boundary.

However, if you are using galvanized steel and high tensile wires, you can get away with spacing your posts further than 12 feet apart.

You need corner posts to help solidify your fence even further, which is why you need to bury them deep.

The general rule of thumb is to bury the post to a depth anywhere between 35 and 50% of the height of your corner post.

So, if you have a 6-foot corner post, you'll be digging a hole between 2 to 3 feet deep. Also, the hole must be three times as wide as the post.

### Land Ownership

Before you erect your fence, find out where your property starts and stops. This way, you aren't throwing away a part of your land or stealing someone else's.

Consider employing the services of a land and quantity surveyor because court battles because of land boundaries can be complex and complicated.

# Chapter 5: Beef Cattle Nutrition and Feeding

Before we get into the conversation about what types of food your cattle should eat, it's important that you understand how their digestive systems work. This will help put things in perspective when we talk about feeding and what kinds of feeds are best for your cattle.

- Ruminant animals such as bovines are efficient at digesting high-roughage feedstuff because of the way their digestive system works. This system consists of:

- Mouth.

- Tongue.

- Salivary glands.

- Esophagus.

- Stomach (made up of four compartments viz: the rumen, reticulum, omasum, and abomasum).

- Pancreas.

- Gallbladder.

- Small intestine (made up of the duodenum, jejunum, and ileum).

- Large intestine: (made up of the cecum, colon, and rectum).

On average, cattle will take between 25,000 to 40,000 prehensile bites each day as they graze. Sometimes, it could even be more. As you can probably deduce, they chew fast and don't chew sufficiently before swallowing.

Grazing for cattle takes up more than a third of their day, while the remaining two-thirds are shared between chewing cud (bringing the partially digested food back up to ruminate) and simply being on the land. Chewing cud takes up about a third of the remaining two-thirds, and the rest of the day is spent resting.

Now, here's what the journey of food from the mouth to the anus in cattle looks like.

When the bovine takes in the forage, it mixes with their saliva, which contains potassium, sodium, bicarbonate, urea, and phosphate. This forms a bolus that travels through the esophagus to the reticulum. The esophagus in cattle works bi-directionally, so it moves food downward, but it also pushes the cud back into the mouth. Once the cud is moved back up into the mouth it is chewed and mixed with saliva a second time before it is swallowed again and moves to the reticulum.

From the reticulum, the solid part of the cud goes to the rumen to ferment while the liquid part goes into the reticulorumen. The solid part remains in the rumen for 48 hours. Now, the reticulorumen (reticulum + rumen) contains microorganisms such as protozoa, fungi and bacteria. These feed on the cud in the rumen and break them down into volatile fatty acids (VFAs). Examples of VFAs include acetate for synthesizing fat, propionate for synthesizing glucose, and butyrate. Cattle utilize these VFAs to produce energy.

Now, let's look at each part of the ruminant digestive system in closer detail.

# The Ruminant Digestive System

### Reticulum

Because of its looks, the reticulum is also called a "honeycomb". Its main role is to move smaller digested food into the omasum and the larger particles into the rumen where these particles are further digested.

The reticulum is also the part of the stomach where heavy objects can get trapped. So, if your bovine mistakenly ingests a wire, nail or any other heavy object, it will most likely get trapped in the reticulum.

As normal contractions occur, the object can pierce through the intestinal wall and move into the heart. This can cause hardware disease, which is why the reticulum is also sometimes called a hardware stomach.

### Rumen

Also known as the "paunch," the rumen comes with papillae, the primary tissues through which absorption takes place. It's mostly a fermentation vat because all the microbial fermentation takes place here. It is an anaerobic environment. There is no oxygen there. It has a pH range of 6.5 to 6.8.

The rumen is also the place where gas is produced, which makes sense since it's where all the fermentation takes place. Gases like methane, hydrogen sulfide, and carbon dioxide are produced in the rumen.

### Omasum

The omasum links to the reticulum via a short tunnel. It is spherical and characteristically comes with many flaps or leaves, which is why it is also called the butcher's bible or "many piles." The omasum is where water absorption takes place for ruminants. In cattle, the omasum is large and well developed.

### Abomasum

Of the four compartments, the abomasum is the actual stomach because it is the most like non-ruminant stomachs. It is highly acidic, with a pH range of 3.5 to 4.0 but the animal is safe because the cells of the abomasum secrete mucus, which protect the abomasum from acid damage.

The abomasum also contains hydrochloric and digestive enzymes such as pepsin and pancreatic lipase, which work together to break down food.

### Small and Large Intestine

In the small and large intestine, nutrients are further absorbed. The small intestine is long (about 150 feet), has a 20-gallon capacity, and is even more acidic than the abomasum. From the abomasum, digested food moves into the small intestine. When this happens, the small intestine becomes alkaline as pH increases from about 2.5 to 7 or 8. The increase in pH is necessary for enzymes of the small intestine to act properly.

Just like in the small intestines of humans, there are villi in the small intestine of cattle. These villi look like fingers and increase the surface area of the intestine to help the absorption of nutrients. As the muscles contract, food is moved from the small intestine to the large intestine.

The main function of the large intestine is to reabsorb water from the food digested while it passes the rest into the rectum.

# Nutritional Requirements of Cattle

There are several nutrient classes cattle need for their bodies to develop and operate properly. Each nutrient class has its own role to play in the body, and an absence or deficiency of them could inhibit growth or cause ill health.

The following are nutrient classes that cattle require:

### TDN (Energy)

It's obvious what energy does in the body of any living organism. This energy gives us the drive to carry out work and, for living organisms, work includes growing, lactating, reproducing, moving and digesting food.

The energy in cattle nutrition is expressed as Total Digestible Nutrients (TDN) and is the most important nutrient that cattle need. They need it in large amounts too.

For cattle, energy sources include hemicellulose and cellulose from grain starch and roughage. They can also get energy from fats and oils, but these only make up a small part of their regular diet.

### Protein

We know proteins to be the building blocks of the body. They form the main components of organs and tissues in the body, such as muscles, connective tissue and the nervous system.

A protein comprises several units of amino acids linked to form chains. When supplied in adequate amounts to the body, it helps normal body maintenance and in lactation, growth and reproduction.

The different components of protein vary in their solubility. There are the digestible proteins digested by microbes in the rumen, and then there are the insoluble proteins that leave the rumen intact to the lower gut.

### Minerals

There are macro-minerals and micro-minerals. Macro-minerals are needed in a relatively larger quantity than micro-nutrients. Examples of macro-minerals include calcium, sodium, phosphorus, potassium and magnesium. Micro-minerals, on the other hand, are also known as trace minerals, include copper, iodine, selenium, zinc and sulfur.

How rich in minerals your cattle's diet is depends on the quality of feed they are consuming. Often, you must fortify their ration with mineral supplements. The type of mineral supplements you choose also depend on the feed your animals are eating, and their nutritional requirements.

Minerals are a critical part of your cattle nutrition, and even though they are only needed in relatively small quantities when compared to other nutrient classes, a deficiency can have mild to moderate to severe consequences. A few of these consequences include poor growth, bowed legs, brittle bones, a fall in conception rates, muscle tremors, convulsions, etc.

### Vitamins

Vitamins are like minerals in their function. For beef cattle, the most important vitamins include vitamins A, D, and E. Fresh foliage is a good source of these vitamins. While older forage contain vitamins, vitamin levels do tend to drop after a while. Silage and grains also have lower levels of vitamins.

Vitamin A ensures normal reproduction, growth and body maintenance. Vitamin D is necessary for the proper development of bones. With selenium, vitamin E ensures that muscle tissue develops properly.

Absent these vitamins, cattle can experience reduced fertility (vitamin A deficiency), rickets (vitamin D deficiency), and muscular dystrophy, and white muscle disease (vitamin E deficiency).

White muscle disease is a common problem with cattle. To prevent this, you may have to inject the calves with selenium or vitamin E at birth. Feeding your cows supplementary selenium/vitamin E or injecting the pregnant cows with selenium/vitamin E can also help.

Vitamin B has little impact on cattle nutrition. The microorganisms found in the rumen already produce this vitamin in sufficient quantities, which the cattle absorb. But vitamin B is essential for calves, as they haven't fully developed their rumen yet. Super stressed cattle might also need vitamin B supplements as stress depletes the microbial population in the rumen and thus diminish the vitamin B.

Now that you know your cattle's nutritional requirements, let's go into the different categories of foodstuffs you should feed your cattle to nourish them with all the nutrients they need.

# Types of Cattle Feeds

### Grain Supplement

Grain is rich in energy and has moderate amounts of protein, but it contains little fiber.

But grain is great for cattle because it facilitates rapid growth and helps to fatten your cattle. Providing grain is a feeding method adopted by most farmers because of its cost-effectiveness.

Grain is also a fantastic alternative for cattle-rearers who live in areas where access to excellent hay is limited. In the winter, too, grain can be a lifesaver for farmers and cattle.

Although grain has excellent benefits, it's important to not let your cattle get too dependent on it. Cattle dependent on supplements reject pasture and hay, which are much better options for them nutritionally compared to supplements.

Examples of grains include barley, corn, and oats.

### Roughage

Examples of roughages include hay, grain hulls, grass and oilseed hulls. Roughage is typically rich in cellulose and hemicellulose (fiber) but pack little energy. It supplies moderate levels of energy. It does contain protein though, depending on the plant from which it is derived and the plant's level of maturity.

Now, since we're here, let's talk a little about hay.

Hay is one of the best feeds cattle can eat. It can single-handedly supply almost every nutrient cattle need, but it must be eaten at the right time or you lose all the dense nutrients. In other words, you should pick it before it dries. Also, proper curing and storage are very important when it comes to feeding your cattle hay.

Hay comes in different varieties, each with the level of nutrition they offer. Alfalfa, for instance, is richer in phosphorus and calcium than grass, but grass hay has high levels of protein. Hence, most experts recommend that you mix alfalfa hay with a bit of grass as against feeding alfalfa exclusively, especially when raising beef cattle.

Alfalfa is great and is even recommended for dairy cattle, but because of its tendency to cause bloating, it is not recommended for beef cattle. So, for your beef cattle, you can mix alfalfa with grass hay, or feed them legume hay, which is protein-rich.

### Forage and Pasture

Pasture and forage crops contain all the nutrients cattle need to thrive. Unless the soil is depleted for one reason or another, or it may be too early in the year for grass to grow lush and rich.

Besides grain, forage crops and pasture are other inexpensive feeding solutions for your cattle, but you must do your due diligence before feeding them just pasture and forage crops. Knowing the fertility of the soil and ensuring good watering is important to ensure the plants are packed with adequate nutrients.

Also, always know what kind of plants your cattle are eating, and their condition and maturity level.

### Oilseeds

Oilseeds are rich in protein and energy, but their fiber content varies. Examples of oilseeds include canola meal and soybeans.

## Byproducts

By-products come with high moisture levels, and their nutritional content varies depending on their source. Examples of byproducts include sweet corn cannery waste, distiller's grains, grain screenings, apple pomace and bakery waste.

# Chapter 6: You Can Still Milk Your Beef Cows!

The cows that bless us with ice cream and the cattle that provide us with delicious steak are different creatures. But people eat *dairy cow meat* and drink *beef cow milk*! Before we venture into *that* conversation, it's important to lay the foundation for this discussion. Hence, we will kick off this chapter by looking into beef cattle and dairy cattle to understand the similarities and differences between these two breeds. We know you're here for the beef, but knowing something about milking and dairy cattle is also important.

## Beef vs. Dairy Cattle

### Beef Cattle

Beef and dairy cattle look characteristically different. Beef cattle look stocky like bodybuilders. They channel all their energy into storing fat and developing muscles. These work together to give you delicious beef; the best is lean meat with marbling for enhanced flavor and texture.

Beef cattle's strong legs help them navigate pastures. Their bellies are also rounded and stocky with thick backs, strong shoulders and rumps, and short necks.

With diet, beef cattle feed primarily on grains and grass, although they eat more grass than grains, especially when they are still young.

You probably already know that beef cattle produce milk because how else would they nurse their calves, right? But as you can also probably deduce, milk production in beef cattle is much lower than in dairy cattle. The logic is simple. Over the years, beef cattle have been bred to do one thing, and that is to produce beef. So, though beef cattle produce milk, they only produce enough to nourish their calves, which only yields about a gallon or two daily.

Beef can come from a steer, a cow, or a heifer, but the best beef comes from heifers and steers.

### Dairy Cows

If beef cattle are like bodybuilders, then dairy cows are like marathon runners. They might look underfed, but that's how dairy cows are genetically wired. No matter how well-fed they are, they remain lean and angular because they channel all their energy into lactating rather than building muscle or storing fat. For cows, milk production and bulking up in mass are mutually exclusive. Therefore, dairy cows and beef cattle are characteristically different in appearance.

Dairy cows produce milk in large quantities daily, up to ten gallons per day usually. To keep her healthy and comfortable, you must milk your dairy cow two or three times a day.

Dairy cows are raised in pastures or free-stall barns where they get access to fresh water and food. They have the same diet as beef cattle, which consists of grass and grains, but unlike beef cattle, they need not navigate the terrain to graze, hence their slight build.

Now, remember that cows will only lactate when they have calves, and cows can have only one calf in a year — beef or dairy. Milking then occurs for roughly 300 days in a year, after which the body takes a break for the remaining 60 plus days as they prepare to calve.

However, let's move into the second part of this chapter. Let's talk about milk production in beef cattle.

# Milk Production in Beef Cattle

While beef cattle are primarily raised for their meat, nothing says you can't milk them when they lactate. The taste differs slightly from what you get from dairy cows, and the quantity is also not as high. Nonetheless, even if it's not for sale, you can still milk your beef cow and enjoy the dairy with your family.

That said, milking beef cows have their benefits and their disadvantages.

### Why High Milk Production in Beef Cows Is Great

If a beef cow produces plenty of milk, her calf will be sufficiently fed and nourished. This is great for the calf's health. It's also great because calves that are fed sufficient milk early in life attain a heavier weight by weaning time. A study by the state of Oklahoma confirmed that more milk translates into an extra 30 pounds of weaning weight for calves.

### Still, High Milk Production in Beef Cattle Has Its Disadvantages

Even with the benefit of a heavier weaning weight for the calves, there are still important reasons farmers might prefer lower levels of milk production in their beef cows.

During times of nutrient deficiency, a cow's body will channel the energy generated into three main areas: body maintenance, lactation, and reproduction. Now, look at these areas as levels of a sort. In other words, if the demands of one level are not met, energy will not be supplied for the next level. Hence, body maintenance is a priority, and only if the energy requirements are met will energy be supplied for lactation. Then, only when energy levels for lactation are met will the cow be biologically prepared to breed.

So, it's easy to deduce from all we're saying that milking-cows need a lot of energy. You'd need to help them keep up by giving them feed in large quantities for them to keep producing milk in sufficient quantities. It's nearly impossible to raise high milk-producing cows in a grass-based, low-input system. Heavy milkers have a poorer body condition when compared with their counterparts producing moderate amounts of milk.

# How to Choose the Best Beef Cows for Milk Production

Picking a beef cow based on her milk-producing ability requires careful thought and consideration. If you go for a heavy milker, you'll get a heavier calf, which is great because they are more valuable. But a heavy milker is way more expensive to maintain than a moderate milker. You must be prepared to provide supplemental feeding, and that will increase your expenses.

Below is an estimate of how much food various cows in the early stages of lactation need:

- 10 pounds of milk daily: approx. 26.5 pounds of dry matter daily.

- 20 pounds of milk daily: approx. 29.0 pounds of dry matter daily.

- 30 pounds of milk daily: approx. 31.5 pounds of dry matter daily.

So, if you're sure you can get cheap surplus feed, then why not invest in a heavy-milking beef cow? But if feed is expensive, it might be better to stick to one that's just moderate in its milk production.

# Dual-Purpose Cattle

As the name probably already suggests, dual-purpose cattle are bred both for their beef and for their milk. In times past, cows were triple-purposed — milk, beef, and draft work. But then horses came on the scene, and cows could take a break.

Dual-purpose cows are not as popular as they once were because farmers preferred more specialized breeds, especially because it confused the breeding purposes. Questions arise such as "What exactly do we want from this cow, and how do we raise her?" Owing to this confusion, farmers manipulated the gene pool to produce beef cattle and dairy cattle specifically through breeding.

Today, there are still a few dual-purpose breeds to be found in the cattle-raising community. But they are limited to small farmers and small farmlands. Dual-purpose cows are not to be found in the specialist dairy industry. They are better suited for the small farmer because they produce more protein, more fat, and more liters of milk, all at lean body weight.

Dual-purpose cows work well for small farms because they make ideal house cows. They will provide enough milk to feed your family comfortably and still make enough to feed their calf. They also hardly ever grow to the standard, gargantuan cattle size. Hence, they are easier to house, and require a less land than regular beef cattle.

You can crossbreed cattle to create a dual-purpose cow. If you do, though, it's important to keep it to the first cross or the second one at the most. Crossbreeding produces hybrid vigor, which gives the offspring the genetic advantage it has over both its parents, but it waters down the more you crossbreed; hence, the reason you should never go beyond the second cross.

# How to Milk a Cow Correctly

### Use Clean Equipment

It's best to use a stainless steel bucket to collect the milk as it's easier to clean and disinfect. Also, always make sure that all your tools and equipment are always 100% clean.

### Tie Up Your Cow

If you don't tie your cow up, she will easily walk off while you milk her in search of the pasture where she can graze or wherever else catches her fancy. A good way to tie your cow in place is to use a neck collar or a halter.

Now, make sure your girl has a snack waiting to be given to her after being a good girl during milking. You can give her hay or a small quantity of grain as a snack so she will cooperate with you and enjoy the experience of being milked.

Also, ensure that her stall is a place where she feels comfortable, so she enjoys going there. It would make your life much easier.

### Prepare the Udder

Before milking, wipe the udder with a warm rag to remove dirt, manure, hair, and debris. This is important to keep the skin on the udder from drying out and cracking. If the udder looks dried out, you can apply a moisturizing dip to rejuvenate the skin, making it easier to milk her when the time comes.

### Strip Each Teat

To confirm that the milk is okay, you can squirt the first few drops of milk into a cup or onto the ground. It's called stripping the teat. Milk should be smooth and white without clumps when expressed.

Now, you want to do this stripping for each teat. Once you've confirmed that the milk is good, you can go to the next step before milking into the stainless steel bucket.

### Apply Pre-Milking Disinfectant

After stripping the teats, apply pre-milking disinfectant to the teats, following the manufacturer's instruction. Once you finish applying it, clean off the disinfectant with a clean, dry towel.

### Express the Milk

Milk from the teats in the front quarters and squeeze them alternatively until they are both empty.

To milk your cow, hold up your hands to the teats in the front quarter first, like you're holding a cup to drink out of. Then hold each teat between your forefinger and thumb and squeeze them to get the milk out. Keep doing this until the udder is empty. You can easily tell the udder is empty because it will become flaccid.

Once you've ensured that you've milked all the teats on that udder, apply post-milking disinfectant. Voila! You're done!

# Chapter 7: Beef Cattle Hygiene, Health, and Maintenance

One very important reason to pay attention to hygiene in your cattle rearing practice is that it has a huge impact on the health of your cattle. In addition, hygienic practices are important for your customer's health.

However, we do acknowledge that many bovine diseases might not result directly from poor hygiene. But whatever the cause, poor hygienic practices can exacerbate the situation.

Whichever way you look at it, it is very important to keep your cattle and their living quarters clean. And as for ensuring that they're healthy, you wouldn't have a practice if your cattle were sickly or dead, anyway.

## Beef Cattle Hygiene

In looking at how to maintain hygiene in your beef cattle practice, we'll be breaking things down into the three commercial life stages of cattle: rearing, housing, and transportation.

### Rearing

There are several practices involved in the rearing of cattle, or what many call cattle husbandry. You'll have to feed them and clean them.

You might also need to perform (or have a professional perform) medical procedures like embryo transfer, artificial insemination, birthing, or castration. All these must be done hygienically. Let's see how.

### Hygienic Cattle Feeding

- The Agriculture and Rural Development Department in Namibia recommends that you wash your cattle's water trough once in three (3) days. As for your food trough, you can wash that out once a week.

- Before you wash your troughs, you must empty them first. You'll need a scoop to get the water out because food and water troughs usually do not have drains. When you're finished getting out the content, spray the trough down, add in dish soap, and start scrubbing.

- If you can afford it, consider getting new water and feed troughs instead of used ones. New troughs stay cleaner longer and are slower to form algae.

- Keep the water in the trough fresh. Algae and amoeba are not things your cattle should be consuming. So, once you notice the water changing colors, it is time to throw it out.

- Keep your water and feed troughs far from each other. If the feed trough is close to the water trough, your cattle could get feed into the water and water into the feed, causing both to become useless quickly.

### Cattle Cleaning

- You can set up a sprinkler system that will spray your cattle with water regularly. You can also set this system up as part of your cattle caretaking system so that all your cattle are sure to pass by regularly.

- But having your cattle sprinkled with water, no matter how regularly, will not be enough. So, you must scrub them once a week.

- Before you scrub any of your cattle, make sure that it is properly held down. For this, you'll need a separate washing head chute so the animal's head is secure while you scrub the body. Be sure that you are not using your regular head chute so it is not perpetually wet.

• Purchase special cattle brushes and shampoos. Do not use all-purpose scrubbing brushes or human shampoo or you can harm them.

• When you wash your cattle, work your way from top to bottom.

• You should also rinse them from top to bottom. And as you rinse, slide your hands down their body to be sure that all the soap suds are gone.

• Cattle prefer to be bathed on a warm day, so consider bathing them when it is warm outside. Not only will they be more comfortable, but they'll also dry faster.

## Hygienic Medical Procedures

If you employ the services of a veterinarian for all your medical procedures, the medical procedures will always be hygienic.

But it doesn't hurt to know what hygienic procedures should look like. Plus, we acknowledge that running a small practice might require you to do medical procedures on your own. So, here are several things to note.

• Make sure that every cow is vaccinated yearly. If you try to breed a sick animal, you're setting your practice up for failure.

• Make sure you always have a first aid kit handy. And sterilize your kit and other items after every use.

• If any of your cattle falls into a ditch and is severely injured or injures itself in another way, immediately tend to the wound. You do not want to risk an infection.

• Create a separate space for birthing. It need not be in a different room if you do not have the luxury of space, but it must be away from the regular living quarters. Also, furnish the space with clean, fresh straw before your cow gives birth.

## Housing

As much as cleaning your own living quarters is important, cleaning your cattle's living quarters is also important. It is probably more important, considering that you don't poop everywhere, but your cattle do!

If you have live-in pets, you might have a little idea of what it takes to clean out your cattle's live-in quarters. With that in mind, let's see what needs to be done:

• One of the most important things you must do in cleaning out your cattle's living quarters is to shovel out the poop. Your cattle should not be living in their own filth. So, it's normal practice to shovel out the poop every day.

• Shoveling out the poop will not be enough, though. You'll have to go a step further to disinfect the floors. Make sure that whatever disinfectant you use is safe for both you and your cattle. You also want to be sure that the disinfectant is versatile (can kill a variety of bacteria) and works quickly. It should also not contain components that are not compatible with certain building materials.

• If you use straw bedding, change it out once every four or five days. If you use sand beddings, dig it out and change the sand when you notice a dark layer of sand across the top.

• If your cattle eat in their stalls, you might need to clear out the stalls every day to rid them of the droppings.

• Make sure that your cattle have ample living space, as squeezing them in will lead to the quick spread of infections, diseases, injuries, and respiratory problems and is generally just uncomfortable.

### Transportation

• You need to make sure that the trucks you use to transport your cattle are regularly cleaned out. You need to clean out your truck after every trip.

• Do not transport sick cows with healthy ones. If you need to take one to the vet because they are sick and another to be vaccinated, you might need more than one trip for that.

• Make certain that your trucks are properly ventilated.

• Make sure that your cattle are not left in the truck for long periods of time and that they have access to food, water, and fresh air. Portable feeders and water bowls come in handy.

• If you are transporting newborns, use a disinfected wheelbarrow or calf taxi. It is best to get a new calf taxi to transport your new calf.

# Beef Cattle Health

While proper hygiene will help keep your cattle healthy and well, vaccinations and an understanding of the health issues cattle are prone to are also important. Both topics are what we'll be exploring in this section.

### Cattle Health Issues

Your cattle could fall prey to diseases, parasites, and food poisoning. Let's look at these specifically:

# Common Cattle Diseases

### Tail Rot

Tail rot is what it sounds like: rotting of the tail. It is most probably a result of an animal continuing to use its tail to swat at flies, although its tail has been injured, broken, or dislocated.

Tail rot is more prevalent in wet areas, and during the rainy season as floors become slippery. It is also more prevalent in places with a lot of trees because cattle can hit their tails violently against trees as they walk past.

**To Prevent Tail Rot:** You must get rid of everything, and every situation that your cattle can hit their tail against or that could trip them. Also, vaccinating your cattle against tetanus will make sure they are not susceptible to tetanus if they do break their tail.

**To Treat Tail Rot:** You must get the animal vaccinated against tetanus. Also, the animal might need to get its tail amputated. If blood flow to the injured part of the tail is completely blocked, amputation might not be necessary as it will eventually dry up and fall off.

### Akabane

Akabane is a disease that causes deformities in cattle fetuses. It is caused by an arbovirus, and it has no clinical symptoms. It is spread by blood-feeding insects (most commonly midges), and it affects the nervous system of a fetus.

**To Prevent Akabane:** The only way to prevent akabane is to kill the midges in your area. Also, exposing a herd to a place where akabane is endemic can help the herd gain immunity.

## Botulism

Botulism is a bacterial disease that affects cattle and is caused by the Clostridium Botulinum bacteria.

The bacteria thrive in decaying plants and animal carcasses and in moist environments. It produces spores that, if in the right environment, will survive for a long time.

An animal can get infected by consuming anything that has been infected with the spores or has come in contact with infected carcasses.

Symptoms include paralysis of the facial muscles and the limbs. And death can occur 1 to 14 days after the first symptoms.

Humans can get a botulism infection, too, but this will not result from contact with an infected animal but from consuming infected food and/or drink.

**To Prevent Botulism:** Make sure your cattle are promptly immunized against botulism. Also, properly dispose of carcasses and bones from your property.

**To Treat Botulism:** If you immediately notice that an animal has consumed an infected substance, purging that animal might work, but the prognosis for botulism isn't good, and infected cattle usually die.

### Stringhalt in Cattle

Stringhalt in cattle is a knee dislocation where the inside ligament hooks over the knee at the top. The affected leg will be straight, and the animal must drag that leg until the ligament releases, and the animal can walk freely.

Stringhalt is almost always genetic, where the animal has an anatomical defect in the leg. And while poor nutrition could make the condition more evident, it is usually not the cause.

If it happens suddenly, stringhalt could result from injury or a phosphorus and calcium deficiency.

**To Prevent Stringhalt:** Do not breed with bulls that have stringhalt. Now, it might be difficult to detect this in cattle that are of optimal health, so you must make a very careful selection when time to breed.

**To Treat Stringhalt:** Many cattle-rearers take their cattle in for surgery to treat the affected knee, but most people put the animal down.

### Three-Day Sickness/Ephemeral Fever

The three-day sickness is a viral disease transmitted by mosquitoes. It is prevalent during the wet season when mosquitoes have ample opportunity to breed.

The three-day sickness usually presents as mild signs like a fever, temporary lameness, and eye and nose discharge, moderately severe signs like swollen joints, depression, and subcutaneous swelling, and severe signs like paralysis and a coma.

Most times, these symptoms disappear after three days, and the affected animal is back to normal, but there is also a significant possibility that the affected animal will die before the symptoms go away.

**To Prevent Ephemeral Fever:** a vaccine can be administered to your cattle to keep them immune. They'll have to take two doses, four weeks apart.

**To Treat Ephemeral Fever:** Seeing as animals usually recover on their own, the best you can do is to ensure that they are comfortable, properly hydrated, and well-fed.

# Common Cattle Parasites

### Ticks

Tick fever is caused by exposure to these blood parasites. Tick fever can be deadly, and if it isn't, it can lead to other complications like abortion of a pregnant cow, infertility for a period with bulls, and eventual financial loss for you.

Cattle that have tick fever might experience a loss of appetite, general body weakness, and/or depression. Cattle between the ages of 18 and 36 months are more prone to a tick fever infection.

**To Prevent Tick Fever:** If cattle are exposed to the parasites between the ages of 3 and 9 months old, they might develop a long lasting immunity against tick fever.

**To Treat Tick Fever:** If you suspect that any of your cattle have tick fever, consult your veterinarian for diagnosis and treatment.

### Worms

If worms have become an issue with your herd, it might be difficult to recognize because the outward expression of symptoms is similar to poor nutrition.

You want to gauge the egg per gram (EPG) of dung. So, if you check your cattle's dung, and there is over 200 EPG, you might have a problem on your hands.

If so, you might have to resort to drenching, which is administering certain chemicals to your cattle to rid their systems of parasites, including worms.

But, seeing as this is a sensitive issue, consider consulting with your veterinarian if you suspect there is a worm infestation among your herd.

# Food Poisoning

### Grain Poisoning

This happens when cattle consume large amounts of grain they shouldn't have eaten for various reasons. It is most likely to occur if you switch your cattle from pasture to grain or if your cattle accidentally gain access to grain.

An animal with a case of grain poisoning may show a few of these symptoms:

- Loss of appetite
- Depression
- Diarrhea
- Smelly feces
- Increased heart rate
- Bloating
- Eventual death

**To Prevent Grain Poisoning:** Slowly introduce grain into your cattle's diet. Start by mixing it in small amounts with what you already feed them.

Then progressively reduce the amount of their old food and reduce the amount of the grains before you completely phase out the old. Also, keep the grain out of the reach of your cattle.

**To Treat Grain Poisoning:** If any of your cattle just ate a large amount of grain and you think there is a risk of poisoning, immediately feeding it hay can potentially help it recover.

Otherwise, you can consider slaughtering, as killing the animal before acidosis develops might be the more financially wise decision.

# Urea Poisoning

Urea poisoning is caused by excess and/or irregular consumption of urea. An animal with a case of urea poisoning will show a few of these symptoms:

- Facial muscles are twitching
- Teeth grinding
- Abdominal pain
- Bloating
- Weakness
- Rapid breathing
- Spasms
- And eventual death (usually near the source of the urea)

**To Prevent Urea Poisoning:** Make sure your cattle do not have access to urea.

**To Treat Urea Poisoning:** You might have to resort to drenching, but this rarely works. Do consult your veterinarian if you suspect that any of your cattle have a case of urea poisoning.

# Cyanide and Nitrate Poisoning

Your cattle can get cyanide and nitrate poisoning from sorghum crops. These crops are generally safe to consume, but they often release toxins in hot weather when they have been stressed.

An animal with a case of cyanide or nitrate poisoning will exhibit a few of these signs:

- Labored breathing
- Bright red mucous membranes
- Muscle weakness

- Convulsing

- Death

**To Prevent Cyanide and Nitrate Poisoning:** If you suspect that any of your cattle is sick with or has died of cyanide or nitrate poisoning, remove any source of cyanide and/or nitrate in your cattle's feed and consult with your veterinarian.

To Treat Cyanide and Nitrate Poisoning: Consult your vet!

# Vaccination

To keep your herd healthy and prevent them from being susceptible to diseases, vaccinate your cattle.

Now, there are several vaccines that cattle need to take for various reasons, and you should consult with your vet to know the ones specific to your herd and location. Generally, your cattle should receive these vaccines:

- **Clostridial Diseases Like Tetanus:** Two shots should be administered 4 to 6 weeks apart as a 5-1 'package.' And you want to make sure your herd gets their first shot as early as 6 months of age. Then you can administer it based on your discretion.

- **Three-Day Sickness:** Two shots should be administered 4 to 6 weeks apart. It is usually too expensive to vaccinate your entire herd, so consider only vaccinating those valuable ones (that is, the ones you want to breed, especially considering you need them to live long enough). Also, you must continue administering the shots every year. Spring is the best time to do so.

- **Botulism:** Depending on the vaccine, you might need to administer one or two shots 4 to 6 months apart. These will need to be administered every year but do not administer this simultaneously you are administering another vaccine.

- **Tick Fever:** A one-time shot. If you are introducing cattle coming from an area where the tick isn't prevalent, administer a second shot to the new cattle. That said, consider administering the shot early, say around 3 to 9 months of age.

Ensuring your cattle's hygiene and health is important for your business, but more important, for the comfort and wellbeing of your cattle. So, pay attention to the things mentioned in this chapter and make sure you have the contact of a trusted vet.

In the next chapter, we go into the specifics of the different genders in your herd.

# Chapter 8: Bulls and Steers

While bulls and steers are both male bovine cattle, they aren't the same. And the difference between them was hinted at in the first chapter. But in this chapter, we'll be expounding on those differences and explaining how they affect your practice.

### Bulls

Basically, bulls are mature male bovine cattle used for breeding. All male bovine cattle are born as bull-calves.

You will then need to carefully examine those calves to decide if they have characteristics you want to see in your cattle.

If they do, keep them intact and use them for breeding your cows. But if they don't, castrate them.

### Steers

Steers are castrated male bovine animals; their testes have been removed while their penis remains intact.

Castrating a male bovine animal that you don't want to breed will keep them from being aggressive, especially when cows are in heat. So, unless it is necessary for you to have bulls, castrate your male cattle.

Now that we've got that settled, let's explore the differences between bulls and steers.

# Bulls Vs. Steers

### Physical Differences

Bulls are typically the biggest of the cattle, and this has something to do with the amount of testosterone they produce.

Because steers are castrated (and so cannot produce so much testosterone) at an early age, they do not grow to be as big as bulls.

In fact, if not for the fact that steers have a penis while heifers have a vulva, it would be difficult to distinguish between them.

Bulls have a more pronounced penis as opposed to steers and are also bushier around the sheath that covers their penis.

### Behavioral Differences

Bulls are generally more difficult to control and keep in check than steers. And things could get even worse if there is more than one bull in the same space. They'll fight one another for dominance and can transfer their aggression to the handler.

Things can escalate even more if there is a cow in the vicinity that is in heat and ready to be bred. Bulls can easily hurt a person that tries to keep them from their precious female.

Now, this does not mean that bulls are impossible to work with. After all, there are practices where bulls are bred. But if you want to raise bulls, special care will need to be taken.

Steers, on the other hand, are generally tamer and easier to handle, especially considering that they are not as big as bulls.

Also, steers have their sexual urges repressed because of the castration. They are less likely to cause fights with other animals or even their handler.

### Handling

Because of the behavioral differences between bulls and steers, the way you handle them is different. You'll need help with anything that requires you to touch the bull.

Your bull will walk through the holding pen just fine, provided you are in its flight zone, but getting it t to enter the squeeze chute won't be so easy. You might need someone else on standby in case you need assistance.

It's important to note that with bulls a head gate might not be enough to hold them still. You must – almost always – couple the head gate with a squeeze chute whenever you are doing veterinary procedures on them.

Now, for steers, it is important to remember that while they have had their testes removed, they are not completely immune from aggressive behavior. So, you do not want to treat a steer as if it is harmless.

However, handling a steer is something you can almost always do on your own unless that steer has a terrible temper.

You might also get away with just a head gate, but if you can afford it, consider buying a squeeze chute – even if you are handling a steer.

### Quality of Meat

Because steers are not used for breeding, they are usually raised for meat. The beef you are used to eating is most likely from steers or heifers.

Now, the difference between the quality of meat from a steer and the meat from a bull is related to the animal's age.

Generally, both a young steer and a young bull (12 to 14 months of age) will offer you about the same quality of meat, which is good. But, as they get older, the quality of beef they produce drops off (which makes sense).

But the quality of beef from bulls actually depreciates faster than that of steers. So, beef from an older steer is more tender and probably juicier than that from an older bull because steers have lower levels of testosterone.

And one more thing! Because bulls are considerably bigger than steers, you'll get a lot more meat from bulls than from steers.

### The Lifestyle of Bulls

Bulls are bred to be breeders. And when bulls are not working, they basically just lounge around eating and generally enjoying themselves.

It is important for bulls to eat well and rest when they are not "working" as they can lose significant weight when they are "working".

However, the first step to breeding is picking the right bull. This is a very important step because calves get a whopping 65% of their genes from their father. So be careful when you pick your bull.

### Picking a Bull

There are two ways to pick a bull: raise your own bull or buy one from outfits that specialize in bulls.

Now, to run a cow-calf operation where there'll be a lot of cows and heifers, it is recommended that you lay off raising your own bulls and buy from a bull specialist or consider artificial insemination in part because of all that has been mentioned about the attitude of bulls.

But a more important reason is the possibility of inter-breeding. If you raise your own bulls and breed them in your practice, a bull might fertilize its sister or aunt or cousin or daughter. And interbreeding isn't a good idea because the calf could end up with a lot of medical complications.

One bull can service up to 25 cows throughout the breeding period (which lasts between 5 and 6 months).

So, if you have a small practice, you should be fine with just one bull. There's no need to over-saturate your farm with bulls and cause a nuisance.

That said, if you have cows of significantly varying sizes, it is to choose a regular or small-sized bull because allowing a big bull to fertilize a small cow can be dangerous for the cow and the calf at childbirth. If all your cows are big, a big bull will be fine.

### Releasing the Bull

The next step is to let the bull loose among your cows. The bull knows his way around a mature cow and will walk up to 10 miles to show himself worthy of the cow.

However, calves are best born during the spring and fall because the weather is just right then. You can use the whole of spring and the whole of fall to allow your bull to fertilize the cows. This should give you a five-month period for the bull to do its work.

### Retiring the Bull

Generally, bulls can breed when they are about nine or ten months and can keep going until they are 11 or 12 years old.

Realistically, your bull might need to be retired after five or six years of active service. Several issues can arise, such as structural problems (like a problem with the hooves that make it difficult for a bull to stand or a problem that prevents the penis from extending properly), which make it difficult for the bull to mate. Then there's also infertility, which makes it impossible for the bull to breed.

So, consider working around 5 of 6 years if you're drawing up a "breeding plan" and maximize that time period as much as possible.

When it is time for your bull to retire, you can either allow it to live its life out or slaughter it. The older the animal, the less the quality of meat it offers.

### The Lifestyle of Steers

That you won't be breeding steers doesn't mean you shouldn't look out for those with good qualities.

If you are starting your own practice, prioritize the propensity for healthy weight gain and the production of tender beef. The reason you want to get the best bull is so your cows can produce the best calves.

So, if you are starting out by purchasing calves, look for the best. Ask to see the father of the calves to be sure.

Now, the life cycle of a steer can be seen in two basic stages: the growing stage and the finishing stage.

### The Growing Stage

If you are starting your practice by buying cows and bulls and then breeding them, you'll start your steer rearing at the growing stage.

The growing stage is basically the time from birth to maturity when your steers are developing physically, mentally, and sexually.

If you are buying your steers as calves, buy them right after they've been weaned to avoid the complications of suddenly switching milk sources.

It is generally less expensive to buy steers as calves than as adults, but a lot more expensive to take care of them because you'll have them longer.

The same goes for breeding your own calves. You'll have to feed them and give them the shots that were mentioned in the previous chapter every year.

However, there are upsides to buying calves or breeding them. Most important, you know what kind of steers you want to breed, and since you've had them from birth you can tailor their food and general care to what you have in mind.

The growing stage (from birth to about 9 months of age) is a very sensitive stage. It is the period when a lot of the illnesses and parasites usually strike.

So, to get quality beef from your steers, pay attention to them during this stage.

### The Finishing Stage

If you would rather not go through the stress of raising calves and are not ready to invest that much money in lifetime care, you can buy a full-grown steer.

It should be mentioned, though, that full-grown adults are a lot more expensive to buy than calves. However, they sure are a lot less expensive to rear than calves.

Steers that are at the finishing stage are basically just adult cattle that need to be fattened to bring in the money when slaughtered, but how effective this stage will be depends heavily on how effective the growing stage was.

Now, unlike bulls, steers do not have to "work". They just must eat, have proper vaccinations, and stay healthy so that when slaughtered, they'll bring in a lot of money.

Now that you can tell the various male folk in your herd and understand what those differences translate into, let's look at the various female folk in the herd.

# Chapter 9: Cows and Heifers

In chapter one, we explained that not all cattle are cows. We also listed the different members of the herding community. In this chapter, just like we did in the last, we will be zeroing in on a pair of herd members: heifers and cows.

As we've seen in the first chapter, heifers and cows are both female, but heifers are female cattle that haven't had their first calf, while cows are female cattle who have had at least one calf. This is a very rudimentary explanation, as you can tell, and there's a lot more to know about heifers and cows. But first, let's find out the anatomical differences between cows and heifers.

## Anatomical Differences between Cows and Heifers

### Cows

Cows are mature female cattle, and the easiest way to spot them in a herd is to look between the hind legs. If there is an udder, then you're looking at a cow.

An udder is a pink sac-like organ that hangs down from the underside of a cow. The udder's four teats resemble cylindrical knobs from which milk is expelled. Usually, you'd almost always find a calf by the side of a cow, except where the calves have just been weaned off their mother's milk.

Now, to their physical appearance. Cows are usually smooth from head to tail. They have no prominent shoulder crests like bulls typically have, and their shoulders and hips are not as muscular as bulls.

Another way to tell if it's a cow is to look under the tail. Cows have a slit below their tail. This is the vulva, and it sits below the anus. It is from here that the cow urinates, mates with the bull during breeding, and pushes out the calves. Although both heifers and cows have vulvas, the vulva of a cow is much larger and much more defined than in heifers.

## Heifers

When defining heifers more precisely, heifers are usually young female cattle that were born female (called heifer calves) and retained their female characteristics through adulthood. These two conditions must be fulfilled for a bovine to be considered a heifer, as there are cases where a calf is born female but grows up to develop secondary male characteristics. Such cattle are not called heifers, but as freemartins.

Most experienced cattle-rearers can easily tell a heifer from a cow just by looking at her. They notice the size and youth of the animal and can immediately tell. For an inexperienced eye, though, it's not as easy. Heifers are typically young cattle grown past the stage of being calves but still on the road to full maturity, which they usually hit by 3 or 4 years.

Anatomically, heifers do not have little hair, a sheath, or a sac between their legs like steers and bulls. They do have udders, but the udders are almost absent, and the teats are nearly impossible to see, even between the hind legs.

Just like cows, heifers have a vulva under their tail, below their anus. It's not as pronounced or as large as a mature cow, though. By the time the heifer is bred and is about to calve, the vulva and udder increase in size, resembling what is seen in more mature cows. The udder still isn't as large as a mature cow until the heifer has calved.

Heifers that have never calved by the time they are older than two years of age are called heiferettes, while a heifer carrying her first calf is called a bred heifer.

### A Word About Raising Cows

You can raise a cow for either of two purposes: for its beef or for its milk. Whatever path you choose, your choice will affect how you raise your cattle. Allow us to chip in a word of advice. For a small scale backyard herdsman, raising a cow for her milk is not a wise investment.

Usually after a cow has had her baby and can produce milk, she will keep lactating if you keep milking her. You can milk a cow for about two years before the udder finally dries up completely, even if she doesn't have another calf during this time. Problems can arise when trying to sell the milk because of numerous rules and regulations surrounding dairy production.

For instance, in 13 states, you're free to sell raw milk in a retail store. In 17 others, you can sell raw milk on your premises, and 8 states only allow you to sell milk through cow-share agreements. A cow share agreement is when cow owners are paid money to board, feed, and then milk their cattle. Still, in 20 states, it remains illegal to sell raw milk straight from the farm and unpasteurized. In these states, you can only milk your cow for personal use.

Now, before you say that doesn't sound like a bad idea, consider this. Maintaining a milking cow is not cheap, and if you're not selling the milk, raising a cow to make dairy for subsistence use only might not make economic sense as you spend more than you save.

True, your cow can give you excess milk, much more than you can consume, and you won't have to buy milk. But how much are you really saving? A gallon of milk is about $3.00. On average, you're buying about two gallons a month, right? That's $6.00. How much are you really saving?

Perhaps, to supplement that, you can process your milk into cheese and butter, so you get to save on those. But on a small-scale, raising cows for their milk still has more drawbacks than benefits.

This is why it's best to raise cows for their beef on a small scale. Like all cows, beef cows will still produce milk, although at much lower quantities, and that will suffice for your family's needs.

### A Word About Raising Heifers — Choosing Replacement Heifers

In a cow/calf operation, everything rises and falls on the selection of replacement heifers. Your female cattle are the future of your herd. If they aren't selected with careful thought, it can be bad news for you.

The first thing you want to consider is weaning weight because puberty and weight are two closely related factors with female cattle. It's best to set apart the heaviest and the lightest calves, think upper 1% and lowest 25%, respectively. While you want heavy heifers, heifers too heavy might be too big for your environment, especially if you're a small-scale farmer.

Now, when selecting, make sure you're choosing based on their actual weaning weight. It's important to do this because you are going to develop their feeding program based on their weaning weight. This will help them reach puberty (about two-thirds of their adult weight) on schedule.

Other factors you want to look into before selecting a replacement heifer is the conformation of its body. Check out her feet, her legs, and her body type. Also, check out her disposition. Don't forget to meet her dam as that gives you a picture of what the heifer is most likely going to look like by the time she becomes a dam herself.

## The Relationship Between Feeding Heifers and Calving Time

Now, what you're about to read may sound super weird and unscientific, but it is tested and proven. To prevent a cow from calving at night, the most practical and the easiest way to make that happen is to feed your cows at night. Experts can't explain the science behind it, but they think hormones might be involved.

Research has been conducted to study the motility of the rumen. From this study, as calving time approaches, rumen contractions are reduced. The fall in contractions begins about two weeks before calving and then falls more rapidly during calving. How does this relate to feeding at night? Well, links have been drawn between nighttime feeding and the rise of intraluminal pressure at night with a decline during the day.

Several studies have proven this phenomenon, but we will focus on one for our discussion today. In Iowa, there were 1331 cows from 15 farms. These cows were fed only once daily and only at dusk. When it was calving time, 85% had their babies between 6.00 am and 6.00 pm. It didn't matter if the cows started the nighttime feeding program a week before calving or two to three weeks before calving time. Most had their calves during the day!

Now, while achieving nighttime feeding for a large herd on a large ranch might be difficult and would require a more sophisticated process, it's easier for smaller farms. Large ranches have it a little tougher. One way to make it easier for large ranches is for managers to feed the cows earlier in the day and leave the nighttime feeding to heifers with their first calves. You want to give priority to the heifers as they require the closest observation during the calving season. It's their first time, remember?

### The Twin Problem

You know the deal with expecting twin calves. If they are different genders, the heifer (freemartin, more correctly) is affected by her twin brother's male hormones. This makes calving unforeseeable in her future, but when the twins are both heifers, there's no testosterone interference. Hence, both heifers should come out just fine with their reproductive abilities intact.

### Replacement Heifers: To Buy or To Raise

The decision between buying and raising your replacement heifer is something many people have attempted to help cattle farmers with, but there remains no one answer. There's only the best answer for you. Here are a few factors you want to consider when deciding between buying or raising your replacement heifer.

### Herd Size

How does herd size affect your choice between buying a replacement heifer and raising one? And which is the more economically smart thing to do? To raise these heifers or to buy them?

For small-scale herdsmen, buying the replacement heifers might be more cost efficient than raising them due to economies of scale. But larger-scale farmers might find it more economical to raise heifers.

But even large-scale farmers still prefer to buy their replacement heifers rather than raise them. This frees up resources and time, which they can channel into other more pressing areas on their farm.

### Facilities and Pasture

Heifers are more demanding to manage than cows, both financially and otherwise. You must consider this too when deciding to buy or raise replacement heifers.

Heifers need to be managed on their own away from the other members of the herd if they are to reach their peak maturity level for breeding. And you need to begin this separate management when the heifer calf is weaned, especially within the first two to three weeks of weaning. During this period, your heifer calf is very vulnerable to illness; hence you must give her extra special attention. If you don't develop your heifers carefully, they won't hit puberty and be ready to breed on schedule, which generally should be when they are between 14 to 15 months old.

Another aspect of raising heifers is feeding. Growing heifers' nutritional needs are different from the nutritional needs of other members of the herd. To wean and develop your replacement heifers properly, you need to provide more pasture. You must get a secure holding pen to protect the heifers from the bull before its breeding season.

Considering all we have just mentioned, it's easy to see that managing heifers is tough, and there are no shortcuts. Taking shortcuts when developing your heifers will only affect their productivity in the long run. But if you buy your replacement heifer instead, you provide more pasture for about 10% more cattle.

### Can You Afford To Raise More Heifers Than Needed?

If you raise your replacement heifers, remember that you can't just raise the exact number of heifers you need because not all of them will stay healthy. A few of your heifers might have to be culled for several reasons ranging from poor structure to poor weight gain.

If you raise your replacement heifer, consider raising at least 45% more heifers than you need. It's going to cost you more and tie up your capital. Best-case scenario, it will be at least one year before you can sell the heifers you don't need and make your money back.

### Herd Health

Despite the difficulty involved in raising replacement heifers, many farmers still raise their own due to health concerns. If you're buying your replacement heifers, you're not sure where these heifers are coming from or to what they've been exposed. You have only the seller's word. There's always going to be a risk of introducing a foreign disease into your herd. A sickly herd is a huge problem you want to avoid. And if we are following the highest level of biosecurity, then you want to maintain a closed herd which means you should raise your own replacement heifer.

But if you'd prefer to buy the animal, then take these steps:

- Ensure you only buy heifers from a reliable source with a clean bill of health. If you're not sure what to look out for, meet with your local vet to give you the health criteria the heifer should meet.

- Always quarantine newly bought animals.

- Always follow through on your vaccination program.

### Genetic Base

The demand for high-quality beef is increasing, and with beef, quality rises and falls on genetics. The genetics of a cow can affect the profitability of your herd for over ten years - up to 14 years, in fact!

This is one area where raising your replacement heifers trumps buying. As a producer, you can select cattle based on specific performance, carcass, or maternal traits to sire your replacement heifers.

Also, and even more important, if you're raising your replacement heifers, you get to select the heavier calves born within the first 60 days in the calving season. Such heifers have a higher chance of hitting their optimal weight by the onset of puberty. Plus, these heifers usually come from the most fertile cows able to conceive in the earliest days of the breeding season. And if there are heifers that fail to conceive, raising your replacement heifers means you get to cull them.

Now, does this mean you can't select fertile females through buying? No, there are many reliable sources from which you buy get good heifers. Just look out for sources that place a premium on strict selection and quality genetics.

If you want to quickly improve your herd's genetics, it might be a great idea to choose your heifer from outside sources. Selecting from outside sources is also good if your gene selection is limited because of heavy culling either due to age or drought.

### Calving Difficulty

There was a study conducted by the Colorado State University and the University of Nebraska Meat Animal Research Center. According to these studies, first-calvers at two years have calving difficulties compared to mature cows at the age of three. This condition is known as dystocia.

Dystocia has two main causes: the small size of the pelvis in immature heifers and the heavy birth weight of calves. Pelvic size cannot be fixed, but something can be done about calves and their birth weight.

Heavy birth weight is usually caused by the sire's genetics. Hence, to reduce it, you can breed your heifer with a low-birth-weight sire or a calving-ease sire. This is an advantage you only get if you raise your heifer.

If you're buying, you might not be able to confirm that the dam was bred with a calving-ease bull, but you can mitigate this by buying your heifer from a trusted supplier.

Now, remember that using a calving-ease bull does not necessarily mean that calving season will be dystocia-free for your heifers. Remember that pelvic size is another contributing factor. So, if the heifer isn't fully mature by the calving season, she could still have dystocia.

Other factors, such as being a first-time calver or incorrect presentation of the calf, can also make your bred heifer experience dystocia.

So, keep these in mind and consider your ability as a producer to handle these issues should they arise. If you can't, it might be better to buy a replacement heifer.

That said, let's look at the advantages of each option for replacing heifers in your herd.

# Benefits of Raising Replacement Heifers

### Greater Genetic Control

Let's assume that your breeding program already involves a couple of generations specifically selected for maternal traits such as milk production, calving ease, fertility, maternal instinct, and stay-ability. In such a case, getting a replacement heifer from elsewhere would be extremely difficult.

Also, finding heifers with the matching genetic profile suited to the environment that maximizes longevity can be quite difficult.

### Greater Control Over Herd Health

If you operate a closed herd system, it's easier to minimize diseases within your herd. Diseases such as bovine viral diarrhea, venereal diseases, and respiratory diseases are more easily controlled when you develop your own replacement heifers on site.

# Benefits of Buying Replacement Heifers

### It Frees Up Your Resources

When you buy your replacement heifers, you buy only as many as you need. In contrast, when raising them, you wind up with more than you need because, in the end, most end up calving. This consumes extra pasture, facilities, space, and feed, which could have been channeled into raising cows that would calve in the end.

### Takes Less Time to Expand Your Herd or Switch a Breeding Program

If you expand your pasture ground or get access to more inexpensive feed, you might increase your herd size. To do that quickly, your best bet is to buy from an external source, as raising new heifers would be time consuming.

It's also possible that a new marketing window involving a different genetic sub-population opens up, and you wish to explore it. Whatever the case, buying from an external source is the fastest way to take advantage of that opportunity.

### Might Be the Only Way to Get Superior Heifers

If you buy from a replacement heifer specialist, you could end up with a more superior heifer than you'd have been able to produce on your own. When buying from a specialist, you can specify the genetic profile of the composite and purebred heifers, the breed cross, and the sire to which the producer breeds the heifer.

Most commercial developers use artificial insemination along with estrous synchronization to increase the genetic merit of the resulting calves and eliminate any chance of transmitting reproductive disease. This technique also makes it possible to develop heifers that will conceive and calf over a shortened time frame.

### May Be the More Affordable Option

It can be quite costly to raise heifers on your own, especially if you don't have access to cheap feed resources. Plus, if you don't grow your heifers fast enough from the weaning stage to the breeding stage several bad things can happen including delayed puberty, low conception rates, an extended calving season, and increased cost to maintain each pregnant heifer. Now, if calving season is extended and most of your heifers are calving late, the weaning weight of your calves could go down, which affects profitability.

# Chapter 10: Cattle Breeding and Reproduction

When it comes to beef production for commercial purposes, no aspect is as important as reproductive efficiency. It doesn't matter whether you crossbreed, whether your cattle have superior genetics or whether you've been managing your cattle well. If reproductive efficiency is only 50%, it will affect your business dramatically. This is why you must learn everything you can about preparing your cattle to have excellent reproductive efficiency.

When you manage your cattle properly, you could have a calf crop that's higher than 90%. The very least you must cover your production expenses is a calf crop of 85%. Anything lower than 75%, and you'd record major losses. A good goal to work toward is a calf crop of 95% within a calving season of 60 days and an average weaning weight of 500 pounds.

## How to Prepare Your Cow to Conceive Successfully

For a healthy pregnancy and a healthy baby calf, your cow will need a lot of tender loving care. Ensure that she's in great shape physically. Also ensure that she's given the proper care for her age and provided with all the preventative healthcare measures to make breeding successful. Here are a few pointers to help you do this.

## 1. Assess Your Cow's Body Condition Scores

An underfed pregnant bovine is prone to several negative consequences, including:

**Malnourishment:** Since most of the already insufficient nutrients are directed to the fetus, the cow ends up malnourished. Malnourishment makes it difficult for the dam to give birth.

**Poor Colostrum Quality:** Poor feeding affects the quality of colostrum the dam produces. This means the calf receives fewer antibodies, which affects the strength of their immune strength.

**Decreased Milk Production:** If cows are not well fed, they don't produce as much milk.

**Slower Rebreeding Rate:** When pregnant cows are underfed, they longer time to rebreed. This means they won't be producing a calf yearly as they should.

Given how important nutrition is to the reproductive efficiency of cows, farmers have come up with a numerical system to assess a cow's body condition. This numerical system is called Body Condition Scores (BCS).

**Body Condition:** Scores refer to a set of numbers that indicate the body condition (relative plumpness) of a cow before pregnancy, and during and after. The thinner the cow, the lower the BCS score; fatter cows will have a higher BCS score.

Here are the 9 points and what they indicate:

1. Means the cow is so weak and emaciated, you can see the bones distinctly. This is a very rare score, and when it occurs, it is typical because the cow is diseased or riddled with parasites.

2. Means the cow is very emaciated to where you can pick out the ribs distinctly. Muscles in the hindquarter and shoulder are also typically atrophied. Nonetheless, such cows are extremely weak.

3. Means the cow is very weak, and there's no fat in the brisket or overlaying the ribs. Cows with a BCS of 3 also have visible backbones, and there's a reduction in the muscles of the hindquarters.

4. Means the cow is only slightly thin with only a few visible ribs (3 to 5) and a visible spine but there's no muscle depletion, and you can see fat on the hips and over the ribs.

5. Means the cow is in moderate condition. So, there's no backbone jutting out, the spine looks smooth, and most ribs are covered with fat except the last two.

6. A cow with a body condition score of 6 is well-conditioned. Such cows usually look smooth all over their bodies with rounded backs. You can find fat covering the tail-head, in the brisket, over the pin bones, and over the ribs.

7. A body condition score of 7 means that the cow has enough flesh, and the brisket is fatty, as is the tail-head. The body has an overall soft and rounded appearance with smooth ribs and only slightly visible hip bones.

8. This means the cow is over-conditioned. Because of the excess fat, the cow's neck looks thick and short, and the back has a squarish appearance. The entire bone structure is covered by fat.

9. A body condition score of 9 is too high and usually means the cow is very obese. Thankfully, just like a score of 1, a score of 9 is quite rare.

So, what's the best score for your cows to ensure a healthy pregnancy and calving? Well, generally, anything between 5 and 6 is fine but for a first-calf heifer, a minimum body condition of 6 is desirable and if they are calving in the winter, then aim for a higher BCS.

To ensure that your cow attains the perfect BCS for calving, you must evaluate her at specific times. So, evaluate your cow once she enters the second trimester, right before she calves, and before she breeds. This way, you can catch any deficiencies in time and make the necessary adjustments to bring your cow to the perfect body condition.

## 2. Pay Particular Attention to the Younger and Older Cows

Pregnancy takes a toll on all cows but not as much as in first-calf heifers, younger cows (≤3 years), and older cows (≥9 years). You need to pay extra attention to these age groups.

### Caring for First-Calf Heifers

A first-calf heifer is still in the process of maturing even as she carries her calf. So, her body is undergoing a lot of stress and, therefore, needs all the help she can get.

If you did a good job selecting or developing your replacement heifer and ensured they were well nourished, your heifer should have successful calving by the time she's two years old. She should also be ready to rebreed in a year and wean her heavy calves. A well-nurtured first-calf heifer becomes a more profitable animal in the long run.

Here are a few tips to help you support your first calf heifer:

• Be Strict With Selecting Your Replacement Heifers

We already showed you how best to go about this in the previous chapter. Kindly go through it again if you need to.

• Feed Stage-Appropriate Feed and Rations

Weaning to Breeding: Your heifers need to gain roughly 1.25 pounds daily. Now, for one reason or another, your heifer might be falling behind and need to catch up to reach the target weight of 65% mature weight. Even in that case, try not to exceed a daily weight gain of two pounds. If your heifer needs to put on over two pounds daily to attain her target weight for breeding, she's probably not a great candidate for breeding.

To achieve a daily weight gain of 1.25 pounds, your heifer would need to eat about 12 to 15 pounds of the dry matter daily. This can be just pasture, provided you're sure that it is high in protein and energy. If not, then supplement pasture with concentrate.

Breeding to Calving: The daily weight gain target for pregnant heifers is 0.8 pounds. So, they need to be supplied with about 20 pounds of the dry matter daily. Remember, they are now sharing with their baby calves, and that's why they need more food to put on less weight.

Now, remember that as heifers approach calving, it's tough to get them to gain weight, and that gets tougher after calving. One way to work around this is to supplement her daily rations with concentrate to ensure she's at a BCS of 6 or 7 before calving.

After Calving: A heifer does not attain full maturity until her second calving, especially heifers of larger breeds that mature late. Even after calving, your heifer is still growing, and you want to keep her at a BCS of 5 or 6. They could make do with the same rations given to other members of the herd. Often, they might be better off continuing to be managed with the first-calf heifers.

- **Breed First-Calf Heifers First**

A good breeding schedule tip is to breed first-calf heifers for two to three weeks before the cow is in the herd because you want the first-calf heifers and the more mature cows to remain in sync if you have to rebreed them all at the same time.

- **Select the Right Sire**

When picking out the bull to breed with the heifers and cows, select one with convenient birth weight. The bull should also come with a calving-ease expected progeny difference (EPD). Both factors tell you how easily the calves from that bull were born. They are also mutually exclusive as the weaning weight of the bull affects his EPD along with other factors like calf body shape. Generally, larger calves tend to cause dystocia.

# Caring for Older Cows

As your cow ages, understandably, her productivity will also decrease. Conception rates will fall, her calves will have a lighter weaning weight, and her ability to forage will be less (probably due to old age).

So, here's how you can support your older cows. If their udders still function such that they can nourish a calf to a desirable weaning weight, it might be a great idea to either manage them with the first-calf heifers or with the more mature 3-year-old cows.

In either of these places, the competition is less, and your senior cow can get all the nourishment she needs.

### 3. Don't Forget the Reproductive Vaccines

Reproductive diseases can negatively affect the health of your cow and the profitability of the herd. They make breeding impossible, abort calves, and tamper with growing and milky.

Here is a vaccination schedule to help you:

**Brucellosis**: Should be administered between 4 months old to 1 year. If you intend to include a heifer in your breeding stock, make sure she receives this vaccination within the aforementioned time frame.

**Leptospirosis:** Cows and heifers should be vaccinated for leptospirosis yearly, at least. If there's been a case of leptospirosis in your herd before, then vaccination might need to be more frequent; twice a year.

**Vibriosis:** Before breeding, your heifer should get this shot twice. Mature cows need booster shots yearly as well.

**Trichomoniasis:** This vaccination is super important, especially if you're on the west side of the US, as trichomoniasis is more common in that part of the world. Confirm with your vet whether your heifers and cows need this vaccine.

**Bovine Virus Diarrhea (BVD):** BVD isn't just a reproductive disease. It also affects the immune, respiratory, and digestive systems. The BVD virus comes in two strains. So, make sure that your vaccination programs cover your cattle from the strain they are likely to encounter.

**Infectious Bovine Rhinotracheitis (IBR):** This does not just attack the reproductive system of cows; it also affects the eyes and trachea. This shot should be administered annually for heifers and cows.

Always ensure that whatever vaccine you're giving your bred cows/heifers is safe to use in pregnant animals.

### 4. Scheduling the Due Date

It's important to have a rough estimate of when your cow is to calve. It helps you care for your cow appropriately at different stages in her pregnancy. Gestation (pregnancy) in cows takes roughly 285 days.

Now, since we're here, how do you confirm that your cow is pregnant? Well, the common method is by palpation. During palpation, the expert inserts a gloved hand into the animal's rectum and feels the reproductive organs for signs of pregnancy.

For highly experienced experts, pregnancy (or the absence of it) can be confirmed 30 days after breeding, but this requires the experience of an expert hand. Generally, 45 days is the more commonly used time frame. In 45 days after a heifer or cow has been bred, pregnancy (or the lack of it) can be accurately confirmed.

# Choosing the Right Bull for Breeding

In the first chapter of this book, we looked at the fact that you should have a goal when going into the beef cattle raising business. If you have a goal for your business, then you can make the best choices. The bull you select should be one able to complement your heifer/cow in her areas of weaknesses.

Here are a few factors you want to consider:

## 1. Is the Bull to be used on a Heifer?

If yes, the top factors to consider are birth weight and calving ease.

## 2. Are You Going to Retain all His Heifer-Calves?

If you intend to retain all his daughters, then choose a bull with a track record of producing cows with excellent maternal instincts. You're looking for traits like fertility, udder conformation, milking ability, as well as mothering ability.

## 3. Are You Going to Sell the Offspring of the Bull as Feeder Calves?

If you intend to sell the offspring from this bull as feeder calves, the weaning weight of the calves should be one of the most important factors to consider.

## 4. Are You Going to Sell the Offspring of the Bull as Beef?

If you're selling directly to consumers as beef, then you want a bull known for its fantastic carcass merit.

## 5. Reproductive Soundness

Conduct a breeding soundness exam before bringing your bull to the heifer/cow to confirm that he is fertile.

## 6. Structural Fitness

The body structure is also important for reproductive efficiency. You want bulls that move confidently, are strong enough to mount cows without tiring easily, are not diseased or injured, have no swollen leg or joints, have good vision, and that his mouth and teeth are in excellent condition.

## 7. Look at Your Bull

Carefully observe the bull for signs easy to miss. Keep an eye out for muscling, disposition, color, and the body condition score. For the start of the breeding season, a BCS of 5 or 6 is best.

## 8. Assess the Bull's Performance

Carefully consider the bull's own performance in key areas such as weaning and yearly weight because that tells you the offspring that would result. More important, learn about the bull's EPD because this goes a long way in determining how easily the mother births her baby.

# How to Care for Your Bull

Begin caring for your bull right after weaning. Once he's been weaned, he needs to hit about 2.5 pounds daily to grow and mature properly, and bulls continue to grow well into their third year, attaining a 1,000-pound weight from 600 pounds weaning weight.

So, ensure your bull has access to food continuously (about 23 pounds of dry matter daily) and has a body condition score of 6. If it's an older bull, then his diet should consist of about 25 pounds to 31 pounds of dry matter (depending on his size) to maintain his weight.

Now, here's an important tip: You should never leave your bull with the cows all year long. Have only your bull with the cows during breeding season and breeding season alone. Typically, this season lasts between 60 and 90 days.

There are several advantages to this. One is that all members of your herd would be at the same production stage (pregnancy, lactation, and rebreeding). Also, you'd have a tight calf crop. All your calves would be about the same age. This allows you to care for your herd and calves more precisely and easily when they all have the same health and dietary needs at roughly the same time.

Leaving the bull with the females all year long is risky because bulls are randy animals. Sometimes, certain heifers attain sexual maturity ahead of the expected time. The bull can prematurely breed such heifers, and that could make things difficult for you.

A bull should be kept in a clean, dry area protected from the elements but also has enough space for him to pasture and exercise. You can put the water trough and feed bunk at opposite ends of the pasture so that he's forced to move around and exercise. Remember, he needs to strengthen his muscles and bones.

Now, don't forget to vaccinate your bull just as you vaccinate the cows. The mature cows and your bull could share the same schedule for vaccinations. Here are the vaccines your bull will need:

Reproductive vaccines, including vibriosis, leptospirosis, and trichomoniasis (possibly).

Respiratory vaccines for bovine virus diarrhea (BVD), bovine respiratory syncytial virus (BRSV), infectious bovine rhinotracheitis (IBR), and parainfluenza-3 (PI-3).

Deworming and aggressive fly-control are also very important for bulls to keep them healthy.

### Going the Artificial Insemination (AI) Route

It's possible to get your cows and heifers pregnant without breeding them with a bull. This process is known as artificial insemination. You're probably familiar with the term. It's where you collect semen from a bull and use it for breeding your cow without bringing the bull to mate her naturally.

Artificial insemination is very popular in the dairy industry in the United States, with about 2 out of 3 dairy cows being bred by artificial insemination. In the beef industry it only about 5% to 10% of beef cows are bred using artificial insemination.

Now, let's examine the good and bad of artificial insemination and see if it's right for you.

### Pros of Artificial Insemination

#### 1. High-Quality Sires

This is the biggest advantage of artificial insemination: access to top-tier AI (Artificial Insemination) sires. Such bulls typically have a proven track record and produce offspring with heavy weaning weights, high carcass merit, and excellent replacement heifers.

#### 2. No Need for a Bull

There's no hiding the truth. Having a bull around can be tough for most herdsmen. So, not having to deal with one would be a welcome relief for most, especially for small-scale rearers.

#### 3. Might Be the More Affordable Option

Artificial insemination might be less expensive than natural service, especially if you have a small herd with only a few cows.

### Cons of Artificial Insemination

#### 1. Conception Rates are not as High

Natural service will always have higher conception rates than artificial insemination. If, after two attempts with artificial insemination, your cow does not become pregnant, it might be advisable to go the natural route.

## 2. AI Requires Labor, Skill, and Equipment

In natural service, the bull does all the work. For AI, it's different. You're going to have to put in the time, equipment, and effort. You might have to go with an AI technician to increase chances of success and to make things easier for you, but it is also possible to do it yourself with the right education.

Now that you know all about cattle reproduction, let's get into the more practical aspect of calving.

# Chapter 11: Calving and Caring For Newborns

Now that you know how to get your cows pregnant, it becomes imperative to know how to care for them in pregnancy and post-pregnancy. You also need to know how to take care of the new calves. And that is what this chapter is about.

But before we go into all of that, here are a few quick facts about pregnant cows:

> • Many people peg the gestation period for cows at 283 days, but it could be from 279 to 287 days. This variation could be because of the gender of the calf. Cows carrying bulls sometimes have a longer gestation period than cows carrying heifers.

> • On average, a cow can get pregnant 55 days after she has calved, but this can take up to 10 days longer if the said cow had calving difficulties or is a first-time mother. Cows that fall ill and lose weight after calving could also take longer before they could get pregnant again.

> • Under normal circumstances, your cow should be able to give birth to one calf every year if she is bred.

With all that said, let's look at what you can do to keep your pregnant cows and heifers healthy.

# Feeding Your Pregnant Cows and Heifers

The goal of proper nutrition with pregnant cows and heifers is to ensure that they remain healthy throughout their pregnancy, deliver healthy calves, lactate well, start their next cycle promptly, and then be healthy and ready when the new breeding starts.

So, it is clear to see that nutrition for your pregnant cows and heifers is something to pay proper attention to.

With that said, the first thing to note is that at the very early stage of pregnancy, their feed need not be changed. What you were feeding them at the breeding stage is what you'll continue to feed them throughout the early stage.

But as the fetus inside them continues to develop, their nutritional needs will continue to increase. This basically means that you must eventually feed them like they are eating for two because they will be.

Two months to when your cows will deliver is when a lot of the fetal developments happen. So, this is the period when you want to improve their nutrition and feed them like they are eating for two.

Now, your younger cows and heifers will need even more protein and better nutrition than the older cows because the younger ones are still growing while still pregnant, but the older cows are no longer growing.

As you increase the foliage you give your pregnant cows, there must be a concurrent increase in the protein they eat.

The reason for this is that your cows and heifers need protein to properly digest the foliage. Also, protein creates the right environment for rumen microbes to grow.

These rumen microbes help the cows extract the energy value from the foliage they are eating. Don't forget that the energy extracted would be really needed, especially when they are pushing.

They also need the foliage to be properly broken down in the rumen so they can maintain a healthy weight throughout their pregnancy and even post-pregnancy. Protein can be instrumental to keep them at a healthy weight.

So, what you want to figure out is how to increase the protein content of your pregnant cow's food. And remember to give the younger cows more than what you give the older cows.

You could increase the protein content by increasing the protein source food in your cows' diet or by adding protein supplements to their meal.

The general rule of thumb is to increase the protein content of your older cows to about 7 to 8 percent while you increase that of the younger cows and heifers to about 8 or 9 percent.

Besides protein, you also want to make sure that your pregnant cows are getting enough vitamins and minerals. Calcium and phosphorus are other nutrients to pay attention to. Consult with your vet to tailor a meal plan for your pregnant cows and heifers.

# Other Things to Pay Attention To

- It is *absolutely important* for your pregnant cows and heifers to get as much exercise as possible. 30 minutes of moderate exercise twice a day should work just fine.

- You could consider massaging your cows' udders for a couple of minutes every day to help increase circulation.

- You'll need a maternity/calving pen where your cow will be delivering her calf. If you can afford it, have a calving pen in a separate barn. But if you can't, just make sure it is as far away from where the other cows are as possible in order not to agitate them.

- Also, make sure this maternity pen is close to a handling facility (headgate and squeeze chute) in case if you need to assist with the delivery.

- You do not want to enter the calving season unprepared. So, make sure that you have a plan for it. Plan your schedule so you always have someone around and consult with your vet to come up with precautions that everyone in the family or practice must take.

- You need to prepare your calving kit. Your calving kit should contain obstetrical sleeves (preferably disposable ones), lubricant (non-detergent soap works well), antiseptic (preferably hypo-allergenic), obstetrical chains (30 and/or 60-inch chains), mechanical calf pullers, and injectable antibiotics.

Now that we are on the topic of calving let's look at what signs tell you your cow is ready to deliver.

# Signs of Calving

- You'll notice that your cow's udders are really full.

- Her birth canal will look really long and squishy, showing you it is preparing for a calf to come out.

- When it's really close to the time, you'll see discharge from the birth canal.

- You'll notice her mood begins to change. She'll be cranky and anxious.

# Preparing for Calving

As your cow approaches her final month of pregnancy, you need to move her into the maternity pen or space to acquaint her with the new area.

And as you notice the signs already mentioned, you need to make sure that the calving space is calf safe. Remove everything that could pose harm to the babies. Also, make sure that the space is clean and dry. Have your vet's number on speed dial, just in case things don't go as planned.

# Calving

- As your cow or heifer enters labor, you'll be able to see the fetus in the birth canal.

- Cervical dilation and contractions start. This should last between 4 and 8 hours. If it goes on for longer than that, call your vet.

- Next, her water breaks, and she goes into active labor, which is marked by straining. The time from when her water breaks to when the calf drops should be between 2 and 4 hours, but for a first-time mother, active labor should last for about 60 to 90 minutes Active labor for older cows is 30 to 60 minutes. If it continues beyond that time without the calf dropping, you need to call your vet. You might have to step in but your vet will tell you what to do.

- After the calf has dropped, your cow should pass the placenta. If this has not happened within 12 hours, it means your cow has retained the placenta, and you need to call your vet.

# Calf Handling

After the calf has been born, it is time for you to step in, make sure that the calf is alive and then take care of it. But before you get to the calf, be careful of the new mama, as she might not take kindly to you touching her baby. So, do not sneak up on her; make sure that she is OK with you taking away her baby. Also, try not to go through the calf handling process alone in case you need help with the mama.

With that said, here are the things you need to do:

- First off, make sure that the calf is breathing. If it is not breathing, try cleaning the calf's nostrils and mouth with wet wipes. The nostrils might be blocked by mucus. You could also try encouraging the calf to breathe by vigorously rubbing its back or tickling its nose with a piece of straw.

- Do not hold a newborn calf upside down as that could squish its internal organs unto its lungs, preventing it from breathing properly.

- Once you've ascertained that the calf is breathing, examine its general wellbeing. The calf should be able to move and the body should be warm within five minutes. It should attempt to stand within fifteen minutes and actually stand on its own within an hour. If it can't meet these milestones, call your vet.

# Calf Nursing

Once you've ascertained that your calf is breathing, the next thing is to ensure that it gets as much colostrum as possible.

When calves are born, they do not have a very good immune system. Colostrum should help them strengthen their immune system. Colostrum is the first milk that mammals produce, including humans. And as the hour passes, the amount of colostrum they produce decreases.

So, if you want your calf to get enough colostrum, ensure that they nurse no more than 30 minutes after they are born. If the calf can't nurse within 30 minutes, you must bottle feed it colostrum.

The colostrum must have been frozen, and then before you feed, slowly thaw it, then feed the calf. The amount of colostrum you feed the calf should be 5 to 6 percent of the calf's body weight. Make sure that the calf is fed colostrum within the first six hours of its life and then 12 hours after it was born.

If the calf is too weak to be fed by mouth, you might have to resort to a stomach tube, but if you encounter this kind of issue, consult with your vet first.

# Calf Health

After your calf has nursed for the first time, it is time to disinfect her navel. Use a 7% iodine solution in a container and then dip the calf's umbilical cord and navel into the solution.

You want to dip it as opposed to spraying because when spraying it is easy to miss a few spots. If you've had a history of navel infections on your farm, consider doing the dip again after 12 hours, just to be on the safe side.

Moving on, if you notice things like rapid breathing, dry muzzle, abnormal posture, lowered head and ears, call your vet because that is not normal.

# Calf Identification

The next thing to do is to ID your calf so you can remember when each calf was born and their parents, but if you have just one calf, you might not need this step.

With identification, you could use physical hanging ear tags, radiofrequency ear tags, or tattoos. Whichever one you use, the ID should be a combination of the year they were born and a number that represents the order in which they were born. It is generally accepted to denote the years as letters thus: H=2020, J=2021, K=2022, L=2023, etc. The letters I, O, U and U are not used.

Therefore, the fourth calf to be born in your practice in 2020 would typically have H4, H04, or H004 as its ID, depending on how many cows you have.

One more thing: IDs are usually attached to the ear. There are two trains of thought when determining which ear. Many people append the ID on the left ear for all their calves because it is easier to see it as the cattle go through the handling facilities. There are those that attach the ID on different ears for different genders. So, if they attach the ID on a bull-calf's right ear, they'll attach the ID on a heifer calf's left ear. This allows them to identify the calf's gender at a glance.

After you've ID'ed the calf, you want to make records. Record the date and time of birth and the mama and papa. You also want to record the calf's weight, which you should take within the first 24 hours of its birth.

# Calf Castration and Implants

This only applies to bull-calves. Castration and implants need not be done that day, especially considering that you need to observe the calf to determine to use it for breeding.

Castration is the removal of the testes, which makes the bull-calf a steer. But a growth implant may be implanted into the steers to make them grow almost as big as a bull. Do consult with your vet, who should help you determine if a growth implant is a good idea for your steer.

Finally, if you castrate and/or insert the growth implant, try to do it before you wean the calf.

Calving might seem scary to you, but it isn't. Mostly, your cow can do the calving herself, and if she needs help, you and your vet can assist her.

# Chapter 12: Expert Tips for Your Beef Cattle Business

It would be easy to think that having all that information on how to set up a proper cattle rearing outfit would guarantee success. However, it takes more than knowing how to run a successful outfit. You need to know how to run a successful business, and this chapter is where we attend to that.

## A Quick Guide for Beginners

### Costs

Setting up a cattle rearing outfit will cost you a lot of money upfront, regardless of the size of the practice you want to run. You'll be spending a lot on everything from the land (if you don't have already), setting up the pasture, erecting fences, and setting up the facilities and equipment that have been mentioned earlier in this book. And this doesn't even include buying the cattle that make up the practice.

Plan properly for it. Having a sustainable source of income before starting the outfit would be a good idea. Still, often it's impossible to get started without a loan. Consider using the services of a financial adviser to better understand your options.

You also want to draw up a budget for your practice. Online budgeting tools and land grant university programs can be found free of charge; take advantage of such options! Also, consider the savings afforded in buying used farm equipment. It not only saves you money, but it is also good for the environment. *(Do try to new feeders, though, as mentioned earlier.)*

### How Much Land?

The minimum amount of land you should aim for is ten acres; with that much land, you should be able to run a small cattle-raising operation. For a standard outfit, start with at least 30 acres. To start small – but are looking to expand later – buy land in an area with prospects where you are sure you can buy more land later, avoiding having to move your practice down the road.

### The Easier Practice

If you are clear on what kind of practice you want to run (that is, feeder or cow-calf), then by all means, do what you want to do. But if you haven't decided yet (or you *have,* but are open to suggestions), you'll want to hear this. As a beginner, you should start out as a feeder practice, and there are good reasons for that.

One, a feeder practice is more affordable to start than a cow-calf because with a feeder practice, you can go right ahead and buy a mature cow and earn money almost immediately. Mature cows are more expensive to buy than babies, but they are also less expensive to care for than babies, seeing as you'll have them for just a few years.

On the issue of cost, with a cow-calf practice, you must set up different facilities for cows and calves while you can use one-size-fits-all facilities for feeders. Furthermore, feeder practice is less stressful to run. This is especially good news for someone with no experience. You won't have calves who are still delicate and require a lot of attention.

Something else to think about is that a feeder practice offers you more opportunity to experiment. To start with two cattle, you can buy two breeds and decide which works best for you. Plus, you won't be stuck for years with a breed you think doesn't work. Still, you may be stuck with a calf till it grows old enough to be sold, unless you want to sell it as a calf and take a loss.

## Breeding

If you've decided to breed, you need to think about how you will go about it. One bull should be all you need for a start-up, but even that one bull can cost a lot of money (more than a couple of cows), especially considering that you'll be looking for one with good genes to be passed on to your calves. If you start with just one bull – and buy it young enough – your bull should be able to service about 25 cows for about six years.

If you'd rather not spend that much, you could swing for artificial insemination (A.I.). But you'll need a backup bull for those cows, which might not take well to A.I.

A more affordable option could be to share a bull with another outfit so you both can split the cost of buying one. You can also consider a leasing arrangement.

## Help

You also want to consider how much help is available to you. If you are starting as a family business, you should have enough hands. Doing it alone is not a good idea!

Hiring additional help will add to your expenses because you must pay them. On the other hand, having to run the entire thing on your own is a lot of work, especially considering that you are not used to the intensity of then work. Weight both options, carefully choosing which works best for you.

If you decide to hire hands, you must think about what aspects of cattle rearing appeal to you the most and then hire out the other aspects. The idea is, if you are passionate about it, it will make doing the work easier and more enjoyable.

It is important to remember that cattle rearing is time and life-consuming as there is a lot of work to be done. You must tend to the cattle while also running a business. So, whether you get help or not, you want to be physically fit and mentally prepared.

# People You Need to Know

If you are starting a cattle rearing practice (whether feeder, cow-calf or a combination of both), you will need the contact information of these people:

- A good large animal nutritionist.

- A reliable veterinarian located near you.

- A good extension specialist.

- An experienced cattle-rearer.

- A good butcher or retailer.

# 21 Tips for Running a Commercially Successful Cattle Rearing Outfit

Whether you're a newcomer to the cattle rearing practice or you've been doing it for years, these tips will help make your practice profitable:

1. When deciding what breed of cattle to rear, consider market trends. You'll want to do a market survey to find out what breeds are in high demand. You can then choose that option or create a niche for yourself if you think you'll be able to get enough customers.

2. More and more people want to buy only grass-fed cattle; consider this option.

3. Try not to skimp on important vaccinations. If you are trying to save costs, there are vaccinations you could do without for many of your cattle, but there are vaccinations that all your cattle must get, and promptly. Prevention is usually less expensive than the treatment or cure. To determine which vaccinations aren't required for your animals and location, you must consult your veterinarian.

4. Don't ever just expect an illness or injury to go away, as things could worsen, and your animal could die. If you notice any of your cattle ill or injured, immediately confer with your veterinarian. Any infirmity greatly reduces the market value of your cattle, and death *cancels it.*

5. If any of your cattle die, know the cause because it could be from something communicable. If you do not know, try to do a necropsy. Once you've been able to ascertain the cause of death, make sure that the rest of your cattle are healthy and safe.

6. Don't just wake up and decide to take your cattle to the market that day without a marketing plan. Developing a marketing plan or strategy involves determining how much your cattle will sell for depending on what the general market price is and the quality of your cattle. It will also include determining the best time to sell.

7. Have a solid network of farmers you do business with. Your network could also include other farmers with whom you could split costs to buy certain equipment or even a bull. Having a solid network can help you get good value for your money.

8. Do everything you can to maintain a good reputation. Cattle rearing exists in a community, and if the people in the community cannot trust you, you won't be able to make much progress.

9. Aside from ensuring that your prices are always legit, patronizing other local businesses for your cattle business will help you maintain a good rep in the community. It could also be your way of contributing to the growth of the community.

10. Do regular analysis and evaluation. It will help you determine what you are doing well and what needs to be improved. It will also help you discover what things you are doing that aren't earning you enough money, which of your cattle isn't bringing in a profit, and which cattle are contributing to the business. Make a plan for the evaluation and decide how often you'll do it.

11. Make sure that you are always up to date with your taxes. Find out if you are eligible for any tax deductions, keeping receipts for every single thing you buy, and invest in a good bookkeeping method; it'll save you a lot of headaches when tax season comes.

12. Make sure that you're always putting effort and money into improving. It is okay if you didn't start with the best equipment and facilities. But as you earn an income from your practice, you'll do well to reinvest and get better equipment and facilities, improve your quality of production and expand your practice if you intend to grow your business.

13. In the same vein, make sure that you are constantly learning about new practices and new technology. Don't experiment with them all, but you'll find something that works for you and gives you good value for your money.

14. Consider livestock insurance. Regardless of how well you plan and how much precautions you take, you might not be able to prevent unfortunate events. Livestock insurance will help cover many of your financial losses caused from cattle accidents, injuries, or illnesses.

15. That you should consult with your vet has been mentioned so often now, but it must also be said that you should be honest with your vet. If they are asking you about your management practices, tell the truth. The truth will help them help you make the right decisions for your practice, at least, as far as your cattle are concerned.

16. Be intentional about your fencing and borders. If you have weak fences and/or porous borders, you could have runaway cattle. Runaway cattle is basically like setting fire to your money unless, by great providence, you can find them.

17. If you are running a feeder practice, consider dehorning your calves. Horns are dangerous and could lead to lots of injuries. And injuries cost money and could reduce their market value.

18. Avoid the craze for modern quick-fixes. Stick with things tested and trusted because cattle cost a lot of money.

19. Buy food in large quantities (as large as a truckful) rather than in small quantities. You'll get better a value for your money when you buy in bulk.

20. Know when it is time to replace your equipment. Old or faulty equipment can become difficult to maintain, and the cost of getting them repaired is ultimately more than the cost of getting a replacement. So, if you've repaired equipment more than twice, you want to think about being financially smart and making a good choice between repairing or replacing the items.

Whatever business you're running, there is a significant possibility that you'll experience a loss. The first time it happens might come as a shock to you, but being prepared for the possibility helps.

# Conclusion

Not all the tips and ideas in this book will come to you easily. A few will, while others will take practice. And unfortunately, still others will take trial and error. But try to be patient with yourself. The more time, effort, and proper knowledge you put into your cattle rearing outfit, the better you'll get. This book is not a one-time read. It is a resource you can always come back to as you meet new challenges in your cattle rearing business.

No amount of reading and gathering of information will make you a successful cattle-rearer. You actually have to start something new or change what you're doing to run a successful practice.

It's time to close this book and start carrying out the ideas and suggestions you've read about! Don't forget to come back to it if you ever find yourself in a pickle. And don't forget to involve yourself in the cattle-rearing community. Good luck!

# Part 4: Raising Llamas

*The Ultimate Guide to Llama Keeping and Caring, Including Tips on How to Raise Alpacas*

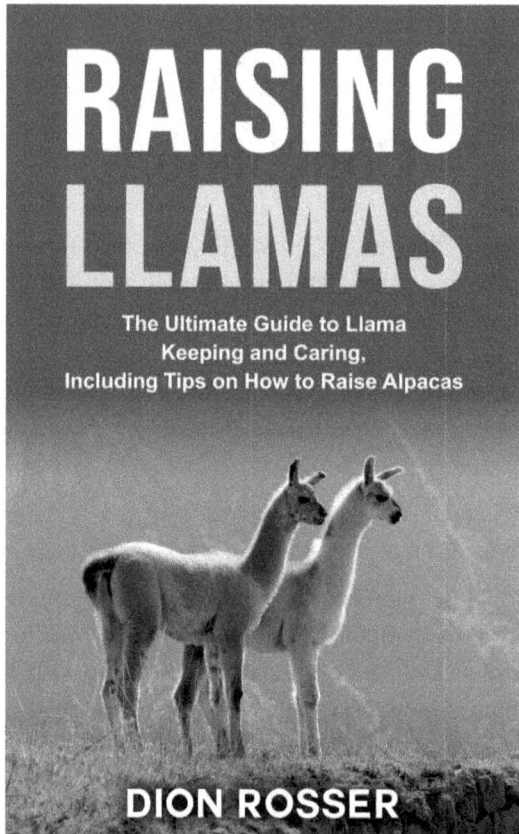

# Introduction

Did you learn about the advantages of raising a llama from a friend, the internet or somewhere else? Are you considering starting a farm? And do you want to enjoy all the benefits of having llamas – or their close cousins, alpacas?

Great! However, you may not know how to go about it and you likely have several questions you want answered.

What are the differences between alpacas and llamas? Can you raise them together? What should you have in place to start a farm? How do you go about buying a llama? What should you know to raise them properly?

This book answers those questions and more.

Or your case might be a little different. You might have raised one or two llamas on your own and then you got stuck. Well, don't fret. It's never too late to improve.

This book will help you learn how to raise llamas, including all the details about their care, behavior, breeds and much more.

We provide all the practical day-to-day information you need to know about llamas and alpacas. Our goal is to ensure that you have all you require in your quest to raising healthy llamas for any purpose, whether for fun or for a business venture.

You might have read other books that promised to give you all the information you need to know but under-delivered. So, you are wondering, what makes this book different? Don't worry! We will tell you.

This book is easy to read, with no scientific terms or facts that are hard to understand. You will also receive the latest information on the correct practices, and since we are experts, all the instructions and methods in this book can be used, have been used, and are still in use.

So, what are you waiting for?

It is time to get all that knowledge about llamas and alpacas you have been yearning for!

# Chapter 1: Why Raise Llamas?

*Quick Fact* - *Llamas were domesticated and used as pack animals in the Peruvian highlands around 4000 to 5000 years ago.*

You may have come across a llama at some point, maybe in your neighborhood or at the local zoo. Their cute looks and hairy body might have drawn you to take a closer look at them.

But suddenly, they were chasing you and spitting at you! What memory will this experience leave you? It's likely you wouldn't want to go anywhere near them again!

Well, believe it or not, llamas are friendly and mild animals that make great pets. Previous mishandling from strangers and intruders might cause their sometimes-strange reactions, but when you keep one, you will discover they are lovely animals to have.

Llamas and their closely-related cousins, alpacas, are one of the oldest domestic animals known to man. They both belong to the camel family and are popular as pack animals. Though similar, they can be differentiated by their size and hair.

Llamas are part of the camelid family, a family that first appeared about 40 million years ago on the Central Plains of North America. It was only about 3 million years ago that the llamas' ancestors migrated to South America. Around 10,000 to 12,000 years ago, the last Ice Age caused the camelid's to become extinct in North America. Now, in Canada and the United States, there are about 100,000 alpacas and 160,000 llamas. And, as a fun fact, it may interest you to know that the national symbol of Peru is the llama, and it can be found on the flags, stamps, coins and other tourist products in Peru.

For farm and ranch owners, llamas and alpacas are an excellent fit for a mixed farming system. They are ruminant animals with three stomach compartments and like cattle and sheep, they also chew their cud. For folks with a small piece of land, you can care for one or two llamas, and although big, they are relatively easy to care for.

If you are a homesteader looking to add a new animal to your livestock herd, then llamas will be a great fit. For folks who need a new pet at home, llamas are popular because of their friendly nature. Now, let's talk about the benefits of raising llamas.

# 8 Major Reasons Why You Should Raise a Llama

### 1. Protection

It is common for livestock like goats, sheep, horses and cows to be hunted by predators. This problem has become a common threat to herders who look for various means to keep predators away. A pack of coyotes is enough to take down big livestock like cows and horses, but you can reduce the risk of attacks from predators by introducing llamas into your herd.

Research by Iowa State University shows that, on average, farmers lose 11 percent of their herd to predators, but this is reduced to 1% when llamas are introduced into the herd. Most farmers introduce llamas into their herd to guard other livestock, mostly using gelded males for this purpose.

They have proven to be an excellent substitute for dogs, requiring less care. One llama is enough to guard hundreds of other animals. Incorporating a llama into your herd is relatively easy because of their quick adaptation. Although some might adapt within hours, others might need 1 or 2 weeks to adapt to other animals completely.

After adapting to other animals, they will chase predators away from the farm. Llamas have good instincts with full awareness of their surroundings and usually draw attention to a stranger (predator) by raising an alarm call. This sound is then followed by chasing, kicking, or spitting at the intruding animal.

## 2. They are great pack animals

How about enjoying an outdoor adventure with a llama carrying all the burden? Sounds great, right?

Llamas have been raised and used as pack animals for thousands of years. They might not be as popular for this purpose as horses and oxen, but they get the job done. Their history traces back to South America, where the animal used to carry loads through the Andes Mountains.

Llamas are suitable as pack animals because of their firm feet and their ability to carry a third of their weight. You need to train your llama for packing before you use it for that purpose. *Alpacas* are not suitable for packing loads because of their relatively smaller weight.

Today, llamas are widely used by campers and adventurers to complement their outdoor activities. Hunters and fisherman have also seen the usefulness of llamas in their daily activities. They usually scout for their food and water while walking, although in harsh environments, you might need to pack food for them.

## 3. A source of fiber

Llamas and alpacas are an excellent source of fiber for yarns and fabric. Though farmers breed alpacas specifically for fiber because of their soft hair, llama hair also has its uses. Fleecing can be done only once a year, though.

Llama hair comprises a fine wool fiber intertwined with coarse guard hairs, but separating the coarse fibers from the fine wool can be quite the task! Once it is achieved, working with the wool becomes easier. This is why llama wools are expensive, generally selling for $2 per ounce.

The coarse hair of llamas is usually used to make rugs and ropes. Alpaca hair is soft, strong and lightweight, containing no lanolin, which makes it easy to be processed and cleaned without using chemicals. They produce more fiber than llamas despite the double hair-coat of llamas.

The fibers produced from these animals are regarded as luxury fibers and can be a superb source of income, given its growing popularity within the fiber industry. Besides the fantastic benefits you stand to gain, it is also a good financial investment.

### 4. Easy care

Feeding llamas is relatively easy compared to other grazing animals. You might think because they are large animals they require large quantities of food, but this is not the case. They are generally happy grazing pastureland and need not be fed much in the way of additional food. However, in the colder months, you will need to supplement their diet with grass and hay.

Given the right care and attention, llamas are generally a healthy breed. However, like most other large farm animals, they require routine checks to keep them in shape.

Proper grooming includes cleaning their feet to prevent lameness, and they should receive appropriate vaccines to prevent them from falling ill. Helped by your veterinary doctor, keeping your llamas and alpacas in good health should not be difficult.

### 5. Suitable for show animals

Llamas make great show animals because of their intelligence and ability to learn quickly. The Alpaca and Llama Show Association has hosted over 150 llama shows, an eventful time when hundreds of owners gather for competition.

The competition awards people for the training and breeding of the animals.

They can be easily trained to run obstacles, like dogs or horses. The show involves llamas navigating courses and running over obstructions like downed trees and rivers. They excel as show animals because of their herd mentality.

They are not shy or scared amidst large groups, especially in competition.

### 6. Small area is not a barrier

Like other animals, llamas and alpacas require adequate fencing, which will serve as protection for them. You don't have to possess a big parcel of land before you can set up where they will live, though; you can use a small space in your backyard to keep one or two.

Any form of shelter (natural or artificial) will suffice. A well-ventilated shelter will help keep them shaded and cool during hot seasons. An adequate shelter will also help keep them warm during the cold season, and the shelter will not cost you much compared to the value it provides your llamas.

### 7. They make great pets

Llamas are well-behaved animals, and they make great pets. They are generally used as pets because of their friendly disposition and cleanliness, making them an ideal companion for your children, provided they are cared for properly.

Some are skeptical about keeping them as pets because they spit, but typically, a llama will only spit when it has a dispute about food or when it feels threatened. Did you know, though – you can train a llama not to spit!

Another reason to keep them as pets is their healthy lifestyle, which requires only mild maintenance.

### 8. They are an excellent investment

Starting a llama and alpaca farm is a wonderful investment. With this addition to your farm, you will enjoy a tax deduction from the federal government; a unique tax benefit to people who train these animals.

A full-grown llama can sell for around $10,000! You will, however, need to be patient because they usually give birth only once a year. But, considering the minimal care and feeding you need to invest in them, you could stand to gain significantly from selling them.

You can make money from the fiber produced by the animals every year. Their hair is an excellent source of wool, and they grow in different colors. One ounce of llama wool sells for around $2.

### Conclusion

Llamas are great animals to raise because of their wonderful personalities. From their companionship, beauty and intelligence, you will enjoy every bit of your experience with them. Knowing and understanding their outstanding characteristics, you should have no doubts about raising one – or even more!

# Chapter 2: Llama Breeds and Alpacas

*Quick Fact* – *The easiest way to distinguish between an alpaca and a llama is size – llamas are typically twice as big as alpacas. Another way to know is by their ears – an alpaca's ears are short and pointy while a llama's ears are longer and stand up straight.*

Llamas and alpacas are often two creatures confused with each other. Differentiating these two creatures is more like telling a turtle from a tortoise.

These two exciting animals belong to a group called Camelids; a broad name given to animals that look like camels.

Animals in this family commonly have long necks. Although they feed on plants, they are not ruminants.

By simply looking at these animals, you can tell they are different. Anyone can spot their long thin legs and necks differ from those of goats, sheep or cows.

Their stomachs are divided into three parts, whereas a ruminant's stomach must have *four* parts.

However, just like ruminants, they also possess two toes. Their toes are unique, though, as they do not have hooves like ruminants. Instead of hooves, their feet's soft pads give them a better grip on the ground.

The animals in this family are a little different from other animals as they are the only mammals known to have oval-shaped red blood cells. All other mammals have red blood cells shaped like disks.

Before you consider the variations between these two beautiful creatures, we need to be clear about something. There are two concepts commonly misused and understanding the two will help you better appreciate the variations between these two animals: the terms are *breeds* and *species.*

Species is a broad term that refers to a group of animals that look alike and can mate to produce offspring.

Let's use dogs as an example. You know that all dogs can mate and produce puppies; you also know that there are different types of dogs. Even with the different types, when you see a dog, you can tell it's a dog, not some other animal. With that picture in mind, the general name 'dog' refers to the species.

But *breeds* are the different types of animals *under the species.* Their appearance is usually different. Using the dog analogy from before, a *breed* would be a Pomeranian.

The Pomeranian and the Husky are different in appearance. Looking at them, you know they are dogs; they both bark and do what most dogs do. Both are of the same species (dogs). However, they are different breeds (Pomeranian and Husky).

Now that you get the picture, let's investigate the differences between llamas and alpacas.

# Differences between Llamas and Alpacas

Nature almost always has two related animals that are hard to tell apart. Animals like toads and frogs, alligators and crocodiles, the list goes on. One of such wonders of nature is the llama and the alpaca.

The two animals look so much alike, it's challenging to tell them apart, unless you are an expert (or have read this book carefully!)

If you see these two animals together, these points will help you tell which is which.

## 1. Face

Starting with the most apparent part of the body, llamas usually have long faces compared with the alpacas. Alpacas usually have short faces with more fur than llamas. Some people think alpacas are cuter than llamas.

## 2. The Ears

The ears of the animals are probably the next noticeable difference. The ears of llamas are usually long, curved and shaped like bananas, whereas in alpacas, the ears are short, straight and typically pointy.

## 3. Size

This feature is a clear-cut distinction between the two animals. Alpacas are smaller than llamas and the average weight for an adult alpaca is between 45 and 70 kg (about 100-150 pounds).

Adult llamas usually grow to at least double that weight. The average weight of an adult llama is between 90 and 160 kg (about 200-350 pounds).

Also, llamas are usually taller than alpacas. The height is typically measured from the shoulder to the ground and, while alpacas rarely exceed 90 cm (35 inches) in height, llamas can grow as tall as 110 cm (45 inches) or even more.

## 4. Animal Fiber

You can also differentiate between the animals by touching them. Alpacas have fluffy, soft, and fine hair, while llamas have a rough coat.

Fiber gleaned from alpacas is used in making hats, shawls, and socks. People do not use wool from llama for making clothes unless it is from baby llamas.

## 5. Temperament

The temperament refers to the moods or general behavior of an animal. While alpacas are usually very gentle creatures, llamas are not.

You've probably heard these animals do spit, but this is usually only when they feel threatened. While it only happens on rare occasions, it's more common in llamas than with alpacas.

Alpacas move together as a herd, like sheep, while llamas are lone rangers, preferring their own company. For this reason and their size, llamas are used for guarding other animals.

Interestingly, they are used to guard alpacas because alpacas are nervous animals. Faced with danger, a guard llama will bravely use itself as a distraction.

### 6. Endurance

Due to their larger size, llamas have more endurance than alpacas, and also have firm feet which give them extra grip. Therefore, they are more suited to walking longer distances than alpacas and are typically used in desert and mountain regions.

Llamas can also carry as much as one-third of their body weight while alpacas are not suited to carrying packs or people.

You will find other differences in how the two animals are used. People usually raise llamas for their meat since their fur is not the best quality. They are also excellent when used as carriage animals or bred as guard animals.

Alpacas are reared mainly for their fur, which is of superior quality and grows faster than llama fur.

By now, you should be able to differentiate between alpacas and llama. Now, let's see the different breeds under the two species of animals.

# Breeds of Llamas

There are four breeds of llamas. They are the classic llama, the Wooly llama, the Silky llama, and the Suri llama. The Classic llama is believed to be a major ancestor of the other three types. The other three are believed to have originated from extensive cross-breeding.

Of all four breeds, the Classic llama is the most common and also the largest. In contrast, Suri llama is the rarest and holds the reputation of being the smallest among the other breeds. The breeds look similar and sometimes differentiating them can be challenging.

All breeds have similar colors, which can be white, black, brown, red or beige; the colors can be plain, spotted or speckled. Therefore, identifying them is often by the characteristics of their fur and by their size.

Here is a brief description of the breeds.

### Classic Llama

This is the most common breed, and the term *classic* refers to the saddle-like pattern of its coat. The hair on its back is longer than the hair on the rest of its body.

Their fleece is rough to the touch, although the undercoat, next to the skin, is fine. When you comb it, you can see the fine hairs are thin.

Llamas do not have as much fiber on their legs, neck and head, but some have hair on their necks, which looks similar to a mane.

The breed is bigger compared to other breeds.

Classic llamas are hardy animals, and they can do well in almost any type of weather. Even in freezing situations, unlike other breeds, classic llamas will thrive, but they will not do well in hot, humid conditions.

This breed of llamas shed their fur when you brush them, so they do not need shearing. However, in extremely hot temperatures, shearing helps keep them cool.

### Silky Llama

These llamas are like the Wooly llama breed, but there are a few differences.

The breed is a cross between the Classic llama and the Wooly llama. They are also called *Medium llamas*. These animals typically have long hair around their body and neck and short hair on their heads, ears, and legs.

Their hair is shiny and has curls that frequently form locks. Their ever-growing hair has two layers; the top part is the guard hair, which is long and rough to touch while the undercoat is soft fleece.

Their shiny, curly hair gives the Silky llamas a beautiful appearance, but their curls and locks quickly get dirty. When they are out grazing in the field, the kinks in their hair can easily pick up lots of dirt – and it gets even worse when left un-sheared.

That can also happen when sheared incorrectly. For instance, barrel shearing, a popular method of sharing llamas, can also lead to dirty hair.

To prevent this, they should be sheared often. Frequent shearing will keep the curls and locks short and clean.

### Wooly Llama

This breed of llama is usually smaller than other breeds, and their name comes from their appearance. They have thick wool covering their body, particularly around their head, ears and neck.

Depending on the individual animal, the amount of fiber can be small, medium, or thick. Its fiber is fluffy, lofty and thick, with curls and a few interlocks. While their fur is like the Silky and Suri llamas, the only difference is that theirs is softer and not as shiny.

The Wooly llamas have just a single layer of fur and do not have an undercoat. Typically, they have only a few guard hairs, which refers to the hair found on the outer coat of an animal. Guard hair is rough to the touch, and it keeps the llama dry by repelling water.

Because of their unique characteristics, their coats can be used as a replacement for alpaca fiber. The hair on Wooly llamas is always growing and, if you decide to raise this breed, you will need to shear them often. Your location will determine how often and the reason for shearing them.

In warmer environments, you must shear them at least once a year. That way, the animal will not suffer from the heat. If you raise them in cold conditions, consider sharing them once in two years. Shearing in colder environments will help prevent the fiber from forming clumps.

### Suri Llama

"*Suri*" as a name was first used in describing alpacas. It became the name for this popular breed when people crossed llamas and alpacas. The word itself translates to the locks found in alpaca fibers.

These locks are a peculiar characteristic of this breed and are typically well defined, starting from the skin and ending at the tip of the hair strands. The locks in the Suri breed can be in different variations; the common ones look like corkscrews, while some are twisted.

When you hear the name, "Suri" the adjective "extreme" should come to mind. The hair on these animals is exceptionally smooth and shiny, short, soft and is similar to that of the Wooly llamas. The only difference is that the hair on the woolly llamas is a little finer than the Suri llama.

One problem with this breed, however, is there are few of them with about 100 in the whole of Europe and breeding is very difficult because there are so few.

# Breeds of Alpacas

Now that you've learned about the different breeds of llamas, let's talk about alpacas. Unlike llamas, alpacas have only two known breeds.

These are the *Huacaya* breed and the *Suri* breed; the Haucayas being the most popular of the two breeds. As of today, there are about 3.7 million alpacas in the world. Almost 90% of this population is thought to be of the Huacaya breed.

Differentiating the breeds can be tricky, even more so than with llamas. Unlike with llamas, both breeds of alpacas are almost the same size, and both have the same preferences in terms of living conditions.

Continue reading to discover the unique characteristics of these two breeds.

### Suri Alpaca

Like you already read, the name "Suri" is mainly used for the alpacas. According to archeologists, the breed is ancient, and research shows it could have existed for over 5000 years. Of the 3.7 million alpacas in the world, only about 370,000 are Suri alpacas.

The distinguishing feature of this breed is its fur. It is typically long with locks at the end, is shiny and dangles freely. Their hair is typically packed densely, is usually soft, and it feels greasy to the touch.

The hair covers the animals from their head to their toes. Interestingly, the hair is locked in all parts of their body, and besides the shiny appearance, the hair on the Suri Alpaca makes them look flat on the sides.

The fiber gleaned from the Suri breed is in high demand, with the highest demand coming from luxurious fashion stores. They use the fibers to produce luxury coats, sweaters, unique designer clothes and the choicest materials for interior decoration. Buyers often look for the shine as the primary characteristic of this quality product.

### Huacaya Alpaca

You might have seen an alpaca that looks like a teddy bear, and it's likely you saw a Huacaya Alpaca breed. Their teddy bear appearance comes from their densely packed wavy hair.

In terms of size, they are not bigger than the Suri breed, but their fluffy hair makes them look bigger.

Their colors are similar to those in the Suri breed, but differ slightly. The hair of the Huacaya breed can come in different shades of gray, while Suri breeds do not produce those colors.

Besides the hair color, Huacaya alpacas do not have markings. Their hair is plain and of almost uniform colors, unlike their Suri counterparts. Suri alpacas always have unique spots on their hair called *Appaloosa* markings, in different colors, sizes and shapes. For instance, you might find a white Suri Alpaca with some dark marks. Those are called Appaloosa marks, and they are generally absent in Huacaya breeds.

The colorful fur of the Huacaya breed is also of high demand, like in the Suri breed. The hair is usually used for clothing worn close to the body, and its fleece is softer than the fleece from sheep.

Though Huacaya alpacas are mainly bred for their fibers, their skin is also in high demand, and is used in producing many high-quality leather products.

The meat from Huacaya alpacas has also become popular recently. The meat is tender, has a mild flavor, and nutritionally, it is one of the healthiest meats in the world. It is high in protein, and low in cholesterol, saturated fat, and calories.

The meat is served in expensive Peruvian restaurants across the world.

# Other Closely Related Species

Just the way you have extended family members, alpacas and llamas have relatives. You might call them cousins.

Whichever name you choose, remember that these species are wild. They are considered wild because they do not stay around humans, preferring to live far away in the bush.

Due to their wild nature, little is known of these two species, known as the Guanaco and Vicuna species. The Guanaco's size lies between the llama and the alpaca and llamas are believed to have originated from them.

Similarly, alpacas are believed to have originated from the Vicunas. The Vicuna is light compared with the Guanaco, more delicate, and their fur commands a higher price. That explains why they are an endangered species in many countries.

With current advanced methods of breeding, some of these species have been crossed, resulting in offspring which have been given various names, often a combination of the parental breed names.

Now armed with all the historical and scientific knowledge about these breeds, let's move on to learning how to raise a llama or alpaca. In the following chapter, you will learn about the facilities and housing you need before obtaining one of these animals.

# Chapter 3: Facilities, Land, and Housing Requirements for Raising Llamas and Alpacas

*Quick Fact* - *The average llama weighs 280 to 450 pounds. They can carry between 25% and 30% of their own body weight so a male llama, for example, weighing in at 400 pounds, can carry between 100 and 120 pounds on a 10 to 12-mile trek without breaking a sweat.*

It's easy to get carried away with the excitement of starting a llama or alpaca farm. However, be sure to consider the one thing that matters most - *where to keep them.*

Note that the original habitat for this member of the camel family is in the arid, high altitude region of South America. However, if you know how to go about it, you can run a successful llama or alpaca farm in *any* area. This book will show you how.

Fortunately, preparing a home for the llamas or alpacas is not as difficult a task as it may seem. If you already have a barn on your property, you can start from there. However, you need to consider the barn's structure and determine if it will work for the animals. If not, you will need to build a new facility to house them.

When planning a new structure to house your new pets, your priority must always be the animal's safety, health, and comfort. As their caretakers, convenience comes into play. Considering these themes when planning and building the structure will result in a thriving farming experience.

# Indoor Housing Requirements for Llamas

Llamas and alpacas, by nature, can cope with most types of weather. However, for health and comfort, they require shelter from the wind, sun and rain. Loving – and needing – shade, large trees on your property will help protect your animals. However, if you have little tree coverage, a three-sided self-built shed will do, serving as a shield from the wind and the sun and providing a good place to train and handle your llamas or alpacas.

When considering the type of shelter needed, remember that freedom is a treasure for llamas and alpacas; they thrive on the freedom to come and go. Therefore, provide a shelter that gives the feeling of openness, using large windows and doors instead of dark sheds, which makes them feel shut in.

During the summer, llamas or alpacas may suffer heatstroke when the temperature and humidity rise so high. For this season, have sprinklers or misters to maintain their body temperature and help them cope with the climatic condition.

When it's the rainy season, and the ground becomes wet and soggy for an extended period, llamas need a place in their shelter where they can dry their feet every day. Also, this place serves as hay storage and water for continuous feeding. Foot-rot, though not common to llamas and alpacas, is caused by standing water, and is slow to heal.

Finally, in any climatic condition, it is best to have at least one stall where you can confine newborn babies and their mothers. The same goes for an ailing member of the herd for treatments. During the cold or damp season, wall-mounted lamps can help keep newborns warm.

Keep a close eye on baby llamas for at least the first two weeks after birth, especially when born during extreme weather conditions. During this period, they learn about their environment and seek comfort.

# Outdoor Living Requirements for Llamas

Llamas or alpacas need enough room to stretch and run. However, the required amount of outdoor space for keeping llamas isn't definite. While some farmers believe you can successfully maintain a llama herd with little or no space and a well-designed barn, some say at least half an acre is needed to give them the freedom they require.

But then, the balance to both schools of thought rests on the number of llamas and the type of farming you practice.

You can keep them indoors throughout the grooming days, and they'll turn out fine. You can also provide them with outdoor space to stretch and run. However, regardless of the type of farming you maintain, you need one or more large gates to allow the free movement of humans and equipment onto the farm premises.

Moving sick llamas or alpacas can be challenging. Therefore, a large gate that will enable the movement of vehicles – like tractors and a transport trailer - in and out is a must.

To offer enough outdoor space for them as a playground, consider a well-drained field. Llamas and alpacas dislike wet areas and will neither stand nor lay on a muddy, wet surface. If possible, raise the outer apron and interior floor with sand, decomposed granite, or crushed rock.

# Indoor and Outdoor Space Requirement

Barn space need not be large. However, you can plan by building a large barn when starting. That's because it's cost effective to have a large barn and allows your herd grow in number easily.

If you build a small barn from the onset, when your herd expands, there will be a non-negotiable need for more room, costing more than you had budgeted for. Best to consider building a larger-than-needed barn from the beginning.

Regardless of the size of the barn you build, it must have enough space to feed them. Also, include a space for catch pens in the barn's layout. Those spaces are reserved for important chores like animal grooming and administering of vaccines. They can also be useful when you need to separate and monitor sick llamas or alpacas and a place for your veterinarian to use during calls.

If you have or can spare some extra space, you can create a compartment to store hay and supplies. This method protects the hay from the weather and other animals and allows it to stay dry.

However, be careful about storing the hay close to the animal's barn; during a fire, excess hay becomes a propellant and accelerant and can promote fire. Smoking and other fire-related activities should be done a safe distance from your hay stores.

The time you spend in planning your llama's shelter is time well-spent; a critical step to the maintenance and growth of happy and healthy llama or alpaca herds.

# Barn and Shed Layout

As previously stated, llamas or alpacas are best kept in a three-sided barn or shelter. Here are a few tips that will help you in constructing this:

- Your shed should face east

The open side of the shed should face the east, as this direction is the most moderate in terms of weather.

- Create more than one door to the outside

Where you have more than a few llamas or alpacas, especially when you have more females, ensure you have more than one door to the outside because the "herd queen" likes to lie by the door. If there's only one door, it can prevent other llamas from accessing the outside. Avoid closing barn doors completely, as they need an escape route in the case of fire.

- Consider proper cross-ventilation

Add enough windows and openings for proper cross ventilation. Besides, a barn with plenty of doors and openings will remain cleaner.

- Cover the barn doors with hanging plastic

In winter months, you can cover the barn doors with hanging plastic, like you see at loading docks. It will protect them from rain, snow, and wind while still allowing them to go in and out without obstruction.

- Install air vents at the peak of the roof

Hot air rises toward the ceiling, so plan a high ceiling design so warm air can rise above the animals. Also, install air vents at the peak of the roof for the free outflow of hot air.

- Install fans for the summer season

Fans installed on the ceiling of barns help move hot air out of the barn and increase air circulation. Therefore, attach the fans to the barn ceiling at strategic points to blow directly at the animals.

- Install automatic heaters and water dispensers

You can include an automatic water dispenser in the barn plan and install a water heater to prevent freezing during the winter seasons. It could be a future installation but provide room for it when designing the barn.

- Use concrete flooring

You can use sand, Ag-lime, or concrete for the barn floor. However, for ease of cleaning, it's best to use a concrete floor as this can be easily cleaned by hosing down regularly.

For cushioning, cover the bathing area with a rubber mat. It also prevents wool from rubbing thin on the animal's knees.

The concrete flooring should have a rough finish to help keep the animal's toenails trimmed. Besides, a smooth surface can become slippery when dirty or wet.

- Consider Ag-Lime as a good flooring alternative

Ag-Lime, also called B-Lime, is another flooring type that works well in the shelter. Though it's a smooth powdery substance, it packs down like a hunk of concrete.

You can also use it in areas where llamas will pace, such as right outside the barn or gate opening. You'll find it useful as it prevents mud, making it easy to clean.

- Build a shallow wooded feeding trough

Along the walls of the barn, build a wood feeding trough – and make it shallow. This allows you to spread out the feed so they don't get too large a mouthful which can be a choking hazard.

Please make sure all animals get equal access to feed. Also, plan for a grain storage area for easy access to animal food.

Use metal storage containers that can prevent raccoons from getting in and gobbling up your grains.

- Use barn dividers

Use a twelve or sixteen-foot tall gate as the barn divider. Mount it on the wall so you can easily remove it if you need to make the area bigger or design it so you can swing it to one side to get a bobcat or cart into the space for cleaning.

- Build a hay feeder

Locate a hay feeder outside of the barn. It will encourage the animals to leave their shelter. However, ensure you cover the hay feeder to prevent the hay from getting wet from rain or overnight dew.

During the wet season, you can feed them hay inside the barn; remember, though, that requires more cleaning.

- Plan an area for storage

Plan an area where you can store halters or head-collars, groom supplies, and medical equipment.

You can also store hay over the llama's pens, but you must plan for an opening that allows you to drop the hay bales directly over the area you need. Again, try to store hay away from the animal barn because it can support fire outbreaks. It's best to keep hay in another barn or shelter and avoid smoking in the barns.

Finally, note that not all the points and items suggested above may be right for you, but these ideas can support how you plan your barn and make your herd management successful.

# Fencing and the Environment

The reason you need fencing around your farm is more about guarding against predators than keeping llamas or alpacas contained. Predators include coyotes, cougars, and dogs.

Dogs cause most of the predator attacks to llamas. Therefore, when planning or fencing your farm, your focus should be to guard against dogs; a fence that keeps out dogs will also keep out coyotes.

Dealing with the cougars is another ball game. A cougar will climb through any fencing if determined to do so; luckily, though, cougar attacks are rare. You should, therefore, focus more on controlling dog attacks, which are more common.

There are several fencing styles, and various types of materials can be used in building fences. However, when deciding the type of enclosure and materials to make your fence, functionality should be your determining factor.

Wire fencing is inexpensive. If you prevent it from getting buried in the soil, it can last for a long time. Border rail fences are also a good fencing option, but you will need to back them up with wire fencing. Combined, these two will effectively guard your farm against predators.

Avoid the use of barbed wire; while it might be adequate to keep predators out, it's dangerous to your herd. Any inattentive or curious llama can run into the fence or rub against it and get injured by the barbs.

A "No-Climb" fence is popular because it is safe, costs less, and has small openings. It's difficult for predators to climb because it's high.

You can install a "No-Climb" fence on metal, wood, or fiberglass post. It's the type of fence that keeps out almost all types of unwanted animals. Even animals that do not directly prey on llamas or alpacas can carry parasites or infectious diseases and should be kept away from your farm.

Another common type of fencing among alpaca and llama farmers is the "Multi-strand high tensile fencing." It is a type of fence that has multiple strands of variably-spaced wires. The wire is concentrated at the bottom and sparsely distributed at the top; this design stops predators from digging for access to the farm and prevents your llamas or alpacas from getting their heads stuck in the wire.

When constructing the fence, use treated wooden posts, metal, or a combination of both, spacing them about 8 to 12 feet apart. A five-foot-high fence is good enough, but remember that a motivated adult llama can jump a high fence. Even if that happens, the llamas or alpacas won't move far from the company of others, and you can easily entice them back with treats.

Cement the posts supporting braces, pulling posts, and corners to the ground. If your farm is on land that's not solid, you may need to cement *all posts*. Remember that it is more economical to build a strong and safe fence from the onset than to mend or rebuild flimsy ones when they can no longer keep predators out of the farm.

# Climatic Demands on Housing and Facilities

There are slight changes in housing and facilities demands as seasons come and go. Therefore, you need to familiarize yourself with the changes and know what to do during each season.

- Winter Requirements

A common misconception is that a llama's native habitat is a high-altitude, cold region. Although the native habitat has proximity to the equator, it provides an average temperature of 20 to 55 degrees F. While the temperature does drop at night, it rarely goes below 10 degrees F. With this in mind, farmers who nurture llamas or alpacas in a cold region will need to protect them.

A large, enclosed barn is the best protection when the temperature falls below 0 degrees. Enclose the barn with hanging plastic to reduce wind.

Llamas or alpacas with less wool will need special consideration during the cold; they must be watched for signs of hypothermia. Consider insulating and heating the barns as commonly done for livestock during winter. However, if you are going to enclose the barn, ensure adequate ventilation. You can install air vents at the peak of the roof for the free in/outflow of air.

Humidity can quickly build up in the barn, causing an outbreak of bronchitis and pneumonia within the herd.

As an alternative to heating the barn, you can encourage body heat by forcing the herd to cluster together in the shed or barn.

- Summer Requirements

In warm climates, shade - either in the form of built shed or trees - is essential, as llamas or alpacas dislike heat; high temps and humidity can cause heatstroke.

Large or normal circulating fans have also proven to be useful when indoor living spaces such as the barn get too hot.

In the heat, llamas and alpacas will stretch out in the sun, but they often find a means of cooling themselves, such as under a shade tree.

You can help them manage the heat throughout the hot summer seasons by providing them with a means of cooling, such as ponds, streams, wading pools, sprinklers, misters, etc. You can also provide a shaded area with sand where they can lay.

It would be best if you had accommodations in place before you consider raising a llama. With the suggestions and requirements outlined above, you should not find it hard to put such facilities in place, and maintain it based on the seasons.

Once you have all your housing facilities, you are ready to buy your first llama. The next chapter will teach you how to make the best choice for you.

# Chapter 4: Buying Your First Llama

*Quick Fact* - *Llamas are incredibly social animals and don't like to be alone. The social structure can change quickly in a herd; a male llama can change position in the herd by winning or losing fights with the herd leader.*

Now you're ready to buy your first llama so you have many factors to consider and steps to take. Llamas and alpacas are spectacular animals, and understanding these animals is important before setting off to buy your own.

Buying a llama becomes more straightforward once you clearly understand these unique animals.

## Things to Do and Consider When Buying Your First Llama

Llama-keeping can be likened to finding a new hobby; there are different aspects you must get acquainted with and rules to keep. Buying a llama isn't a decision to make because you're feeling blue or lonely, or on a whim. It must be a slow, thoughtful, and knowledgeable process. Here's a list of suggestions to help you in this important decision.

## 1. Research

Researching the animal and its care is crucial before investing in one. It's essential that you digest all the available information and possibly visit a llama farm to acquaint yourself with what owning one might be like.

It will also help you discover if the space where you intend to house them in is wide enough, or if you'll be paying a farm to house and care for it. After your research, you can determine if llama-keeping is a venture you are capable of undertaking.

## 2. Determine Why You Are Buying Llamas

Don't buy a llama just because you feel like it, or because you like how they look. You might be setting yourself up for more than you bargained. If you're looking to breed llamas, then you should look for females rather than geldings.

You'll need to determine how old your llama should be and what it weighs, if you will keep them as pets, for parking, or cart driving. In all, you should have a specific reason in mind for buying one, as it will help you decide what you need.

## 3. Where You'll Be Buying From

The excitement of owning a llama, after months – or maybe years – of waiting, should not make you jump on the first opportunity to buy one. Where you're buying your llama is as important as how you'll care for it. You need the history of the llama's life and behavior.

A random llama seller might not provide you with all the information you need to care for it. That's why it's best to buy from a trusted breeder rather than brokers or an auction. You risk not getting the type needed for the purpose you intend, and worse, it could be sickly.

## 4. Space

Like any other herd animal, llamas need sufficient space and room to roam. If your backyard space isn't very large, you may still house two llamas there. However, if you love llamas but you don't have enough room to accommodate them, then you can consider boarding them with the local breeders near you.

Some ranches may house them, so all you need to do your homework before purchasing your llama. If you can't find one available, your seller might board your animals, so you can still a proud llama owner – even if you're short on space.

### 5. Consider the Herd-Nature of Llamas

It's okay to fall in love with these intelligent animals and want to bring them home. However, note that they are only at their best when other llamas are around.

So, if you are thinking of buying a llama, you will probably need to go home with at least two same-sex llamas. You can also board them with others until you buy your next llama.

You may buy just one, only if it'll be serving as a guard to your sheep herd.

### 6. Time and Care

One secret behind the calmness of llamas is attention and care. It will help if you have plenty of time to care for its needs. These animals need at least one monthly routine vet check, regular fur-shearing, and nail-trimming.

When you're getting a llama, you need to pour all the love you can into its care. Your llama will feel more confident around you when it receives care and attention from you.

Ensure that you have the time to check up on them to ascertain they are in good condition. If you're too busy and can't get someone to do these things in your absence, then you might want to reconsider keeping one.

# Dos and Don'ts When Buying Your First Llama

There are so many things to consider when you want to buy llamas. The rules may seem overwhelming at first, but it's all for your sanity and the wellbeing of the animals you're buying.

There are certain dos-and-don't that will help make your purchase go smoothly. Here is a list for your consideration:

• Never buy a llama without educating yourself

Knowing all you need to know about llamas puts you at an advantage when you eventually buy one. You need to have the right knowledge as you risk trouble if you purchase without adequately understanding these unique animals.

- Never buy your first llama without observing it

Observing it doesn't mean lifting it, turning its back down and legs up, to do a thorough check. It means spending time visiting a llama farm to watch how llamas live, how they are taken care of, and how they behave.

Observing means you know everything that goes on around the farm every time you visit. See how the animals are led, trained, haltered, and managed. It will show you what you're venturing into and help you imagine yourself doing the same thing.

- Don't forget to ask questions

You need all the information you can get; therefore, it's essential to visit the farm as many times as possible. You'll be able to ask questions about anything that you don't understand, and possibly spot the llama or llamas you wish to buy.

You'll need to ask questions about the health records of the animals as they give a possible indication of the health status of your prospective purchase. Ask about how they are vaccinated, how often, about the vet, and what to expect after buying one. Some farms will offer free breeding, follow-up, or even delivery. Do not pay for a llama until everything is fully spelled out.

- Do a pre-purchase examination

Have a vet help examine the animals before you purchase; it's always easier to take a professional's word than that of the person looking to sell the llama. A pre-purchase examination by a vet makes the whole process easier and even helps to spot problems that the seller might be unaware of.

- Don't purchase your first llama from an auction

It's usually unwise to purchase your first llama from an auction. It's a risky venture for many reasons. Purchasing your first llama from an auction won't afford you the privilege to observe, check, and ask questions like you'd have done if you were buying from a farm. A lot might go wrong with the animal after purchasing it, and you might not have access to its health records. Plus, you might never get to know if the animals were auctioned due to an underlying problem. Finally, it will be difficult to ascertain if the animal is the best fit for what you had in mind.

- Pay attention to the personality of the llama you're buying

Like humans, llamas also have their unique personalities, strengths, and weaknesses. Seek to discover those and possibly ask the seller once you spot a pair of llamas want to take home. Don't fall for the trick of believing that there is a perfect llama. Your job is to get acquainted with the possible difficulties buying a particular type might bring and ask yourself if *you're willing to deal with them.*

- Never buy just one llama

Llamas hate to be alone, turning mean and depressed when out of the herd. You don't want an unhappy llama around you. So, never buy a single llama!

Any seller willing to sell only one to you, despite knowing that you've never owned one, should be avoided. They are probably interested in your money and not in your sanity, much less the llama's wellbeing.

- Don't buy a pair (male and female)

The possibility of buying a male and female might seem like a juicy idea, especially if you're looking to raise a herd to sell later. However, consider that a male and female kept together will repeatedly breed, a practice that will eventually lead to infections for both animals. If you're looking to breed, it's better to buy same-sex pairs.

There's no point purchasing opposite-sex pairs if you aren't interested in breeding in the first place.

- Don't buy a llama you've never seen

It's normal to get deals off the internet and even be furnished with enough information to help you make a decision. However, it's better to seek a seller if they are around your locality. Please don't buy a llama off the internet that you've never seen, touched, or observed.

- Visit several llama farms

You deserve the best deal for your money and won't possibly get that visiting only a single breeder. Visit many llama farms, observe their practices, and familiarize yourself with their terms before buying.

- Don't purchase a llama without a written contract

A written contract keeps the seller accountable for all the post-sales services promised. Having the agreement in writing makes it easier to refer to the terms when things go wrong, rather than guessing what was agreed upon.

You can more easily hold the seller responsible to fulfill his part of the contract when it's written in a contract.

# How to Spot a Good Llama Breed to Buy

Now that you know all you need to do and not do when buying your first llama, you're ready to go! These crucial points will help you know the right llama breed to buy.

### 1. The Reputation of the Breeder

The breeder's reputation will help determine what breed of llama to buy. Therefore, it is essential to check with many breeders and observe their practices. A breeder of repute will be a member of llama associations and have their animals registered on the international llama registry.

The breeder will also breed young llamas responsibly without mass-producing them like dog pups. Anywhere you find more than a maximum of five *crias* (baby llamas or alpacas) in a breeding farm, it indicates that the breeder may not be caring for their animals properly.

### 2. The Seller has Good Knowledge and Record of the Animals

How a seller engages with his llamas will reflect the quality of care they've received and helps you to decide if the investment is worth it. How much knowledge the seller displays about the animal's health and history will also help to determine the choice you make.

A good breed will reflect a long history of attention and care from the seller, and the risk of future problems after purchase will be minimal.

### 3. Quality of Veterinary Attention

The quality of veterinary attention that the llama breed has received over time will help you determine what quality you're paying for. If the llamas are regularly vaccinated, routinely checked, and have an overall record of good health, then you know you've found a good breed.

### 4. Excellent Conditions from Observation

What you observed during your visits will also determine if you've found the right breed. Consider whether the animals look healthy or underweight, have clean bodies, have sores or other apparent indicators of how well they were cared for.

Were you able to take them for a walk? How did the animals respond to being led or haltered? Have they been trained? These steps provide necessary indicators for determining if you've found the right breed or if you should continue looking, depending on how you intend to use them. If they look sickly, malnourished, unkempt with untrimmed nails, and un-sheared fur, those might be the red flags for considering looking for a new place to buy from.

### 5. The Llamas are Independent

Now, the llamas may develop a liking for you when you show up around them consistently; still, they shouldn't be following you about!

When the animals are too friendly around you, then you shouldn't go for those breeds. It's dangerous for them to always want to be around you; they are livestock, not dogs.

When the llamas are friendly yet independent, consider them. The seemingly too-nice ones can turn out quite mean – especially when they don't get the attention they expect.

### 6. Sufficient Weaning and Milking

First, go for breeds weaned appropriately in five to six months. Breeds weaned earlier may be underweight, prove dangerous, and prone to infection and diseases later.

If you're looking for a female and intend to breed her, it's essential to find one whose mother milked well. If the mother was a light milker, she might also be a light milker which can pose problems for you later.

### 7. Good Genetic History

An expensive llama with an excellent genetic history will yield more overall benefits than a cheaper one with a history of genetic problems. Therefore, it's essential to ask your breeder about possible genetic problems in your prospective llamas.

# How to Get a Good Deal on Your First Llama

Finally, it's time to get your first llama, but you're not sure about pricing; you can get a good deal on your first llama without emptying your purse.

Llama prices will always fall within three categories - cheap, moderately priced, and expensive. These animals vary in price due to quality of care, age, and individual breeder ratings. Some breeders offer an all-inclusive post-sale service, which might also create higher prices.

A free or cheap llama often has several reasons for being inexpensive, and you should find out why they are being sold for less.

On average, llamas should cost between $1500 and $5000. Finding a llama way lower than that amount shouldn't excite you so much as make you *curious*. Once you've been filled in on the condition of the llama and you are content with dealing with all the possible outcomes from that purchase, then you can move ahead.

Many factors determine your moderately-priced purchase. These factors include the age, quality of breeding, healthiness, weight, and strength of the llama. Checking prices with several farms will help you note if a seller is unreasonably hiking prices. But generally, well-bred llamas won't cost a fortune.

Some llamas will cost more, especially if you'll be boarding them with the seller because of lack of space or herd. You'll need to pay for all the care, feeding, and medical care. A pregnant llama will cost more than a non-pregnant female.

Carefully consider all the factors underlying your purchase as it determines how much you pay. Llama prices are relative from place to place, but ensure you're looking out for quality animals when seeking the best deals.

### Conclusion

Buying a llama is not child's play, and you must be ready to undertake all the sacrifices in exchange for the thrill of owning these intelligent animals. Remember, if you are coming home with your first llama, it shouldn't be with just one llama, *but two.*

Ensure you have all it takes to host two or more llamas and prepare yourself mentally and financially for your new furry friends. Now that you know how to purchase and house a llama, you must learn their behaviors.

# Chapter 5: Llama Behavior and Handling

*Quick Fact* - *Llama's rarely bite. However, they will spit when upset or agitated, but usually at one another, not at people. They also neck wrestle and kick each other when upset, but they don't tend to attack humans - unless you upset them.*

You need to know everything about llama behavior to properly care for them. It's important to be able to predict and understand their reactions. Interestingly, llamas are easy animals to care for, especially when you know how they behave.

In this chapter, you will discover everything you need to know about their behavior and ways to handle them. Now, let's dive in!

## What Behaviors Does a Llama Exhibit?

A llama is an intelligent animal that can be easily trained; with one to five repetitions, they will learn and remember many skills. You can instruct them to do lots of things, such as accepting a halter and being led on a lead.

They can quickly adapt to training like pulling a cart, carrying a pack, and getting into and out of a carriage vehicle. Llamas are friendly animals, but they need the companionship of their kind.

Llamas are gentle, shy and curious animals; they are calm and have common sense, making them easy for anyone, even children, to handle. Llamas are enjoyable animals, and they are fun when doing things; however, most are not attention seekers and do not like to be handled excessively.

# Do Llamas Spit?

Yes, llamas can spit, and it is one way they communicate with each other and display anger. Other means of communication with each other include ear position, humming, and body language.

Llamas usually spit at other llamas to establish dominance, but do not spit at people. If llamas spit at other llamas while in the barn, it is usually at feeding time when personal space gets invaded.

Llamas also spit as a defense mechanism. However, before they spit, they usually elongate their necks and heads upwards to show displeasure – that's their warning sign. If you read this body language correctly, you can steer clear!

Llamas won't spit at you unless they feel confined or perceive that they are in danger. Like dogs don't bite people without reason, these animals only spit when provoked as a defensive mechanism.

Llamas make a "mwa" or groaning sound to show anger or fear and put their ears back when agitated. You can also know how agitated the llama is from the content in the spit. When they are very disturbed, they draw materials from their innermost stomach, bringing up green, sticky cud from its depths. Try not to get caught in the path when llamas spit because it can get incredibly nasty!

When you train these animals correctly, llamas will rarely spit at a human. They might sometimes spit at each other to discipline lower-ranked llamas, as they are social herd animals. Llamas can climb the social ladder in their ranks by picking fights. You'll mostly witness these fights between male llamas to get the alpha position.

These fights between llamas can be entertaining. They spit, ram each other with their chests, wrestle with their necks, and kick to knock the other off balance. The female llamas usually spit to control other herd members.

You remember we talked about the llamas' need for the companionship of its kind. Now let's talk about companionship.

## Companionship

As a herd animal, a llama needs other llamas. Therefore, you should have, at the very least, at least two llamas in your pasture. It is sad to see a llama alone, and even if you want the llamas to guard your sheep, get at least two for that purpose, as they are more effective when working with a companion. Their keen eyesight helps them remain vigilant of their surroundings and they have a natural curiosity, which makes them want to see and sniff everything.

## Berserk Males

One cannot discuss llama behavior without touching on Berserk Male Syndrome, also known as "Novice Handler Syndrome" or "Berserk Alpaca Syndrome." It is a behavioral syndrome caused by humans when they incorrectly interact with young males (llama). The llama can exhibit aggressive behavior and humans misinterpret the aggressive behavior as friendliness.

## Fast Runners

Llamas can run fast. The average dog can move at about 30 to 40 kilometers per hour; a llama, when it gets a sprint on, can move at over 60 kilometers an hour. This a great protective mechanism as it means they can outrun many predators.

## Mating

When discussing llama behavior, mating is a topic you will hear a lot about. You should not hinder an aggressive male during mating as he will be preoccupied with completing his task and you could easily get hurt.

When you add the elements of different environments and females, you will see more differences in the llama male temperament. However, it is not only llama males with temperament variations. Female llamas also exhibit moodiness, and an untrained female llama's personality might change when a male approaches for mating. Even the crabbiest llama can turn sweet and docile during the mating session.

There are always llamas watching as spectators during mating. Any untrained female will lay close to the mating couple while the trained females will usually stay back and watch as if the process is for their entertainment.

### Pregnancy

Pregnant llamas also change their personality. A friendly llama can become aloof, while a quiet and quirky llama can become spunky. They are affected by the change in hormones, and you can see it in the dramatic shift in their behaviors.

# How Do They Communicate? Llama Sounds

Being herd animals, llamas communicate using several sounds.

### 1. Llama Humming

These animals use this sound to communicate from birth, similar to human humming. Llamas make this sound when worried, distraught, tired, anxious, or curious. A mother llama may also hum to welcome her newborn. This sound helps them communicate and stay connected.

### 2. Clucking

This sound is like a human clicking their tongue on the roof of their mouth. When llamas cluck, they typically hold back their ears. This sound expresses concern or signals friendliness, use it to greet new llamas or flirt with females.

### 3. Llama Ogling

This sound is like a person is gargling. Male llamas make this sound when going close to a female for breeding. It continues to sound that way until the copulation completes, and may go on for twenty minutes to an hour.

### 4. Llama Alarm Call

Llamas make this call when they sense fear or get surprised by something. The sound is loud, high-pitched, and rhythmic, and alerts others in the herd that a predator is nearby (especially dogs).

Llamas travel in herds when they are in the wild. When one animal notices a predator, they make this sound to alert the others.

### 5. Snorting

Llamas will snort when another llama is invading their space, usually as a warning message to move away. Not all llamas snort, but the ones that do snort often.

### 6. Screaming

When a llama screams, it is as if someone is blowing a siren next to your ear because they are loud! Llamas will scream only when they are not handled correctly. They also communicate their moods with a series of tail, body, and ear postures.

Just like humans, llamas are unique. Not all are smart, nice, or agreeable, and figuring out the core behavior of a llama will help you modify their behavior, or at least accommodate it.

# Llama Handling

Although llamas are not animals to be overly-pampered, there are still guidelines you need to follow when handling them. To an extent, llamas are emotional animals and, as members of the camelid family, they have several traits similar to the camel. This means you can use camel treatment guidelines to handle your llamas.

Llamas are herding animals, making them averse to separation. One way to handle such a situation is to keep dividing the llamas into smaller groups. You will need to repeat this process until you select the one you need from a relatively small group. Be careful so as not to threaten or scare the animals, avoid sudden movements.

If you must remove just one llama from its herd for treatment or another purpose, specific procedures must be followed.

### How Can I Separate One?

Try to approach the llama slowly and get hold of its head. Do not be forceful, but try to ensure a firm grip using your arm and shoulder. The llama may try to keep you from taking it – and sometimes in a forceful manner but there are a few tricks you can use in restraining it.

You can apply the earing technique: press down the head of the llama and firmly hold its outer ear. This technique is commonly used on camels and horses.

Also, you can press down the shoulder of the llama, placing your hands firmly at the neck base.

The midline catch is another brilliant way to catch them. The llama should be in a position where it aligns with the pen with its head in a corner. This positioning gives a smooth and steady movement from a place behind the eye. Place the back of your hand on its lower neck and then slide the hand up behind the ears as you step in to bring the other hand under the chin. Place your forefinger and thumb into the groove of the lower jaw, giving you a *bracelet hold* on it. The grip helps to keep the animal steady.

Some llamas can be cornered and grabbed around the neck for husbandry, but are likely to make a run for it. You can use a catch rope and wand to catch the animal without trapping it and entering its flight zone. When you do, the llama stands still. At that point, you can move closer. However, be aware of the llama's body position, then approach.

With the rope around its neck, you will be at a vantage point to help the animal gain balance and behavior properly. Maintain a safe distance from the llama. With this stance, you will not be a threat to it.

In handling llamas, you will need equipment that can be easily bought or improvised. Ropes are the most common equipment.

Do not use the rope for holding the animal still; instead, keep it tight enough to shut off its escape route. It might trigger the flight instinct in the animal, so it's best to use the pen as containment for the animal – not the rope.

Put your arm around the neck to maintain its balance; being pulled off balance by a handler creates panic in the animal. A llama in balance will carry about 67 percent of its bodyweight over the front. The remaining 33 percent will be over the rear legs with the head held in line over the neck and shoulders.

### How Do I Treat Llamas?

The above procedures will allow you to complete your examination without unnecessary stress. Injections can be given in the triceps, or in the angle of the neck and shoulder but, when injecting the llama, lean over the animal so movement will not displace the needle.

When you carry out a blood test on your llama, crouch down to do it as this position will conceal quick and sudden movements that might frighten off the animal.

Llamas pose handling challenges because of their size and strength. Those with less-dense fleece are easier to examine, but if a llama cannot stand still for necessary procedures such as brushing, it likely will not be calm during veterinary processes.

In such cases, you can apply the techniques explained earlier, to give the animal the chance to stand independently.

### How Do I Fix a Halter for Llamas?

A well-designed halter is recommended to help your animals balance effectively. It is a comfortable and useful tool used in communicating with camelid animals, especially the llama.

Camelids breathe through their nose. For this reason, you should use halters that do not slip forward on the nose, compressing the nasal cartilage. To prevent such incidents, tightly secure the crown piece behind the llama's ears. The halter you choose must be comfortable. You will know it is comfortable when there is enough room in the nose cavity for the llama to eat and ruminate. A perfect halter sits comfortably on the llama's head rather than on its nose.

Sometimes, it may seem impossible to conduct an examination, and thus, you require alternative plans. Do not chase your frightened animal; you may be risking an injury to yourself and/or the llama.

If necessary, reschedule examinations rather than putting your animal (or yourself) at risk. Get assistance from more experienced handlers or, in more serious cases, sedate it.

With these simple procedures in place, handling them will not be a problem. Taking time to study llamas will help you know how to deal with them in any situation.

# Chapter 6: Llama Nutrition and Feeding

*Quick Fact* - *Llamas are vegetarian, and their digestive systems are incredibly efficient. They have three compartments in their stomachs - the rumen, the omasum, and the abomasum. They regurgitate their food and re-chew it several times to completely digest it, a process called chewing the cud.*

Llamas belong to a group of animals called the New World Camelid. Nutrition and feeding are unique because they have a significantly different digestive system from that of a typical ruminant, with a higher digestibility coefficient.

In this chapter, we will explore the llama digestive system, their nutritional requirements, and feeding recommendations, briefly exploring things you shouldn't feed them.

## The Llama Digestive System

You might be wondering why it is essential to understand their digestive system. Llamas are not considered true ruminants. They are a modified ruminant because they have one stomach with three compartments compared to the true ruminants, which have four compartments.

Llamas only chew their food enough to mix it with saliva to lubricate the food and help it pass down the esophagus to the first compartment called the rumen. The esophagus is directly connected to the rumen and, in adult animals, may be as long as four feet.

The first compartment is about 83% of the total stomach volume; it is full of bacteria, and it is where the fermentation process begins. This bacteria is crucial to their nutrition, so if you upset the population of the bacteria, it can negatively affect their health.

You must be careful what you feed them and how you make changes to their diet. There is a water-like substance in this compartment which breaks down the cells of the plants and absorbs the nutrients; an imbalance might spell trouble for your llama's digestion.

The substance in the first compartment moves to the second compartment for further fermentation. Little activity happens here, and the second compartment is about 6% of the total stomach volume.

The third is full of stomach acid, which aid in the digestion of food. The stomach acid splashes on the cell membranes of the substance eaten, and once the cell bursts, it disperses the nutrients and energy from the food.

The bacteria that aided the fermentation process in the first and second compartments will be digested in the third compartment. It provides protein and is also a major source of amino acids.

The pH in the first and second compartments is neutral, while in the third compartment, it is acidic. Therefore, llamas can develop ulcers if they are not adequately fed. The nitrogen balance in their stomach is also crucial. They recycle urea so the bacteria in the stomach can synthesize the protein.

Llamas chew their food in a figure-eight motion. Once llamas chew and swallow their food, it goes to the other compartments of the stomach. The llamas then regurgitate their food and chew it again, repeating the process up to 75 times.

If you closely observe your llama, you will notice a bubble-like lump (known as the cud) moving up its neck. Therefore, regurgitating is known as *chewing the cud.*

It is essential to keep their digestive system in balance. Llamas needs microorganisms to break down cellulose, protein and urea and to keep them healthy; the microbe's population must not be upset.

What does this mean? If you are taking them to another farm or a new environment, provide them with the food they were used to eating and then slowly add new feed to its diet. If they will be doing strenuous activities, it is crucial not to change their diet. You can also add probiotics to ease their stress. A balanced and healthy microbial population in the stomach equals a healthy llama.

# Digestive Disorders in Llamas

Digestive disorders are diseases or disorders associated with the digestive tract, also called *gastrointestinal* disorders. The clinical signs are anorexia, abdominal distension, depression, increased pulse, subnormal temperature, and colic.

However, these signs are not diagnostic, so additional tests should be done to confirm. Some gastrointestinal disorders are explained below.

### Mega-esophagus

Mega-esophagus is a digestive disorder in which the esophagus dilates (gets larger) and loses motility (the ability to move food into the stomach). When this happens, food substances accumulate in the esophagus and have difficulty moving on to the stomach.

Dilatation of the esophagus is relatively common in llamas, especially after instances of choking. Common signs of mega-esophagus are chronic weight loss and postprandial regurgitation of food. The exact cause of this disorder is unknown and there is no treatment. Some animals can maintain the condition for an extended period, while others will continue to lose weight.

### Stomach Atony

Stomach atony is a rare gastrointestinal disorder in llamas, and the cause of this disorder is unknown. Common signs are reduced or complete cessation of food consumption, depression, and loss of body condition. Other gastrointestinal problems, like diarrhea, may also occur. Fluid consumption is one way to correct this disorder.

### Ulcers

Ulcers in llamas develop in the third compartment because of the stomach acid present there. Common signs are decreased food consumption, depression, and intermittent to severe colic and stress is also a significant factor. No particular treatment is recommended, but is usually based on clinical signs and history. Administration of omeprazole can help reduce acid production. Stress reduction, parenteral antibiotics, and other supportive therapy can aid the recovery process.

### Hepatic Disease

Hepatic disease is a relatively common problem in llamas. It can be caused by stress or abrupt change in the diet or feed. Common signs are diminished growth, ill thrift (when their growth rate is slower than expected) and acute death. Treatment is usually based on specific symptoms, but increased serum bile acids and enzyme concentrations can aid the recovery process. The mortality rate in untreated animals is relatively high, so if you notice the signs, you must give them the appropriate treatment.

### Diarrhea

This gastrointestinal disorder is not common in llamas. The primary causes of diarrhea include cryptosporidium, rotavirus, coronavirus, and enteropathogenic strains of Escherichia coli. Some crias (baby llamas) may also experience transitory diarrhea 2–3 weeks after birth, but diarrhea in older llamas is usually caused by infection or associated with a change in feed.

### Constipation and Indigestion

Clinical treatment is recommended for this gastrointestinal disorder and diet modification. In young llamas, bladder rupture, retained meconium, and clostridial enterotoxemia should be considered.

### Bloat

Bloat is a gastrointestinal condition of hyperacidity from grain overload, traumatic reticuloperitonitis and abomasal displacement. This gastrointestinal disorder is not common in llamas.

# Prevention and Treatment Therapy for Gastrointestinal Disorders in Llamas

The treatment for gastrointestinal disorders in llamas is similar to that of domestic ruminants. However, when signs of acute abdomen disorders are observed, it should be treated as an emergency condition requiring immediate care.

With ulcers, transplantation of the stomach contents from another llama or cow can be helpful. Using mineral oil, vinegar and bicarbonate can also help, especially when the atony is related to grain overload.

Most of the gastrointestinal disorders are caused by their diet. Llamas should be fed mostly legume pastures and mixed grasses. You can also add a concentrate supplementation if your llama requires a lot of energy, especially pregnant/lactating and packing llamas.

### Nutritional Requirements for Llamas

You must know the llama's nutritional requirement as it is essential to raising a healthy producing herd. The dietary requirements will affect their reproduction, the health of their crias (baby llama), heat stress, wool quality, and milk production.

The nutritional requirement may vary slightly depending on what purpose your llamas are serving, your location, and the pasture you provide for them. But generally, the llama's diet should consist of fiber, protein, salt, calcium, phosphorus, minerals, and vitamins.

### Fiber and Energy

The major sources of energy in their diet are pastures and hay. Good leafy grass hay that is not dusty or moldy will provide the fiber and energy required. A grain like corn is also a high-energy source, and it can be added to their diet to help them get the energy they need to stay strong and healthy.

However, it should be added in the right proportion. Llamas in late gestation or early lactation can have 3/4 lb. of cracked corn added to their diet to give them the energy they require. Cracked corn can be added to the expectant mother's diet about four to six weeks before the delivery date.

You can also continue the feeding it after birth, especially if the mother loses a lot of weight after giving birth. She will also require higher energy, as she will be feeding her cria.

You should, however, note that grains like oats or corn should be used only as supplemental high-energy sources and not as the primary energy source in their diet. Grains should also not be given in extremely hot weather conditions.

## Protein

The protein requirement for llamas is relatively low. Usually, good leafy grass hay will provide the required protein intake for your llama. However, where protein supplement is necessary (lactation or cold weather), you can add 50% alfalfa hay to their diet. However, it must only be fed as a supplement, not as their main feed because of the high level of protein in it. Alfalfa hay is the most likely culprit for fat pads in the mammary tissue, and it negatively affects the crias by adding excess fat during their primary growing season.

Also, excess calcium obtained from alfalfa hay will upset the Calcium (Ca) – Phosphorus (P) balance, which is vital for the rapid growth of your crias. The deficiencies and imbalance of calcium and phosphorous can cause abnormal bone growth formation, like bowed legs. This happens when the mother or crias eats too much alfalfa.

Be careful with the amount of protein you feed your llamas. A 6-10 percent protein content is recommended, though crias may have a higher requirement of about 16 percent. The quality of the pasture and the protein content is higher in the spring when plants are growing actively.

### Salt, Vitamins, Calcium, and Phosphorus

Salt, vitamins, calcium, and phosphorus are also a good supplement (feed). These nutrients are essential for their wellbeing, but you must regulate how these supplements are fed, ensuring they are administered evenly.

The most efficient way to feed and control their dietary needs is by providing them the supplement by way of a pellet only. Mixing the minerals and vitamins as powders, loose grains, and pellets do not allow for a controllable and consistent diet.

The ingredients will not be evenly distributed, as most of it will fall to the bottom of the bag. Keep the pellet size at about 1/8 inches to prevent choking. If your llama chokes while feeding on the pellet, stop feeding it for a couple of days. You can then slowly introduce the pellet back into its feed.

The supplement usually contains all the vitamins, minerals, and salt. However, you need also to give them a loose trace mineral mix as the absence of a trace mineral like selenium in their diet can cause problems. Your animals might experience weak crias, growth problems, white muscle disease, lactation, and even reproduction issues.

Check the selenium level of your animals at random when you take their blood for a periodic checkup. If the selenium level is above 150 to 200, it is normal. However, anything below 150 is cause for concern.

Llamas also need a lot of Vitamin E in their diet. The Vitamin E in dried forages is not sufficient so give them supplements; lack of or insufficiency of Vitamin E in llamas shows up as crooked legs and the development of weak crias.

Ensure you feed them a balanced diet in hot, humid weather as it will help them fight the heat stress. You might also have to up the dosage of supplements when your animals are in late gestation, early lactation, and in freezing weather.

While understanding the nutrition of llamas can be complicated and a bit confusing, it is essential knowledge to breed a healthy and strong herd. They can eat different feeds without you watching them and still appear to do fine. However, the problems will eventually show up. It can be in birthing problems, costly veterinarian bills for sicknesses – or even death.

Provide routine checkups to monitor the health of your animals. Perform their blood tests regularly and randomly check the llama's selenium level. Checkups should include calcium and phosphorus balance tests, and protein levels with a CBC.

Occasionally, you can do an IgG (immunoglobulin) blood test to see what their zinc and copper levels are. Also weigh them periodically and keep a record to ensure you know their overall health and wellbeing.

# Feeding Recommendation for Llamas

Llamas are adaptive feeders, eating grasses, shrubs, forbs (herbaceous broadleaf vegetation, non-woody) and trees. They are herbivores, grazers and browsers. They need fiber, energy, vitamins and protein to remain healthy and they receive energy and fiber by eating hay, corn, pasture and oats.

For protein sources, you can feed them alfalfa hay, grass hay, and geldings. Llamas also have a high requirement for vitamin C, which can be obtained from pellets or powder. Also, water always needs to be available.

Alfalfa hay is a good choice of hay. However, avoid using it all time for feed, complementing it with mixed pastures like grass and legumes. You can also supplement their diet with grain or concentrates if they will be used as pack animals.

An adult llama will consume about 2 percent of its body weight per day. That can increase to 3 percent if they are packing, pulling carriages or any other activity, or to 4 percent if it's pregnant or lactating. On average, llamas require about one bale of hay a week or a pound of hay a day.

You can feed approximately three to five llamas per acre depending on the quality of the pasture. You can also practice rotational grazing of llamas to help utilize the pasture to a greater extent. Using fields to meet most of their nutritional requirements is cost effective because pasture is less costly than purchasing supplemental hay or grains.

An essential factor in the feeding and diet is regularity and consistency. The suggested daily feeding proportions are 1 lb. supplements (grain), 5 lbs. from pasture and hay, plus some free trace minerals.

# Things to Avoid Feeding Your Llamas

### 1. Cantharidins (Blister Beetle Poison)

Cantharidin is a toxic terpenoid substance secreted by blister beetles and can harm or kill your herd, and with only a tiny quantity ingested, your animal will be in danger. Llamas can ingest cantharidin in alfalfa hay infested by blister beetles.

Therefore, inspect the alfalfa hay thoroughly before you feed it to them. When the alfalfa hay has an oily-looking substance, then it's likely that blister beetles have infested it. Do not feed that hay to them.

Llamas that have eaten a large amount of this toxin will show signs of shock, and, unfortunately, die within hours. Symptoms of cantharidin poisoning are depression, elevated temperature, diarrhea, frequent urination and increased pulse.

If you think they have eaten cantharidin, contact the veterinarian immediately. If the antidote is given to the animal immediately, maybe it will survive. However, if the animal has eaten a large amount, it may not survive.

### 2. High Copper Content Feeds

A high copper content can be harmful to your llama, and some studies show that feeds with high copper content can cause spontaneous abortion. Feeds such as cow minerals, pig minerals, or chicken food may lead to copper toxicity. When your animal has copper toxicity, it will have copper-colored urine and a sweet smell.

### 3. Too Many Grains

You should not give them too many grains, as it can lead to grain overload or poisoning. This results from the carbohydrates fermenting in the animal's stomach instead of getting digested. Lactic acid is produced, which causes dehydration and slowing of the gut – sometimes death.

Barley and wheat are the biggest causes of grain overload, along with excess oats and lupins. Also, a sudden switch of your llama's diet to grain can cause grain overload; therefore, regularity and consistency are essential with their nutrition and feeding.

### 4. Feed with a High Level of Protein Content

High protein content in their diet can lead to complications, primarily adding fat to the mammary pads and obesity. Plus, crias ingesting too much protein will gain excessive weight quickly, which is detrimental to their health. In breeding females obesity can add to heat stress, a lack of milk production and dystocia, which is otherwise defined as a "difficult birth."

### 5. Sweet Feed

Avoid feeding them sweet feeds as high amounts of sugar and starch can cause digestive upsets like acidosis and bloat.

# Chapter 7: Llama Health and Disease Prevention

*Quick Fact* - *A llama is a hardy animal and can easily navigate harsh environments. They are sure-footed and can traverse difficult terrain at high altitudes. However, although they make great pack animals, they do know their limits. Try to put too much weight on a llama and it will simply refuse to move or lie down.*

As hardy as they are, llamas and alpacas get sick and their diseases can be difficult to spot. While some conditions are easy to recognize, many others are not detectable until they are severely ill. Often, a sick animal behaves just like a healthy one.

Unlike you, your llama or alpaca cannot talk. Even if they are in pain, they cannot communicate their displeasure to you in words. To identify changes in their normal behavior, you must be observant and understand the animal's normal behavior so you can spot anything outside of the ordinary.

In this chapter, we will examine diseases that affect lamas and alpacas. We also will look at ways to prevent them from getting sick.

# Dangerous Diseases that Affect Llamas and Alpacas

You have probably heard about communicable and non-communicable diseases, and we'll be looking briefly at both.

But first, what causes diseases? A lot of things can make an animal sick. Animals are comprised of chemical and biological systems, and in a healthy animal there's a balance between these systems. An animal becomes ill when this delicate balance is disturbed. In other instances, the cause of the disease is genetic.

But diseases can be caused by the intake of chemicals (or drugs) that act as a toxic agent to tip the delicate balance of health.

In genetic and chemical causes, the disease is noncommunicable, meaning that it cannot be transferred to another animal.

Other times, the animal's body is invaded by a virus, parasite, fungi or bacteria; living things that feed off your animal and disturb the internal balance. These can live on the inside or the outside of the body; either way, they can cause serious problems.

These living invaders often multiply on their host and release harmful secretions, and sometimes sick animals can pass these living organisms to other animals. These diseases are called communicable infectious diseases.

The following are diseases that affect llamas and alpacas.

### Anemia

Anemia is causes the skin to become pale and is easily spotted by checking the animal's lower eyelid to see what color the membrane is.

It should be bright pink in a healthy animal, while anemic animals eyelids will be close to white. Their coat will look dull or shabby, they will be tired and weak and may have a poor appetite.

Anemia is more of a symptom than it is a disease. It happens when there is a reduction in the number of red blood cells which can occur because of severe parasitic infestation on the animal's skin, including fleas, lice, ticks, and other similar parasites. Internal parasites, such as worms, can also cause anemia.

In addition, anemia can be caused by severe blood loss from an injury or childbirth or by feeding llamas a poor diet, specifically a diet lacking in the trace amounts of copper they require.

Treating anemia can be easy, depending on the cause and severity of the illness. In the early stages, consider changing their diet to one rich in protein, which helps rebuild the red blood cells. Also give them iron supplements, vitamins, minerals, and probiotics.

In severe cases, the animal might need a blood transfusion and left untreated, anemia can lead to death. Whatever the case, if you notice any of these signs, contact your vet immediately.

### Bottle Jaw

This is a caused by severe case of anemia, evidenced by a pronounced swelling in the lower jaw. The barber pole worm is one of the most common causes of bottle jaw. This deadly condition requires immediate veterinary attention when the symptoms are noticed.

### Anaplasmosis

This disease happens when the red blood cells of your llama or alpaca are infected. The condition is rare, non-communicable and is transmitted by insects, such as ticks and flies, depositing a parasite into the animal's blood.

Since this disease is an infection of the blood, the first sign to look out for is anemia. The animal will seem weak and pale, and your animal will have a fever. The mucus membranes of the nose and mouth will also turn yellow.

As the infection becomes severe, the animal will reject its food and, along with dehydration, you will notice severe weight loss.

Anaplasmosis is a dangerous disease in llamas and alpacas. Even though there are treatments for the disease, it weakens the animal, leaving it with a defective immune system and weak stamina. If you notice any of the above signs, contact your veterinarian immediately.

### Barber Pole

The barber pole worm is one of the most dreadful worms that can affect llama or alpaca. The worm stays in their stomach, piercing the walls of the stomach and sucking out the blood.

The blood-sucking process quickly leads to anemia and can be dangerous. Signs of the disease at the initial stage are pale eyes, weight loss, and tiredness.

Subsequently, you will notice bottle jaw (an area of edema under the chin), or the animal may collapse. If diagnosed early enough, the barber pole worm can be treated by veterinarians. As a preventive tip, make sure you deworm your animals regularly.

### Coccidiosis

Coccidiosis is caused by a microscopic parasite called Coccidia. This parasite lives in the cells of the animal, causing damage in the small intestine.

Younger llamas and alpacas have a higher risk of infection; however, adult llamas and alpacas can get infected but gain immunity from the infections.

This disease is common with animals kept in non-sanitary conditions. Stress and overcrowding can also make animals vulnerable. It is very contagious, so infected animals must be isolated from the herd.

At the start of the illness, you will notice mucus-filled diarrhea. If unattended, the stool becomes bloody, potentially leading to dehydration, weight loss, anemia and stunted growth.

While the condition is treatable, prevention is usually best. You can always prevent the disease by keeping the animal's environment clean and not housing too many together.

You can also take fecal samples to a vet's clinic to check for dangerous parasites.

### Foot Rot

Foot Rot is a common livestock disease, not just in llamas and alpacas. It is a bacterial infection that affects their feet.

The leading cause of this disease is zinc deficiency, but it can also occur when the animal is kept in muddy wet conditions for too long.

It starts with swelling between the toes of the animal, and you may see lumps on the pads of their feet. They will likely walk with a limp because the swelling is usually painful.

When the condition is left unattended, their feet decay gradually, producing creamy fluids with a foul odor, leading to nerve and tissue damage in the affected foot.

You can treat foot rot at the initial stage by cleaning the affected area and removing the rotten parts. Once the area is thoroughly cleaned, apply iodine and antibiotics.

Luckily, the infection in llamas and alpacas is not as severe as sheep and goats since they have toes instead of hooves. However, care must still be taken because it is contagious, especially in the first seven days.

If you spot the above signs, contact your vet.

### White Muscle Disease

This disease is common to sheep, llamas, and alpacas and occurs when they consume a diet poor in vitamin E, selenium, or both.

The disease can affect the animal's muscles, heart muscles, or both.

When it affects the heart muscles, you will notice the animal struggling to breathe and you may see blood or mucus leaking from the nose.

If it affects their muscles, they will look arched and their back will seem stiff and hunched over. The disease leaves the animals with a weakened immune system.

Both vitamin E and selenium deficiency are common in animals that graze. Vitamin E deficiency develops when the animal ingests grass low in vitamin E, whereas a selenium deficiency occurs when the animal feeds from soil lacking the mineral.

While treating a deficiency is easy, white muscle disease must be treated by a vet. If you suspect a deficiency in your animals, give them supplements, but if you suspect white muscle disease, talk to your veterinarian.

### Urolithiasis

We've all heard of kidney stones; some of us have been unlucky enough to have them. Llamas and alpacas can also get these blockages in the urinary path, usually when there is an imbalance of phosphorus and calcium in their diet. These minerals will then form solid crystals that will block the path of urine.

The disease is common in males, especially when fed a grain-heavy diet. It can also happen when they consume too much alfalfa.

Animals with this disease are easy to spot as they do not urinate often. When they do urinate, they will appear to be in distress, and sometimes the urine will come out in a trickle instead of a strong flow. The animal might also not want to walk or will walk stiffly or stand with their hind legs stretched out.

The condition is serious, as death can occur in a few hours. If you notice these signs, call your vet immediately.

Generally, it kidney stones occur more often in sheep than in llamas and alpacas. In the same vein, it happens more in male llamas and alpacas than it does in females.

On a general note, you can prevent the disease by letting animals graze on their own so they can select healthy foods. Alternatively, you can feed them with forage products.

Care must be taken when giving llamas concentrate foods - foods rich in protein and carbohydrates like grains, legumes, and so on - as this can quickly tip the mineral balance in their body.

### Arthritis

Yes, you read that correctly! They can also have arthritis, and while many things can cause this, the fundamental cause is aging. Other causes of arthritis in llamas include malnutrition, infection, tight confinement, and injuries.

Just like in humans, arthritis in llamas and alpacas is not a transmittable disease. Animals with arthritis will have limited movement due to pain, and you might notice them lying down often. They might also lose weight, develop swollen joints, and dull coats.

Treating arthritis is usually done by treating the root cause. Therefore, if you suspect that your animal has this disease, you must seek the advice of a veterinarian.

### Pink Eye

There are two types of pink eye disease in alpacas and llamas: infectious and noninfectious. The infectious type is caused by viruses or bacteria and transmitted between animals via flying insects.

The non-infectious type usually results from vitamin A deficiency, stings from insects, scratches, or toxins.

Depending on the cause, pink eye can be a severe problem. The infectious type initially appears as red, swollen eyes with discharge and, then you will notice the transparent covering of the eyes becoming thick and visible. If not treated early, the animal can become blind and in worse cases, the infection can spread to the animal's brain, leading to death.

The moment you spot pink eye in any of your animals, segregate the animals immediately, protecting the sick llama and preventing the spread of the infection to the rest of the herd.

The non-infectious type can be treated easily using eye ointments. However, to be sure, consult a veterinarian for a proper checkup to determine the cause.

### Sore Mouth

This disease is caused by a virus closely related to chickenpox. Just as in human chickenpox, this disease is contagious in llamas and alpacas. The condition usually penetrates the skin via cuts in the skin.

Young llamas can contact the disease while their mothers are nursing them and it is dangerous to the younger animals; not only will the disease pass on to them, they won't be able to feed properly.

The disease usually runs its course within 3 - 4 weeks. During this period, blisters will develop around the animal's less hairy body parts, such as the lips and inside the mouth. With time, these small blisters become bigger as they turn into scabs.

When you spot these signs, separate the sick animals from the healthy. Your vet will prescribe ointments you can apply to the affected parts. Take your time and clean out everywhere the animal has been before you separated it and treat the sores, so they do not get infected with bacteria.

Just like in humans, a survivor becomes immune to the disease. While this is good news, it calls for caution. The survivors, although immune, can still carry the disease and transfer it to other animals.

There is no known cure for this infection. The animal is managed while the disease runs its course.

# Health Care Practices for Disease Prevention in Llamas and Alpacas

Their health is non-negotiable; they depend on you to help keep them safe healthy.

Four factors contribute to disease in any animal: lack of immunity, disease-causing organisms, environment, and stress.

An animal whose immunity is not compromised is unlikely to become sick, or at least not seriously. The same applies to animals that do not come into contact with a disease-causing organism, but the right environment will protect them and reduce the risk of disease.

Stress refers to conditions that can make an animal predisposed to illness. They include injuries, malnutrition, inappropriate use of medication, and so on.

For an animal to remain healthy, all these factors must be kept in check. Here are a few tips to help you do that:

### 1. Understand your Animal

You must first understand what normal behavior is *to be able* to spot abnormal behavior. Notice that your animals are unique individuals and will behave differently. For example, alpacas are shy animals and might not be as active as llamas. It would, therefore, be wrong to judge both animals on the same scale for activity.

Even among alpacas, you will have some friendly animals and some that don't mingle so well. The idea is for you to understand e*ach* one of them by observing and learning their usual behavior.

Every morning, before you feed your llamas, check on them, looking for animals not responding well. While feeding, look out for those that won't eat or appear to be less interested in eating, and check for animals that isolate themselves from the herd.

Animals with excessive salivation, discharge from the nose, bloody stool, diarrhea, or teary eyes require immediate attention. If you spot sick animals, remove them from the herd immediately to avoid the spread of any potential disease.

## 2. Restrict Human Contact

Humans are one of the biggest carriers of animal diseases. If you own a llama or alpaca farm, always restrict how often people access your farmland and your farm animals, including the vet.

If it's a must that you have visitors, find a system for disinfecting them before they enter your farm. You can make use of foot dips made of water and a strong disinfectant placed at the entrance to your property and have disinfectant hand washes ready too.

If you have a sick animal, take it to the vet or have the vet visit your premises as soon as possible; make sure they see the animal separately from the rest of the herd.

## 3. Proper Feeding Is Important

Llamas need to eat well, not just the right amount of food but the proper quality of food too.

The best way to feed llamas and alpacas is to let them graze and select their own food. Where that is impossible, you must provide food of the highest quality, balanced and containing all the essential nutrients. It should be clean and presented in clean bowls, and your llamas and alpacas should also have access to clean water at all times.

## 4. Vaccines and Other Medications

Ensure your animals are given all the necessary vaccinations and keep in touch with your vet to make sure any boosters or yearly vaccines are given at the correct time.

As crucial as vaccines are, regular deworming is just as important. Speak with your vet to arrange a deworming schedule.

Also, give your animals multivitamins that will boost their immune systems, keep them active and reduce stress.

## 5. Keep an Ideal Environment

The ideal environment for your llamas and alpacas is clean, uncrowded, and kept at a comfortable temperature. This will eliminate or at least significantly reduce the risk of potentially dangerous disease-causing organisms.

You should have no more than seven alpacas or four llamas on one acre of land, and you will need a barn or shed to ensure they can escape harsh weather. Last, your llamas should be sheared at the correct time to ensure they do not overheat or suffer from the cold.

# Chapter 8: Llama Breeding and Cria Birthing

*Quick Fact* – *Baby llamas are called crias, a Spanish word that translates to "baby". Female llamas usually have just one cria at a time; twins are possible, but very rare. A llama pregnancy lasts for around 350 days and a cria will weigh 20 to 30 pounds when born.*

## Llama/Alpaca Reproductive System

The species of llamas and alpacas today originate from South America and share a common feral ancestry. Their reproductive systems are similar but distinct.

### Female

The female llama or alpaca ovary is not so different from that of a mare, but it resembles a cow. Relative to body size, the reproductive tract is small when the llama or alpaca is not pregnant.

The ovum is small and cannot be detected clearly by ultrasound instruments, at least not the ones we have today. However, antra follicles can be detected, which are small, measuring about 1 to 2 mm in diameter. Several fluid-filled follicles are also present.

Between 10 to 12 months after birth, ovarian activities will begin in the llama or alpaca. Ovarian follicles assume a peripheral cortex arrangement, and any area on the surface of the ovary can accommodate ovulation. Corpus luteum (CL) and large follicles in llamas and alpacas are visible and palpable. Corpus luteum is a bundle of cells formed in the llama's ovary and is what produces the progesterone hormone in the early stages of pregnancy.

### Male

Relative to their body sizes, the llama and alpaca have relatively small testes. The llama's testes usually measure at least 3 X 6 cm at birth, while the alpacas' testes are usually at least 2 X 4 cm. The testes are typically close to the body of the animal and the prepuce (sheath) adheres to the penis in young males, not detaching until around 2 to 3 years of age. An unstimulated prepuce not stimulated is usually caudo-dorsally directed; it points towards the back of the tail, which explains why they appear to urinate backwards. Compared to other livestock species, the llama and alpaca testes are small.

The penis points forward. The prepuce is attached to the penis. When the animal reaches 1- 1/2 to 2 – or even three – years old, the penis will detach.

Not all the animals will reach sexual maturity at the same time. Most males breed at 18 to 24 months old while some may become fully sexually mature when they reach 30 months. Generally, a llama may attain sexual maturity and become fertile earlier than the alpaca.

The cranial, lateral, and caudal preputial muscles in the sheath aid erection. They also have roles to play when the animal displays mating behaviors.

Llamas and alpacas usually have a low quantity of semen, making it very difficult to evaluate. This is a common problem in the camelid family.

The ejaculations of fertile males are inconsistent. Some people resort to training their animals to mount on a dummy, preparing it with an artificial vagina to give the male the feel of climbing a real female.

Usually, they sedate the animals, and they may introduce electro-ejaculation, although this isn't always efficient. Another option is to collect the semen from the vagina of the female after mating.

# Llama/Alpaca Reproduction

Reproduction in llamas and alpacas begins at puberty. The female llama and alpaca attain sexual maturity between 10 to 18 months of age and can begin breeding. However, following a veterinarian's advice, some people do not let their female llamas and alpacas breed until they weigh up to 90 kg (200 pounds) for llamas and 40 kg (90 pounds) for alpacas.

Alternatively, they can breed when they weigh two-thirds of their mature body weight. This precaution is taken because of the relatively small size of the female alpaca and llama and it also helps to avoid challenges associated with early breeding, such as dystocia.

When puberty begins, the animal experiences follicular waves, developing a follicle in the interval of 12 to 14 days. The male llama and alpacas breed between 18 to 24 months of age, and by that time, the penis is no longer attached to the sheath and the testes will have grown significantly.

Ovulation in the female llama and alpaca occur when it has been mated because they are induced ovulators. Before mating can occur, the receptive female will assume a position that allows the male access into her and, while the male is mounting her, he will start "orgling," the sound they make while mating. The common belief is this sound will help the female ovulate.

Ejaculation lasts for between 5 and 45 minutes, although the average is about 20 minutes, accruing to a relatively small volume of 2 to 5 ml. After mating for 24 to 30 hours, the semen can still induce reflex ovulation.

A pregnant llama or alpaca will not be receptive and will reject the male's advances. After 2 to 3 days of ovulation, there will be a CL (corpus luteum). Then, about seven days after mating, the fertilized oocyte will be present in the uterus.

There will be implantation by 30 days into the gestation period. A hyperechoic embryo will be there to show that the llama is pregnant 21 days into gestation, and at 45 days into the gestation period – perhaps a bit more – you can perform rectal palpation to know if the llama is pregnant. For alpacas, it will be difficult given their size, but if the person has relatively small hands, palpation may be possible. This is best left to a veterinary doctor, though.

The gestation period for llamas is around 345 to 350 days. Usually the dams deliver one cria, although sometimes they deliver twins - but this is rare.

# Reproductive Problems and Management

Like other animals, llamas and alpacas face some challenges with their reproductive systems. In males, these problems may include:

## • Acute Scrotal Swelling

This problem can be caused by heat stress, infection, trauma, and so on. There can also be penile swelling from injury to the penis and urolithiasis.

Symptoms of penile swelling can obstruction of the free flow of urine. Depending on the extent of swelling and injury, surgery, flushing, and cystotomy may be recommended.

If surgery is the option, you have a significant role to play afterward. The animal will need extra care to recuperate fully, while therapies and drugs should be provided.

## • Heat Stress

This problem affects the llama or alpaca's penis and animals suffering from a penile injury may present with hydrocele (scrotal swelling) and experience scrotal edema.

The effect of heat stress can cause the animal to become uninterested in mounting the female. They may experience reduced fertility for, lasting up to two months or more, even years and sometimes, the animal can become permanently infertile.

When the case is severe, the animal may become depressed and have a muscular weakness while other symptoms are excess salivation, dehydration, etc.

There are several ways you can protect them against heat stress; the most obvious is by providing shade. Animals should not be in the sun for long periods of time, and if a male has been exposed to the sun for an extended period, he should be cooled immediately, until he regains normal body temperature.

When the animal is dehydrated, he should be rehydrated. Don't allow him to gulp huge amounts of water as this can lead to problems such as a diluted sodium level in the blood which can cause weakness and even convulsions in the worst case. Shearing is also recommended. If the condition is severe. Take the animal to the veterinary clinic for proper care, and when necessary, the veterinarian may have to administer medication. In times like this, you should not subject the animal to a long, rough transport. This situation may require a house call from the veterinarian.

• Testicular Hypoplasia

Another reproductive problem that male llamas and alpacas can have is testicular hypoplasia, caused by a bridge in the sexual development of the animal. This causes the size of the testes to be disproportionate to the size of his body. The testes do not develop as they should and become smaller than they should be for the age of the animal.

Sometimes, this situation can be caused by poor nutrition, like zinc deficiency. It can also be an effect of cytogenetic and endocrine abnormalities or may occur where the germ cells are insufficient.

Hypoplasia of the testes results from irregular progressive sclerosis and degeneration. It usually becomes glaringly obvious after puberty, but when both testes are of equal size, it's difficult to recognize.

If one of the testes is smaller than the other, it's called *unilateral hypoplasia*. It will be easy to detect because you can compare the contralateral testis.

If the situation is not complicated, the animal may just have low sperm morphology. However, in extreme cases, he may be aspermic.

There are preventive measures you can adopt to avoid this situation. Be careful not to allow breeding between affected animals because if the cause is genetic, it may be transferred to the cria.

Castration is another viable treatment option. Also, you may want to slaughter the animal for its carcass value.

Female llamas are more likely to have issues because their reproductive system is more complex than males. Some of the most common issues are:

- **Dystocia**

One challenge llamas and alpacas may have during delivery is dystocia (difficulty in giving birth.)

Dystocia can occur because of several factors.

If your dam is having dystocia, there will be signs. Usually, with delivery, you must be vigilant. Any slight inconsistency should be checked. If there is a delay at any stage, be concerned.

All may not be well if the dam remains in the first stage of labor more than is reasonably expected. If she spends up to four hours or more in the first stage, there may be a problem. Also, if the fetus is visible, but the dam has not delivered it for up to 30 minutes or more, there is definitely a problem.

- **Uterine Torsion**

Uterine torsion is another problem that may cause a difficult a delivery. This situation is where the uterine is twisted; the delivery may not progress from the first stage to the second. This condition typically occurs in the last month of the pregnancy when the dam is exhausted.

In the second stage of delivery, there may be a delay if the fetus assumes the wrong position. It can also happen if the birth canal is not patent enough (sufficiently opened) to allow the fetus through. Sometimes, the fetus is larger than the birth canal. This problem is one reason why some people do not crossbreed llama and alpaca. Llamas are usually bigger than alpacas. When there is crossbreeding, the fetus may be too big for the alpaca to deliver.

Situations where the fetus assumes the wrong position is common among camelids. This problem should be corrected before delivery and can be fixed manually or spontaneously. Without this correction, the dam may not have a normal birth.

You will know if your dam has uterine torsion when it displays symptoms such as depression and colic (abdominal pain.) You will know if the dam has colic if she kicks at her abdomen.

A veterinarian should check on the llama or alpaca to know how twisted the uterus is. He/she will note the direction in which it is twisted and resolve it. Resolution may involve medicating the dam to calm her down so the process will succeed.

The dam assumes a position of lateral recumbency. The dam will be held in place, and the process will be performed. The uterus and fetus will be held in a static position. It can be done with hands or by placing a plank on the dam's abdomen. After this, the dam will be rotated to the direction opposite which the uterine is twisted; this process can be repeated depending on how twisted the uterine is.

If this procedure is done up to three times, and the situation is not resolved, the dam must undergo surgery.

### Cria Birthing

Cria birthing is the delivery of a newborn.

### Labor Signs

Labor signs may begin earlier in some dams than others. Therefore, monitor the llama or alpaca when it is about 330 days into gestation. At this stage, check on it often – every few hours – which enables you to know when labor is approaching.

Llamas and alpacas do not necessarily experience labor in the same way, but some signs are common among them. These signs are:

### • Fuller Udder

The llama or alpaca's udder will become fuller as the day of delivery draws near. Two to three weeks before birth, the milk will start to flow. And by 3 to 4 days before delivery, the teats will have a telltale sign of being waxy.

### • Vulva Size

A few days before delivery, the vulva will increase in size, swelling and becoming more pronounced.

### • Restlessness

One common sign of labor among most animals, including llamas and alpacas, is restlessness. The dam may move, shift, or hum, she may roll about, lying down and rising again, and so on. Sometimes, she will lose her appetite and refuse to eat, but will instead chew her cud.

### • Unusual Behavior

When delivery is near, the llama or alpaca will display unusual behaviors. Anything the dam does not do before pregnancy; she may do now. If you notice any behavior out of the ordinary, it is likely a sign of labor.

# Stages of Labor

Before delivery, the llama will go into labor. There are three stages of labor.

- **Stage 1**

During this period, the animal will urinate frequently. She will separate herself from the herd, make a humming sound continuously. These behaviors will persist throughout the first stage of labor.

At this stage, the uterus contracts and the cervix dilate. The cervix assumes the same width as the vagina, and the fetus moves into the pelvic inlet. This stage can last from 1 to 6 hours.

- **Stage 2**

This stage begins from the rupturing of the membrane to the birth of the cria. It takes 30 minutes or more. You may see the female lying down and standing up continuously, the abdomen is strained, and the water bag or amniotic sac may be visible at the vulva; you may even see it rupture. The female will obviously have contractions and the contractions be close together in time. If you see her resting between contractions and you think that things are going too slowly, don't panic at this stage – she is getting tired by the contractions and wants to rest.

- **Stage 3**

This stage lasts for four hours or more – up to six and is the stage where the placenta is passed. Know, unlike many other species, the mother does not ingest the placenta and typically will not lick the newborn cria, either. Examine the placenta and make sure it is intact, filled with fluid and has no tears in it. Dispose of it carefully, wearing gloves (do NOT use bare hands) as it can attract nearby predators.

These stages of labor usually last longer in first-time deliveries.

**When to Get Veterinary Help**

Call for veterinary assistance when:

- Stage 1 goes past 5 hours and there are no signs of contractions.

- Stage 2 goes past 30 minutes and the birth is showing no signs of progression.

---

- Stage 3 – if the placenta has not been passed within 8 hours after the birth or, if the dam gives birth at night, by the next morning.

## Cria Birthing

Cria birthing occurs in the second stage of labor, and the placenta follows within a few hours. Before the birthing begins, get a birthing kit, which should include:

1. Flashlight or torch

If the llama or alpaca gives birth late in the day, which is unusual, as most give birth between 8 am and noon, you may need light to see what's happening and you will need to note the time of delivery.

2. Towels

You will cover the bedding with clean towels during the birth, and when the new cria arrives, you will need the towels to dry it off and clean the birthing fluids.

3. Scissors and dental floss

You will need these to cut and tie the umbilical cord.

4. Iodine and bottle

This is used for dipping the end of the umbilical cord. Use an empty pill bottle and a 7% iodine tincture.

5. Betadine surgical scrub and sterile lubrication

You will need it to sterilize your hands and birthing supplies, especially if you need to assist the veterinarian.

6. Rectal thermometer

It is used for checking the newborn crias temperature, especially if he or she seems to be lethargic or weak.

7. Sterile lubrication

Just in case you need to help the llama with the birth.

8. Feeding bottle and nipple

If the cria cannot nurse immediately, you will need to feed it.

9. Supplement

If the cria cannot nurse immediately after birth, a multi-species colostrum supplement must be given – this is critical.

10. Milk replacer

A multi-species milk replacer is given where the cria cannot nurse properly – choose one with a minimum 24% protein.

11. Electrolytes

It is used to rehydrate the dam and reverse the effect of fluid loss in the cria after delivery.

12. Disposable bags

These are used to dispose of the afterbirth, soiled towels, and other things you need to throw away.

Newborn llama cria weigh between 20 to 30 pounds at birth, and they are usually larger than alpaca cria, which typically weigh between 15 to 20 pounds at birth.

# How to Care for a Newborn Cria

Caring for your newborn cria begins before the cria is birthed. The period of waiting for your newborn cria is packed with several emotions, so you need all the tips you can get!

Naturally, some things will go as they are meant to. However, you have a role to play. Knowing what to do and how to do them will help you better handle whatever situation may arise. Some ways you can better care for the newborn cria include:

- **Preparing for a Smooth Birth**

If the birth is not smooth, the newborn cria may not do well. Before the due date for delivery, ensure that the llama or alpaca has a clean and appropriate place to deliver. A leveled grassy area will do fine in good weather, but the site should be safe. There should be no sharp objects or unneeded items to clutter the area.

If the weather is not favorable, the llama or alpaca should be delivered in a clean, well ventilated stall and have comfortable bedding.

Prepare the birthing kit and have it readily available for when you need it. Make sure it contains all the items listed above.

- **Immediately After Birth**

When the cria is born, check it is healthy. The dam should be in a clean, warm, room - weather permitting.

Ensure the cria is breathing properly. Sometimes, the cria has difficulty breathing because the nose or mouth is blocked, so make sure you clean all the birthing fluid off its face, paying particular but gentle attention to the eyes, nose and mouth.

Check if the cria's temperature is okay - it should be 35 C or 95º F. If it is less, the cria is too cold and must be warmed up.

One hour after birth, the cria should be able to stand. Two hours after birth, it should be able to nurse, but if these do not happen, you can assist it.

If you try, but nothing happens, contact the veterinary doctor.

• **Medical Care**

Although the medical care for the cria begins before birth, it is necessary during and after birth.

Routine medical checkups for both the cria and dam are necessary. Crias born between October and March should be given a vitamin D supplement, as they are unlikely to be out in the sunlight to receive it naturally.

Vaccinate the cria for Tetanus and Clostridium Type C and D, and vaccinate against diseases they are prone to contracting. You will need to check with your veterinarian what diseases are common in your region.

Your veterinarian can guide you against harmful practices and advise you on the right steps to take to care for your new herd member.

Don't be scared when you have a pregnant llama; with the proper preparation, you can help your llama during pregnancy and the birthing process.

### The First Few Days – Feeding

The most critical time for your newborn cria is the first 18 to 24 hours. You should see him start nursing within two hours of birth. This will provide him with all the nutrition he needs but should the dam die, is in distress, or is having other problems nursing her young, you must have bottles with spare nipples and nutrition on hand.

A mother in good health will produce colostrum, a yellowish thick milk which gives the cria's immune system a kick-start and provides it with antibodies not passed to it during the pregnancy. The cria's body has a unique design; its intestines can absorb these antibodies into its bloodstream, but this can only happen for the first 12 to 18 hours after birth. This gives your cria the very best start at a healthy life because those antibodies are specific to your llama's surroundings and herd.

If your cria does not nurse within a couple of hours or you are concerned that he isn't nursing sufficiently, you can provide a colostrum supplement, but you must do it quickly. Feed the supplement every 3 to 4 hours using a bottle and continue for up to 48 hours after the birth – follow the package instructions carefully.

After the first 48 hours, if your cria still isn't nursing properly, swap the colostrum supplement for a milk replacement. Make sure it is at least 24% protein. This will ensure he continues to receive the right nutrition to grow and develop properly... Try not to handle the cria too much while you are feeding – this will minimize the potential for behavioral issues.

The process of the birth exposes the cria to lots of microorganisms and pathogens that can lead to digestive distress; this can lead to diarrhea and dehydration. Whether the dam is feeding her young or you are, you must supplement with electrolytes. Be sure you provide the electrolytes in a separate feeding from milk products.

# Chapter 9: Training Your Llama

*Quick Fact —* *Llamas are one of the smartest and easiest animals to train but patience is required. They have long been used for guarding other animals, like flocks of sheep and sometimes alpaca herds and require little training to be effective at guarding an area or other animals.*

Training cats and dogs is relatively easy and some of us have done it often. We efficiently train them to do the basics, the things we want or need them to do, and stop them from doing things we don't want them to do.

Few llama and alpaca owners know the possibility of training their pets. Many owners ask if it's possible to train their llamas by themselves. The simple answer to this is yes. Be able to teach one by yourself if you have plenty of free time and patience. You'll have to learn llama and alpaca body language, understand normal and abnormal behavior and then follow the tips and tricks below to train them.

Note that if you are the type of person that gets nervous around animals, you may find it challenging to train them yourself, and "do-it-yourself" training is definitely not for people with a short fuse.

If you get frustrated by the aggressive or sluggish behavior of animals, you shouldn't try training one yourself. Even though llamas or alpacas are trainable, only a particular type of temperament can successfully do it; otherwise, you may do more harm to the animal than good.

Many llama farmers try to train their creatures incorrectly and then become angry with the llamas when it doesn't work. Instead of changing their approach to training, they keep trying the same things repeatedly. Ultimately, they give up and conclude it's impossible.

Most llama farmers are of the belief that it's impossible to train llamas by themselves are those who have tried and failed at it. The important thing to remember when training a llama is that when it isn't working, stop. Please consider what you are doing wrong. It isn't the llama's or alpaca's fault. And just like when training a dog, you should never end a session on a low note–the animal will remember and will associate training as unpleasant and be even less cooperative.

You'll need to understand how to re-educate these llamas. Essentially, you must learn to train a broken llama. The llama has equated humans with suffering and pain, and to get it back on track requires re-education. That's why it best you don't try to train them before you learn how to do it properly.

This chapter will take you through basic knowledge about training llamas.

So, let's get started.

# What You Should Teach Your Llamas or Alpacas

Many people believe dogs are fast learners, and probably the quickest learners of all pets. But, when you compare llamas to dogs, it might interest you to know that llamas will learn more rapidly than dogs that walking without a leash is the best. Your focus should be to get them to walk by your side without a leash.

There are three categories of llama-training. You decide the level you want to take your llamas or alpacas to; in this respect, your decision depends on the reason you keep your herd.

If your goal for keeping a llama herd is simply for llama wool, then you may only need to teach them the basics to make the shearing process easy. If your llama will be a pack animal and has to follow you into the mountains, you must conduct lessons geared towards carrying a pack.

You can also train them to drive carts, obey commands such as sit down or get up, and much more. You decide what you want them to know and train them accordingly.

Let's look at the levels of llamas training and lessons under each group.

- **Basic School**

At this level, you teach them what constitutes "socially acceptable behavior."

For example, the law demands that any llama *not* on your property be kept under physical control via a lead and halter. This law implies that you must train each llama to be willing enough to take on a halter. Each llama or alpaca must also understand the basic concept of leading. This is non-negotiable training every llama must have.

Their physical needs demand you groom them, trim their nails, and inspect their body for any medical conditions. The implication is that you must train them to be calm enough for you to carry out these activities. They must know how – and be willing to – stand when tied, stand still without restraint, and lift their feet when asked to.

These are the essential schooling requirements for any llama or alpaca training. However, you can also take the practice to a more advanced level, which we explain next.

- **Elementary School**

At this level, you train them on specific skills that make for an enjoyable human-animal companion. Taking them through elementary school lessons is not only enjoyable for the llamas but also for you, as the handler.

Llamas and alpacas enjoy regular walks, so you need to train them to avoid trauma and trouble during these periodic excursions. Each llama must understand simple navigation concepts, such as the proper protocol to negotiate through gates. It should be able to follow behind on a narrow trail and understand how to respond in traffic.

Not only that, but you must also train each llama or alpaca on crossing vehicle and pedestrian bridges. They should even know how to negotiate mud, close trees, bush, shallow water and jump over low barriers such as falling logs, and human-made obstacles like ramps and steps.

Finally, when you need to load them into a vehicle, it can be a challenging game to play if you do not train them for such beforehand. You, therefore, must prepare them on how to load into vehicles readily.

They should also be trained on how to travel well in the sense they know how to take advantage of periodic "rest stops." Such training prevents them from soiling their traveling accommodation.

This level aims to train them to walk on a loose lead and rely on visual and verbal cues.

### • Occupational Schooling

This level is for those willing to make their llama an enjoyable working partner. It will be best if you had more than the basic knowledge of llama training to get them to work for you. No llamas will naturally or willingly give themselves up for primary or elementary training.

However, performance llamas earn their keep by doing the following: packing, driving, and showing.

Packing refers to using llamas for loading and unloading. Such llama must be trained to stand untied anywhere, carry and maneuver loads around objects or obstacles, doing it alone by string or verbal direction.

Did you know llamas and alpacas can be trained to drive a cart? That's what driving means. It requires the use of distinct gaits and verbal commands like run, walk, jog, and ground drive commands like start, turn, and stop. Therefore, you must train the llama about these things and how to accept different types of llama-drawn vehicles, driving on roads, backing out of narrow spaces, etc.

Under this training level is housing llamas as pets. A pet llama must be trained to negotiate all types of in-house structures, obstacles, and restrictions such that you can easily find on the floor, in hallways, elevators, etc. It must know how to bring its head down for easier access and to be "spook proof."

### • High School

Learning at this stage is the peak of llama training and this is where you train your llamas for show. If you want your llama to participate at a competitive level, you will need to prepare it to negotiate various obstacles defined by the show associations regulations.

# Training Facilities and Safety

It's vital to consider where you are going to train your llama(s). The best place to do so is in a catch pen as it will willingly enter and can be held safe and secure.

If you are dealing with more than one llama and plan to train them all, you can't teach them together. You will need a small area for an individual llama as you start the beginner halter training. The training space shouldn't be too big, yet big enough to catch the llama and move it through the space safely.

Also, plan to have a double gate system that will allow you to maneuver the individual llama into the pen and secure the gate. Not only that, but the system also helps to create a small triangular-shaped pen with a smaller room. This design allows you to stay outside the pen but still handle the llama if needed.

Keep all the leads and halters within your reach. That way, you can access what you need for that session with ease without needing to leave the llama you are training. The llamas will also become used to seeing the leads and halter whenever they come into the barn.

# Training Equipment

Though you need little equipment to get them through elementary school, you need to be sure you have the correct equipment to hand for the training session.

It is best to have a halter that fits and a good rope to serve as the lead. Other items include a stick to help guide the llama where you want it to go, a bag to carry a small portion of reward feed, etc.

It is useful to have these items at hand, but they are not essential. You could spend a fortune on them if you wanted to. However, if you must pay for a stick, you will have the same results using a PVC pipe or a pure bamboo cane, and you can use a cheap self-made bag to hold feed.

Just know that what matters most is the quality of the *training*, not how much you spend on equipment.

# Trainer and Llama Safety

More important than training is the safety of both the llama and you. When preparing the facilities and equipment for training, ensure there are no sharp edges from which you or the llamas can get injured and no items around the training ground in which you or the llama can get entangled.

A good healthy llama is a powerful animal that delivers a quick and painful sidekick. Therefore, remember that whenever you are in the pen, do not stay in a compromising position where you can get kicked.

Remember that whenever a sidekick happens, it's most likely your fault and not that of the llama. A llama will naturally react when you touch it in an uncomfortable or unexpected place. Therefore, if you are unlucky enough to be side-kicked, note where you touched it animal – and learn from the experience.

Llamas and alpacas are good jumpers, especially when spooked. Be alert and do not lose concentration whenever you are around them. Anytime a llama jumps out of the pen, you need not fret; bring it back in, calm it down, and start again. Still, evaluate what you did that made the llama spook and jump away.

# Bond of Trust

Every animal has the instinct to preserve themselves. While a dog will bite to defend itself and a cat will use its claws, a llama will run away as a form of protection.

Llamas and alpacas will do anything possible to protect themselves from danger; therefore, room to room is their friend. They will also do anything to protect their area. Their body language usually conveys the message, "This is my space, and I don't want you here. If you try to get into my space, I will either spit on you or run away."

You can use this knowledge to your advantage as a trainer; to earn a llama's trust enough to allow you into its space, you must be meticulous. Start by going into the pen the first couple of days to feed it, change its water, and clean its environment. Don't pay attention to it and don't try to corner it.

The idea is to let the llama know you are not a threat. That way it can be comfortable with you around.

The next step is to talk to the llama and move close to it slowly. If you move close and it wants to run away, don't stop it. Let it move. After a few days, you can take a PVC pipe or a sorting pole into the pen. Use it to rub its back gently. The llama will probably move; let it run but keep in contact with the pole and be careful not to corner it.

Continue to do this until you no longer need to use the pole to touch its back. Over time, it will discover that the rod is not a threat. When that happens, you can come close and touch its back with your hands.

Do undertake the process gently. Remember, you read earlier that "a llama will naturally react when you touch it in an uncomfortable or unexpected place." Therefore, touch from the shoulder, work your way to its neck, around its head, and under its belly.

Talk to your llama quietly while you do the touching. When it remains still while standing, walk out of the pen. Don't leave until it is standing quietly, which means you may have to back off and ignore it until the llama feels comfortable. Continue until it lets you touch the entire body, including the head. Then introduce it to a halter.

Rub the llama's neck and around its head, then gently put the halter on it. Remove it and put it on again. Repeat several times till you determine that the llama is comfortable with the process.

Don't make the mistake of starting halter-training the first time you put it on the llama. If you do, you will make the llama think the halter is a restraint and count it as an enemy. Your aim should be to make training a fun thing so the llama willingly goes for a walk with it on.

# Tips to Train Llamas Successfully

The things you've been reading may sound easy to do, but that's only if you do it the right way. Here are tips you need to train your llamas or alpacas yourself, successfully:

• Be patient and don't rush the training

Here is the golden rule to training any llama or alpaca. You can easily get tempted to rush things when you start to make progress but that is a big mistake.

Also, know that llamas have different personalities. When you're training more than one llama, some will learn fast, while others will be slow to learn - have some patience with the slower ones.

- Repetition is key

Any llama will naturally resist training, and they won't get it at the first attempt. It is your duty as the trainer to get the llama comfortable doing whatever you want or need them to do.

Be it haltering, leading, brushing, desensitizing, fitting a pack, trekking, etc., they won't be comfortable with it on the first attempt. You must repeat the process until the llamas are happy about it.

Other things to consider include:

- Keeping the session short and simple
- Devote the right quantity of time
- Never get angry in front of your llama or alpaca
- Recognize failure and know when to withdraw
- Reward llamas when you make progress

All these constitute the attributes of a good llama or alpaca trainer. If you have trained them yourself, then you must learn to implement these attributes.

One reason you should train them is because a trained llama will earn you more on the market. Do you want to make money from keeping llamas? Check out the next chapter on tips for running a llama business.

# Chapter 10: 10 Tips for Your Llama or Alpaca Business

Starting a business can be difficult for any entrepreneur but, it shouldn't be for you. If you follow this step-by-step journey, you can get started on your llama or alpaca business quickly. And even to raise them for the fun of it, you can still learn a thing or two.

## 10 Tips for Starting an Alpacas and Llamas Business

These tips will help you set up business with no stress and enjoy the dividends quickly.

### 1. Learn about Alpacas and Llamas

As with any new business venture, lots of research needs to be done so you don't struggle at any point in your journey.

During your research, decide to raise alpacas, llamas, or both. It will help to learn about their differences, feeding patterns, when and how to shear them, the best location for your farm, etc.

There are so many mistakes that can be avoided if you do your homework!

## 2. Get Advice From a Mentor or the Competition

A mentor is experienced at raising llamas and will show you what they've learned. , he or she is already in the llama business and can serve as a guide for you. And if your farms are far enough apart, they won't see you as a threat to their business.

A mentor may be of immense support, especially in the early stages of the business. They will tell you what to do and what pitfalls to avoid and they are the people you can always turn to if you encounter a problem.

The competition is someone who might not want you in. They have been in the business longer than you, are experienced and may even be located near to you.

As much as you might not like it, it would help to learn about the competition – what their strengths and weaknesses are, the services they offer, what makes them unique, etc.

Leverage their weaknesses and provide that service.

For example, if your competition does not offer washing and drying of fiber, include that in the services you offer.

## 3. License and Registration

Before starting any business, you must register it with the proper authorities; there is usually one where you live or close by. Be sure you understand the terms and conditions. It is highly recommended to obtain a membership in AOA (Alpacas Owners Association).

You might also require a business plan (or proposal) that shows your current and long-term plans.

It is essential to talk to a business or tax consultant to guide you through the process. If you plan to sell the fleece from the animals, you will require a license from the state.

## 4. Funding

Funding is crucial to the survival of any start-up. At the initial stage, a lot of costs are incurred - buying the land, fencing, getting supplies, seeing a vet, licensing and registration, etc., and a lack of funds can delay the process.

Money is also needed to pay for manual labor around the farm.

You could apply for a loan from the bank if personal funds are not sufficient. There are government grants that cater to the needs of alpaca farmers.

### 5. Get Property

If you already have land, skip this step. However, you must make sure that the land is fit for the alpacas and llamas to graze. If not, consider expanding or buying a larger plot of land. Alpacas and llamas are social animals and love company.

Raising 6-7 alpacas needs about one acre of land. The land should be filled with plenty of healthy grass for grazing.

### 6. Check that the Location is Safe

The location of the farm should be safe from wild animals, parasites, and poisonous grass.

Build a fence around the farm site to make sure that the llamas don't wander away. You also need to check that the grasses are right for the animals to eat.

Some plants are toxic to alpacas, such as oleander, tobacco, poppies and buckwheat. Rid your farm of those.

### 7. Build Shelter

Although the animals will stay outdoors for most of the day, you still need a barn to keep them safe during extreme conditions.

A barn can be a simple structure; it need not be elaborate. However, it should be capable of serving as a windbreak and keeping the animals safe.

### 8. Get Other Tools and Equipment

Besides a barn, you will need other equipment on your farm. These include tools and supplies required for practical work including gloves, boots, hay-elevators, toe-trimming and teeth-cutting equipment, and shearing tools.

It is crucial to shear the animals once a year. If the animals are not sheared on time, the fiber may get too tangled and difficult to remove.

If you don't want to shear them yourself, you can always pay someone to do it for you.

### 9. Employ the Services of a Vet

You will require the services of an experienced veterinarian to help you cater to the health challenges of the animals. As time goes on, you might be able to handle health issues and routine care yourself under the guidance of a vet.

The number one killer of alpacas is parasites. You must ensure they are tested and dewormed regularly.

### 10. Make Provision for Feeding

Alpacas need a highly nutritious diet; they should be fed a healthy green diet. If you need to buy hay, it should be fresh.

Old, dusty, or moldy hay will not be the right choice for your animals, even though it may be the cheaper option. Also provide mineral supplements besides their hay.

# Other Managerial Skills Required for Business

If you have gone into the llama and alpaca business, you have made a smart choice. Several people are thriving in the trade, but this success is not without planning and organization.

If you want your business to be lucrative, you must take strategic steps to make sure your progress is successful. In this section, we will introduce you to some tips you need to be abreast of. If you set your budget right and use the right managerial skills, you will succeed in this specialized business.

# Budget and Management Tips

There is money involved in all businesses – llamas and alpacas inclusive. With the right budget and management guide, you are good to go. We have explained some areas you must check.

Your budget is the amount of capital you have envisioned to spend on your business, at least as a startup. Approach budgeting from the perspective of what your startup costs will be - consider the size of your business and how much money will be required to make it work.

First, consider how much money you can afford to put into the business and make sure your budget covers every area, including the following:

- **Starting Up**

Here, you must consider how much money it will cost you to purchase the first set of llamas and alpacas.

How many llamas and alpacas are you buying to get started? Take note that the number of animals you have determine how many crias will be born. It will also determine the amount of fleece.

When planning your budget, allocate a decent amount for necessities. While you are not trying to go beyond what you can afford, get the number of animals that best meets your business needs.

The number of llamas and alpacas you have determines the size of your ranch or farm. Consider the amount of hay you need to buy if you do not plan to engage in outdoor grazing. These items take space and money.

- **Location**

Also consider the best location for your llamas and alpacas. You will spend some amount of money on your ranch or farm, and its structure and organization will determine how well you can run the place. The movement and arrangement of animals is an important consideration.

The essential factors to be considered involve the number of animals you intend to have. Do you have enough grazing land or are you intending to feed your animals hay daily?

What will be the style and construction of your farm? Do you want to fence it permanently or create removable demarcations? Remember, you must have sections for cria birthing. Or do you plan to use a part of your barn?

If you have a robust budget, you may want to dig a well or provide a tap at your location. If otherwise, considering proximity to the source of water when creating your farm is wise.

If you plan to supplement their feed with pellets or grains, you need space for keeping large storage bins. In designing the management of your farm, give this factor ample consideration.

You must shear them yearly. Do you propose to do them on your ranch or elsewhere? If on your ranch, make room for it.

Fleece processing is another area that will influence your choice of location. Do you plan to process the fleece yourself? If yes, do you have enough space to accommodate the processes? Know that you must wash, dry, dye, and package it all.

You may need to perform other activities depending on what you want, so make sure you have sufficient space for whatever you need.

You may decide not to process the fiber yourself, so your budget must cover the processing cost. Remember that it is an expense you must make each time you shear them, mostly yearly.

The amount you allocate to location depends on the answers to these questions; take care to consider each area carefully.

- **Feeding**

This factor is crucial when budgeting for your business. How do you plan to feed your herd? You could provide them with hay every day. If this is your plan, have you factored the additional expense into your budget?

A viable plan is to locate a way of getting it at a relatively lower cost; is there a co-op close by? Could you barter some of your services in exchange?

Another option is to have a grazing area. If you provide for pasture, then you should have a tangible plan on how to manage areas in terms of irrigation, weeding, fertilization, etc.

Aside from pastures and hay, they will need supplements. These are essential for keeping their mineral and vitamin qualities in balance. Feed your animals pellets or grains.

What is your plan in this regard? Some people buy in bags and replenish as the need arises, while others buy it in bulk because it is cheaper. It saves time in going to buy often and some money.

Bulk-buying poses the question of storage. Large bins will be needed for storing the feed, and your budget should accommodate this expense.

Your herd will also drink water. Can you fetch water daily? If no, then will you have a well or tap close by?

- **Electricity**

You must have electricity on your farm. With the change of weather, you will need to warm the llama barn when it is cold (think of winter). If the weather is warm and they need to keep cool, you will need a fan to do the job.

Your source of water might also use electricity. When winter, and you have freezing waters, your water tank must be kept flowing.

If your dam delivers a cria and its temperature demands assistance, electricity will be vital then.

- **Manure**

Manure management is an important area to consider. They will produce manure every day and their living areas must be kept clean of it. A tangible plan on how to get the waste out is vital.

- **Trailer and Equipment**

Effective management of your farm depends on the availability of the essential equipment. Your budget should cover tools and the vital equipment you need to run your business successfully. Equipment like manure spreaders, elevators, UTVs, tractors, and so on is crucial.

You also need a trailer for easy mobility and a vehicle to transport them to veterinary checkups.

When going for AOA show and games, you will require a vehicle to tow your trailer. The distance you travel and the number of animals you transport at a time will determine the size of the vehicle.

- **Insurance**

Consider getting your farm and animals insured against liability. You can insure your llamas and alpacas against mortality and theft, and, on average, the cost of insurance is valued at 4.25% of the llama's value.

- **Miscellaneous**

There should be room for any unforeseen expenses that may come up, particularly emergencies.

Overall, you need a business plan to ensure the success of your business and a good plan will help your budget.

# Writing Your Business Plan

Management begins with a business plan and coming up with one requires excellent management skills. This is a blueprint for your business and while it will take some thought to come up with one, it will guide you on the right steps to take and what to do.

Without a business plan, there are larger chances of failing in business. Proper planning will make sure you make the right choices and avoid mistakes. A business plan is essential for a newbie and even seasoned businessmen and women.

A business plan will help you determine the capital you put into the business, and also help you structure your budget properly to accommodate the necessities.

There are essentials for a business plan:

### 1. Analysis/Description

You must analyze your business and what it entails. It shows what you do, what you bring to the table, and your target market and is a pointer to your future activities.

### 2. Mission Statement

You state why you have a farm and where you are going with it. Your mission statement details your future goals and where you are aiming to be in, say 5- or 10-years' time.

### 3. Competitors

Your competitors are the farmers in the same business as you, including local and national farms. If you know about your competitors and how they operate in the market, you can make strategic moves to boost your brand and excel.

### 4. Market Opportunities and Threats

You must know how the market works and what is going on at any given time. Information is the key to opportunities here. Know what others are doing and how to do it better.

Market threats are factors that can hinder your business. These factors include your environment, the economy, resources, authorities, competitors, and so on and knowing what can pose a threat and how to deal with them will be of great help.

### 5. Income Sources and Goals

State the channels and strategies for earning your income. You can earn through llama and alpaca sales, sports, events, fiber sales and processing, and other side activities.

Your income goals refer to the amount you envision making from your llama and alpaca business and you can set weekly, monthly and yearly plans. Doing this will keep you focused on your priorities and strategize on how to hit the mark.

### 6. Expenses

You should have an idea of your business expenses. The crucial costs include the cost of starting up and maintaining your farm. Routine and eventual medical checkups and farm activities like shearing and processing must also be accounted for.

### 7. Marketing and Advertisement

This section includes how you envision promoting your sales. You could go down the traditional means of advertising, such as adverts in newspapers, magazines, and other prints, and you can also use the radio and television.

In the today's world, almost everything is online, and you should have a website for your business to ensure it is visible to the world. If you have your target market outside of your locale, then make your website all-encompassing.

Use several languages and offer translation in different languages. Social media platforms are also a viable means of advertisement; Twitter, Facebook, Instagram and other media are popular platforms for businesses.

A Facebook business page is another way of having a virtual office. Word of mouth has always been a viable option, and businesses thrive on referrals. Recommendations are good for business awareness and growth.

Explore clubs, shows and events that promote llama and alpaca sales.

The price tag attached to these areas differs according to the geographical location. Your taste also determines how much you spend; if you want a top-notch construction be ready to spend a LOT, or consider a lower-priced but functional structure.

### 8. Milestones

These are significant events that drive your business so indicate the ones you want to achieve to boost your business quickly. Any activity geared towards building your business should be part of your plan.

In this section, your plan should cover activities like llama and alpaca herd acquisition, building a website, fencing, constructing barns, etc.

# More Tips on Management

A successful business hinges on successful day-to-day management. With adequate management, your business will cross borders. Areas to note are:

- **Accounting**

The accounts department is vital to any business and keeping income and expenditure records is essential. These will show you if you are making money or where you are spending more than necessary.

Since you are just getting started, you need to spend less and save more. With time, you can hire an accountant or bookkeeper, but meanwhile, several applications can aid you here. Most people use WAVE accounting, QuickBooks, FreshBooks, or something similar but reputable.

- **Associations**

Belonging to a relevant association is essential to business growth. It is an opportunity to network and meet people in the trade, and you can also learn from people who have been into the llama and alpaca business for some time.

There are several associations to join, like the Alpacas Owners Association, Inc. (AOA). Get licensed and identify with the association and observe local and national ordinances and regulations on owning a llama and alpaca business.

- **Tax**

You will need to pay tax and you can prepare your taxes yourself or have someone to do it for you, but you must consider the cost if you choose the latter.

- **Labor/Help**

For the smooth running of your business, you may have to hire help. If you cannot afford permanent staff at the initial stage of the business, hire temporary help.

- **Marketing**

Spreading the news about your business and increasing traffic is essential for business growth. Manage your website and social media handles yourself or hire a marketer or someone who is social media savvy.

- **Repairs**

Have the money to repair all broken equipment, taps and water lines, fencing, etc. to run your business without stress.

## Areas Where You Can Make Money

There are several areas you can generate an income, including:

- **Sales**

The first thing that comes to your mind when going into llama and alpaca business is the prospect of selling them for money. You can also go into breeding and sell the crias.

- **Manure**

They will produce manure every day. What will you do with it? You can use it on your field or pasture as practical sources of fertilizer or sell it on to other farmers.

This source is a dual advantage for you. You get to make money by keeping your animals' living areas clean. It may interest you to know that llama poop is virtually odorless and is commonly known as "llama beans". It is one of the best fertilizers, completely natural and eco-friendly. Historically, dried llama poop was burned by the Peruvian Incas as a form of fuel.

- **Fiber**

You must shear them yearly. It not only benefits them health-wise, but it also yields money, and some people prefer buying raw fiber while others prefer to buy it processed.

While you may choose to process the fleece, be aware that washing, drying, dyeing, up to the point of delivery, may be hectic and with every stage comes financial commitment. However, every bit of money you put into processing the fleece will yield you more profit.

The yarn produced by processing llama fiber is lightweight and soft. It is also very warm, which is why the softer undercoat is used to produce handicrafts and garments. The coarser undercoat is typically used to make rope and rugs.

- Events and Shows

You can make money from your llamas and alpacas by taking them to animal shows and events where they participate in sports and work.

# Strategies to Prosper in the Alpaca and Llama Business

There are strategies you can use to excel in your business, including:

- Get Information

Ask people questions about everything. Learn more on top of what you know already because you can never have too much information. Always seek to understand why, how, what, and where.

- Take Notes and Pictures

You may have a unique arrangement in mind, but you can learn from others. Visit other farms and take notes and pictures. Add ideas from other businesses to create a unique and comprehensive style.

- Work in Conformity with your Local Authorities

Check with your local authorities to learn what is allowed and what is not. If you have chosen a site to locate them, make sure that it is authorized.

- Customers Feedback

Encourage customers' feedback. Your business will grow if you please the market and satisfaction, quality, and consistency are essential to business growth.

# Mistakes to Avoid in Business

Anyone new to any business may make mistakes. It is why a guide is necessary. If you know the paths to avoid, you will not have to walk them, at least not consciously. Some mistakes to avoid are:

- Unsafe Purchase

There are many people out there looking to sell their animals. Being a newbie in the business, you may want to jump at the cheapest sale you can find, but sometimes these purchases may turn out not to be beneficial.

It is safer to buy your animals from the general market. If you are buying from an individual, endeavor to scrutinize the animal to decipher its health status. Do not buy animals that look malnourished and sick. Enlist the services of a veterinarian to be on the safe side.

- **Negligence of Health Care**

Mother Nature will play a massive role in the birth and growth of your cria. However, you should not mistakenly leave them entirely alone. If you do not have the time and amount of commitment needed to care for them, then you have no business owning them. It is that serious.

Get help. Many people looking to start their farms will be glad to get the experience while earning on the side.

- **Overlooking The Authorities**

The ordinances in your location bind you, and you must conform to these rules. If you locate your farm or have your animals grazing where they are not allowed to, you are violating the rules. The consequences of this action may be serious for your business.

Do not mistakenly violate the rules.

- **Overlooking Necessities**

When it involves money, you may be tempted to overlook it. Please do not. Do not forget necessities like repairs, purchases, replacements, etc.

# Bonus Chapter – Llama Terminology

To succeed in your llama or alpaca business, there are several terms you must understand:

- **Alarm Call** – the sound male llamas make when they feel their herd is under threat. It sounds like a turkey call, an engine turning over or a combination thereof.

- **Artificial Insemination (AI)** – a process where semen is taken from a male and placed manually into the uterus or cervix of a female llama.

- **Banana Ears** – a term describing llama ears that curve inwards and look similar to the size and shape of a banana.

- **Berserk Male Syndrome** – a condition describing a male llama that imprints on humans the wrong way and, when reaching puberty, becomes aggressive towards humans. Once it starts, this behavior cannot be changed.

- **Body Score** – a value given based on how thin or fat an animal is. The values range from 1 to 9, where 1 is emaciated, 5 is optimal and 9 is obese.

- **Bone** – a term describing the size of the llama's skeletal frame – those with large frames are said to have "a lot of bone."

- **Colostrum** – the first milk a female llama produces around the time of birth, rich in antibodies that the cria needs in the first 24 hours after birth.

- **Concentrates** – a supplemental feed dense in energy and lower in fiber. This includes multiple types of grains that are combined into a feed.

- **Cria** – describes a llama from birth to weaning.

- **Dam** – a female llama that has given birth.

- **Dung Pile** – an area where llamas defecate and urinate – they usually decide the area for themselves and there may be several areas in a pasture or field.

- **Dust Pile** – an area where llamas roll.

- **Embryo Transfer (ET)** – where early embryos are taken from a female and transferred into another.

- **Forage** – a food component that is lower in energy and higher in fiber, including hay, legumes and grasses.

- **Gait** – locomotion or movement. Llama gaits include walk, trot, pace, gallop, and pronk.

- **Gallop** – three-beat gait where the four feet are never on the ground simultaneously – the fastest of all gaits.

- **Get of Sire** – a llama show class where three llamas with the same sire and two or more dams are shown in a group – the judge wants to see consistency in the sire's influence.

- **Going Down** – when the female is receptive to the male she will drop to a 'kushed' position, known as "going down" for the sire.

- **Herdsire** – a male llama on a llama farm used purely for breeding – also called a stud.

- **Humming** – a sound made by llamas when they are hot, stressed, tired, concerned, curious, uncomfortable or tired.

- **Knock-kneed** – a llama condition whereby the front knees are angled inwards, known medically as carpal valgus. The condition causes incorrect movement in the llama and can lead to degenerative disease in the joints. These llamas also 'wing' when walking – see below.

- **Kush** – a term describing a llama lying down and is also the command used to get a llama to lie down.

- **Lama** – the genus llamas and alpacas are classified in.

- **Maiden Female** – an unbred female, usually too young for breeding.

- **Open Female** - a female that isn't pregnant.

- **Over-conditioned** – the polite way to say that a llama is fat.

- **Pace** – a two-beat gait where the rear and front limbs on the same side move backward or forward simultaneously. A medium speed, it is the least stable.

- **Packer** – a llama that can carry large loads to travel over long distances, usually with a lighter wool cover and larger than an average llama.

- **Paddling** – a term describing faulty movement where the llama's front feet swing out from the body as the leg moves forward. Usually caused by the llama having too wide a chest, sometimes genetically, but more typically in overweight llamas with a lot of fat in their chests.

- **Produce of Dam** – a class in a llama show where a pair of llamas with the same dam but different sires are show together – the judge wants to see consistency in the dam's influence.

- **Preemie** – a premature cria.

- **Pronking** – a term describing a gait where a llama bounces stiff-legged into the air, usually when playing or escaping from predators.

• **Rolling** – an activity llama do a lot; they lie on their sides and roll several times, either completely over or halfway, They do it to keep their fibers open, creating air pockets that provide extra insulation.

• **Sickle-hocked** – a llama fault where the hind feet go forward too far, creating a sickle shape at the hind quarters when the llama is seen from the side.

• **Sire** – a male llama that has sired at least one cria.

• **Stud** – see Herdsire – a male llama used for breeding.

• **Three-in-one** – commonly used to describe a female llama, sold when pregnant and with a cria. Effectively, you are getting three llamas for the price of one – the dam, the unborn cria, and the unweaned cria.

• **Tipped ears** – a term that refers to llama ears not quite erect. This is caused by cartilage in the ear tips that isn't strong enough to stand and can be genetic, caused by frostbite or by prematurity. It is not considered a major llama fault.

• **Topline** – commonly used to describe a llama's back when seen from the side. The ideal topline is level from the withers to the tail.

• **Trot** – a two-beat gait where the diagonal rear and front limbs move backward or forward simultaneously. A medium speed, it is a stable gait.

• **Underconditioned** – used to describe an underweight llama.

• **Walk** – a four-beat gait where three feet maintain ground contact at any one time. It is the slowest of all gaits.

• **Weanling** – a llama of less than 12 months old - already weaned.

• **Winging - used** for describing faulty movement. When it moves one front foot forward, the front feet swing in and then away from the llama's body before being placed back on the ground. Typically, this is seen in knock-kneed llamas and is worse in those that are severely knock-kneed.

• **Woolies** – sometimes used to describe llamas with a very heavy wool coverage.

• **Yearling** – a llama between one and two years old.

# Conclusion

Let's take a quick recap of all that you have learned from this book.

You learned why you should raise llamas or alpacas in the first chapter. In the second chapter, we explained the differences between llamas and alpacas, and now you should find it relatively easy to identify the breeds.

You should also know how to design facilities for them from our guidelines in the third chapter. Your first purchase of llamas and alpacas need not be a disaster because we have provided all the details you need to buy your first pair of same-sex llamas in the fourth chapter.

Spitting llamas should not be a strange phenomenon to you, as you now understood all the behavior and handling of these animals from the fifth chapter. You also learned what you can and cannot feed your llamas in the sixth chapter.

The seventh chapter covered what you need to know about the health, care, and prevention of diseases in llamas and alpacas. Birthing new life comes with its challenges in all animals, even humans. We have helped you understand the birthing process and how to care for the baby cria (baby llama).

You might not have realized that llamas can learn to do many things before you read this book, but now you know how to train your llamas or alpacas to do various, important tasks.

Are you ready to start your llama business now? Our last chapter provided tips that will help you ensure your business is a success.

This book is not one for you to read and forget. You can always refer to it while on your llama or alpaca journey.

You have a vital tool for raising llamas in your hands. Use it wisely!

# Part 5: Raising Pigs

## *The Ultimate Guide to Pig Raising on Your Homestead*

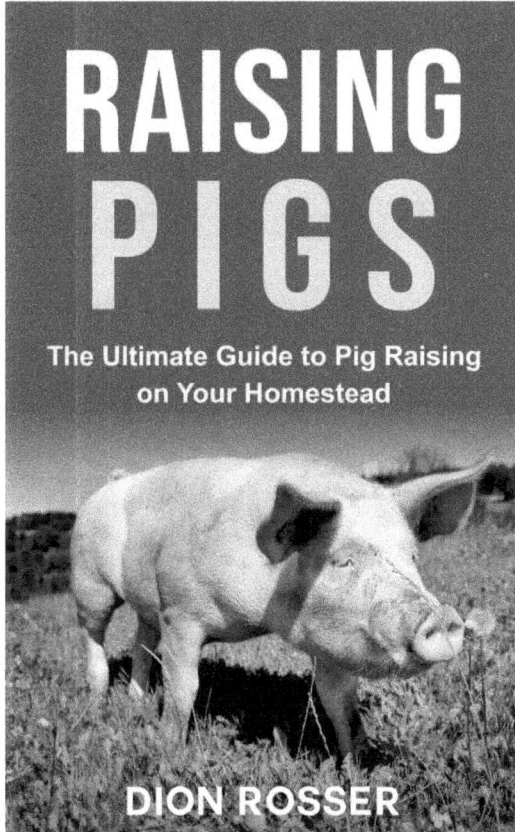

RAISING
PIGS
The Ultimate Guide to Pig Raising
on Your Homestead

DION ROSSER

# Introduction

Raising pigs is a profitable venture made easy with this guide in hand. Each chapter provides detailed information to help both beginners and experienced pig farmers in their journey raising pigs. By simply following the recommendations in this book, it is possible to enjoy life while raising pigs, unburdened by the challenges that most pig keeper's face.

Some books on the market claim to have in-depth knowledge to pig keeping. This book is up to date, featuring all the modern practices associated with modern-day farming. This book has been written in easy to understand language for both beginners and experienced pig farmers.

Raising pigs requires a hands-on approach. For this reason, this book contains hands-on methods and instructions using accessible and relatable language. Additionally, the book meets the needs of various pig farmers from across the globe. Whether you are in the United States or South Africa, this book's practical actions are beneficial to all pig keepers, regardless of the size of your pig operation or location.

# Chapter 1: Why Raise Pigs: Meat, Compost, or Pets

Despite their reputation, pigs are not "filthy" or "dirty" animals. In fact, they are clean animals that roll in the mud as a cooling mechanism in a hot environment. Pigs that live in cold climates need not roll in the mud, and as a result, stay "clean." Pigs are great domestic animals that can be kept as a source of food or as pets. The following are facts that will help you to understand pigs better.

## Facts About Pigs and Their Purpose

### History

Pigs, also known as hogs or swine, are domesticated animals whose meat is popularly consumed worldwide. Historians started documenting the breeding of these animals in Europe, Asia, and the northern parts of Africa about 9,000 years ago. Since then, many farmers raised pigs, and by the late 20th century, pigs were a household name, owing to the then improved breeding and feeding techniques.

There are many species of pigs, including the wild boar, which is an uncastrated male domestic pig. The term boar is generally used when referring to a wild pig. A pig can weigh from 300 lbs. (136 kg) to 1000 lbs. (454 kg). On average, a swine can grow up to 2.5 feet (70 cm) long.

Today, there are over two billion domestic pigs worldwide. These animals are distributed across different parts of the world. They can survive in different habitats, and scientists have attributed this incredible resilience to their high intelligence levels. But pigs are comfortable in colder environments and hot climates.

### Environment

Contrary to popular belief, pigs are relatively clean animals. Rolling in the mud helps them regulate their body temperature because they cannot sweat biologically like humans or other animals. And it allows them to create an unfavorable environment for parasites. These fascinating creatures keep their waste secretions far from where they live or eat.

### Intelligence

Pigs are intelligent animals. People that work with pigs know that they are very smart animals. For instance, did you know that pigs can remember objects, places, and other items to help them navigate their environment? They have excellent memories and can recall information for years. And they can also perceive time! Pigs are curious and like to forage while exploring the ground.

### Social Capabilities

Although it doesn't always seem like the first choice, many people keep pigs as pets. Being quite playful, along with their social attributes, pigs have been described by many people as great pets due to the variety of characteristics these animals display.

They prefer to travel in close groups known as sounders, made up of females and their young offspring. These groups help them keep warm during the cold seasons. Pigs must be kept in their social circles since isolation causes stress and discomfort, but when they are pregnant or sick, isolation is the go-to strategy.

### Communication and Defense

Pigs communicate using grunts and squeaks. A pig's grunt depends on the animal's "personality" and exposure to danger. Grunts and long squeals are a pig's way of alerting others about imminent threats. In such a case, a pig's primary defense mechanism will be to flee, and you'll be surprised to discover that pigs are well-known sprinters. They can run as fast as ten miles per hour (17 km/h), and wild pigs can run at speeds of up to 30 miles per hour (50 km/h). This short outburst of pace is not sustainable as they tire out quickly. If running is not an option, pigs can use their tusks as weapons if they feel threatened. Some have sizable tusks that are razor sharp and can inflict significant damage. Show caution when handling sows with piglets, but pigs are generally not aggressive animals.

### Reproduction

A pig takes about four months to reproduce. This is by far a desirable feature in livestock, especially compared to a cow which gestates for approximately nine months. Additionally, a swine can have a litter of about six to twelve piglets compared to a cow, which gives birth to one or two calves at most at a time. Unlike any other livestock animals, a piglet can double in size a week after its birth. You'll find that newborn piglets quickly learn to respond to their mother's voice, and usually the mother uses grunts to communicate with her offspring while nursing them. This is why in the past, farmers would prefer to raise pigs more than any other animal as they can produce a lot of meat at a much faster rate.

### Vision and Hearing

Last, pigs do not have good vision. They can distinguish between colors, but their range of vision is limited. To make up for it, they have a great sense of smell and hearing. You will quickly notice that pigs are not comfortable around loud sounds. Prolonged exposure to such noises startle pigs and can cause them a lot of stress, so consider maintaining a quiet approach. Don't enter piggeries slamming doors or making loud noises. As pets, they enjoy listening to soft music and getting occasional massages.

# Reasons for Keeping Pigs

### Meat

Raising hogs for commercial meat is one of the most profitable farm ventures, regardless of the farm's size. Globally, keeping pigs for commercial purposes is quite a lucrative business. For instance, China has the largest number of pigs of any country, with over 310 million, followed by Europe, the USA, and Brazil.

## Advantages of Keeping Pigs for Commercial Meat

Pig products such as pork and bacon are always in demand. There is a growing demand for both from traditional farm-kept pigs. Approximately 35% of all meat consumed by humans is pork. And what's even better is this percentage is growing at a steady rate every year. There could not be a better era to raise pigs for meat as the global production output has fallen by approximately 7% because of the crisis in 2020, and an additional 2% decrease in the worldwide production of pork courtesy of the African swine flu, which plagued the Asian market. This has seen farmers expand their herds to cope with the increasing demand for pork.

Keeping hogs for meat is relatively straightforward and basic. Most farmers already have a rough idea of the kind of meat they would like to sell or keep for personal consumption. For many people, pig options revolve around bacon and pork; some niches require a special kind of pig product. Here, you must use unique methods to meet this demand. Popular options include pork sausages, pork burgers, pork chops, and bacon.

Pigs are relatively cheap to maintain, especially compared to other animals such as cows. This is why farmers prefer to breed pigs for commercial meat because of their relatively low maintenance cost, coupled with their ability to produce a lot of meat quickly. Pigs, unlike most farm animals, can eat just about anything. They are omnivorous animals. These animals have a unique reproduction ability that will see your investment quickly reap the rewards. A sow can give birth twice a year to a litter of up to twelve piglets. Within a short period, you are almost guaranteed to double your pig-count on the farm.

While a cow needs pastures and fields where they can graze, pigs will more or less eat just about anything you throw at them. For instance, you could give them kitchen waste or even food scraps to eat. They are versatile animals that can be raised anywhere in the world on organic waste. Additionally, the feed to meat conversion ratio is more desirable than any other livestock. This means that the more food they eat, the more they grow and convert this food into flesh. Such factors combined make raising pigs a worthy investment.

### Challenges of Keeping Pigs for Commercial Meat

Raising pigs for meat requires a decent amount of processing. For small scale farmers, this might present a significant challenge. For instance, in the United States, small scale farmers reported this challenge in Minnesota. Approximately 17% of all farmers reported adequate access to processing. Consider having sufficient access for processing your meat if you are planning to distribute it to a particular market directly. Alternatively, consider setting funds aside to cover processing fees for your hogs.

Another challenge that farmers encounter when keeping pigs for commercial meat is dealing with a pig carcass. Many farmers, both large- and small-scale, struggle to distribute pork, including the whole carcass. Capturing the full value of your hog will remain a constant challenge. In most markets, especially in the USA and Europe, pig carcass components, including byproducts, do not contribute to the overall earnings that a farmer receives. Here, you should sell pigs as a whole if the opportunity presents itself.

### Raising Pigs for Compost

If you run a farm, one thing that you must deal with is manure. Raising pigs is a great way to help you turn waste into compost for your plants and garden. Compost, also known as "black gold," is beneficial as it adds nutrients and beneficial organisms to the soil. Furthermore, it is good for the overall environment, just like composting and recycling kitchen and yard waste.

Early farmers used to till the land with pig manure to allow it to decompose into critical nutrients for the next batch of crops. Today, this practice is uncommon as pig manure carries a host of harmful bacteria and parasites. Pig composting is one of the key reasons you should raise pigs on your farm.

### How to Use Pig Manure for Compost

The key to effective composting is mixing the right ingredients at a high temperature. One way to comfortably work around this is by adding pig manure to a compost pile consisting of vegetable waste, dead leaves, weeds, and dried grass and allowing the mixture to decompose. Also consider heating the pile of compost as temperature and fertilizer go hand in hand. The temperature should be between 30-60 degrees Celsius. The heat will destroy unwanted living organisms, including seeds and potential weeds. And the heat helps the pile of manure turn into compost quickly.

One crucial aspect of composting involves aeration. Allow air to flow in the mixture for the pile to turn into compost. Frequently turning the mix using a rake, shovel, or pitchfork is a great way to increase air flow into the pile. Drive any of this farm equipment into the bottom of the pile and bring them to the top. Consider repeating this movement at least once every three weeks. The compost should be ready for use after approximately four months but the longer the compost stays, the richer it becomes.

Moisture is key to activating the compost. If the fertilizer is too dry, all the nutrients and micro-organisms living inside will die, failing to activate the compost effectively. Consider adding a fair degree of moisture into the pile. One way to quickly check for moisture in your compost is by putting your hand in it and squeezing. If you don't get a damp sponge-like feeling, then your pile is reasonably dry.

### Challenges of Raising Pigs for Manure and Composting

If you do not heat the pile of pig manure and vegetable waste well or long enough, it will cause a rather unpleasant smell. Additionally, it might take even longer to break down and turn into compost. This is one challenge that farmers, especially small-scale farmers, encounter when turning pig manure into compost.

And excess moisture only causes a foul smell, flies, and creates a breeding ground for harmful bacteria and living organisms. This happens when a person adds fresh material such as vegetables and leaves without the right balance.

### Keeping Pigs as Pets

Pigs are intelligent, engaging, and social animals. All these qualities combined make pigs one of the best animals to keep as pets. Pet pigs are also called "mini-pigs" or miniature pigs. Common breeds of pigs kept as pets include the Ossabaw Island pig. The number of mini pig owners is increasing with each passing year. For instance, Canada and the United States had over 200,000 mini pigs back in 1998. This figure has since skyrocketed to more than a million in recent years.

Rightly so, these animals are fun to be around—their average lifespan ranges from 10 to 15 years. Pig keepers should consider a few factors before keeping a hog as a pet.

## Legal Considerations

While you may consider a pig as a pet, they are legally recognized as farm animals in most countries across the world. Fortunately, some states grant permits that allow residents to keep pigs as pets. You must observe the rules and regulations surrounding the domestication of these animals, depending on your country and location. For instance, Scotland does not allow residents to walk their pigs on a leash like a dog.

Check with your local authorities before keeping a pig as a pet. Additionally, keep all records, including vaccinations, medications, trips to the veterinary clinic, etc., to avoid legal complications.

## What do pet pigs eat?

Just like cats and dogs, pigs have their dietary requirements, and this differs from other pets. When feeding a pet pig, it is essential to remember these animals have one of the best feed to meat ratio, which means they quickly grow with increased food consumption. To prevent obesity in your pet pig, consider feeding them with regulated commercial diets.

However, most pet pigs enjoy feeding on sow nuts, which are readily available from many farm suppliers. Consider giving the animal a handful every morning and every night, and . consider supplementing the diet with fruits and vegetables as pigs also enjoy these options. Please note that most countries do not advocate feeding pigs with any waste or scraps. In fact, many consider it illegal.

Last, your pet, just like us humans, requires a decent amount of water every day. The amount of water that a pig needs will vary with the size of the animal. For instance, a "mini-pig" or a miniature pig can drink up to five liters of water daily. But your pig will require access to fresh and clean water every day. Remember that pigs like to forage and will occasionally put their feet and body inside a water trough, making the water dirty. As a result, you might have to change the water several times a day to keep it fresh and clean.

## Welfare

As mentioned above, pigs are intelligent animals. Their cognitive, physical, and social enrichment is a vital part of their well-being. Consider giving your pigs durable toys to play and forage with, and consider keeping them in pairs or groups for their social well-being.

Mini-pigs require decent housing and shelter. It should be dry, safe, ventilated, and well maintained. Fortunately, pigs are usually clean and restrict their toilet activities to one area. Consider giving your pigs a decent shelter to make a home. Also remember that young piglets are vulnerable, so consider keeping them in a warm and safe area for the first few weeks.

## Challenges of Keeping Pigs as Pets

Pigs present several challenges to pet owners. First, there is no way to predict the extent to which the pig will grow. Most pig owners buy these animals when they are relatively young and small. Pigs can grow to enormous sizes, and as mentioned above, their food to meat ratio is relatively high. A pig can grow and weigh up to 450 kg, which makes it challenging to maintain as a pet. There are specific breeds such as the Ossabaw breed, Göttingen mini pigs, and Juliana pigs that do not grow to these astronomical sizes. But it is still somewhat hard to determine the extent to which the pigs will grow when you first get them.

Pigs require significant care. For instance, as they grow, they will need new housing or shelter because of the considerable increase in size. Second, mini pigs need oiling before they can go out in the sun because of their sensitive skin. Third, poor diet and nutrition can lead to seizures and arthritis, which are challenging to treat in pigs. They are also vulnerable to dog attacks. In many ways, these animals need extra care, attention, and time, which pet owners might not always have.

Pigs are naturally foragers and explorers. Their natural rooting behavior might destroy property, including household items such as furniture or outside items, including flowers and gardening equipment. If they are bored, their curious nature will lead them to explore neighboring environments. In the process, they might get lost or hurt if they encounter animals such as dogs.

Sows (female pigs) will come into heat a few weeks after they are born, and this process will continue every three weeks. If they have children, sows become aggressive and territorial. The same goes for the boars. Aggressive behavior can lead to injuries or the destruction of property. Consider a friendly and calm demeanor when handling these animals to reduce any chances of anxiety or aggressive behavior.

Most of these pig challenges can be avoided with a more profound understanding of the animal. Pigs are fun to be around and have proven to be loyal companions. In-depth knowledge of these animals will help you avoid most of these challenges in your quest to become a mini pig owner.

# Chapter 2: Choosing the Right Breed

Pigs are intelligent animals. They are quite beneficial to have around and are considered social animals. They are all omnivores, meaning they feed on plants, animals, and almost everything else. Domesticated pigs are raised for commercial purposes to produce pork, ham, or bacon. Other pigs are kept as pets, such as Kune Kunes.

There are different kinds of pigs available. You can pick either male pigs, commonly called *boars*, or females, known as *sows*. These pigs come in many colors, such as brown, white, tan, red, gold, ginger, cream, and black. You will need to choose whether you want all sows, or a mixture of sows and boars, depending on your commercial or domestic needs and capabilities. This can be challenging, but you can pick whatever suits you best using the list below.

## Different Breeds of Pigs

Pigs come in many shapes, sizes, and colors. This can be overwhelming for any farmer when they want to make the best purchase. The list below will help you get to know the different types of pigs, the differences, and the ease of rearing each one of them.

The main types of pigs are commercial and heritage pigs. Commercial pigs are reared in factories in large numbers. The primary purpose of raising these pigs is to provide meat. They require a lot of feed and are not as fat compared to heritage pigs.

Heritage pig breeds are the best option for small scale farmers. They are easy to rear and provide delicious meat. They are relatively easy to manage as they feed on pasture.

Here are the best breeds to rear in your backyard:

### 1. Wooly Mangalica

The Wooly Mangalica is famous for its wooly coat; no other pig fosters this feature. They come highly recommended by small-scale farmers. They produce high quality and tasty meat. Their meat is tender and retains delicious fat juices. It provides fantastic bacon.

### Pros

- They are low maintenance
- They have manageable temperaments
- They don't rely heavily on protein
- They can adapt quickly to the winter season
- They have high returns

### Cons

- They produce a lot of fat, which can be overwhelming

### 2. Red Wattle

The Red Wattle is one of the most amiable pigs alive. They have a humble demeanor, which makes them a great companion. They are red with spots across their body. They can be quite heavy and large. Why should you buy this pig?

### Pros

- They have a high growth rate
- The meat is tender, lean, and non-fatty
- The sows are very motherly, reducing your work significantly
- They have a high birth rate

The Red Wattle is a great pig to rear for a first-time farmer. They are straightforward to manage and are non-aggressive. They are very friendly and will give you an easy time when breeding. They also help the soil by foraging. They are great in small confinements, so no need to expand your pen. They can go up to 1,000 pounds, which can bring outstanding returns after a few months.

### 3. Gloucestershire Old Spots Pigs

This pig is white with large black spots across its body. It is known for its docility and intelligence.

### Pros

- High maternal instincts
- High birth rate
- They are best suited outdoors
- High-quality meat

### 4. Kune Kune

Kune Kune is known for its docile nature, sweet meat, and excellent temperament. They are medium sized and are great when confined. Why should you buy this pig?

### Pros

- Their smell is not overwhelming
- They are calm and quiet
- They make great crossbreeds

### Cons

- They do not have fur, so they need shelter when it rains
- They need particular feed

### 5. Chester White

The Chester White is the most common pig in most homesteads. Here are some of the reasons why farmers like them:

### Pros

- They have extensive life spans
- The sows are very motherly
- They are bulky and muscular

- They require minimal maintenance

## 6. American Yorkshire Pig

The American Yorkshire pig is a popular member of different homesteads. The pretty pink skin is common all over farms in many locations. Here are the reasons you should have one.

### Pros

- They have a high growth rate
- They have a high birth rate
- They are muscular
- They are affordable to rear
- They have tasty meat
- The sows are incredibly motherly, reducing your monitoring rounds

## 7. Berkshire Pig

These are small black pigs with white socks, white tip on tail, and prick ears. The Berkshire pig is a popular choice among small scale farmers, and they are the oldest breed. Why should you buy a Berkshire Pig:

### Pros

- They have very delicious meat
- They are active foragers
- They have a high growth rate
- They are very friendly

## 8. Large Black Pig

They are also known as the Devon or Cornwall. They tend to have an elongated form. Most small-scale farmers buy them because:

- They are easy to manage
- They are great producers of bacon
- They are adaptable
- They are resistant to sunburn

### 9. Hampshire Pig

The Hampshire pig is easily identifiable with the white belt on its shoulders and front legs. They have large ears. They are very active and are known for their erect ears.

#### Pros

- They have a high growth rate
- They have a high birth rate
- They are generally large
- They have good temperament
- The sows have a high maternal instinct
- 

#### Cons

- They do not weigh as much compared to other pig breeds
- They have smaller hams

### 10. Landrace

It's a great pig for rearing indoors or even outdoors. The pig's carcass is exceptional for bacon and pork. Landrace has white skin with black hair. It also has drooping ears with a slight slant forward. They have long middle forequarters.

#### Pros

- They have excellent ham development
- Sows have a high birth rate
- The piglets have a high growth rate
- High-quality lean meat
- It's ideal for crossbreeding

#### Cons

- They are prone to sunburn due to the coat and skin color

### 11. Duroc

The Duroc is usually called Red Hog. It has a large frame with small droopy ears. It's quite a muscular pig with medium length. The head and the neck are light in complexion. Duroc has hard skin with a solid red color.

## Pros

- They can survive extreme temperatures
- Succulent flesh with a lot of muscles
- They are extremely friendly

## Cons

- They take time to mature

### 12. Large White

It is well-developed for the outdoors. It is a long, large pig with white skin, white hair, and long ears that stick up.

## Pros

- They can withstand extreme weather
- They have high birth rates
- They have high milk production
- The sows have a high maternal instinct
- Prone to sunburn due to lack of pigmentation

## Cons

- Their hams are of less quality.

# How to Select the Best Breed

Selecting the correct breeding stock for your farm is crucial for your farm's success. It is essential to consider the litter growth, size, and feed efficiency before making any purchase. Several traits of a pig should also be considered, such as long life, adaptability to different housing and temperature, carcass quality, resistance to diseases, and ease of rebreeding.

If you are a first-time farmer, remember these different factors. The availability of food supply means dealing with pig output, local beliefs (religion), availability of the pig breed, local requirements, local and global market conditions, and the local diseases prone to pigs. These factors are instrumental in guiding the type of pig you will select and the sustainability.

These steps will help you in the selection process:

### Why Do You Want to Raise Pigs?

There are several reasons farmers raise pigs. This could be for personal consumption, for sale, as a pet, or even for breeding. The reason as to why you are raising pigs changes the requirements you will have. Pigs intended for sale will require a more routine structure with high maintenance from the farmer. Pigs intended to be petted will need a less monitored environment.

### How Big Are Your Facilities?

Small scale pig farmers are at an advantage compared to those having a large farm. This will be easier for maintenance. This is a significant element of pig rearing.

### What Are Your Preferences?

Pick pigs you like, whether you want spotty ones, brown, white, black or prefer small, medium, or large. There are many friendly pigs available in the market.

### What Are Your Capabilities?

Large pigs require a lot of work. If you are active and free, you can choose the large pigs. Choose small pigs if you do not have as much dedicated time, especially if you are starting pig farming. This will enable you to grow at your own pace, acquiring knowledge and experience.

After answering the above questions, you can easily identify the next factors.

# Select from A Proper Farm

Pig breeders are very common, and it can be a daunting task to find the right farm to buy your pigs. The quality of the breed is affected by the environs. An adequate farm should manage its breeds with a high level of cleanliness and pre-planned programs. The lifespan of a particular pig that is confined can stretch up to ten years. This depends on its management and genetic composition.

Pigs have different character traits that are easily identifiable. You can rate the performance of the breed by checking on the maternal ability. The maternal pig should be able to nurse the piglets to the weaning stage, check on the number of piglets, and the rate of weight gain.

A good breeder will not only sell the pigs to you, but they will follow up after the sale. They will answer any queries and give more information regarding the pigs. Some will even offer free delivery to your proposed location.

### Choose Registered Pigs

Always select registered pigs, as this will ensure that you get the quality purported by the breeder. Without registration, it will be difficult to gauge the different aspects of the pig. The ear-notches or tags easily identify a pedigree pig.

Selecting the best breed is easy once you have established the traits. The following are vital things you should check before settling for any purchase.

### Check the Characteristics of the Best Breeds

Before buying any swine, make sure that the pigs are of high standard. Generally, you can gauge their health by checking their alertness; their eyes should be bright, and they should show ease of movement. You can also check how quickly they devour food and whether their ribs are visible. Be able to check whether the pig is active or dull. A malnourished pig will be dull and withdrawn.

Check on the temperament of the pig. Do not choose an aggressive or timid pig. Aggressive pigs are not suitable for rearing, especially for a first-time farmer. Go for pigs that are young as opposed to older pigs; buy pigs about ten weeks old.

### Body Features

The neck should be longer than average. This will make the shoulders appear to have a downward slope. When standing, the pig should appear to have slanted forearms.

The pastern is the location between the pig's hoof and the joint with the dewclaws. This area should have a gentle forward slope. The toes of all the legs should be moderately large.

Check on the buttocks as well. This is called the *rump*. The top line should appear flat-like, with the tail fixed high on it. The hind legs should be straight but curved after the knee joint.

The hock joint is located at the "heel" of the foot. This is an important area to be wary of before purchasing. Check on the shape or form of the hock joint to establish if it is healthy.

Also check on the teats of the pig. A healthy pig will have well-spaced breasts that are long and slender. Pigs have almost 32 teats running parallel on the underside from the groin to the chest. The average pig will have 10-14 pairs of teats projecting milk. The number of teats is essential, as it will dictate how many piglets it can feed at once.

### What to Consider

Inspecting a pig before a purchase is extremely important. First check the teats of the pigs. If they do not project outwards from the skin, then the mother will not be able to feed the piglets, as the mammary glands will dry off after birth, becoming useless. The pigs with extra teats are also not a good buy; the teats will not deliver milk after birth.

Check the report the farm has on the different pigs. Note the birth rate of the pig, the maternal performance, growth rate of the sows, and the presence of genetic deformities, if any. Any mother that weans less than ten piglets at a time should not be bought. Check on the rate of mastitis in the sows. This is an infection that occurs in the mammary glands of the mother pig. Also, check for metritis, an infection of the uterus, and agalactia, which is a lack of milk production.

When purchasing the pig, go with someone with a lot more experience in pig rearing. They will help you identify the best breeders and pigs for breeding. An experienced breeder will easily spot defects in their pigs. Remember, the pig price is an important factor to consider. The price tends to be different from one breeder to the next. Younger pigs are generally less expensive, whereas boars and sows are more expensive because they have proven to be fertile.

It is essential to check if they have been vaccinated against any diseases. Pigs rarely have routine medication, but there must be basic injections against common pig diseases such as Erysipelas. Obtain all the registration documents from the breeder. You will need them as proof of vaccination.

### Selecting Pigs Intended for Cross-Breeding

If you are a small-scale pig keeper looking to upgrade your existing stock, you must be vigilant in the selection process. Important factors to consider when crossbreeding pigs include cost and time. The most crucial factor is that they do not lower the standards of the existing stock or introduce diseases. You must consult your veterinary doctor before embarking on any purchase.

Get information about the disease history of the pigs and the current health status. Examine the health reports of the pigs and get to know a detailed medical history of the animals.

Remember the market acceptability, the genetics, availability, and the quality of the incoming pigs to your farm.

# Chapter 3: Housing, Fencing, and Facilities

During the sunny days, when the nights are short and the days are hot, pigs may sleep out under the sun. Regardless, you will need to provide housing and accommodation. Before purchasing your pigs, make sure there is a dry and cool house, safe from the threats of harsh temperatures and other animals. For their overall wellbeing and productivity, these animals require adequate space, and access to water and food.

There are many pig houses on the market, and you have many options to choose from. Failure to build the proper housing for your pigs can lead to severe problems that affect your pig's overall wellbeing and productivity. When housing pigs, carefully consider the following factors.

### The Environment and Site Location

The location in which you erect the pig's housing should be elevated or slightly raised. Such a location is necessary to avoid flooding when it rains. And the site should be protected from the sun to provide shade. The area should be cool, with fresh air to keep the pigs cool.

### Temperature

As mentioned, high temperatures make pigs uncomfortable as they cannot sweat and cool their bodies. To achieve the best productivity from your pigs, consider observing a specific temperature range. For instance, the most favorable temperature for newborn piglets ranges between 27 C and 35 C, but temperatures above 27 C are deemed unfavorable for most pig breeds.

Pigs can tolerate cold temperatures, but they are not comfortable in drafty areas. A drafty area is an enclosed space in an open area characterized by a lot of currents, usually of cold air. Consider having the housing location moved to a cool area free from winds or currents of cold air. If such a location is not an option, it would be best to check where the drafts are coming from and put a stop to them.

### Hygiene

The overall hygiene of the house will affect the pig's health and productivity. Many diseases are caused by unsanitary conditions, which create a suitable environment for the growth of harmful living organisms. These micro-organisms inhabit the pig's gut causing stunted growth and problems with manure.

### Water and Drainage

Freshwater supply is essential for raising pigs. Consider having a year-round supply of potable water for animal consumption and sanitization. Water will come in handy when diluting lagoons or putting out fires. Where groundwater is not sufficient, consider using additional sources such as ponds and community water systems.

If the pig house is in an area with significant rainfall or snow, think about constructing a slope or a runoff around the house to reduce the amount of water near the location. Runoff water can be contaminated, jeopardizing the health of your hogs. Additionally, high water tables impact the construction of buildings and manure storage.

### Manure Management

When selecting a site for raising pigs, consider one with adequate space for manure management. Depending on where you live, there will be different guidelines on the basic acreage required based on the nitrogen requirements for growing crops. However, the location you raise your pigs must be large enough for manure spreading. Avoid steep or high areas that could lead to manure runoffs, causing water and land pollution to adjacent environs.

Consider a rectangular pit measuring 10' x 8' x 6'. For 50-70 fully grown pigs, this pit will take approximately five months to fill.

### Security and Safety

Pig safety and security is an essential factor when it comes to site location. Remember that there are issues of theft and vandalism across the world. Also, visitors can infect animals with life-threatening diseases, so consider an area with limited human access to control diseases while reducing interference with other farm operations.

### Feeding and Drinking Area

Pigs should have these areas built systematically, preferably in a line, within the structure. It is advisable to have each pig have its own feeder but a general drinking area they can all share. The recommended size of the feeding trough should measure approximately 12" x 12" x 6". Although these measurements are standard, younger pigs might not require such large feeding areas.

### Space Requirements

As raising pigs is a worthwhile investment, it would be wise of you to remember that they might double in size after a relatively short time. Different animals require different housing facilities. The following are housing suggestions for different pigs.

### Fattening Pigs

The fattening phase of a pig commences as soon as the piglets start maturing (usually between weeks 8 and 15). This period does not stop until the pigs are brought to slaughter after they attain a minimum weight of 85 kg to 170 kg. For such pigs, consider a minimum space of 0.5 sqm (5 square feet) to 1 sqm (10 square feet) for each pig. This will give you adequate space for feeding, stabling, and anti-stress solutions.

Consider using a housing/spacing model with a flat solid floor made from concrete, hard soil, or cement. The floor should be slightly inclined to make it easier to clean with fresh water.

### Pregnant Sows

Pregnant sows require a quiet and peaceful environment. Remember that the house should be free from all types of elements that could stress these animals, such as temperature, ventilation, hygiene, and noise. With that said, every pregnant sow requires at least 1.5 (approx. 16 sq. f) sqm to 2.0 sqm. In hot climates, consider keeping sows in groups of two or three.

## Lactating Sows

There are many factors regarding productivity and efficiency that affect sows. One of them is inadequate housing and feeding programs. Lactating sows need to be fed more than twice a day for the best results. The importance of a proper house in removing wet and spoiled feed from the feeders should not be overlooked. Additionally, these animals need a quiet environment.

Therefore, it is advisable to use individual pens. These pens should have provisions for farrowing pans, cooling, heating a piglet nest, and a starter feed for piglets. The recommended housing size for each sow is approximately six square meters.

## Weaner Piglets

Weaner piglets are usually small but grow to about 25 kg in six to seven weeks. Each piglet will require about 0.3 to 0.5 sqm. The floor housing should be made of concrete to make it easier to maintain or clean. It should not be polished to avoid slipping. Just like the other pens, the floor should be slightly inclined to facilitate cleaning with water.

## Breeding Boars

Housing requirements for breeding boars are often overlooked. If the conditions are not optimum for these animals, they will "break down," limiting their overall output.

Breeding boars require a strong and well-insulated pen for sleeping and feeding. Breeding boars are usually kept alone and are prone to temperature variations. And mature boars have little fat cover to insulate them when it is cold. In the winter seasons, consider giving these animals increased bedding to provide them with extra warmth.

Areas with high temperatures also affect a boar's performance. Libido is usually affected before there is an impact on sperm quality. If prolonged high temperature occurs, sperm quality can be affected for approximately six to eight weeks. All these factors suggest that housing for breeding boars is crucial to their productivity and overall performance.

The floor housing for the boars should be made from cement to make it easier to clean. It shouldn't be polished because the pigs will often slip, risking serious injuries.

The size of the pen should be at least seven to eight sqm (3 x 3 or 2.3 x 3). The gates and overall structure of the pens should be strong to prevent the boars from escaping. When they are in heat, they might find ways of escaping the pen to secure a mate.

# Building Plans for a Good Pig House/Shed

As a small-scale farmer, there are several good options you should consider for housing your pigs. First, you must consider the accommodation type required for the different classes of pigs.

### Construction Plans for a Single Pig

Consider using locally available materials. Not only are local materials cost-effective, but you will have an easier time assembling these materials.

• The floor of the house/pen should be at least 9 sqm (3 m x 3 m)

• The floor of the house should be raised at least 0.6 m (1.9685 feet/ 60 cm)

• Consider spacing the floorboards (at least 2 cm).

• The roof should be made from water-resistant materials; should be water or rainproof.

• The house should be constructed so it shades sunlight to protect the pigs. The house could have provisions to allow a little sunlight in the house, but there should always be shade in the house.

### Construction Plans for a Pen Housing Sows

The smallest unit you can build is a pen housing a sow and her piglets. These pens can be used for a sow and her litter, two litters of weaned piglets, about four gestating sows, nine piglets, or one boar.

### Construction Plans

• Length- 4 meters with 1.4 meters allocated for manure management

• Width- 2.7 meters

• Height-3.4 meters (highest) or 1.1 meters (lowest)

• 60 cm raised off the ground. You can build the floor using either cement, wooden poles, or wooden slates and bricks.

• Two troughs (Although with one boar or fattening pigs, consider using one)

• Most of the area should be allocated feeding; creep management

• There area should be slightly raised to allow for drainage when cleaning with water

### Fencing Plans

Pigs can pose credible challenges when it comes to fencing. As mentioned above, these animals are intelligent and curious by nature. That means they will occasionally look for weak areas in the fencing system as they try to break free and explore other areas. Having a sound perimeter is important as you will be avoiding liability problems with hogs, especially when they run to neighboring areas to wreak havoc.

Should you build a permanent structure to serve you for the foreseeable future, then the best course of action will be to use a medium grilled rolled wire fence. This option is great as this material is tough and can withstand efforts from the pigs to cut loose.

Pigs usually escape through the bottom of the fence. There is no need to build the fence over four feet tall (48 inches). If it is within your budget, consider adding electricity inside the fence. Should the pigs come too close, the electric shock will quickly have them retreating. Keep checking the state of the electric fence as certain items could disrupt the flow of the current, risking the pigs escaping.

If electricity is not an option, then the bottom wires should be meshed closely together to prevent both mature and baby pigs from escaping.

# Effects of Bad Housing

### Parasitic Infection

Failure to erect proper housing for the pigs can lead to the contraction of diseases and infections. As a pig keeper, consider providing an optimal environment necessary for the safety of the animal, reducing the chances of hospitalization by disease-causing agents. For instance, sows may contract mastitis (which is characterized by a reduction in milk production, loss of appetite, and high body temperature) if the housing is wet and unhygienic. Furthermore, poor housing can lead to the spread of contagious diseases to both pigs and humans.

## Economic Losses

The housing can negatively affect your investment. For instance, if the house is not strong enough, the pigs will escape because of their curious nature. Also, poor housing will affect the production of meat negatively as conditions will not be favorable for developing the animals, and may lead to stunted growth - not desirable for the overall production of meat.

# Chapter 4: Pig Behavior and Handling

Gaining a good understanding of how a pig behaves is vital for ensuring the animal meets its daily needs. Natural behavior can be observed when it's in its natural habitat or even in the wild. A pig's performance is altered depending on the location and many other factors. Here we outline the various behaviors to expect. This will significantly affect how you handle a pig and its production quality. Once you gain a proper understanding of how a pig behaves, you can:

- Facilitate animal handling

- Reduce stress and frustration

- Reduce risk to the handler

- Reduce loss due to fatigue, injuries and bruising

Of course, it much easier to handle calm pigs than agitated or stressed ones! If a handler uses basic handling practices, the pigs will be less likely to become agitated. The handler should take into account:

- Point of balance

- Fight zone

- Senses

# The Fight Zone

This is the area a pig considers as its individual space. Pigs actively try to maintain a certain distance between the handler and themselves. The distance differs from one pig to the next. The more threatening the handler appears to be, the more distance the pig requires. When a handler becomes too frightening, the pig gets defensive, and their body language immediately changes. As a handler, you must recognize the cues from stressed pigs and establish more distance or back off until they are calm again.

# Point of Balance

The pig uses this to gauge the direction they should take when they are moving away from the handler. The point of balance is usually located at the shoulder but adjusts depending on the environment. Different conditions spark different reactions from the pigs. To achieve optimum results, the handler must work ahead of the pigs. For example, if a handler wants to get the pigs through the gates, they must avoid stroking the pig's rear while standing in front. The handlers should not block, move, or interfere with the pigs from the front position. Pigs tend to balk when coerced to move past people.

### Sense of Hearing

A pig utilizes their sense of smell and hearing to situate itself in different environments. They use their sight to complement the two senses. They have a blind spot that does not allow them to see the rear; the eyes are on the sides, giving them 310 degrees coverage. Pigs have an uncanny ability to spot any threat or pressure. They always make sure their handlers are within their line of sight, and they also use their hearing to track the movement of people they cannot see. A handler must know the vision span of pigs to facilitate their movement effectively. Their sense of touch is also essential.

### Pig Behavior

You can establish what a pig pays attention to by observing their ears, head, eyes, and body language. Handlers should note the directions pigs are looking, how they twist their bodies, turn their heads, and position their ears. Pigs tend to track their handlers even more when they feel threatened. Pigs will become more stressed in confined areas. The pressure from the handler during this time will make the pigs draw closer as opposed to pulling away. When they become agitated, they lie in a group and refuse to move. The body language of pigs change as they become more excited.

### Releasing Pressure

This is any action intended to reduce the level of frustration of a pig. It involves giving the pigs a lot of time and space. Here are some ways of reducing pressure:

- Step back and avoid constant contact with the pigs
- Pause and allow the pigs to move away
- Ease your body language to make the pigs feel safe
- Allow the pigs to circle past you
- Stop making too much noise
- Look away from the pigs
- Reduce the group size—this depends on the size, environment, door, and the aisle.

Pigs can effectively communicate their emotions through their heads, ears, eyes, and body movements. Here are signs that the pigs are fearful when moving them:

### Calm Pigs

Calm pigs will have these qualities:

- Ability to maintain a safe distance from the handler to relieve pressure
- Heads and ears are usually low, and the body is relaxed
- Attention is usually directed forward
- Vocalization is very minimal and in low tones

### Mild Stressed Pigs

Here are reasons/signs that your pig is showing mild fear:

- A handler is getting too close to the pigs and not giving them enough release from pressure
- The heads and ears are always rising
- The pigs will move away but fix their attention on the handler

- The fighting zone is expanding

- The pigs will increase their speed briefly

- Releasing pressure from the pig will calm them

- If you continuously sustain the pressure, they become fearful

### Defensiveness in Pigs

Here are reasons/signs that a pig is experiencing heightened fear:

- The handler is administering too much pressure and is getting too close

- Their full attention is on the handler

- The pig adopts different tactics as opposed to moving away—stopping, backing up, or turning back

- The pigs shut down and refuse to move, showing signs of fatigue

- Releasing the pressure will calm the pig down with time

- Escalating the pressure will make the pig escalate their tactics

- They tend to bunch up and refuse to separate

### Extreme Defensiveness

The signs that a pig is experiencing intense fear:

- Panic

- High pitched vocalization

- Willing to run over the handler bunching up and difficult to separate

# Herd Behavior and Group Patterns

Pigs seek solace in one another for protection. The extent to which pigs associate with one another depends on their fear level, their attention, and the available space.

### Flowing Herd Behavior

This is what occurs when pigs move together. The flowing movement occurs when:

- Pigs are drawn to the movement of other pigs

- Calm pig response

- The attention is towards moving and staying with the herd

- Movement of front animals encourages movement from the rest

- Animals are loosely spaced

- The handler is not coercing movement from the pigs. The pigs are clear from obstructions

### Disrupting Flow

The movement and distractions ahead or from the sides can take the pigs' attention, preventing them from moving. Factors like excessive noise, pressure, and crowding will also stop the movement. These changes can affect the pigs' movement:

- Footing/traction

- Temperature

- Lighting

- Floor surface

Other factors that may affect the pig's movement:

- People on their path

- Drafts or wind

- A beam of light shining through a crack

- Equipment, trash, or objects in the path

- Loud or sudden noises or activities

- Water puddles

- Shiny or reflective objects

- Change in color of equipment

- Moving or flapping objects

- Other animals

- Change in the height of the flooring

Handlers who can read these signs with ease keep their pigs calm by giving them space and time. Take time to remove all distractions from the environment before buying a new breed. Pay attention to the body language of the pigs. When the pigs are getting more afraid, the handler needs to release the pressure.

Most handlers get agitated when transporting and unloading the pigs, because of the new personnel that will receive, count, tattoo, and move the pigs. It is vital that the transporter minimizes the contact with the pigs, give them ample space and time to get into the truck.

### Bunch Herd Behavior

This occurs when pigs remain still when the group is stopped. Bunching is a defensive response by pigs to stop movement, especially during ear tagging or vaccination. It is caused by anything that traps, crowds, stops, or confuses the pigs. It occurs when the pigs are facing away from the handler. They tend to be closely paced and listen intently.

You can easily identify this early by checking on the ears or crowding of the group. Pigs will opt to stay in a bunch as opposed to leaving the bunch to steer away from the handler. When a handler increases pressure or aggressiveness, the pigs will tighten the bunch.

### Handler's Bubble

The handler's bubble can also be regarded as the *flight zone* for handlers. The bubble takes up real space that leads to crowding. It changes depending on the pig's level of fear or the handler's pressure. It acts as a real barrier that moves with the handler.

Pigs move according to the arc of the bubble. Handlers can note the movement of the pigs to actualize the arc of the bubble, using this information to direct the pigs properly. Small pigs tend to pile away to get away from the bubble. Large pigs hold still within the bubble. You can use large animals to face a particular direction so that the rest can follow.

### Rooting Behavior

This is where the pig uses its snout to push something repeatedly. The pigs root to find food like truffles, grubs, and roots. Rooting is regarded as an exploratory behavior need. This is a great activity, especially if you need your land to be cultivated or weeded; however, it can pose a challenge to those with gardens. A nose ring is inserted on the septum to prevent this behavior.

Lack of proper feeding regiments increases the frequency of rooting. The different levels of rooting depend on the nutritional needs of the pigs. On average, the sow spends at least a quarter of its life rooting. This can be an advantage to those with larger tracts of land needing cultivation.

If you want to reduce rooting, you can opt to plant root crops on the land, but this is not the best alternative compared to nose rings. You can use edible enrichments to prevent damage to the paddock. Sows prefer branches and peats as rooting materials.

### Environmental Enrichment

This refers to providing pigs an opportunity to root, play, and investigate its environs to make it more comfortable. This is usually seen when you give pigs a long straw, and they play with it then store it for later use. You must implement this with regard to the requirements of the pigs. Enrichment can stimulate foraging if used appropriately. Through it, piglets tend to rise high in the social status of the pen. You can identify the need for enriching by spotting injuries on the neck, ears, and head of the pig.

Pigs usually use rooting behavior as a way to find food and obtain nutritional balance. The pigs generally use their snout and mouth to root. Even without the reward of food, they will root. Farm pigs spend a lot of their time investigating and manipulating the environs – an excellent way of establishing the health status of the animals. Failure to provide a distraction to keep the pigs occupied can lead to tail biting.

Enrichment highly affects weaners as opposed to the much older pigs. All pigs still prefer having a stimulant that will draw them away from harming each other.

### Maternal Behavior

There is a recurring behavior among sows that undergo isolation, community integration, and living. Farrowing the environment greatly affects the sows. Female pigs need to construct their own nest and farrow the environs; this is done most often when the sow is in distress.

### Isolation

This stage lasts two days before giving birth to the first piglet. The sow tends to isolate itself from the group and looks for a nest. The sow can walk up to six kilometers investigating the environs to find the perfect spot. Sows choose areas far from the group, as well as sloping ground. She constructs the nest using straw and makes sure that the walls of the nest are strong.

### Nest Building

This process occurs in stages as the sow must check on various factors before settling on the new area. The sow must make sure the spot is about four inches deep before proper construction. Then she looks for grass, leaves, and roots to line the nest for comfort. She puts large branches over the nest and covers with light materials to form a roof.

### Farrowing

This is done after building the nest. The sow is usually very passive during the process. She sniffs and investigates the piglets that are born. The sow barely gets up to help the piglets from their membrane. The umbilical cord detaches itself when the piglet moves to the udder. The sow's inactivity is due to the numerous piglets it has birthed, but it usually regains its energy after two days of rest. It's a great adaptation that prevents the sow from crushing its newborn.

### Nest Occupation

This occurs a week after farrowing. The maternal instincts of the sow dictate the nursing routine. The sow can initiate by lying on its side or by the squealing piglets. The sow grunts a lot during this period. As the grunts become more rapid, the piglets become quiet and continue to suckle. This is followed by piglets butting and nosing at the udder. Some piglets detach themselves and go on to sleep or play. The sow can end the nursing by standing up or rolling over.

### Social Integration

The piglets are not introduced to the rest of the herd until they are one week old. In the first two days, the sow does not eat as much as before, but as time goes by, the sow moves farther away from the nest and eventually re-joins the herd. The litter takes a few more days and then joins the herd as well. The sow introduces its offspring to the herd, establishing their relation immediately. In the first seven days, the litter maintains proximity to the sow. The litter gradually starts interacting with other piglets in the herd. The litter shouldn't be integrated with the rest of the herd until it's at least fourteen days old.

### Weaning

The frequency of nursing decreases after the first week. Piglets begin to wean four weeks after birth. In eight weeks, the piglet only consumes solid food in its diet. Different litters have different weaning stages, but it usually ranges from eight to seventeen weeks postpartum.

### Mixing and Fighting

Once pigs are mixed, they go through a phase to establish social relationships. Some pigs dominate, while others become subordinate. It is crucial to be certain that the pen is socially stable. Establishing social relationship requires some pigs to fight. Pigs that do not fight are consequentially subordinate.

During these fights, the pigs do not eat. They decrease in weight significantly (the newly weaned pigs are not affected as they do not eat as much as the others.) The subordinates suffer the most as they do not feed as much as they would like. The old pigs, which are reserved when it comes to eating, tend to experience significant weight loss due to the disruption.

The size and age of the pigs determine the effect of the fight. The larger the pig, the more damage it causes. It is vital to avoid putting large pigs together as they can cause irreversible damage and injuries. If you spot a smaller pig being harassed, it is essential to relocate it to another pen.

# Pig Handling

People handle pigs for various reasons, from medicating, transportation, weaning, or even birthing. Animals appropriately handled are gentler and more productive. Rough handling can cause lower production. Therefore, the persona must manage the pigs not to perform painful procedures as it may hinder the production.

Animal welfare has a lot to do with the way the pigs are handled. If the pig is improperly managed, it is induced with stress and fear, which can affect the quality of meat. It may also reduce the safety of the pig and the handler. Meat from a pig improperly handled tends to be pale or exudative. Proper handling can increase animal welfare, the quality of meat, and safety.

For an outdoor system, pig handling and care will require a lot of observation. Unlike indoor systems kept at a specific temperature, the outdoors offers a different experience to the pigs. It is, therefore, essential to note this will affect the behavior.

A stock person must develop a routine checkup on all pigs daily. Inspect the animals by walking through them gently. This is a vital exercise to detect animals that are sick or lame. Petting the pig through friendly stroking is also a significant factor to consider as it will help the pig gain more trust. It is also essential to check the drinkers.

Following are best practices for proper handling of pigs.

### Handlers

It is not an easy task to handle pigs, for both the handler and the pigs. Being gentle and patient can ease the process by reducing the stress levels. Always remember that despite the high IQ of pigs, they do not fully understand what you want them to do. When you need to move them, it will be much easier if they are calm than excited. As a handler, you must move slowly and quietly so as not to disturb the pigs.

A handler should familiarize themselves with the pigs first. New handlers are not recommended, especially when moving the pigs. You are also required not to rush or yell at the pigs. It can be frustrating to move pigs as they may not be in the mood, but do not allow this to get to you. Practicing patience will bring more positive results. Never be quick to use aggressive methods simply because the pigs want to explore the environment.

# Handling Tools

Handling equipment is used to provide barriers and stimuli, such as physical barriers, visual barriers, visual stimuli, and auditory stimuli. Several farm tools are friendly to pigs and may pose no danger or harm to them.

Using a nylon flag, cape, plastic ribbon, or sorting boards to move pigs or give them direction is highly recommended. Handlers should never use electric prods. These will make the pigs more aggressive and induce stress, therefore, affecting the quality of meat. Sorting boards are more effective when moving pigs.

Prodding animals is not recommended as it causes fear and stress. The electric prod raises the temperature of the pigs and the heart rate. Never prod a pig in the eyes, testicles, anus, or nose. These are extremely sensitive areas that may cause fatalities or health issues.

Here is a detailed view of the acceptable equipment mentioned above:

### Nylon Flag

This is excellent equipment to stimulate pigs visually. The nylon flag is especially effective amongst large pigs. It is used to block the optical path of a pig or get its attention.

### Matador's Cape (Witch's Cape)

The cape is useful in acting as a visual barrier with all pigs. It creates an illusion that the pig has reached a dead end.

### Plastic Ribbons on a Stick

These provide visual stimulation when flapped or waved. It can create a proper distraction to move the pig in the correct direction.

### Plastic Rattle

The rattle is quite a useful tool in providing auditory, visual, and physical stimuli. As a handler, you can also improvise and use shaker cans or bottles. The noise shouldn't be too loud and continuous, as this will inhibit the movement of pigs. Short spurts are quite effective in controlling the pigs.

Rattle paddles are also an efficient way of pig handling. Do not raise them above the shoulder when tapping the animals. The hit should be very gentle to prevent frightening the pigs. A simple touch of the pig with a rattle draws its attention. Pigs tend to move towards the paddle and brace it.

Avoid repeated contact and noise as they will prevent the pigs from moving. Paddles are very efficient in providing the pigs with visual aids. Do not move the paddle too much as this may stimulate the pigs negatively.

### Sorting Board

This is the most versatile tool available on the farm. It is also known as a sorting panel that comes either as a single panel or bifold. The sorting board can be used as a visual aid or a physical barrier.

### Electric Prod

This tool is not recommended during pig handling. There are cases where there are strict guidelines provided that may require its usage. There may be a situation whereby pigs are in a bunch at a doorway, and the electric prod may be needed to move them on.

When you shock the lead pig, it will jump and pave the way for the rest. Shocking the lead pig does not necessarily mean that the other pigs will move in the intended direction. The pig that follows may be scared and retreat to prevent being shocked. In this instance, do not shock all the pigs; simply give them time. After the pig realizes the lead pig is unharmed, the pigs will follow and enter the pen.

Using the prod is the last resort when all other tools have failed and should be put away immediately.

### Mixing Pigs

When transporting pigs to a new pen, you must be very meticulous. Be sure the pen is not overcrowded, poorly ventilated, or fostering broken or sharp equipment. Mix all pigs simultaneously in a completely new pen. Mixing them at different times may cause the newcomers being beaten. It is advisable to mix many pigs at the same time, as opposed to a few pigs. The latter will also result in a lot of fighting.

Make sure the pen you have built has an escape route. This is a safety measure when a fight breaks out in pen. It is also not recommended that you group large pigs into standard weight pens.

As a handler, it is essential to know the signs of a stressed pig. You can easily tell if a pig is under duress if it has blotchy skin, stiffness, muscle tremors, reluctance to move, squealing, and panting. These indicators are useful in establishing the comfort of a pig and change to better tactics.

### Training Animals

Pigs need to be trained to foster their safety and that of handlers. Pigs should be accustomed to handling to minimize stress. Pig handling occurs at different stages during the pig's stay. Handlers may need to clean the pen, showing and preparation, transportation, movement in the environment, and husbandry procedures. These activities will require a lot of handling that may stimulate the pigs negatively or positively. It is, therefore, vital to set up a routine that will help the pigs accustom.

Routines will train the animals efficiently and help them acquire good habits.

### Protective Equipment

To determine what equipment you will need, you can assess the tasks in loading, transporting, and unloading the pigs. It is essential to note down the injuries you may encounter during the process of protecting yourself. The minimum equipment a handler should have is a sorting board and safety boots. Handlers who travel inside the truck with the pigs must also consider wearing knee pads, shin guards, and bump helmet to protect them. Head injuries are prevalent amongst handlers traveling in the trailers. It is easy to get head bruises, cuts, and bumps.

Other equipment is necessary for day to day handling of the pigs include:

- Hard hats
- Shin guards
- Eye protection
- Hearing protection
- Dust mask
- Gloves
- Sort Boards
- Knee pads

# Chapter 5: Pig Nutrition and Feeding

Pigs, just like most farm animals, require essential nutrients and vitamins to meet their sustenance needs. Failure to provide pigs with such nutritional requirements increases their risk of stunted growth, poor reproducing, lactation, among other functions. Good feed is a necessity for these animals. You can use locally available feeds that are affordable.

Remember that feed is the biggest cost factor in the raising of pigs and can amount to about 60% to 80% of the total cost of production. Pigs can be fed using kitchen and vegetable waste. The food must be of the right quantity and mixture. And focus on valuable sources of energy rather than achieving feed efficiency or growth rate. However, their nutritional requirements can be divided into five categories; carbohydrates, fats, proteins, minerals, and vitamins.

## How do pigs digest food?

Pigs consume food with their mouth, where the digestion process begins. Pigs are omnivorous animals with one of the best feeds to meat ratio. As piglets, they are born with needle teeth. As they grow, boars grow tusks and canines, which they use as weapons if they feel threatened. Their molars have numerous tubercles, make them ideal for crushing food.

Food is chewed into smaller bits, which is then mixed with saliva, making it easy to swallow. Food then passes through the esophagus and into the stomach, where it is broken down further by other enzymes to form chyme. This chyme is later broken down in the small intestines and absorbed. It doesn't stop there as food particles make their way into the large intestine (cecum and colon) where water and remaining nutrients are absorbed into the pig's body. The colon forms the feces, which are expelled through the anus.

# What can you feed your pig?

### Grains

You can comfortably feed your pigs commercially prepared or locally made grains. Cereal grains are the world's leading source of energy in foods in both humans and animals. For your pigs, consider a total feed mixture constituting approximately 55% to 65% of grains. Grains are primarily energy-providing foods, but they also contribute to approximately 20-50% of all protein content in the food mixture.

For instance:

- Broken rice contains approximately 8% protein.

- Maize is also a great feed option that is high in digestible energy. It can be the primary source of energy in the feed mixture. Maize is an affordable food option in many countries, especially in South America and Africa.

- Oats are good energy sources but cannot constitute over 40% of a mixture for growing pigs and less than 60% in mature pigs.

- Sorghum has properties like maize. Consider using one as a substitute for the other.

- Wheat (feed grade) is also a great source of energy and protein that can be used in the feed mix. It is a great alternative to maize but is slightly more expensive compared to maize. Yet, using wheat could potentially save you a lot in food expenses, as you might not need to buy more protein.

- Barley is an energy source high in dietary fiber, which is excellent for digestion. Consider keeping the barley content in the feed mix less than 70%.

There are grain by-products such as maize bran, wheat bran, and maize cobs used to lower the digestible energy of the food mixture. Additionally, such brans are rich in protein and are relatively affordable. The most popular grain by-product is wheat bran. It is cost-effective and rich in protein. However, it does have a laxative effect on pigs.

### Fishmeal

Fishmeal is a brown powder/flour derived from the cooking, drying, and crushing of raw fish. Fish is a well-known source of protein. Pig keepers widely use fishmeal in feed mixtures across the world.

### Blood and Carcass Meal

Blood meal is a form of animal feed made from the blood of cattle or hogs as a by-product of the slaughterhouse. It is high in protein and is one of the highest non-synthetic sources of nitrogen. But its dense nutritional value does not warrant extensive use of this meal because the blood meal is unpalatable. Consider limiting blood meal to 5% in the feed mixture.

### Vegetables and Fruits

You will notice that most pigs are fairly happy eating broccoli, tomatoes, oranges, kale, spinach, cabbages, melons, potatoes, beets, carrots, apples, and cucumbers. Most vegetables, fruits, and even bread scraps (that have not been tampered with) are pig treats. If they are by-products, they should be cooked properly.

Lucerne is a common plant option used in feed mixtures. It is high in fiber but low in digestible energy. As a result, consider limiting Lucerne in the feed mix. Other common plant options include soya bean oil cake meal and sunflower oil cake meal, which are high in plant protein.

Soybeans can act as a protein supplement for pigs above 25 lbs. (approximately 11 kg). Growing pigs have a limited ability to process the complex proteins usually found in soybean meals. Additionally, developing pigs may develop allergies to certain proteins found in this meal.

# Sources of Minerals in Pigs

In pigs, minerals play a vital role in their development, performance, and overall well-being. Minerals are helpful in the formation and development of bones, lactation in sows, and certain chemical reactions in the body. For such reasons, pigs require about 13 different minerals. Out of the 13 minerals, the following should be routinely added to their feed mixture—calcium, zinc, iodine, manganese, phosphate, copper, sodium, iron, and selenium. Minerals for pigs are divided into two groups: trace (micro) minerals and macro minerals.

• Calcium is one of the most deficient major minerals in diets comprising of oilseed meals and grains. Additionally, calcium affects the absorption of other minerals, such as zinc. Feed lime is a great and affordable source of calcium, but it does not contain phosphate. For this mineral, consider giving the pigs bone meal.

• Sodium is essential as it helps with nerve function. The deficiency of this mineral leads to impaired growth and loss of appetite. The grains listed above are great for energy but poor in mineral supplementation. This problem can be solved by simply adding salt (sodium chloride) to the food. If the food is too salty, consider providing adequate water to reduce the toxicity. Failure to do so can cause weakness, seizures, or even death of the pigs.

• Iron is required for the synthesis of hemoglobin necessary for oxygen in the red blood cells. Piglets are born with high concentrations of iron in their livers. Lactating sows usually need iron as their milk is the only way piglets can get their nutrients and it doesn't contain iron. Consider giving these pigs iron supplementation in the form of injections or tablets administered through the feed mix. Iron deficiency in pigs leads to these symptoms; pale mucous membranes, enlarged heart, spasmodic (contraction of the trachea) breathing, reduced immunity, and lowered immunity.

• Selenium is an important mineral used in developing enzymes that protect cells against oxidative damage. In the United States, most areas lack this mineral in the soil, while few locations have it in abundance. For this reason, check the soil in which your farm or pig's husbandry is located. Deficiency signs of selenium include muscle dystrophy, sudden death, especially in growing piglets, impaired reproduction, and liver necrosis, among others.

• Zinc is a major mineral necessary for the development of normal skin and many enzymes. Deficiency symptoms include rough, cracked, or scaly skin, loss of appetite, and impaired sexual development. Zinc concentration is low in plants and grains; however, this mineral is abundantly found in animal products such as a bone meal.

• Just like zinc, copper is an essential mineral needed for the formation and function of a couple of enzymes. Also, this mineral is necessary for the absorption of iron from the intestinal tract and liver. Most crops have a sufficient supply of this mineral. Copper supplementation is necessary as it stimulates growth and feeds intake in pigs, especially weaning pigs. Copper deficiency symptoms include heart enlargement, stunted growth, nervous disorders, poor development of bones, and hemoglobin-deficient red blood cells. But exposure to high levels of copper include impaired growth, anemia, and in extreme cases, death.

• Manganese is necessary for enzyme function influencing bone development, metabolism, and reproduction. Signs and symptoms of manganese deficiency include a general imbalance in developing pigs, lactation problems in sows, enlarged hocks, and stunted growth (which includes irregular legs), among other things. Manganese does not occur naturally in grains, and thus it is advisable to supplement this mineral in the pig's diet.

# What should you not feed your pig?

Most pig owners are not aware that feeding pigs certain foods might be harmful to the swine or even illegal. For instance, feeding pigs meat or meat products in Australia is illegal. Feeding pigs these food substances could potentially introduce deadly diseases to both pigs and other livestock present on the farm. The following are foods you should not feed your pigs.

### Meat or Meat Products

You must not feed pigs meat or meat products. This is illegal in some countries. Additionally, the CSIRO Australian Animal Health Laboratory testing on pork products showed in 2019 that out of 418 tested samples, 202 tested positive for the African Swine Fever (ASF). Pig related studies and surveys have shown there is a direct relationship between ASF and meat or meat products. Avoid feeding meat to pigs to reduce the chances of an outbreak of the African Swine Flu. If you notice any unusual death in pigs, be quick to contact local authorities.

### Food Waste and Scraps

Food waste or scraps that have potentially been in contact with meat or meat products may carry dangerous viruses, including the African Swine Flu. As a result, these viruses could provide an entry point to infect other farm animals. It is advisable to avoid such products because many viruses can survive comfortably for long periods in meat or meat products. Some say that the outbreak of foot and mouth disease back in 2011 in the UK had its roots in waste products fed to pigs. The waste food products contained meat products that carried the virus.

Refrain from feeding your pigs kitchen scraps, food from retailers including supermarkets or bakeries and rubbish dumps, meat, blood, or bones form other mammals, birds whether cooked or raw. If you don't know whether any food product has been in contact with meat or meat products, you should not feed it to pigs.

### Traditional Pig Feeds

There are certain foods that pigs need to eat to meet their nutritional requirements for growth, reproduction, and overall well-being. The following are traditional foods you can give to your pigs.

- Rice Bran- Great for energy. It also contains 11% protein.

- Maize- Best source of energy, it is very cheap, and has 9% protein.

- Soy beans- Has a high nutritional value and contains 38% protein. It should be cooked with other foods such as rice bran or maize.

- Broken Rice- Another great alternative for energy. It contains about 8% protein.

- Wheat bran- Contains important dietary fiber with significant proportions of proteins, carbohydrates, minerals, and vitamins.

• Root Crops- As the name suggests, root crops are underground plant parts frequently consumed by both humans and animals. They should never be over 30% of the feed mix. They should be washed, peeled, sliced, and dried because of the toxic substances found on root plant skins.

• Fruits- Fruits can be given to pigs *fresh*. If they have been tampered with during transportation, consider boiling them before feeding the pigs. Suitable fruits include bananas, papaya, melons, and apples, just to mention a few.

• Screened restaurant or kitchen waste- Waste can be given to pigs but it needs to be screened first because of potential contamination. Either way, consider boiling or properly cooking such food items before feeding the pigs.

• Vegetables- Vegetables can be given while still fresh. If they are damaged or tampered with during transportation, they should be boiled. They are supplementary feeds for pigs, i.e., spinach, cabbage, morning glory, and lettuce, among others.

• Ipil-Ipil- These are locally available tree crops. These plants are nutritional and are rich in protein. Consider mixing them with other feeds before feeding the pigs.

• Banana Stem- Pigs enjoy eating banana stems. Consider chopping them down into small bits and adding salt before feeding the pigs.

• Cola-Cassia- This plant is rich in crude protein, calcium, iron, thiamine, phosphorus, vitamin C, niacin, and riboflavin.

• Green Soya Bean Plant

• Pumpkin- They are an excellent source of vitamins, including vitamin B. Be careful when preparing pumpkins as many vitamins are lost during the preparation process.

• Other plants you should feed your pig include water hyacinth, clovers, alfalfa, mulberry, chayote, and winter melon.

# Pigs and Their Feed Requirements

### Boars

When feeding boars, it is important to remember that they must not be fat or too lean. Consider feeding your boars 2 kg of feed mix daily. Keep a close eye on them; if they grow too thin, consider adding extra feed every day. If they grow too fat, consider reducing the daily feed. If the boar is regularly used for breeding, then increase the feed to about 2.5 kg daily.

### Dry/Pregnant Sows and Gilts

After the weaning process, consider giving the sows a feed mixture of approximately 2 kg daily. Keep the sows in good condition during this period i.e., just like the boars, monitor the weight and fat of the pregnant sows. The weaner meal should be about 0.25 kg extra for every suckling pig.

### Lactating Sows

Lactating sows (sows with piglets) require a lactation mixture, especially those with many piglets. Additionally, they should not lose weight or lose as little weight as possible. A sow in good shape should be fed more than 2 kg., with sows with over six piglets should be fed at least 6 kg of feed and lactation mixture every day. Also, they always have access to clean and fresh water.

### Young Piglets (Up to 10 Weeks Old)

When feeding young piglets, it is important always to make their feed dry (creep pellets). Consider using a self-feeder so that no feed goes to waste. Remember that pigs in this stage need to eat as much as possible to stimulate quick growth. The feed should be approximately 0.25-100 kg per day after seven days up to the day they start weaning.

### Growing Pigs (11 to 13 Weeks Old)

After the pigs have been weaned, they will grow at an incredible rate. Growing pigs are excellent for good quality meat with low-fat percentage. However, just like the young piglets, always consider feeding these pigs with a self-feeder.

Remember that pig appetite is important to their overall growth and development. Pigs are clean animals who eat fresh and clean meals as opposed to stale or even contaminated meals. You should clean their feed and water troughs frequently; also remember that maintaining adequate feeder space is important to allow the pigs to feed whenever they want.

# Chapter 6: Pig Health, Care, and Maintenance

Pig's welfare is an important aspect that directly affects the quality of meat. The welfare of a pig includes its physical wellbeing, mental wellbeing, and natural living. These aspects can be compromised by extended periods of being confined, barren environments, or mutilation. Transporting pigs over long distances can also affect their welfare negatively.

This chapter will show you how to care for your pig properly, and the diseases they are prone to, as well as the currently available treatments. The topics help to provide the best care for your pig for quality meat.

## Diseases and Welfare of Pigs

### Pig Welfare

A pig's welfare is not merely an issue of health and diseases; their welfare also involves the *ethical aspect* of farming. This is especially true in terms of slaughter and transport. There are different perspectives on animal welfare, depending on cultural backgrounds. In small farms, pig production is directly influenced by welfare practices. Their productivity and health will be improved as the treatment improves.

### Transport and Slaughter

Poor transportation creates stress in pigs. Pigs do not have sweat glands; hence they become very susceptible to heat, especially during transport. Many pigs die every year while being transported.

### Welfare Issues of Castration

Most farmers castrate pigs without giving them pain relievers or anesthetics. This causes the pigs to suffer short-term and long-term pain. Castration also makes the pigs more susceptible to infections due to the open wound. Most farmers administer no pain relievers due to the extra time and costs involved.

The anesthetic should be administered one hour before the procedure. Make sure that the anesthetic is non-aversive. NOTE: There are some countries, such as Switzerland, that have banned castration.

### Tooth Clipping

The teeth of the piglets are usually clipped immediately after being born. The purpose is to prevent injuries from occurring. This happens frequently when they are trying to locate the teat of the sow. Sows are not always able to cater to the growing litter due to their poor health, or if the litter is simply too large to handle. To increase the survival rate, tooth clipping is crucial, or the strongest pigs will overwhelm the rest.

The teats located at the front of the body have the most milk. The teats, located at the back, have progressively less milk. Once a piglet has chosen a teat, they will defend it at all costs.

### House of Fattening Pigs

Pigs intended for meat production are kept in crowded and barren conditions. This is usually in slatted concrete floors with no rooting devices. The pigs cannot access the outdoors and have not experienced fresh air nor daylight. They do not behave naturally and tend to be frustrated and bored. They are usually fighting and biting each other, leading to injuries. Pigs also experience tail cutting that causes stress, infections, and conflicts.

### Farrowing Crate

A sow or gilt is moved to a farrowing crate before the date of giving birth. This is often confused for a sow stall. The significant difference is space for the piglets. The bars in the crate prevent the sow from crushing the piglets. Just like sow stalls, the movement of the sow is highly restricted.

The sow cannot roam freely to build a nest for the piglets, nor is she able to retreat from the piglets when they bite her teats.

Farrowing crates are allowed in most countries, but the practice is banned in Sweden, Switzerland, and Norway.

### Sow Stalls

As much as it is common to put a pregnant sow in a stall for 16 weeks, this practice can be quite harmful. The stalls serve as a mental cage for the sow. They are usually bare concrete floors that are narrow, preventing the sow from even turning around. The sow can only lie down or stand up – and with a lot of difficulty.

Sow stalls prevent the sow from her natural behaviors. They cannot socialize, forage, exercise, or explore, and they prevent the sow from going outside. Pigs naturally love to explore the environs; caging them makes them frustrated and stressed.

Sow stalls increase abnormal behavior in pigs. They tend to bar-bite, indicating very high-stress levels. Many researchers have likened their behavior in a stall to clinical depression. The feed is customarily limited during pregnancy, thereby increasing the frustration levels of the sow.

The stalls are banned in UK and Sweden but are popular in the rest of the world. They are encouraged when the sow is still weaning the previous litter until the end of four weeks of pregnancy.

# Diseases

The most crucial factor when starting your pig farm is to be sure the pigs you are purchasing are of good health. You must obtain the health reports of each pig to establish their condition and wellbeing. You can ask your veterinary doctor to accompany you during the purchase for assistance in understanding (and assessing) common diseases pigs are prone to; many can be fatal. Below are common pig diseases, along with their symptoms and preventative steps.

# Pre-Weaning Stage Diseases

### 1. Exudative Dermatitis

This is also known as *greasy pig disease*. It's an infection brought on by a bacterium called Staphylococcus hyicus. Its primary symptom is skin lesions which look like black spots on the skin, spreading and becoming flaky and/or greasy. The disease can be fatal, should it be left untreated.

You can easily treat this infection with a series of antibiotics, autogenous vaccines, and skin protectants. To prevent the disease from spreading or occurring, make sure the hygienic standards of the pen are high. Consider avoiding teat dipping during the healing process. Reduce the chances of skin abrasions to prevent the infection from entering the skin system. Abrasions may occur due to sharp equipment and rough floors.

### 2. Coccidiosis

An incredibly prevalent parasite among suckling pigs caused by three types of coccidia. The primary symptoms are diarrhea with bloody spots in piglets over 21 days of age. Extreme conditions can be remedied with coccidiostats and fluid therapy. Due to damage to the intestines, pigs are prone to secondary infections.

The sows should be treated to prevent the spread of the disease. The feces of the sows can pose a huge risk as they carry many types (and much) bacteria. The best way to prevent this disease from occurring is to maintain a clean and dry environment for the pigs.

# Post-Weaning Diseases

### 1. Respiratory Diseases

It is easy to identify a respiratory disease among pigs, as they will cough, sneeze, experience heavy breathing, stunted growth, and, in extreme cases, death. You must administer antibiotics either through water, food, or injectable substances. Inadequate ventilation can also increase respiratory diseases.

Some strains of pneumonia can be curtailed by administering vaccines, so it is crucial to identify the type of strain present to fight it efficiently. Overcrowding and unhygienic housing are also critical factors for respiratory infections.

## 2. Swine Dysentery

Pigs with this type of infection often have diarrhea with traces of blood in their feces. This infection is caused by a bacterium known as Brachyspira hyodsenteriae. Pigs that have completed weaning have a reduced growth rate or even death when infected.

The infection can easily be treated by antibiotics administered through food, water, or injectable substances. You can reduce stock density to minimize infection and you can easily improve the hygiene of the pen and control the rodents in it. The disease is prevalent when new stock is bring introduced to the pen.

# Breeding Stage Diseases

### 1. Mastitis

A bacterial infection prevalent in sows that causes an infection in the mammary glands, resulting in skin discoloration. The significant symptoms of mastitis are reduced milk production, loss of appetite, and increased body temperature. Mastitis can be treated efficiently by anti-inflammatory drugs or antibiotics.

The best way to prevent this disease is by increasing the standards of hygiene. It is essential to maintain healthy nutrition during the late stages of pregnancy. Stress can also cause this disease, especially if the teats are harmed by the housing facilities.

### 2. Porcine Parvovirus

This disease mostly occurs in pregnant sows and is common in gilts, affecting reproduction immensely. If present in pig litters, they will suffer an increased decline in size due to mummification and stillbirths. This disease is fairly challenging to diagnose as its symptoms are crosscutting on other reproductive diseases. The parvovirus can exist outside the host for several weeks.

There are no treatments of this disease, hence the need to take preventive measures.

# Other Diseases

### 1. Malnutrition

This is a common pig disease that is very easy to identify. The symptoms are stunted growth and visible thinness. Healthy pigs are not bony; the only bones visible are the shoulder blades. If the farmer can also see the backbone, ribs, or hips, then the pigs are too thin. Pigs grow rapidly over a few weeks; if they are growing slowly, then consider malnutrition as the foremost factor.

Malnutrition is caused due to poor quality feed. Piglets that have completed weaning require high quality of feed compared to adults. Lactating sows also need high-quality feed to produce milk.

### 2. Lice and Flies

Lice and flies infestation can cause the spread of infectious diseases. It is easy to spot the lice on pigs as they are unusually large. They lead to blood loss and bacterial infection. Flies are a threat because they can land on open wounds and result in diseases. Spraying the pigs can reduce the flies and lice. You must maintain high hygienic standards and use fly traps.

### 3. Parasites

Pigs are prone to many parasites including roundworms and tapeworms. Roundworms live in the gut and look like a worm. Pigs with parasites experience sudden weight loss. Young pigs are the most prone to parasitic infections. If not treated, parasites can block the entire gut, leading to death. Dewormers are efficient in flushing them out of the intestinal system.

Tapeworms usually reside in the muscles of the pigs resulting in pig measles. Pigs usually have pain and difficulty moving. It is not advisable to eat meat infested with tapeworms as it can cause human health problems. There is no cure for infected pigs, so farmers should take measures to prevent the pigs from wandering around the farm.

### 4. Self-Poisoning

This occurs due to improper feeding. Feeding pig's food from various restaurants may not be ideal. The pigs may experience blindness, lose balance, vomit, and experience seizures. Farmers should always check on the quality of the food they give their pigs.

### 5. African Swine Fever

It is caused by the Asfarviridae family of viruses, which differs from the classical swine fever; the fever can be caused from contaminated feed, lice bites, ticks, other infected pigs, and contaminated medical equipment.

There is no treatment for this disease, and it is, therefore, essential to prevent it in the first place. Infected pigs should be isolated immediately after the disease has been detected.

### 6. Foot and Mouth Disease

This is caused by picornaviridae aphthovirus. Its symptoms are excessive salivation, fever, loss of appetite; it can be deadly.

A farmer should routinely take his pigs for vaccination to protect the breeding stock as it is a prevalent disease during the winter. Other farm animals will only spread it.

### 7. Rabies

This disease is transferable to humans. Its symptoms are nerve disorders, aggression, paralysis, and often leads to death. The symptoms evolves very quickly in pigs, and they tend to become shaky, aggressive, shriek, quickly attack, and have a hoarse voice. Rabies is usually fatal and has no cure.

# Tips to Prevent Diseases in Pigs

As a farmer, you must know the measures you should take to prevent diseases from infecting your breeding stock. There are some treatable diseases, but others can be very damaging to the breeding stock. When preventing diseases, consider the following approach;

• Pigs must be enclosed in spaces with good hygiene levels. The area should not be prone to overcrowding and poor ventilation.

• The farmer should constantly communicate with the vet to prevent looming diseases, identify existing ones, and cure health problems. They should be notified upon any death.

• All pigs should be purchased from registered sources. Make sure the area is clean and properly managed.

• A farmer should know of what he feeds the pigs. It is not advisable to feed the pigs with general waste from restaurants or households

- It would help if you also complied with the regulations of pig welfare. This is crucial, especially when transporting the swine.

- It is vital to collaborate with veterinarians to avoid any hiccups. This will ensure a smooth transition when examining the pigs medically.

- Make sure the fresh meat you sell or consume is examined by veterinary experts to avoid serious repercussions.

- Neutralization units or local authorities should handle the bodies of dead animals or infected pigs.

# Medicines

Medication can be administered in different ways, depending on the medicine. Some can be fatal when injected and hence need to be administered orally. Other medications can be applied only topically and absorbed through the skin. The following are some of the conventional methods of administering medication:

### Oral

Most antibiotics are administered through the mouth.

### Topical

The medicine is applied to the skin. A farmer can use a spray to apply on the surface.

### By Injection

The injection can be intradermal, intramuscular, subcutaneous, or intravenous.

### Via Uterus

Antibiotics can be inserted into the anterior vagina when infected.

### Via Rectum

This is not a common method of administering drugs. It is used on pigs that suffer from salt poisoning.

Use the information on the bottle to guide you on the method of administration. If you are having trouble, always consult a veterinary doctor.

# Taking Care of A Pig

Pigs are intelligent animals, and if brought up clean from birth, they will not deviate. There are different stages of pigs as they grow; starter, grower, finisher, and breeding. When raising the pigs, it is cleaner to raise them on concrete as opposed to other environs. The concrete reduces exposure to parasites. Your swine need a lot of shade and protection from the rain, wind, and snow.

Being exposed to too much heat can cause the pigs suffering from heatstroke. The exposure can cause salt toxicity, especially if there is no water. You should provide clean and fresh water. Add water every thirty minutes till the pigs have drank their fill. Lack of proper hydration may cause brain issues.

The size and age of the pigs will determine the space requirement in pen. Provide the sow with a crate while farrowing to prevent it from lying on another pig. As the pigs grow, make sure they have three feet of space.

The nutrition of the pig depends on the ages. Growing pigs require different feeds to provide them with more energy. Their feeds require more high energy content.

There must be treatments of external and internal parasites. The type of housing and history affects the inoculation. The sow is treated before breeding and a fortnight before farrowing. Treat the growing pigs, especially if they are on a dirty floor. Take a fecal sample from the growing pigs to determine the proper product to deworm. Human food scraps, especially the ones that contain meat, shouldn't be fed to pigs.

Do not feel pressured to vaccinate the pigs, especially during the hot season as this can be a source of additional stress. Administer the vaccination individually to the pigs to prevent hiccups. Use the weight of the pigs to determine their overall health.

When transporting pigs, you must obtain health certificates for the swine. Be sure to have the pigs' bill of sale in your records. It is a requirement in some states to provide such documentations when slaughtering or selling. A health certificate is crucial when traveling across different states. Using pig notches and tattoos has proven an essential aspect of identifying the pigs.

# Pig Care During Different Seasons

Pigs and sows experience extreme heat during the summer as they decrease feeding, grow, and produce milk. They also suffer just as much during the winter season. Cold seasons result in slow growth, reduced feed efficiency, high infection rate, loss of body fat, and high mortality rate.

When it's too cold, pigs try to keep warm by minimizing heat loss; they shiver to increase metabolic heat production and increase food intake. However, when a pig is stressed, they avoid eating. It is essential to keep them warm, especially two weeks after arrival.

You can utilize these specific mechanisms to reduce heat loss. Tackle their legs beneath their body and huddle them together. Piglets and young pigs can change their sleeping and dunging to obtain warmth from their excretes. These steps will help you to ensure your pigs are always kept warm:

• It is crucial that you can identify when pigs are cold. They tend to huddle together and tuck their feet beneath their body. The pigs will develop long rough hair and become skinny.

• Make sure the pigs are dry and that their bedding is replaced frequently.

• Reduce the ventilation in the room during the cold months. Always make sure that the doors and windows are closed.

• Insulate the walls and ceilings.

• Utilize zone heating such as headlamps, creep boxes, and heated mats.

• Avoid multiple stressors. Vaccinating, weaning, castrating, transporting, changing the environment, and changing feeds can induce chilling.

# When Should You Contact A Vet?

Disease prevention is still a significant challenge among farmers, and new diseases are continually cropping up in pigs. The condition is a threat to the pigs, and the food supply on the farm. Some measures are taken to prevent diseases: food safety and adopting suitable pig farming activities. However, the most important is biosecurity. It is an important management tool to curtail the spread of disease.

Veterinarians are involved on a day-to-day basis in taking of the pigs. Their role today has evolved beyond merely treating sick pigs. They are useful when being consulted, managing, and even constructing a new farm.

Veterinarians are crucial in taking medicine inventory, considering weather and feed, taking lab samples for testing, managing disease outbreaks, and calculating withdrawal dates. The following are examples of when a pig farmer should consult a veterinarian:

- Testing for viruses and administering vaccinations
- Oversee health management plans
- Assessing sows individually
- Ensuring safe delivery of the newborn and take care of new moms

The basic needs of a modern pig are to increase production and efficiency. For maximum profitability, a veterinary doctor is key. A routine monthly checkup can save you from a lot of problems. The monthly visit should be instrumental in creating more awareness of the farm-related problems and develop procedures to solve them. A veterinary doctor increases efficiency, contributes to the management, educates the farmer, controls diseases, and prevents diseases.

A farmer must accompany the vet in his routine checkups to give observations. It is vital that during this time, the farmer discusses with the vet the weaknesses and strengths of the breed. Obtain a written report for evidence. It will serve as a reminder of the discussions and a highlight of the recommendations.

# Chapter 7: Pig Reproduction and Breeding

Reproduction is an important factor with profitability in the pig industry. This is because the number of pigs, sows, and weaning pigs every year is crucial for the profits of many investors in the pig industry. This number is heavily reliant on the total number of pigs per litter reproduced by a sow. The reproduction of weaning piglets depends on the breeding of these animals. The piglets must be able to grow fast in a short period while producing quality carcasses, with low fat and plenty of meat.

It is essential you buy breeding animals of high quality. The pigs should come from a farm with high standards of nutrition, hygiene, and overall management. If it is your first time, consider having a professional or experienced individual to help you make the right choice. This topic will help you further understand pig breeding and reproduction.

A breed can be defined as a group of animals who share the same ancestry with identifiable traits. When this group of animals mate, they produce offspring with the same qualities. The main purpose behind breeding is to achieve desired traits deemed as profitable.

# Pig Mating or Breeding Systems

As mentioned above, breeding pigs requires significant knowledge or experience handling such practices. When buying breeding pigs, consider ones that have been well fed and kept in sanitary conditions. If you are running a small-scale farm, then consider the following selection criteria when selecting boars, gilts, and sows:

- Consider buying above average purebred boars. Pure breeding involves breeding pigs of the same breed. The main purpose of pure breeding is the identification and propulsion of "superior" genes to be used in the commercial production of meat.

- When buying boars, consider buying prominent breeds used in your country.

- When buying gilts or young female pigs, it is crucial to purchase them from a reputable vendor who keeps records of the pigs. Gilts can be used as purebreds or cross-bred pigs. Also, consider buying gilts from the same vendor. It is important to seek expert opinion on such matters to help you identify the appropriate breeding policy.

- Should you choose to select your own gilts, apply strict measures and keep accurate growth and feed conversion records.

- Your selection of a gilt should be based on the size of the litter, i.e., consider choosing a gilt with 12 teats to serve a large litter.

- Consider choosing gilts at least eight months old and approximately 120 kgs (264 lbs.) before their first service.

- Gilts chosen from sows that wean approximately eight to ten piglets for every litter are linked with good motherhood. The sows should have their first farrowing after a year and the second farrowing seven months from the first.

- The choice of gilt or boars should be based on their ability to grow fast. In the foreseeable future, this will prove less costly to keep, as they consume less as they gain healthy weight with reasonable body fat.

- Consider choosing gilts with proper teats; i.e., not inverted or having fat deposits at the base of the teats

- It would be best if you chose gilts with well-developed hams. Before you start the mating process, consider exposing the gilts to the heat of about two to three days. However, for gilts, they should mate after the first day of their heat period while sows should mate on their second day of the same.

- Boars should be well developed, with sound feed, proper hams, and a good overall length. Additionally, these developments should extend to the teats; they should have 12 primary teats to increase the chances of passing on this desirable trait.

- Consider the biggest boar from the litter to use as a sire. If castration is to be done, it needs to be four weeks after the breeding process has been completed.

- Just like the gilt's age considerations, the boar should also be at least eight months old before their first service.

Breeding and mating systems are methods used for pairing boars and sows (and sometimes gilts) to achieve profitable and desired traits in the offspring. Genetics play a massive role in the overall productivity and performance of the pigs. Pig farmers are urged to be familiar with such methods.

It involves two primary strategies; positive assertive mating and negative assertive mating. With positive assertion in mating, breeding occurs to increase the chances of achieving desired traits while reducing the odds of undesirable odds. Negative assortative mating involves breeding two different pigs to rectify the expression of a certain trait. The following are common breeding systems that pig keepers.

### Outbreeding

Outbreeding involves mating pigs of the same breed but with slight relations to the average breed. It is also known as outcrossing. Simply put, there shouldn't be a common ancestor among the mating pigs for a couple of generations.

### Inbreeding

This breeding system involves linking two closely related pigs within the same breed. The relationship could be anything from mother and son, daughter and father, or siblings with siblings. As a result, one can concentrate common and desirable genes in the offspring. However, expect a reduction in the litter size. The following are other effects of inbreeding

# Effects of Inbreeding

• Inbreeding increases mortality rates in pigs. You will notice certain limitations in the overall physical function with instabilities. Additionally, when the sow cannot move, the risk of mortality is significantly increased.

• Inbred boars tend to have low sex drive.

• Separation of the offspring or parents severely affects the pigs. The main purpose behind breeding is to create desirable traits in pigs for commercial purposes. Once the male or female piglets are taken away, the stress might affect the remaining pigs or piglets negatively.

• Breeding between siblings might not always bring out the desired outcome.

• Approximately 25% to 50% of the piglets are usually born smaller and weaker compared with the first sow. Additionally, some of the piglets are born dead.

• The overall number of piglets in a litter is significantly smaller.

### Cross-Breeding

Cross-breeding involves a careful and planned approach to mating pigs. It entails mating two pigs with different backgrounds. This results in heterosis, which is the improved productivity and performance of offspring, especially when compared to the previous generation. Heterosis occurs when different breeds of pigs are mated with each other as a correction mechanism of traits exhibited in the earlier generations.

# Cross Breeding Strategies

• **Terminal System**

This system of breeding is one of the most common systems used across the United States. Pig farmers running large scale commercial operations frequently use a terminal cross-breeding stem. The terminal system involves a terminal that provides the desired genetic traits to maximize pig growth, development, feed efficiency, and the quality of the carcass. The terminal sire could either be a purebred or a cross-bred.

Terminal systems result in developing "superior" pigs that should meet the demands of your audience or target market. This simple system has created genetically uniform groups of hogs annually in the United States. Also, this system brings out hybrid vigor in all the females and their offspring.

Hybrid vigor is the tendency of offspring to exhibit superior genetic traits, especially when compared to the previous generation. One major downside associated with terminal systems is the perennial purchase of boars and gilts. You will be forced to replace all the gilts and boars after selling them to your target market. This process may be costly. Additionally, some pigs may introduce pathogens, causing diseases to the remaining herd of animals.

- **Rotational Systems**

If you consider your farm operations small scale, then consider using a rotational system. Just like terminal systems, rotational systems are also simple and efficient. It is also known as the back-crossing system or the two-breed rotational system, which includes only two breeds. This system is cheap and affordable for most small-scale pig keepers. Unlike the terminal sire systems, rotational systems do not maximize hybrid vigor. But with technology and the purchase of semen, some of these barriers in rotational systems have been significantly reduced.

- **Combination System**

As the name suggests, this strategy of cross-breeding combines the functionality of the two methods mentioned above. For instance, a small group of the herd is kept in the rotational system to produce female pigs for the entire farm. Afterward, the gilts are serviced with terminal sires to ensure that most (if not all) of the offspring's genetic traits are easily sellable in the market. For a small-scale farmer, this system can be hectic because of the insufficient labor. And this method requires meticulous management and record-keeping for success.

Breeding systems influence the genetic make-up of your pigs; such methods play a vital role in the carcass quality and overall performance of your pig. Because of the perks of heterosis, cross-breeding countries like the United States have become popular. For small scale pig keepers, rotational systems are the most affordable and practical system to use, especially when using artificial insemination.

# Effects of Cross Breeding

• Leads to piglets with local sows.

• Brings about piglets with exotic sows.

• The local sow can bear bigger and healthier piglets.

• Piglets borne from cross-breeding are strong, healthy, and grow fast.

• From a financial standpoint, cross-breeding is profitable as most piglets are sold, and a few are selected for cross-breeding.

• The stronger and healthier pigs are sold or castrated for meat purposes leaving behind weak piglets that cannot be used for further cross-breeding

• Negative breed selection results in smaller and weaker piglets, 50% of which will die during or after birth.

• Negative selection results in a small litter size.

### Line Breeding

Passing undesirable traits results from negative selection inbreeding. The closer the relationship of the parents, the higher the risk of passing on undesirable traits in the next generation. The traits are *phenotypic*, meaning that results will affect the pig's health, productivity, and overall wellbeing. This breeding method is like breeding, but it focuses on a particular characteristic.

This is not easily achievable as the genetic pool can be limiting. Fortunately, technology has helped pig keepers identify the relationship between pigs. Furthermore, you can use artificial insemination to help you reduce the risk of using related boars in the breeding process. One mistake that breeders make is using multiple boars from the same litter for the siring process. Consider a maximum of one boar from each litter; otherwise, you might be reducing genetic diversity not only in your farm but also your country.

### Random Mating Within a Breed

Random mating involves selecting pigs with no considerations, i.e., relations, genetic make-up, etc.

# Mating Types

### • Pen Bred

Pen mating is one of the three mating types that pig keepers commonly use. This process involves putting boars and sows or gilts in the same pen for a specific period of time, usually 20 to 40 days, without close supervision. This method is usually cost-effective as pig keepers get to save on labor. However, it will affect the farrowing rate.

### • Hand Mated

This method of pig mating is used by small to medium-sized pig operation farms. Hand mating is the placement of a female in heat with a boar in the same pen, with the close supervision of a stock person. This stock person will assist the boar's penis as it enters the sows or gilts vagina. Using hand mating is effective in increasing the performance of the sows and boars.

### • Artificial Insemination

Artificial insemination of swine is a common practice across the world. In Europe alone, most pigs have been bred by artificial insemination over the past few decades. Artificial Insemination is very helpful as it reduces the risk of diseases and weak genes by introducing desirable and "superior" genes.

# Common Signs of Heat/ Estrus in Pigs

Heat, also known as estrus, is the physical manifestation of a biological need to mate because of increased hormones in pigs. Heat detection is the process of observing and identifying the pigs receptive to mating. A mature female pig that is not lactating or pregnant should cycle after three weeks. As a result, the heat cycle should last approximately 3 weeks. Signs of heat include:

- General unease or restlessness.
- White, slimy, and sticky mucus discharge.
- A general desire to mount or be mounted on by other pigs; can be spotted mounting other pen mates.
- Twitching ears.
- Rigid (legs and back), also known as being *locked up.*

• In females, the vulva becomes swollen and red in color.

• The female will not sit still but she will stand still if pressure is applied to her back. If someone applies pressure on her back by simply pushing down or sitting on her, the sow will stand still.

• Pigs may frequently squeal or make their voices heard.

# Inducing Heat in Pigs

### Stimulating the Boar, Sow, and Gilt

Boars are usually stimulated in preparation for artificial insemination. Remember that boar stimulation requires physical contact, including the occasional sniff or nudge, to arouse the female pig. Caution should be applied; consider using fence line contact.

After farrowing for the first time, a sow may take time to come into heat. Consider these techniques used by stock persons to induce heat;

• Gently stroke the sow's vagina/vulva using a freshly cut papaya stalk in the morning. Do this for three to five days.

• Bring the sow next to the boar's pen. Also, bring them before they feed. Consider bringing the sow to the boar every day for a short while just before the heat period is expected.

• You should not mate these animals during the heat of the day. Pick a time best for the boar to serve twice within 24 hours, ensuring an interval of about 12 to 14 hours between each service.

• Spray the guilt's or sow's pen with urine belonging to the boar. Do this every morning for approximately three to five days.

• To avoid boar fights and injuries, keep them in different pens/housing facilities. Consider taking the sow to the male for mating.

• Before service, have the sows/gilt consume an extra one or two kilos (approx. four pounds) of extra feed daily. After service, prolong the extra feed for another week.

• If the sow or gilt does not conceive, she will come into heat in about 21 days' time.

• If the sow or gilt manages to conceive, consider giving it an extra 0.5 kg (lbs.) extra feed mix every day. A week before farrowing gradually reduce this amount, substituting with plenty of water to prevent the congestion of the sow's/gilt's gut.

- If the sow had her first farrowing, remove all her piglets early when they grow six weeks old. All the piglets must be removed at once. Take the sow to a pen/ housing facility hosting dry sows.

- Put the sow in a location close to the boar in such a way to enable them to make contact i.e., they can smell and see each other.

# How to Provide Assistance with the Mating Process

Occasionally, young boars may need assistance, as they might struggle with lining up the sow. Before you start, make sure you clean your hands and wrists. It will also help if your fingernails are short and clean.

The mating process is a slow one. The boar should take about a minute and a half before reaching the ejaculation point. To improve the conception of the sow/gilt, consider crushing one kilogram of semen nelumbinis, also known as the *lotus seed*, into the pig's feed mixture. Give this feed to the pig twice a day for about three to five days.

### Culling

Culling is a term used to describe low productivity and fertility in pigs because of age or certain problems such as diseases or physical injury. Consider selling the sows that are difficult to impregnate. Also, if such sows have small litters, they should be sold off. Consider replacing them with replacement gilts or nulliparous sows (females that have never given birth, or have given birth to stillborn piglets). On the other hand, boars that are infertile should be culled, including those that are slightly fertile.

# Reasons for Not Conceiving

### 1. Infertility

In the United Kingdom alone, infertility is the leading cause of high costs of pig production. In the United States, conception rates are above 92%, with 90% farrowing rates. Anything below these standards is considered a fertility or performance problem. There are a couple of things that lead to infertility in pigs as explained below.

- **Poor Heat Detection**

Heat detection is an overlooked process of pig reproduction. Most pig keepers who fail to record their first and second heat cycles risk missing out on the third cycle when sows are at their best productive cycle.

It is important to observe and record the pig's heat cycles. It is advisable to watch the pig for approximately 18 to 25 days for the first, second, and third heat cycles for the same intervals when the sow/gilt is ready to be served. It is not advisable to introduce the sow/gilt to the boar or inseminate artificially before the pig is accurately identified as standing estrus—the period in which the pig demonstrates sexual receptiveness.

Consider mating the two pigs later in the third heat cycle when the pig stands firm without moving forward. Fertility levels are high when the sow is served six days after weaning. Sows will show signs of heat before three days, but servicing them only leads to undesirable results.

- **Bacterial/ Parasitic/ Viral Agents**

Numerous agents could potentially cause infertility in sows and gilts. For instance, mycotoxins are caused by molds and fungi normally found in feed mixtures, including grains. Normally, all pigs are susceptible to these toxins, but in breeding pigs, it is detrimental as it causes damage to the reproduction system, causing abortion and stillbirth. Other agents include brucellosis, eperythrozoonosis, bacteria in semen, erysipelas, porcine reproductive, and respiratory syndrome (PRRS), among many others. Consider a good vaccination protocol to prevent such infectious agents from rendering your sows and gilts infertile. Also. a high-quality and stable environment will prevent seasonal infertility.

- **Nutritional Deficiency**

As mentioned earlier, nutrition plays a massive role in a pig's performance and ability to reproduce. Deficiency of certain minerals, vitamins, proteins, and fats can affect the pigs' ability to conceive.

- **Poor Management**

Management plays a crucial role in the fertility and overall performance of the pig. From weaning to mating, the entire process of growth and reproduction should be planned and properly supervised. Evaluation of reproductive soundness should be carried out when the pig is fairly young (two-and-a-half weeks old). There are other criteria you can use when evaluating the pigs for reproductive soundness, as explained in the following sub-topic.

- **Unfavorable Temperatures**

Recent studies have shown that temperature extremes are linked to low fertility in sows and reduced desire in boars.

### 2. The Sow is Overweight

If the sow is too fat or overweight, its ability to conceive is compromised.

### 3. The Boar is Too Young

There are optimal ages for breeding pigs, as explained above. Mating pigs at a young age, i.e., when they are below five to six months old, could lead to the inability to conceive. It is advisable to avoid premature mating in a bid to optimize reproduction as much as possible.

### 4. The Boar Has Been Over-Used

Over-mating a boar affects its ability to make a sow pregnant. Overworking a boar could mean mating it over five times in a week.

# Factors Affecting Pigs Productivity

## Genetics

A pig's genetics can have a major influence on the productivity of the pig and, eventually, the profitability of the business. The combination of nutrition, environment, and management will eventually have a major influence on productivity, size, and carcass quality.

The most common breeds of pigs include the largely white, landrace, and duroc. When selecting a boar, consider choosing such prominent breeds used worldwide, but preferably in your parent country. But commercial producers use a mix of these main breeds to take full advantage of the positive effects of cross-breeding. There are genetic improvement programs that will take account of various performance traits, including feed to meat ratio, carcass quality, and milking abilities, among others.

## Nutrition

Nutritional requirements must be met for your pig to perform at an optimum level. Different pigs have different nutritional requirements, as explained in the previous chapters. For instance, boars require a different diet to lactating sows for their performance and overall output. Additionally, the quantity of the feed will influence the pig's fat levels. For optimum productivity, pig nutrition must not be overlooked.

## Disease

Closely related to nutrition are diseases. Health and nutrition are two of the most critical factors affecting both the physical and economic performance of the pigs from the weaning stage until their slaughter. It is easy to argue out that good nutrition can act as a prevention for most diseases. Additionally, a good diet goes a long way in maintaining a healthy weight for pigs regardless of the stage of development.

Diseases are associated with weight loss, depending on the severity. Diseases affect the productivity of pigs in these ways;

• Certain diseases have been linked to a decrease in the insulin-like growth factor, which plays an integral function in the growth and development of pigs.

• Cytokines are a large group of proteins usually secreted as part of the pig's immune response to diseases. Cytokines are associated with the suppression of certain growth hormones. This is detrimental to the pig's growth rates and overall body size.

• Certain diseases or anorexia due to specific pathogens that compromise the pig's immunity. As a result, diseases may affect the pig's ability to eat and convert feed to meat.

• When the body is fighting pathogens, causing infections and diseases, it redirects nutrients away from tissue growth to support the body in its fight against the disease.

## Environment

The environment is an important factor to consider when assessing possible outcomes to meet the intended goals regarding meat production in pigs. Too much heat will stress the pigs causing them to roll in mud as they try to cool off. And if the environment is noisy, the pigs will be continuously stressed, affecting their ability to eat and, ultimately, convert feed to meat.

Individual housing of these social animals could be very stressful to them and could ultimately compromise their welfare and productivity. It is essential to consider environmental enrichment. Remember that pigs are sensitive and intelligent animals that require special care for optimum productivity. Consider using absorbent bedding materials that create a clean, comfortable, and most important, dry environment.

Certain factors in the environment could potentially affect the pig's sense of exploration and appetite. For instance, hanging bottles, playful balls, and other things need to be changed after a while to keep the pigs interested. It is important to note that a pig's metabolism is affected by behavioral activities.

### Management

When raising pigs, it is essential to note it is possible to increase their growth while reducing mortality through improving facilities and specific management practices.

# Care and Management of Boar

A high degree of care and priority should be given to boars introduced to the breeding herd. The management of such animals is influential to the overall reproduction efficiency. Remember that good care and management yield reproduction and high meat quality.

• The boars should be well fed. After testing and examination of these animals has been done, the next step will be to feed them adequately. A good diet will provide the boar with sufficient energy for the mating process. Additionally, good feed will prevent the boar from becoming excessively fat. Feeding the boar goes a long way in assuring the animal remains sexually active without physical implications.

• After testing them, it is important to be cognizant of the fact that these animals' main purpose is reproduction. As a result, they should be managed and treated accordingly. It is crucial to conjure physically hardening processes for the pig, besides sexually stimulating procedures. Consider changing the boar's location, providing ample female contact through the fence line method, especially when the boars show aggressive behavior towards the females.

• The boar should be at least seven to eight months before they can be considered for breeding. The evaluation should be done before this age to make it easy to cull problematic boars.

• Observe the pig's libido. The desire to mate is crucial to breeding. Observe its aggression when mating because some may need assistance at least once in their mating life. The same goes for mounting as some may be physically injured or diagnosed with arthritis, preventing them from the successful mounting.

# Chapter 8: Farrowing and Piglet Care

Good management and care can influence the health of the piglets born and their numbers. It will also affect their production levels later in life. Most deaths occur due to starvation and pre-weaning. This is common in the first few days of the piglet's life.

An excellent caretaker must know newborn piglets and their characteristics. This makes pigs overly reliant on proper care and management. Piglets are born without antibodies, and their bodies have a fat content that can last them only one day. Piglets can regulate their body temperature for only a few days. They must be taken care of and guarded against diseases that can compromise their health.

## The Farrowing Process

It is necessary to know the anatomy of the pelvis and the reproductive tract for easing the farrowing process. When farrowing begins, the vulva enlarges and the vagina, leading to the opening of the womb. Lubricate your arms before inserting it into the vagina to avoid causing damage. The neck of the cervix leads to two long horns that contain the piglets.

The umbilical cord of the piglet ends at the placenta that is attached to the surface of the uterus. The cord carries the nutritional value that supplements the piglets. The placenta encloses the piglet in a sac that carries its fluids and waste products. The placenta and the sac are known as the afterbirth.

### The Beginning of Farrowing

Once the piglet reaches the final stage of maturity after 115 days, farrowing begins. The pituitary and adrenal glands are activated by the piglet to produce corticosteroids. The hormones are carried via the bloodstream to the placenta. The placenta is stimulated to produce prostaglandins transported to the ovary. They are responsible for terminating the pregnancy; thus, the hormones initiate farrowing.

### Length of Farrowing

The minimum period of farrowing is 115 days. Gilts have a shorter time span compared to the sows. The duration is affected by the environment, litter size, breed, and time of year.

# The Farrowing Preparation

The process occurs in three stages:

### Stage 1: Pre-Farrowing Period

Preparing for farrowing should start fourteen days before the day of giving birth. The teats start to enlarge, veins in the underside stand out, and the vulva swells. Farrowing reduces the appetite of the sow, and they become restless. Twelve hours to farrowing, the mammary glands of the sow can be stimulated to secrete milk. This is the best sign of farrowing. You may also spot a small mucous discharge on the vulva and around pellets of feces present. The pellets indicate that the piglet is secreting. An examination must be conducted.

### Stage 2: The Farrowing Process

The process can last up to eight hours with a variation of 20 minutes between; you must check on the sow and litter in case of any harm. The gap between the first and the second sow can run up to 45 minutes. Most pigs are born headfirst, but some come out in reverse. You will notice the twitching of the tail of the pig when it is ready to give birth.

### Stage 3: Delivery of the Placenta

This can last up to four hours as an indication of the farrowing process is complete. The sow will appear to be at peace, and the shivering and movement of the hind legs stop. There is usually a heavy discharge after birth for five days. At times, bacteria enter the uterus leading to inflammation commonly known as endometritis.

# Farrowing Problems You Are Likely To Encounter

## Step 1

The sow will be having difficulty if one these problems present itself. You will notice the lack of piglets, slow panting, and distress or blood in the vulva region. Failure to deliver the piglets can lead to these conditions:

- Rotation of the womb
- Illness of the sow
- The inertia of the womb
- Mummified pigs
- Dead pigs in the womb
- The nervousness of the sow
- Over-fat sow
- 

## Step 2

It helps to internally examined the sow using warm water and a mild antiseptic. Avoid using detergents as they can irritate the sow. Make sure your hands are washed properly, and your fingernails are short. Examine the sow as they are lying down on their side.

# Problems You Might Encounter During Farrowing

### Uterine Inertia

This is whereby the womb stops contracting, and two or three piglets are just beyond the cervix. If the piglets are in anterior position with legs overhead, then you can easily pull them out. In a breach pregnancy, the piglets can be delivered by raising the hind legs and clamping the hands around using the first and second fingers.

### Difficult Presentations

There are certain occasions when a large piglet is daunting to birth. You can use a piece of cord and loop the center around the third finger. Use plenty of lubricants to pass the cord into the vagina. The cord is placed between the right and left ear, then secured at the jaw. Traction can help to secure the piglet.

### Rotation of the Horns of the Womb

This occurs when large litters are present. The crossover between the horns distorts the cervix. Passing the hand through the cervix, you will feel the pig by reaching downwards. You must use full arms to remove the piglets.

### Stimulating a Piglet to Breathe

If a piglet is delivered and it doesn't breathe, take a straw and gently poke it up its nose. This will make the piglet to cough and remove the mucus blocking the windpipe. Place your third finger across its mouth with its tongue pulled out. Place your hand around the head and swing the pig downward to remove mucus from the throat.

### Step Three

If you examine the sow and detect uterine inertia, you can inject oxytocin to help it contract. This can be avoided as the arm in the vagina will stimulate more contractions. Grown pigs are capable of this venture. However, small pigs may prove difficult and result in stillbirth. You can place a piglet on the teat of the sow to help stimulate contractions.

### Step Four

Once you have completed the examination and farrowing, administer antibiotics to each piglet. Penicillin is adequate to prevent any form of infection. If death occurs among the piglets, it is crucial to put antibiotics in the cervix of the sow.

### Step Five

Monitor the sow for 24 hours to detect any signs of infection.

# How to Care for Piglets After Birth

Caring for newborn pigs will require a good environment, adequate nutrition, and safety from diseases and crushing. Individual attention from the handler to the pigs reduces the mortality rate significantly. Labor directly affects the time you spend in the farrowing house.

# Different Categories of Piglets

There are two categories that piglets are born into, normal and disadvantaged. A caretaker must know how to identify each to provide proper care. Normal piglets are born quickly and can manage a few steps. They suckle after fifteen minutes of birth. If the sow is in good condition and the farrowing environment is great, then the piglets will thrive.

Disadvantaged piglets are lightweight, foster congenital defects, are colder, and are slow to locate a teat. The longer a sow takes to farrow, the worse the condition of the piglets. They tend to be oxygen-deprived and have experienced physical trauma. The weak state of the piglets makes them unable to compete with other piglets. Chilled piglets have an low temperature that increases the mortality rate.

These techniques will help you care for your piglets.

# Attended Farrowing

According to research, proper farrowing can increase the survival rate of the piglets and the number of piglets being weaned. Being present at the farrowing stage is vital to identify piglets that may need more attention.

### Prevent Chilling

Farrowing quarters must reflect two climates. The sow needs a cool temperature of 65 F, and the piglets require 80 F. You can maintain the room at room temperature and provide heating for the piglets.

Makes sure you monitor the litter's responses to set the specific temperature for their thermal requirements. You will see the piglets move away from the heating zone if the temperature is too high. The temperature of the zone should be set 24 hours before farrowing. You can use heat pads, radiant heat, and headlamps to provide the necessary heat. Be careful not to place the headlamp at the rear of the sow during farrowing to reduce mortality.

### Colostrum Intake

The initial milk from the teats is known as colostrum. The milk is rich in antibodies that help the piglet's fight infections. The piglets must ingest this milk for their general wellbeing. Here is a tactic to be sure the piglets get enough colostrum:

- Regulate the temperature, so the piglets stay warm and active.

- Split suckles to ensure all the piglets get enough time to feed. You can separate the strong ones from the teats for one or two hours. This is a great technique to be sure there is a high colostrum intake of the piglets.

### Cross Fostering

This is a great strategy to reduce pig mortality by reducing litter-weight variation. It is also a great way of determining the number of functional teats. A good cross-fostering will help determine that the health status of the piglets is high and increases milk supply. Tips for effective cross-fostering:

- Be sure the piglets obtain the colostrum from their dams. This should be a minimum of six hours after birth.

- It is essential to cross foster the piglets 48 hours after they are born. Piglets identify the pig they will suckle and stick to them until weaning. This is crucial to reduce competition and to fight at the udder. When teat fidelity is not established, the piglet suffers from weight loss.

# Processing Piglets

Processing piglets start from teeth clipping, clipping and treating the umbilical cord, tail docking, iron administration, treating splay-legged piglets, castration, and providing supplemental nutrients. These processes can either be performed by a specialist or a caretaker, depending on the preference. It is recommended these activities take place four days after birth to reduce the stress levels of the newborns.

### Equipment

Arrange all your equipment on a trailer on wheels. The supplies and equipment must be disinfected. Gather the side cutters, supplemental iron, syringes, needles, and plastic clips on the tray.

### Disease Transfer

Minimize the chances of infection while transferring piglets. Process the sick litter last, clean and disinfect the box or carts after transferring the piglets.

### Persona Safety

Sows are extraterritorial after giving birth to the piglets. The sow may bite you while protecting the litter so make sure there is a partition between you and the sow.

### Holding the Piglet

When trying to clip teeth, tail, and umbilical cord, hold the pig firmly. Beware of not chocking the piglet while trying to perform these processes. You can support the piglet's weight by placing your fingers under the jaw. If this is too hard on you, place the piglet on your knee carefully.

### Umbilical Cord Care

The umbilical cord can foster bacteria and viruses if not taken care of properly. The cord is important to help the fetus obtain nutrients and expel waste during pregnancy. It is possible the bacteria can lead to excessive bleeding from piglets.

If there is excessive bleeding from the cord, tie it off with a string or a clamp. New-born piglets do not require their cord clamped or tied. However, if the cord is short, it can cause excessive blood loss and, eventually, death.

## Needle Teeth Clipping

A newborn piglet has eight needle teeth, commonly known as wolf teeth. They are located on the sides of the upper and lower jaw. Most caretakers prefer clipping the teeth within 24 hours after birth to reduce laceration among each other. It is crucial to perform this if there is greasy pig disease or when sows are not milking well. Here are tips to assist you.

• Use cutters without blades when clipping. Do not use regular wire cutters and replace side cutters.

• Cut out one-half of the tooth. Avoid removing the whole tooth and do not crush or break it. This will prevent the piglet from nursing properly.

• Cut the tooth flat and not in an angle. The chances of the piglet causing trouble with the teeth flat are less.

## Tail Docking

Tail docking is crucial to reduce cannibalism and tail biting. The process must be performed 48 hours after farrowing. This is because it can be stressful on the piglet. This age is crucial so the litter does not nibble the newly docked tail and farrowing quarters are clean. Dock the tail about an inch from the tail joint. If cut too short, the muscle activity around the anus is primarily affected. Use sterilized cutters to perform this procedure. Avoid extremely sharp objects such as a scalpel as it may lead to excessive bleeding.

## Supplemental Iron

Anemia in piglets must be prevented. Iron deficiency develops rapidly in nursing pigs as there is not enough to sustain them in colostrum. There are low reserves in the newborn piglet, minimal interaction with the soil, and rapid growth.

Iron can be administered by injection or orally. The injection is a more efficient way of administering iron as it is absorbed faster, reducing the deficit. Oral iron may cause enteric disease, as it is necessary for the growth of microorganisms in the digestive tract. You can give the piglets iron when they are three days old. Try not to overdose; 200 mg is enough for them.

### Creep Feeding

In addition to milk from the sows, pigs require a *creep* (supplemental food) offered to maximize weight gain during weaning. You should issue creep feed the first week away from the sow. The ration should be high-quality and ready to eat. The creep rations can be mixed at the farm or purchased. Use high energy feed that meets the nutrients of the pig.

### Castration

This is the surgical removal of the two testicles and is considered routine practice for piglets meant to be slaughtered. Boars or un-castrated piglets tend to produce a bad odor during slaughtering if not removed. The best time for castration is when the piglet is two weeks old. It is easier to castrate piglets as they are easier to hold and bleed less. It is not recommended to castrate earlier because it may lead to scrotal hernias.

Examine each piglet carefully before castrating them. The scrotal hernia will make a loop of an intestine in the scrotum. Hold the piglet upright allowing the scrotum to fall, then squeeze the hind legs together. If you spot enlargement in one of the scrota, the piglet has a hernia. Avoid castrating the piglet unless you are professional and can treat the hernia properly. Most hernias are genetic.

# Post-Castration Care

You must regularly check on the castrated animals for bleeding or infected tissue. Try applying pressure on the wound for two minutes to prevent further bleeding. You can consult a professional to confirm that the wound is healing well.

### Record Keeping

It is highly recommended that caretakers use records to establish the strengths and weaknesses of the pigs. Reproductive traits are heritable to the piglets, and it is crucial to take that into account. It is a great way to establish superior sows. This improves the lactation performance of the sows. Consider the birth date and cause of death, pedigree information, number of piglets weaned, and the weaning weight. Record remarks of any unusual characteristic of the piglets.

# Prevention of Spread of Diseases Among Piglets

Ensure that the piglets are safe and healthy. Consider the source and handling of primary and replacement breeding stock, rules governing the movement of people, the layout of the farm, and the location of the new farm and cleaning the farrow quarters. The most critical period in the pig's life cycle is the time between birth and weaning. Two pigs per litter are lost during this dire period. Poor management is the leading cause of death. The piglets can die due to crushing, bleeding from the navel, starvation, anemia, and disease.

# Chapter 9: Homestead Butchering and Processing

*Disclaimer: The chapters above have promoted the raising of pigs in an ethical and animal-friendly way. The following chapter contains graphic details about the butchering, slaughtering, and processing of pigs. Needless to say, the topic might not be for everyone. Some may find the information disturbing and alarming. If you plan on raising pigs for pets and nothing more, then you might consider skipping this chapter.*

The crisis that brought the world to its knees in 2020 caused major disruptions to supply chains across the world. Nearly all commodities in the market, including items in the pig industry, have seen their supply and distributions chains suffer. Many people keeping pigs have been forced to seek alternative options to market or distribute their products, and customers have also been forced to look for alternative options for sourcing their meat.

One option that seeks to reduce production costs involves butchering at home. Pig keepers with a ready market can sell pigs (alive or dead) directly to consumers. The following is intended to help you understand the proper techniques used in slaughtering pigs at home. As inhumane as butchering sounds, there are procedures that, when followed, result in a humane slaughter followed by the safe production of meat. If not done appropriately, it can increase personal safety risks, animal welfare, and meat safety.

# Skills and Necessary Equipment Needed for Butchering a Pig

Before butchering a pig at home, there are several skills and equipment you should have.

• Knowledge of how to handle a firearm. Slaughtering a pig starts with taking away its life. Most people prefer using a 22-caliber rifle to do this. Whatever the case, you must know how to use a firearm.

• Your ability to handle knives should be impeccable. It doesn't stop there; there are other sharp tools such as saws you should fully know. Knowledge of handling knives will help you slaughter the pig quickly and effectively. For instance, did you know that a blunt knife is more dangerous than a sharpened one? Dull knives require added pressure when cutting. This increases the risk of injury to both you and your loved ones.

• You should know how to deal with animals in a humane way. It is imperative you learn how to restrain the pig safely. It would be best if you learned how to restrict the pig's movement because failure to do so makes it much harder to stun the hog in a humane way.

• It would be best if you learned the correct procedures before starting. There is a certain degree of patience and attention to detail you need to observe to ensure that both the animal and carcass are handled in the right way.

Skills and knowledge of handling animals and relevant equipment are an absolute must when it comes to handling pigs. Once you have built these skills, then the next step is to evaluate your equipment inventory.

• Firearms and Stunning Equipment

Electrically stunning the pig with a captive-bolt stunner renders it immediately unconscious. Once the pig is no longer conscious, shooting it with a 22-caliber rifle is the most humane way to kill it.

• Knives

It is advisable to have a couple of sharp knives. From skinning knives to bone saws, consider having a few knives measuring at least six inches.

• Constant supply of water

You should consider having a metal barrel to heat the water. If a metal barrel is out of the question, consider a different heating source capable of heating water to about 150° F (65° C). Slaughtering pigs requires a decent amount of water.

- Chains and Ropes

These are used in transporting the animal after it has been killed. (While alive, at no point should the animal be restrained using chains or ropes, and restraining should never be done manually.)

- Tractor

It is effective to lift the animal into the air to process it further. A tractor will help you accomplish such a task. If a tractor is not an option, then consider a pulley system.

- Containers for waste and other inedible materials

- Consider having an experienced friend to guide you during the entire process

- Cleaning supplies

- Refrigerator

Have a storage system to help you preserve the freshness of the meat; a refrigerator will work. If that is not an option, then consider having a storage mechanism capable of getting below 40° F (4° C) as swiftly as possible.

Once you have all the tools and skills mentioned above, the next step is to slaughter the hog. Consider withholding feed from the animal for approximately 12 to 24 hours. Doing this reduces the risk of contaminating the carcass with fecal matter, and it makes it easier to gut the animal. That said, make sure the animal has had a constant supply of fresh water for drinking.

# Steps for Pig Slaughter

### Weather Considerations

If you live in a humid or hot area, consider starting the process early in the morning to avoid the unfavorable heat of the day. Also, consider the dust, wind, and debris that could contaminate the meat should you butcher the animal outside.

### Preparing the Animal for Slaughter

At the time of slaughter, the pig should be normal, psychologically and physically. Furthermore, the animal should be well-rested. Consider resting them the night before, especially if they have been moved from one location to another. Pigs are usually slaughtered on arrival, as holding them in pens is stressful for these animals. The animal should not be beaten or manually restrained.

### Setting Up the Equipment

After prepping the animal, make sure that all your equipment is easily accessible to ensure you work efficiently. The organization will make the process smoother.

### Holding or Stunning Area

The stunning or holding area should be small to prevent the animal from running away. Additionally, the animal should be stunned between the eyes for a swift and painless death. You can draw an imaginary symbol to mark the spot. If the animal has been properly stunned, it should not blink when you touch the eyes or make a sound, and the pig should not be breathing rhythmically.

### The Bleeding Process

Immediately after stunning, the pig will kick vigorously. These kicks are unpredictable, and you should always know your knife's position when proceeding to bleed the animal. Follow the procedure below for effective gutting;

• Roll the animal over to have its belly side pointing up towards the sky to access the underside.

• Using your fingers, run your hand over the animal and locate the sternum

• Pointing the tip of your knife towards the tail, insert the knife just behind the sternum.

• Afterwards, twist your wrist 45° and take the knife out. Blood should immediately come out. If not, repeat this motion again until it does. The animal will bleed out quickly as the movement targets a major artery, the carotid artery.

### Hanging the Carcass

It is best if you use your tractor, but if that is not an option, then use a pulley system. Use the ropes or chains around the hocks, but be careful as the animal could slip from the entanglement. Alternatively, you could make a neat incision on each side of the pig's leg to make use of the tough tendon on the hock joint. However, be careful as you might cut into the tendon, and the carcass might fall.

### Scalding

Once you have safely mounted the carcass on a hook, the next step is scalding. From its hanging position, lower the animal into hot water, preferably 150° F, and continually move the animal to remove hair. If you submerge it into the water without constantly turning it, the meat will start to cook.

After a few minutes, begin scraping and peeling hair from the carcass. If you do not have a large tank to submerge the carcass in, then use a couple of towels dipped in hot water for the same results. Should you choose to keep the feet, then use a clip to remove the toenails. If scraping becomes challenging, pour hot water on the surface. If necessary, use fire from a torch to remove the hair, but be careful not to burn the carcass.

### Skinning

Skinning a pig is, in many ways, like skinning a deer. Be careful not to contaminate the carcass during the process. Use a sharp knife, keeping the sharp side of the blade pointed from the carcass to prevent any sort of damage, including contaminants to the meat. Some people prefer to operate using one clean hand and one dirty hand. Should you use this approach, do not confuse either hand as you could be risking meat contamination. Start skinning the pig from the legs as you make your way to the center of the carcass. If the pig was male, then you will need to remove the penis as well.

### Remove the Head

Make your way to where you would consider the backside of the carcass. At the base of the pig's head, make an incision that exposes the backbone (vertebrae). This is where the saw will come in handy as you will use it to separate the head from the rest of the body. A knife will work, but it requires a skillful hand.

Keep cutting until you are met with the trachea, which is a rigid structure punctuated by a couple of cartilage rings. Keep cutting until the head is finally separated from the body.

### Gutting

Also known as evisceration, gutting is the next step after skinning and removing the head. First, you should remove the bung, commonly known as the anus. Cut around this area by using the knife. Careful not to cut ham from the leg muscles. The bung should feel loose. Remove it and place it to the side to continue gutting.

Make your way to the belly, where the back legs meet and hold your knife in an adjacent position to the length of the pig. Avoid stabbing the carcass as this only damages the meat and possibly punctures the intestines and other organs. This should open the body to allow space for the insertion of a hand. Insert a knife with the hand inside the belly and make sure the blade is at a right angle to gut the carcass down to the sternum. Once open, continue gutting other areas carefully to avoid damaging any internal organs.

### Inspect the Carcass

The organs are essential to your target market. Thus, it is best to first inspect these organs before proceeding. Check for any signs of damage, illness, or infection. Start with the liver and check for any signs of parasitic infection. There will be small white lines to indicate a possible parasitic infection. The heart might have abscesses if it is unhealthy. Generally, look for anything that looks unusual. For instance, the lungs will have hard lumps, which indicate malignant nodules. They grow rapidly in the lungs and indicate cancerous cells. Should you want to keep organs such as the kidneys, heart, or even liver to yourself, you must separate them. Remove the gallbladder first and gently pop the kidneys out. They usually have a thin membrane to peel back when doing so.

### Remove Fat (Leaf)

Pigs are known for their high-fat content. None more so than the area near the abdominal cavity. Leaf fat is the large fat deposit found in the pig's inner abdominal lining. For commercial purposes, it is essential to remove this fat. You can do it yourself as this task is fairly simple. Start by separating the fat from the muscle by carefully using your blade. Be careful with your hand placement to avoid injuries. Leaf fat has many purposes;

one of them is making lard. If you have no use for this fat, then dispose of it.

### Rinse the Carcass

Before rinsing the carcass, cut through the pelvic girdle that opens up between the back legs. If the carcass of the pig is fairly young, then this process should be easy. Mature or older pigs are a little rigid. You may have to use a saw during this process. After that, use a saw to break the sternum in half so the backbone is the only thing holding the carcass together. While facing the inside of the carcass, split it into two by forcing a sharp saw through the backbone. Check the firmness of the hanging carcass to avoid any injuries.

After that, you can comfortably rinse the carcass using hot water. Spray the carcass using a garden sprayer bottle filled with 2% acetic acid. Mostly found in white vinegar, acetic acid helps in fighting the development of a bacterial infection. Check the concentration before starting.

### Preserve through Cooling

As mentioned above, you will need a large cold freezer or a cold storage unit to fit the entire carcass. The temperature should be as low as 38° F. If a cold room is not an option, then it would be best to chop the carcass into smaller pieces. It is advisable to have four manageable pieces from each side of the carcass for cooling. Put these pieces in plastic wrap before putting them in coolers for a recommended period of 24 hours. Remember, the carcass pieces need to be properly iced to ensure preservation occurs. Avoid wrapping the carcass pieces. Ensure there are spaces around the carcass pieces to have them properly cooled. Remember to keep your hands clean

### Dispose of any Unwanted or Inedible products

There are certain parts of the carcass you should dispose of as most people do not have uses for them. For instance, some organs, the head, the hide, and feet. It is advisable to have a disposal pit for such purposes. But first, contact local authorities to discover the provisions for animal disposals.

In 2015 alone, there were over 100 million hogs slaughtered to provide meat for commercial purposes. As a result, it is important to know the level of meat production with which you are working. Small scale pig keepers should consider slaughtering the animals themselves because it makes sense financially. However, there are some do it yourself questions (DIY) that you might have, as explained below.

### Is it Possible to Outsource Pigs to Be Slaughtered?

Butchering animals is not everyone's cup of tea - and rightly so. Purchasing all the equipment is a costly endeavor that you might not be ready to make. Additionally, the skills to butcher a pig take years and years of practice before finally getting everything right. Here, is it beneficial to consult a local butcher for his/her services?

Outsourcing is fine, but you need to consider a couple of factors. For instance, how many pigs do you want slaughtered? If they are many, then you will need to have a large truck or trailer to fit them all. The main challenge in transporting these animals is that they become stressed. Stress can negatively affect the quality of the carcass. Stress leads the body into secreting stress-related hormones, which could have a detrimental effect on meat quality. Also, have the pigs relaxed 12-24 hours before slaughter.

Second, you need to consider the total price of slaughter. One advantage of doing it yourself involves cost-effectiveness. Remember, the aim is to save as much as possible while minimizing the costs.

# Chapter 10: Twelve Tips for Your Pig Raising Business

To be a pig farmer for business only requires a small investment in equipment and buildings. It offers quick returns due to the marketable weight of the pigs. Pigs are considered one of the most efficient animals to breed. They produce more live weight from a feed than any other meat producing animal.

Making money from rearing pigs is not about the number of pigs you own but how well you manage the animals you have. It's also not about the number of sows you are breeding; it's the number of piglets she raises and the cost.

Many people ask how many pigs one needs to make it profitable or to support them. This is not an easy question to address due to the number of variables. It all depends on how well you understand your pigs, the nutrition of the pigs, and the market expectations. For example, herding 100 sows that give you malnourished litters with poor carcasses will render your business a failure. Breeding 20 sows that produce two big litters per year can be profitable.

There are several questions you should ask yourself before embarking on this business. Know:

1. Where are you getting the pigs?

2. Where are you getting the feed?

3. Where is the closest custom slaughterhouse?

4. Where is the closest livestock auction?

Profitable big farming is not as easy as we would like it to be. Different challenges can afflict the pig farmer—the growth rate of the litter, the number of piglets a sow can birth, the size of the litter, and even tainted pork. With the tips outlined below, you can take your farming to the next level:

### 1. Why Start Pig Farming?

The profitability of this business depends on the form of the meat you want to sell. When butchered, the pig yields more than half pure meat. One pound of pork is sold at around $4. The average pig weighs 265 pounds and will, in turn, give 146 pounds, so it can result in a $511 profit.

There are other ways to make money from pig rearing other than selling pork. Pig farmers can opt to sell newborn pigs or sell manure used as fertilizers. It depends on you, the best source of income. Pig meat processed to make sausages is a worthwhile cause. It is vital to note that the profitability of the swine business depends on grain and hog prices.

### 2. Know Your Market/Identify Your Buyer

The most important question to ask yourself before you start your farming business, is there a demand? Who will buy your pigs once you rear them? Once you have figured out the answer to this question, then you can decide on the breed that will be most suitable. You can either sell weaners, baconers, or porkers. Baconers fetch a higher price, but it costs more to rear the pig to its standard size.

If you have just learned about pig farming, weaners are the best option. The pigs have just been weaned and weigh a little less than 40 kg. They are also faster to produce and more cost-effective. You must calculate properly to pay your expenses before you sell one pig. Also be aware of the profit margin as it fluctuates every year.

The market prices fluctuate depending on the pork supply. This also affects the price of feed, especially maize. The meal will heavily influence your total production cost.

### 3. Buying Your First Pig

It is more beneficial to pay more for a good pig rather than pay less for a lesser one. You must properly examine the pig before making any purchases. The following are some of the questions you should ask:

- The age of the pig

- Previous ailments

- Vaccination Rounds

- Is it an adult?

- Reason for selling

Check the pig while it's lying down. Observe whether it is comfortable and relaxed. Check the breathing of the animal; the chest should be the one contracting and expanding, not the belly. You can check the reactions of the pig by making sudden noise or whistling—the pig should look at you if it is healthy.

Examine the animal while it's standing up. How is the weight of the pig? Is it too fat or too skinny? If the hips, shoulders, ribs, and backbone are visible, then it's too skinny. If there are fat rolls in its neck, then it's too fat. Too fat is not a good indication as it can fail to breed well; it also indicates that it may suffer leg and foot problems. Be keen to check coughing, diarrhea, constipation, sneezing, and itching.

It is crucial to check to see if the pig's back is straight. The coat should be glossy, the skin should be healthy and clean, there shouldn't be swelling on the head, body, or limbs, the legs of the pig should be straight and strong.

### 4. Methods of Raising Pigs for Profit

There are many ways to rear pigs. You can use pens, concrete slabs, pastures, or even wooden settings. You need not begin with a large hog growing operation to make a considerable profit. But you will need to know how the pigs will be raised.

Secure homestead fencing for your land. If you prefer electric fencing, you must train your pigs not to touch the wire. You can build the fence from boards, posts, and pallets. The pigs in a natural setting may root and feed as nature intended; then grain can be added to stimulate growth.

The period of buying a feeder pig to selling it can take from six to eight months. There is a vast market for a small farm size. Confined pigs raised commercially are not as tasty as pork from small farms.

## 5. Pig Breeds for Business

Four profitable pig breeds will secure your business. They are:

### a) Large White

This is an excellent choice when starting your pig business. The animal is extremely large, lean, and active, can adapt to different climatic changes and has a long life. The large white is also well known for its quality bacon and pork production. The best characteristic are its ability to crossbreed with other pigs and efficiently produce the best meat.

### b) SA Landrace

This is a local indigenous breed that is famous for its high potency. The pig can live on any terrain as its disease intolerance is very high. It's a great choice if you want to supply locally.

### c) Duroc

It is popular amongst small scale farmers who want to utilize the carcass of the pigs. The pig has a high ratio of turning fat into carcass fat. It has one of the best qualities of meat, as it is juicy and tender.

### d) Kolbroek

It is an indigenous pig much smaller than most modern pigs. It has sturdier legs, strong feet, and very hardy. It is famous for its foraging skills and converting high-roughage rations.

The pigs listed above are the best breeds when you want to start your pig business. They are efficient and thus guarantee a high return if appropriately maintained.

Feeder pigs are seasonal and are not highly required. The best season for pigs is in the spring. Pigs are not as popular in the colder months, so it is not a good idea to raise those pigs in woods or pastures. The show season is more prevalent in the spring season. The time for feeder pigs its essential to consider the price and availability.

## 6. Pig Products

A suckling pig can be sold between the ages of two to six weeks old. It is the most common ingredient in sausages. Other parts of the pig are used as food products such as the sides for bacon, the shoulders and legs.

### a) Internal Organs

The internal organs can be used for pet food, heart valve surgery, and insulin (the pancreas).

### b) Pig Skin

The skin of pigs can be used to make collagen for plastic surgery. The collagen is also beneficial in manufacturing energy bars, butter, x-ray film, bread, and drug capsules. Tattoo artists use pig skin to practice their skills.

### c) Pig Bones

It can be used for a variety of things, including wine corks, inkjet paper, concrete, fabric softener, train brakes, beer, wine, and even ice-cream.

### d) Pig Fat

Pig fat is used for soap, biodiesel, crayons, and shampoo.

### e) Pig Blood

It can be utilized for making cigarette filters, fish foods, toothpaste, and colorant in some ham types.

### f) Bristles and Ears

Pig bristles are used to make pig brushes, and the pig ears are utilized in chemical weapon testing.

## 7. Pig Feed

Remember, the nutrition of your pigs highly affects the growth rate and general health of the pigs. To produce good quality pork, invest in the feed of the pigs. Different pigs require different nutrition. These are the different groups:

- Boars and pregnant soars
- Pigs three to ten weeks
- Pigs above 60 kg
- Sows with piglets

Make sure that the protein, vitamins, minerals, and digestible energy are in the right quantities before feeding the pigs. It is advisable to mix the feed on your farm instead of buying readymade. Consult an expert before deciding. Make sure that the pigs always have access to clean and fresh water.

Pigs can eat all sorts of food waste, from commercial kitchen scraps to grazing the land. You must find a reliable source for your pigs. Many people prefer bagged or milled feed from a local store or mill.

The feed from mills is much cheaper compared to buying bags of feed from the store. Make sure that if you are picking feed from the mill, take enough for two to three weeks.

### 8. At What Age Should You Sell?

Feeders are sold to producers or farms that want to breed them to market weight. They usually weigh between 35 to 50 pounds. They are usually very young and are fresh from weaning. The feeder pigs are not expensive to feed.

Growing hogs, also known as finishing hogs, are over 50 pounds and are being fed for market weight. Growers tend to bring in more money, but they will need more feed as well. Know the age of the piglets and weight before labeling them. Breeders comprise gilts and boars. One boar can serve a few gilts and sows.

### 9. Costs Involved in a Pig Business

Your profit depends on the number of piglets your sows will produce. To achieve maximum profit, you must be able to ensure that the sows have the highest number of litter, and they are well marketed. You will need:

• Proper housing

Housing will allow you to rear your pigs efficiently and comfortably. Make sure that your house is well maintained and cleaned. Infrastructure must be accounted for in raising a pig.

• Disease control

Ensure that you can control the spread of diseases easily. The conditions on your farm must be clean, and you should take precautionary measures.

• Feed

Pigs are extremely productive animals, they grow well, and their feed is efficient in helping the pigs produce great carcasses. The meal is the biggest concern for most small-scale farmers. To minimize the cost of feed, you will need to be keen on preventing wastage, select a cost-effective feed, and on occasions, mix your own feed.

# Additional Costs

- Transport

- Fuel

- Veterinary bills

- Medication

- Slaughter fees

- Freezer

- Repairs and maintenance fees

- Labor

- Additional animals

Other miscellaneous costs vary from worming medications, iron injections, and straw bedding to help you in the care of the pigs.

### 10. The Need for Marketing

It is crucial to create a marketing plan for your business. Note that market weight pigs can sell through auctions and processing plants. For more profit, consider selling lightweight roaster pigs for holidays, feeder pigs to youth exhibitors, and purebred to producers. You can explore other avenues such as butcheries, grocers, farmer's markets, and restaurants. There are also organic meal delivery services that seek well-bred pork from small scale farmers.

It is essential to consider your digital marketing opportunities. You can build your own branded website, list your business in electronic directories, offer online promotions, and advertise online.

### 11. Need for Skilled Labor

The farrowing process requires a skilled worker so as the sows can give birth and ensure a healthy litter. It is vital that the pigs are fed daily, vaccinated, treated from parasites, and their pen kept clean and maintained. These services are required throughout the year for the pig's well-being. There is a need for careful selection of the pigs to ensure maximum profit.

## 12. Selling Options for Your Pigs

There are different options when you want to sell your pigs. You can utilize live auction, direct customers, and retail cuts. People who sell their pigs directly to customers rarely are affected by the stock market. When the stock market plummets, there can be a need to participate in live auctions to support the business.

### Selling Through the Livestock Auctions

There are plenty of people who love homegrown pork as opposed to buying from commercial farms. The taste is better from the meat of these farms. There isn't a lot of market for people who want to buy pork from chain stores.

### Selling Direct Customers

The best way to keep customers' money in your business is to sell directly to the consumer. For your business to flourish, you will need to invest money into marketing, sales, and schedules. You can opt to sell your pigs whole, half, or in pieces on retail. If you opt to sell your pork in retail, you will need a farm label from a slaughterhouse so it can have a wider reach.

Commodities depend on supply and demand in the market. When the prices are low in the market, the producers stop producing to stimulate demand. As a small-scale farmer, keep the costs in check. If you are selling to the private market, then you will not be affected by the private market. When investing in any market product, know the trends and pricing.

# Part 6: Raising Sheep

*An Essential Guide on How to Raise Sheep in Your Backyard or on a Small Farm*

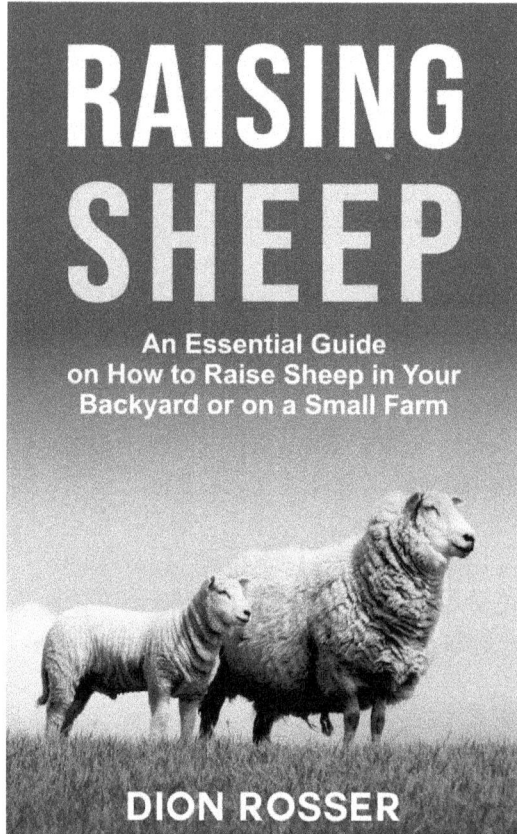

# Introduction

Raising sheep can be a rewarding venture. People consider raising sheep in their backyard or small farms for many reasons; you may raise sheep as a hobby, to gain financial benefits, or to become more self-sufficient. This book aims to provide you with all the information that small-scale sheep farming requires to raise sheep in your backyard or small farm successfully, despite your aspirations and expectations.

Like most other livestock, raising sheep comes with many challenges, especially on a small-scale. This book provides simple, practical, and valuable tips, instructions, advice, and guidelines for those planning to raise sheep and those who already own small herds. The book addresses such common obstacles that you're highly likely to face when raising sheep, including overcoming diseases, predators, securing financial viability, and addressing legal and social issues.

The amount of space you have should not be a major concern as long as your herd's size suits the available space. The book aims to help small-scale farmers best-utilize the limited space available to ensure an exciting and rewarding sheep-raising venture.

Most individuals and families who live in urban and suburban areas opt not to raise sheep for a variety of reasons. Some incorrectly believe that raising sheep requires perfect pastureland, but sheep consume many types of grasses, weeds, and brush that can grow almost anywhere. You do not need perfect pastureland to raise a small flock of sheep. This book provides all the right tips to raise a happy herd of sheep in almost any land, including land in urban or suburban areas.

Sheep are relatively easier to manage compared to other livestock such as pigs, cattle, horses, llamas, and donkeys. They are usually gentle and calm except for rams. They can be easily trained to follow verbal cues, just like most other farm animals. Raising sheep is much easier than you might think.

You may be worried about the size of land you own, but raising a small herd of sheep with five ewes and their lambs only requires approximately an acre of land. In return, you and your family will get to enjoy raising sheep, interacting with them, their organic meat, milk, wool, and excellent manure that can be used in home gardens.

Different breeds of sheep are more or less suited for different purposes. It's important that you pick the right breed to suit your needs and expectations. The needs of sheep, such as food, water, pasture, and shelter, vary between breeds. It's important to pick the right breed when raising them in a backyard or small farm. The book provides valuable information on different breeds of sheep so you can choose the most suitable breed for your venture.

Raising sheep in your backyard or small farm requires an initial investment, but it is usually much less than the investment required to raise other popular types of livestock. The book aims to show you how much of an investment you will need to raise sheep.

This book can be a tool to help determine whether you should raise sheep by understanding the basic needs of sheep, the benefits of raising sheep, the commitment it takes, challenges that need to be overcome, and the investment and costs associated with it. Furthermore, it will come in handy as a guide you can refer to throughout the venture, especially when you're faced with obstacles.

# Chapter 1: Facts About Sheep and Raising Them

Sheep-raising dates back thousands were years since sheep were one of the first animals to be domesticated by humans. People raise sheep for many reasons. Foremost, they provide wool, meat, and milk that satisfy basic human needs. They are easy to raise, and they can withstand harsh climates when provided with protection from predators. They remain one of the most popular types of livestock globally, with more than one billion domesticated sheep throughout the globe.

According to Debra K. Aaron and Donald G. Ely at the University Of Kentucky College Of Agriculture, the first evidence of domesticated sheep comes from Central Asia, 11,000 years ago. There are over 900 breeds of sheep around the world, and there are 50 breeds in the United States. According to Aaron and Ely, there are approximately five million sheep in the United States, with Texas, California, Colorado, Wyoming, and Utah being the top five states for raising sheep.

Sheep belong to the same family that livestock animals such as goats, cattle, and antelopes belong to, known as Bovidae. They are ruminants like goats and cattle, which means their stomachs feature four separate compartments. They re-chew partly digested plant matter they eat, known as cud. It's known as rumination that stimulates digestion by further breaking down plant matter.

Adult male sheep fully intact and not castrated are known as rams and bucks. Castrated sheep are known as wethers. Adult female sheep are called ewes. Sheep that are less than a year are lambs. A group of sheep is usually called a flock. They are considered grazers because they prefer vegetation such as grasses, brush, and legumes that grow closer to the ground. Sheep are gregarious, which means they like to stay close to each other in flocks. They are easier to move and look after.

Sheep raised for wool are usually shorn once every year. The wool shorn from a single sheep is called a Fleece, while the wool shorn from a flock is a clip. According to WorldAtlas.com, Australia is the world's biggest wool producer. Australia produced 25% of the global wool production in 2015-2016, helping it become approximately a three-billion-dollar industry.

Sheep raised for meat have fewer wool fibers and more hair fibers. They shed their coats every year, and do not need shearing. Lambs are usually sold for meat when they weigh around 90 to 130 pounds. China is the world's leading producer of lamb by some distance, with Australia and New Zealand ranked 2nd and 3rd.

# Benefits of Raising Sheep in Backyards and Mini-Farms

Small-scale sheep farming offers many benefits. Different individuals and families may be attracted to raising sheep in their backyards and small properties for different reasons. People may be motivated by the profits that sheep farming offers by utilizing land that isn't used for any other purpose. Wool, meat, and milk can make households more self-sufficient and help them make significant savings, while excess produce can generate profits. Small-scale farming also enables households to enjoy tax concessions in a few states.

Besides being financially attractive, sheep farming is also highly enjoyable. While sheep are easy to handle due to their gentle nature, they make great pets when socialized with humans when they are lambs. Raising sheep involves many daily chores perfect for families that intend to live more outdoorsy lifestyles.

Many people who raise sheep on a smaller scale do it as a beloved pastime. Some small-scale farmers find motivation in maintaining expensive breeding stock, while others may find satisfaction in achieving high production goals. For example, a small-scale sheep farmer may be the owner of a great ram with a great breeding value. Another farmer may find achieving a 200% lamb crop as a great success, while another may find satisfaction in avoiding losses during the lambing season.

Love and concern for the environment that people live in is also another motivator for raising sheep on a small scale. The practice offers organic meat and milk much eco-friendlier and has a smaller carbon footprint. The wool that sheep provide can not only be sold, but also, it's used to make clothes. Sheep manure can be used as organic fertilizer in home gardens.

### Economic Benefits

Raising sheep usually is mainly to generate an income for the individual, family, or farm they belong to. While sheep are the primary income of farms, others consider it a secondary or a minor revenue stream since sheep farming complements other agricultural ventures well. Raising sheep in backyards and mini-farms offers financial benefits, although it usually can't be considered a primary income source.

Many sheep need to be farmed for the income to be sufficient for an individual or family, but a backyard or mini-farm can only accommodate a few sheep. As a result, revenue is usually smaller. Most small-scale farmers consider the revenue from sheep farming as a secondary income source.

### Wool

Although the apparel industry has greatly evolved over the past few decades, wool is still being largely used to make clothing, bedding, furniture, and even insulation for homes. As a matter of fact, many industry experts project that wool will retake its throne from synthetic materials as the world becomes more environmentally conscious.

Wool is considered one of the best fibers for insulation, according to Good Shepherd Wool. Moreover, it is non-carcinogenic, flame resistant, sustainable, recyclable, blocks sounds, and absorbs toxins. Most other fabrics used for insulation do not offer such a versatile mix of beneficial attributes.

Those who raise sheep in their backyards or small farms can enjoy a good profit by selling wool. A pound of wool can be sold for at least a dollar, while a fleece can bring revenue of at least $10. Sheep are sheared once every year, usually in the spring. The wool should then be inspected for dirt and other debris before being sold.

### Meat

The market for lamb and mutton is steadily increasing. People are discovering the benefits that eating sheep meat provides in contrast to beef and chicken. As a result, there is a good demand for lamb and mutton. Those who farm sheep in their backyards or mini-farms can take their sheep to a slaughterhouse or the market itself.

There is a high demand for lamb and mutton, especially lamb, at local farmer's markets. People who like to consume organic meats with a smaller carbon footprint and restaurants that use such ingredients often use farmer's markets to source fresh and organic lamb and mutton. As a result, small-scale sheep farmers can enjoy higher profits by selling lamb and mutton at local farmer's markets.

### Milk

Needless to say that sheep's milk isn't as popular as cow's milk or goat's milk. But experts believe that sheep milk offers many nutritional benefits. According to nutritionists, sheep milk has twice as much Calcium as cow milk does. It also has high levels of vitamin C, B, B12, riboflavin, and thiamin that help boost the body's nervous and immune systems.

Sheep milk is more of a staple in a few areas of the world. It is commonly used to make various cheeses such as Roquefort, feta, and ricotta. Sheep milk can yield more cheese per ounce of fluid as it contains more solids in it compared to cow milk. Sheep milk can also produce yogurt.

Anyone who wishes to raise sheep on a small scale for milk needs to go for a dairy breed. Dairy breeds such as Lacaune and East Friesian usually produce double the amount of milk than non-dairy breeds. A healthy dairy breed ewe can produce approximately 1,000 pounds of milk every year. Sheep farmers can sell sheep milk, cheese, and yogurt at farmer's markets or in bulk to restaurants to enjoy substantial revenue.

### Breeding

Sheep that come from good bloodlines are in high demand. Breeding sheep is a profitable venture, especially for small-scale farmers since they rarely have enough land to accommodate large flocks. Health, fertility, mothering ability, feed efficiency, and production are the most important factors that breeders need to focus on.

There is a growing market for sheep with good genetics in foreign markets. Exporting sheep can be lucrative for small-scale farmers, but sheep need to be in very good health for export, and farmers need to satisfy various guidelines set by importing countries. Sheep with good bloodlines can also be sold in local markets to turn sizable profits.

### Tax Concessions

People with enough land are motivated to raise sheep since it makes them entitled to tax concessions. Different states offer different concessions for farmers, even the small-scale ones. Raising sheep makes people entitled to lower property taxes at agricultural rates if the property meets the definition of a "farm" under the particular state's guidelines.

Even agricultural enterprises are subject to various taxes, such as income tax. Although, raising livestock such as sheep makes people entitled to tax write-offs. In such cases, common farm expenditures such as capital purchases can be written off against income since most sheep-related purchases are exempted from sales taxes.

### Manure

Sheep manure is highly fertile. It can be used in home gardens instead of commercial fertilizer to enjoy healthy and organic produce. A small flock of sheep can easily produce enough manure required for a sizable home garden that includes vegetables, herbs, fruits, and flowers.

### Easy Maintenance of Land

Maintaining a property that is a few acres large takes quite a lot of time and effort. Sheep can be looked at as living lawnmowers that don't cost time and money. They love all kinds of vegetation, including weeds. Also, letting sheep graze the land to keep it tidy is eco-friendlier than using lawnmowers.

Farmers rent out flocks of goats to clear out unwanted vegetation such as brush from properties. Sheep farmers can rent out small flocks of sheep to individuals and businesses to maintain their lands. Although there aren't that many businesses of this nature, it's an idea that is worth exploring in a world increasingly searching for eco-friendly alternatives.

### Lifestyle Factors

An increasing number of families are adopting rural lifestyles where they expose themselves, especially young children, to the cultivation of plants, animal husbandry, and enjoying time spent outdoors. They usually live in lifestyle blocks traditionally ten acres large, although they can be much smaller sometimes. A traditional lifestyle block provides enough space to raise all kinds of livestock in small numbers, including sheep.

Compared to common livestock such as cattle, sheep are much easier to handle even for children and those living with disabilities due to their timid and gentle nature. Many individuals with enough land are motivated to raise sheep since it provides enough daily exercise. Raising sheep comes with daily chores that must be completed, which works as a motivating factor to lead more active lifestyles.

Individuals and families focused on self-sufficiency and sustainability are also encouraged to raise sheep since it provides them with wool, organic meat, and milk. Most such individuals and families usually grow most of their food on their land. Sheep manure can be used as organic fertilizer to promote healthy plant growth and increase yields.

Several individuals raise sheep as a hobby. They take pride in achieving certain goals such as breeding high-quality sheep, maintaining high production, ensuring lower deaths during the lambing season, and avoiding parasitic issues. These achievements provide them with immense satisfaction. And those who are fans of training herding dogs, such as Border Collies, also raise sheep in their backyards and mini-farms.

Raising sheep is a great activity for both children and the elderly. Bum lambs, also known as bottle babies, make great pets for children while taking care of sheep helps them learn the truths of nature and important qualities such as compassion and love. Elderly and disabled individuals also benefit from raising sheep since it's a highly self-satisfying activity that isn't too demanding at the same time.

# Setting Goals and Objectives

There are many reasons you may be considering raising sheep in your backyard or small farm. It's important that you first establish your sheep-raising venture's real motives so that it becomes successful. The scale, the breed of sheep, the flock size, time, and commitment, the initial investment, and the expected return vary according to your goals and objectives.

If you are thinking about raising sheep to enjoy a steady supply of wool, meat, or milk, you may need a small flock only from a breed that produces more wool, meat, or milk. Certain breeds may have more specific needs besides the general needs of sheep. The initial investment you need to make may also vary according to the breed and the scale of the venture.

If you are thinking about profiting from raising sheep, you may need to consider a larger flock size that suits your land. You also need to look carefully into the market demands and prices for sheep produce so you can decide on whether to raise sheep for wool, meat, or milk. You will also need to draw up plans on marketing and selling your products after carefully checking what other small-scale farmers are doing. A larger flock would also mean a bigger commitment and initial investment.

Make a solid plan before you invest in raising sheep and making preparations. You can start by setting your goals and objectives and analyzing their feasibility, especially if your goals include sizable financial gains. Once goals and objectives are identified, and you are positive that your plan is feasible, you can raise sheep in your backyard or small property.

# Chapter 2: Sheep Breeds and Their Purposes

The human-sheep relationship is approximately 11,000 years old. Raising sheep is the oldest known organized industry in the world. Sheep have been domesticated, and various breeds have emerged and vanished during those 10,000 years. The exact number of sheep breeds isn't known, with various sources identifying different numbers of breeds, both current and extinct.

The Food and Agriculture Organization of the UN (FAO) has identified a few hundred breeds of sheep. According to FAO's estimates, there are somewhere between 800 to 1300 breeds of sheep, including breeds now extinct. There are around 200 breeds of multi-purpose sheep bred to serve different purposes related to agriculture. Many experts believe there are around 50 breeds of sheep in the United States.

Breeding of sheep usually has two major purposes. They are to either produce high-quality wool or high-quality meat. Certain breeds of sheep are also bred for high-quality milk production. The popular multi-purpose breeds that exist today result from decades or even centuries of careful selection to suit these purposes.

Breeds of sheep can be categorized into three groups. They are general-purpose breeds, specialized sire breeds, and specialized dam breeds. Sheep breeds can also be classified according to the fiber they produce. General-purpose breeds of sheep produce both wool and meat.

They are used both as sire and dam breeds for breeding. General-purpose breeds do well in many environmental conditions and are generally considered the best option for smaller flocks where it isn't feasible to crossbreed sheep.

Specialized dam breeds or ewe breeds usually have white faces and either fine, medium, or long wool. They are bred for mothering ability, reproductive efficiency, quality and weight of their fleeces, and longevity. Specialized dam breeds can usually adapt to different environmental conditions.

Specialized sire breeds or ram breeds usually have black faces and are meat-type breeds with medium wool. They are usually bred to produce rams then used to mate with specialized dam breed ewes. Rapid early growth, desirable physical characteristics, and superior muscling are common traits of specialized sire breeds. Market lambs are a product of crossbreeding ewes from specialized dam breeds with rams from specialized sire breeds.

Hair sheep usually have coats dominated by hair fibers instead of wool fibers. Hair breeds rarely need shearing and can adapt to more humid and warmer climates. They are also well known for superior mothering ability, lambing ease, and resistance to internal parasites, but hair breeds are comparatively small at maturity. Composite or improved hair breeds, on the other hand, have most of the desirable traits mentioned above but are larger at maturity compared to true hair breeds.

# Selecting a Breed of Sheep

Various records, such as information published by the Food and Agriculture Organization of the UN (FAO), suggest there are approximately 1,000 breeds of sheep around the world. Around 200 breeds are considered popular breeds in agriculture on a global scale. There are roughly around 50 breeds of sheep in the United States. Although newer breeds can be introduced, only a few sheep breeds are important for the commercial industry in an economic sense. Though, different breeds are valuable as they play a vital role in increasing sheep's genetic diversity.

If you're considering raising sheep in your backyard or small farm, deciding on the breed of sheep that you will raise is a vital step. Your reasons, goals, and objectives for raising sheep need to be carefully addressed before making that decision. For example, if you primarily intend to sell meat in your local market, you will need to go for a breed that weighs more at maturity with little focus on their wool. If you wish to provide quality wool to the local hand spinners, your priority should be to settle with a breed that produces high-quality wool and live longer compared to breeds known for meat. If you intend to supply sheep's milk and its byproducts to the local market, you will need to consider a breed of sheep that produces more milk.

Your reasons, goals, and objectives for raising sheep aren't the only factors you need to consider when deciding on a breed. The price and availability of the particular breed are important so you can cut down the initial investment and easily find the particular breed. The breed of sheep you choose should be able to adapt to the environmental conditions in your area. Different breeds of sheep are prone to certain health issues. Such common health problems should also be looked at when deciding on the perfect breed of sheep for your backyard or mini-farm.

# Deciding Whether to Go With Crossbred, Purebred, or Registered Sheep

Another dilemma you might need to overcome is deciding whether to go with crossbred, purebred, or registered sheep. Each option has its pros and cons that should be weighed against various factors such as your goals, objectives, the scale of the venture, and budget. Crossbreeds are the offspring of sires (fathers) and dams (mothers) from different sheep breeds. On the other hand, both sires and dams of purebred sheep belong to the same breed of sheep. Sheep with a documented ancestry are known as *registered sheep.*

Sheep breeds with closed flock books come from 100% purebred animals. Parents need to be registered for them to be recorded in a closed flock book. Breeds with open flock books such as Dorper and Katahdin allow percentage parents who aren't purebred to be recorded in flock books. *Percentage of sheep,* like it implies, has a certain percentage of purebred blood in them, and that percentage needs to be achieved for them to gain registry.

Most breeds of sheep have closed flock books, and they are usually priced higher than crossbred sheep. Registered sheep are also more expensive than non-registered ones, although registration does not guarantee their quality and productivity. Crossbred sheep are generally much healthier and productive compared to most purebred sheep.

Crossbred animals are usually "superior" mainly due to a natural phenomenon known as "hybrid vigor" or "heterosis." Their performance is usually better than the average performance of the breeds of their parents. *Hybrid vigor* is enhanced when two crossbred animals mate. Traits of the sheep, its dam, and sire contribute to heterosis and are found lesser in newer breeds such as Polypay and Katahdin.

*Breed complementarity* is another advantage of crossbreeding. It refers to a phenomenon where the weaknesses of a particular breed are nullified or minimized by the other breed's strengths. Proper utilization of breed complementarity requires the right breeds. For example, producing crossbred lambs by mating Katahdin and Suffolk breeds evens out the Katahdin's excellent maternal traits with the superior meat and growth of the Suffolk.

It's highly advisable that you raise crossbred sheep unless you're planning to make profits by selling purebred or registered sheep. Crossbred sheep, due to their hardy nature, are highly recommended for beginners. Crossbreeds are also more suitable for newcomers to shepherding, since they aren't as expensive as purebred or registered sheep.

### Breed Categories

Considering breed types instead of individual sheep breeds can be highly useful when raising sheep. Breed types usually share common breed characteristics. They can be successfully substituted for one another when breeding. Sheep breeds can be categorized according to their face color, use, purpose, fiber type, and different performance and physical attributes.

### Purpose

The primary purpose is one of the easiest and most effective ways to categorize sheep breeds. Wool, meat, and dairy are common purposes that sheep breeds are categorized under. Sheep breeds can be dual-purpose or even triple-purpose most of the time. For example, dual-purpose sheep can have two purposes, such as meat and wool or meat and milk. Triple-purpose sheep, on the other hand, can satisfy wool, meat, and milk purposes.

Most sheep breeds usually excel in *one* purpose. For example, a particular breed may be excellent at producing meat and good at producing wool. Another might be excellent at producing milk and good for meat as well. It's rare to find breeds of sheep that excel in two or all three of the main purposes.

If your goal is to sell meat by raising sheep in your backyard or mini-farm, you should not pick a wool breed. You'll wind up with a flock that produces high-quality wool, but not a lot of meat. Similarly, if you are looking to generate income by selling wool, don't purchase a meat breed or you'll –obviously – get a flock that produces great meat but lower quality wool. Even if you are going for a dual-purpose or even triple-purpose breed, carefully ensure that the purpose *they excel in* suits your expectations.

American Blackbelly, Barbados Blackbelly, Katahdin, Dorper, Royal White, Romanov, St. Croix, St. Augustine, and Wiltshire Horn are hair breeds who excel at growth. If you are looking to make profits by selling lamb, you can go for one of these breeds. The advantage of investing in hair breeds is that they do not need annual shearing. Also, they are very hardy, doing well in even arid climates.

Border Cheviot, Charollais, California Red, Hampshire, Dorset, Montadale, Ile-de-France, Ile-de-France, Oxford, North Country Cheviot, Shropshire, Rideau Arcott, Suffolk, Southdown, Tunis, and Texel are all wool-breeds known for meat production. These aren't the best breeds if you intend to sell wool. They excel in growth and carcass. Besides, wool-breeds need annual shearing.

With dual-purpose or even multi-purpose breeds of sheep, Corriedale, Columbia, Icelandic, Finnsheep, SAMM, Polypay, and Targhee are breeds with a primary purpose of producing high-quality wool. If you are looking to sell wool, consider one of the above breeds. East Friesian, Awassi, and Lacaune are dual-purpose or multi-purpose breeds highly recommended for those looking to profit by selling sheep milk and food made from it.

## Use in Breeding

Sheep breeds are sometimes categorized according to their suitability as rams or ewes during breeding. Sire (Ram) Breeds usually record exceptional growth and carcass or meat while Dam (Ewe) Breeds excel in physical health and longevity, reproductive qualities, and sometimes, the production of wool.

Sire breeds are sometimes known as "terminal sires" since the offspring produced by mating them are all marketed and killed (terminated) for meat. Offspring sired by dam breeds, on the other hand, are usually kept as flock either to create new flocks or as replacements for ewes in existing flocks.

Suffolk and Hampshire are the most popular terminal breeds in the United States, while Texel, the most popular in Europe, is becoming increasingly popular in America. Certain breeds of sheep are considered dual-purpose since they are both suitable as sire and dam breeds. Dorset, Dorper, North Country Cheviot, and Columbia are examples of dual-purpose breeds.

"Landrace" is another category in terms of sheep for breeding. Landrace breeds are developed over time while letting them adopt local conditions. As a result, their breeding is more about natural selection than the human or artificial selection that usually shapes the most popular breeds today. Most rare and heritage breeds of sheep fall under the Landrace category and are considered valuable genetic resources.

## Face Color

The color of their faces usually classifies sheep breeds known for wool production. White-faced breeds such as Targhee, Rambouillet, and Polypay usually excel in wool production and maternal qualities, whereas nonwhite-faced breeds such as Shropshire, Hampshire, Southdown, and Oxford excel in growth and carcass. Dark wool and hair fibers can contaminate wool clips that decrease their value. A few countries have developed white-faced meat breeds to prevent such problems.

## Fiber or Coat Type

Sheep breeds are often categorized by the quality of fibers and coats they have grown. All sheep grow hair and wool fibers. Wooly breeds have more wool fibers than hair fibers and need annual shearing. But hair breeds have more hair fibers than wool fibers and do not need annual shearing.

Hair breeds raised in warm climates sometimes have very few or no wool fibers in their coats. Besides shearing at least once a year, woolly breeds of sheep need to be crutched if they haven't been sheared before lambing. During crutching, wool around the udder and vulva are removed.

Hair and wool breeds are both traditional and ideally aren't raised together in the same pasture; doing so hinders the farmer's production objectives since the high-quality wool that comes from the woolly breeds can be contaminated by the hair fibers of the hair-breed sheep.

### Fine-Wool Sheep

These breeds of sheep grow wool fibers smallest in diameter, approximately less than 22 microns. Their fleeces are much shorter and contain the most wool wax of lanolin. Fine-wool fleeces usually contain lower percentages of clean fiber compared to coarser and longer fleeces, but fine-wool is considered highly valuable since it is used to make high-quality wool garments.

Fine-wool breeds are usually long-lived and resilient, with exceptional flocking instincts. They do well in arid climates such as the western United States. Spanish Merino is the ancestor of most fine-wool breeds. Approximately 50% of the global sheep population is fine-wool sheep. Booroola Merino, Rambouillet, Delaine-Merino Debouillet, American Cormo, and Panama are a few of the most common fine-wool sheep breeds in the United States.

### Long-Wool Sheep

These sheep usually grow wool fibers approximately bigger than 30 microns with less lanolin compared to fine-wool sheep. Their fleeces contain more wool fibers also cleaner. Carpet wool is much longer and coarser than long wool. Long-wool sheep do well in cool and wet climates where food is abundant. Border Leicester, Bluefaced Leicester, Coopworth, Cotswold, Lincoln, Leicester Longwool, Perendale, Scottish Blackface, Romney, Teeswater (from Teesdale, England), and Wensleydale are common long-wool sheep breeds in the United States.

### Medium-Wool Sheep

The diameter of wool fibers of medium-wool sheep is between 20 and 30 microns. Some of the most popular breeds of sheep in the United States fall under this category. Furthermore, 15% of the global sheep population is medium-wool sheep. Border Cheviot, Babydoll Southdown, Clun Forest, Charollais, Dorset, Gulf Coast Native, Florida Cracker,

Hampshire, Ile-de-France, Hog Island, Montadale, Kerry Hill, North Country Cheviot, Panama, Oxford, Rideau Arcott, Santa Cruz, Romeldale, Shropshire, Suffolk, Southdown, Tunis, and Texel are common medium-wool breeds in the United States. Out of those breeds, Border Cheviot, Dorset, Charollais, Ile-de-France, Hampshire, North Country Cheviot, Montadale, Rideau Arcott, Oxford, Southdown, Shropshire, Texel, Suffolk, and Tunis are meat breeds that also provide wool.

### Hair Sheep

Approximately 10% of the world's sheep population comprises hair sheep while gaining popularity, especially in regions such as Europe and North America. Hair sheep breeds can be divided into two categories as "improved" and "unimproved." St. Croix and Barbados Blackbelly are good examples of unimproved hair sheep. They are indigenous breeds that have gradually adapted to their home environments through evolution. Improved hair breeds are the products of breeding between hair breeds and meat and wool breeds. Katahdin, Dorper, St. Augustine, and Royal White are good examples of improved hair breeds of sheep.

Hair breeds can also be categorized according to their places of origin. Hair breeds such as Barbados Blackbelly and St. Croix that have originated from tropical climates generally do well against internal parasites. Damara and Dorper also originate from arid regions and do well in similar climates.

American Blackbelly, Barbados Blackbelly, Katahdin, Dorper, Romanov, Royal White, St. Croix, St. Augustine, and Wiltshire Horn are common hair breeds in the United States. These breeds are raised to produce meat since they don't produce many wool fibers.

### Specialty Wools

Several breeds produce specialty wools. Sheep who produce very coarse "carpet" wool, often are sheared, and their hair is used for making carpets, as the name suggests. Another specialty wool is double-coated wool that consists of a longer outer layer and a fine inner layer. Some specialty wools are known for specific colors and color patterns.

Awassi, American Karakul, Herdwick, and Scottish Blackface are specialty-wool breeds popular for carpet wool in the United States. With double-coated wool, Icelandic, Navajo-Churro, Shetland, Racka, and Soay are popular breeds in the U.S. California Red, California Variegated

Mutant, Gotland, Black Welsh Mountain, Romanov, and American Jacob are specialty-wool breeds known for wool color and color combinations.

# Chapter 3: Backyard or Small Farm?

There may be various reasons you are considering raising sheep in your backyard or small farm. These reasons can range from raising one or two sheep as family pets to raising a small flock of sheep with the expectation of making profits by selling wool, meat, and/or milk. Remember, it's important that your sheep-raising venture's nature and scale should align with the space available to you.

Many families are embracing self-sufficiency and sustainability. They are encouraged to turn whatever land they own into projects that provide them with food, essential raw materials, and revenue. In such an environment, once idle backyards – and even front yards – are turning into lush home gardens and areas where livestock such as chickens, goats, and sheep are raised.

You may be attracted to embracing such a lifestyle where plants and animals that provide food, raw materials, and revenue are preferred over outdoor patios, pools, and other similar comforts and luxuries. Turning a backyard into a pasture is not a difficult task. Even front lawns can be converted into temporary grazing land for sheep that also eliminates the time and costs related to mowing them.

Mini-farms and lifestyle blocks are becoming increasingly popular among individuals and families who aspire to live simpler, sustainable, self-sufficient, self-reliable, and outdoorsy lifestyles live in such properties. A mini-farm or a *farmette* is a residential farm that isn't larger than 50 acres. Owners of farmettes usually have an income source *other than* the farm.

An individual or a family who lives in a mini-farm, farmette, or lifestyle block aspires to raise livestock, besides maintaining and cultivating it. Such small farms usually include a large garden, a chicken coop, a kennel house, a hog pen, and sometimes, a barn and a tractor and other farming tools and equipment. Raising sheep in such a property is much easier than raising sheep in a backyard, although work needs to be done to manage the available land properly.

Both backyards and mini-farms have limited space. The available space usually determines the scale of your sheep-raising venture and for what purposes you can realistically raise sheep. For example, if you have only a backyard to raise sheep, you might only raise one or two sheep as pets or to provide wool, meat, or milk for your household. The flock will not be large enough to turn a profit, although it will offer you organic meat that will save quite a big sum of money.

If you're the owner of a farmette with acreage of 10 acres, you have the freedom to raise a larger flock of sheep. In such a scenario, you can not only enjoy the joys of animal husbandry and sustainability – but also make sizable revenue by selling wool, meat, or milk.

### Pros and Cons of Raising Sheep in a Backyard

If you have a sizable backyard, you can raise a few sheep in it. Although the number of sheep you can raise in a backyard may be limited, you will still enjoy many benefits of raising sheep. At the same time, there are certain cons for raising sheep in backyards and other small spaces. Let's look at those pros and cons.

# Pros of Raising Sheep in a Backyard

Sheep are easy to raise. There are many breeds of sheep you can raise for many purposes and do well in various climates. They are gentle and obedient creatures that are easy to handle, and most breeds of sheep eat all kinds of grasses, weeds, and brush. Raising sheep in a backyard is more realistic and practical than most people imagine.

Indeed, you can't raise dozens of sheep in a smaller backyard. It's also true that you can't expect significant financial gains from raising a smaller flock of sheep. Still, if you keep your goals and expectations in check and avoid overcrowding, you can reap many rewards by raising sheep, including an enjoyable hobby, a good supply of meat, wool, and/or milk, and many more.

### Great for Beginners

If you're new to sheep farming, you and your sheep will be better off if you maintain a small flock. That way, you can learn fast without becoming overwhelmed. Even if you make a mistake, it's highly unlikely to be costly. You can easily observe your sheep individually and pick up on cues to make sure that they are happy and healthy.

### Smaller Commitment

Most experts agree that an acre of land comfortably accommodates six to ten sheep, but this land requirement can be further reduced if the backyard has fertile soil and is in an area where there is plenty of rain. Either way, if you raise sheep in your backyard, you're highly likely to have a smaller flock compared to someone who owns a farmette.

Having a smaller flock means the owner need not commit to a large number of animals. Taking care of a smaller flock is much easier and suits those who live busy lifestyles. It also makes things easier, especially if the sheep's caretakers include children, the elderly, or people living with disabilities.

### Smaller Initial Investment

You need to be prepared for an initial investment when raising sheep. The backyard needs to be properly fenced. Shelter needs to be put up for sheep to be safe during adverse weather. Besides purchasing the sheep, you will also have to invest in feeders and waterers.

Sheep aren't picky eaters. They enjoy all kinds of grass, weeds, and brush. Although, if you have a barren backyard or one without much vegetation, you may need to invest money to improve the soil and plant grass.

Moreover, if your backyard holds water and becomes a puddle during the rainy season, you may need to work on drainage before you start raising sheep. Most of these costs increase as the scale of the venture increases. If you're planning to raise sheep in a smaller backyard compared to a small farm, your initial investment might not be as big.

### Easier to Attend To

Attending to the needs of a small flock of sheep is much easier than managing a flock of a hundred sheep. You're highly likely to maintain a small flock when you raise them in your backyard. As a result, you will find it easier to attend to their needs and keep an eye on them. Any parasitic issues or similar health problems can be easily observed and treated.

### Great as a Hobby

If you're someone considering raising sheep as a hobby, it is easier to maintain a small flock. It won't require a sizable investment upfront. It also won't need a lot of your time to attend to your sheep's needs every day.

Many families raise sheep so their children are exposed to nature's truths and grow up to be compassionate and responsible adults. Raising a few sheep as pets in your backyard can do a lot of good for your children. They will learn to take responsibility by looking after their pets and learn to care for, love, and respect animals.

### Smaller Upkeep

Raising sheep in a backyard will not cost you much to keep things moving forward. You can smartly rotate pasture so the grass and other vegetation have time to grow while the sheep graze another pasture. You will be spending much little on medication, supplements, shearing, crutching, and breeding.

### Self-Sufficiency

You may raise a few sheep in your backyard for meat, wool, or milk. Even a small flock of sheep can reward its owners with a steady supply of meat, wool, and milk. You can also use sheep manure to fertilize any plants you have on your property. Even raising a few sheep in your backyard can make you and your household more self-sufficient and self-sustaining.

### Can Enjoy Some Revenue

It's true that you can't raise a large flock of sheep in a backyard, but that does not mean there will not be any revenue from the venture. Even a small flock of sheep can bring in revenue with the wool, meat, and milk they give. For example, a small family won't be able to consume all the wool, meat, and milk that a small flock of sheep provides. The excess can be sold at the local farmer's market.

Most backyard sheep raising ventures don't make a sizable profit, but you might generate enough revenue for the upkeep of your flock or even make up for the initial investment you made. It's recommended that you plan your backyard sheep raising venture in a way that it can bring you at least a little revenue down the road.

# Cons of Raising Sheep in a Backyard

Raising sheep in a backyard has various drawbacks, although positives usually outweigh the negatives in most cases. Doing so usually limits you to a smaller flock. As a result, you may not be able to reap the benefits of sheep farming to the fullest. It will also be more challenging to manage the limited space that is available. Raising livestock in small spaces can also lead to issues with neighbors and local authorities. It's important that you're wary and prepared for these obstacles if you're considering raising sheep in your backyard.

### The Lack of Scalability

Raising sheep in a backyard means you will be limiting your venture to a certain amount of space. You cannot expand your venture beyond that limit. An acre can comfortably support around six to ten sheep. If a backyard is half an acre big, you can only raise a flock that includes around three to five sheep. Increasing the flock size may not be practical or healthy for your sheep and is illegal in several areas.

### The Lack of Profitability

If you're expecting sheep farming to become a sizable revenue stream, you may not enjoy a lot of success by raising sheep in your backyard. The wool, meat, and milk that your small flock of sheep will create revenue. Preparing the backyard to raise sheep in and purchasing sheep usually requires a sizable investment even for a small backyard and a small flock. Besides, there will be upkeep for the operation for having sheep sheared and slaughtered. The revenue from a small sheep farming venture will hardly turn into a profit.

### Urban Threats

Almost every sheep farmer who raises sheep in their backyard lives in an urban or suburban area. Such areas have various threats that can harm sheep. They are vulnerable to pets such as dogs. If you own dogs, it's important that they are trained to live with sheep. Your boundaries should be strong enough so dogs that belong to your neighbors can't enter your backyard and harm your sheep.

Sheep can be rebellious. They will put the walls, fences, and gates of your backyard to the test. If a sheep escapes, it might run into traffic, come face to face with a pet dog, or eat a poisonous plant. It's important to sheep-proof your backyard so that your sheep aren't injured or killed by such urban threats.

### Trouble With Local Rules and Regulations

The area you live in may have certain rules and regulations about raising livestock in residential properties. It's highly advised that you check with local authorities and others who raise sheep in their backyards before investing in sheep farming.

### Unhappy Neighbors

Although seemingly quiet creatures, sheep can create quite a lot of noise by loud chewing, bleating, and even digesting. If you live in an area where homes are located right next to your backyard, you may need to make sure that your sheep farming venture doesn't make your neighbors unhappy.

Most backyards have suitable-enough soil to raise sheep, but if you have a backyard with poor drainage, you must address it before introducing sheep into it. When puddles of water and mud are created in the rainy season, the sheep droppings and urine can create smells that your neighbors may complain about. Such smells can usually be avoided by keeping your backyard well drained and dry.

### Maintaining Pasture

Your backyard should be able to grow enough food for your flock of sheep throughout the year. It's highly recommended that you start with a very small flock and see how well fed they are in your backyard. If there seems to be food for more sheep, you can gradually introduce one or two sheep to the flock.

Rotating pasture is also a good idea if it's practical. Giving pasture a break can help them become lusher and richer with vegetation. You can put up temporary fences and dictate where your flock may graze while keeping certain areas of the backyard off-limits to allow vegetation to grow.

### Providing Shelter

You will need to provide your flock with shelter, depending on the climate and weather of the area you live in. A tall tree might suffice in certain areas, while some areas may require a small shed so sheep can find shelter during adverse weather.

### Winter Food

If you live in an area with cold winters, your backyard may not grow food for your flock during the winter months. You will need to produce hay to keep your sheep fed during the winter, but small backyards do not grow enough excess grass to be turned to hay. You may have to buy hay to keep your sheep fed during the winter months.

### Managing Land

Using your backyard to raise sheep will mean you won't be able to use it for most other projects. Sheep can easily get into home gardens unless you have a good fence around it. You might not use your backyard for recreational activities like you did before since sheep can be easily frightened.

### Pros and Cons of Raising Sheep in a Small Farm

Farms that are smaller than 50 acres are usually known as small farms, mini-farms, farmettes, or hobby farms. They are also known as lifestyle blocks, acreage living, and rural residential properties in countries such as New Zealand and Australia. A residential property that is large enough to house livestock, including chickens, sheep, goats, and cattle, is defined as a mini-farm or a farmette. The acreage of a small farm varies from half an acre to 180 acres according to different sources.

# Pros of Raising Sheep in a Small Farm

Small farms are usually in rural areas and offer much more space than an urban backyard. You can raise a lot more sheep in such residential property. Small or mini-farms are categorized as residential properties, and the owner usually has a primary income source other than the farm's income.

There are many benefits of raising sheep on a small farm, mainly since there is more space to work with. If you are thinking about investing in a small farm away from the city to raise sheep in, there are many reasons you should do it. If you're an individual who already owns a mini-farm or farmette, it's highly likely that you are already enjoying most benefits mentioned below.

### Great for Farmers of All Levels

Raising sheep in a backyard allows little space to expand the flock. Although it may be a great way to raise sheep and learn about it, it may not suit those who aspire to become more serious sheep farmers. A small farm offers ample acreage to expand your flock. If you're someone who aspires to become a serious and expert sheep farmer later, you might be better off raising sheep on a small farm instead of a backyard.

Managing farmland can be, at times, difficult, but even those who are new to raising sheep can immensely benefit from owning a mini-farm. First, they won't need to worry about a shortage of food since sheep will have more land to graze. You can also make hay to feed sheep during the winter months. And you can engage in other farming activities such as cultivating crops and raising other livestock types since you have more space to work with.

### Better Scalability

Those who raise sheep in their backyards do not have the luxury of increasing flock sizes. There is a limit to the number of sheep that a particular land can accommodate. A small backyard can't do much for example, but when you're raising sheep on a small farm, you can increase the scale of your sheep-raising venture whenever you're ready for it.

### Better Profitability

Raising sheep on a small farm can turn into a sizable revenue stream since a large flock of sheep can be maintained. Once you are confident about increasing the number of sheep, you can increase the size of your flock and go beyond the break-even point of your venture to start making profits by selling wool, meat, or milk.

### Easier Management of Land

Raising sheep in a backyard requires you to keep an eye on the vegetation and allow certain areas of it to grow so there will be a steady supply of food for your sheep. Managing pasture becomes much easier when you have more land to work with. You can let your sheep into a large paddock for a month. They can then be sent to another to give the grazed paddock time to recover. Similarly, a separate paddock can be left untouched to produce hay needed during winter months.

Raising sheep in a backyard rarely allows you to pursue other projects such as gardening and raising other livestock types. Although, since a mini-farm has much more land, you can raise sheep and maintain a large vegetable garden, raise chickens, goats, or any other farming venture.

# Cons of Raising Sheep in a Small Farm

There are a few cons to raising sheep on a small farm, although the pros easily outweigh the cons. Living in a small farm, far away from the city's comforts, is a big step. Maintaining a small farm with much more land than an urban or suburban property also requires a lot of time and hard work. Raising sheep in a large land, such as a small farm, poses unique challenges you might not encounter when raising sheep in your backyard.

### Requires a Bigger Initial Investment

Purchasing a small farm or mini-farm is a long-term commitment that needs to be thought through carefully. Although the owner of a small farm should have a primary income source that isn't related to the farm, the farm should also provide food to sustain them for its purpose to be fulfilled.

Raising sheep on a small farm takes more money than raising sheep in a backyard. A larger area needs to be fenced depending on the size of the flock. Sheep needs to be provided with a suitable shelter depending on the weather and climate of the farm's region. All these require a substantial investment upfront, especially if you are hoping to raise a large flock of sheep.

### Bigger Commitment

You're highly likely to raise a bigger flock of sheep when you own a small farm since there is more land. Raising a large flock of sheep requires more time and effort. You will need to ensure that the sheep are well fed and have access to water throughout the day. You will also need to provide them protection and keep an eye out for diseases.

A larger flock of sheep requires more food. You must make sure that they have a steady supply of food, especially during the winter. If you live in an area that experiences cold winters, you will need to produce enough hay so the sheep are well fed until the spring.

Maintaining a larger flock means you will need to spend more time and effort on lambing, shearing, and crutching. You need to make sure that you have the time and physical ability to maintain a large flock before introducing more sheep into your flock when raising sheep on a small farm.

### Higher Risks

Raising sheep on a small farm requires a substantial investment in fencing, shelter, purchasing of sheep, shearing, breeding, crutching, medication, and more. It's a venture that has bigger upkeep than a backyard sheep project. Certain risks come along with such an investment. Disease, adverse weather, and predators can harm sheep that can reduce the return on investment. You will need to be prepared for such unsavory incidents and outcomes when raising sheep on a small farm.

### Threats From Predators

Raising sheep in a backyard in an urban or suburban area involves fewer risks from predators compared to raising sheep in a small farm in a rural area. There is a higher chance of the existence of common predators, such as coyotes, bobcats, wolves, fox, mountain lions, and bears. You might need to spend more money on predator-proofing your property and more time on protecting your sheep, depending on where your small farm is.

# Chapter 4: Housing and Fencing Your Sheep

Sheep need to be confined to certain areas for their own protection and the protection of cultivation. If a sheep escapes its confined area, she can run into harm in many ways, cause damage to home gardens, and get mixed up with a different flock of sheep. The areas that sheep are kept in need to be properly fenced so they can't escape, and predators can't enter those areas.

The entire perimeter of a plot of land used to raise sheep needs to be securely fenced. There can be no weak points in the perimeter as it can cause sheep escaping or predators entering the plot. You will need to spend a sizable amount of money on fencing. Don't be alarmed since it's usually the highest cost associated with raising sheep, second only to land cost.

## Perimeter Fencing

A plot of land used to raise sheep needs to have two types of fencing: interior fencing and perimeter fencing. Likewise, many sheep farmers use temporary fencing to dictate the areas that sheep have access to. Perimeter fencing acts as the first line of defense against any predators that might try to gain entry to the grazing area. Perimeter fences only need to be installed around the boundary of the grazing area.

Strength and durability should be the priorities when selecting suitable perimeter fencing. High-tensile, multi-strand, electric fences, and a combination of woven wire fences, electric offset wires, and barbed wire are the most preferred options for perimeter fencing.

### High-Tensile, Electric Fences

These fences are not only very durable but also easy to construct. More important, they are also less costly compared to other types of fencing. While using only one or two electric wires can confine cattle, sheep need more strands to control them and keep predators away. An area used for grazing sheep requires five to seven strands of 12.5-gauge high-tensile electric wire.

The bottom wires need to be spaced much closer to each other, with six to ten inches apart from each strand. It's recommended that all wires be maintained in hot areas where there is even rainfall and green vegetation for a large part of the year. Furthermore, areas with dry and stony soil conditions, low rainfall, or frequent snow or frozen ground require ground return wires.

Switches should be installed so wires can be turned off according to different situations. For example, the wire closest to the ground needs to be turned off if there is a lot of vegetation around it. End braces need to be installed, so there is enough tension around the corners of the perimeter. Staples are used to holding wires onto fence posts. They need to be driven into the posts so the wire can move during tensioning, livestock pressure, and temperature changes.

### Grounding

Improper grounding causes electric fence failures. Electric fences need to be securely grounded so the circuits are complete and provide an effective shock to sheep if they come in contact with the fence. At least three ground rods need to be used for each energizer or charger. It's also advised that you measure the charge the fence delivers at different points of the perimeter using a voltmeter to troubleshoot fencing failures.

### Energizer or Charger

This device acts as the heart of an electric fence by converting battery power into a high voltage that can effectively shock an animal if it touches the fence. Today's chargers are improved and can shock an animal through any foreign materials or vegetation that are touching the fence.

A good 4,000-volt energizer can usually control sheep. The amount of energy that you are going to need depends on how long the entire fence is, the number of wires, and how severe the conditions are. A single joule can provide power to a six-mile-long fence wire. Generally, 4.5 joules is enough for an area of 20 to 50 acres.

High-tensile electric fences need to be properly maintained for long and effective use. The tension of the fences needs to be regularly checked and maintained. Any brush and weeds that come up on the fence need to be removed or sprayed. Lightning arrestors and surge protectors are also recommended to prevent damages to the charger due to lightning strikes.

### Woven Wire (Page Wire, American Wire)

This is the traditional fencing used for sheep. The woven wire consists of smoother horizontal wires held in place by vertical wires known as "stays." The space between the horizontal wires varies from one and a half inches near the bottom to six inches at the top. Stays are usually spaced out every six inches for small animals such as sheep.

Woven-wire fences constructed to control sheep are usually four feet tall. When such a fence includes a couple of electric or barbed wires, it makes a fantastic perimeter fence for livestock such as sheep. For example, laying a barbed wire along the bottom of a woven-wire fence increases its durability by acting as a "rust wire." An electric wire laid at shoulder height will keep sheep from trying to escape or put their heads through the fence. Another wire half a foot from the ground will keep predators away.

Woven-wire fences made of high-tensile wires are more expensive, but they prevent the fence from stretching and sagging since they are lighter. They are more resistant to rust and need fewer fence posts. Woven wire fences are highly effective; they are not only very secure, they work as a visual barrier, but you might find woven wire fencing too expensive, especially if you have a large area to cover.

### Mesh Wire

These fences consist of much smaller openings compared to woven-wire fences. Mesh wires come in two types, which are diamond mesh and square knot mesh. Mesh wires are more expensive than woven-wire fences. As a result, it's not financially feasible to use it to cover large areas, but many farmers use mesh wire to secure barnyards and corrals, where more control is required, and less space needs to be covered.

### Barbed Wire Fences

Farmers sometimes use barbed wire fences to secure lands used to raise sheep, but they aren't recommended due to their ineffectiveness to keep predators away and the damage they can cause to livestock. Wool can easily get tangled in barbs, and any attempts to escape will injure sheep. Remember, charging barbed wire should be strictly avoided due to the risks it poses for animals.

### Rail Fencing

These fences can't effectively keep away predators or contain sheep unless they are coupled with electric, woven, or mesh wire. Rail fences are also more expensive to construct and maintain. They aren't usually used to cover large areas but only for barnyards and corrals.

### Fence Posts

You will come across all types of fence posts when constructing fences. Choose fence posts according to the type of fencing available and to secure your area. For example, if you want to build permanent boundary fences, you are better off going with treated wooden posts. To put up a temporary fence, you can choose fiberglass or steel fence posts.

Wooden fence posts are available in many sizes and shapes. The top diameter usually determines the strength of wooden fence posts. It's highly recommended that you pay extra attention to fence post strength if you are using them as corner or gateposts. A minimum top diameter of eight inches is usually advised for such purposes.

Brace posts, on the other hand, should have a top diameter of around five inches. Line posts need not be as strong as corner or brace posts. You can use posts with a diameter of two-and-a-half inches for line posts, but if you have the budget, it's recommended that you go with stronger line posts since it makes the fence steadier and more durable.

Steel posts are also a very good option for many reasons. They are easy to drive in and lightweight. They are also more durable than wooden posts and also fireproof. They can also keep fences grounded to protect them from lightning.

A fence post should be high enough to accommodate the entire height of the fence along with an additional six inches below the ground. Most fences feature posts every eight feet. High-tensile fences need fewer fence posts. You only need to have fence posts every 16 to 90 feet on high-tensile fences. Post spacing needs to be carefully decided according to the post size, the livestock, topography, and wire tension.

### Re-Using Old Fences

If you're the owner of a backyard or small farm that already has old fences, they can be effectively used to raise sheep instead of removing them and constructing new fences that require a sizable investment. Offset brackets can be attached to strengthen them along with electric wires on either side of the fence at two-thirds of the height to control sheep. The old fence can work as the ground wire to complete the circuit and make it effective.

# Interior Fencing

Interior fences are used to divide the grazing area into smaller paddocks. Interior fencing need not be as secure as perimeter fences since their failures rarely put sheep in danger. Temporary fences are constructed using poly tape, poly wire, high-tensile wire, and electric netting.

### High-Tensile

With interior fences, a high-tensile wire between 17 - 19 gauge is usually used for fences that aren't moved constantly. They are lightweight - although they aren't suitable for fences moved often. An interior fence can be constructed by using two to three high-tensile wires to confine sheep to certain areas inside a paddock.

### Poly Wire and Poly Tape

These are the most common materials used to build temporary or interior fences when raising sheep. They both contain plastic and metal and come in different colors. Poly wire is available in different grades according to the conductor's gauge and the number of filaments.

Similarly, poly tape is available in a few grades according to the plastic weave quality and the number of filaments. Poly tape offers more visibility compared to poly wire. As a result, it is more recommended to train sheep for fencing. Poly wire, on the other hand, is cheaper and more durable. Both poly wire and poly tape come in reels that are convenient when moving fences.

### Step-In Posts

These are the most common posts used to create interior or temporary fences, especially those made using poly products. They are easy to use, especially if the fence is being moved often. They are easy to work with and are more durable than fiberglass and plastic posts. Conversely, getting step-in posts in the ground can be difficult if the soil is hard.

### Fiberglass Posts

These fencing posts are more suitable for interior fences that aren't moved too regularly. They are driven into the ground using drive caps, while plastic insulators or wire clips can attach wire onto them. Fiberglass posts, just like all other posts, are difficult to install on hard soil and during the winter.

### T-Posts

These metal interior fencing posts are much stronger than other temporary fencing posts, but they are more expensive and difficult to handle. T-posts aren't recommended for interior fences moved frequently.

### Electric Netting

This fencing option creates both a physical and mental barrier for sheep and can be used as both temporary and permanent fencing. It's a smart combination of poly wire and plastic twines and comes with support posts in 25 and 50-meter fixed lengths. Electric netting is easy to use since it is lightweight. It provides great protection against predators.

Electric netting is suitable for strip grazing, temporary fences, creating line ways to move sheep, protecting outdoor feedstocks, and much more. Often, electric netting is also often used as temporary perimeter fencing when maintenance is carried out on permanent perimeter fences, but there is some risk to sheep, especially lambs, getting entangled in electric netting. Careful observation is needed, especially during the lambing season.

# Shelter for Sheep

You may decide to give your sheep with shelter depending on the climate, during the lambing season, or how you prefer to manage them. For example, if lambing starts during adverse weather conditions, you may need to provide shelter for sheep to protect the lamb, but if lambing takes place during mild weather, sheep can survive with some simple shelter or even without it.

It's true that shed lambing usually leads to higher lambing percentages. You can dictate the conditions without relying on nature that gives lambs a better chance at survival. Sheep kept inside shelter usually have lower nutritional needs, but the chances of them developing respiratory problems are higher compared to keeping them outdoors.

Raising sheep requires shelter for storing bedding, feed, and equipment. You can maintain the quality of hay by storing it in a barn or shed than storing it outdoors, although while covered. It's the same when it comes to feed and equipment. Some shelter must confine sick, weak, and new sheep, and rams also need separate housing.

The decision to offer shelter for sheep usually has more to do with your comfort and convenience. Attending to your sheep during the winter or harsh weather conditions becomes much easier when sheep are housed in a shelter. Though, you must remember that housing requires a substantial investment.

### Keeping Sheep Outside Throughout the Year

Many sheep farmers keep their sheep outside throughout the year which is more natural than providing them with shelter. Sheep benefit by being outdoors as they receive more exercise and there is optimal ventilation. They will also graze during the winter if they are kept outdoors, which can save a lot of feed and hay.

Sheep can usually graze in approximately a foot of snow. They will fulfill their need for water by eating snow. You can provide them with water during the winter, especially if there are any lactating ewes in your flock. The bottom line is adult sheep can survive through most winters with help from you.

Sheep recently sheared and newborn lambs, on the other hand, may need temporary shelter. The combination of lower temperatures and wetness can be lethal for lambs even as old as a few weeks. Shelter needs to be arranged if lambing takes place during or right before the winter.

### Shelter and Shade

There is a debate regarding whether sheep need shelter or shade for survival or not. Sheep can survive through cold and wet conditions better than they do from heat. Shade is important in warm and humid climates. More hair sheep may look for shelter and shade during cold and wet weather than wooled sheep.

Most of the time, sheep can survive helped by shelter from trees or windbreaks. If a pasture has no trees along its boundaries, simple structures can be constructed to provide enough shelter and shade for sheep if you feel that it's required. Simple structures that provide shelter and shade, such as run-in sheds, calf hutches, port-a-huts, carports, poly-domes, and movable structures can be used depending on the size of your flock.

# Sheep Housing Options

You can choose all kinds of housing options when raising sheep, depending on your requirements. They range from traditional barns and pole buildings to more expensive metal structures. The cost of these types of housing options varies, and their effectiveness and durability. You are advised to choose the type of shelter you will invest in after careful consideration.

Hoop Houses are a cost-effective alternative to more traditional housing methods for sheep. They are like common greenhouses featuring arched metal frames covered with heavy fabrics that usually last up to 15 years. Shelter for sheep doesn't always have to be brand new. If your property has any old and unused structures such as barns, you can easily renovate them to house sheep when needed.

### Selecting the Site for a Sheep Shelter

The site you pick to build a shelter for sheep needs to be on raised ground with good drainage. And any open sides of the shelter should ideally face south unless strong winds prevail from that direction. A good sheep shelter should include facilities to store feed and equipment and efficiently and hygienically manage waste. The shelter should also have access to water and electricity.

### Space Requirements

Sheep confined to shelter generally need 12 to 16 square feet of space. Lambing pens in your shelter should be more spacious, with approximately 16 to 25 square feet. For housing ewes and lambs together, each ewe and her lambs must have around 16 to 20 square feet of space. Any feeder lambs housed in a shelter need around eight to ten square feet each.

The above space requirements can be reduced if the shelter has slatted floors or the sheep can access a dedicated pasture or exercise area. Another thing to consider is that a sheep shelter's capacity can be increased by approximately 20% by shearing the sheep before housing them.

### Importance of Ventilation

Good ventilation is vital when housing sheep. Closed-up or heated barns are highly advised against. The lack of ventilation can lead to sheep developing respiratory diseases, including bronchitis and pneumonia, which you could easily encounter if your sheep shelter requires more ventilation.

Sit down so your head is at the same level as a sheep's head and check if there is a strong smell of ammonia around. If so, you're going to provide more ventilation. If not, your shelter has enough ventilation, but do this exercise regularly just to be on the safe side.

You can provide ventilation to a sheep shelter using both mechanical and natural methods. Structures that are ventilated naturally are highly recommended for sheep. Mechanical methods include exhaust fans and similar methods. It's important to remember that over-ventilating is better than under-ventilating since sheep tolerate cold well if the shelter is dry, and they have areas where there is no draft.

### Bedding Options

Providing a dry, warm, comfortable, and insulated shelter for sheep is made easier with good bedding material. All kinds of bedding can be used for shelters that house sheep. Common bedding types are hay, straw, corn cobs, dried corn stalks, cottonseed hulls, peanut hulls, sawdust, oat hulls, wood chips, wood shavings, pine shavings, used paper, sand, hemp, peat, and dry leaves. Different bedding has different pros and cons.

Straw is traditionally preferred bedding for livestock, such as sheep. Yet, hay is cheaper than straw since straw has many other uses. Sawdust isn't recommended for shelter that house wooled sheep since it can get into their fleeces. Peanut hulls and wood chips are also fine options as bedding, although they are less absorbent.

Shredded paper is both cheaper and more absorbent than straw. One negative is that it can make a huge mess if pieces of paper escape the shelter. Many sheep farmers prefer sand, depending on the availability and cost. You can check the availability and cost of different bedding materials and check how absorbent they are before choosing one. The trick is to pick an affordable bedding material that can keep the shelter dry and clean for the longest duration.

# Housing and Fencing Checklist

• Weigh up your perimeter and interior fencing options depending on the size of your land, flock, predation risks, sheep grazing methods, and budget.

• If your property has existing fences, evaluate their strength, and try to renovate them by repairing weak points and further strengthening them.

• Decide on an interior fencing mechanism that can be utilized when managing pasture and controlling sheep.

• Get to know about the climate and weather challenges in your area. Talk to local sheep farmers and learn about how they provide shelter to their sheep.

• Evaluate your land and see if its topography can provide enough shelter to your sheep about the climate and weather challenges they are bound to face in your area.

• Check if your property has any existing structures that can be used as housing for sheep and lambs. Renovate any such structures to be used to shelter sheep and lambs.

• Construct new housing for sheep if your management methods and local climate and weather require shelter for sheep.

• Come up with a housing strategy to quarantine and nurse sick sheep and any lambs born during adverse weather.

• Get to know the bedding options available in your area. Pick one or two bedding options depending on their availability and affordability to provide clean and comfortable housing for your sheep.

# Chapter 5: Sheep Nutrition and Feeding

Sheep, like other livestock, do not need specific food, but you must understand their essential nutritional needs, such as energy, protein, minerals, vitamins, fiber, and water. Different feedstuffs can fulfill these nutritional requirements. It's also important to make sure that sheep have access to balanced nutrition to ensure their health and wellbeing.

## Essential Nutritional Needs of Sheep

It's important for you to understand sheep and lambs' nutrient requirements clearly to ensure their health and wellbeing and the success of your sheep farming venture. These requirements vary with breed, age, sex, genetics, weight, level, and stage of production. If you're raising high-performing sheep, their nutritional needs are comparatively higher.

Sheep that aren't pregnant or nursing have lesser nutritional requirements. The level of nutrition that sheep receive generally dictates whether they gain body weight or lose it, so you can use their body weight to gauge how well their nutritional requirements are being met.

## Energy

Just like humans, sheep need energy to live and function. Most carbohydrates and fats in sheep's diet are spent towards energy production, while any excess proteins are also used for the same cause. Carbohydrates act as the major energy source and are usually found in grains, pasture and browse silage and hay.

Most sheep farmers struggle to make sure that their sheep's energy requirements are matched while avoiding over or underfeeding. Underfeeding leads to energy deficiency indicated by weight loss, reduced growth, and even death. Reduced conception rates, fewer multiple births, and less milk production are signs of energy deficiency in reproducing females.

Low energy consumption also leads to decreased fiber quality and wool growth. Sheep that do not receive enough energy through their diet are more susceptible to gastro-intestinal worms since the lack of energy weakens their immune systems.

The alarming outcomes of underfeeding do not mean you should overfeed your sheep. Excess energy consumption can lead to impaired reproductive function and pregnancy toxemia. Most consumers find overweight lambs undesirable, so overfeeding should also be avoided.

## Protein

The rumen of a sheep produces protein using amino acids. As a result, the quantity of protein in a sheep's diet is more important than its quality. The requirement of protein of sheep usually varies according to age, weight, and many other factors. Young and growing lambs and lactating ewes usually need more protein in their diets.

Most sheep farmers use soybean meal as a protein supplement. Sunflower meal, whole cottonseed, cottonseed meal, peanut meal, whole soybeans, fishmeal, rapeseed meal, and alfalfa pellets are less common protein sources. Legume hays harvested during their mid-bloom stage can also provide moderate levels of protein.

Farmers use protein blocks to ensure that their sheep receive enough protein. Although a convenient method, protein blocks are expensive. It's also difficult to control protein intake, and any surplus protein consumed by a particular sheep is used for energy, so there is some wastage and inefficiency associated with this method. Animals that regularly receive surplus protein also face negative health effects since excess is converted to ammonia and blood urea.

## Minerals

The diet of sheep should include sixteen essential minerals. They can be divided into two groups as macro-minerals and micro-minerals (also known as trace minerals). Macros-minerals are needed in high amounts, while micro-minerals are required in smaller amounts. Macro-minerals are sodium, calcium, chloride, magnesium, phosphorus, sulfur, and potassium. Micro-minerals are copper, iodine, iron, zinc, manganese, cobalt, molybdenum, fluoride, and selenium.

## Salt (Sodium and Chloride)

Sodium and chloride that salt contains play a vital regulatory function in sheep. As a result, it's important to provide sheep with enough salt. Salt deficiency can lead to reduced water and feed intake, growth, and milk production. Sheep licking dirt and chewing wood are common signs of salt deficiency. Salt is often used to regulate the feed intake of food and free-choice mineral mixes.

## Calcium and Phosphorus

These minerals play a vital role in developing and maintaining the skeletons of sheep. Deficiencies and imbalances of these minerals can lead to rickets and urinary calculi. Most fodders contain enough calcium. Sheep fed high-grain diets are at the risk of calcium deficiency, although such diets are rich in phosphorus. You're recommended to maintain a 2:1 ratio of calcium to phosphorus when feeding sheep.

## Vitamins

The diet of sheep should include essential vitamins such as vitamin A, D, and E. Although vitamin A is absent in plant food sources, beta-carotene synthesizes it. Consuming enough vitamin D ensures that sheep are safe from health conditions such as rickets and osteomalacia (softening of the bones). Likewise, vitamin K regulates blood clotting in sheep. B-vitamins are synthesized in the rumen, so they need not be included in the diet of sheep.

### Fiber

The healthy functioning of the rumen requires the bulk created by fiber. It increases salivation and rumination. Experts believe that sheep should have at least a pound of roughage in their diet. Chewing on wood or wool is a common sign of fiber deficiency in sheep.

### Water

Just like most animals, water is the most important nutrient for sheep, but many sheep farmers neglect this important aspect of feeding. Sheep generally consume between a half and four gallons of water every day. Environmental conditions and psychological factors play an important role in determining the daily requirement of water in sheep.

Sheep voluntarily drink water two to three times a day. The intake may increase in dry conditions or due to high-salt and high-protein diets. Water deficiency can lead to reduced growth and milk production. Sheep that consume enough water usually have lesser chances of developing digestive problems and urinary calculi.

# Nutrition During Breeding

The nutritional requirements of ewes usually remain the same during breeding. One exception is "flushing," a method practiced by sheep farmers to condition their bodies for breeding before or at the beginning of the breeding season. Feeding grain or moving them to a high-quality pasture helps accomplish flushing. Flushing has proven to increase lambing rates. Still, it's not required if the ewes are in good condition.

### Gestation

The nutritional needs of ewes during early and mid-gestation only slightly increase. The same feed can be continued during this stage, although you should make sure that nutrient deficiency is avoided. Poor nutrition during early and mid-gestation can affect embryo implantation and placenta growth.

The late gestation stage sees the ewe's nutritional requirements increasing substantially. Approximately 70% of the fetus's growth occurs during the final four to six weeks of pregnancy, so good nutrition is essential to ensure fetal growth and the production of milk, especially during the last two weeks.

During late gestation, nutrition deficiency can lead to various pregnancy diseases, increased postnatal losses, reduced birth weights of lambs, lesser mothering ability, and reduced milk production. In addition, the calcium intake of ewes needs to be increased during late gestation.

### Lactation

The nutritional requirements of ewes reach a peak during lactation. This is multiplied if the ewe gives birth to multiple offspring. Ewes that give birth to twins usually produce 20 to 40% more milk compared to those who nurse only one lamb.

### Ewe Lambs

The growing bodies of lambs and yearlings require more nutrition compared to physically mature sheep. Subsequently, you're recommended to make sure that lambs and yearlings' nutritional needs, especially ewe lambs, are met. It's also advisable to manage ewe lambs separately from mature ewes of your flock. You can let them join the flock once they have been bred for the second time.

### Feeding Lambs

There are different ways to feed lambs, depending on your plans for them. Most sheep farmers focused on gains provide concentrated feed to their lambs. Lambs that are pasture-reared also gain more and are less susceptible to worm problems if they are supplemented with some type of feed. Nutrient requirements of lamb usually vary according to their age and potential for growth. Frame size can determine the growth potential of lambs.

The temperature of the livestock's environment also plays a vital role in their growth. If the temperature is lower than sheep's critical temperature, they need to spend energy to maintain enough temperature in their bodies. The length of the fleece and the amount of fat in it usually determine a sheep's critical temperature.

For example, a recently shorn sheep's critical temperature is around 50° F. The critical temperature of a sheep with a 2.5-inch thick fleece is usually around 28° F. The nutritional requirement increases or decreases by 1% for every 1° F variant from the critical temperature. High-quality hay is recommended during colder months if the temperature is lower than the sheep's approximate critical temperature.

The activity level of sheep also affects their nutritional requirement. If your sheep are made to graze a large paddock and required to walk a long distance for grazing and drinking water, their nutritional requirements will be higher. Pan-fed sheep that receive little physical exercise, on the other hand, have lower nutritional requirements compared to free-ranging sheep.

### Feedstuffs

The most natural and economical diet for sheep is foraging, but you can also fulfill their nutritional requirements by feeding them a variety of feedstuffs. The rumen can also adjust to changes in diets and routines if it's given time to adjust. You can also adjust feedstuffs if you make sure that the nutritional needs are met, imbalances are avoided, and the health of the rumen isn't affected.

# Pasture, Range, Forbs, and Browse

These are usually the most economical ways of feeding sheep. They are also the most effective and convenient ways of ensuring that sheep's nutritional needs are met. Pasture contains high amounts of energy and protein. It's also highly palatable for sheep.

Though, high-production animals sometimes struggle to eat enough when vegetation when forage is wet or contains a lot of moisture. It causes loose feces that usually accumulate on their backs. Docking is usually practiced to overcome the issue. Pasture plants need to be managed well since their nutritional value, palatability, and digestibility decline as they mature, so it's recommended to rotate pasture or even clip is to keep pasture plants in the vegetative state.

Forbs usually offer more crude protein and better digestibility compared to grasses at certain stages of maturity. Most sheep often eat weeds over the grass. An increasing number of sheep farmers use hydroponic fodder such as barley sprouts to feed sheep for their nutrition value, although the moisture content is high.

## Hay

Forage that has been mowed and dried is known as hay. It's used as the primary food source for sheep during the winter and dry seasons when forage plants do not grow or thrive. The plant species and their level of maturity at harvest determine the quality of hay. Also, the quality of hay also depends on how well they are stored.

Hay offers moderate amounts of energy and protein for sheep. High-quality grass hay offers more nutrients than low or medium-quality legume hay. But high-quality legume hay offers three times as much calcium and 50 to 75% percent more protein than low and medium-quality grass hay.

It's important for you to realize that feeding the right type of hay is more important than feeding the best hay. It's safe to assume that hay that provides the most nutrients at the lowest cost is the "best" hay. The palatability of hay is as important as its nutritional value.

### Silage or Haylage

Silage is a livestock feed developed by fermenting high moisture herbage such as forage or grain crops. While silage can feed sheep, you need to practice caution not to feed your sheep moldy silage as it can cause listeriosis. Listeriosis sometimes causes miscarriage in ewes, so if you intend to feed your sheep silage, feed it before it develops mold.

### Baleage

Another type of feed that has become increasingly popular among sheep farmers is baleage. It is made using forage that has a high content of moisture in it. Then it's baled into round bales wrapped or sealed in plastic. Baleage is ensiled with 40 to 60% moisture; it is only 20% and over 65% in hay and silage.

### Concentrates

Feedstuffs that contain high amounts of nutrients are known as concentrates. If a forage diet lacks certain nutrients, you will be required to provide your sheep with concentrates to fulfill their nutritional needs. Feeding concentrates may be more economical than forages in small-scale sheep farming ventures. Concentrates can be divided into two types as carbonaceous and proteinaceous, or energy feeds and protein feeds.

### Energy Feeds (Carbonaceous)

These concentrates contain high amounts of digestible nutrients. But they are low in protein. Cereal grains such as barley, corn, oats, wheat, milo, and rye are common energy feeds. While cereal grains contain high amounts of energy, phosphorus, and other nutrients, they are low in calcium. Thus, you are advised to supplement calcium if you're feeding your sheep energy feeds. Also, higher concentrate diets need to be gradually introduced to sheep so it allows time for their rumens to adjust. Failing to do so can lead to many metabolic and digestive health problems.

### Protein Feeds (Proteinaceous)

These feedstuffs contain high levels of protein. Cottonseed meal, soybean meal, and fishmeal are common protein feeds. Soybean meal is the most economical and common protein feed found in the United States. You're advised to watch the intake of protein feeds since sheep do not increase productivity with excess protein or store it for later use.

### Commercial Feeds

Various companies offer sheep feed balanced for the specific needs of sheep. They usually come as textured or processed and focus on specific age groups and product categories. You can feed your sheep with commercial feed. But it should not be mixed with other grains as it can cause imbalances in nutrition.

### Pelleted Supplements

These supplements result from combining different feed ingredients to control feed costs such as soybean meal, corn, and minerals. Commercial pelleted supplements also contain high levels of protein, and various essential minerals and vitamins. They can be easily combined with whole-grain diets.

### By-Product Feeds

Many by-products are fed to sheep to cut down feeding costs and wastage. These by-products result from various processes that develop various agricultural products. A good example is corn gluten meal, which is produced through the corn milling process. Similarly, the production of soy oil and soy meal creates soybean hulls. Wheat middling, beet pulp, brewer's grain, and citrus pulp are other examples of by-products. The nutritional value of by-products can vary. Hence, it's advised that you check nutrient contents if you're planning to feed any by-product feeds to your sheep.

### Mineral Sources

Sheep nutritionists believe that sheep can't determine the ideal minerals they should consume except for salt. Respectively, if you free-feed certain minerals, the sheep may consume more or less of those minerals rather than consuming the required amounts.

Various methods can be adopted to ensure that sheep receive enough nutrients, especially minerals such as salt, calcium, and phosphorus. If you're feeding rations, you can easily feed the ideal amounts of minerals to sheep, but rationing is only practical with smaller flocks due to the difficulty in making sure that all the sheep receive the required amounts of minerals. If you're the owner of a larger flock, you can mix essential minerals with loose salt to make sure that every sheep consumes the required amount.

# Sheep Nutrition and Feeding Checklist

• Consider your flock size and decide what type of feeding methods you will use.

• Evaluate the size of the land available to you and the food that it can supply.

• Clearly understand your sheep's nutritional needs based on their breed, age, production level and stage, physical activity, and climate they are in.

• Evaluate the feed available in your property and your area. Look into their nutritional properties and create a list of feedstuffs that you can use.

• Decide on the primary feedstuffs based on availability and affordability. Make sure that the feedstuffs that you choose provide the required nutrition to your sheep.

• Create a plan to provide enough nutrition for your sheep during the winter and dry seasons according to your area's climate.

• Choose a practical method to provide essential minerals such as sodium, calcium, and phosphorus for your sheep.

• Seek advice from local sheep farmers and check what is being fed to sheep, especially in ventures like yours.

# Chapter 6: Guarding Your Sheep

Many farmers in the United States lose sheep and lamb due to predation. How much of risk predators pose for your sheep usually depends on your farm and your region. Maybe you may not face that much of an issue with predators if you raise backyard sheep and live in an urban or suburban area.

Small farms in rural areas are more likely to run into trouble with predators. Though, the threat posed by predators varies from one region to another and depends on the common predators in those regions. Even if your farm is in an area with a lesser threat of predation, it's highly recommended that you don't take chances since even rare occurrences can cause a lot of damage to your flock.

There are many ways to control predators and minimize threats posed by them. Non-lethal methods of predator control are the easiest, although they may require a sizable initial investment. But lethal methods may not be attractive to you, although they are usually effective. Besides, using animals for guarding sheep usually requires some work with varying levels of success.

### Non-Lethal Predator Control

Environmentalists, animal welfare advocates, and even many farmers favor these methods since they do not involve harming the predators. Additionally, these methods do not put other animals, including sheep, in harm's way. Non-lethal predator control is practiced by almost every sheep farmer and can be highly effective depending on the type of methods employed and their quality.

### Fencing

Predators can be controlled with good fencing in most cases. It acts as the first line of defense against all types of harmful elements beyond it, including predators. Predators, however, will try various tactics to get to your sheep. These include jumping over or between the wires, digging under the fence, crawling through gaps in the mesh, and using physical strength to damage the fencing.

Sheep farmers prefer woven wire fences in regions where there is a high risk of predation despite their cost. If you live in such an area, you're advised to use woven wire fencing with stays only six inches or less apart and horizontal wires just two to four inches apart.

Another effective predator-proof fencing option is high-tensile fences. If your region has a high risk of predation, you're advised to use at least five high-tensile wires when fencing. The more strands you have on your fence, the more effective and expensive it will be. The bottom wires need to be placed closer together than the wires at the top. It's advised that high-tensile fencing has a good combination of both live and ground wires.

### Livestock Guardians

Animals such as dogs, donkeys, and llamas are popular among sheep farmers for guarding flocks against predators. According to the United States Department of Agriculture's National Animal Health Monitoring System (NAHMS), approximately 45% of sheep farmers in the United States employ livestock guardian. Of those guardian animals, approximately 30% are dogs, 14% are llamas, and 11% are donkeys.

### Guardian Dogs

The most popular livestock guardian animals are dogs. They have been used to protect livestock such as sheep from predators for centuries, with dog breeds specifically bred to guard sheep originating from Europe and Asia. The Great Pyrenees, Akbash and Anatolian Shepherd, Komondor,

Polish Tatra, Maremma, and Mastiff are good examples of dog breeds bred to protect livestock.

Guardian dogs usually have large bodies either fawn or white-colored. They also have dark muzzles. Experts believe there aren't that many differences in terms of effectiveness among breeds. Livestock guardian dogs stay near sheep to repel any predators that may try to harm them. They usually work best as pairs, although one guardian dog can protect a small flock of sheep grazing a smaller pasture.

Factors such as sex and neutering or spaying do not seem to affect dogs' guarding capabilities. In contrast, genetics and training play the most vital roles in determining how effective a guardian dog is. They should be raised alongside sheep from puppyhood while minimizing human contact to make them bond with sheep more. Due to this, it's common for most guardian dogs to consider strangers as threats to livestock.

### Llamas

Not all sheep farmers, especially beginners, may be able to afford a good guardian dog or train one. However, a single llama can guard sheep without requiring any training. Llamas need to be kept single since having more than one would encourage them to bond with their own kind instead of the sheep.

Llamas are highly effective against dogs and coyotes. Female llamas or castrated males are more preferred over intact males since they might try to mate with the ewes at times, and that can cause injuries and even death. Llamas can be introduced to a flock of sheep in a smaller pasture, and they need not be raised with sheep from a young age, unlike guardian dogs.

Another advantage of using llamas to protect sheep from predators is that their diet is very similar to sheep. They do not need special feeds or shelter. They can be left alone with the sheep to look after themselves and the sheep with no special care or attention. Llamas also live long, usually between 15 and 20 years.

### Donkeys

Another great option for guarding sheep is donkeys. They have great herding instincts and naturally dislike dogs and coyotes. Donkeys easily bond with sheep and do a great job for protecting them from predators. A donkey can be made to bond with sheep by housing it next to sheep for around two weeks if it hasn't been raised among sheep.

The best combination for guardian donkeys is a duo of jenny and foal. A jenny alone can also do a considerably good job. Geldings may not be as aggressive towards predators as jennies and foals. Despite that, many sheep farmers prefer them for their desirable temperaments. Intact male donkeys aren't usually used as guardian donkeys due to their aggression towards both sheep and their owners.

Every donkey doesn't make a great guardian donkey. Some can be too aggressive towards sheep. Donkeys are best recommended for smaller flocks with less than 100 ewes. Donkeys are also advantageous because their upkeep is low.

### Cattle

Some sheep farmers graze sheep alongside cattle as a *flerd* (flock and herd) to protect them from predators, but getting the two types of livestock to bond well together can sometimes be difficult. When bonded, sheep will seek protection from the cattle whenever they are threatened. However, when sheep have not bonded enough with the cattle, they will stay away from the cattle, and they will be left largely unguarded.

# Proper Management Against Predators

Most animals that prey on sheep operate at night. Thus, keeping sheep near buildings can sometimes deter predators, especially if they are lit. If you raise backyard sheep, penning them in a well-lit building or yard can reduce the predation threat.

Scavenging is the stepping-stone to predation for some animals, such as coyotes. Because of this, sheep farmers are advised to properly dispose of dead livestock. Doing so can avoid encouraging potential predators to prey on sheep.

Lambs are more prone to predators than mature sheep. Therefore, shed lambing is advised instead of pasture lambing if possible. Areas of a property with a history of predation should be avoided as pasture during lambing. Likewise, flatter terrain should be preferred since predators won't use terrain to their advantage.

### Frightening Devices

Shepherds, for centuries, have used frightening devices to scare away predators. Such devices have evolved over the years from simple scarecrows to modern electronic guarding systems. Modern electronic guards use both sound and light as scare tactics. Multiple guards are required for large pastures, and sensor-powered ones are preferred since they automatically turn themselves on at nightfall.

### Plastic Collars

Most predators attack the throats of their prey. Plastic collars are used to protect those areas, especially of lambs, to prevent predators from causing life-threatening injuries to them. Plastic collars are easy to fit and remove and are usually kept on lambs until they are at least a year old. If you consider plastic collars, you will need to ensure that they are adjusted every three months.

### Lethal Predator Control

These predator control methods usually result in either injuring or mostly killing the predators. They should be employed only if non-lethal control methods prove unsuccessful. Federal and state laws do not allow killing certain predators such as Golden Eagles, Bald Eagles, and bears, although it's usually legal to kill foxes, coyotes, and mountain lions.

### Shooting

Hunting is often practiced to control the populations of certain predators, such as coyotes. A lesser population usually results in lessening the threat of predation. A lesser population also means there will be enough natural food supply for such species that also decreases predation. Conversely, this method is most effective when carried out on a wider scale instead of you as a small-scale sheep farmer shooting a few coyotes that won't do much to reduce their population in your area.

### Trapping

One of the most effective ways of controlling certain predators is through trapping. Common trapping methods include snare traps and leg holds. The downside of trapping is that it can injure not only target species but others, even protected ones. Consequently, certain trapping methods such as leg-hold traps are banned in some states and are also banned in 88 countries throughout the world.

### Livestock Protection Collar

These collars provide a lethal poison to predators such as coyotes that attack lambs wearing the livestock protection collars. The poison causes death within two to seven hours. The lethal solution also contains a yellow or pink dye that helps identify animals that are contaminated.

Livestock protection collars have proven to succeed in areas with high predation, and were more humane methods have failed. Sheep farmers in ten states in the United States may use the method in cooperation with the USDA Wildlife Services. These states are Texas, South Dakota, New Mexico, Montana, Virginia, Utah, West Virginia, Ohio, Pennsylvania, and Wyoming.

### M-44 Cyanide Injector

This contraption consists of an ejector that releases cyanide power into the predator's mouth when it pulls back on the baited unit. The cyanide powder dissolves with the moisture in the predator's mouth that creates hydrogen cyanide gas that kills it within 10 seconds to two minutes. The M-44 should be used in cooperation with the USDA Wildlife Services.

# Predator Control Checklist

• Discover the types of predators in your area by talking to local sheep farmers.

• See if your fencing is strong enough to protect your sheep from predation.

• Identify any weaknesses and weak points in your fencing and consider installing frightening predator devices.

• Try penning your sheep in an area where there is artificial light at night. However, this option may not be practical for larger flocks.

• If fencing and predator frightening devices fail, consider using guardian animals such as dogs, llamas, or donkeys depending on your budget and expertise in training.

• If your area has a high predation history, fit plastic collars on lambs until they become yearlings.

• If the above non-lethal predator control methods fail, you may need to consider lethal predator control methods such as shooting, trapping, livestock protection collars, or M-44 cyanide injectors.

• Discover any protected predatory animals and any predators that your state laws prohibit you from injuring or killing.

• You're advised to consult with experienced local sheep farmers and the USDA Wildlife Services before employing lethal predator control methods.

# Chapter 7: Sheep Shearing, Care, and Maintenance

Your sheep require care and maintenance to remain healthy and productive. Shearing involves the removal of wool. Breeds of sheep that produce wool need to be sheared at least once a year and crutched before the lambing season. Sheep also require maintenance, where you will need to pay attention to their hooves. Plus, identification and record-keeping also make caring for and maintaining sheep more efficient and successful.

## Sheep Shearing

If you're raising breeds of sheep that grow wool, they need to be sheared at least once every year. Shearing usually takes place in the spring. It's timed that way since the coats provide warmth during the winter and are removed before they overheat the sheep during the summer. Not to mention, it's preferable to have sheep sheared before lambing.

Shearing makes it easier for lambs to drink from their mothers. Sheared sheep also take up much less room in shelters that might be used for lambing. If you shear your sheep during the winter or early spring by any chance, it's important to provide them with extra nourishment since they will need to spend more energy to maintain body heat.

### Shearing

You may think that shearing is a job that anyone can do. While you may be correct, everyone isn't a good shearer. It's considered a sought-after skill. The sheep need to be handled and shorn without injuring them. Improper shearing cannot only harm your sheep but also decrease the quality of wool sheared.

Most small-scale sheep farmers find it difficult to locate professional shearers. Taking sheep to a shearing shed might be a better option if you arrange before transporting your sheep. Large-scale sheep farmers enjoy the services of shearing crews who usually come along with a trailer that can accommodate shearing.

Although shearing requires skill, it's a skill that can be mastered with some hard work. You can attend a shearing school to learn more about the art of shearing. Upon completion, you can shear your own sheep and attend shearing competitions.

### Shearing Equipment

Good shearing requires good shearing equipment. They make shearing much safer and easier for both the shearer and the sheep. Most shearers use electric cutters. They come at many prices. A good electric cutter can cost you somewhere between $250 and $500. It's also important to keep a few extra cutters with you since they can become dull. Shearing with dull tools is highly advised against since it can be dangerous.

### Preparing Sheep for Shearing

First, arrange to have your sheep sheared. If you're planning to have a professional shearer do the job, make an appointment beforehand. If you are taking your sheep to a shearing shed, you will need to gather them up and take them, being sure to confirm with the shearer.

If you are doing the shearing yourself or if a shearer is coming to your property to do the shearing, have your sheep penned. Divide rams, ewes, lambs, and yearlings into separate groups according to their breed or grade. It's also recommended that you refrain from feeding your sheep before shearing so that the shearing floor is much cleaner.

Sheep sometimes find shearing discomforting if their stomachs are full. Sheep should be dry when shearing, and it's important to keep the shearing floor clean and dry. It should also be swept after shearing each sheep so that a clean surface is available for the next one.

### Skirting Fleeces

Tags and belly wool need to be separated from the rest of the fleece after shearing. Lay the fleece with the flesh side facing down. Remove any wool that is off-color or dirty, short or matted wool, tags, and any other contaminated areas. Finally, roll the two sides of the skirted fleece toward the middle and nicely roll it from one end to the other. The flesh side should be facing out. Skirting is an important skill to have as it makes wool more appealing to hand spinners and other buyers.

### Packaging Wool

You can package fleeces in plastic garbage bags or cardboard boxes. It is important not to use poly feed sacks and burlap bags to package wool since they can contaminate it. Large square bales are used when packing a lot of wool. Clear plastic wool bags are the preferred packing option for wool.

Package tags, belly wool, off-color, seedy, burry, cotted, chaffy, stained, and dead wool separately. Correspondingly, any black wool should be kept and package separately from white wool. All bags containing wool needs to be labeled according to what they contain. Store wool in a dry and clean place before they are sold. Properly sorting and packaging wool can cause your wool selling for a higher price.

### Hair Sheep

If you have hair sheep in your backyard or small farm, they should be kept separately from wool sheep. The existence of hair fibers in wool fibers reduces wool quality. Any hair wool crosses need to be the last sheep to be sheared. Their wool should be kept separately from the fleeces of wool sheep.

### Crotching or Crutching

Crutching is a type of shearing where only the area around the vulva and udder are sheared. If you are shearing ewes before lambing, you can get them crutched simultaneously. Crutching makes sure that the area is dry and doesn't attract disease like a blowfly strike.

# Sheep Hoof Care

One of the most important parts of sheep management is hoof care. Various hoof diseases can have significant negative effects on the health and productivity of sheep. Therefore, you're advised to regularly check your sheep's hooves for signs of diseases and excess growth. Culling might be required if your flock includes sheep that ail from recurring hoof diseases and excessive hoof growth that do not respond to treatment.

### Hoof Trimming

Factors such as genetics, breed, nutrition, management, and soil attributes such as moisture content determine hoof growth. Sheep that graze on soil with high moisture content and free of rocks need regular hoof inspections. Also, sheep housed may need more hoof maintenance than free-range sheep.

When trimming hooves of sheep, first remove any dirt, stones, or manure stuck in them. If you notice a rotten smell, it might be a sign of foot rot. The dirt and junk can be cleaned out using a small knife. The perimeter of the hooves then needs to be trimmed.

Trimming should be stopped at the first sign of pinkness. Trimming should start from the heel and go towards its "horny" area. You can familiarize yourself with what a properly trimmed hoof should look like by inspecting the hooves of newborn lambs. Hoof trimming can be combined with other management tasks such as vaccinating or shearing and should not be carried out in hot weather or late gestation.

# Diseases Affecting the Hoof

Many diseases can affect the hooves of sheep. Lameness is a sign of hoof diseases and should not be ignored since some can be very serious.

### Bluetongue

Biting insects usually contribute to the spread of this viral disease. It's a non-contagious disease that can be easily diagnosed by identifying the presence of a reddish or brown colored band around the coronet.

## Foot Abscess

Swelling of the soft tissues located immediately above the hoof and draining abscesses in the areas between the toes are signs of a foot abscess. It's caused by the bacterial infection of food tissue that is damaged. Foot abscess mostly affects the front legs and can be treated with anti-bacterial compounds.

## Foot Rot

This is one of the worst diseases known to the sheep industry around the world. It causes loss of production and the need to cull animals. It also costs a lot of money to provide treatment, especially for labor. Foot rot, a disease caused by two anaerobic bacteria, is present wherever there are sheep.

The bacteria that cause foot rot are introduced to farms through infected animals. Once introduced, they spread in warm and moist conditions. Though, these bacteria can only last in the soil for two to three weeks.

Healthy sheep that walk on the ground or manure infected with the bacteria can develop foot rot. It will then continue to infect the entire flock unless the infected animals are culled, or the bacteria are effectively destroyed using early diagnosis and treatment.

Maintaining properly trimmed hooves is one of the best ways to avoid the development of foot rot. Still, excessive or aggressive trimming should be avoided as it can aid the development of the disease. It's also advisable to soak the feet of sheep in a 10% zinc sulfate solution.

Vaccination can also help prevent the development of foot rot, but it does not guarantee complete immunity from the disease since vaccines do not cover all the foot rot strains. Any sheep that do not respond to treatment or have a history with the disease need to be culled. However, it is more economical to control the disease through prevention since vaccination can be expensive.

Always treat each new addition to your flock as a sheep infected with foot rot. Isolating new animals for a month, trimming their hooves upon arrival, treating the feet upon trimming, and regular inspections of the feet during quarantine are great ways to safeguard your healthy flock from introducing foot rot. You're also advised not to purchase sheep that have been infected with foot rot and not to buy animals from sale barns.

### Foot Scald

White, blanched, red, and swollen tissue between the toes of sheep is a sign of foot scald, which is a non-contagious disease. It's much easier to treat compared to foot rot. Placing sheep on drier pasture, the topical use of copper sulfate or zinc sulfate, and footbaths of 10% zinc sulfate solution can easily treat foot scald.

# Sheep Identification and Record-Keeping

It does not matter how small your flock of sheep may be; proper identification and record-keeping make things much easier and contribute to your venture's success. Record-keeping is a great way to identify the ideal lambs to keep as replacements, best-performing ewes that need to be kept and those who need to be culled, and which rams produce the best lambs.

Besides, the National Scrapie Eradication Programs require you to maintain records regarding animal disposition. Maintaining records regarding health products such as antibiotics and anthelmintics is also becoming increasingly important.

### Animal Identification

You must first identify sheep in your flock so record-keeping can begin. You can choose from different identification methods depending on the number of sheep in your flock, your preferences, needs, and budget. Sheep identification should ideally be loss and tear-resistant, easy to apply, and easy to read and understand.

### Ear Tags

Many sheep farmers use ear tags to identify their sheep. There are all sorts of ear tags made in various sizes, designs, and materials such as aluminum, brass, and plastic. Rotary tags, button tags, looping tags, and swivel tags are the most common in the United States.

Brass tags are perfect for newborn lambs as they are lightweight. One minor difficulty is that you will need to catch lambs to read their tags. Although metal tags are a cheaper option, they can easily be ripped out of the ears, which can cause infections. Looping and swivel tags are not only durable but also more readable than brass tags. Temple tags usually have the least risk of ripping out, but you need to punch a hole in the ear to insert the tag.

### Scrapie Identification

The United States Department of Agriculture (USDA) has made it mandatory for all sheep and lambs to have proper identification in the form of ear tags before leaving their farms, despite the flock size. Every ear tag should carry the premise identification number and the sequential identification number. You can use the sequential number for your record-keeping purposes. And the USDA dictates you keep records of sheep for five years after they are sold.

You can get your premise identification number and metal ear tags for free by calling the toll-free number 1-866-873-2824. That said, the USDA does not provide free plastic ear tags unless you're requesting them for the first time. Sheep farmers participating in the Scrapie Flock certification program need to identify all their sheep that are older than a year using a tamper-proof identification method such as ear tags, microchips, or tattoos.

### Tattoos

Although difficult to reach without catching the sheep, tattoos are a permanent identification method. Tattooing an animal does not decrease its value. Once they are tattooed, the identification remains for their lifetime.

### Ear Notching

This method is more of a differentiation method rather than identification. For example, some sheep farmers use ear notching to easily identify sheep that need to be culled.

### Electronic ID

Many sheep farmers are starting to use electronic IDs to easily identify their sheep. The method uses radio frequency identification technology. The ear tag used in this method contains a microchip and a tiny copper antenna within the tag. Electronic ear tags can be easily applied and removed.

# Sheep Shearing, Care, and Maintenance Checklist

• Evaluate how often your sheep need to be sheared depending on their breed and purpose.

• Decide how you will have your sheep sheared. If your flock is small, you might need to visit a shearing shed. If you have a larger flock, you might need to ask shearers to come to your small farm.

• Get in touch with local sheep farmers and shearers to find the best way to have your sheep sheared.

• If you're interested in learning to shear, find a good shearing school you can attend.

• Create a schedule to carry out hoof inspections and trimming.

• Check hoof rot and other similar diseases are common in your region.

• Come up with a plan to quarantine and treat any sheep that have signs of hoof diseases and ways to stop the disease from spreading.

• Create facilities to quarantine any new sheep you purchase for a month before inspecting them and introducing them to your flock.

• Consider different sheep identification methods and choose a suitable method depending on your budget and needs.

• Maintain records of all the sheep you own. It's highly advised that you maintain records electronically while maintaining back-ups of your original files.

# Chapter 8: Sheep Reproduction: Understanding Rams and Ewes

The next level of raising sheep in a backyard or small farm is breeding them, but you may not need to breed sheep if you are raising them for wool. However, if you're raising sheep for meat or milk, you need to breed your sheep to sustain your flock. Breeding takes a lot of work. Breeding requires you to accommodate an intact male associated with certain risks.

There's also the option of seeking the services of a ram owned by someone else. Either way, breeding is a viable option for anyone who raises sheep and wants to expand their flock without purchasing new animals.

Breeding should be carefully done upon careful consideration of your purpose. Are you looking to maintain optimal breed standards? Or are you trying to produce lambs with desirable characteristics belonging to different breeds? Breeding is a complex topic, and first make yourself familiar with it before you proceed.

# Reproduction in the Ewe

Ewes are considered to have reached sexual maturity upon having their first heat. Genetics, breed, nutrition, size, and birth season usually determine the age of puberty. Ewe lambs usually reach puberty when they are between five to 12 months old. Ewe lambs born in the spring usually reach puberty in their first fall, and lambs that were born later may take longer to do so.

And single-lambs reach puberty much sooner than twin or triplet-born ewe lambs. Meat and hair sheep breeds also reach puberty much sooner than wool breeds. It's also normal for crossbred ewe lambs to reach sexual maturity sooner than purebred ewe lambs.

### The Estrus Cycle (Heat Cycle)

The estrus cycle's length that regulates the reproduction in sheep usually varies from 13 to 19 days. It consists of four phases, known as proestrus, estrus, metestrus, and diestrus. Ewes usually respond to rams and mate during the estrus. It usually lasts for around 24 to 36 hours.

The ovulation usually occurs during mid or late-estrus. It's when the ovary releases eggs. Metestrus usually lasts for three days and begins as the estrus ends. The corpus luteum that maintains pregnancy in ewes' forms during metestrus. The corpus luteum is fully functional by the time diestrus begins.

Proestrus usually starts as corpus luteum regresses and remains until the start of the next estrus. It usually lasts for nine to eleven days, where rapid follicular growth occurs. The state where the normal cycle stops is known as the anestrus.

Different seasons affect estrous cycles depending on the number of hours that the sheep's eyes are exposed to daylight. Most sheep reach estrus as the length of the day decreases. As a result, October and November are the most natural times to breed sheep in the United States and Canada.

Breeds such as Dorset, Marino, Rambouillet, Karakul, Finnsheep, and hair sheep breeds are less seasonal and can breed throughout the year or have extended breeding seasons. Flocks located closer to the equator usually have longer breeding seasons compared to others.

It's usually difficult to read the signs of estrus in sheep unless a ram is around. Mature ewes in heat usually seek the ram and stand still, allowing him to mount them. They may also wag their tails fast or even try to mount the ram. However, young ewes rarely exhibit such behaviors.

### Gestation

This stage usually lasts for around 150 days upon mating. It's important that you keep track of the dates so that you can start feeding ewes with a grain a few weeks before they are expected to start lambing and carefully observe them during the last days of gestation. You're advised to start with one pound of grain per ewe and gradually increase the amount. The maximum amount of grain that should be fed during late gestation usually depends on the breed.

The ewes also need to be crutched as the gestation period ends. Vaccines also need to be administered four weeks before the expected date of lambing. You can also deworm your ewes around the same time.

# Reproduction in the Ram

You're advised to treat the ram as the most important member of your flock. Sadly, many sheep farmers neglect the ram, although he's the one who contributes most of the genetics to their flocks. The wellbeing of your ram will contribute to breeding and the eventual success of your sheep-raising venture.

### Puberty

The age at which a ram's reproductive organs become functional, he's ready to mate, and secondary sexual characteristics develop, known as puberty. Ram lambs usually reach puberty when they are five to seven months old and upon achieving 50% to 60% of their mature body weight.

The time it takes a ram to reach puberty usually depends on genetics, breed, and nutrition. Prolific, meat, and hair breeds usually reach puberty much sooner than other breeds of lambs, wool breeds, and especially those who consume low-nutrition diets.

### Spermatogenesis

The production of the male reproductive cell or sperm is known as spermatogenesis. It usually takes about seven weeks for rams to produce sperm. Experts believe that the larger scrotum size and firm tail are signs in rams that usually indicate good sperm production and reserves.

Nutrition plays a vital role in sperm production. With that in mind, experts recommend that you provide a nutrient-rich diet to rams, especially two months before breeding takes place. Although, avoid overfeeding since it can reduce sperm production in rams.

# Seasonal Effects on Reproduction

Sheep that live in more temperate climates are more seasonal breeders, although they are less affected compared to ewes. A ram's ability to mate and produce sperm usually varies depending on the season of the year. Their breeding capabilities reach a peak in the fall, where the traditional breeding season takes place.

Some breeds such as Rambouillet, Dorset, Polypay, Merino, Romanov, Finnsheep, and hair breeds are usually less seasonal to breed capabilities and behavior. Temperature plays a vital role in determining the fertility of rams. For example, experts believe that even a half a degree variant in body heat can affect libido and spermatogenesis.

### Mating

Ewes in heat usually seek the rams. They sniff, chase, and even try to mount the ram. It's normal for rams to fail a few times before mounting the ewe, and they may also mate with the same ewe more than once. Some rams select older ewes or ones of their own breed over younger ewes and ones of other breeds.

Some sheep farmers only use one ram for a group of ewes. When multiple rams are used, the older rams may dominate the younger ones and hinder less dominant rams from breeding. Such behavior can cause fights. Another issue is that it is difficult to identify which rams are superior or inferior at breeding in multi-sire scenarios. Therefore, a single ram is recommended for smaller groups of ewes.

### Libido

A ram's willingness to mate is known as libido. The ram's testosterone level usually determines its libido. Different rams have different libidos. Some can be seasonal while others maintain the same libido throughout the year. Age and health are also determining factors of libido.

Some rams naturally inherit poor libidos. According to experts, some rams are homosexual and may refuse to mate. A ram's libido can be determined using a Serving Capacity Test. It involves exposing the ram to estrus ewes and recording their mating activities over two or more weeks. Serving capacity tests are often used to identify high-performance rams.

You can also simply determine a ram's libido by exposing him to estrus ewes and carefully observing its mating behavior. A marking harness or raddle paint can be used for careful monitoring. The marking crayon of the harness or the paint's color should be changed after 17 days. A ram that fails to mate with ewes, even after marking and monitoring, needs to be replaced with a better-performing ram. If a ram re-marks ewes after a 17-day cycle, it's an indication of a sterile or sub-fertile lamb.

# Ram Management

It's natural for a lamb to lose approximately 15% of his body weight while breeding. That's why you're advised to ensure that the rams are in optimal physical condition prior to breeding. Thin rams struggle to impregnate ewes, while fat rams may be too lazy to breed or sub-fertile, especially in hot weather. Rams should be sheared, dewormed, put on a high-nutrient diet, and have their hooves trimmed two to four weeks before breeding begins.

### Ram to Ewe Ratio

Breeding experience, age, pasture-size, terrain, and the number of ewes in the group are factors that determine how many ewes a ram can breed during a breeding season either 34 or 51 days long.

A good ram can usually mate with three to four ewes every day. Experts recommend that you use one ram per 35 or 50 ewes. Using one ram per 100 or even 150 sheep is also common. The percentage of rams becomes higher for larger flocks.

# Breeding Systems

The systematic approach where the genetic value of livestock is evaluated and then taken forward is animal breeding. A breed of sheep is a group of sheep showcasing homogeneous characteristics, appearance, and behavior distinguishable from other sheep.

### Pure-Breeding

Facilitating the mating between sheep of the same type or breed is known as pure-breeding. Such a flock can be easily managed as a single flock since all rams and ewes belong to the same breed. Pure-breeding aims to safeguard superior genetics considered valuable.

Improvements to genetic traits of purebred sheep need to be documented with performance records. The National Sheep Improvement Program (NSIP) collects that data. In return, breeders receive across-flock Expected Breeding Values or EBVs.

An EBV provides estimates the genetic merit of a particular animal in relation to a particular genetic trait. It provides a comparison between the expected performance of the particular animal and the average performance of that trait within the breed.

### Out-Breeding

When animals of the same breed, which are at least four to six generations apart, are bred, it's known as out-breeding. It is the more recommended breeding practice.

### Inbreeding

When closely related animals are bred, it's known as inbreeding that includes son to the dam, sire to daughter, and brother to sister breeding systems. This breeding is focused on the higher frequency of the pairing of similar genes. Inbreeding is only recommended for qualified operators. You should avoid allowing or facilitating inbreeding within your flocks.

### Linebreeding

This breeding involves sheep that aren't closely related as they are in inbreeding. Instead, it may look to breeding systems consisting of mating between cousins or half-siblings to ensure that their offspring are related to a highly priced ancestor.

### Crossbreeding

When rams and ewes from different breeds or types are mated, it's known as crossbreeding. It's a systematic approach where desirable genetic resources are made to create commercially valuable and productive offspring. Breed complementarity and heterosis are the main advantages that are crossbreeding offers.

### Breed Complementarity

Different breeds have distinct strengths and weaknesses. Breeding systems usually aim to maximize the strengths and minimize weaknesses using superior genetic traits. For example, if you want offspring with great reproductive efficiency, lower maintenance, heavy-muscled, and fast growing, it will be hard to find a breed that matches all those traits. However, you can crossbreed Polypay ewes are known for their moderate maintenance and reproductive efficiency with Suffolk rams, which are more heavy-muscled and fast growing.

### Heterosis

The term heterosis refers to the superiority of offspring compared to their parents that were crossbred. It's measured by the difference between the offspring's performance and the performance of their purebred parents. Crossbreds are more fertile, fast growing, and vigorous compared to their purebred parents.

# Sheep Reproduction Checklist

• Consider your purpose for breeding sheep. Explore if you have space, time, and resources to successfully breed sheep.

• Evaluate the profitability of breeding sheep and how you will market the offspring.

• Decide on the breeding system you are going to use to breed your sheep. Different types of breeding systems are suitable for different purposes of raising sheep.

• Decide whether you have space, time, and resources to raise a ram. The ram should be looked after well and kept healthy for breeding. Rams are also more difficult to handle compared to ewes and wethers.

• If you don't have enough land to raise a ram, you can seek the services of a good ram. Talk to local sheep farmers regarding rams available for crossing.

• If you are bringing a ram into your farm for breeding, make sure that he arrives with ample time to quarantine him to ensure that he's not carrying any diseases.

• A ram requires a dedicated pasture until ewes are ready to mate. Have a pasture that is large enough and has enough food for the ram.

• Make sure that the ram's diet is nutrient-rich starting from two months before breeding while making sure that they are not too thin or fat by the time breeding begins.

• Trim the hooves, deworm, and shear the ram two to four weeks before breeding.

• Observe the behavior of ewes and identify when they have reached estrus. Let the ram into the pasture that the ewes are in.

• Monitor how well the ram mates with the ewes. If you own the ram, it may be beneficial to keep track of his performance by using cradle paint or a marking harness.

• A single ram can mate with as many as 150 ewes. If you have a larger flock, you may be required more than one ram.

• Once mating is completed, and the ewes reach metestrus, remove the rams.

• Gestation usually lasts for 150 days upon mating. Keep track of the dates that the sheep mated so you can estimate when lambing will begin.

• Start grain-feeding ewes a few weeks before the expected date of lambing. You're also advised to crutch and deworm ewes before late gestation.

# Chapter 9: The Lambing Process

Thanks to evolution over thousands of years, most ewes have little difficult lambing. The process is regulated by a sequence of hormonal changes guiding the lamb to decide when time to be born. You must have a thorough understanding of the lambing process so you know when ewes are about to give birth and provide help if necessary.

As a ewe gets closer to lambing, she may stop eating, her teats and udder will be swollen, and vulva dilated. First-time mothers will find the process a little confusing, especially yearlings. You need to be prepared when ewes get close to lambing. You should have lambing facilities ready along with lambing supplies. Ewes also need to be carefully managed and fed, leading to lambing.

## Pasture vs. Shed Lambing

Both these methods have their own pros and cons. It's up to you to weigh those pros and cons in relation to your operations so that you will be able to provide the ideal conditions efficiently and economically to safely deliver lambs. Feed costs, climate, labor availability, predation, risk of disease, and market highs and lows are key factors that you will need to consider.

# Shed Lambing

Sheep farmers in the United States who own small flocks usually practice shedding lambing. So, it's suggested that you should follow the same approach after evaluating the pros and cons associated with it. Shed lambing allows early or out-of-season lambing that can usually fetch higher revenues. Lambing will take place in a structure such as a barn where even winter lambing can be carried out.

You can manage lambs more when delivered in a shed compared to pasture. You can control losses more effectively. Tasks such as treating ewes and lambs, vaccinating, and weaning become much simpler.

A lambing barn should generally have the capacity for 10% of your flock. Some ewes can be housed in the barn until the grass is available outside, while others can be moved outside upon successful lambing. Most lambing barns are constructed with drop pens. The availability of a few drop pens lowers the chances of ewes stealing lambs or mismothering.

Most lambing barns also feature jugs. Each jug can house a ewe and her lambs. Tasks such as deworming, tagging, and banding can take place in each jug while each family is confined. The families are then sent into a mixing pen after 24 to 48 hours, where they will bond with the flock.

Sometimes a few lambs will need bottle-feeding so it's important that a lambing barn or shed has a dedicated area for it. Shed lambing makes things easier for you since you'll be able to easily take lambs from their mothers if they can feed no lambs. You will have the luxury of either giving the lambs to another ewe or keep the family in a jug longer to make certain that they are doing well.

The downside of shed lambing is the high initial investment that lambing barns, corrals, pens, and feeding equipment it requires. Lambing barns also need more labor since you will need to make sure they are clean and dry. If lambing occurs during the winter, you must spend more on feed compared to spring lambing.

You will need to check on ewes and lambs at least every few hours and feed animals in each pen. You will also have to regularly change the bedding to maintain clean, dry, and comfortable surroundings in the lambing barn. A lambing barn should be free of the draft, so the risks of pneumonia are minimized.

## Pasture Lambing

You do not need a sizable initial investment or intensive labor for pasture lambing. Ewes can feed themselves by grazing, and pasture need not be cleaned, unlike lambing barns. However, pasture lambing is only recommended in temperatures above 45° F. Most newborn lambs can survive with sufficient natural shelter. Still, you will need to have plans to provide shelter in case of adverse weather.

Ewes are usually healthier when lambing takes place on pasture since they receive enough daily exercise. The chances of mismothering are also decreased since ewes have ample space to distance themselves from others while lambing. Pasture lambing also doesn't require you to check ewes and lambs after dark since ewes tend to lamb when there is some natural light available.

However, pasture lambing makes it difficult for you to offer assistance and treatment during lambing. Deworming, bottle-feeding, weaning, and record-keeping are also harder due to the difficulty of catching lambs on pasture. Newborn lambs also face significant threats from predators when they are born on pasture.

## Lambing Facilities

If you choose shed lambing, getting the facilities ready becomes as important as prepping ewes for lambing. The barn area should be clean with fresh bedding. You will also need to check for drafts and eliminate them beforehand. The drop area should at least have 12 to 14 square feet for each ewe.

It's advised that you set up lambing pens before the first ewe starts lambing. It's recommended that you have enough lambing pens for 10% of your flock. However, more is better since concentrated lambing is always possible. Smaller ewes can do with 4 ft. x 4 ft. pens, but larger ewes need 4 ft. x 6 ft. or 5 ft. x 5 ft. pens.

## Lambing Supplies

You will be more involved in the lambing process if you adopt shed lambing. In that event, you will require a list of supplies that will enable you to provide a helping hand to your ewes during lambing. Keep a stock of rubber or latex gloves for helping with difficult births and when handling newborns. Difficult births may also require OB lubrication, snare or leg puller, nylon rope, and disinfectant.

You may have to use a bearing retainer, prolapse harness, or ewe spoon to hold the vaginal prolapse in. Keep a warming box or heat lamp to warm up chilled lambs. It's also advised that you have the required antibiotics and needles and syringes for giving shots during and after lambing.

A thermometer comes in handy when diagnosing problems. Betadine or gentle iodine must dip naval chords. Some newborn lambs will require help feeding. Therefore, keep an esophageal feeding tube, frozen colostrum, and colostrum replacement handy. You're also going to need lamb milk replace, lamb nipples, and a lamb bar to feed multiple orphan lambs. You can also administer 50% dextrose for weak lambs.

An oral dosing syringe and an S-curved needle for suturing can also be handy. You can tag and maintain records of the newborn lambs during shed lambing. However, keep your choice of ear tags, an applicator, docking, and castrating tools, hanging scale, weigh sling for newborn lambs, and a pocket notebook for record-keeping. A head stanchion can also be helpful to graft lambs to encourage ewes to accept their own lambs.

# Dystocia or Assisting With Difficult Births

Difficult births are one of the leading causes of lamb death, according to experts. Various factors can cause dystocia in your flock, including miscarriage, malpresentation of the fetus, the disproportionate size of the lamb and ewe, cervix failing to dilate, deformed lamb, and vaginal prolapse. The biggest challenge you will face during lambing will be to determine when to assist the ewe or when to call for help.

You're advised to check on the ewe if she has been straining for an hour with no sign of the lamb. You must clean the ewe's backside and wash your hands using warm water and soap before entering her. Wear clean gloves whenever you examine a ewe and lubricate your hand all the way up to your elbow using a non-irritating lubricant.

Fold your fingers, creating a cone shape, and insert the hand into the ewe's vagina. You will feel the lamb's nose if the cervix is open. It should be gently resting on the front legs of the lamb. If the lamb is presented this way, the ewe should deliver without requiring your help unless the lamb is too big for the ewe's pelvic opening. If the lamb seems too big, gentle assistance is recommended.

Avoid pulling the hand in and out of the ewe and avoid changing hands without cleaning them again. You can also try to elevate the ewe's hindquarters or get her to stand up, so there is more room for repositioning. If you're unsuccessful in your attempts for half an hour, call the vet. It's highly advised against excessive pulling. Delayed delivery and excessive pulling can cause serious injuries to the ewe and lamb.

It's important that you never attempt to deliver a lamb when the birth canal isn't fully dilated since it can seriously injure the ewe. Lambs usually assist with their own birth to some extent. Be sure there are no more lambs remaining in the uterus after each delivery. It's advised that you provide a long-acting antibiotic injection to every ewe that you assist with delivery.

### Backward Presentation

Sometimes the lamb may present itself with its hind legs first. There is no need to turn the lamb since it can cause injury or death to the lamb and damage the uterus. The lamb can be born normally with some assistance. Backward presentation is common with twins and triplets.

### Elbow Lock

A lamb in the normal position can sometimes have its knees locked inside the birth canal. If you sense such a position, gently push the lamb back so the legs are extended.

### Leg Bent Back

If you feel that one of both legs of the lamb is bent back, gently reach the hoof and cup it in your palm. Then move it forward. If you can't straighten the legs, you may need to use a lambing rope on one or both the legs and push the head back so the legs can be straightened.

### Head Back

If the head is positioned back without resting on the front legs, gently push the lamb back. Then slowly turn the head to the correct position. It's advised that you attach a lambing rope to both legs so that you can locate them after pushing the lamb back. Don't pull by the lamb's jaw – which can injure it. Gently use the eye sockets for leverage to pull the head forward.

### Tight Birth

Disproportionate size causes lambing difficulties most of the time. You can assist by providing good lubrication and gentle yet firm pulling. Use the skin above the head of the lamb for leverage and extend one leg at a time.

### Breech

When a lamb is positioned backward with its tail near the opening and legs tucked under, it's known as a breech. Gently bring the lamb's rear legs forward. Provide assistance and ensure that the lamb is delivered quickly. The umbilical cord usually breaks before the lamb is born in this position so the lamb can suffocate if the delivery is delayed.

### Swollen Head

The lamb's head can become swollen if it has been outside the ewe's vulva for some time with the tongue sticking out. Lambs can usually survive in this position for a long time, although they may look cold and dead. Ensure that the head is clean by washing it with warm water and pushing it back into the uterus. Provide plenty of lubrication and determine the position before providing assistance in delivery.

### Simultaneous Births

Ewes belonging to flocks with higher lambing rates can often run into this problem; twins. These lambs will have their legs intertwined. You will need to first determine which leg belongs to which head. Then untangle the legs and push back one lamb so that the other has enough room to be delivered. Triplets are usually expected in simultaneous births.

### Dead and Deformed Lambs

Delivery and removal of dead or deformed lambs usually need the assistance of a vet. Such lambs rarely pass through the birth canal. Lambs dead for a while will need to be removed in pieces, and freshly dead lambs can be extracted normally.

### Ring-Womb

This condition takes place when the cervix fails to dilate. A caesarian section is usually required, as ring-womb doesn't respond to manipulation or medical treatment. You should not breed ewes that have experienced ring-womb before.

### Disinfecting Navels

Infectious agents can get into the newborn lamb through its navel. If the navel cord is over two inches long, you will need to clip it closer to the body. Disinfecting navel stumps soon after birth can avoid infections. You can achieve this by dipping or spraying the navel area with betadine or gentle iodine.

# After Lambing

You need not interfere with the ewe after a normal lambing since it can take care of the newborn lambs. Simply wipe away any mucus that may be stuck on the lamb's nostrils, and then the ewe will claim her lambs, allowing them to nurse. Most lambs will be up and nursing within an hour after birth.

### Colostrum

The "first milk" that ewes produce after lambing is known as *colostrum*. It contains high amounts of essential nutrients and antibodies key for the lambs' future health and performance. It's critical that the lambs drink enough colostrum within 18 to 24 hours from their birth, especially when it comes to receiving antibodies since they do not receive antibodies that are in the ewe's bloodstream before birth.

Thankfully, lambs can naturally absorb high amounts of antibodies during the first 18 to 24 hours from birth. You're advised to ensure that a lamb receives at least 10% of its bodyweight worth of colostrum during this time. Although lambs can survive without colostrum, the chances of disease and death are higher if they don't.

### Weaning Lambs

This is an important part of raising and breeding sheep. Weaning is the process of separating lambs from their dams, giving up their milk diet and adjusting to a plant-based one. It's usually a stressful time for both the lambs and ewes. Consequently, you need to provide an easy transition that causes minimal stress.

### Timing

According to surveys conducted by the USDA, the weaning age of lambs in the United States is usually around four months. There isn't an ideal time for weaning since it's determined by many factors, including the availability of pasture or feed supplies, facilities, and target markets. Some lambs are weaned earlier than four months while others are left to naturally wean, which usually takes six months.

### Early Weaning

This usually refers to weaning lambs anywhere between 21 and 90 days from birth. Lambs can be successfully weaned early, given they are consuming enough dry feed, preferably one pound every day, and drinking enough water. Size can also determine if lambs are ready to be weaned. Many sheep farmers wean their lambs either at 60 days from birth or when they reach 45 pounds.

Lambs weaned early can generally convert feed efficiently into lean tissue. It's more economical and beneficial to feed grain to lambs since the conversion of feed into gains is much greater than converting milk into gains. Early weaning also reduces the stresses involved with lactation of ewes, especially young ones.

Lambs weaned early can also be placed in dry pastures for finishing. It also allows farmers to sell culled ewes earlier, usually for higher prices. Early weaning also enables lambs to be marketed much earlier in the year when the prices are usually high. Contrarily, that does not mean weaning lambs too early is a great idea since it puts lambs and ewes under immense stress.

### Weaning Orphan Lambs

Aim to wean orphan lambs when they are 30 to 42 days of age or when they reach 25 to 30 pounds in body weight. Most farmers prefer abrupt weaning, although some farmers provide them with a diluted milk replacer. Dry lots are more favored when weaning orphaning lambs unless you have a high-quality pasture available.

### Late Weaning

You also have the option of letting lambs wean naturally. It usually takes them around four to six months from birth. Spring-born lambs usually take longer than winter or fall-born lambs to weaning naturally. You're also advised not to let spring-born lambs on pasture with dams until they are ready to be sold.

Late weaning is more natural and less stressful on ewes and lambs. The milk production of ewes naturally decreases by the time late weaning takes place, which decreases any risk of mastitis. Late weaning also allows you to fully use available forage by feeding it to lambs while easily managing both ewes and lambs as a single group.

Weaning naturally can result in ewes and lambs competing for forage, especially high-quality forage. The risks of parasitism and infection with worm larvae also increase with late weaning. Late lambing also requires you to castrate male lambs before they are three or four months of age.

### Weaning Environment

Lambs go through more stress during weaning than ewes. They are separated from their dams and required to feed themselves without relying on the milk diet they are used to. Accordingly, ewes should be taken away from the lambs instead of lambs being removed. Remaining in the same location can reduce the stress that weaning causes, as lambs already know where the water, feed, and minerals are located.

You're advised to keep ewes and lambs far apart so that they don't hear each other. Also closely monitor lambs during weaning because they are more susceptible to parasitic diseases and enterotoxaemia caused by overeating. Enterotoxaemia prevention can be accomplished by vaccinating against it when lambs are six to eight weeks old, and then following it up with a booster two to four weeks later.

# Chapter 10: Sheep Diseases and Healthcare

Many diseases can affect sheep and lambs. While we'll summarize some of the most common diseases in the United States, remember that certain regions or states may have different common diseases. Ergo, it's important that you seek advice from local sheep farmers and an animal veterinarian regarding diseases, treatment, and prevention methods to ensure that your flock remains healthy.

### Miscarriage

Miscarriage leads to the termination of pregnancy and losing lambs. It can also result in ewes giving birth to deformed or very weak lambs that die soon after birth. Although it's usual for miscarriage to occur in some ewes, you need to be concerned if your flock's miscarriage rate is higher than 5%.

Many factors can cause this issue; therefore, good management and hygiene are highly advised to protect your sheep. Providing antibiotics in late-gestation and vaccinating against Vibrio and Chlamydia before breeding can reduce the risks of miscarriage in ewes.

### Caseous lymphadenitis (CL)

This condition affects the lymphatic system in sheep that results in the formation of lymph node abscesses. CL is a highly contagious disease that severely affects the internal organs if untreated. There is a vaccine for CL that can decrease the number of abscesses, although it can't prevent the disease from infecting sheep. However, there is no need to vaccinate flocks without CL.

### Foot Scald and Foot Rot

These two diseases are the most common hoof diseases that affect sheep and have caused huge losses to the sheep industry worldwide. *Foot scald* takes place when the tissues between a sheep's toes are infected, while *foot rot* refers to the infection of the hoof's underlying tissue.

Both foot scald and foot rot can be very difficult to control and eradicate. The most effective measures include proper hoof maintenance or trimming, foot soaking, foot inspections, topical treatments, administration of antibiotics, and isolation of new or infected animals. Culling might be required if certain animals don't respond well to treatment for the protection of the flock.

Although vaccinations are available for foot rot, they do not cover all the strains of the disease – and they may not prevent the disease from occurring. Therefore, proper hygiene and management of your flock are advised regardless of vaccination status.

### Internal Parasites

The most common health issue that affects sheep throughout the world is internal parasites. Many parasites can infect sheep, varying by region, year, and farm. The most common parasites include flatworms such as flukes and tapeworms, roundworms or nematodes, and protozoa or single-cell organisms.

The barber's pole worm (also is known as Haemonchus contortus) causes anemia or blood loss and bottle jaw. Coccidia are protozoan parasites that damage the intestines and cause ill thrift (like "failure to thrive") and poor weight. It's important that you control internal parasites to maintain a healthy flock of sheep. It requires you to use a combination of treatment and management tools.

### Good Management

Parasitic problems can be minimized with proper management of your sheep and using common sense. Providing clean water, feed, feeders that are clean and constructed in a way to avoids easy contamination, avoiding overstocking pastures and shelters, and isolating newly-acquired sheep are some fine examples of proper management of sheep.

### Providing Clean Pastures

The pastures you provide your sheep should not contain worm larvae. Pastures that haven't been grazed for 6 to 12 months by sheep or goats, fields where silage or hay crop has been removed, land grazed by cattle or horses, and pastures rotated with field crops are examples of clean pastures ideal for sheep.

### Pasture Rest and Rotation

Many sheep farmers misunderstand how rotating pasture can help control or worsen parasitic problems. Rotating your flock using smaller paddocks increases the chances of them being exposed to parasite larvae. A pasture requires at least three months for the level of infectivity to become low. Therefore, you must provide enough rest for pastures, and pasture rotation will be fruitful only when such rest is provided.

### Grazing Strategies

Experts believe that around 80% of parasite larvae are found within the first two inches of grass. You are advised to avoid making sheep graze forages that are less than three inches in height. Experts believe that browsing (eating the leaves and young twigs of trees and shrubs) also leads to fewer parasitic issues.

### Alternative Forages

Experts advise that making sheep graze forage containing tannin-rich plants lower parasitic issues than sheep that graze grass pastures. Condensed tannins can deworm sheep and reduce the development of larvae in feces and the hatching rates of worm eggs. Forage species such as birdsfoot, chicory, trefoil, and sericea lespedeza are highly recommended as alternative forages.

### Nutritional Management

Sheep and lambs on nutrient-rich diets usually have better immune responses against internal parasites. Higher protein consumption has also been proven to help with parasitic problems in sheep, especially in ewes after lambing.

### Proper Anthelmintic Use

The use of anthelmintics (a group of antiparasitic drugs that expel parasitic worms and other internal parasites from the body by either stunning or killing them and without causing significant damage to the host – also called "vermicides") can help you control parasitic diseases.

Though, they are mostly used to enhance treatment effectiveness and slow down the rate of drug resistance developed by worms. You also need to accurately measure the weight of sheep to provide them with the right dosage. Under-dosing should be avoided since it can backfire by making worms resistant to the anthelmintics used.

It's recommended that you use oral drenching when administering anthelmintics while delivering it over each sheep's tongue. It results in the close of the esophageal groove that bypasses the medication to the sheep's rumen. Anthelmintics are more effective when the sheep's gut slowly absorbs them, so you are advised to fast the sheep for at least 24 hours to enhance deworming efficiency - but the sheep should be allowed to drink water.

Any newly-acquired livestock needs to be dewormed with at least two-to-three different anthelmintics families. Moxidectin and Levamisole are preferred due to their superior potency. It's recommended that you release the dewormed sheep into a "wormy" pasture so that the medications can dilute any resistant worms that are present.

### Ovine Progressive Pneumonia (OPP)

OPP affects many systems in the sheep's body resulting in various symptoms. This viral infection is one of the most common causes of death in sheep. One common symptom of OPP is a hard bag. It's a form of mastitis where both sides of the udder are affected, resulting in decreased milk production (or *no* milk production) that causes the death of lambs. Ewes with hard bag are also usually culled since they can infect other ewes.

OPP is very difficult to eradicate – or even control – since there is no treatment or cure for the disease. Blood tests need to be carried out on ewes that show symptoms and need to be isolated or culled if they are found to carry OPP. Lambs need to be removed and isolated from infected ewes. In such cases, you will need to feed them with colostrum and milk that are heat-treated.

### Respiratory Disease

Pneumonia – caused by bacteria, viruses, and the environment – affects the digestive tract of sheep. Affected sheep often refuse to eat due to depression, while showing signs of respiratory distress that includes coughing. Respiratory disease can be treated using anti-inflammatory drugs and antibiotics, but there is no effective vaccine to prevent respiratory disease. You can minimize the risks of respiratory disease by providing sheep - especially those who are housed – with good ventilation.

### Scrapie

This fatal disease attacks the central nervous system of sheep, gradually developing over years before symptoms finally appear. Scrapie is usually transmitted during lambing via the placenta, and blood tests are usually recommended to identify sheep and lambs infected with it. The sheep industry has worked hard to eradicate this severe disease, and the USDA requires all sheep to have an ear tag of tattoo to assist in locating the live animals born where another animal was diagnosed with scrapie.

### Sore Mouth

This is the most common skin disease known to the sheep industry. Sore mouth is caused by a virus that belongs to the pox family with symptoms such as blisters and lesions on the lips, noses, mouths, and other body areas. Lambs and yearlings are more susceptible to sore mouth, while humans can also be infected with it. Sore mouth can be controlled using vaccines in your flock if there is an outbreak. Infected sheep can be treated with antibiotics and WD-40 sprays.

### Biosecurity

The measures taken to minimize or prevent exposure to diseases is known as *biosecurity*. It is highly recommended that you introduce strict biosecurity measures into the way you manage your flock so they remain free of diseases. Spreading of diseases can cause harm to sheep enterprises of all sizes, so, seriously consider using biosecurity methods - even if your flock is small.

### Acquisition of New Animals

Diseases can be introduced to your healthy flock accidentally when acquiring new livestock; and it's one of the most common ways that diseases spread from one farm to another. Sheep carrying diseases will often look healthy from the outside, so you must not underestimate the importance of taking strict biosecurity measures when purchasing new sheep.

First, make sure that you are buying healthy animals, and they come from a healthy flock. Always inquire about the farm's disease status and health program before purchasing animals. You're also advised to only purchase animals from reputable breeders, although they may be more expensive. Reputable breeders are more likely to have good health programs in place. Therefore, the likelihood of ending up with disease-carrying animals is very low.

Purchasing sheep from closed flocks – a group of animals that haven't been exposed to another flock for at least three years – is also highly advised. Experts do not recommend buying sheep from sale barns, stockyards, or public livestock auctions, as diseases can spread quickly among animals under such environments.

### Isolate Newly-Acquired Sheep

Experts recommend that you isolate or quarantine new sheep for at least a month to verify that they are free from diseases. Doing so greatly minimizes the likelihood of introducing diseases to your healthy flock through newly-acquired sheep. The quarantine area should be ideally 100 feet or as far away from your flock as possible.

It's advised that you trim the sheep's hooves while they are in isolation and inspect them for foot rot and foot scald. Soaking their feet in a 10% zinc sulfate solution is also highly advised. You should also deworm the animals with all three classes, so prevent introducing drug-resistant worms to your farm.

### The Risks of Sheep Showing

There are some risks associated with showing sheep at sheep exhibitions and shows. If you show your sheep at such events, avoid any direct contact with other sheep, sharing of equipment, feeders, and waterers. Remember to disinfect any equipment you borrow from event organizers or lend to other farmers during such events. Also, it's important to isolate your show animals for a month upon returning from sheep exhibitions and shows.

### Shearing

There's a chance of diseases spreading through shearing. Shearing equipment needs to be disinfected when animals being sheared belong to different flocks. Small-scale sheep farmers may have to take their sheep to shearing sheds, especially if they only have a handful animals. In such situations, quarantine your animals upon returning and inspect for any signs of diseases before releasing them to graze your land.

## Proper Management

You're advised to properly manage your farm no matter how small your flock may be. Poor management of your farm can lead to the spreading of diseases through rodents and other wildlife. Proper management of waste and secure storing of feed can usually help you avoid attracting rodents. Take steps to control rodents if there is a rodent problem on your property.

If you have cats in your farmstead, make sure that they are kept away from your grain and hay storages. Vaccinating and neutering cats is also highly advised, so the cat population in your property remains healthy and stable. Immediately remove and properly dispose of any dead carcasses to avoid the spread of diseases to healthy sheep. You should never feed dead carcasses to dogs or other animals or leave them out to be eaten by wildlife and rodents.

# Chapter 11: Selling Sheep Products: Wool, Meat, and Dairy

The purpose of raising sheep may be to make significant profits. Even if making profits isn't a high priority for you, having revenue from raising sheep will help you with the upkeep of your flock. Sheep farming ventures have the potential to make money by selling lambs, meat, wool, and dairy. You will need to market your sheep products accordingly; each product has its pros and cons.

### Lamb and Mutton

Meat that comes from sheep less than a year old is known as a lamb, while mutton comes from older sheep. Consumers prefer lamb since mutton tends to have a stronger flavor. Teeth are good indicators of their age if paperwork, tags, or tattoos are unavailable for confirmation.

The lower jaw of lambs usually has eight milk teeth. A yearling has two cut permanent incisor teeth while a sheep has two pairs. The front shanks of a lamb carcass usually have two break joints that are red, porous, and moist. Mutton carcasses have two spool joints, while a yearling's carcass features at least a single spool joint.

## The Demand for Lamb

According to the Journal of Food Distribution Research, the current per capita consumption of lamb is approximately a pound per person, per year. It's still considered a specialty product in the United States, with approximately 30% of citizens having never tried lamb. Only 24% of the population consumes lamb at least once every year - *much less* than countries such as Australia and New Zealand.

## Lamb Grading

Various standards are maintained when grading lambs. Lamb is graded according to the carcass, live lambs, feeder lambs, age, sex, and weight, and shrink or drift. These quality grades usually indicate the eating characteristics and palatability of meat. Prime, Choice, Good, and Utility are the USDA lamb grades.

## Carcass and Live

The yield of quality of meat is sometimes used to grade lamb. Fatter lambs are more likely to be graded as Prime. There's also a comparatively good demand for lamb graded as Good in ethnic markets, as they prefer leaner or lighter lamb. Lamb is given a yield grade standard according to the percentage of external fat found in the carcass. The leanest lamb is graded as 1 while the fattest is graded as 5. USDA grades live lambs with the same grades used for the carcass. Some states have different split grades for live lambs.

## Feeder Lambs

These lambs only weigh around 60 to 90 pounds and are mostly sold to grazers or feed lots. Feeder lambs are sold as large, medium, and small, determined by their weight and frame. Some states have unique grading standards for feeder lambs. These grades are becoming less important, according to experts since they are considered as potential slaughter lambs. Ethnic slaughterhouses now purchase feeder lambs to cater to markets that prefer lighter and leaner lamb.

## Age, Weight, and Sex

The age and weight of lambs when harvested varies. The average weight of lamb harvested in the United States is around 135 pounds, although weights vary between 30 pounds and 200 pounds. Lambs are harvested in the U. S. when they are between two to fifteen months of age.

Consumers rarely have a considerable preference for meat that comes from ewes, wethers, or rams. Meat from rams has a strong flavor that most consumers dislike, but some ethnic markets have a preference for meat from intact males.

### Shrink or Drift

The weight that lambs lose while being transported to the market is known as *shrink* or *drift*. Shrink is usually due to losing stomach contents during the first 20 hours after departing the farm. The body then compensates for the decreased water and feed by utilizing nutrients and moisture in the tissues that cause weight to shrink further.

According to experts, length and mode of transport, temperature, diet, and age of lambs are some factors that determine shrink. Lambs are also highly likely to shrink more if they are taken off feed the night before the day of sale. So, under those circumstances, you are advised to provide the lambs the same diet the night before and sort them on the day of sale.

# Marketing Options for Meat

There are many ways you can market your lambs. Lamb marketing methods can be divided into two main groups as commodity and direct. It's also important to understand that sheep marketing methods and practices vary according to the region and the size of the operation. Because of this, you're advised to select the most suitable option when selling your lambs.

### Commodity Marketing

Most lambs are sold into various commodity markets that include public livestock auctions, buying stations, and abattoirs. Commodity markets are for producers who sell generic products in bulk and favor larger and low-cost producers, especially those whose farms are located closer to terminal markets. Lambs are slaughtered soon after purchase at terminal markets.

### Public Livestock Auctions

Most lamb producers sell their lambs at public livestock auctions at sale barns. Some sales grade lambs into large lots where lambs from different producers can be mixed in different lots. Some sales, on the other hand, sell each producer's lambs as separate lots.

Many sheep farmers prefer selling lambs at sale barns since it's a very convenient option. There are also more opportunities since most sales barns have sales every week. Payment is also usually prompt.

But there are disadvantages to selling lambs at sale barns. You won't know the price, and it can vary from one week to another, depending on the local supply and demand. Sale barns usually involve fees, commission, insurance, and yardage costs.

# Dealers, Brokers, and Order Buyers

You can also sell lambs to livestock dealers, brokers, or order buyers who act as middlemen. This method usually helps you save costs associated with selling your lambs at sale barns. The price is negotiated before the sale, and transportation is sometimes arranged.

### Abattoir (Slaughterhouse)

You also have the option to market your lambs directly to a slaughterhouse or meat processor. Lambs can be sold either on a carcass basis or live. Pricing methods also vary from forwarding or formula prices to spot cash prices. You can also benefit from value-based marketing and grid-pricing when you sell directly to a processor.

Value-based pricing involves pricing lambs based on the individual value of each lamb, while grid-pricing is based on carcass weight, quality grade, and yield. Lambs closer to the grid are valued higher, while those who "miss the grid" are valued less.

### Direct Marketing

When you sell sheep products directly to the consumer, it's known as direct marketing. Direct marketing of sheep products takes various forms, such as selling products at farmer's markets, selling over the internet, freezer lambs, on-farm sales, and selling products to retail outlets and restaurants. The main difference between commodity and direct marketing is the volume. The volumes involved in direct marketing are usually much lower than in commodity marketing.

Direct marketing of sheep products is advisable for small-scale farmers since profits are usually higher. At the same time, costs such as transportation, processing, and labor can also be high. Direct marketing may be the best option for you if you live near a city where people favor small businesses instead of products that come from commercial farms.

### Selling Carcasses

The most common way of direct marketing lamb is by selling whole carcasses or half-lambs. These are also known as "freezer lambs" since consumers usually buy a whole carcass or half of it and keep it in their freezer. You can sell animals by their hanging weight if you use a federally inspected plant to process the meat according to the customer's preferences – and at their expense. The meat will be stamped as "not-for-resale."

There is a higher demand for grain-fed lamb due to the milder flavor, while the market for grass-fed lamb is also on the rise since they are believed to be much healthier. Customer preferences also vary according to the age, size, and diet of the lambs. If you have a good meat processing plant nearby, selling "freezer lambs" is highly recommended.

### Farmer's Markets

A growing number of small-scale farmers are selling lamb at farmer's markets. Farmer's markets are becoming increasingly popular as consumers look to purchase local produce, preferably from smaller enterprises. If you wish to sell lamb at farmer's markets, you will need to process carcasses at a plant inspected by the USDA. The meat will come labeled. Some farmer's markets and states may require licenses and insurance to sell lamb at farmer's markets.

# Marketing Options for Wool

Selling wool is the primary income source of certain sheep-raising enterprises. If you raise wool sheep, selling wool can help you earn revenue to keep your flock going or even make profits depending on the size of your flock and the wool's quality. Some wool breeds can be sheared twice a year. The wool produced by certain breeds is also of high value. Wool harvested also needs to be stored, prepared, and packaged correctly to maximize earnings.

# Characteristics That Determine the Value of Wool

The wool value is determined by various characteristics such as the yield, crimp, fiber diameter, purity, color, staple strength, and length. The fiber diameter of wool, which is also known as its *fineness*, refers to the thickness or diameter of wool fibers, which, in turn, determines the thickness of the yarns it makes.

Different parts of a fleece usually have different diameters. Higher variation of wool fibers is undesirable with wool, with more uniform fibers being more valuable. As a result, the average fiber diameter is one of the key factors that determine the value of wool.

Wool fibers usually have a natural bend or waviness, which is known as *crimp*. Hair fibers usually have no crimp, and coarser wools have less of it. Fine wools usually have more crimp. Yield refers to the amount of wool that is left after washing, which is known as *scouring*. Lanolin or wool grease, dirt, dust, sand, and vegetable matter all amount to the "shrinkage" in wool. The yield of different wools usually varies between 40% and 70%, with bulkier fleeces usually indicating higher yields.

Colored fibers are highly *undesirable* in the wool market, primarily since they can't accept the dye. Certain niche markets, however, may have a high demand for colored wool. Some weavers and hand spinners who prefer to work with naturally colored wool may pay high prices for colored wool. Still, finding such consumers is difficult compared to selling wool in the commodity market.

The *staple length* refers to the length from the base to the top of an unstretched wool fiber. Wool with longer staple lengths is usually more valuable. Staple strength determines how well the wool can withstand cleaning and manufacturing; thus. stronger wools are valued higher.

### Marketing Options for Wool

Australia, China, and New Zealand dominate the wool market, with China also acting as the world's largest wool consumer. The United States – compared to these giants in the wool trade – is only a minor player. Super-fine-wool has the most demand globally as it is used to make high-quality clothing and fashion products. Ways you can market wool can be divided into two categories: as a commodity and via direct marketing.

## Commodity

These markets are generally more suitable for large wool producers. However, that does not mean you can't market wool in the commodity market. You're advised to weigh your options and select commodity markets if you find them convenient and profitable.

## Wool Pools

Large producers of wool have enough produce to directly market to wool mills and warehouses. However, most wool producers, especially small-scale farmers, rarely have enough wool to do so. Wool pools are large stocks of wool that consist of contributions of multiple producers.

Countries, regions, and states operate them so there is enough wool to directly market to warehouses and wool mills. Wool is classed at wool pools before being sold according to their quality and type – and there has been a reduction in the number of wool pools in recent times. You can explore this option if there is an operational wool pool in your region.

## Wool Warehouse

Both private and cooperative wool warehouses play the role of the broker when marketing wool. The Roswell Wool warehouse in New Mexico is the largest wool warehouse in the U.S., while the oldest wool warehouse in the U. S. is Ohio's Mid-States Wool Growers Cooperative Association.

## Fiber Co-Ops

Cooperatives of varying sizes have been formed to maximize the value offered to wool by producers of different scales. These alliances usually have international partners and can market different amounts of wool.

## Direct Marketing

You can market wool directly to consumers in different ways. The most common direct marketing method is to sell whole fleeces to weavers, hand spinners, and other craftsmen. Different consumers usually have different preferences. Therefore, you need to understand what such consumers prefer before marketing your wool.

The preferences of hand spinners usually vary with type and color. Longwools are generally the most popular among them since they are easier to spin. Some hand spinners prefer more variety as they use different types and colors of wool.

Almost every hand spinner prefers clean wool, so, you'll need to *skirt* the fleeces (remove "junk" wool, second cuts, stains, or vegetable matter before processing.) It's common for some farmers to cover their sheep to make sure that their fleeces remain as clean as possible, which usually fetches higher prices.

You also have the option to market wool as *rovings*, which are made by washing and combing wool into twisted clumps. Rovings are used for felting, spinning, padding, stuffing, and crafts. You can also go a step further and make yarn from your wool. Some small-scale sheep farmers market many finished products made using the wool their sheep produce, including rugs, outerwear, garments, bedding, and more.

# Marketing Options for Seed stock

Every sheep-raising enterprise need not expect revenue from marketing wool, meat, and milk. You may raise sheep to breed sheep as a hobby or as a profit-making enterprise. There is a high demand for both purebred and crossbred seed stock. You can also market both registered and unregistered rams and ewes.

It's important that you do enough market research to identify breeds and breed crosses that are in high demand in your region. Certain breeds and breed crosses have established markets, while some may have niche markets. These markets usually vary geographically. Appropriately, you're highly recommended to do a proper market analysis before breeding, especially if you wish to earn an income by selling seed stock.

### Important Traits for Seed Stock

With dam breeds, fertility, early puberty, mothering ability, prolificacy, pounds of lamb weaned, milk production, easy-care, efficiency, resistance to foot rot, parasitic problems, and other diseases, fleece traits and longevity are key traits. Libido, lamb survival, lamb vigor, feed efficiency, carcass traits, post-weaning growth, and resistance against Scrapie are traits that are important for sire breeds.

### Breed Registries

Breed associations set the standards for specific breeds. Those standards determine the eligibility for registration of purebred sheep. Thus, breed registries are very important to production and marketing of high-quality seed stock.

### Standards of Health

Sheep farmers who sell seed stock must maintain high health standards so their animals are more desirable to other farmers. Your stocks need to be closed or mostly stocked for biosecurity reasons. Breeders are highly advised to enroll in the Voluntary Scrapie Flock Certification Program. It will help later by making your seed stock more attractive to potential buyers due to resistance against Scrapie.

Your seed stock should also be free from many other common diseases, especially foot rot, sore mouth, pinkeye, epididymitis, and caseous lymphadenitis. You're also advised to test your flock for caseous lymphadenitis, ovine progressive pneumonia, Q fever, and Johne's disease.

# Performance Record-Keeping

You are highly advised to maintain detailed flock records of your sheep when producing seed stock. Birth records, weaning weights, and the rate of gains after weaning are very important. You're also recommended to adjust weaning weights according to the sex of lambs, type of birth, rearing, and the dam's age.

If you produce terminal sire breeds, you're advised to collect carcass trait data. You can use ultrasound scans to determine features such as back fat and loin depth. Like other data, you need to adjust carcass data so proper comparisons can be made. Also consider having your flocked enrolled in the NSIP that calculates EBV, a measure of animals' genetic value.

You can also use Central Performance Tests as an alternative to NSIP. These tests are conducted by evaluating the performance of rams by bringing them to a central location. Central performance tests are especially recommended for terminal sire breeds such as Suffolk, Hampshire, and Texel.

### Advertising

An easy way of advertising seed stock is by putting up signs at your property's entrance and on your vehicles. Newspapers and magazines provide effective advertising options as well. Also consider web directories, a website of your own, and maintaining a presence on social media to market seed stock. Another common method to promote seed stock is by exhibiting your best animals at sheep fairs, shows, and festivals.

### Export

According to the United States Livestock Genetics Export, Inc. (USLGE), the export market for sheep genetics from the United States is growing. Yet, exporting seed stock involves a lot of work, especially in terms of animal health. Different countries have regulations and requirements you will need to abide by and fulfill. Diseases are the biggest barriers to the international trade of seed stock. Therefore, exporting semen and embryos are becoming increasingly popular.

# Marketing Options for Sheep Dairy

Although the demand for lamb and wool is much smaller than the market for sheep milk and dairy products, it is steadily increasing. People looking to eat healthily and purchase locally may buy sheep milk and dairy products from you. Sheep milk can also be marketed to local enterprises that produce sheep dairy products such as cheese, yogurt, and ice cream. You can use resources on the Specialist Cheesemakers Association website when you do market research before raising sheep for milk.

You might discover direct marketing options to sell cheese, yogurt, and ice cream to consumers themselves or restaurants that usually value quality over price. You might also find opportunities to market sheep milk and dairy products to local retailers if there is a market for them in your region.

### Marketing Methods

The market for sheep milk and dairy products is a niche market. It's recommended to maintain a strong presence online with a good website and social media pages. It's also advisable that you advertise on local farming and culinary media such as newspapers and magazines to give enough exposure to your products.

# Chapter 12: Showing Sheep

Showing sheep is great for those who raise sheep as a hobby and breed sheep. If you are passionate about sheep and showing sheep, take part in sheep shows, exhibitions, and festivals despite your experience or scale of the enterprise. Most principals of showing sheep are universal, although there can be certain regional principals.

### Maintain a Show Schedule

Preparation is a key ingredient of successful sheep showing. Know when the next event is and have a clear plan on how you will prepare for it. Maintaining a show schedule will certify that you prepare well for sheep shows. It makes tasks involved with sheep shows, such as washing, trimming, and transportation timing more organized and effective.

### Preparation

It's advised that you do a rough shear approximately two to three weeks before a show so that your sheep will be easier to wash and slick shear. Doing so will also make your sheep appear much fresher, cleaner, and attractive. Showing meat breeds require "cutting out" about a month ahead of a show. It involves slick shearing most of the sheep's sides and torso, so there is enough time for wool regrowth. It also makes final preparations much easier and quicker.

Card, curry, and finish trimming needs to be done a few times on the days before the show, so the wool has a firmer and smoother finish. Also arrive on time for sheep shows, and the hour before showing should be spent brushing, applying hide conditioner, and slick brushing.

Showing meat breeds require shearing the belly area around two weeks before a show. It ensures that your sheep look cleaner and more attractive in the show ring while allowing the wool to regain its color to provide a natural appearance. Blocking (a very close shear without the blades touching the sheep's skin) is also recommended a few days before a show.

Sheep breeds aren't washed for shows to allow the evaluation of natural wool. Still, cleanliness is very important when showing sheep, so pay attention to your sheep's ears, eyes, nose, and other areas, wiping them down to remove any debris or dirt before your class is called.

### Train Your Sheep

It takes time to train sheep for show. Most sheep farmers, especially beginners, use sheep halters to break and show their lambs. It needs to be done before the date of the show. Those who plan on showing sheep without a halter are still advised to train their sheep using a natural gait so they perform well in the show ring.

Also spend time training your sheep to be in a "Set Up" position. Ensure that your lambs are comfortable having their legs touched or re-positioned. It avoids incidents where lambs panic while in the show ring.

### Your Dress Code

Showmanship matters when showing sheep. It's recommended that you carefully check each show for specific dress codes, and wear appropriate attire. If no dress code is mentioned, dress professionally anyway; tie your hair up so that you can maintain eye contact with the judges. Pay careful attention to smaller details regarding your appearance.

### The Importance of Arriving on Time

You should not only avoid being late to your show class but also avoid arriving too early. Arriving late will make things stressful for you and interfere with your final preparations. Arriving too early will cause you to wait around with your lamb and create congestion at the ring entrance, resulting in your animal becoming tired and stressed. Hence, you are advised to check the show order for your show class in advance so you can arrive with enough time to be ready to enter the show ring five minutes before your class is called.

### Pay Attention to the Judge

Maintaining eye contact with the judge is something that many beginners forget to do. It allows you to be wary of the judge's position in the ring and the directions he or she may provide the showmen. It's sensible to avoid becoming too preoccupied with positioning your animal.

It's important for you to be aware of what is always happening in the show ring, including the judge's position in the ring and the positions of other animals and their showmen. Being aware of their positions will help you prepare to brace your lamb, creating a great impression of your animal and to avoid missing any directions provided by the judge.

Paying close attention to the judge's position is paramount in showmanship classes to ensure that your movements allow an unobstructed view of your animal. Finally, maintaining eye contact and putting on a smile can go a long way towards helping you – and your animal - make a good impression.

### Setting Up and Bracing Your Lamb

You will be asked to line up so the judge can evaluate the animals in the ring upon entering it. Different judges work differently. Watching a few classes in the event before your class is called is important, giving you a clear idea of how animals are set up and evaluated. Most judges are consistent with the way they do things, so being familiar with how they work can help you set up and move your animal most pleasingly.

### Setting Up Lambs for Shows

When showing sheep, positioning their hooves so they look more balanced, natural, and squarer while standing is known as *"setting up."* It's important for you to realize there isn't a "correct" position for all sheep. Some lambs may look more attractive with their feet set up wider in the rear, while some may look better with their feet stretched out. You can get advice from 4H leaders and experienced showmen at shows and fairs. You can then practice those tips on your trimming stand as you prepare for the show.

Generally, most sheep are set up with their feet sitting squarely under the corners of their body. The hocks on the rear legs need to be half an inch beyond a perfectly vertical position. The front legs should be positioned squarely under the shoulders. The sheep should appear straight when the judge evaluates both from the front and rear.

The animal's head should be set up in a natural-looking position with the nose pointing forward. Place your hand under the sheep's chin extending towards the neck. It allows you to hold the head high while checking that the nose comes down just enough so the jaw remains level with the back.

### Bracing Your Lamb in the Show Ring

The judge will handle your sheep at least once to check the animal's conditioning, thickness, length, and structure. Proper bracing makes certain that your sheep can be comfortably handled, giving you an advantage over your competitors. The best bracing position requires you to position your knee against the animal's chest while gently pressuring the animal's head held high. Doing so encourages the animal to slightly push back against you while flexing its muscles.

Practice bracing before attending sheep shows, and get help from another person. Your lamb must be comfortable with bracing so it doesn't become frightened when the judge eventually handles it. A frightened animal is very difficult to judge, and the results rarely go in your favor.

Beginners take time to learn how to brace animals. With experience, you can get any sheep to brace correctly. NOTE: You're highly advised to avoid lifting the lamb or twisting its neck in attempts at bracing.

# Part 7: Raising Goats

*An Essential Guide on How to Raise Healthy Goats and Tips on Starting a Goat Farming Business from Scratch*

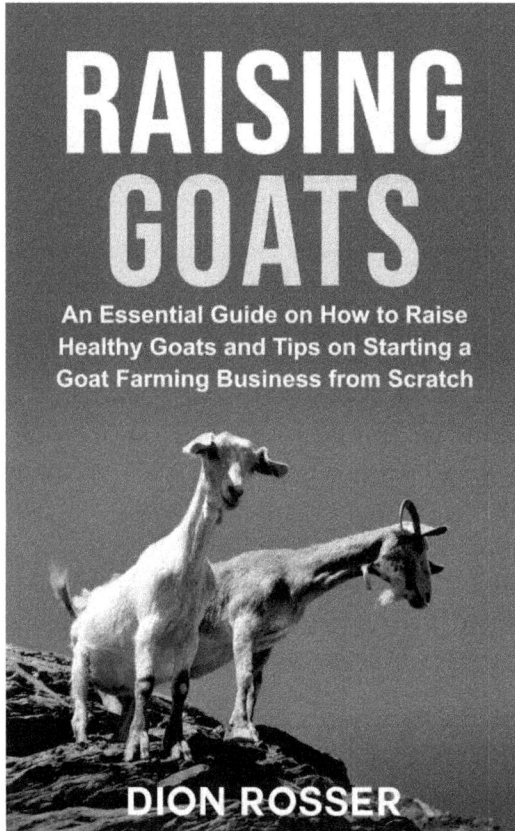

# Introduction

This book will help you understand everything you need to know to raise a healthy goat. You will learn all the aspects related to raising a goat successfully at home, understanding the pros and cons, behavior, basic care, housing, diet, and health needs of the animal.

The breeding and selling of animals has happened for many thousands of years, but many modern people are unaware they can raise a farm animal on their land. Lately, though, the methods and manners governing the process have evolved. This book provides all the step-by-step information you will need to raise goats properly.

Like any other domesticated animal, a goat is a precious mammal that needs care and love from humans. Like many other pets, they can share a bond with their owners, but there are also possible pitfalls. You may have a dog or a cat as a pet, but having a goat is very different. Goats can be tricky to handle; many new breeders, companies, or individuals face multiple issues when raising goats for the first time. If you are, by any chance, looking to buy and raise baby goats, then please read this book carefully.

This book will provide you with the common problems, tricks, and caring methods required to raise a baby goat into an adult. It will also give you knowledge and ideas to take care of them as individual creatures and give them the best environment to thrive and grow to be healthy, fit, and active. Whether you want to start up a business, set up a homestead or a farm – or if you just want an unusual pet – this book provides a detailed guide to every aspect of raising, caring, and handling your goats. It also covers all the potential mistakes, common and uncommon, that a new owner may make.

After reading this book, you will have all the knowledge you need before buying a goat and bringing it home. You will also learn various tricks and tips for success; these will be a quick guide when looking for different ways to have fun with your pet. You can expect to learn their basic behaviors, eating habits, shelter requirements, grooming, and training techniques.

In short, the book will help you to be a better owner by learning everything about the animal. This will help you form an everlasting bond with the pet. I am sure you will find many things that surprise and delight as you begin the journey toward understanding these unusual creatures. I'm pleased to have your company as we start our exploration of the remarkable, intriguing—and often downright hilarious—world of goats.

Now, let's get started!

# Chapter 1: Why Raise Goats?

Knowing what you would like your goats to help you accomplish is the first step toward determining which breed of goat is right for you. Goats are within the classification, which is known as ruminants. This designation includes those animals that possess four stomachs.

Goats should not be kept alone; they need to be part of a herd. Since they can live longer than seven years, if you are considering getting a herd of goats, be prepared to take care of them over this amount of time.

Goats offer several benefits—food like milk or meat, clothing in fiber or skin, and fuel such as manure.

These animals also offer indirect benefits. One such benefit is how goats have a habit of helping us realize where our food comes from. By being aware of your food source and how to improve it, you can increase your level of self-sufficiency.

Dairy goats can help you reduce or even eliminate your need to purchase dairy. Your goats will need to have kids to provide you with milk. Once this occurs, they will be available for milking for another three years without the need to have further kids.

You must stop milking pregnant goats at the end of the pregnancy during the last two months to help them provide enough nutrition for their kids.

One normal-sized dairy goat can provide three or four quarts of milk per day. Cheese can also be made from the milk. This process usually yields around one pound of cheese for each gallon of milk.

Besides saving money, you will have full control over the quality and safety of the milk and dairy foods you eat by producing your own dairy. And goat's milk is an excellent option for those who may find themselves lactose intolerant. As long as you abide by your local laws, you should be able to sell the excess milk to make a profit or help with the cost of raising your goats.

Goat meat is also rising in popularity. It has always been popular in developing countries due to goats being less expensive than cows. But, as more people move from these countries to more developed countries and bring their customs and recipes with them, goat meat grows in popularity worldwide. Another benefit of goat meat is it is a lean protein source.

When you raise your own goats, you can also control how they are raised. Too often, animals farmed in a confined space may not exercise or eat fresh grass. For peace of mind, raising your own goats for their milk or meat will allow you the benefit of knowing what they consume and any medications they have taken.

Your goats can serve as an alternative source of income, but it is important to do your research before jumping into such an endeavor.

Investigate whether there's a demand for goat meat in your area. This can be done by visiting local auctions or checking your newspaper's agricultural section for current prices.

Next, it is crucial to determine how many animals can be kept on the land you have available. This will be necessary so you can calculate your potential profit.

To raise meat goats, you will first need to go through the purchase process. This means you should check to see how much it costs to procure your initial goats.

There are several ways the slaughtering of your goats can be performed. You can do it yourself, sell them in an auction, have someone come to your farm, or you can take your goats to a slaughterhouse. If you need to take them somewhere, proper transportation must also be considered. Not all slaughterhouses are created equally and identify your nearest USDA-certified facility. Laws and finances will play a big part in your decision-making regarding slaughter methods.

Fiber is another reason to raise goats. Different breeds of goats produce different kinds of fiber, including cashmere, mohair, and cashgora.

Adult angoras can provide anywhere between 8 and 16 pounds of mohair every year, while a young goat, called a kid, can provide around 3 to 5 pounds.

Goats producing cashmere and cashgora cannot provide as much fiber as angoras, but the fiber is worth more. Fiber goats produce fiber, which is used to make things like blankets, clothing, and headwear.

Many people believe there's a breed of goat called cashmere, but this is not the case. Cashmere, instead, refers to the downy hair from certain breeds. Central Asia is the main region where cashmere is harvested. These sweaters are so expensive because you need the fiber from four goats to make one sweater.

Goats can also prove to be handy landscapers. It is common knowledge they are skilled in eliminating weeds. They prefer rough plants. People even rent out their goats to be used by cities to eliminate blackberry bushes and weeds that have taken over a piece of land.

Goats not only eliminate pesky weeds, but they can also reduce the need for herbicides, improve the fertility of the soil, widen the range of plants in the area and reduce the danger of a fire breaking out.

Other animals, like cows or sheep, can coexist with goats in the same area.

Even if you intend to use them for other purposes, they can still be handy when it comes to clearing land. Just keep them safe by using fencing or by having a guard animal.

Goats eat weeds, not grass. Sheep are much more suited to eating grass.

Breeding is usually a big part of owning goats. If you are using them to provide dairy, you will need to breed them to produce enough dairy in the long run. Goats sold or slaughtered will also need to be replaced, which is most easily achieved through breeding.

Money can also be made from selling kids. Another potential income earner is providing a bucking service. Bucking is when you lease out your buck for breeding purposes.

People hire this service for several reasons. Many don't have space or don't want to deal with the complications that result from keeping their own buck. Others are looking for certain genetic aspects that can only be gained through breeding with outside bloodlines.

Besides profit-earning potential, goats make excellent companions.

Miniature goat breeds have grown in popularity, especially among city dwellers. These breeds include pygmy, Nigerian dwarf, and a variety of other miniature dairy breeds. Goats are intelligent creatures that can also serve as comic relief.

Many miniature breeds can be house-broken – and car-broken! By taking them out with you, you are likely to meet new people and can help educate others on the wonderful characteristics of goats.

If you consider keeping one as a pet, it is important to understand they are herd animals. This means you should always have at least two.

Goats can also be leash-trained and can go for walks just as a dog might. This can provide socialization and exercise for both you and your goat.

Once a goat has established a bond with you, it will enjoy spending time with you. They can go hiking with you and help carry your things. They can find food in nature most of the time and are helpful without asking much in return.

Those seriously considering taking their goat packing should select a large, sturdy breed and spend plenty of time training them for the journey.

Goats can even make great therapy animals. They should be specially trained for this kind of work. These animals have been known to help autistic children. Goats can also help improve sensory and social skills in the young and old alike.

Teaching children how to care for and maintain them is a good way for them to learn responsibility. Caring for a goat requires chores twice each day, and children caring for them can be a part of a 4-H project.

Children who participate in a 4-H project involving goat care should expect to create a budget, make a speech, and write reports. They should also demonstrate ordinary care like hoof-trimming, participating in a fair, milking a goat, cheese-making, leash-training, and creating a piece of work for a goat news source.

Before getting a goat, make sure it is the right choice for you. This can be determined by researching them and their habits. And you should spend time with a few goats to get a feel for them and their personalities.

Goats can live upwards of 15 years. If you are buying them as companions or for dairy, be prepared to be responsible for them for that long.

At the minimum, goat owners should spend 30 minutes with them in the morning and again at night. If you have a larger number of goats or are using them for their dairy, meat, or fiber, you will need to spend even more time with them.

They should be fed hay and grass they would typically find in a pasture and should be provided with plenty of water. Time spent with your goats should include cleaning, watering, feeding, and making sure they are safe and healthy. You will probably want to spend as much time as you can with them as you enjoy their personalities.

Those without flexibility in their work schedules still need to handle emergencies, and someone must be available to check on them when you are away.

If you get a goat as a pet, there are a few things you should look out for when selecting your animal—sociability, tameness, and choosing goats without horns. A buck should never be kept as a pet. Instead, get a wether (a buck that has been castrated.) A doe can make a good pet, but wethers require the least maintenance and tend to be sweet.

City dwellers should get miniature goats. Miniatures are easier to handle and are good for those with a physical disability.

Laws and ordinances in your area often regulate keeping goats as pets. Always check these first before buying one. They may be prohibited, and you may receive complaints from neighbors.

Neighborhood dogs can also serve as a threat. If your neighbors are vehemently opposed to having goats in the neighborhood or have an aggressive dog, consider whether owning a goat is a feasible choice. It is always a good idea to familiarize your neighbors with your goats and involve their children in projects with the animals. The more comfortable they feel, the less likely you are to have a problem.

# Goat Terminology

**Doe** - a female goat, also called a doeling when it is young. The term *nanny* is not a proper term for a female goat anymore.

**Buck** - a male goat, also called a buckling when it is young. *Billy* is no longer an acceptable term for a male goat.

**Brood doe** - a female goat with desirable genetic traits, kept for breeding.

**Kid** - a goat less than a year of age.

**Yearling** - a goat between the ages of one and two.

**Wether** - a male goat that has been castrated.

**Herd** - several goats.

**Ruminant** - an animal with four stomachs and chews cud.

**Udder** - the organ producing milk. Goats have one.

**Teat** - what you use on an udder to milk a goat. Goats have two.

**Dam** - the mother of a goat.

**Sire** - the father of a goat. This term can also be a verb.

Goats are mammals and, as such, have certain common features with other mammals.

Terms referring to the body parts include—cannon bone, chine, escutcheon, pastern, pinbone, stifle joint, thurl, and withers.

The withers refer to the shoulder area of the spine. The height of a goat is determined by measuring from the withers to the ground.

The thurl refers to the hip joint. Goat aficionados often discuss the levelness of the thurls. The pinbone is the hipbone.

The stifle joint is the knee.

The pastern refers to the flexible portion of the bottom of the leg.

The escutcheon is the area where the udder is on a doe.

The chine is located directly behind the withers on the spine.

The cannon bone refers to the shin.

Because goats are ruminants, they also rely on a plant-based diet. It is important to understand how a goat's digestive system works to make sure your goats are healthy.

Goats are herd animals, so they evolved to live and feed together in a group. This is the environment in which a goat is most happy, and it's important to remember when deciding on how many you should get. At a minimum, you should have two goats. I recommend three, so if something happens to one, you still have the minimum recommendation of two.

While goats are cute, adorable, and very social, they aren't domestic pets, and I don't recommend raising them that way. This doesn't mean you can't love your goats like pets—by all means, do. Even though they can form bonds with humans, they should never be raised alone as a single goat. Humans aren't part of their herd. Though single goats may live happily with other hoofed animals (horses, sheep, etc.), there's no guarantee they will accept other species as part of their herd, so it's important to have two goats.

No matter how affectionate and attentive you are, studies have shown that goats raised without others can become lonely, depressed, and stressed. A stressed or unhappy goat is more susceptible to sickness.

My neighbor used to have a goat as a pet, and she would walk the goat on a leash through the neighborhood. It was adorable until you heard the goat bleating all hours of the night whenever she left the house. The poor thing sounded like it was being tortured. So remember, goats are like cookies - you need more than one!

# Which Breed is Right for You?

There are three classifications of domestic goats: dairy, meat, and fiber goats. A few breeds are multipurpose, which means they can be good for both dairy and meat or meat and fiber. Each breed has its area where it shines. Your needs or goals determine the breed you will want to raise, and this section highlights the best in class for each type of goat. We'll also cover other considerations, such as size, cost, and how and where to buy your goats. In the end, you'll be equipped to decide for your homestead or farm business.

# Selling Fiber

When we think of fiber animals, the first thing that comes to mind is sheep. Although sheep's wool may be more popular, fiber from goats is considered more luxurious and extravagant. Their fiber is soft, durable, long-lasting, and is used in fine garments.

Selling the fiber is just one of the many ways you can use goats to sustain your self-sufficient life and make money from home. Besides monetizing your herd by selling fiber, you can also save money by making your own clothes. Try your hand at using a spindle and loom or even knitting. You can make beautiful clothes from your goat fiber. Handmade items are also in high demand at artisan stores and markets.

The average cost of wool in the United States is $1.75 per pound, whereas fiber from goats can range from $40 to $190 per pound. Many sheep farmers have raised sheep for meat while raising goats for fiber to make more money.

# Fiber Types

There are three different types of fiber you get from goats: mohair, cashmere, and cashgora. Let's take a look at each and discuss the differences between each.

Mohair is the fiber most used in the goat textile industry and comes from Angora goats. It is a strong, beautiful fiber. Turkey was the original producer of mohair, but the demand exceeded its supply, and now the United States is the biggest producer.

Cashmere is the most luxurious textile and highly sought after and, because of its qualities, cashmere also commands higher prices. Many goats, including Pygora and Nigora goats, produce Cashmere.

Cashgora is a happy result of crossbreeding mohair and cashmere goats. Because of this crossbreeding, not every cashgora goat can produce high-quality fiber. Sometimes it's the luck of the draw. Because of this lack of consistency in breed quality, cashgora is considered rare and in demand.

# Shearing

When raising fiber goats, you have one of two choices for shearing time: do it yourself or hire someone to do it. Hiring out the task, of course, costs more money. Depending on the type of goat and your location, you can expect to pay an average of $16 to $25 per goat.

But learning how to shear well takes practice. It's not something to be done in a hurry, and you have to have extreme patience. A well-trained shearer can accomplish this task in minutes, while a novice shearer can take one to three hours, which can be stressful on the goat.

Like sheep, Mohair goats need to be shorn twice a year to get their fiber, but cashmere goats must be brushed, making the process more time-consuming.

If you plan on shearing your herd, I suggest hiring a professional for the first time and taking good notes. This way, you can see the process and the techniques they use. Meanwhile, here are a few general tips:

- Expect to harvest 5 to 10 pounds of fiber per adult goat per shearing.

- Angora goats should be shorn in the spring right before kidding season and in the fall before mating season.

- Goats can be sheared when their hair reaches 4 to 6 inches long.

- Have good lighting and your first aid kit handy, including the product Blood Stop.

- Goats need to be cleaned and completely dry before shearing.

- You can use shearing scissors or an electric livestock shear (one designed for sheep).

- Place a drop cloth or tarp down, then your stanchion on top of it to keep your goat in place while shearing.

- Work on one side of your goat at a time.

- Shave as close to the skin as possible without cutting the skin.

- Have two catchment containers available, one for the discarded hair and one for the fiber you need to process. The discarded hair is any coarse or undesirable hair. Use a breathable bag for the fiber for processing.

- Label and tag your bag with the date, age, weight, and name of the goat.

# Processing

Once you have fiber from your goats, it has to be made into something for resale. You can sell raw fiber, as many new homesteaders want to do the processing independently or the ready-to-use product. The first step in processing is washing. You need to wash the hair to remove dirt, grease, or impurities. You can wash your goat fiber in the washing machine, but I recommend doing it by hand.

# How To Wash Goat Fiber By Hand

Skill Level: Beginner | Estimated Material Cost: $20 | Time: At least 30 minutes

# Supplies, Tools, and Steps

- Cloth mesh wash bags
- Washtub
- Hot water

- Detergent or Dawn dish soap

- Drying rack

1. Place the fibers loosely in the wash bag. Do not pack it tight.

2. Fill the tub with water between 145 - 160°F.

3. Add laundry detergent (a quarter cup per pound of fiber) to the water and mix.

4. Gently add the bag of fibers to the water and soak for a couple of minutes.

5. Squeeze out the water.

6. Repeat steps 2 through 5.

7. Once the fiber is clean (dirt-free and bright), you will need to rinse the soap out by following the same processes in steps 2 through 5 (without detergent).

8. Lay the mesh bag on a drying rack to continue draining the water.

9. Once the water is drained, you can remove the fiber and place it on the drying rack until completely dry.

### Troubleshooting

Be careful not to wring the fiber or use the agitator in the washing machine. Doing so will cause the fibers to felt (turn felt-like), which is not a good practice.

# Spinning

After you wash the fiber, you card or comb it; this straightens the fibers out and removes any debris that the washing may have missed, so the fiber is ready to be spun into yarn.

To spin fiber into yarn, you can use a drop spindle or a spinning wheel. A drop spindle looks like a stick the size of a wooden spoon. It has a spin top on the end and a small hook. It's lightweight, easy to store, and inexpensive, and can be bought for under twenty dollars or so. It is a fun way to learn how to make yarn.

If you plan on processing fiber on a large scale, a spinning wheel might be a better option. Many people sell used spinning wheels online. You can plan on spending a couple of hundred dollars on a spinning wheel.

# Selling

As I mentioned earlier, you can sell raw fiber not washed or carded to those wanting to do the processing themselves, large textile corporations, or you can do the processing and sell the completed product. Mohair generally sells for $25 for a four-ounce skein; however, cashgora and cashmere sell for more. Ideas for where to sell your fiber include specialty shops, online marketplaces such as Etsy, local knitting or crocheting clubs, artisan stores, and more.

# Additional Services

Here are other strategies for making money with your four-legged livestock. When deciding what kind of business you should set up, it's important to think about your market and how big your products' demand will be. For example, when we lived in the city, we were the only show in town. I could, within reason, create my own market. I would sell my products and farm supplies for top dollar, and my eggs and honey always had a waiting list. To put it simply, it was a matter of supply and demand. Then I moved to the country, where everyone in town raised livestock, and I couldn't give the stuff away. We moved away from our target demographic. So, know where your customers are. There are many places to find customers, including homeschooling groups, health food stores, food co-ops, farmers markets, restaurants that source food locally, other farmers, or online. What is available in your area may inform you of which of these ventures best suits you and your herd.

**Selling Your Kids:** (goat kids, that is!) Resale value is one reason we decided we wanted a registered herd. With papers, we can sell our registered Nigerian Dwarf does for $200 to $700 each. I would get around $150 for an unregistered goat. Bucks tend to sell for less than does, and wethers go for the least amount since they are not used for dairy or breeding purposes. For the past year, we have focused on growing our herd to increase our milk supply. Now that we have done enough in advance, all the new babies will be sold this year. If you have four does and each doe kids two offspring, you can make anywhere from $1,600 to over $5,000 in one kidding season. Now you can see the math adding up and the potential to make money from selling kids.

**Buck Service:** If you own a registered buck, you can charge anywhere from $30 to more than $100 per buck service. If your buck comes from show-quality goats, meaning he or his parents won places in goat shows, you can command a higher fee. A one-year-old buck can service ten ladies per season or month. Providing the buck is in good health, a two-year-old buck can service twenty-five females a month, and a three-year-old buck can service up to forty females.

**Fertilizer or Compost:** Goat pellets or goat berries are great for the garden. They make wonderful fertilizer you can sow directly into the soil. Because of its composition, it doesn't burn your plants, and you don't have to wait a year to apply it. There is hardly any odor, and it doesn't attract flies like cow manure. Gardeners or farmers who work organically are interested in this fertilizer. A farmer friend collected goat manure, then dried it, bagged it into eight-ounce bags, and sold them for $7.95 each plus tax online and at their local nurseries.

**Weed Control:** All over the country in fire-prone areas, people are singing the praises of goats' ability to clear brush and help prevent the spread of forest fires. Depending on where you live, you may be able to rent goats for weed control and clearing brush. A reasonable price would be a $200 base price, then $125 per week to clear one acre, plus food, travel fees, and other related costs. I've seen others advertise around $1,000 per acre to clear. One important note: because goats are browsers and foragers, not grazers, they do wonders for keeping the brush and weeds at bay but are little good for mowing the lawn.

**Goat Therapy:** Many animals are used for therapy, helping bring joy, calmness, relaxation, and comfort to humans. Goats are one animal that people use to help them feel better. Goats offer much-needed joy for people who have special needs, seniors, and those with PTSD. Your goats need not be certified to work as therapy animals; they just need to be friendly and enjoy being around people. Another way people are using goats for therapy is by offering goat yoga. All you need are yoga mats, a yoga instructor, and a bunch of bouncing baby goats. People are charging around $45 for a one-hour session to stretch with goats.

**Farm Tours and Goat 101:** From garden groups to school field trip groups, people of all ages love to visit farms and petting zoos. A goat breeder friend used to offer farm tours and charged $3 per person. She would walk them around the farm, let them pet the goats, observe milking, and even give goat milk samples. Once you have experience under your belt, you can offer classes to other would-be goat owners in goat care, milking, cheese making, goat soap, and much more. Cheese-making classes are $50 to $100 per person, and one-on-one goat mentoring can be offered at $50+ per hour.

**Say Cheese:** Who doesn't love an adorable spring picture with a baby goat in a field? Spring is the perfect time of year to book photoshoots on your farm with your new baby goat kids. Photographers and individuals alike will love to book photo sessions with your baby goats during the kidding season. Generally, photo sessions start at $50 per hour for photos with baby goats.

# Chapter 2: Goat Breeds, Types and Purposes

Breeding goats is an art, but you will need to learn the skills. Knowing what makes one breed distinct from the next helps you deal with a situation should this situation happen.

## Miniature Goats

Not all registries recognize miniature goat breeds. We get miniature goats when we crossbreed varieties such as Cashmere, field goats, Angora, Nubian, and others. This goat breed's main traits are that it has a gentle and adorable nature with a high intelligence level. Breeding this variety brings your life a lot of fun and excitement. Miniature goats eat little and require little space. They like to spend their time outdoors and have a good life expectancy of 20 years or more if you care properly for them. They produce a lot of milk for their size, so they are a good investment.

Another significant aspect of miniature goats is how they bond with other farm animals such as cattle and horses. You can allow them to graze together on the field. Goats prefer the company of humans, and so they make good pets. Miniature goats do not develop health problems if there's a change in the weather. As long as you conduct regular health checkups and give them enough food to eat, they will remain healthy. It is possible to buy miniature goats at the tender age of 4-12 weeks. Bottle-feed the kid until it is ready to eat vegetation.

### Nigerian Dwarf Goat

The miniature goat breeds do not produce much milk. The Nigerian Dwarf is one such goat with its origins in Africa. They have a very sociable personality, and their coats come in a variety of colors. They produce better-than-average amounts of milk and have a height between 17 and 21 inches. The bucks are 19 to 23 inches in height with a weight of around 75 lbs. We see numerous quadruplets and quintuplets in this breed. They have a maternal attitude and seem to enjoy their kidding experience. The amount of milk from the Nigerian Dwarf is approximately 1 gallon each day. They make a lot of noise and so may not be suitable for city dwellers. Though the meat is edible, people rarely eat them because they are costly and produce little meat.

### Pygmy Goat Breed

Another miniature goat is the Pygmy goat. These are stockier and shorter than the Nigerian Dwarf goats. They are not considered dairy goats, but they do produce a fair amount of milk. They have problems kidding due to their stocky nature. The size of the Kinder goat is between that of a Nigerian Dwarf and a Pygmy goat. This goat produces both fiber and dairy. The mini goat is a crossbreed derived from a Nigerian Dwarf buck with a doe from any breed you want to miniaturize. This is useful for those who want to raise goats but do not have enough space for regular goats. Regular de-worming is needed for this breed, along with the trimming of the hooves.

Though the minis will have fewer kids, they will still have triplets and quadruplets. Minis are a great option for people living in the city because of the volume of milk they produce. For an urban lifestyle, the best-suited breeds are Mini Mancha and Oberian because they are the quietest.

### Dairy Goats

To get a good dairy goat, use any standard breed. People raise the Pygmy Goat for dairy. For a goat to qualify as a standard breed, the doe must have a minimum weight and height. Their height must be between 28 and 32 inches, but this varies from breed to breed. The bucks must be between 30 and 34 inches in height. All standard goats produce ½ - 1 gallon of milk every ten months. The milk production will be slow initially but build up in speed and then drop back to a low level.

### Alpine Goat Breed

Alpine goats are wonderful dairy goats. They are large, and their coats are multicolored. Their ears stand up straight, and because of their big size, they are also used as pack animals. The La Mancha, which is also a dairy animal, has very small ears by contrast, and in a few cases, the ears will appear to be missing. This breed came to the US from Mexico, and we see two types—gopher and elf. These are friendly goats.

### Nubian Goat Breed

Nubian is another popular breed of goats. Their ears are floppy, and they increase in numbers through breeding. Nubian goat milk has a good amount of butterfat. They also produce a large amount of milk, so these goats are ideal for making cheese. The Oberhasli is a type of Alpine goat. Their size is medium, and they have upright standing ears. Their coat is reddish and has a black marking. A few will have all black coats. People like this variety because they have sweet temperaments and enjoy being milked.

### Other Dairy Oberian Dairy Goats

The colors of the coat of the Sable and Saanen breeds vary. It is not often that you get a dairy goat with a nice coat. Saanen goats have a white coat. These two are the largest of all goat varieties, they give a large amount of milk, and they have a relaxed temperament. They have difficulty keeping their white coats clean, and often, the Saanen goats suffer sunburn. We can recognize the Toggenburg goats by their fawn to chocolate-colored coats. They are the oldest of all dairy breeds. They do not produce a large quantity of milk, and their butterfat content is also average at best.

# Meat Goat Breeds

The breeder has as many choices of meat goats as they have with milk goats. Here, the leader of the pack is the Boer. The Boer is sturdy, with its origins in South Africa, and bucks will grow big reaching 300 lbs. in weight and does reach 220 lbs. Boers are usually all white with a brown head but can also be all-brown or all-white. They have long ears and grow fast and gain weight rapidly. Being very fertile, they will produce multiple kids. By nature, they are docile, so it is easy to care for them. This makes them the ideal choice of a goat raised for meat.

### Mountain Goats

The Mountain goat is a breed you find in North America. They have a size as big as large wolves and can climb rocky slopes easily. For this reason, they are also called antelope goats. They have a life span of 12-15 years. Because they are big, people rear them for their meat. The adult goat can weigh as much as 220 pounds.

If you want meat goats, the consideration will be different. About 75-80 percent of people in the world eat goat meat. Not all meat goats produce milk. Only the Spanish goat is good for both meat and fiber. We can use meat goats to clean the land. Due to the feral nature of most, they are self-sustaining. We need not spend much time looking after them.

### Boer Goat Breed

Boer goats have floppy ears and are large. The bucks weigh between 250 and 360 pounds, while the doe is smaller and weighs between 200 and 250 pounds. Boers are costly and originated from the southern parts of Africa. They are highly adaptable but have many genetic differences, such as abnormal testicles. The Tennessee fainting goat gets its name because it falls down when surprised. Breeders encouraged this defect, so it became popular. The muscles become rigid when the goat falls, so over time, these muscles become strong. That is one reason they make such good meat goats. They are smaller, have a sweet attitude, and weigh between 50 and 70 pounds. Meat goat farmers with limited space will find this goat ideal for him.

### Kiko Goat Breed

Kiko is a New Zealand goat, which is a newer breed. It is a meat goat, and it gains weight without feeding. They are even harder than Boer goats. Spanish goats have long horns and are medium-sized. It has a long history, being brought over to the US from Spain during the 16th century. Even though Kiko is a hardy breed, there are fewer breeders, so an effort is needed to preserve them.

### Kalahari Red Goat New Moatcashier Red Coat Breed

With origins in South Africa, the Kalahari Red Goat is a meat goat that figures among the top breeds developed like the Savana and Boer goat breeds. Being a new goat breed, it's now quickly gaining recognition in South Africa and other neighboring countries as one of the better meat goats. The first part of the name comes from the Kalahari Desert, while the second part is from its red coat. The Kalahari Desert is spread over vast stretches of South Africa, Namibia, and Botswana.

Many people suspect that the Kalahari Red is a derived breed originating from the Boer goats because of their uncanny resemblance. But blood testing proved that the Kalahari Red is a distinct goat species, not related to any other breeds. The Agricultural Research Council of South Africa conducted this testing. On a comparative note, the Kalahari Red has many advantages over the Boer. We can see this in their camouflage, the kids' survival rates, the goat's hardiness, and the meat's tenderness. Due to its superior meat quality, it is raised extensively in South Africa. This breed is also raised in places like the United States, Brazil, and Australia.

### Characteristics of the Kalahari Red

The Kalahari Red is a beautiful animal with a glorious appearance. The breed is large-bodied with a red coat. You might have lighter shades of red and even white but they are not preferred since these colors do not give the goats the needed protection in their native habitat. They have strong herding instincts that serve to protect them. Their ears are long and floppy, and the skin in their neck area is loose. The skin is pigmented, and they have sloping horns that are moderate in size.

They forage throughout the day, even when it is hot. The teats and udders of the doe are properly attached. You can crossbreed any other goat to increase the carcass size and improve the hardiness. The bucks are bigger than the does and have an average body weight of 250 lbs. The doe weighs an average of about 165 lbs.

Use: The biggest use of the Kalahari Red is for meat goat farming. It grows fast and produces very good meat.

Other special properties: the Kalahari Red is a hardy animal that can survive the harsh conditions prevalent in most South African regions. Being very adaptable, they breed well. They are also terrific foragers, feeding on a wide range of plants, grains, and grass. The Kalahari Red will go to vast distances in search of food and water. They require little management because they are resistant to most parasites and diseases. Due to this, one may raise them organically. If you do so, you will get lean meat with excellent texture and taste. They give birth to kids twice every two years, and they do care for the kids carefully.

The kids are born with a strong urge to suck and are strong. The kids grow rapidly, gaining weight at a rate of approximately 3.3 pounds every week. This gives the breeder an excellent profit on his investment.

# Other Goat Breeds

Crossover breeding increases the potential of the goats. Examples of these varieties are Savanna, Moneymaker, and Texmaster. Crossbreeding Nubians with Saanens produced the Moneymaker breed in California. Boers were crossbred with Tennessee Fainters to produce the meat goat called Texmaster in Texas.

The Savanna originated in South Africa. It is a new breed that can resist heat well and needs little water. This makes them suitable for breeding in drought-prone regions. These animals are survivors and can adapt to a wide range of oppressive conditions easily.

### Fiber Goat Breeds

The fiber goats need more care than the other goats. The size of these goats ranges from small to medium. One type of fiber goat is the Angora, with a coat with long fiber. The fiber is called mohair, which is usually white. Breeders try to make Angora goats in other colors too. One fully-grown Angora will give 8-16 pounds of fiber. This breed is from Turkey, but the United States produces the most Angora fiber. Because they do not have a hardy nature, they must be protected from the elements and extreme cold and heat. They have problems kidding because the does are not naturally maternal.

### Cashmere Goat Breed

Cashmere goats are a type of goat rather than a breed. Any goat that produces Cashmere fiber is a Cashmere goat. You can get the starter goats for your Cashmere fiber from Australia. You can use them as meat goats or as fiber goats. Cashmere goats are medium-sized but hardier than Angoras. A buck weighs about 150 pounds, and a doe weighs about 100 pounds. Every December, Cashmere fiber is removed from the goats. Cashmere needs exposure to light for it to grow. The yield is about 4 pounds per year per goat.

Breeding miniature meat goats is not economically viable, but you can find two miniature fiber goats in the US. Crossing a Pygmy with an Angora gives us the Pygora that produces almost as much fleece as an Angora. Many people have them as pets but not for fiber. Even then, it is preferable to shear the fiber twice a year. Then, we have the Nigora breed of goats obtained by crossing a Nigerian Dwarf with a Pygmy. We get both milk and fiber from these goats. But, being a new breed, they are only recently gaining in popularity.

# Chapter 3: Housing and Fencing Options

Proper fencing for goats is crucial. Goats are like most animals because they are curious and like to roam. They like their open spaces—the bigger, the better. So, if given a chance to exploit a weakness in their enclosure, you can be sure they'll take it. A strong buck or doe will have little difficulty leaning on the goat fence panels you put up, so much so they will eventually push them down enough to walk over them. It's important to make sure that the ground for your fencing is firm and the materials you use are strong enough for a goat enclosure.

## Goat Fencing Basics

Decent options for goat fencing are chain link and woven wire. Remember, if your fence is next to greenery, it will be put to the test, and the goat will push on the fence to get to their food. This type of fence is ideal for young goats and in larger areas.

If using an electric goat fence, the common suggestion is to use one that has seven strands. If it is what you want, you can train your goats to respond well to goat pens with fewer strands. A common modification is to make a typical New Zealand goat fence of only four strands.

Another option is goat pens featuring woven wire-style electric fencing. Most of the feedback is generally positive. There are stories of animals getting tangled in these goat pens and being shocked repeatedly.

To properly utilize electric goat fencing, train the goat by first introducing it to the fence in a smaller surrounded area. This is because if you first introduce the goat to it in a larger area, it will have enough room to charge and get through it as opposed to simply backing away. In a smaller area, the goat will learn to respect the fence because it won't be able to charge through it like it would in a bigger space.

Panel fences are another option and are typically available in three different sizes. The smallest available are Hog panels, which have a height of 3 ft. A pen using this type of panel is best suited for kids since they are not developed enough yet to climb or jump over them. They are also great because the owner can reach in and out of the pen easily.

Another option, and probably the more popular for smaller yards, is cattle panels. These panels are best suited for adolescent and adult goats because of their height (4ft), and they are hard for the animal to jump over. But, when it comes to kids, because of the panel's uniform spacing of 6", some goats may wriggle their way between the panels.

The combo panel is the best panel you can use if you can spend the extra money. It is great because it combines the hog panel's tight spacing at the bottom and the cow panel's hard-to-jump height of 4 ft.

The one catch, and the fence's weakest point, will be the gate clip. You'll want something that you can open easily, one-handed optimally, but, at the same time, you need a clip strong enough to withstand pressure from a goat that wants to escape out of the pen. A lot depends on how many goats you have in the pen, testing its strength. A latch may seem like a good option, but clever goats can open them with ease.

You can try a bungee cord as a quick fix and short-term solution. But they can break down quickly with the pressure goats can put on them and be chewed through with little trouble. Another option and one that is inexpensive and easy to replace is using bailing twine. Remember that you will have a few goats whose sole mission will be to undo the knots with their dexterous little mouths!

### Electric Fencing

The following are a set of basic tips for a strong and well-functioning electric fence:

1. Hidden shorts in the electricity can be caused when a staple is hammered through the insulation layer in insulated fences. So, take care when attaching your staples.

2. Bottom wires can ground out if they are too close to snow or grass that is wet, or at the least, their charge can be low as a result. Your best resolution is to be able to shut down these bottom wires.

3. Think twice before running a new fence in tandem with an old one. It's tempting but can cause undesirable shorting out.

4. It goes without saying, but if you're using an electric fence charged by solar panels, make sure they are in a position where they face the direct sun.

5. Use good quality insulators with your fence. Since your fence will face a lot of exposure to the elements, namely the sun, it's important to use an insulator that has been treated to reduce its potential of breaking down.

6. You should make sure to keep at least a 5" gap between wires so they do not cross.

7. Use one type of metal. Electrolysis will corrode your wires. Mixing something like steel and copper wire is likely to do this.

8. Ground your fence properly using many galvanized rods, ideally 6 to 8 ft in length.

9. Fix any damage to the fence as soon as you can. Any sections of wire that get flattened or kinked can wear down and break. Splice your damaged sections by using a square knot tied by hand or a dedicated fence splicer.

10. The spacing of ties and posts is important. If there are too many and they are too tightly spaced, the fence won't stand up to the goats' abuse. There needs to be a little elasticity in the fence.

11. You need to have a fence with a good "kick" to it. A fence using a thin wire that doesn't carry a good charge won't do much to deter your goats much from overcoming it. Even with thicker wires and more expensive insulation, an electric wire fence is still one of the cheaper options to create a perimeter for a big area.

12. Use a voltmeter to check the fence's charge rather than using your hand.

# Shelter for Your Goats

The main thing you need is to protect your goats from is the wind and the rain. Otherwise, goats are resilient in terms of both high and low temperatures. If you make sure your goat has shelter from these two elements, you've done your job, and the goat will be happy. This means you can get away with using almost any structure—from a doghouse to a barn, as these will do the job nicely.

A calf hut isn't a bad option because of its low cost, mobility, and ease with which they can be cleaned. There are a couple of cons, though; they deteriorate quickly from the constant exposure to the sun, and they can also be a nightmare to maneuver in when you have to catch your goat.

If possible, a barn with a mix of a concrete floor for human traffic and a slightly lower dirt floor for the goats is probably the best scenario. The dirt floors provide absorbency for waste and make it easier to clean up, while the concrete paths make it a mobile space for owners.

Goats are also great because they don't mind being near each other. But that doesn't mean you need not provide space for them in their living quarters. It is recommended to have about 16 square feet for every fully-grown goat you have. This is to make sure that waste is spread out and will help to maintain cleaner bedding. If adequate space isn't provided, the risk of different diseases like parasites increases dramatically.

# A Word About Flies

I think it goes without saying that wherever there's livestock, there *will be flies*. But that doesn't mean you shouldn't do what you can to reduce their numbers. Flies are naturally attracted to the ammonia present in the waste of animals. They lay their eggs and become grown in only a short time; within a single summer season, you're likely to run through many generations of flies.

Your best bet against flies is a mixed approach where you might employ home methods along aided by a pest control expert. The easiest way combines sticky flypaper and flytraps. These will contain a liquid attractant, and the top allows the flies in but not out again, so eventually, they will drown. With the various birds, bats, and insects that are the natural predator of flies, you should hopefully be able to keep them at bay.

Having a good enclosure and shelter for goats is important and something that you should put a little forethought and research into. Go for quality when selecting materials to construct your fence, whether you go electric or not, as any feeble fence's weakness will be exploited by your goat's tenacity. When dealing with shelter, the idea is the same. Do the best with what you've got, but remember that the less expensive options usually come with their inherent flaws.

# Chapter 4: Building Your Goat Barn

Our goats need a safe place to call home, a place that protects them from the elements and predators. A goat shelter—or what we like to call a goat manger—can be as elaborate or as simple as you want it to be. You may need to set up a temporary shelter when you first get your goats, but long-term housing plans should begin before you purchase your herd.

## Essential Components of a Shelter

Your goat shelter needs to keep your goats dry, give them somewhere to go out of the elements and keep them safe from predators. At the very least, this means goats need a roof and three walls. Recall, too, that no matter what your shelter looks like, each goat in your herd should have at least 20 square feet of living space inside the shelter. Let's take a closer look at the essential components.

Roof: Every goat shelter needs a roof free of leaks.

Walls: The walls should be sturdy enough to keep out wind and rain.

Flooring: The best flooring for a manger is dirt or gravel. Concrete is too cold, and wood absorbs odors. Dirt and gravel allow the manure to disperse and decompose. On top of this, you need a couple of inches of hay, wood shavings, or straw to help provide warmth and absorb smells.

Room and board: If you plan to breed goats or keep both does and bucks, you need separate living quarters. The dividers need not be fancy, but they must be goat-proof, meaning they separate your goats, so they don't have access to each other. You can use wood pallets, wire fencing, wood planks, or tin to divide stalls.

Birthing area: If you plan to breed goats, you'll need a birthing area separate from the main living quarters, away from the rest of the herd. This area provides mama with privacy, safety, and time to bond with her kids. This area should be at least 4 ft by 6 ft, well-insulated with hay, straw, or wood chips, and is free from drafts and the elements. You will also need room for feed and water buckets.

### Sleeping and Bedding

Bedding helps keep your goats dry, absorbs ammonia from their manure, and provides warmth. You want something absorbent, soft, and cost-effective. Common bedding materials include:

Hay or straw. This is my preference. It's not as absorbent as the other two, but I always have it on hand to feed the goats and pigs.

Pine shavings. Make sure it's pine and not cedar since cedar can cause issues with goats.

Wood pellets. These are the same pellets used for horse bedding or wood pellet stoves.

Add a couple of inches of bedding to the entire floor, and on any shelf they lie on.

### Keeping the Shelter Clean

How many goats you own and the season will determine how often you need to clean out the shelter. We have nine Nigerian Dwarf goats, and we clean out their shelter every other week in the summer to help keep the fly population under control. We use the deep-bedding method in the winter, which means I just keep adding fresh bedding to their existing bedding without removing the old bedding. The decomposition of the old bedding gives off heat, which helps keep the goats warm in the winter months.

Your goat shelter should smell "goaty" or musty. It should never smell like ammonia or burn your eyes. If it does, it is time to clean your goat shelter and replace the old bedding with new bedding.

# How to Build a Temporary Shelter

Skill Level: Beginner | Estimated Material Cost: $100 or less | Time: 2 hours

This plan is for a shelter that should be used only for temporary housing until the permanent shelter can be built. You may also need a temporary shelter when moving goats from one area to another on your land or when separating goats. This shelter should have a dirt floor.

### Supplies, Tools, and Steps

- 2 (4' × 16') welded wire cattle panels

- Heavy-duty zip ties

- 5 (4') T-post stakes

- 1 (16' × 20') heavy-duty tarp

- Hammer

1. Lay both cattle panels flat on the ground side by side to cover an 8 × 16–ft area. Then push one panel over the other, so they overlap by 4 in (one square of the panel). Use the zip ties to secure the panels together every three squares.

2. Using two of the T-posts, drive down each post into the ground about 1 ft deep where you want one side of your shelter. Make sure the posts are firm and solid in the ground and on either end of the 8-ft section.

3. Place the shorter end of the cattle panels up against the T-posts secured in the ground. (It's easier if you have a helper.)

4. Hold the opposite end of the cattle panels and slowly walk the end toward the side, pressing against the T-post. This will form the panels into an arch.

5. After the arch is made (arch should be about 9 ft wide), one person continues to hold the arch in place while the helper drives the two remaining T-posts into the ground on the outside of the panel to secure the loose side.

6. Cover the arch with the tarp and secure it to the panels with zip ties. Completely cover the back and sides of the shelter, leaving the front open.

7. Add straw to the floor and place a wood shelf or folding plastic table inside for your goats to lie on.

### Troubleshooting

Goats are curious characters, and they like to eat things they shouldn't, including the tarp for their housing. Try to make sure that you secure all loose ends and have no overhang that is not secured, or they will eat it.

# How to Build a Permanent Shelter

Skill Level: Beginner | Estimated Material Cost: $500 or less | Time: 2 days

This shelter considers the long-term needs of your goats and will accommodate a bigger herd. You'll start by framing three sides. Next, you'll work on the roof. The 2" × 4" × 10' boards are your roof rafters. The roof will be elevated in the front to help with runoff, and you will have a 1-ft overhang on the front and back. This shelter will be wide enough you can divide it into separate living quarters if needed. If you build this shelter using wood screws instead of nails, it is possible to disassemble the structure and move it if you need to. This shelter should have a dirt floor.

### Supplies and Tools for the Framing

- Disposable paintbrush
- Tar
- 3 (4" × 4" × 8') wood posts
- 3 (4" × 4" × 10') wood posts
- Post hole digger
- Level
- Measuring tape
- 2 (2" × 6" × 16') boards
- 1 box (3½") decking screws
- Electric drill
- 4 (6' × 8') wood fence panels

### For the Roof

- 10 (2" × 4" × 10') boards
- 6 (1" × 4" × 16') boards
- 8 (26" × 10') tin roofing sections

- 1 bag screws

## To Make the Frame

1. Measure and mark off an area for your shelter. Each side will be 8 ft long, and the front and back will each be 16 ft wide. Choose a flat and level place with the opening facing south, if possible.

2. Using the disposable paintbrush, paint the bottom 2 ft of each 8-ft and 10-ft 4" × 4" post with the tar, and then discard the brush. The tar protects the wood post from rotting in the ground.

3. If you are looking at your goat shelter, you will start your building at the back-left corner.

4. Using the posthole digger, dig a hole 2 ft deep. Place one of the 8-ft posts, tar-side down, in the hole.

5. Use the level to check for plumb on the side and front of the post. Once you are plumb, backfill the dirt and pack it firmly around the post. Check for plumb again.

6. From the post's outer corner, measure over to the right 8 ft for the second hole. Repeat steps 4 and 5, placing the second post at 8 ft center (the center of the second post should be 8 ft from the outer corner of the first).

7. From the center of the second post, measure out 8 ft to the right. Repeat steps 4 and 5, using the last 8-ft post.

8. Pull the measurement from the third post's outer edge to the first post's outer edge; the total measurement should be 16 ft.

9. Measure from the outer edge of the first post forward 8 ft. Repeat steps 4 and 5 using a 10-ft post. This will become the corner post for the front of your shelter.

10. Measure from the outer left corner 8 ft. Repeat steps 4 and 5 with the second 10-ft post, placing it at 8 ft center.

11. From the center of the second post, measure out 8 ft to the right. Repeat steps 4 and 5 using the last 10-ft post.

12. You now have six posts in the ground. The three back posts are 6 ft high, and the three front posts are 8 ft high.

13. Position one 2" × 6" against the backside of the 4" × 4" posts, flush with the top of the posts, and secure it with the decking screws; this is the shelter's back cross support.

---

14. Secure the remaining 2" × 6" board at the top of the front 4" × 4" posts.

15. The top of each 2" × 6" board should be flush with the top of your 4" × 4" posts.

16. Install the fence sections to the back and sides of the 4" × 4" posts using decking screws. You now have all three walls installed in your shelter.

### To Make the Roof

17. Starting with the front left, lay the first 2" × 4" on top of the two 16-ft cross-support boards, leaving a 1-ft overhang on both sides of the shelter (front and back). Secure it with decking screws. Make sure to line up the outer edge of your 2" × 4" with the 16-ft cross support's outer edge.

18. From the outside left side of the first rafter, measure over 2 ft and install the second 2" × 4" as you did in step 1. Repeat this process with the remaining 8 (2" × 4") boards until you have ten rafters.

19. Next, install the tin supports, which lie lengthwise across the rafters. Install the first 1" × 4" board flush with the front edge of the front rafter and secure with decking screws.

20. From the front edge of this first tin support, measure backward 2 ft and install the second 1" × 4" board and secure it with decking screws. Repeat this process with the remaining 4 (1" × 4") boards until you have six tin supports.

21. Secure the tin roofing sections to the supports using tin screws.

### Troubleshooting

The roof must be watertight. The tin screws have a rubber gasket on them to help prevent water leaks. You can add silicone caulk to the outside of the screws for an extra level of water protection on the roof.

# How to Clean Your Goat Shelter

Skill Level: Beginner | Estimated Material Cost: $10 per month per 8' x 16' shelter | Time: 30 minutes

### Supplies, Tools, and Steps

- Dust mask or respirator
- Gloves
- Shovel

- A large trash can or wheelbarrow

- Fresh bedding (pine shavings)

1. Put on your mask and gloves, and make sure all the animals are out of the goat shelter.

2. Shovel out the old bedding, placing it into the trashcan or wheelbarrow for composting.

3. Remove any spider webs and inspect for rodents.

4. Once you've removed all the used bedding, let the shelter air out for about 1 hour.

5. Add a couple of inches of new bedding. Compost the manure and old bedding.

6. Rinse off the shovel and spray with a disinfectant such as bleach.

# Chapter 5: Feeding Your Goats

In the wild, goats are browsers rather than grazers. Wild goats eat mostly trees and other food sources that are off the ground. These plants often have deep roots that bring minerals up from the subsoil. We can learn from this and arrange it so our goats can eat mineral-rich food, which is off the ground in a backyard environment. When we learn from nature and apply it to the backyard environment, our goats can enjoy healthy lives free from parasites and diseases.

Goats are highly prone to parasites if they eat their food too close to the ground. For grazing goats, the pasture should be at least 16 inches (15 cm) high if you want them to eat any of it. Hay and other brought-in foods will need to be kept off the ground too, either with a hay feeder or manger or with cheap hay bags or rubber tubs that can attach to the fence. Hay bags can be found wherever you can find horse supplies. Avoid the net style if your goats have horns.

The strict butting order in goat herds and the amount of time that they spend eating means that you must make sure each goat can access food when they want to. Providing a separate hay bag or tub for each adult goat will achieve this, as will a large manger with more than enough space for your entire herd at once.

Goats can be very fussy with hay. Lucerne, clover, and other legume hays are usually easy to find and favored by goats (avoid red clover hay for white goats, it may be too high in copper for them). Second-cut grass hay, carefully made from fertile pastures, can be acceptable. If horses are fond of the hay you're looking at, your goats will probably be as well. They will also favor grain crops that have been baled as hay well before the seed heads are mature while the grass is still soft.

If you're unsure about hay, it's best just to buy one bale and offer your goats a little to see if they like it. Never feed them moldy hay, and try to keep it out of direct sunlight in a well-ventilated area. The traditional hayloft of a barn is the ideal place to store hay as it gets plenty of ventilation. Garages and carports are also fine for storing hay.

If you have the storage space and the money upfront, it is worth arranging to get a year's supply at harvest time rather than buying small amounts throughout the year. Many farmers will run out before the next lot is ready, and it can be stressful going on a wild goose chase trying to find another supplier. During our time living in rental properties with goats, we always just bought two to three weeks of supply at a time. We've had to put up with very expensive hay at certain times of the year and would have preferred to avoid this, but at least our goats got fed.

The amount of hay that your goats will eat depends on whether they have other food. If you're feeding them hay only, without grazing, two adult goats will generally go through between one and two small rectangular bales every week, usually around three bales every two weeks. This depends on the quality of the hay and how tightly it has been baled.

The dry weight of food that a goat will eat is estimated to be between 3.5 and 5 percent of their body weight each day, so for a 143 lb. (65 kg) goat, this works out to be between 5 lb. and 7.1 lb. (2.27 kg and 3.25 kg) of dry food per day. All food has some moisture content, so its actual weight will be higher than the dry weight. If your goat eats a lot of scraps, fresh pasture, and leaves, it will work out to be more in weight than if she was only eating Lucerne. If the food they're eating is low in nutrients, they may eat more, and if it is nutrient-dense, they will eat less. Observation is always best—if your goat seems hungry, then he/she probably is. It's always best to allow free choice access to staple foods such as Lucerne or tree branches. Goats will adjust their own food intake depending on their energy and nutrient needs.

Goats are ruminants, which means they have four stomachs, one of which contains bacteria that ferment their food to digest it. Because of this bacterium, it's important to allow goats time to adapt to any new feed given to them. Feed them garden scraps in moderation. Upsetting the goat's digestion by introducing too much new food at once can lead to serious health problems, even death.

### Feeding Scraps

Goats enjoy most fruit and vegetable scraps such as apple cores, orange peels, banana skins, the limp outer leaves of cabbage, broccoli stems, pumpkin skin, and vegetables we don't eat. They also enjoy scraps from bread and other baked goods. Goats should be fed no meat, nor anything poisonous such as potatoes that have gone green or anything moldy. Individual goats seem to have different preferences for scraps. One goat I look after thinks that banana peels are the best things ever, but the other goats won't touch them.

### Feeding Trees

Goats love to eat tree branches and leaves. If you have access to suitable trees, you may be able to get away with not buying any hay. Goats generally love nitrogen-fixing trees like acacias and tagasaste. They are fond of most maple leaves (although red maple is poisonous), tree ferns, other ferns species (not bracken though), willows, apple trees, and pear trees. They like ash, elm, oak, poplars, and pines.

Goats have a good sense of what they can and can't eat, so if you're unsure about whether something is a suitable food for them, you can give them a small amount, with plenty of their usual food to eat. This way, they are not forced into eating only the new stuff, and you can see their reaction to the new food. I have found that goats prefer different trees at different times of the year, and some prefer different plants to other goats.

In earlier times, "tree hay" was often made in the summer from ash, elm, ivy, and oak. If you have storage space, you can cut small branches off these and other goat fodder trees and dry them in bundles hanging from the rafters. Nettles and other leafy plants can also be treated in this way. If the tree hay branches you collect are thin enough (around 1 cm - 1/2" thick), goats will often eat the whole thing, branch and all.

Goat fodder trees can often be found on public land, so if you don't have many trees at your own house, you can always go for a daily stroll with secateurs or a pruning saw to gather branches.

### Poisonous Plants

Rhododendron and azalea are highly toxic to goats. Many other garden ornamentals are a bit suspicious as well, so make sure that before you feed anything to your goats, you've looked it up first to check it's not toxic to them.

There are lists online of plants that can be toxic in high enough doses, but goats will often eat small amounts of these with no problems. The key to avoiding poisoning is always to have plenty of food accessible that they will eat. Before feeding any new plant, make sure you've identified it and that it's safe for goats. Before tethering a goat, check that there's no rhododendron in reach, that bracken ferns have been thoroughly stomped down or removed, and that there's plenty of food within reach that the goats are eating at this time of the year.

Plum, peach, nectarine, and cherry leaves can be toxic to goats, so try to make sure you don't have these trees anywhere near your goat paddock. Many believe that the leaves of other plants aren't good for goats, but from my experience with sycamore maples, as long as there's plenty of other food for them, it's not a problem.

### Growing Food for Goats

In a backyard, it is best to either keep plants separate from goats and bring small amounts to them or to offer controlled grazing, either by tethering them nearby for short periods or by growing plants against the outside of their fence so a few leaves can be accessed from the goat paddock, but the goats can't gobble the entire plant up or eat all the bark off the trees.

Goats appreciate access to comfrey, either a couple of leaves offered in their feed each day or being tethered near comfrey for a short time (with plenty of access to their other favorite plants in the same place).

Roses are good as a remedy for scouring, and goats also appreciate the taste of them.

A variety of kitchen herbs and "weeds" can be grown and offered to the goats with other feeds. Goats might choose to eat at certain times and not others, but a variety of food is good for their health, so it's worth growing a few extra herbs to share.

### Minerals and Supplements

Copper is the most important mineral to add to goat diets in areas where it is deficient in the soil or where the water is high in sulfur, iron, or calcium. Darker colored goats have a higher need for copper than white goats, and you can often tell when a darker goat is deficient in this, as their coat will become lighter. Loss of hair on the tip of the tail to give it a "fishtail" appearance is another sign of copper deficiency. In *Natural Goat Care*, Pat Coleby states that she's never encountered a goat with worm problems when their diets have been supplemented with copper. Copper sulfate can be bought in animal feed stores, and it's often found with horse supplements. The easiest way to add it to the diet for milking animals is to mix one teaspoon per goat into the "treat" rations each goat receives. Another way is to place it in small containers available to the goats all the time, but make sure they are kept indoors, or they will be ruined every time it rains.

Copper oxide is more difficult to find than copper sulfate but is a safer option for those worried about copper toxicity.

I had never heard or read anything saying it is possible to feed too much copper to your goats until recently, and there is still no definite upper limit for it. I found when I was feeding my Toggenburgs copper sulfate every day (around half a teaspoon a day—over three times more than what I recommended above), they were very healthy and had no parasite problems. Here in Australia, the soil is often low in lime minerals and copper, and our goats benefit from the extra copper, but if you have healthier soil, keep to 1 teaspoon a week for copper sulfate or to feed them copper oxide instead.

If sulfur is deficient in your soil or notice skin problems or external parasites on the goats, it might be worth offering gypsum or yellow dusting sulfur to them. You can do this as a free-choice mineral or sprinkle it into their food.

Kelp (seaweed) is an excellent natural supplement that supplies a wide range of minerals, especially iodine, which is essential for absorbing all other minerals and vitamins and especially important if you're feeding your goat's Lucerne. Kelp is best-given free-choice, either by having a container on a wall out of the rain for the goats to eat as they choose to or offering it to the goats at milking time twice a month to see if they are interested. I like to sprinkle a small amount on top of their treat-feed every day. Sometimes they will eat large amounts of it, and other times they are either not interested or will only eat only a small amount. If they have never had kelp before, you may find they eat a lot at first.

Selenium is an important mineral for goats. Kelp, wheat, oats, and sunflower seeds are good sources of this (as long as the soil they're grown in is not deficient), so your goats may already get the right amount via their milk treat. If you're concerned about the mineral levels of any goats that don't get grain, give them a handful of sunflower seeds regularly. Sulfur is needed to absorb the right amount of selenium, so supplementing with Sulfur if the soil is deficient or acidic is a good idea.

Salt is essential for goats if you are not feeding kelp, but you may find they get enough of it from their regular feed. Goats know when they need salt and when they don't, it's best to offer it free choice (preferably as kelp).

Goats will sometimes eat a lot of salt when they need potassium, so adding cider vinegar to their water can add extra potassium to the diet. Goats can be fussy about licking from a block of salt that another goat has been licking, so loose salt is preferred to blocks, or get one block for each goat. I have used Himalayan salt, but any natural unrefined salt without additives will do the trick. Instead of having a salt lick for the goats to lick when they want, you can give them handfuls of coarse salt to nibble at now and then, either out of your hand or a bowl.

Calcium and magnesium are very important for dairy goats. Dolomite lime, either offered free choice or around a tablespoon per day added to the treated feed, will supply both of these minerals.

Potassium is important for pregnant does as kidding time approaches. Apple cider vinegar added to the drinking water is a good source of this and is an excellent supplement throughout the year to boost immunity and digestion.

Pregnant and lactating goats need a supplement, too. Usually, this is a mixture of locally grown grain. Barley is said to be especially good for dairy animals, as it increases the amount of milk. This supplement is best fed as a treat at the milking stand. Feeding a pregnant goat like this every day will get her used to coming to the milking stand and will make milking a lot easier once she has kidded. Avoid goat pellets at all costs. Goat pellets turn to something like mushy cardboard inside the goat's belly, and goats need more fiber than pellets provide. Also, try to avoid anything with molasses in it or sweetened, as sweet foods make them more prone to insect attacks. To buy prepackaged "treat" feed, dairy meals designed for cows, made from cracked and rolled grains, can be an acceptable choice, or just buy a large bag of whole wheat and a smaller bag of sunflower seeds and mix them together, or even just plain wheat or plain barley is good. Soaking whole grains in water with a splash of cider vinegar overnight or for 24 hours will enhance their nutrient availability and make them more digestible. I usually soak one batch of barley in the morning each day. Some of it is fed in the evening, and the rest of it the next morning. Before feeding the barley, I drain the soaking water and then mix in the daily rations of copper sulfate, yellow sulfur, and dolomite lime into the grain.

Before you get your goats, research soil mineral deficiencies in the area you'll be buying hay from and try to offer these minerals as a free choice. Alternatively, carefully add small amounts to their treat feed. Offering minerals as a free choice makes it easier for the goat to correct her own nutrition when she needs to, but you'll need a way of keeping these out of the rain. If the goat isn't interested in the minerals, you can try sprinkling a little grain over the top to encourage her.

For Australia, where our soils are mostly acidic and deficient in copper, Pat Coleby recommends a basic stock lick made from 12 lb. (6 kg) of dolomite, 2 lb. (1 kg) yellow dusting Sulfur, 2 lb. (1 kg) copper sulfate, and 2 lb. (1 kg) kelp. These minerals can be found in animal feed shops and horse supply stores. Dolomite is easily found in any garden center.

### Hoof Trimming

Goats are from mountainous areas where their hooves are worn down from daily wandering and jumping on rocky ground. We can imitate this to a certain degree by having large rocks for the goats to climb on in their paddock, but you still need to keep an eye on their hooves, which generally need to be trimmed every eight weeks. Specialty hoof trimming shears (also called footrot shears) designed for sheep or goats are the best tools for this job, but garden sheers can also be used, or a sharp knife if you have enough confidence and a goat that stays still. If you don't trim their hooves on time, the hooves can grow long and curl around over the base of the foot, trapping mud and goat poo, which may rot and cause health problems.

When trimming a hoof, it's better to start by trimming a small, even slice all around the hoof first, then trimming another small amount until you are very close to the foot. Everything should appear to be even, clean, and comfortable. It's possible to trim too closely, and the goat can get cuts on their skin from doing this, so it's better to try a little at a time, and if there's any doubt about whether you've trimmed enough off or not, it's better to err on the side of caution and not trim off anymore. It's good to do this on the milking stand with a bowl of treats for the goat to eat. Depending on the personality of your goat, you may need someone to help hold its leg still. You may need to do the hoof trimming over two or four days, especially if you've been milking the goat on the stand before you start, as they might decide they've eaten enough treats and that it's time to go back to the paddock.

## Milking Stands

This isn't essential right away, but it will make life a lot easier when you need to milk your goats or trim their hooves. There are free instructions available online for making them out of pallets and other wood. They can occasionally be picked up second-hand from sellers on Craigslist, Gumtree, and other classifieds. A good milking stand will have a means of securing the goat to the stand, usually by having her head go through an opening that can be closed into a size big enough to be comfortable around her neck but small enough she can't move her head back through. Another way is to have the goat on a leash secured to the milking stand or a wall beside it.

## Water

Goats need clean water available at all times, and for a small backyard herd, this is easy to manage. I've found it easiest to provide this in sixteen-liter (three-gallon) buckets. I use one or two in winter and three or four on hot summer days. It's important to check up on it twice a day to make sure they haven't drunk it all or that it hasn't frozen in winter. We attach one of these buckets to a clip at the end of a rope attached to the fence. My husband can reach over the fence to lift it up and down using the rope so we can easily refill the water without going in and out of the paddock. Refilling the buckets via a watering can is another quick option, but you must still remove the buckets when they need to be cleaned. Rubber or flexible plastic tubs designed for horses work well for goats. Cheap plastic buckets can be used but will not last long.

Always check to make sure your goats haven't defecated in the water. If they have, it should be changed right away. Try to keep a couple of buckets in different places in the paddock. It's less likely the goats will knock them all over or defecate in them simultaneously.

If you live in a climate with very cold winters, you will need to either insulate the water container or use a heater system.

Goats appreciate warm water in winter and cool water in summer. You can put ice cubes in the water on very hot days, and on cold days, they will appreciate a bucket of warm water if you can manage it.

# Chapter 6: Milking Your Goats

### How to Milk a Goat

Before you begin, make sure you have everything ready you need for the milking and straining. The straining cloth should be boiled, the jars and funnel sterilized (see the next section for information about doing this). Fill a food bowl with your treat feed and place it in the milking stand's feed bucket area.

The amount of treat feed to give a goat will depend on how much milk she gives. Some goats will handle higher amounts of grain than others. Some goats produce more milk with higher amounts of grain, while other goats seem to do better with less grain. Approximately two cups of grain is a good amount to start with. Have your milking bucket close by, but not anywhere that the goat can easily knock over or anywhere else that it can easily be knocked over or contaminated. I keep a small table near the milking stand for the bucket and jars.

Walk the goat up to the milking stand, guide her head through the headgate and secure it around her neck. You will now need to clean her udder. Either brush it with a dry cloth or the back of your hand to remove stray hairs and dirt, or if she's very messy, you can wash her udder with a wet clot. Rub it gently with a very dry towel, making sure she is dry, as you're far more likely to get sick from dirty water dripping into the milking bucket than you are from a few stray hairs or bits of dirt.

If you're washing and drying the udder, you will need to use a separate cloth for each goat. Few goat books recommend following the first method (my preferred one) for udder cleaning and prefer the more thorough washing and drying approach. A lot of the belief in washing goat udders comes from milking cows, as they seem to be attracted to the muddiest part of the paddock and can have very dirty udders. On the other hand, goats will find the driest place possible and don't seem to get dirty often. The simple method works for my family, as we keep our goats clean and dry with lots of straw, but if your goats are covered in muck, washing and drying is the best option. My mention of the simple method might be a controversial approach, but it is far easier to brush the udder quickly than to wash and dry the udder. If you're in doubt, or can't chill the milk quickly, or are sensitive to food contamination, wash and dry the udder, making sure you dry it thoroughly.

Make sure you are seated comfortably. I sit on the edge of the milking stand, but plenty of people use stools instead. You should be able to sit there milking the goat with no need to bend your back and without stretching your arms out awkwardly to reach the teats.

Take two squirts of milk from each teat, milk it onto the milking stand, ground, or a separate dish. By discarding the first squirts of milk from each teat, you decrease the risk of contamination from anything lurking on them. Once you have discarded these first squirts and your goat's udder is clean, place the milking bucket close to the udder and begin milking into it.

To milk a full-sized goat, first place your thumb and index finger around the top of the teat where it meets the udder and close it off, then close your middle and ring fingers (or just the middle finger if her teats are small) around the teat to squeeze the milk out of it. Repeat this with one hand after the other until it becomes more difficult to get the milk out of the teat. Remove the bucket, and then massage her udder or mimic the action that a kid uses on it by pushing against it with your hand, then place the bucket back under her and continue milking as you were before. This helps her to let down as much milk as possible.

If your hands get tired using that method of milking, you can alternate with another method where the thumb is not used, and just the index finger is used to close off the top of the udder. This method uses different muscles to the usual milking method but can't usually be done until the udder has emptied a bit.

To get the last of the milk, "strip" the udder using both hands on one half of it at a time. Gently squeeze the milk from that half of the udder into the teat and then out into the bucket. When it's time to stop milking, she will be giving the tiniest milk (or none at all).

It's easiest to watch someone else milking to learn and if you don't have anyone nearby, try searching for videos online. To get your hands used to the action of milking, go through the motions of milking on your thumb. It's a good idea to learn to milk while the kids are still drinking their mother's milk because the kids can help drink the rest of the milk, and your doe is not at risk of udder problems or drying up as long as someone is taking the milk. Once you are in a good milking routine with your goat, milking will take less time than straining and cleaning. I take around five minutes to milk a goat with a good udder – a bit longer if her milk is slower to flow.

When you've finished milking your goat, leave her on the stand to finish her meal while you strain the milk. This extra time on the milking stand helps the teat close before any bad bacteria can get into it. To strain the milk, place a funnel over the top of a glass jar, then cover the funnel with a sterilized thin cloth, such as butter muslin or cheesecloth, and pour in enough milk to fill the funnel. If it's taking a long time to go through the cloth, you may need to find a thinner or more loosely woven cloth for next time. Alternatively, gather the edges of the cloth in your hands and tilt them around carefully to get more milk through. The creamier the milk, the longer it will take to strain.

### A Milking Routine

- Boil the straining cloth (or boil it the night before)

- Assemble everything you need during and after milking (e.g., clean jars and funnel on the table, clean milk bucket near the milking stand)

- Bring the goat to the stand, clean her udder, milk her

- Strain the milk

- Take the goat back to her paddock

- Repeat for other goats

- When you've finished milking all the goats, wash the straining cloth and hang it up to dry, sterilize the bucket and funnel

## Milking Equipment and Hygiene

When the milk is in the udder, it is sterile and is a perfect food for baby goats to drink. You rarely hear of baby goats getting sick from their mother's raw milk in the same way that the media sensationalizes cases of humans getting sick after drinking raw milk. Due to its neutral acidity, any milk out of the udder, raw or pasteurized, is an easy medium for bacteria to grow. This can be beneficial when we encourage good bacteria to make cheese, yogurt, and other fermented foods, or it can be bad. If you're drinking the milk right away, hygiene is not much of an issue. The longer you wish to store it, the more careful you need to be about the storage conditions and the likelihood of anything coming into contact with the raw milk.

There are two main approaches to preventing contamination by the wrong bacteria on milking equipment. The most sustainable and healthy option is heat sterilization. Any containers used for the milk must be heated to a safe temperature first, then the milk can be added. The other main method is with chemicals.

After the equipment has been sterilized, it needs to be kept away from anything that could contaminate it. I recommend milking buckets with lids. That way, you can keep the funnel and the bucket's interior away from potential contaminants. I use a bucket with a 7 quart (7 liters), but around half this size is sufficient. Empty the bucket as soon as you've milked each goat to avoid it being kicked or stepped and losing the milk. Buckets larger than seven liters will be difficult to fit underneath the goat, so search for a small stainless-steel bucket with a lid. It's tricky to find, but it's something that only needs to be purchased once, so it's worthwhile getting the right one to start with. A stainless-steel stockpot can be used instead of a bucket. Try to find one without air holes in the lid, and you will have something that works just as well as a bucket with a lid.

Heat sterilization can either be done with boiling water or in the oven. Using boiling water can cause injuries (and rude words), so the oven is preferable. To use the oven, everything you put in it should be metal or glass. Plastic can dry after being boiled once the oven has been turned off, but anything put in for long enough to sterilize it should be able to withstand the heat, so I recommend stainless steel milking buckets, stainless steel funnels, and glass jars.

To sterilize using the oven, place your clean bucket and jars in it upside down, and switch it on to 230ºF (110ºC). Don't use ovens with visible (orange-glowing) electric elements for sterilizing glass, as the glass can crack. Leave the oven to heat up, and once it's been fully hot for at least five or ten minutes, test it by touching something sterilizing in there—it should be very hot to the touch. Turn it off, close the door, and leave it to cool down. First, jar lids and plastic funnels should be submerged in boiling water for 30 seconds, and then the water drained off. Place them in the oven as it cools down to dry them and keep them sterile until you need to use them. Be careful that your plastic will stand up to this as some plastics are flimsier than others, but the plastic Ball mason jar lids will without any problem, as do good funnels designed for jam.

For the straining cloth, I rinse it and hang it out to dry after every milking, and then boil it when we're ready to begin milking the next time.

If you need to sterilize everything with boiling water, boil enough so you have plenty to pour over everything that needs to be sterilized. The aim is to heat the jar, funnel and bucket surfaces to kill off any potential nasties that might be lurking there, so slowly pour plenty of boiling water over all the surfaces.

The jars should be wet (but with no standing water) before adding boiling water so they don't break. Pour the water into the jars, filling them to around one-third of the way, and put the lids on. Turn the jars on their sides and rotate until the water heats the jars and you can't comfortably handle them. These days I rely on a wood cooking stove that's often slow to boil water in the mornings, so at night I put the straining cloth in the bucket with the funnel and leave it all submerged in the boiling water overnight, draining it all in the morning.

Every time you empty a jar of milk, rinse it twice with a little cold or lukewarm water and leave it until you're next ready to sterilize jars. Leaving jars sitting with a little milk in them makes it hard to remove it later.

### Handling and Storing Milk

Once the milk is in the jars (if you're not drinking it right away), you should chill it quickly. I surround each jar of milk with ice-filled containers (I use the "ice bricks" made for coolers). You can even chill the jars before you milk, so the cold jar begins chilling the milk as soon as it is strained. After the milk has been chilled, it's important to keep it at a low temperature and not to let it fluctuate. Many people keep their milk in the refrigerator door, but this is not a good place for longer-term milk storage. Only store it there if you will be using it in the next 24 hours. The temperature fluctuates too much in the fridge door, and it's also the warmest part of the fridge. It is best if the milk is on a shelf in the fridge, preferably toward the back. Avoid leaving the milk sitting out at room temperature for entire mealtimes or similar periods unless you plan on drinking the rest of the jar soon.

Don't place warm containers of leftovers or anything else next to the milk. If you're adding a lot of room temperature and warmer things to the fridge at once, add ice-filled containers right next to the milk to make sure that it stays cold.

The quicker you'll be drinking the milk, the more relaxed you can be about its storage. Bacteria need both the right temperature and the right amount of time to multiply to dangerous levels.

Now that I rely on a small off-grid system without a fridge, I find that in winter, we drink all the milk within around 24 hours, so the temperature of an unheated room out of the sun (50°F/10°C) is cold enough for it, even without ice bricks. In summer, there is a lot more milk to handle. On the hottest days, anything that doesn't get purposely fermented into cheese or yogurt begins to ferment on its own within 24 hours unless I'm super careful about switching the ice bricks around.

1-quart (1-liter) mason jars and 22 ounces (650 ml) Passata bottles are good sizes for storing fresh goats' milk. To make the easiest "chèvre" from milk warm from the udder, it is worth having a 2-quart (2-liter) jar for this purpose.

### Excess Milk

If you're lucky in your search for goats, and the goats you thought would only give one liter (one quart) a day each instead give two liters or more, you may find you have more milk than you can use for drinking and cheese-making. Depending on local laws, selling or giving away the excess milk is one option. A herd-share arrangement may also work. The legalities of selling raw milk vary depending on the country and state, so check before you sell.

Another option is to feed the milk to animals. Pigs can drink the milk as it is. While chickens will drink the milk, they will gobble it up in its solid form far more readily if you make "ricotta." Milk left sitting at room temperature for too long will often begin to turn to cheese on its own and can be fed to animals.

Goat's milk is great for the skin. You can either add it to baths or dilute it and use it on your skin. Fresh goat's milk applied to a sunburn and other skin conditions can be soothing and healing. Goat's milk soap can also be made.

Diluted raw milk sprayed onto pasture or garden plants works as a great anti-fungal and fertilizer. This is my way of making lemonade from lemons when a goat puts her foot in the bucket—at least the garden is getting a drink.

Excess whey from cheese making can be fed to pigs and chickens and made into whey cheeses such as gjetost. Whey with live cultures from chèvre and hard cheese (not acid-curdled whey from ricotta or paneer) is great for adding as a starter culture to fermented vegetables like sauerkraut and pickles. Whey can also be used instead of water in stock and bread, as soaking water for grains, and as cooking water for vegetables, grains, and pasta. Whey from cultured cheeses (not acid-curdled ones) can be diluted (one-part whey to nine parts water) and used to water plants.

# Chapter 7: Goat Grooming, Health, and Hygiene

Keeping a goat healthy requires you to keep its digestive system healthy. A goat's diet is plant-based because they are ruminants. The goat has three fore-stomachs, so each has an omasum, rumen, and reticulum. The true stomach is the fourth one and has the name abomasum. When the goat eats hay, it is digested in the forestomach. The abomasum helps break down the protein, carbohydrates, and fats, and it resembles the human stomach in this way.

## Parts of the Digestive System

Every part of the stomach does unique work. Among the forestomach, the rumen is the largest, with a capacity of one to two gallons. It has bacteria that help ferment the hay and break it down. This hay is regurgitated, chewed, and swallowed again. In the process, methane gas is produced. Rumination causes belching, which has a strong odor indicative of a healthy rumen. There is heat produced in this process that helps keep the goat warm.

The second part of the forestomach is the reticulum, and this is close to the liver. This stomach compartment works with the rumen and helps break down the food the goat eats into smaller units to absorb and use for its blood circulation, breathing, and other metabolic processes. All bigger pieces of food get stored here. The reticulum pushes the easy-to-digest food to the mouth for chewing as *cud*.

### Chewing and Digestion

This chewing and regurgitating process will continue until all the food is small enough to comfortably enter the omasum. The food is broken down even more by the action of enzymes in the omasum. The abomasum is the only place where the digestion of the food items such as milk and grain occurs, as they do not need bacteria. The broken-down food is sent to the intestine, where the useful material is absorbed and the waste eliminated.

# Other Parts of the Goat

### Hooves

One has to understand the role that hooves play for the goat. Hooves play an important part in the movement of the animal. If the hooves are injured, it affects all the other parts. The goat will feel pain, will limp about, and if not rectified, it can lead to a shorter lifespan. Care for the hooves will keep the goat happy. Trim the hooves to avoid scald and rot since it could lead to death. The hooves help the goat climb the high, steep, rocky terrain. Spanish goats have a feral nature, and so they need little care for their hooves. A good, well-cared-for hoof will have the shape of a rhomboid.

### Teeth

The goat's teeth differ greatly from those of other animals. It has a hard pad on the top of the mouth in the front. There are no teeth there; it has teeth only at the bottom. There are teeth on top and bottom in the back of the mouth used to chew the cud. Like all other animals, baby teeth fall out with age. They grow adult teeth, and this helps establish whether the goat is an adult or not. Vets check for the growth of the teeth on the lower jaw in the front of the mouth. By the time they are five years old, the goat must have all eight adult teeth in place.

### Beard and Pupil

Several varieties of goats have beards that are more prominent among males. Sheep do not have this beard. Goats use this beard during mating to attract the female because the beard has a scent. In dairy goats and pygmy goats, we find the wattle, which is attached to the neck. The eyes of the goat can be confusing because they have many shapes and colors. The main difference is that goats have a square-shaped pupil instead of a circular one.

This peculiar shape of the pupil helps goats see in the dark, which is important because goats need to stay away from predators. The color of the eyes ranges from blue to brown and yellow. Angora goats have hair over their eyes, and this hampers their ability to see properly.

### Difference Between a Sheep and a Goat

You can spot a sheep from far off because the tail will stay down while that of the goat will stay up. Also, the horns of the goat will be straight, while sheep have curved horns. Sheep will not have beards, but goats may have a beard. While grazing, the goat tries to be independent, and the sheep will try to follow others.

# Visual Inspection

You can tell a healthy goat by the shine in their eyes and their coat. They will be playful if they are healthy. They will play around until it is time to chew their cud or sleep. They will have good posture, standing tall with tails, head, and ears upright. If the goat is sick, it will have a droopy posture. The sick ones try to relieve pain in the stomach and other parts of the body by stretching. If a goat is trying to stretch or urinate excessively, it is a sign it is not well.

### Keep a Record of Good Health and Behavior

To keep up with your goat's health, know how your goat behaves when it is in peak condition. Observe how it jumps around and interacts. If there is any deviation from this behavior, you must act. Although you do not have to respond to their every call because goats make lots of sounds, tend to them when they ask for food or water. If you make the feeding time fixed, it will help you understand their cry perfectly.

And, if your goat is not feeling well, it will moan or keep silent but will not cry out. The doe may cry when they are in heat, while bucks in a rut will make peculiar noises. It does make noise while giving birth. The sound is more like a whine than a cry, but the cry will become distinct and loud when it is pushing time. The cry of a goat trapped or in pain will be frantic and plaintive. You can give them enough care once you recognize the different types of cries.

### Keep the Goat Warm

The goat's internal temperature is around 102°F, although there might be a one- or two-degree difference from one goat to another. On hot days, their temperature will be higher. If there is a profound change (more than one degree) in their temperatures, it is a sign of illness. When a goat has issues with the rumen, it will show a low temperature. You must warm it, or it will die. To do this, buy a coat made for goats to keep them warm. If you cannot get one, make one with human sweaters or other clothes.

When you are in charge of goats, record their normal behavior and state. Take the goat's temperature throughout the day and note this along with the time. You can compare the readings in the future using this. Check the type of thermometer you use; either a digital or glass thermometer is okay. Always shake the glass thermometer well before you use it. Tie the thermometer with a piece of string so you can pull it out if it goes in too far.

# Taking the Temperature of a Goat

To get the temperature of the goat, hold the goat still. If it is a fully-grown goat, you may need a stanchion to hold it. Use petroleum jelly to lubricate the thermometer and then place the thermometer inside the rectum. Keep it there for two minutes. Remove it slowly and note the temperature. Clean and sanitize the thermometer using alcohol. Cud chewing is normal, and every healthy goat must be doing this (ruminating). So, watch your goat and see whether it is ruminating. You can check the rumination by looking at the abdomen of the goat. Listen on the left side, and you will hear a growling sound along with a bit of movement once every two minutes. You may also use a stethoscope to listen to this sound.

### Measuring the Pulse and Respiration

Goats rest during the early afternoon period. This is ruminating time for them, and if you find any who aren't, then check them to see if they are unwell. The easy way to do this is to discover their pulse rate. Ordinarily, they should have a pulse rate between 72 and 85 beats per minute. Kids will have twice this rate. Before taking the pulse, make sure the goat is resting. Place your finger below the jaw, and you will feel a pulse. Take the count for 10 or 15 seconds and multiply the number by 6 or 4 to get the beats per minute.

It is possible to discover how healthy your goat is by measuring its respiration rate. For an adult goat, this will be between 12 and 30, whereas, for a kid, it will be between 22 and 38. You can measure this easily by looking at the goat while it's resting and counting the number of times its side rises and falls. By the time the goat is two years old, it is almost fully grown. They continue to grow until they are three, but the growth won't be so rapid then. On average, all goats live between 7 and 12 years, but they can live much longer.

Wethers have a longer life expectancy, and people often raise them as pets. The main cause of death here is urinary calculi. For the does, death is more often due to kidding problems. It is customary to stop kidding after they turn ten because this will lengthen their life span, and they may even live another ten years or more.

# Preventing the Onset of Disease

Most diseases come with newly purchased animals. This may come through the clothing and footwear of the people handling them. Other pets, birds, and mice might also bring in germs that cause disease. To prevent this, one has to clean the shelter, vehicles, footwear, and mats with a bleach or disinfectant such as Virkon S. You could also use chlorhexidine, an antiseptic.

The deficiencies of nutrients in the diet, including copper, selenium, calcium, zinc, or protein, could lead to poor health. The breeders must check the soil to make sure that all nutrients are present and plentiful in the pastureland.

### Keep an Eye Out for Symptoms

When goats sneeze, cough, or look lethargic and do not keep up with the herd, it means something is not right with them. This indication gives you a warning 3-4 days before something happens. Use a stethoscope to check the heart rate and measure respiration. If you check your goats' health daily, do it at the same time.

# Major Diseases

It can be hard to diagnose a disease because many have the same symptoms. It is better to work with veterinarians and use their treatment recommendations.

### Caprine Arthritis Encephalitis

This viral infection affects the lungs, joints, mammary glands, and brains, which will spread to the colostrum once the goat is infected. The signs and symptoms will not all show up at once. Test the bucks and the semen because it can spread to the does.

### Caseous Lymphadenitis

This is a contagious disease spread by bacteria through the lymph glands. You can control this disease by culling.

### Contagious Ecthyma

This is the sore mouth disease you can see on the lips of kids. It spreads through contact, and scabs will appear on the vulva, teats, scrotum, face, and lips. Lesions will disappear in two to three weeks. There is a chance for the animals to get a secondary infection. Wear gloves since this is a zoonotic disease.

### Footrot

This is another contagious bacterial infection that occurs in the soft tissue of the toes. You will see swelling, pus, and redness in the toes of the goat. It has many forms, so it is better to have a swab analyzed at a laboratory.

It is necessary to trim the hoof when needed. Give the goats high-quality zinc with the mineral mix. To help prevent footrot, encourage the goats to walk on rough surfaces to make their hooves stronger. Also, pay attention to the feet of the animals during selection.

### Listeriosis

This bacterial infection causes paralysis of the trigeminal and facial nerves with discoloration of the eyes, fever, and depression. This bacterium will last for years. Infection occurs when the goats feed on silage. You can treat it with off-label drugs.

### Overeating Disease

A bacterium named clostridium perfringens causes overeating disease. This bacterium is found in the soil and the intestinal tract. When the goat is not acclimatized to the feeding land of the pastures or wanders into bushland with fast-growing cereal crops, this increases the chance of infection.

You can prevent the spread of this disease by vaccinating the doe three weeks before they kid, so the bacteria is not passed on through the colostrum. Vaccinate the kids six weeks after this.

If the goat gets infected, it will stay sick for several weeks, while the kids may die before the symptoms are even noticed. They will have no appetite and will have intermittent diarrhea.

### Pneumonia

Pneumonia manifests in many forms in goats. This is linked to fungi, bacteria, parasites, or viruses. Before you begin the treatment, it is important to know which form of the disease you are dealing with.

## Goat Polio

This is a Vitamin B1 deficiency that can be cured by giving your goat thiamine (Vitamin B1). The symptoms appear if there is any change in the diet of the goat. This includes moldy grain or hay, improperly formulated rations, sudden feed changes, and giving molasses-based grain that has mold. If you don't treat the goat immediately, it will die within 1-3 days.

## Leptospirosis

This abortion disease can be avoided by vaccinating before you begin breeding. Since this disease is contagious, you have to wear gloves when handling dead fetuses.

## Urolithiasis

When stones form in the male urethra, it causes urine retention. This condition is called urolithiasis. It comes with abdominal pain and may cause bladder rupture. There is no specific reason for this, as it is not dependent on season or feed. The bucks sometimes break their penises while breeding. This condition is not treatable.

## Bloat

This occurs when you feed the goat pellets, milkweeds, hay that is wet and moldy, or alfalfa straight. The goats cannot burp, and this causes serious problems. At times, this problem is caused due to an obstruction in the esophagus. Offer baking soda to the goat to regulate the working of its rumen. This will help remove the gas naturally.

## White Muscle Disease

You will see sudden trembling and stiffness when white muscle disease afflicts the goat. When the pastureland doesn't have enough selenium, it can lead to this disease. Increase the Vitamin E and selenium supplement in the mineral mix to overcome this problem. Kids must be given a shot as soon as they are born if the pasture is deficient in selenium.

## Scrapie

It is a form of degenerative disease fatal to goats. It attacks the nervous system and is a form of transmissible spongiform encephalopathies. The deadly mad cow disease can be possibly transmitted to humans through this Scrapie disease. Remove afterbirths fast, then clean and disinfect buildings where kidding takes place.

### Infections by Parasites

When parasites infect your goats, they will show decreased appetite and loss of weight. Common parasites include the Brown Stomach worm and the Barber Pole worm. Use a chemical de-wormer if you think the goats have worms. Check the insides of the eyes.

Additional parasites include Razor worms and Brown Stomach worms. They reduce appetite, cause diarrhea and weight loss. Compare the color of the inside of the eye with the FAMACHA scorecard, and it should be pink.

# What is the FAMACHA Score Card?

FAMCHA is derived from **FA**ffa **MA**lan **CHA**rt and is a method used in South Africa by goat breeders when they spotted that, although they were regularly worming their herds, the worms were not disappearing, but instead getting worse. They discovered that the worms were building up resistance to the chemical de-wormers that the herders were giving their goats constantly. Once the worms were resistant, there was no way to get rid of them, and the result was the gradual loss of their goats.

So, what do we use FAMACHA for? It is used to determine parasites in sheep and goats and to detect anemia caused by them. A scorecard is used, with a scale of 1 to 5 – lower scores indicate fewer anemias, which means less risk of parasites. Always use this scorecard – if you try to score by memory, you risk serious issues if you miss-score an animal.

Your local vet should be able to provide you with the FAMACHA scoring cards. You can also get in touch with the American Consortium for Small Ruminant Parasite Control to learn more about the FAMACHA scoring training.

### How to Use the Scoring System

This will require a scorecard, another person to help you, and a holding stand.

You need to check the membranes of your goat's eyes in natural lighting – sunlight gives the best chance of accuracy. Also, make sure that your shadow doesn't shield the eye you are looking at.

A method to remember how to check the membrane is this:

- **COVER** – the eye must be covered with the top eyelid

- **PUSH** – push the eyeball – not hard, just enough that the top eyelid's eyelashes curl backward over your finger
- **PULL** – pull the lower eyelid down. If you do this right, you should see the inner membrane

Now, quickly check the membrane's color, looking at the pinkest part against the FAMACHA scorecard. You must do this quickly because if you take too long, the goat's eyelid will dry out, and the membrane will turn red.

So, what do these scores mean? The scores are from 1 to 5. The lower the number, the less chance of parasites. If your goat scores 1 or 2, there's no need to worry about worming right now. However, a score of 4 or more needs immediate treatment because not doing so could lead to death. If your goat scores 3, you need to make a judgment call on whether to worm them or not. If you have a few goats and they all score 3, it may be best to worm them to stop the problem from worsening.

Some people think it's easier to forget about the FAMACHA scoring and just worm their goats anyway; this can be dangerous, as we explained earlier, because the worms develop resistance. If you are at all unsure, consult your vet.

# Chapter 8: Goat Breeding and Kidding

If you hadn't realized yet, the only way to get milk out of a goat is to breed her and let her have babies. She will produce no milk until that has happened, and the process is known as freshening. To succeed at breeding your goats, you might be interested to know these facts about a goat's breeding cycle:

Bucks, or male goats, can start breeding from as young as seven weeks old. This does not mean you should allow it, just that they are sexually active and can get their sister or mother pregnant. Separate the bucks away from the does before they are seven weeks old.

Bucks can breed at any time and will go 24/7 if allowed, unless there are extreme weather conditions. They will not breed for fun, though, only when they can smell that a female is in heat.

Bucks go into a "rut." This means they get a real surge of hormones and are ready to breed before the female is ready. Occasionally, when a buck goes into a rut, it can make the does go into heat. During the rut, bucks can be very dominating and will do crazy things, some of which will make you laugh, others that will make you cringe! They will snort, spit, and urinate on themselves to make themselves smell worse and may even drink their own urine.

A doe goes into heat on a 21-day cycle, and each heat lasts between 1 and 3 days. There are breeds, like the Nubians, Spanish, Boer, Fainting, Pygmies, and Nigerians, that can breed all year, but most dairy goats are seasonal. This means they will only go into heat in the fall, between August and January.

A full-size goat can breed at about eight months or when they reach 80 lbs. in weight. Try for the year mark before allowing them to breed, just to be on the safe side.

Signs that your goat is in heat are a wagging tail, fighting, trying to mount another doe, or letting one mount her, clear discharge from the vagina, or bleating for no apparent reason.

Gestation for a goat is five months—approximately 150 days, give or take one or two.

Goats can give birth to five kids in any one litter, although the average is two to three.

Many people allow their goats to breed once a year to stop the milk supply from drying up.

You can milk a pregnant doe, but it is best to let her dry up around two months before the birth. This will allow her body to rest and build up nutritional reserves for her kids.

A doe will breed for as long as she is alive, generally around 10 to 12 years, but the older they are, the more chance complications will occur.

A doe can also become pregnant she is lactating.

# Breeding Season

The fall is breeding season. All does want to breed and will have no qualms about communicating this desire to you but you need to remember that only your best specimens should be bred no matter how much they try to tell you otherwise. Goats can breed as early as two months, but the typical time is around four months. Most goats will experience their heat cycle in the fall. The safest time to breed is after the seven-month mark, with an approximate kidding time of around one year.

A few maintenance-related items need to be taken care of before breeding season. You will want to make sure they have had a Bose shot if your region is known to be selenium-deficient, trim their hooves, and conduct both a fecal analysis and a CAEV test. You will also want to clip at least their stomach region. Not only will this make your breeding season easier, but it will also allow you to give your goats one more once-over before they breed to make sure they are healthy and not demonstrating any symptoms indicative of disease. If they feel a bit thin, you can also take this time to address any deficiencies in their diet.

Most goats breed seasonally, but several miniature breeds can reproduce throughout the year. Even when this is the case, heat is still most apparent in the fall. As the daylight decreases when summer turns into fall, it will begin to go into heat on a three-week cycle. If your doe has continuously short cycles, you need to contact your vet to see if there is an issue. As the daylight decreases, the males begin to get into a rut. These changes will cause your goats to become a bit restless. As you see this happening, make a breeding plan to be well prepared when the time comes.

A doe in heat will have a red and swollen vulva with vaginal discharge. They will also wave their tail rapidly. Does in heat will also be very vocal and act more like a buck than they usually would. Also, expect your doe to produce less milk during this time.

The odor associated with bucks in rut originates from the buck urinating onto his face and into his mouth. The reason they do this is to attract the does and allow the does to find them. They will also make very distinct faces and sounds. The fighting amongst other bucks increases in frequency during this time. Mounting also becomes more frequent. Bucks become concerned with nothing other than mating, which includes a lack of concern for eating. Make sure to supplement their diet to make sure they maintain their health.

Once a doe has shown signs of being in heat, you can place her with a buck. They will dance around each other, urinating and making sounds a little at first. Once they mate, it lasts only for a few seconds. They should do this a few times to make sure that the doe is impregnated. You then watch to see if she goes into heat. If not, you will know it succeeded. Sometimes, a doe simply refuses to mate with a specific buck. This can happen when an adult doe is put with a young buck. Once kids are born, the buck will need to be separated from the doe and the kid. For one thing, his presence increases the risk she will be re-bred far too soon.

Because bucks need to be separated during certain times and can be a pain during other times, many goat owners simply choose not to have one. Instead, they will pay for buck service to get their doe's bred. There is paperwork required for this arrangement, but it is fairly common.

Knowing whether your does are in heat is a bit more challenging when there are no bucks present. One solution is to use a buck rag. This cloth has been rubbed onto a buck in a rut and then stored.

If the doe is in heat, she should become excited and make noise and rubbing against the rag. This will let you know when the best time is to have a buck brought in. Alternatively, you can bring her to the buck or have her artificially inseminated. If you are having a buck brought in, one method is to lease the buck. If you plan to do things this way, you will need a separate enclosure for the buck away from your does. The buck then stays with you and your doe for as long as you feel necessary. The cost of leasing a buck should be much lower than that of keeping one all the time. The minimum amount of time the buck should spend with you is around three weeks. This allows them to experience an entire breeding cycle. If this does not suit you, you can often find buck owners who will allow your doe to come and stay with them. For those who do not have the luxury of time, there is always driveway breeding. This involves a prior arrangement with a buck owner to be available once your doe comes into heat. Then, when she shows signs, you bring her to the farm where the buck is. Upon arriving, you exit your vehicle with the doe on a leash, and the process happens without even removing the leash so you can quickly load the doe back into the car and head back home.

Artificial insemination requires the collection of semen from the buck and proceeding to put it into the doe's reproductive system. This is convenient because the semen can be frozen and ready for the doe whenever needed rather than coordinating schedules, but this is not typical practice due to the cost. Still, high-quality breeding will occur this way. The cost can be managed by going in with other breeders and sharing the equipment. There are also semen collectors who can pass through and can retrieve the semen for you.

Immediately after breeding, there is not much to do. It does do not even show much during the first three months of the pregnancy, and milking can continue during this time. Her feed can stay the same initially as well. After three months, it will need to be adjusted. Goats gestate for around 150 days. This being said, it can vary slightly, so it is a good idea to mark your calendar 145 days out just in case. Know false pregnancy, a somewhat common occurrence in goats. This is when the goat exhibits all the signs of being pregnant, but when it comes time to give birth, fluid is released, but no kid is birthed. This is frustrating but not necessarily dangerous.

The majority of pregnancies only require basic care, like good nutrition and clean shelter, but there are still instances in which complications overrun a pregnancy. This can cause an abortion where the pregnancy cannot continue to completion. If the pregnancy continues until term, but the kid is dead at birth, it is called a stillbirth. These two things can happen for a variety of reasons.

If a kid will be born with genetic defects or malformation, they are typically aborted in the early stages of the pregnancy. They often occur so early on that you may not have even realized the goat was pregnant. There is nothing you can do to prevent this from happening. An overly stressed goat will also experience problems having a healthy pregnancy. Stress can occur because of anything from the weather to a lack of nutrition. You have more control over this cause of abortion and should work to eliminate anything stressful by making sure your pregnant goat is protected by a clean shelter and well-fed with a balanced diet. You should avoid moving your doe toward the end of her pregnancy, which is likely to cause her significant stress. Half of all goat abortions are thought to be due to infections. Not only can an infection affect one pregnancy, but it can also spread throughout the entire herd and affect other pregnant does. If multiple abortions occur, you will need to take the fetus to the vet to be tested with a necropsy process. An unsuccessful pregnancy may also be due to poison or injury. If a goat consumes the wrong plant or medication during pregnancy or is butted in the wrong place, it may abort.

Hypocalcemia occurs when a goat experiences a calcium deficiency from not receiving enough calcium in its diet to support itself and the kids it is carrying. This happens to a doe near a pregnancy's culmination or even during the lactation phase. A heavier producer of milk is more likely to experience this condition. Goats experiencing hypocalcemia will no longer wish to eat anything, especially grain. The doe becomes weak by not taking in enough food and may run a fever or become depressed. Here, weakness is caused by a lack of calcium in the muscles. This can be avoided by ensuring the doe is consuming a proper diet throughout the pregnancy and lactation. Offer alfalfa to help boost calcium. You may need to watch how much grain is given to make sure she takes in enough alfalfa. The ratio should be around two to one in favor of alfalfa. You can provide alfalfa in the form of pellets, so they can be fed alongside grain.

If you discover your goat is experiencing hypocalcemia, you will need to administer Nutridench as soon as possible. This will provide the energy needed to continue the pregnancy or continue providing milk. After this, you will want to contact your vet to develop a more long-term recovery plan. This usually includes a prescription with potassium, calcium, phosphorus, and magnesium. If the doe is dehydrated, it may also require intravenous fluids. Once the goat's heart rate returns to its usual state, you will know it is on the road to recovery. You will probably need to continue administering the medication throughout the duration of the pregnancy. Does who are within a week of kidding and do not quickly recover can be given a prescription called Lutalyse, which will induce birth.

Hypocalcemia is often accompanied by a condition called ketosis, in which a goat is not getting enough energy. This happens when a goat stops eating, which causes a metabolic imbalance causing the body to release fatty acids. The liver typically employs these fatty acids, which produce by-products known as the ketone bodies. Overweight goats experience this condition more often and may experience it during the early stages of the pregnancy. A key identifier for goats experiencing ketosis is a sweet odor from their breath, compounded with hypocalcemia's usual symptoms. Ketosis should be treated with Nutridench.

The final few weeks of a doe's pregnancy will require added care and maintenance to guarantee a smooth birthing. To reduce the risk of abnormal labor and white muscle disease, anyone living in a region known for selenium-deficiency should administer a BoSe shot. Those who vaccinate their goats should administer a CDT shot. This will allow the kids to build up immunity from both tetanus and enterotoxaemia. The tail area will need to be trimmed and the area around the udders. This helps the doe remain clean and makes it easier for feeding. You should not milk your doe during the final two months of her pregnancy. Make sure to be subtle about any changes to diet during this time.

A kidding pen will need to be set up and ready a few days before day 145 of the pregnancy. The pen should be sanitized using bleach and water. A new layer of wood shavings or straw should be put down as bedding. It is also helpful to have a clean, sanitized bucket nearby. You may also choose to place a baby monitor near the kidding pen so you can be alerted of the birthing process.

Preparation will make the birthing process much less stressful. To make sure you have everything you need and know where to find it, you may want to put together a kidding kit. The kit should have 7% iodine, a prescription bottle, flashlight, floss, bulb suction, towels, surgical scissors, gloves, and a syringe. It is also helpful to have a list of important phone numbers for people like your vet or other goat friends who can help. Betadine surgical scrub should be procured to help you while washing the goats, and an obstetrical lube is always a good idea. Do not forget to have an empty bottle with the right teat if bottle-feeding becomes necessary. When the time comes, you will need a bucket of hot water or a hot water source near the kidding pen. If the doe needs assistance, dish soap can be used for your hands and the doe's vulva to clean off the lubrication.

Usually, the doe can birth with no help from you, but you will still want to be around if an emergency occurs and to make sure the birthing process goes as smoothly as possible. When your doe is nearing the time for birth, its tailbone changes shape as it rises, and the ligaments connecting the pelvis stretch. If a hollow area forms on the sides of the tail, this could indicate that birth is near. The most accurate measure of how soon the birth is likely to occur comes from feeling the ligaments on the side of the tail. Typically, these ligaments are firm, but they will become soft and will not be perceivable. Once you can no longer feel them, you can be fairly certain the birthing will happen within the next 24 hours. When they become soft, move her to the kidding pen. When a doe is getting ready to kid, you will also experience a few behavioral changes. The doe will isolate itself, have vulva discharge, lose its appetite, become aggressive or restless, and its udder will become firm and shiny. Once the process has begun, you can leave the baby monitor on and allow her to focus on kidding.

# Basic Kidding

If you are a new goat owner or have had your goats for a year or two and just bred them for the first time, you may be worrying about them getting through kidding safely. The main thing to remember is that having a baby is normal and, most of the time, it will go just like nature planned.

Goats usually deliver their kids between 145 and 154 days. Use 150 days to estimate kidding, but keep a close eye on your doe starting at about 144 days.

According to David MacKenzie, from *Goat Husbandry*, as long as you can see the kid(s) as a bulge on the right side and see movement, the goat is unlikely to kid within the next 12 hours. Kidding, or parturition, is divided into three stages:

- The first stage of labor is when the uterine contractions dilate the cervix by forcing the placenta, fetus, and amniotic fluid against it. This can last up to 12 hours in first-time moms but is often faster for those who have previously kidded. Again, every doe is different.

- The second stage of labor is when the doe pushes the kid(s) out. It usually lasts less than two hours but can be longer.

• The third stage of labor is the expulsion of the placenta and the reduction of the uterus back to its normal size. Usually, the placenta is passed within an hour or two after birth, but it can take hours in rare cases. The uterus does not reach its pre-pregnancy size until about four weeks later.

The first stage starts with estrogen secretion by the ovaries, which causes the uterus to contract.

You will not feel the kids moving. The bulge in the doe's right side will change, and the rump will slope more. This may not be visible to any but the trained eye.

You will see restlessness begin in the doe. If you have a clean kidding pen prepared, now is the time to move her there. Like all mammals, goats like a quiet, safe place to have their kids. It should be lit well enough (or have access to light) so you can see what you are doing if you need to help but dim enough to be comfortable. The area shouldn't be too small, so she can move around as the labor progresses.

Avoid putting water in the pen, as kids have been known to drown in it. To give the mother water, make sure the water is warm and once she is finished drinking, remove the water from the pen.

Around this time, you may see a thick discharge. This means that the doe has lost her cervical plug. You will likely see a change in discharge as labor progresses. It thickens and changes color and can be blood-tinged; this is normal.

What is not normal is thick, rusty-brown discharge, which may indicate a dead fetus. If you have questions, contact your veterinarian or an experienced goat breeder.

Your doe, at this point, will probably reposition herself regularly, trying to get comfortable. She may lick herself or objects, "mama-talking" (a special talk reserved for welcoming kids), or with a very spoiled goat, demand you stay there and pet her throughout.

The second stage of labor is where the real work begins. The babies have lined up for birth, and the doe pushes them out, in sync with the uterine contractions. The contractions become stronger and closer together.

Some goats deliver standing up, while others prefer lying down. The doe might cry out at this point. It depends on how stoic she is. The first sign that tells you the labor is progressing is what looks like a balloon at the vaginal opening. This is the membrane surrounding the baby.

The doe may start licking in earnest between pushes, sometimes situating her body so she can lick up the amniotic fluid. With more pushes, you may see two little hooves and a little nose, which indicates that the baby is positioned properly. The kid is moving down the birth canal.

If you see just the nose and no legs, and the birth's progress seems to have stopped, insert a thoroughly washed finger in to feel for bent back legs. You sometimes need to pull just one of these gently up to help the baby get out; with others, it may take two. If you pull one leg slightly forward, it will decrease the shoulders' width, and the kid should come out easily now with just another push or two.

Anytime you have to help a goat and put your hand in her vagina, it is important to have clean hands and short nails. Ideally, also wear gloves. Often goats, especially minis, are born in a breech position - back feet first - with no problems. Frank breech position, where the hind legs are folded underneath the kid, is potentially a bigger problem, but small kids can also be born this way. Otherwise, it will need to be corrected before birth, which you can do by gently pulling the feet and then the kid out. This prevents it from accidentally inhaling amniotic fluid and getting aspiration pneumonia or drowning.

Another presentation problem I have encountered only once out of hundreds of births is crown presentation. This is where the kid's nose is pointing down toward the body, with the top of the head presenting. Because I didn't know what I was feeling and the vet's hands were too big, we had to perform a c-section. (That kid was born four hours after his brother and did just fine.)

Another unusual position is transverse, where the kid is sideways. This will always stop the birth, and the kid has to be turned with back legs coming first and gently pulled out. Once a kid is born, wait for the umbilical cord, if it hasn't already broken. Once the cord breaks on its own or collapses when the blood flow stops, you can tie it off securely with dental floss in two places: an inch or two from the kid's belly and an inch past that. Only now should you cut it.

During this time, the mom will be licking and cleaning the baby. If the doe does not want to get up or can't reach the kid, you can fetch it for her. She will continue with this behavior until the next kid is ready to be born, which can be quickly or can take another hour. Longer times may be a sign of malposition, so if a placenta has not been delivered yet, and you aren't sure if there are other kids, you may want to check. Remember to err on the side of not intervening unless needed. This is where experience comes in.

There are a couple of ways to check for more kids: First, you can check inside the doe with a finger. That will at least tell you whether another kid is in the birth canal and needs help with positioning. If that tells you nothing, you can "bump" the doe. Stand behind her, and with your hands on the doe's abdomen, lift up quickly to feel for another kid. An effective but more invasive method is to check inside the uterus with a well-washed, lubricated hand and forearm. I have found that having a bucket of soapy water helps this effort immensely. Wash the perineum and be gentle with your exploration. A loose-feeling uterus will contain no other babies.

I have had to do this only once in my seven years of kidding experience. There, the doe had a ring womb, which means the cervix will not dilate enough, and I had to slip the cervical lip around the large kid's head. Usually, you will know that doe is through kidding.

If you deliver a kid that is not breathing and seems very weak, you can try baby CPR or simply hold tight to the kid (one hand on the leg and one on the neck to stabilize the head) and swing it back and forth in a 90-degree arc to clear the mucus. This is what I did with the "c-section" kid, born four hours after his brother. If the kid cannot suckle, you may need to tube feed it.

Once the kids are born, the mother should nurse, which causes a release of oxytocin—also known as the bonding hormone. It not only helps mother and baby bond, but it stimulates uterine contractions that lead to the delivery of the placenta and closing of the cervix. You will sometimes need to help the kids find the teats to nurse; in rare cases (once in my experience), the mothers will not know to nurse their young. Breeders who pull the kids at birth should milk the goat, as this has the same effect. There is normally only one placenta for each litter, and it comes out after the birth. I understand that more than one placenta may exist with some goats, and it may be expelled between deliveries of kids. Expect to see that the doe has a bag of amniotic fluid attached to the umbilical cord hanging from her vagina. The weight of the fluid helps to pull out the placenta after it detaches from the uterine wall.

Failure to deliver the placenta may indicate that another kid is still inside the doe. Never pull on the membranes to remove the placenta as it can cause ripping and lead to problems later. The placenta is not considered retained in a goat until at least 24 hours have gone by. You may obtain a prescription from a veterinarian for oxytocin for a retained placenta, but do NOT routinely use it. Do not assume that if you found already-born kids and did not find a placenta, it is retained. Goats, like all mammals other than humans, typically eat the placenta.

Once kids are born, dip their navels in 7% iodine to prevent navel problems. Make sure they are thoroughly dried, especially if the weather is inclement. They need to receive colostrum within the first hour, if at all possible. Once mom has completed her job, I have a ritual of bringing hot oatmeal with molasses and a bucket of hot water to offer her. The water replenishes her system, and the oatmeal is a great treat with the added benefit of being galactosemic (helping to produce milk).

# Chapter 9: Seasonal Herd Care and Maintenance

In the world of livestock, goats are the easiest to care for. Given the right conditions and the right feed, your healthy goats may seem self-sufficient. Although they may be easy to raise, they still require care. In this chapter, you will learn what care is required for raising and maintaining healthy and happy goats, from trimming their hooves to castration.

### Grooming

We brush our teeth and hair, take baths and eat right, so why should our goats be any different? There are two different types of grooming. One is grooming for health and wellness. Routine grooming will help you develop a bond with your goats and allow time for health inspections. The second type of grooming is for shows. Grooming for shows is a lot more involved—regular brushing, bathing, and shaving—since they need to look their absolute best. This section focuses primarily on everyday grooming.

### Petting Your Goat

Your goats will beg you to give them a good scratch, just like Fido does. Just remember, goats don't like being petted on the head. They get spooked when you try to pet them on the head because they can't see what you're doing. Try petting your goat on the back, chest, or neck. Besides avoiding the top of their head, try not to push against their forehead. While it's funny and cute when they are little, they are training to knock you off your feet when they get big enough to establish dominance.

### Brushing and Bathing

Goats love to get a good back scratch. You will see them brushing up against a tree trunk, a wire fence, or the side of a barn to scratch that itch. We like to take the heads off stiff-bristle brooms and screw them to trees so the goats can brush up against them, and they love it.

When you spend time brushing your goats, you create a grooming bond, similar to the one a mother makes while grooming her young. You can also take this time to inspect your goat for injuries, abnormalities, and hooves in need of trimming.

During the colder months, goats grow a winter coat. You will see what looks like dryer lint close to their skin. This is their winter fluff. Don't try to brush this out when it's still cold, as they need it to keep them warm, but you can help groom them in the spring when they start to shed their winter coat.

To brush your goats, you need a stiff brush and a soft brush. The stiff brush helps get all the old winter fluff off, while the soft brush is used for daily or weekly brushing. Brush their fur in the direction in which it is growing, and try to brush their chest, back, and legs.

If you are raising goats for livestock only, there is little need for bathing unless a goat is sick or gets stuck in the mud, or you just want a better-smelling goat. I recommend reserving the task only for times when it is absolutely necessary. Too much bathing can interfere with the natural oils that keep their skin and coat healthy.

Remember, goats hate water. Bathing your goat is not a fun task for either you or your goat, but they are creatures of habit, and if you bathe early, they will get used to it.

If you do want to bathe your goat, I suggest using a collar with a short leash and tethering them to a fence or a milk stand (stanchion) for this task. This holds them still while you remove dirt and shampoo them.

Bucks smell worse than does do due to the buck "cologne" they create during mating season. This is a sticky, smelly residue that is quite hard to get off. You want the cologne to remain during the mating season since the ladies go wild for it. The buck smell does dissipate after the mating season has ended.

Use goat milk soap or livestock shampoo sold at farm supply stores. Wash your goat on a warm day when they will have plenty of time to dry in the sun before nightfall. Avoid cold, wet, or windy days for bathing.

## Hoof Care

As daunting as it may seem, I recommend that all goat owners learn to trim their herd's hooves. You can hire this job out to trained people, and that may be the best choice for you, but this is a task I am confident you can learn to do on your own with practice.

When a goat lives in its natural environment, rocks, forage, tree bark, and the like keep its hooves trimmed. When you place a goat in a fenced-in pasture, performing routine tasks to care for their hooves is essential in protecting their health. Overgrown hooves can lead to leg, joint, muscle problems, and footrot, which happens when bacteria is trapped in the fold on the hoof.

Think of a goat's hooves as you would think about your fingernails. The growth past the skin is what you need to keep trimmed and clean. Goats have cloven hooves and one dewclaw (on the back of their ankle). How often you must trim your goats' hooves depends on the individual goats and their living conditions. It is best to check your goats' hooves weekly to help determine how fast they grow. A general rule of thumb is to trim them every two to four weeks.

When you buy your goats, ask the breeder to show you how to trim hooves on one of their goats. Take pictures or notes about the process so you can refer to them as needed. If your breeder cannot demonstrate, you can contact your goat vet to help you through the process until you are comfortable trimming them yourself. Goats are very skittish and jumpy. The last thing you want to do is cut your goat or yourself. Be calm, talk to your goat through the whole process, give it time and be patient. Do a few practice rounds before performing the real deal by walking your goat to the stanchion, securing them, lifting each hoof and trimming it, and then returning them to their usual pasture.

### How to Trim Goat Hooves

Skill Level: Beginner | Estimated Material Cost: $10 or less | Time: 10 minutes per goat

### Supplies, Tools, and Steps

- 1 cup of warm water
- Small stiff-bristle brush
- Stanchion or a collar and leash
- Feed or treats, as needed
- Stool or bench

- Clippers or hoof trimmers

- Antiseptic spray

- Styptic spray or powder

1. If the goat's hooves are muddy, soak them in warm water and use the brush to remove any mud.

2. Secure the goat to the stanchion. Offer the feed or treats to keep them occupied during trimming. Place the stool beside the goat (not behind), working on just one hoof at a time.

3. Using warm water and a brush, remove any dirt, and clean the hooves.

4. Spray the clippers with antiseptic spray. Do this between each trimming to prevent spreading infection or disease from hoof to hoof.

5. Grab the hoof and bend it back toward you; do not raise the leg forward to trim.

6. Using your clippers, trim any excess growth away from the pad of the hoof. The pad is soft and pliable, and the outer edge is the part you will be trimming. Make sure the hoof is level and straight. Any curves should be trimmed.

7. If you accidentally cut the goat, use the antiseptic spray and the styptic spray or powder to stop the bleeding.

8. Dewclaws need not be trimmed often, usually only on older goats or when the dewclaws start to curl into the goat's skin.

### Troubleshooting

Not cutting enough or cutting too much can affect the way the goat walks and can cause issues. It's important to make sure their hooves are trimmed nice and level.

### To Dehorn or Not to Dehorn

Dehorning is the act of removing a goat's horns permanently. Dehorning goats is the subject of much debate among goat owners, and both sides have compelling arguments. I have been, and I still am, on both sides. I have goats with horns, goats that have been dehorned, and naturally polled goats, and I've even owned a goat with scurs — we'll get to that in a minute. Let's start with the basic pros and cons of horns.

### Horn Pros

Horns help goats defend themselves against predators and protect the herd. This ability is diminished in dehorned goats.

Horns help goats establish a natural pecking order. A goat with horns will dominate a goat without horns.

Horns help regulate body temperature. Certain goats, such as Angora goats, should never be dehorned because, without their horns, they could overheat and die.

You avoid the risks associated with dehorning. If not done properly, dehorning can cause permanent brain damage or infection.

### Horn Cons

Horns can get stuck in fences and cause injury. This risk is diminished in dehorned goats.

Horns can injure you and others. Dehorned goats are less dangerous to humans.

Goats with horns are often harder to sell than dehorned goats.

Goats with horns rarely are allowed in shows. If you plan on showing goats in the future, your goat needs to be dehorned.

Dehorning, or disbudding, is usually done when the goat is just a couple of weeks old. This is a medical procedure during which a hot iron is used to burn the horn buds (horn buds are the beginning of the horns forming) off their head. If you want a goat without horns, let your breeder know before purchasing your goat or contact your vet to perform the procedure.

Polled goats are naturally hornless. A polled goat comes from a parent or parents that are polled. No disbudding or dehorning will ever be needed if you have a polled goat.

Sometimes dehorned goats develop scurs or partial horns that grow after a goat has been disbudded or dehorned. This can happen months or even years later. Generally, these scurs break off naturally, but sometimes they will continue to grow, which is fine. I don't recommend removing the scurs during older age unless it is causing a health issue, and if that's the case, it's time to contact a vet.

# Chapter 10: Selling Meat, Dairy, and Other Goat Products

## Running Your Side Business

If you plan to sell goat meat, it's important to market your meat to reach your buyers. You have likely seen products with labels like "organic," "all-natural," and "grass-fed." As these labels become more popular, so do the licensing requirements and regulations to use them. You can no longer say something is organic without being a licensed organic farm, which requires fees. If your farm is organic, but you don't pay the fee, you can't call your products organic.

There are still honest marketing approaches you can use without paying to reach your target customer. For instance, my farm friend who lives out West, where there are many devastating fires, advertises, "These goats were raised to maintain a fire-safe environment," which appeals to her local market.

There are lots of ways you can market your product to find your own niche and draw in the crowds. Here are selling points you can think about for marketing your goats:

- Family-farm raised
- Pasture-raised

- Free-range

- Humanely-processed

- All-natural

- Locally-produced

- Farm to table

Although goat meat is widely consumed in other parts of the world over beef or poultry, it is fourth on the list in the United States, except for ethnic and specialty markets. Certain ethnic groups—such as those with heritage from Asia, the Middle East, Latin America, Africa, and the Caribbean—will probably be your largest consumers.

Religious celebrations where goat is on the menu for celebratory or ceremonial meals will often encourage a spike in demand. Thankfully, there are many celebrations throughout the year, giving your business a year-round market. A few of these holidays include:

- Chinese New Year

- Greek Orthodox Easter

- Rosh Hashanah

- Islamic New Year

- Start of Ramadan

- Passover

To find your customer base, you need to go where they are. Start by advertising at specialty stores, farmers markets, local restaurants, religious centers, and even livestock auctions. Create a desire in people you already know by inviting them over for dinner and letting them see how good the goat tastes. Once people see and experience the difference in farm-raised meat treated ethically and humanely, you can create your own market. Help educate those in your community about goat meat's benefits, how lean it is, how sustainable the livestock is, and the importance of cutting out the middleman and getting their meat direct from the source.

Remember that on-the-farm slaughtering for sale is illegal, and you can only sell the live animal—what we call "on the hoof." The purchaser can then transport the animal to the slaughterhouse or have a mobile butcher process it.

# Chapter 11: 7 Deadly Mistakes New Goat Owners Make (and How to Avoid Them)

Over the past few years, I have encountered people who had made a mess of enormous capital invested in goat farming. Investing so much is not the problem, but the problem is when you are beginning to lose everything you have invested without the desired output over the years. My parents made mistakes while raising animals; it was as if everything was going against us, and at that time, we thought it was a spiritual attack to jeopardize our efforts. When you are not well equipped with updated knowledge of raising an animal, you will likely lose the animal and lose your investment.

Is making a fortune your driving force toward goat farming? This marks the beginning of failure in the business. Instead, focus on quality production, and you will make good profits.

The business's failure rate will be reduced by at least 70% if you avoid these mistakes that first-timers make in goat rearing.

### 1. Getting Started with a Single Goat

Goats are peculiar creatures - they are social, curious, and intelligent. Just as most humans do not enjoy being alone for very long, goats easily get bored and lonely. Goats are not dogs or other animals you can rear singly. It is never a good idea that you begin a goat business with one goat. At least two goats are required to get started. Apart from the mating aspect, goats love the company of other goats around them.

You can begin with a doe and a buck or even a doe and wether but make sure they have at least one companion.

Goats are herd animals. They depend upon staying together for safety. They have few natural defense mechanisms but many predators.

A lonely goat will try to escape or climb and get into your garden, which can lead to devastating effects.

Note that a single goat will be a noisy goat, as it will always call for a companion.

If you purchase a goat, be prepared to add a companion goat.

## 2. Combining a Buck with a Milking Goat

Bucks are generally stinky and have a characteristic odor for about half of the year. Remember this before buying a buck; the buck's smell will undoubtedly get into the milk. Smelly milk will undoubtedly influence the market value of your milk and its derivative products.

I have received several complaints from goat farmers about the milk quality, while some complain that the milk has a foul taste. The first question I ask is if they have combined a buck with a milking goat. Most of the time, I get a YES response. The solution is straightforward as it lies in separating the buck from the milking goat. If you keep a buck with a milking goat on the same farm, then it must be spacious enough to keep them well separated.

## 3. Poor Breeding Technique

Inadequate knowledge of breeding can lead to an extremely undesirable output. When breeding, avoid breeding a larger-framed male goat (buck) with a moderately sized female. When a female goat is not sexually matured enough, avoid breeding it against a matured buck as this can cause complications during the birth of the new kid. Again, the young doe could die during the process of parturition due to tears. I recommend first-time goat farmers consult a professional when they want to embark on the breeding process.

### 4. Poor Market Research

For any business anyone wants to delve into, intensive market research is a key to profitability and sustainability. Before purchasing a goat, it is compulsory to determine the demand for goats in your locality. If you are rearing a goat to make money, you must see goat farming as a business and treat it.

Whenever I receive complaints of poor sales of goats and their products, I ask if thorough market research was done before embarking on the business. If the market demand in your locality is very high for meat, you shouldn't focus on raising milk-producing goats. More importantly, you shouldn't seek advice from other breeder producers different from yours, as applying their techniques to your herd will cause health problems for your goats.

Also, you need to check your zoning regulations and whether it permits goat rearing where you are not living on a farm out in the country. You may not be allowed to rear goats. This is one reason why proper research is needed before delving into the business.

### 5. Inappropriate Breed for an Environment

Goats are primarily dry climate animals, although there are breeds that show more resilience and seem more adaptable to varying climatic conditions than others. It is imperative to find a breed of goat that fits your climate and other environmental factors.

A goat that does well in a particular region does not mean it will do well in all areas.

### 6. A Jack-of-All-Trades in Goat Business

I tell first-timers going into the goat business that a goat business is not as simple and easy as many think. It is crucial for someone new to goat farming to study the various breeders according to the economic and market demand. To start a goat business on a small scale, do not try to produce breeding stock, show goats, or slaughter goats all at once, as you will get frustrated eventually.

When a client approaches me to help them set-up a goat farm, I evaluate many factors and then come up with a recommendation. One recommendation is to start with one aspect of goat breeding and become well acquainted with the particular breed's modus operandi. When you become familiar with a breeder, you can easily maximize their potential to your advantage.

### 7. An Urban Approach to Raising a Goat

If you are considering rearing goats with an urban approach, then do not try it. I have had many years in the integrated and sustainable agricultural system, and I can tell you from experience that animal farming is much more complicated than crop farming; therefore, you need to understand how to do things and not rely on your intuition as it likely will fail.

I have seen cases where novices in the goat farming business attempt to confine their goats to a particular spot to avoid them moving around. In other cases, some restrict their goats to a small building. Goats were not created to stay indoors, so give up on your urbanite approach to goat farming.

I need to reiterate that goats are typical livestock. They are not cats or dogs, so they are not meant to live in the house with you - they are created to live outside. The consequence of confining goats is that they become unhealthy and die due to worm infestation and disease.

## Important Notes for Goat Farmers

• Goats don't like getting wet, and because of this, they do not thrive well in moist, swampy areas. They require a dry shelter and dry paddocks.

• Dairy goats get upset when you frequently change their routine. They do not like it when you rearrange the milking stands too often.

• Goats are typical browsers; they prefer hay, bushes, and trees to grass. Do not expect them to mow your lawn.

• Aside from goats being clean eaters, they eat a lot. They do not eat contaminated food, and they do investigate what they eat. Prepare a sufficient budget to meet their feeding demands before importing them to your farm.

• Goats of different breeds have distinct personalities and traits, so do not expect all breeds of goats to behave the same way. Always do proper research before purchasing a goat, so you know their distinct behavior and determine which temperance suits your preference and personality.

- Goats are good listeners. If they trust you and are inclined toward you, they will respond to your call and can also call out to you whenever you appear.

- Pasturing a buck with a milking goat is a wrong move. The smell of a buck can make the milk taste bad.

- If you keep a milking goat, milk it at least once in 24 hours. You cannot afford to leave a milking goat and go on vacation.

- Check local zoning regulations to know if you can have goats out of a farmyard in your country.

- Before you embark on the goat farming business, take your time to locate sources of medical help closest to you because this will save you time when you need a prompt response from a goat vet.

- From experience, any species that experience sexual maturity too early, short gestation, and multiple births are likely to die earlier than envisaged, no matter your intervention.

- Call a vet doctor during emergencies.

# Chapter 12: Tracking Your Business's Progress

Several factors control the beneficial activity of goat farming. A privileged position to enter goat farming is a specialized showcase, unlike the most cited and used farm animals such as beavers, pigs, and chickens, which means there are less committed competitors. Raising goats also requires less funding than other four-legged farm animals and will give a higher profit. Another thing is that you can create multiple products to choose from. Is it true that you are interested in selling dairy products like milk and cheese? How about selling your hides to the calfskin industry? Goat meat is also a decent decision, especially for the increasingly extravagant market, which requires goat meat as a must. The sale of goats can produce big profits. Regardless of what market you hope to be in with that goat business, here are tips for a productive goat farm:

Breed—First, know which exact breed of goats is best suited for the goat-breeding barn you want to have. Even though they are all goats, they are not all are the same. Some goats are even bred for certain purposes, such as meat creation, while others are better at producing dairy products. So, it is better to have a Boer goat if you are concentrating on milk and not on meat. After the basic purchase, go for acceptable quality goats. Choosing the right breed is the pathway to your business success.

Appropriate consideration—Learn to handle your goats properly and raise them well. A goat shelter and pen are a necessity, so look at it as an investment and insurance. Also, feed your goats with common food or food proper for their purpose and job. For example, use feed specifically indicated for a kid or lactating goats. The benefit of using feed is that the nutritional requirements are already taken care of, and you don't have to worry about overfeeding, but there are more expenses and even hardware needed for feeding. Going for little by little characteristic foods is an increasingly beneficial goat breeding technique, but you still need to know that what you're feeding your goats is safe for them and still healthy. What's more, never neglect to use a veterinarian's services to make sure that your animals are in the best shape and protect them from any disease.

It is very important to have business plans for goats if you decide to invest in this market. The investment required to raise goats is much less compared to other larger animals, such as sheep and bulls, and the yields that can be produced from this are realistically acceptable. Running a goat farm is not a walk in the park, but it is achievable, especially for those who are smart enough to prepare and know what they're doing to keep things running smoothly. For those interested in this business, we will see a step-by-step strategy for a livestock business plan:

• Before thinking about investing in goats, sheep are versatile animals, so you need to know the negative factors when raising goats. The goat is a good source of many things, such as:

• Meat: Very popular in some target markets.

• Dairy products: Milk and cheese. Usually, the more distinct something is, the more expensive it can be, thanks to supply and demand.

• Fiber: Goatskin is truly an incredible source of textiles, such as cashmere.

• Goats: Why kill them if you could sell them? Goat farming is an industry in itself. Goats are easy to breed, and a single goat can have a high value on the market, depending on their condition and breed.

• After choosing the type of goat for sale, it is time to move on to the next step in your goat breeding business. Choose a goat breed that matches your needs because not all goat breeds are the same. For example, if you like meat, choose Boer goats because they are bred specifically for that purpose. If you want them to produce fleece, look for cashmere goats, but if you are in the early stage of crossbreeding, go for Kiko goats. The list goes on. Choose carefully because this is an important factor in the success of your goat business.

- The next step is an urgent step to implement business plans for raising goats.

Before you begin, think about your current financial plan or how much you can afford to invest. Besides the initial capital, raising goats requires a large field, goat barn, and goat food.

The establishment of a goat farm favors the continuous development of livestock activity. When you start a goat farm, learn about the types of goats you have.

Evaluate the nature of the goat that fits the bill for the delivery of the meat. Gather those who are suitable for this field. Some goats can produce fibers. For the goats used to create milk, they must be set up in the farm area with maintained drainage tools. Goats to be used for meat delivery must be properly cared for. The goat slaughter and slaughter program must be respected to allow the creation of immaculate and high-quality meat. Improper feeding, aging, and slaughter of the creatures will lead to the taste of the cooked meat being unpleasant.

Choosing goat farming may feel extreme at first. Yet, with the best possible information, commitment, and hard work, a goat farming business can be a wonderful thing.

# Conclusion

Raising goats is not for everyone. Let's face it, what sounds like a great idea, in theory, can often end up becoming overwhelming in reality. If you don't have the time, or the ability to commit yourself, or the discipline, then goats might not be for you. There is no shame in recognizing your limitations, and only nobility in avoiding actions can eliminate trouble for yourself and other living beings.

But if you have the time to commit, have space and money to spend on the fencing and feed, and the time to build a shelter, raising goats can be very rewarding. If you love animals, you know how gratifying it is to see your animal happy and contented, thriving and enjoying your interaction. Goats love company and are very social creatures. They are generally glad to see you when you enter their enclosure and rarely resort to the head butting you see in the cartoons.

As more people leave cities and move to rural areas, consciously wanting to reconnect to the land and the old ways of doing things, more people are raising farm animals like goats, chickens, and even pigs. While some may find it was a great notion that didn't pan out, others may find great contentment, an inner peace that can only come from becoming connected to the land on which you live. Raising goats can be a great way to do that. In a few months, when you're pouring goat's milk onto your cereal one morning, milk that came from goats you raised, cared for, and milked, you will feel a tremendous sense of accomplishment and completeness. More and more, that sense of completeness is missing from daily life for most people, but for those who get back to the land and try something new, like raising goats for milk or fiber, it is a different story.

The path to true happiness does not always lie in more advanced technology. Talk to people who've raised goats and see what they say about it. You may be surprised.

# Here's another book by Dion Rosser that you might like

DION ROSSER

# OFF THE GRID LIVING

How You Can Live Off the Land and
Become Self-Sufficient through Homesteading
and a Backyard Guide to Raised Bed Gardening

# References

8 Tips to Prepare for Goat Breeding Season. (2019, July 22). Hobby Farms. https://www.hobbyfarms.com/goat-breeding-tips-prepare/

12 Popular Goat Breeds. (2015, August 5). Successful Farming. https://www.agriculture.com/family/living-the-country-life/12-popular-goat-breeds

Building the Goat Barn | GottaGoat. (n.d.). http://www.gottagoat.com/gottagoat-goats/building-the-goat-barn/

Cleanliness Is Next To Goatliness. (2015, April 21). Modern Farmer. https://modernfarmer.com/2015/04/cleanliness-is-next-to-goatliness/

DIY: Make a Free Goat House from PALLETS. (2017, August 5). Weed 'em & Reap. https://www.weedemandreap.com/make-free-goat-house-pallets/

Goat Care and Maintenance of Healthy Goats. (2020, January 23). Timber Creek Farm. https://timbercreekfarmer.com/goat-care-and-maintainance/

GOAT FARMING AS A BUSINESS: a farmer's manual to successful goat production and marketing For the Department of Livestock Production and Development Supported by: SNV -Netherlands Development Organization. (n.d.). https://snv.org/cms/sites/default/files/explore/download/goat_farming_as_a_business_-_a_farmers_manual.pdf

Goat Farming (how to start & make money) by Business Tips Zambia. (2017, August 22). Zambia Farmers Hub, Zambia Farmers hub. https://zambiafarmershub.wordpress.com/2017/08/22/%E2%80%8Bgoat-farming-how-to-start-make-money-by-business-tips-zambia/

Goat Reproduction Preparing for the Breeding Season – Goats. (n.d.). Goats.Extension.org. Retrieved from https://goats.extension.org/goat-reproduction-preparing-for-the-breeding-season/

Hot Weather Tips for Goat Enthusiasts. (n.d.). Brazosfeedsupply.com. Retrieved from https://brazosfeedsupply.com/blog/5950/hot-weather-tips-for-goat-enthusiasts

Housing, Fencing, Working Facilities and Predators - Goats and Health - GOATWORLD.COM. (n.d.). Www.Goatworld.com. Retrieved from http://www.goatworld.com/articles/fencing/fencing1.shtml

How a young farmer developed a goatmeat business. (2018, January 22). Farmers Weekly. https://www.fwi.co.uk/livestock/how-a-young-farmer-developed-a-goatmeat-business

How to Build a Goat Barn ★ThePlywood.com. (2018, August 14). ThePlywood.com. http://theplywood.com/goat-barn

https://www.facebook.com/thespruceofficial. (2018). The Spruce - Make Your Best Home. The Spruce. https://www.thespruce.com/

Keeping Goats Warm in the Winter. (2018, October 31). The Hay Manager. https://www.thehaymanager.com/goat-and-sheep-round-bale-hay-feeders/keeping-goats-warm-in-the-winter/

MorningChores - Build Your Self-Sufficient Life. (n.d.). MorningChores. https://morningchores.com

Planning, G. F., & says, S. Y. N.-B. G. P. G. (2017, May 9). My top 3 picks for goat fencing that is secure and safe. Simple Living Country Gal. https://simplelivingcountrygal.com/goat-fencing-101-everything-you-need-to-know/

Preparing and Caring for Your Goats in Winter. (2015). Mannapro.com. https://info.mannapro.com/homestead/preparing-caring-for-goats-in-winter

Raising Goats: Keeping their barn clean - Boxwood Ave. (2018, October 9). Boxwood Ave. https://boxwoodavenue.com/raising-goats-cleaning-barn/

ROYS FARM | Modern Farming Methods. (n.d.). ROYS FARM. https://www.roysfarm.com/

Top 10 Mistakes Made by Goat Owners. (n.d.). Www.Lambertvetsupply.com. Retrieved from https://www.lambertvetsupply.com/wellpetpost-top-10-mistakes-made-by-goat-owners.html

Top Ten Mistakes Made by Goat Producers. (n.d.). Www.Tennesseemeatgoats.com. Retrieved from https://www.tennesseemeatgoats.com/articles2/toptenmistakes06.html

Want to Become a Successful Goat Farmer? Here are the Excellent Tips, Benefits of Rearing Goats & Making Maximum Profit. (n.d.). Krishijagran.com. https://krishijagran.com/animal-husbandry/want-to-become-a-successful-goat-farmer-here-are-the-excellent-tips-benefits-of-rearing-goats-making-maximum-profit/

Wolford, D. (2019a, July 18). Goat Breeding 101 - Weed'em & Reap. Weed 'em & Reap. https://www.weedemandreap.com/goat-breeding-101/

Wolford, D. (2019b, October 19). A Simple Guide to Raising & Milking Goats. Weed 'em & Reap. https://www.weedemandreap.com/raising-goats-milking-goats/

*5 Questions to Ask Before Keeping Sheep.* (2016, March 1). Hobby Farms. https://www.hobbyfarms.com/5-questions-to-ask-before-keeping-sheep-3/

*6 Reasons To Raise Sheep • Insteading.* (n.d.). Insteading. https://insteading.com/blog/why-raise-sheep/

*13 tips for lambing outdoors.* (2020, January 4). Farmers Weekly. https://www.fwi.co.uk/livestock/husbandry/livestock-lambing/13-tips-for-lambing-outdoors

*A beginners guide to lambing...* (2015, February 26). Indie Farmer. https://www.indiefarmer.com/2015/02/26/beginners-guide-to-lambing/

*Breeding Sheep -What You Need to Know.* (2018, July 23). Timber Creek Farm. https://timbercreekfarmer.com/breeding-sheep-on-a-small-homestead/

*How to Raise Sheep on a Small Acreage for Profit.* (n.d.). Small Business - Chron.com. Retrieved from https://smallbusiness.chron.com/raise-sheep-small-acreage-profit-55996.html

*How to Show Sheep: 7 Sheep Showing Tips for Any Level.* (n.d.). Raising Sheep. Retrieved from http://www.raisingsheep.net/how-to-show-sheep.html

Mckenzie-Jakes, A. (n.d.). *02 Fun Facts About Sheep Fact Sheet II.*

*Pasture Vs. Shed Lambing.* (n.d.). EcoFarming Daily. Retrieved from https://www.ecofarmingdaily.com/raise-healthy-livestock/other-livestock/pasture-vs-shed-lambing/

Serban, C. (2018, November 22). *10 Most Popular Sheep Breeds raised for Meat, Fiber and Dairy.* Seradria. https://seradria.com/blog/most-popular-sheep-breeds.html

*Sheep 101 Home Page.* (2019). Sheep101.Info. http://www.sheep101.info/

*Sheep Shearing: How to Shear Sheep (Beginner's Guide).* (2018, May 8). ROYS FARM. https://www.roysfarm.com/sheep-shearing-information-guide/

*The Different Breeds Of Sheep - TheSheepSite.com*. (n.d.). The Sheep Site. Retrieved from https://www.thesheepsite.com/focus/5m/87/the-different-breeds-of-sheep-thesheepsitecom

*Welcome*. (n.d.). 2020 Scottish Smallholder Festival. Retrieved from https://ssgf.uk/exhibitors/beginners-guide-to-showing-sheep/

Board, N. P. (n.d.). *Safe Animal Handling*. Pork Information Gateway. http://porkgateway.org/resource/safe-animal-handling/

Cooperative, S. S. (n.d.). *5 Great Pig Farming Tips | Southern States Co-op*. Www.Southernstates.Com. https://www.southernstates.com/farm-store/articles/5-great-pig-farming-tips

*Feeding The Pigs*. (2014, April 2). The Elliott Homestead. https://theelliotthomestead.com/2014/04/what-to-feed-a-pastured-pig/

*Handling and Restraining Pigs*. (2019, October 8). Thepigsite.Com. https://www.thepigsite.com/articles/handling-and-restraining-pigs

*How To Butcher Pigs (At Home On The Farm)*. (2014, October 14). The Elliott Homestead. https://theelliotthomestead.com/2014/10/how-to-butcher-pigs/

*Is Pig Farming Profitable Business? 2020 Market Analysis*. (2019, September 19). BusinessNES. https://businessnes.com/is-pig-farming-profitable-business-market-analysis/

Norris, M. K. (2015, March 13). *10 Reasons To Raise Pigs*. Real World Survivor. https://www.realworldsurvivor.com/2015/03/13/10-reasons-to-raise-pigs/

*Pig Breeds: A Handy Guide to Choosing the Best*. (2019, April 19). Reformation Acres. https://www.reformationacres.com/2018/01/choosing-pig-breed.html

*Pig Pens or Pig Pastures*. (2014, July 25). Timber Creek Farm. https://timbercreekfarmer.com/pig-pens-or-pig-pastures/

*Raising Pigs: Pros & Cons*. (2014, December 11). The Prairie Homestead. https://www.theprairiehomestead.com/2014/12/raising-pigs.html

*Reproductive Biology 101*. (2003, February 15). National Hog Farmer. https://www.nationalhogfarmer.com/mag/farming_reproductive_biology

Snyde, C. W. (n.d.). *How to Butcher a Homestead-Raised Hog - Sustainable Farming*. Mother Earth News. https://www.motherearthnews.com/homesteading-and-livestock/how-to-butcher-a-homestead-raised-hog-zmaz82sozgoe

---

*What are the Benefits of Raising Pigs? | White Mountains Livestock Blog.* (2019, January 23). White Mountains Livestock Company. https://www.whitemountainslivestock.com/blog/swine-blog/general-tips/what-are-the-benefits-of-raising-pigs/

*A guide to handling camelids.* (2019, September 24). Veterinary-Practice.Com.

*Alpaca Digestive System.* (n.d.). Apple Mountain Alpacas. https://www.applemountainalpacas.com/mentoring/alpaca-digestive-system/

*Alpacas and Llamas: What They Are & Why You Should Keep Them - Hobby Farms.* (2016, August 8). Hobby Farms. https://www.hobbyfarms.com/alpacas-llamas-what-they-are-and-why-you-should-keep-them/

*Alpacas as a Business.* (2017, December 13). Alpacainfo.Com.

*Breeds of Livestock - Llama — Breeds of Livestock, Department of Animal Science.* (n.d.). Afs.Okstate. Edu. http://afs.okstate.edu/breeds/other/llama/

Carmen. (2013, June 20). *5 Important Reasons You Should Add Llamas To Your Livestock Herd - Off The Grid News.* Off the Grid News. https://www.offthegridnews.com/how-to-2/5-important-reasons-you-should-add-llamas-to-your-livestock-herd/

Dohner, J. (n.d.). *Selecting a Guard Llama.* Mother Earth News. https://www.motherearthnews.com/homesteading-and-livestock/selecting-a-guard-llama-zbcz1404

*Herd Health of Llamas and Alpacas - Exotic and Laboratory Animals.* (n.d.). Merck Veterinary Manual.

*How to Buy A Llama?* (n.d.). Www.Shagbarkridge.Com.

*Labor and Delivery.* (n.d.). The Alpaca Hacienda.

*Llama Behavior.* (n.d.). Fancycreekllamas.Com. http://fancycreekllamas.com/llama-care/15-llama-behavior

*Llama Habits & Behavior.* (n.d.).

*Llama Housing & Fencing International Llama Association Educational Brochure #5.* (n.d.).

*Llama Shearing.* (n.d.).

*Llama Training: What You Should Teach Your Llamas.* (2009). Llamas-Information.Com. http://www.llamas-information.com/llama-training/llama-training-what-you-should-teach-your-llamas/

*Successful Business with Alpacas and Llamas.* (n.d.).

Taylor, M. (2018, July 23). *You Can Actually Adopt a Llama or Alpaca as a Pet.* Good Housekeeping. https://www.goodhousekeeping.com/life/pets/a20706815/get-a-pet-llama/

Twitter, T., & LinkedIn, L. (n.d.). *A Guide to Llamas, Alpacas, Guanacos, and Vicuñas.* ThoughtCo.

Amaral-Phillips, D., Scharko, P., Johns, J., & Franklin, S. (n.d.). *Feeding and Managing Baby Calves from Birth to 3 Months of Age.* https://afs.ca.uky.edu/files/feeding_and_managing_baby_calves_from_birth_to_3_months_of_age.pdf

*Beef Cattle Behavior and Handling Understand Behavior to Improve Handling.* (n.d.). https://extension.msstate.edu/sites/default/files/publications/publications/p2801.pdf

*Best Healthy Feed for Beef Cattle.* (n.d.). Arrowquip. https://arrowquip.com/blog/animal-science/best-healthy-feed-beef-cattle

Blake, E. 'Skip.' (n.d.). *Cow psychology: Handle them by getting into their heads.* Progressive Dairy. https://www.progressivedairy.com/topics/herd-health/cow-psychology-handle-them-by-getting-into-their-heads

*Breeds of beef cattle | Breeds | Beef | Livestock | Agriculture | Agriculture Victoria.* (2018). Vic.Gov.Au.

Candi Johns. (n.d.). *6 Reasons to Raise Your Own Meat and How Long it Takes - Farm Fresh For Life Blog - GRIT Magazine.* Grit. https://www.grit.com/animals/livestock/6-reasons-to-raise-your-own-meat-and-how-long-it-takes-zb0z1601

*Cattle Breeds From England.* (n.d.). Beef2live.Com. https://beef2live.com/story-cattle-breeds-england-89-106430

*Cattle housing equipment.* (n.d.). En.Schauer-Agrotronic.Com. https://en.schauer-agrotronic.com/cattle/cattle-housing-systems

*Cleaning a Cow: How to Clean a Cow (Beginner's Guide).* (2018, March 14). ROYS FARM. https://www.roysfarm.com/cleaning-a-cow/

*Cows and heifers calve better later.* (2017, May 3). Farm Progress. https://www.farmprogress.com/animal-health/cows-and-heifers-calve-better-later

Gadberry, S., Jennings, J., Ward, H., Beck, P., Kutz, B., & Troxel, T. (2016). *Beef Cattle Production - MP184.* https://www.uaex.edu/publications/pdf/mp184/Chapter3.pdf

---

*Handling Facilities for Beef Cattle.* (n.d.). The Beef Site. Retrieved November 5, 2020, from http://www.thebeefsite.com/articles/912/handling-facilities-for-beef-cattle/

https://www.facebook.com/CloverValleyBeef. (2016, September 27). *27 Amazing Facts About Cows That Will Impress Your Friends.* Clover Meadows Beef. http://www.clovermeadowsbeef.com/amazing-facts-about-cows/

*Milk Production in Beef Cattle.* (2017, March 14). Homestead on the Range. https://homesteadontherange.com/2017/03/14/milk-production-in-beef-cattle/

Niman, N. H. (2014, December 19). Actually, Raising Beef Is Good for the Planet. *Wall Street Journal.* https://www.wsj.com/articles/actually-raising-beef-is-good-for-the-planet-1419030738

*Reproduction in Cattle.* (2019). Peda.Net. https://peda.net/kenya/css/subjects/agriculture/form-3/lsab/ric

*Seven Fencing Tips for Cattle | Ag Industry News - Farm and Livestock Directory.* (n.d.). Farmandlivestockdirectory.Com. https://farmandlivestockdirectory.com/seven-fencing-tips-for-cattle/

*Steer Vs. Bull.* (n.d.). Animals.Mom.Com. https://animals.mom.com/steer-vs-bull-3150.html

*Top Ten Considerations for Small-scale Beef Production.* (n.d.). Small Farm Sustainability. https://www.extension.iastate.edu/smallfarms/top-ten-considerations-small-scale-beef-production

www.ingramcontent.com/pod-product-compliance
Lightning Source LLC
Chambersburg PA
CBHW071854090426
42811CB00004B/603